Foundations of American Education

Third Edition

L. Dean Webb

Arizona State University

Arlene Metha

Arizona State University

K. Forbis Jordan

Arizona State University

Merrill,
an imprint of Prentice Hall
Upper Saddle River, New Jersey   Columbus, Ohio

Library of Congress Cataloging-in-Publication Data

Webb, L. Dean.
  Foundations of American education / L. Dean Webb, Arlene Metha, K.
Forbis Jordan.—3rd ed.
      p.   cm.
  Includes bibliographical references and indexes.
  ISBN 0–13–923871–9
    1. Education—United States.   I. Metha, Arlene.   II. Jordan, K.
Forbis (Kenneth Forbis),   .   III. Title.
LA 217.2.W43   2000
370′.973—dc21   99–25023
                                                                        CIP

Editor: Debra A. Stollenwerk
Editorial Assistant: Penny S. Burleson
Production Editor: Mary Harlan
Design Coordinator: Diane C. Lorenzo
Text Design and Production Coordination: WordCrafters Editorial Services, Inc.
Cover Designer: Dan Eckel
Cover art: © Stephan Schildbach
Photo Coordinator: Nancy Harre Ritz
Production Manager: Pamela D. Bennett
Director of Marketing: Kevin Flanagan
Marketing Manager: Meghan Shepherd
Marketing Coordinator: Krista Groshong

This book is set in ITC Garamond Light by The Clarinda Company and was printed and bound by R. R. Donnelley & Sons Company. The cover was printed by Phoenix Color Corp.

© 2000, 1996, by Prentice-Hall, Inc.
Pearson Education
Upper Saddle River, New Jersey 07458

Earlier edition © 1992 by Macmillan Publishing Company

Printed in the United States of America

10   9   8   7   6   5   4   3

ISBN: 0-13-923871-9

Prentice-Hall International (UK) Limited, *London*
Prentice-Hall of Australia Pty. Limited, *Sydney*
Prentie-Hall of Canada, Inc., *Toronto*
Prentice-Hall Hispanoamericana, S. A., *Mexico*
Prentice-Hall of India Private Limited, *New Delhi*
Prentice-Hall of Japan, Inc., *Tokyo*
Prentice-Hall (Singapore) Pte. Ltd., *Singapore*
Editoria Prentice-Hall do Brasil, Ltda, *Rio de Janeiro*

Photo Credits

(All photos copyrighted by the individuals or institutions listed.):
Anne Vega/Merrill, **p. 2;** Scott Cunningham/Merrill, **p. 13;** Anne Vega/Merrill,
p. 14; Scott Cunningham/Merrill, **p. 20;** Anne Vega/Merrill, **p. 34;**
Anthony Magnacca/Merrill, **p. 40;** Anthony Magnacca/Merrill, **p. 46;**
Carolyn Salisbury/NEA, **p. 52;** Todd Yarrington/Merrill, **p. 62;** Corbis/Bettmann,
p. 76 (left); Anne Vega/Merrill, **p. 76 (right);** Anne Vega/Merrill,
p. 78 (left); Corbis/Bettmann, **p. 78 (right);** Corbis/Bettmann, **p. 82 (left);**
Anne Vega/Merrill, **p. 82 (right);** Scott Cunningham/Merrill, **p. 90;** AP Wide
World Photos, **p. 96 (left);** University of Chicago Archives, **p. 96 (right);**
National Library of Medicine, **p. 103 (left);** PhotoDisc, Inc., **p. 103 (right);**
Michael Greenberg/Sunbury Valley Schools, **p. 113;** Courtesy of Nel Noddings,
p. 114 (left); Courtesy of Maxine Greene, **p. 114 (right);** AP Wide World
Photos, **p. 118;** AP Wide World Photos, **p. 120 (left);** AP Wide World Photos,
p. 120 (right); Courtesy of Michael Apple, **p. 122;** Corbis/Bettmann, **p. 130;**
United Nations, **p. 141;** Todd Yarrington, **p. 149;** Corbis/Bettmann, **p. 154;**
Corbis/Bettmann, **p. 166;** University of Virginia Library, **p. 171;**
Corbis/Bettmann, **p. 182;** Corbis/Bettmann, **p. 190;** Arizona State University,
p. 199; Corbis/Bettmann, **p. 204;** AP Wide World Photos, **p. 214;**
John F. Kennedy Library, **p. 221;** Corbis/Bettmann, **p. 225;** AP Wide World
Photos, **p. 231;** Anne Vega/Merrill, **p. 240;** Gail Zucker, **p. 244;**
Scott Cunningham/Merrill, **p. 255;** Silver Burdett Ginn, **p. 262;** Barbara
Schwartz/Merrill, **p. 268;** Anne Vega/Merrill, **p. 274;** Scott Cunningham/Merrill,
p. 277; Tom Watson/Merrill, **p. 281;** Scott Cunningham/Merrill, **p. 283;**
Woodfin Camp & Associates, **p. 287;** Todd Yarrington/Merrill, **p. 301;**
Barbara Schwartz/Merrill, **p. 308;** Barbara Schwartz/Merrill, **p. 316;**
Scott Cunningham/Merrill, **p. 320;** Gail Zucker, **p. 331;** Frank Siteman/Stock
Boston, **p. 340;** Supreme Court Historical Society, **p. 369;** Lisa Berg, **p. 373;**
Ulrike Welsh, **p. 379;** Michael Newmann/Photo Edit, **p. 383;** AP Wide World
Photos, **p. 388;** Scott Cunningham/Merrill, **p. 395;** Shelley Boyd/Photo Edit,
p. 403; Scott Cunningham/Merrill, **p. 419;** Tom Watson/Merrill, **p. 428;**
Ulrike Welsh, **p. 440;** Anne Vega/Merrill, **p. 444;** Anne Vega/Merrill, **p. 450;**
Barbara Schwartz/Merrill, **p. 456;** Scott Cunningham/Merrill, **p. 468;**
Mike Penny, **p. 471;** Bob Daemmrich/Image Works, **p. 480;** Anne Vega/Merrill,
p. 491; Scott Cunningham/Merrill, **p. 498;** Scott Cunningham/Merrill, **p. 517;**
Scott Cunningham/Merrill, **p. 527;** Scott Cunningham/Merrill, **p. 529;** NASA,
p. 536; Anne Vega/Merrill, **p. 543;** Gail Zucker, **p. 544;** Anne Vega/Merrill,
p. 549.

Preface

Interest in education reform has contributed to a renewed emphasis on the critical role of the teacher in American education. As a result of various reforms such as decentralization and site-based decision making, members of this rewarding and challenging profession play a greater role in making the decisions that affect their lives and the lives of their students. The movement toward the professionalization of teaching is being advanced by the development of national certification programs.

In writing this third edition, our primary goal has been to provide current and useful information that will help persons interested in careers in elementary and secondary education develop an understanding of the philosophical and historical roots of education, current educational structures and practices, and projections for the future. With this understanding and knowledge, they can make informed decisions about their professional and career goals. There is general agreement about the need for able persons in education; however, the decision to become a teacher should come only after careful deliberation. Before making the decision to enter teaching, individuals need to understand the complexities of the teacher's role, the many and diverse duties and responsibilities of the profession, and the commitment of time and energy required to be a successful teacher.

Orientation of the Text

To help the student develop an understanding of education, this book follows a sequenced presentation of major topics: the recent and contemplated changes in the role of the teacher; the philosophical foundations and historical background of education; the relationship between schools and society; educational responses to an increasingly diverse and multicultural society; the particular challenges of working with diverse populations and at-risk youth; the law and its effect on schools; the organization and financing of elementary and secondary schools; the current and evolving process of teaching and learning; and projected demographic, social, and economic changes and their impact on education. In this interdisciplinary approach, we have given attention to both the theoretical and the applied aspects of education. Our goal has been to prepare a text that includes a balance of past, present, and future applications of education in a context that students will find both readable and challenging.

Interdisciplinary Emphasis

One of the strengths of the text is the extensive use of relevant concepts from the social sciences. The philosophical roots of education have been identified and discussed. Historical materials were used in developing the extensive discussion of the evolution of schooling for the past several centuries. Disciplines such as sociology, economics, politics of education, political science, public administration, finance, and law have been used to provide an understanding of the current and developing context of education. Research from the field of psychology is used extensively in the discussion of teaching, learning, and meeting the needs of at-risk children and youth.

Theoretical and Applied Aspects of Education

Through the use of current research, we have emphasized the connections between theory and research and the applied world of teaching. Unlike many foundation texts that concentrate primarily on pedagogical knowledge and academic skill domains, this text provides a comprehensive application of research and theory to actual classroom/teaching situations and practice. Through margin notes, special features, and discussion questions, the educational implications of research and theory are reinforced in ways that will be understandable to both practicing and prospective teachers.

New to This Edition

In order to provide an integrated and more current perspective, this edition:

- Discusses the leadership roles for teachers in the school reform era.
- Integrates philosophy, educational theory, and history in a cohesive and unified manner.
- Provides a context for critical analysis of the relationship between the school and society.
- Suggests a variety of educational remedies designed to achieve educational opportunity and equity in a diverse and multicultural society.
- Presents a review of the research on protective factors and resiliency and its impact on at-risk behaviors.
- Provides increased attention to women and minorities.
- Reviews the concepts underlying school improvement models.
- Highlights the relationships among the curriculum, teaching, and learning and their philosophical and theoretical antecedents.
- Emphasizes the educational implications of demographic, economic, and technological developments.

Pedagogical Features

Several features have been designed to help the student use the text for study and review.

Vignettes

The basic concepts of each chapter are reflected in the opening vignettes. They present teachers in real-life situations that reflect the many challenges and rewards of teaching. They may be used to stimulate interaction between teachers and students using this text.

Objectives

Each chapter begins with a series of objectives to be achieved through study and discussion. They may be used as guides for class discussion and also are a good tool to use in studying and reviewing the material.

Margin Notes and Key Terms

Notes in the margins of each chapter help students identify and understand key concepts. Key terms are identified in italic type in the text, referenced at the end of each chapter, and defined in a glossary at the end of the book.

Discussion Topics

At the end of each chapter, discussion questions provide an overview of the basic concepts. They may be used as oral or written assignments, topics for class discussion, or review topics.

Figures and Tables

Figures and tables have been used to enhance and supplement the text and add additional content. These visual features not only give an additional dimension to the chapters but also help students develop a better understanding of major concepts.

Summary

The key points are summarized at the end of each chapter. These can be used as guides for class discussion and in study and review sessions.

Internet Resources

The Appendix lists a number of World Wide Web sites where information may be found on a broad range of topics related to education and educational issues. In addition, at the end of each chapter, students and instructors are directed to Web sites related to key topics and individuals discussed in the text.

References

References at the end of each chapter provide bibliographic information for all citations. The reference lists can be used in further study to develop a better understanding of specific topics and as beginning points for identifying sources and topics for research papers.

Glossary

A glossary at the end of the book defines the terms identified throughout the book. It ensures consistent definitions in the use of terms throughout the book and will help the student better understand the key concepts.

Special Features

Each chapter contains pedagogical features designed to enrich the learning opportunities by including historical notes and discussion stimulators drawn from current and past educational developments, current issues, or applications of educational principles in real-life situations. Special features include the following topics:

- *Historical Notes* provide background information about specific educational developments that have resulted in changes in education or about individuals who have exerted leadership in some aspect of education. They supplement the other content of the text and illustrate the educational contributions made by various role models.
- *Ask Yourself* features are designed to stimulate reflective thought that will help students develop a better understanding about teaching as a career. They contain a series of questions that expand upon the text and stimulate exploration of specific concepts and issues in greater depth. These enrichment activities can be used by groups of students or by individuals.
- *Controversial Issues* present a dichotomy of arguments, pro and con, about a variety of educational issues. As students reflect on and discuss these controversies, they will address a range of values and beliefs concerning important educational concepts.
- *Personal Reflections* are direct quotations from Teachers of the Year from various states. They provide focused thoughts and advice based on experiences with students, parents, their peers, and administrators.

Ancillaries

The following ancillaries have been developed for the instructor and the student:

- An *Instructor's Manual* that contains an instructional resources section with chapter outlines, student objectives, lecture and discussion guide, guide to the use of transparencies, extended projects and assignments for students, test bank, and an annotated list of instructional media (videos).

- A *Custom Test Manager,* a computerized version of the test bank for the instructor, available for IBM PC and Macintosh compatible computers.
- Transparency masters that accompany each chapter.
- A *Companion Website* (see pages x-xi) provides the instructor with a *Syllabus Manager,* an online syllabus creation and management resource, and provides the student with chapter objectives, interactive self-quizzes, a *Results Reporter* that computes a percentage grade and analysis of the quizzes, a message board, Internet searches with links to key terms, and links to WWW sites that relate to chapter content.

Acknowledgments

The authors wish to recognize the many persons who have contributed to the preparation of both this and the previous editions of this text. First, we give special recognition to the teachers and other educators who work each day to provide learning opportunities for the youth of America. Second, we wish to acknowledge the diverse scholars who have provided the past and present record of the development of elementary and secondary education and the researchers and policy analysts who are charting the future. Third, we express our appreciation to our students and professional colleagues for their critical comments and suggestions about ways to improve the third edition.

We extend our special thanks and appreciation to our editor Debbie Stollenwerk and her most valuable assistant Penny Burleson, and to the production editor, Mary Harlan.

To the various reviewers of the second edition, we extend our sincere thanks for their constructive comments. Their efforts helped us improve the text in this third edition. For their participation, we extend our thanks to Judy Arnold, Lincoln Memorial University; John Bertalan, Hillsborough Community College; JoAnn Hohenbrink, Ohio Dominican College; David A. Joyner, Old Dominion; and Mary E. Reeves, Northwestern State University of Louisiana.

L. Dean Webb
Arlene Metha
K. Forbis Jordan

Discover Companion Websites:
A Virtual Learning Environment

Technology is a constantly growing and changing aspect of our field that is creating a need for content and resources. To address this emerging need, we have developed an online learning environment for students and professors alike—Companion Websites—to support our textbooks.

In creating a Companion Website, our goal is to build on and enhance what the textbook already offers. For this reason, the content for each user-friendly website is organized by chapter and provides the professor and student with a variety of meaningful resources. Common features of a Companion Website include:

For the Professor—

Every Companion Website integrates **Syllabus Manager**™, an online syllabus creation and management utility.

- **Syllabus Manager**™ provides you, the instructor, with an easy, step-by-step process to create and revise syllabi, with direct links into Companion Website and other online content without having to learn HTML.

- Students may logon to your syllabus during any study session. All they need to know is the web address for the Companion Website, and the password you've assigned to your syllabus.

- After you have created a syllabus using **Syllabus Manager**™, students may enter the syllabus for their course section from any point in the Companion Website.

- Class dates are highlighted in white and assignment due dates appear in blue. Clicking on a date, the student is shown the list of activities for the assignment. The activities for each assignment are linked directly to actual content, saving time for students.

- Adding assignments consists of clicking on the desired due date, then filling in the details of the assignment—name of the assignment, instructions, and whether or not it is a one-time or repeating assignment.

- In addition, links to other activities can be created easily. If the activity is online, a URL can be entered in the space provided, and it will be linked automatically in the final syllabus.

- Your completed syllabus is hosted on our servers, allowing convenient updates from any computer on the Internet. Changes you make to your syllabus are immediately available to your students at their next logon.

For the Student—

- **Chapter Objectives**—outline key concepts from the text
- **Interactive Self-Quizzes**—complete with hints and automatic grading that provide immediate feedback for students

After students submit their answers for the interactive self-quizzes, the Companion Website **Results Reporter** computes a percentage grade, provides a graphic representation of how many questions were answered correctly and incorrectly, and gives a question by question analysis of the quiz. Students are given the option to send their quiz to up to four e-mail addresses (professor, teaching assistant, study partner, etc.).

- **Message Board**—serves as a virtual bulletin board to post—or respond to—questions or comments to/from a national audience
- **Net Searches**—offer links by key terms from each chapter to related Internet content
- **Web Destinations**—links to www sites that relate to chapter content

To take advantage of these resources, please visit the *Foundations of American Education* Companion Website at www.prenhall.com/webb

Contents in Brief

Contents

Part Three
Historical Foundations of Education   129

Part Four
The Schools and Society   239

Special Features

Historical Note

Ask Yourself

Controversial Issues

Part One

The Teaching Profession

Chapter 1

What most determines whether students learn is not family background or even dollars spent per pupil, but the talent, the ability, and the dedication of their teachers.

President Bill Clinton
January 21, 1999

Status of the Profession

> *Dr. Flynn enters the room of a patient who was recently admitted to University Hospital complaining of severe abdominal pain. Several interns follow Dr. Flynn to the patient's bedside. Dr. Flynn begins to ask the patient a series of questions. After the patient responds, Dr. Flynn turns to one of the interns and asks for a diagnosis. The intern gives a diagnosis. Dr. Flynn follows with a series of questions related to the basis for the diagnosis and possible treatment.*

The ABC Corporation has just initiated a new data management plan. All middle managers have been told to report to the conference room at 8:30 A.M. on Monday. Upon arrival, the director of human resources introduces Ms. Dominguez from Data Resources, the retailer of the software supporting the new data management plan. Ms. Dominguez distributes a packet of materials and spends the remainder of the day with the managers, reviewing the materials in the packet, presenting additional information using a computer presentation platform, and showing a video related to the data management plan.

Mr. Pell stops at Amy Black's desk and answers a question. He moves to the desk of another student, observes the student writing in a workbook, points to something the student has written, and then, in a low voice, tells the student that the response is not correct and explains why. He continues around the room, stopping at almost every desk to make some remark. After about 10 minutes he goes to the front of the room and says, "Class, it appears that several people are having problems with this assignment. Let's review how to divide one fraction by another fraction." Mr. Pell walks to the blackboard and begins talking.

Which of the individuals, Dr. Flynn, Ms. Dominguez, or Mr. Pell, is a teacher? Why? What defines the act of teaching?

Teaching has been considered by some to be the most noble of the professions. H. G. Wells went so far as to say that "The teacher, whether mother, priest, or schoolmaster, is the real maker of history." Perhaps you are asking yourself, What is a teacher? What is this profession of teaching all about? And, perhaps most important, Should I become a teacher? This chapter presents an overview of the teaching profession. After studying the chapter you should be able to:

- Provide a demographic overview of America's teaching force.
- Evaluate your motives for becoming a teacher, as well as those commonly cited by others.
- Describe a typical teacher preparation program.
- Identify the most common strategies being used to recruit minorities into teaching.

- Discuss current issues related to teacher certification, including testing, alternative certification, emergency certification, recertification, and interstate certification.
- Discuss the current status of the movement to institute national certification for teachers.

- Compare projected data related to teacher supply with that projected for demand, and explore the factors contributing to supply and demand.
- Identify the major elements of teacher compensation, including incentive pay and supplemental pay.
- Discuss the public's views of the schools and student's ratings of teachers.

The Teacher and Teaching: Definitions

Put most simply, a teacher is one who instructs another. A more formal definition from Good's *Dictionary of Education* (1973) defines a teacher as "a person employed in an official capacity for the purpose of guiding and directing the learning experiences of pupils or students in an educational institution, whether public or private" (p. 586). Teaching is defined in another work as "the process of helping pupils acquire knowledge, skills, attitudes, and/or appreciations by means of a systematic method of instruction" (Shafritz, Koeppe, & Soper, 1988, p. 468). A well-known educator and writer in the field of education, B. O. Smith (1987), provides five definitions of teaching:

1. The descriptive definition of teaching: Defines teaching as imparting knowledge or skill.
2. Teaching as success: Defines teaching as an activity such that X learns what Y teaches. If X does not learn, Y has not taught.
3. Teaching as intentional activity: Defines teaching as intended behavior (i.e., paying attention to what is going on, making diagnoses, changing one's behavior) for which the aim is to induce learning.
4. Teaching as normative behavior: Defines teaching as a family of activities, including training, instructing, indoctrinating, and conditioning.
5. The scientific or technical definition of teaching: Defines teaching by the coordinating propositions; teaching is not explicitly defined, but its meaning is implicated in the sentences where it occurs (e.g., "The teacher gives feedback.").

Do you believe that teachers are "born not made"? In your experience as a student have you been exposed to teachers who were "artists" in the classroom?

Perhaps the most provocative definition defines the teacher as an artist and teaching as an art. According to Eisner (1994), teaching can be considered an art from at least four perspectives:

First, it is an art in that teaching can be performed with such skill and grace that, for the student as well as for the teacher, the experience can be justifiably characterized as aesthetic. . . .

Second, teaching is an art in that teachers, like painters, composers, actresses, and dancers, make judgements based largely on qualities that unfold during the course of action. . . . The teacher must "read" the emerging qualities and respond with qualities appropriate to the ends sought. . . .

Third, teaching is an art in that the teacher's activity is not dominated by prescriptions or routines but is influenced by qualities and contingencies that are unpredicted. The teacher must function in an innovative way in order to cope with these contingencies. . . .

Fourth, teaching is an art in that the ends it achieves are often created in the process . . . teaching is a form of human action in which many of the ends achieved are emergent—that is to say, found in the course of interaction with students rather than preconceived and efficiently attained. (pp. 154–155)

To consider teaching an art does not negate the necessity of establishing a scientific basis for the art of teaching and for developing a theoretical framework for teaching that addresses what we know and believe about intelligence, the conditions of learning, and what defines the effective teacher. The stronger the scientific basis, the greater the potential to improve teaching.

Profile of the Teaching Profession

Whatever definition is used, there is little argument that the teacher is the central element in the educational system. It is of interest to review what we know about the teacher in American society today. Table 1.1 presents some characteristics of public school teachers.

Table 1.1: Selected Characteristics of Public and Private School Teachers, 1996

Teacher Characteristics	Public School Teachers
Sex (percent)	
Male	25.6
Female	74.4
Race/ethnicity (percent)	
White	90.7
Black	7.3
Other	2.0
Average age (years)	44.0
Highest degree (percent)	
Bachelor's	43.6
Master's	54.5
More than master's	1.7
Average years teaching experience	15.0
Average number of students per full-time classroom teacher	
elementary	24.0
secondary	31.0
Average number of hours per week spent on all teaching duties	
elementary teachers	47.0
secondary teachers	52.0

Source: U.S. Department of Education, National Center for Education Statistics. (1997). *Digest of education statistics, 1997.* Washington, DC: U.S. Department of Education.

Table 1.2: Historical Summary of Public Elementary and Secondary School Statistics: United States, 1869–70 to 1996–97

	1869–70	1879–80	1889–90	1899–1900	1909–10	1919–20
Total enrollment (in thousands)	6,872	9,867	12,723	15,503	17,814	21,578
Total instructional staff (in thousands)	—	—	—	—	—	678
Total teachers, librarians, and other nonsupervisory staff (in thousands)	201	287	364	423	523	657
Men	78	123	126	127	110	93
Women	123	164	238	296	413	585

As indicated in the table, the teaching force is predominantly female and white. Less than 10% of the teaching force is minority, down from 13.5% five years earlier. The data also attest to a trend toward greater numbers of teachers attaining higher degrees: 54.5% of teachers held a master's degree in 1996 compared to 42.1% in 1991. And, continuing a trend that began in the 1980s, the average class size of secondary teachers was larger than that of elementary teachers. Secondary teachers also reported spending more hours per week on their teaching duties than elementary teachers.

The number of teachers and other instructional personnel employed in the public school systems of the United States has grown over the years as enrollments have increased. Table 1.2 gives a historical summary of public elementary and secondary school enrollments; number of instructional staff; and number of teachers, librarians, and other nonsupervisory staff. As can be seen, in the years since 1950 the total number of teachers, librarians, and other nonsupervisory staff more than tripled. The growth in staff reflects not only enrollment increases, but the steady reduction in pupil-teacher ratios, legislation requiring increased services and specialized personnel, and the increased utilization of teacher aides, librarians, guidance counselors, and other instructional support personnel.

Why Become a Teacher?

There are many reasons why an individual might choose a career in teaching. Very few teachers would be able to identify a single reason for entering the profession. Many were positively influenced by former teachers. For others an important reason might be a practical consideration such as job security, or something as forthright as the fact that their first career choices were blocked (i.e., they didn't

Table 1.2: Historical Summary of Public Elementary and Secondary School Statistics: United States, 1869–70 to 1996–97 *(continued)*

1929–30	1939–40	1949–50	1959–60	1969–70	1979–80	1989–90	1996–97
25,678	25,434	25,112	36,087	45,550	41,651	40,543	45,251
880	912	963	1,457	2,286	2,406	2,986	3,008
843	875	920	1,393	2,195	2,300	2,860	2,842
140	195	196	404	711	782	—	—
703	681	724	989	1,484	1,518	—	—

Source: U.S. Department of Education, National Center for Education Statistics. (1997). *Digest of education statistics,* 1997 (Table 39). Washington, DC: U.S. Government Printing Office; National Education Association. (1997). *Estimates of school statistics.* Washington, DC: Author.

make it into medical school or into professional sports). Others may be attracted by the long summer vacations or a schedule that allows them to spend more time with their families. A less positive reason might be that teaching is a good temporary job while waiting to prepare for or be accepted into another career.

All of the above are indeed motives for becoming a teacher, but they are not the primary motives. Over the years, numerous researchers have asked teachers what attracted them to the profession. The three reasons given most consistently are (1) a caring for and desire to work with young people, (2) a desire to make a contribution to society, and (3) an interest in a certain field and an excitement in sharing it with others.

The reasons one has for becoming a teacher have a significant effect on the ultimate satisfaction one finds in the job. For this reason, Herbert Kohl (1976), elementary school teacher and well-known educator, suggests that prospective teachers question themselves about what they expect to gain from or give to teaching. Several sets of questions suggested by Kohl to guide you in this inquiry are found on page 8.

Satisfactions and Dissatisfactions With Teaching

Just as each individual has his or her motives for becoming a teacher, each individual will find certain aspects of the position satisfying and certain aspects dissatisfying. In fact, it is possible that a particular aspect may be both satisfying and

Do I Want To Be a Teacher?

1. What reasons do you have for wanting to teach? Are they all negative (e.g., because the schools are oppressive, or because you need a job and working as a teacher is more respectable than working as a cab driver or salesperson)? What are the positive reasons for wanting to teach? Is there any pleasure to be gained from teaching? Knowledge? Power?

2. Why do you want to spend so much time with young people? Do you feel more comfortable with children? Have you spent much time with children recently, or are you mostly fantasizing how they would behave? Are you afraid of adults? Intimidated by adult company? Fed up with the competition and coldness of business and the university?

3. What do you want from the children? Do you want them to do well on tests? Learn particular subject matter? Like each other? Like you? How much do you need to have students like you? Are you afraid to criticize them or set limits on their behavior because they might be angry with you? Do you consider yourself one of the kids? Is there any difference in your mind between your role and that of your prospective students?

4. What do you know that you can teach to or share with your students?

5. With what age youngster do you feel the greatest affinity or are you most comfortable with?

6. Do you have any sex-based motives for wanting to work with young people? Do you want to enable them to become the boy or girl you could never be? For example, to free the girls of the image of prettiness and quietness and encourage them to run and fight, mess about with science and get lost in the abstraction of math? Or to encourage boys to write poetry, play with dolls, let their fantasies come out, and not feel abnormal if they enjoy reading, acting, or listening to music?

7. What kind of young people do you want to work with?

8. What kind of school should you teach in?

9. How comfortable would you be teaching in a multiracial or multicultural setting? Do you feel capable of working with a culturally diverse student population?

dissatisfying. Long summer vacations are satisfiers, but the reduced salary is a dissatisfier. Working with children can be both satisfying and frustrating. Although each individual will find his or her own satisfactions and dissatisfactions with teaching, it is of interest to look at what practicing teachers have identified as the satisfactions or attractions of teaching, as well as the dissatisfactions or challenges of teaching. Prospective teachers in particular need to know and prepare for what they will encounter when they enter the classroom.

Understanding the satisfactions and dissatisfactions of teaching is also important for those making policies that affect teachers, since teacher satisfaction has been found to be associated with teacher effectiveness which, in turn, affects student achievement (U.S. Department of Education, 1997b). The good news for those considering entering the teaching profession is that the majority (54%) of those in it rate their job satisfaction as "very high," up 10% from a decade earlier, and only 12% are "very dissatisfied," down from 21% a decade earlier (Louis Harris and Associates, 1995).

What exactly is it that teachers find satisfying and dissatisfying about teaching? We have already mentioned what teachers most often identify as the major satisfactions of teaching: the joy of working with children and the feeling that they are making a difference in the life of a student and in the larger society. Teachers often talk about the sense of accomplishment they feel and the reward it brings when they watch children learn and progress. In a comprehensive Metropolitan Life survey of American teachers, when asked what they liked most about their job, 89% identified such intrinsic rewards as watching a child develop and making a difference in a student's life (Latham, 1998).

Many teachers find the autonomy they exercise in their classroom and the control they have over their own time to be attractions. For others it would be the opportunity to have a lifelong association with their subject field. And for yet others the security of the position and the feeling of comaraderie and cooperation they share with their colleagues are important attractions. Teaching is one of the few professions where competition is virtually nonexistent.

Among the extrinsic factors that have been associated with teacher satisfaction and dissatisfaction are salary, level of support from parents and administrators, availability of resources, degree of student misbehavior, and school safety (U.S. Department of Education, 1997b). And, while very few teachers are motivated by salary to enter teaching, salary can influence teachers' level of satisfaction or dissatisfaction in the position, as well as their desire to remain in or leave teaching.

Teachers are no different from other professionals in wanting to have input into the decisions that affect them and to have control over their immediate environment. And, while teachers feel they are in the best position to recognize the needs of their students, they often are excluded from participation in the decision-making process regarding their students. Fortunately, an increasing number of districts nationwide are adopting site-based management (see Chapter 13), allowing teachers a greater role in the decisions that affect their professional lives.

Lastly, inadequate resources, the constant bane of teachers, inhibit the ability of teachers to meet the needs of individual students and prepare all students for higher levels of educational attainment or successful participation in the workforce.

Perhaps the ultimate indication of teacher job satisfaction or dissatisfaction is whether, given the opportunity to make the decision again, a person would become a teacher. A U.S. Department of Education (1997b) survey that asked teachers this very question found that 64% of public school teachers said they "certainly" or "probably" would. Only 4% said that if given the opportunity to make the decision to teach again they "certainly would not."

Teacher Preparation

There are a number of ways to become a teacher. The most traditional is to complete a four-year baccalaureate teacher education program. At some institutions, undergraduates majoring in fields other than education are able to accumulate enough teacher education credits to qualify for certification. An extended, or five-year preservice, teacher education program has been implemented at a number of institutions. These programs typically emphasize field experiences, and most award a master's degree upon completion. For the increasing number of individuals who have noneducation college degrees and want to enter the profession, the two options are (1) enrolling as a post-baccalaureate student and taking only enough courses to obtain a teaching certificate, or (2) enrolling in a master's degree program leading to teacher certification. In the next section we will review baccalaureate teacher education programs, the most common avenue into the profession.

Program Characteristics

The formal education of teachers takes place in about 1,200 different departments, schools, or colleges of education in the United States. Teacher education programs usually consist of four areas: (1) general studies, (2) content studies in a major or minor, (3) professional studies, and (4) off-campus clinical and laboratory experiences. The general studies or liberal arts portion of the program, as well as the academic major portion, are generally similar to those required of other students at the college or university. The most recent standards of the National Council for the Accreditation of Teacher Education (NCATE) (1995) call for the general studies to include courses in the arts, communication, history, literature, mathematics, philosophy, sciences, and the social sciences.

Preparation programs for elementary school teachers are somewhat different from those for secondary school teachers. Depending on the organization of the institution, students completing preparation programs for secondary school teachers may have a major in education or a major in the subject field to be taught. The number of hours in the major will usually constitute two thirds of the hours taken in the upper division, with the other third in the professional education sequence. Some variations, though not usually significant, may exist for the preparation of secondary vocational education, physical education, and art teachers (Goodlad, 1994).

How did you determine your preference for elementary or secondary teaching?

Although some institutions require that students preparing to be elementary school teachers have a minor in a content area, elementary education is considered their major. At most institutions it is assumed that students know the content of the elementary school curriculum and need no further instruction in it (Cruickshank and Associates, 1996). Consequently, they commonly take courses that cover both the content thought desirable for teachers to know and the methods for teaching reading, science, math, social studies, language arts, and so on (Goodlad, 1994).

The professional studies component of the teacher preparation program is that specialized body of knowledge and skills required by the profession. This component of teacher education has been the most controversial, and it has been the subject of the greatest criticism in the various reform reports addressing teacher education (Tom, 1997). Since the 1985 report of the National Commission on Excellence in Teacher Education (NCETE), *A Call for Change in Teacher*

Education, the 1986 report *A Nation Prepared: Teachers for the 21st Century* (Carnegie Forum on Education and the Economy), and *Tomorrow's Teachers: A Report of the Holmes Group* (the Holmes Group, 1986), more than three dozen books and reports have been published on teacher education. However, these reports have disagreed over the nature and amount of preservice needed before teachers begin to practice. Today, the typical professional studies component includes courses in the foundational studies in education (e.g., introduction to education, history and philosophy of education, educational psychology and sociology, comparative education, and multicultural education) and the pedagogical studies, which concentrate on teaching and learning theory, general and specialized methods of instruction, and classroom management (Cruickshank and Associates, 1996).

The fourth component of the teacher preparation program, what NCATE labels *integrated studies,* includes on- and off-campus clinical, laboratory, and practicum experiences designed to provide students the opportunity to "relate principles and theories from the conceptual framework(s) to actual practice in classrooms and schools" (NCATE, 1995, p. 7). For most teacher education programs, these experiences include

> *observation,* where preservice teachers observe in K-12 classrooms but do not engage in teaching; part-time *participation,* where engagement in real teaching is limited to trying out selected teaching abilities . . . *apprenticeships,* where preservice teachers learn by practical experience under the guidance of skilled teachers; and finally full-time *practicum* or student teaching, where preservice teachers work in a classroom for an extended period of time and are expected to assume most, if not all, responsibility for teaching. (Cruickshank and Associates, 1996, p. 28)

Student teaching, or the practicum experience, is required for certification in almost every state. The number of weeks required varies in length from six to eighteen ("Teaching Quality," 1997). Typically, the student teacher is assigned to a cooperating teacher selected because of his or her reputation as an "expert" teacher. A college or university professor is assigned to supervise the student teaching experience and makes periodic observations and visitations with the student and the cooperating teacher. During the student teaching experience the student gradually assumes greater responsibility for instruction under the guidance of the cooperating teacher. While the amount of time the student teacher actually spends teaching may vary considerably, in part a function of the demonstrated ability of the student teacher and in part a function of the nature of the classroom, the average student teacher will spend about 60% of his or her time teaching. The remaining time is spent observing, record keeping, and assisting in various classroom activities. The student teaching experience is consistently rated by practicing teachers as the most important part of their preparation program.

Figure 1.1 graphically depicts the typical preparation programs for elementary and secondary teachers and gives the percentage of each program devoted to each area. As indicated, the general studies and student teaching requirements are approximately the same for both programs; they differ in the percentage of

Figure 1.1: Elementary and Secondary Education Program Requirements

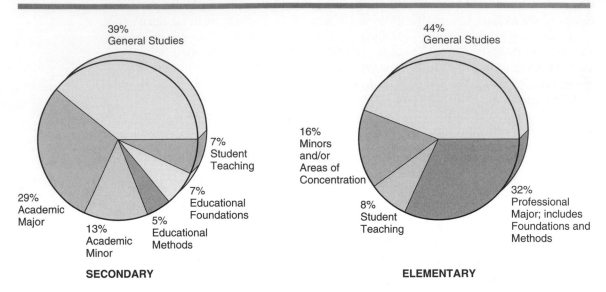

39%
General Studies

7%
Student
Teaching

7%
Educational
Foundations

29%
Academic
Major

5%
Educational
Methods

13%
Academic
Minor

SECONDARY

44%
General Studies

16%
Minors
and/or
Areas of
Concentration

8%
Student
Teaching

32%
Professional
Major; includes
Foundations and
Methods

ELEMENTARY

time spent in professional studies and in other academic studies. Overall, secondary education students average 10 semester hours more to complete their program than elementary majors.

Minority Participation

Minority teachers are needed in the schools for a variety of reasons, perhaps the most important being their presence as role models for all students. Minority children, the majority of whom come from impoverished backgrounds, derive an obvious benefit from seeing minorities in professional positions. But it is also important that all children see minorities in professional roles, rather than overly represented in nonprofessional roles. Otherwise, they will be implicitly taught that majority people are better suited for positions of authority than minorities (Villegas & Clewell, 1998). Yet, one of the major concerns of teacher preparation programs today is that fewer minority students are entering the programs. What once was one of the few professions open to minorities must now compete with all the professions for capable minority students.

The decline in minority enrollments is especially distressing because it has been occurring at the same time that minority enrollments in the public schools have been increasing. It has been predicted that by the year 2020, 50% of the students in our nation's schools will be minorities. Yet, as we have seen, minorities make up only 9% of the current teaching force, a figure that is projected to continue to decline. The need for minority teachers is so intense that officials in some states fear that a child could complete 12 years of schooling without having one minority teacher (Haselkorn & Fideler, 1996).

Practicing teachers rate their student teaching experience as the most important part of their preparation program.

Qualified minorities are not choosing education as a career for a number of reasons. One is that teaching must compete with professions with higher status and salaries for the pool of available talent. Another is the increased testing requirements in many states which disqualify disproportionately larger percentages of minorities. Yet another is the heavy reliance on loans in the financial aid package at many postsecondary institutions, a situation that "deters racial/ethnic minority students from choosing a career in a relatively poorly paid profession such as teaching, since many of these students already have considerable financial responsibilities at home" (Villegas & Clewell, 1998, p. 122).

Strategies for Increasing Diversity

In an attempt to address the critical shortage of minority teachers, educators, and policy makers at the local, state, and national levels have initiated a number of programs aimed at eliminating obstacles to participation and recruitment. Strategies aimed at removing obstacles to participation include increasing scholarship, loan, and loan forgiveness programs; increasing support services and retention

Minority enrollments in the public schools are expected to increase at the same time the percentage of minority teachers is expected to decrease.

How old were you when you first became interested in teaching? How likely would you have been to attend a magnet high school for prospective teachers if one were available in your location?

efforts; and ensuring that testing and evaluation programs minimize the influences of race and ethnicity on entry to the profession.

A number of strategies designed to increase the number of minorities in teaching go beyond traditional recruitment efforts to strategies aimed at increasing the pool of teacher education students. One such strategy involves identifying and encouraging interested students before their senior year in high school. This is done through future educator clubs, "teacher cadet" programs, and even magnet schools that offer a college preparatory program for students interested in becoming teachers (e.g., the High School for the Teaching Professions in Cincinnati, Ohio, and the Austin High School for the Teaching Professions in Houston). Most programs targeting junior or senior high school students are operated by colleges or universities who cooperate with local schools to provide on-campus and in-school experiences for interested students. Such programs often provide financial aid, support services, and in some cases, transferable credits that may be taken while in high school.

An increasingly popular recruitment strategy operated as a joint venture between a college or university and local school districts is the "grow your own" program for paraprofessionals. Under the typical program, teacher aides or other professionals continue in their regular jobs, taking courses in flexible scheduling arrangements after school, on the weekend, and during the summer. Some districts provide time off with pay to attend classes. Tuition is often at a reduced rate or paid for by the district. And, perhaps most important, graduates are guaranteed employment in the district upon successful completion of the program and certification.

Teacher Certification

Successful completion of a teacher training program does not automatically qualify an individual to teach. To become qualified for teaching, administrative, and many other positions in the public schools and many private schools, individuals must acquire a valid certificate or license from the state where they wish to practice. The *certification* or licensure requirement is intended to ensure that the holder has met established state standards and is therefore qualified for employment in the area specified on the certificate. The certification process is administered by the state education agency. The certificate can be obtained in one of two ways: assessment by the state agency of the candidate's transcripts and experiences against a particular set of course and experience requirements, or, more typically, the "approved program approach." In this case, candidates who have graduated from a teacher preparation program approved by the state to prepare teachers are automatically certified upon graduation (Zimpher, 1987). The certificate, when issued, may be good for life, or more commonly, must be renewed every three to five years.

While specific state certification requirements may vary, they typically include a college degree (all states require a bachelor's degree as a minimum), recommendation of a college or employer, minimum credit hours in designated curricular areas, a student teaching experience, evidence of specific job experience, "good moral character," attainment of a minimum age, United States citizenship, the signing of a loyalty oath affirming support of the government, and in recent years, the passing of a state-prescribed competency exam. There has been a recent movement among the states to require a college major in a field other than education in order to be licensed. This has been a response, in part, to the findings of the National Commission on Teaching & America's Future, the National Education Association, and others, on the high number of teachers not licensed in their main assignment fields or teaching in a subject area in which they do not have at least a minor ("State Teachers by the Numbers," 1997).

Competency Testing

The number of states requiring some form of competency testing as a requisite for initial certification has increased dramatically in the past decade and a half, from 13 in 1980 to 44 in 1996 (U.S. Department of Education, 1997a). The increase in the testing of teachers grew out of the reform movement and the debate over the quality of education and the quality of the teaching force. Testing for

*Have you com-
pleted a precerti-
fication exam?
Do you believe
the exam made a
fair estimate of
your knowledge
and skills?*

certification was seen as a necessary accountability measure to ensure that prospective teachers are qualified to enter the classroom. Several states have developed their own competency test for prospective teachers. However, the most commonly used test is the National Teacher Examination (NTE), which is made up of (1) a core battery of tests in general knowledge, communication skills, and professional knowledge; (2) specialty area tests; and (3) a professional skills test. A new and more rigorous version of the NTE called the PRAXIS series is being transitioned into user states as they move to new core battery and specialty area tests. In addition, a new general pedagogy test, Principles of Teaching and Learning (PTL), has been introduced to replace the professional knowledge test.

Alternative Certification Programs

In response to the shortage of qualified teachers in some teaching areas, 36 states have adopted *alternative certification* programs to certify candidates who have subject-matter competence without completion of a formal teacher preparation program (AACTE, 1997). These programs hope to attract to the teaching profession qualified recent college graduates or persons with at least a bachelor's degree from other professions who may voluntarily wish to re-career or who have been the victims of layoffs and downsizing in the private sector or the military. Although many programs were originally intended to address the shortages in math and science, most are open to those with majors in any teaching field.

*If noneducation
graduates can
prepare for
teaching in one
year of study,
why can't educa-
tion graduates
also be prepared
in one year?*

Alternative certification programs may be offered through the hiring school district, a college or university, or a partnership of the two. The typical alternative certification program includes (1) a rigorous selection process to ensure the selection of qualified applicants; (2) preservice training in methodology, classroom management, and human development; and (3) a structured, supervised internship that includes the guidance by a mentor teacher (Duhon-Hayes, Augustus, Duhon-Sells, & Duhon-Ross, 1996). Studies of alternative certification programs have found little difference in command of subject matter between those completing alternative certification programs and those completing traditional teacher education programs. However, an equal number of studies have found that alternatively certified teachers may lack the pedagogical skills that, along with subject matter expertise, are necessary for effective instruction. One positive finding is that alternative certification programs tend to attract more men and minorities than traditional teacher education programs (Bradshaw & Hawk, 1996).

Emergency Certification

Forty-nine states have some provision for granting *emergency* or *temporary certificates* to persons who do not meet the requirements for regular certification when districts cannot employ fully qualified teachers. Emergency certificates are issued with the presumption that the recipient teacher will obtain the credentials or will be replaced by a regularly certified teacher. In every state, before the emergency certificate is granted, the vacancy must be confirmed by the district or state superintendent (AACTE, 1997). While the spread of alternative certification programs has reduced the rate at which emergency certificates are issued, nationwide 50,000 individuals enter teaching each year on emergency or temporary licenses ("Teaching Quality," 1997). In California, more than 29,000 teachers are working with emergency credentials, many with no teacher training or experience (Streisand & Toch, 1998).

Unlike alternative certification, emergency certification does not require any professional education training prior to the assumption of teaching duties and normally does not require the passage of a subject matter test (although some states do require the passage of a basic skills test). Many professional educators question the ethics and safety of hiring untrained persons to teach: What other state-licensed profession would issue "emergency" certificates to untrained persons? However, despite the recognition that this practice must stop if teaching is to become a genuine profession ("Teaching Quality," 1997), given the growing shortage of teachers discussed later in this chapter, is seems unlikely that the practice will be abandoned any time in the foreseeable future.

In your mind, what sort of emergencies could justify issuing teaching certificates to persons who have no training in education?

Recertification

Acquiring certification once does not mean that a teacher is certified for life. One of the reform efforts a number of states have adopted in an attempt to upgrade the quality of the teaching force is to raise the requirements for the recertification of experienced teachers. To obtain recertification a teacher is typically required to earn a specified number of continuing education credits (CEUs), which may be earned by taking approved college courses or by attending workshops, in-service training, or other acceptable activities. In three states (Texas, Arkansas, and Georgia) passage of a competency test is required for recertification.

Interstate Certification

A matter of concern related to state certification for any profession is whether the certification granted by one state will be recognized by another. The increasing mobility of teachers has encouraged state certification authorities to establish *interstate reciprocity,* which allows teachers who are certified in one state to be eligible for certification in another. It is to the advantage of each state to facilitate the employment of qualified educators and to increase the availability of educational personnel, not to establish barriers to employment. To this end, 32 states, the District of Columbia, and the overseas dependents schools have entered into interstate certification agreement contracts to permit certification reciprocity.

National Certification: The National Board
for Professional Teaching Standards

The prospect for some form of national certification has been enhanced by the efforts of the National Board for Professional Teaching Standards (NBPTS) not only to develop professional standards for teaching (discussed in Chapter 2), but also to develop certification in more than 30 fields. The certification fields are

Figure 1.2: National Board for Professional Teaching Standards: Areas of Proposed Certification

<table>
<tr><th></th><th>Early Childhood Ages 3–8</th><th>Middle Childhood Ages 7–12</th><th>Early Adolescence Ages 11–15</th><th>Adolescence and Young Adulthood Ages 14–18+</th></tr>
<tr><td>Generalist</td><td>■</td><td>■</td><td>■</td><td></td></tr>
<tr><td>English Language Arts</td><td></td><td>■</td><td>■</td><td>■</td></tr>
<tr><td>Mathematics</td><td></td><td>■</td><td>■</td><td>■</td></tr>
<tr><td>Science</td><td></td><td>■</td><td>■</td><td>■</td></tr>
<tr><td>Social Studies/History</td><td></td><td>■</td><td colspan="2">■</td></tr>
<tr><td>Art</td><td colspan="2">■</td><td colspan="2">■</td></tr>
<tr><td>Foreign Language</td><td colspan="2">■</td><td colspan="2">■</td></tr>
<tr><td>Guidance Counseling</td><td colspan="2">■</td><td colspan="2">■</td></tr>
<tr><td>Library/Media</td><td colspan="2">■</td><td colspan="2">■</td></tr>
<tr><td>Music</td><td colspan="2">■</td><td colspan="2">■</td></tr>
<tr><td>Physical Education</td><td colspan="2">■</td><td colspan="2">■</td></tr>
<tr><td>Health</td><td colspan="2">■</td><td colspan="2">■</td></tr>
<tr><td>Vocational Education</td><td colspan="2">■</td><td colspan="2">■</td></tr>
<tr><td>English New Language</td><td colspan="2">■</td><td colspan="2">■</td></tr>
<tr><td>Exceptional Needs/Gen</td><td colspan="2">■</td><td colspan="2">■</td></tr>
</table>

Source: © National Board for Professional Teaching Standards. (1998). http://www.nbpts.org/nbts/standards.

structured around student development levels and subject areas (see Figure 1.2). Teachers with three years of teaching experience who hold a state teaching license can start the certification process upon payment of a fee. The process involves preparing a professional portfolio containing videotapes of classroom teaching, samples of student work, and a written commentary, and coming to one of the board's assessment centers for a full day of written exercises and performance assessments. If the candidate is successful, he or she is deemed *board certified,* a term commonly used in other professions. Such certification is not a substitute for state certification or license, but is a public acknowledgment that the teacher possesses not only the requisite knowledge but the demonstrated ability to teach in the areas or levels of certification specified. As noted in Chapter 2, a major incentive for teachers to undertake this process is that a number of states and school districts are offering financial rewards or other incentives to teachers who receive board certification.

How likely are you to seek national board certification?

Teacher Supply and Demand

The increased demand for teachers that began in the mid-1980s is expected to produce a demand for 220,000 new teachers a year between 1998 and 2008. As shown in Table 1.3, the size of the teaching force is expected to increase from 3.1 million in 1998 to 3.5 million in 2008. The projected demand for additional teachers is a result of projected increases in enrollment (see Figure 7.2), as well as the record number of vacancies created by the retirement of the first of the "baby boomers." One third of the teaching force is 48 years of age or older and many are beginning to retire (Barrett, 1998). And, the problem of teacher attrition from retirement is compounded by teacher attrition resulting from career changes. In urban districts, up to one half of new teachers leave within the first five years (Streisand & Toch, 1998).

The continued lowering of pupil-teacher ratios has also contributed to an increased demand for teachers. Pupil-teacher ratios in the public schools have declined from 19.6 at the elementary level and 16.2 at the secondary level in 1983, to 18.6 and 14.5. respectively, in 1996, and are projected to decline to 17.0 and 13.8 by the year 2008 (U.S. Department of Education, 1998).

While the demand for teachers is expected to increase, the projected supply of new teachers is not expected to be sufficient to meet the demand. The supply of newly hired teachers is a function of (1) the number of college graduates entering teaching for the first time, (2) the number of former teachers reentering teaching, and (3) transfers from one state or district to another. In recent years first time teachers have come to represent an even larger percentage (46%) of newly hired public school teachers. However, over the last decade a smaller

Table 1.3: Projections of Total Number of Elementary and Secondary Teachers, by Control of Institution: 1998–2008 (in thousands)

Year	Total			Public			Private		
	K-12	Elementary	Secondary	K-12	Elementary	Secondary	K-12	Elementary	Secondary
1998	52,718	35,006	17,712	46,792	30,418	16,374	5,927	4,588	1,339
1999	53,112	35,227	17,885	47,143	30,612	16,531	5,970	4,616	1,354
2000	53,445	35,396	18,049	47,439	30,756	16,683	6,006	4,640	1,366
2001	53,736	35,513	18,223	47,698	30,852	16,846	6,038	4,661	1,376
2002	53,987	35,495	18,492	47,924	30,824	17,100	6,063	4,671	1,392
2003	54,153	35,408	18,745	48,075	30,737	17,338	6,078	4,671	1,407
2004	54,308	35,215	19,094	48,221	30,566	17,655	6,087	4,648	1,439
2005	54,426	35,025	19,401	48,335	30,405	17,930	6,091	4,620	1,471
2006	54,457	34,877	19,579	48,368	30,281	18,088	6,088	4,597	1,491
2007	54,425	34,797	19,628	48,342	30,213	18,130	6,082	4,584	1,498
2008	54,268	34,775	19,492	48,201	30,196	18,005	6,067	4,579	1,488

Source: U.S. Department of Education, National Center for Education Statistics. (1998). *Projections of education statistics to 2008* (Table 32). Washington, DC: U.S. Department of Education.

percentage of these new hires have come directly from college, while a growing number have come from substitute teaching and from fields other than teaching. Returning teachers make up 23% of the newly hired teachers, while transfers comprise about one third of the new hires (U.S. Department of Education, 1996). One of the major unknown factors in projecting teacher supply and demand is what percentage of these individuals would enter teaching if salaries and working conditions were improved and the status of the profession were enhanced. What is known about the supply of teachers is that it is greatly impacted by the salaries and working conditions of teachers compared to other occupations, as well as the cost of preparing to become a teacher compared to the cost of preparing for other occupations (Murnane, 1995).

While a shortage of teachers is expected nationwide, supply and demand will vary among states, school districts, and disciplines. States in the South and West with growing populations will have a greater demand for teachers. For

Teacher testing for certification has become increasingly rigorous as states adopt various measures aimed at promoting teacher quality.

example, Florida officials anticipate 10,000 public school vacancies per year to the year 2010 (Drummond, 1994). High-poverty and rural districts will also experience teacher shortages and will need to hire 350,000 teachers by the year 2002 (Mellander, 1997). Shortages are also expected in such fields as special education, foreign languages, bilingual education, art, music, physics, mathematics, gifted and talented, and physical sciences.

Salary and Other Compensation

Historically, teachers' salaries have lagged behind not only those of other professionals with comparable training and responsibility, but also those of many of the technical and semiskilled occupations. However, with renewed public interest in the quality of education, teacher compensation has generally improved. Beginning in 1986 teacher salaries increased at a higher rate than inflation. Figure 1.3 depicts the trend in average annual salaries of elementary and secondary teachers since 1970 in constant dollars (adjusted for inflation). As can be seen, over the last several years salaries have decreased slightly in constant dollars. This may be

Figure 1.3: Average Annual Salaries of Public School Teachers (in 1997 constant dollars)

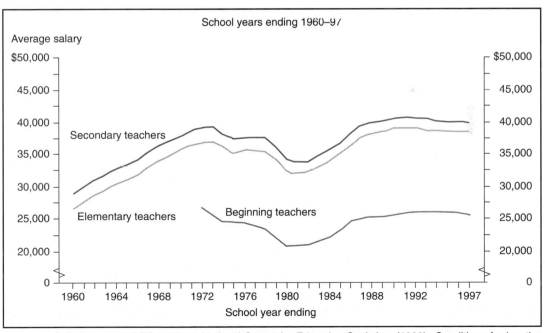

Source: U.S. Department of Educational, National Center for Education Statistics. (1998). *Condition of education 1998.* Washington, DC: U.S. Department of Education.

due to the fact that salaries are losing ground to inflation, or it may be due to the fact that, as National Education Association (NEA) researchers point out, the first wave of baby boomer retirees are being replaced by younger, lower-paid teachers, thereby bringing down the average salary. In 1997 the average teacher salary in the United States was $38,921. Salaries ranged from over $50,000 in Alaska and Connecticut, to under $27,000 in South Dakota (National Education Association, 1998).

The specific salary a teacher will receive depends on a number of factors including supply and demand, union activity, the prevailing wage rate in neighboring districts, and perhaps most importantly, the wealth of the district (or state) as determined by the tax base. School districts with a higher assessed value of property per pupil will typically pay higher salaries than those with lesser assessed value of property per pupil. However, many poor districts, in terms of assessed valuation, have chosen to levy higher tax rates in order to pay competitive salaries.

Salary Schedules[1]

More than 90% of teacher salary schedules across the nation are based on the *single salary schedule* format. The single salary schedule pays equivalent salaries for equivalent preparation and experience. The trend toward the adoption of a single salary schedule for teachers began in the first quarter of the twentieth century, and before the end of the third quarter had come to dominate direct compensation. The position system it replaced based salaries on positions within the school system (elementary teacher, secondary teacher, librarian, counselor, etc.). The single salary schedule has not always been favored by teachers' groups, but it is popular with boards of education because it is easy to understand and to administer.

There are two basic dimensions to the single salary schedule: a *horizontal dimension* made up of columns that correspond to levels of academic preparation (e.g., bachelor's degree, master's degree, master's degree plus 30 hours, doctorate degree), and a *vertical dimension* of rows of "steps" that correspond to the years of teaching experience. There is no standard number of columns or rows in a teacher's salary schedule, although there are usually more rows than columns so that the schedule tends to form a vertical matrix (see Table 1.4).

Initial Placement

The initial vertical placement of a new teacher on a specific vertical step on a scale is determined by several factors, the most common of which is previous teaching experience. To receive credit for any previous years of teaching, the teacher usually must have taught for 75% of the school year. Most school districts place a limit on the number of years of teaching experience credited toward

[1]Discussion of salary schedules is based on Educational Research Service. (1987). *Methods of scheduling salaries for teachers.* Arlington, VA: Educational Research Service.

Table 1.4: Tempe Union School District Teacher Salary Schedule 1998–1999

	BA	BA+18	MA BA+36	MA+15 BA+51*	MA+30	MA+45	MA+60
1	24,259	25,471	26,684	27,897	29,110	30,323	31,536
2	25,350	26,618	27,885	29,153	30,420	31,688	32,955
3	26,442	27,764	29,086	30,408	31,730	33,052	34,375
4	27,533	28,910	30,287	31,664	33,040	34,417	35,794
5	28,625	30,056	31,488	32,919	34,350	35,782	37,213
6	29,717	31,203	32,689	34,174	35,660	37,146	38,632
7	30,808	32,349	33,889	35,430	36,970	38,511	40,051
8	31,900	33,495	35,090	36,685	38,280	39,875	41,470
9	32,992	34,641	36,291	37,941	39,590	41,240	42,889
10	34,083	35,788	37,492	39,196	40,900	42,604	44,309
11	35,175	36,934	38,693	40,451	42,210	43,969	45,728
12	36,267	38,080	39,893	41,707	43,520	45,334	47,147
13	37,358	39,226	41,094	42,962	44,830	46,698	48,566
14	38,450	40,373	42,295	44,218	46,140	48,063	49,985
15	39,542	41,519	43,496	45,473	47,450	49,427	51,404

*Only for specialized Masters programs with approval of Director of Human Resources

Note: A doctoral degree in the individual's area of specialization or in the field of education, which has been granted by an accredited university shall result in an additional increment equal to 4% of the base salary.

Special Note: The Governing Board may present economic awards of excellence to selected staff members for outstanding performance.

Source: Tempe (Arizona) Union High School District No. 213.

initial placement on the salary schedule. Factors that bear on this decision are whether the experience is in or out of the district and in or out of the state.

Other factors that are considered in making the initial placement on the schedule are credit for related experience, credit for military service, and credit for other experience. Some districts recognize related experience such as public library experience for librarians or recreational experience for physical educators. Others grant full or partial credit for military service or for experience in the Peace Corps, VISTA, or the National Teachers Corps.

Advancement

Horizontal advancement across columns in a salary schedule is dependent upon earned academic credit beyond the bachelor's degree. Vertical advancement from one step to the next within the scale is normally automatic after a stipulated period of time, usually one year, although longer periods may be required for advancement to the higher steps. Although teachers' groups have continued to advocate automatic advancement, in an increasing number of districts certain restrictions are being placed on vertical advancement. For example, advancement at specified points may be made contingent on (1) the attainment of additional units of academic credit or completion of in-service training programs or (2) satisfactory performance or merit.

To provide for teachers who have reached the maximum number of steps in a particular scale, some salary schedules also provide for supermaximum or long-term service increments beyond the highest step in the scale. Whereas in most instances the awarding of this increment is based solely on the attainment of a specific number of years' experience above the highest number recognized on the schedule, in some cases a performance or merit evaluation is required before the award is made.

Performance Pay Plans

Teacher performance *incentive pay* plans have been perceived as a strategy that will both attract and retain good teachers and motivate them to greater performance. Incentive pay plans are of two basic types: performance-based programs in which differential pay is awarded to individuals with the same job description on the basis of their performance, and differential staffing programs that in effect pay teachers more for different kinds or amounts of work (e.g., master/mentor teacher plans or career ladder plans). Programs of the latter type are discussed in the following chapter. Discussion here will focus on performance-based plans.

Should performance-based rewards based on student achievement go to individual teachers or the school as a whole?

Performance-based programs may be based on the performance of the individual teacher or the performance of the school as a whole. Merit pay programs are the most common form of the individual performance-based program. While merit pay programs have been around for a long time, the experience of many school districts with merit pay has been more negative than positive. This is no doubt in large part a result of the incentives often being too small to really make a difference, that too few teachers received awards, and that the teaching staff was not involved in the development of the program. As a result of their negative experiences, many school districts abandoned the merit pay programs. In numerous other districts they are operating successfully. The typical plan involves an evaluation conducted by the principal with teacher input into the process. The major arguments for and against merit pay are presented in the Controversial Issue presented on page 25.

School-based performance reward programs provide financial rewards to individual schools that meet certain prescribed standards or outcomes in such areas as student achievement, dropout rates, graduation rates, or absenteeism. Depending on state guidelines awards given to the school meeting the prescribed standard may be used for instructional purposes other than salaries (e.g., South Carolina's Campus Incentive Program), or for salary bonuses to the staff (e.g., Kentucky's Instructional Results Information System).

Compensation for Supplemental Activities

In addition to their base salary, approximately one third of the public school teaching force receives compensation during the school year for supplemental activities such as coaching, student activity sponsorship, or an extra class or

Controversial Issues

Merit Pay

Several reform reports have advocated merit pay for teachers—that part or all of a teacher's pay be based on performance. However, while the public supports the practice, teachers, as a whole, do not support merit pay. The reasons often given in favor of or against merit pay are:

Reasons For

1. Merit pay would reward good teachers and provide the incentive for them to stay in education.
2. The public would be more willing to support the schools if they knew that teachers were paid according to merit.
3. Rewarding performance is consistent with the standard applied to other workers and professions.
4. Teachers would be encouraged to improve their performance and students would be the beneficiaries.

Reasons Against

1. There is little agreement about what is good teaching or how it should be evaluated.
2. Evaluation systems are often subjective and potentially inequitable.
3. Competition creates morale problems for people doing the same job.
4. Research has identified the ingredients of effective teaching, none of which are directly linked to merit pay.

Why do you oppose or favor merit pay? Are you familiar with a school system where merit pay is in operation? What effect has merit pay had on education in that system?

---

evening classes. At one time extracurricular activities were considered normal duties that teachers had to assume as part of their work. In the 1950s, as teacher salaries began to lose ground in a rising economy and as many teachers sought to supplement their incomes by working second jobs, teachers' organizations became more aggressive in seeking additional compensation for time spent in extracurricular activities (Greene, 1971). Now it is common practice for districts to provide supplemental pay for a variety of extracurricular assignments.

Do you have any interest in becoming involved in any extracurricular activities? Which?

The amount of the supplemental pay normally depends on some consideration of the activity involved: the more student contact hours involved, students involved, and equipment and budget involved, the larger the supplement. For example, the supplement for a senior high football coach or band director may be 8–10% of a fixed point on the teachers' salary schedule, while that of the chorus director or cheerleading coach may be 4–5%.

Salaries for Administrative and Support Personnel

Many teachers begin their educational careers in the classroom and then move into administrative or supervisory positions or into positions such as counselor or

Table 1.5: Mean Salaries Paid Personnel in Selected Positions in the Public Schools, 1997–98

Superintendents (Contract Salary)	$101,519
Deputy/Associate Superintendents	90,226
Assistant Superintendents	82,339
Directors, Managers, Coordinators, and Supervisors for:	
Finance and Business	67,724
Instructional Services	73,058
Public Relations/Information	57,224
Staff Personnel Services	71,073
Other Areas	61,161
Subject Area Supervisors	60,359
Other Central-Office Administrative and Professional Staff	50,777
Principals	
Elementary	64,653
Junior High/Middle School	68,740
High School	74,380
Assistant Principals	
Elementary	53,206
Junior High/Middle School	57,768
High School	60,999
Classroom Teachers	40,133
Counselors	46,162
Librarians	44,310
School Nurses	34,619

Source: Educational Research Service. (1998). *Salaries paid professional personnel in public schools, 1997–98,* Part 2. Arlington, VA: Educational Research Service.

librarian. Most of these positions are 10- to 12-month positions and command significantly higher salaries, even on a monthly basis, than classroom teachers. As the data on Table 1.5 indicate, the average salary of superintendents in 1997–98 was $101,519. Superintendents in districts with over 25,000 enrollment often earn a salary of over $125,000 per year. Principals, the administrators closest to the teacher, earn 161% to 185% of the average salary of classroom teachers. However, it must be noted that most administrative and supervisory positions do require higher levels of educational preparation and experience than is required of classroom teachers.

Indirect Compensation: Employee Benefits and Services

Indirect compensation, commonly referred to as fringe benefits, is an important part of any teacher's compensation package and costs the district an average of

Professional Reflections

"To be a teacher is to make your profession your passion. It is a profession where possibilities capture the imagination. It consumes you, commits you to making a difference. In teaching there is no half-way, no motive other than the pursuit of excellence . . . in yourself, in your students."

Maureen Spaight, Teacher of the Year, Rhode Island

". . . teaching is not a job, it's a lifestyle."

Anne Jolly, Teacher of the Year, Alabama

30% of wages. Certain benefits, namely Social Security and worker's compensation, are required by law. Other benefits, including health and hospitalization insurance and long-term disability insurance, are not required by law but are voluntarily provided by the school district. And, almost all school districts provide medical insurance (96%), and 73% provide life insurance (Educational Research Service, 1995).

A third category of benefits includes retirement and savings plans. In most states retirement benefits are financed jointly by teacher and public contributions. In several states, in an attempt to increase compensation but not increase state aid to education, school districts pay the employee's share of retirement as well as the employer's share. This benefit has great appeal to employees because it has a significant impact on net income while not increasing gross taxable income. Consequently, in an increasing number of school districts this provision has become a popular item for negotiation. Also becoming increasingly popular are tax sheltered annuities, which allow employees to invest part of their salaries, before the computation of taxes, in an annuity, allowing employees to not only reduce current taxes, but also supplement any state retirement plans.

Employee services enable the employee to enjoy a better lifestyle or to meet certain personal obligations at a free or reduced cost. Such services include credit unions, employee assistance programs directed at improving employee mental and emotional health, wellness programs, childcare, or subsidized food services.

Rating the Schools and Teaching

Each year the public's perceptions of the schools and issues related to the schools is assessed by the Gallup Poll of the Public's Attitudes Toward the Public Schools. The poll "has become a barometer, closely watched and debated each year by educators and policymakers" (U.S. Department of Education, 1991, p. 82). In 1998, the Gallup Poll results indicated that 46% of the public surveyed gave their local schools grades of A or B, a somewhat higher proportion than the mean of the previous decade. Table 1.6 shows the ratings given to schools in the

Table 1.6: Ratings Given the Public Schools, 1998

Ratings	Nation's Public Schools	Public School Parents	Nonpublic School Parents	Local Public School	Public School of Oldest Child
A&B	18	16	12	46	62
A	1	2	4	10	22
B	17	14	8	36	40
C	49	52	52	31	25
D	15	13	19	9	8
Fail	5	4	7	5	3
Don't know	13	15	10	9	2

Source: Rose, L. C., & Gallup, A. M. (1998). The 30th annual Phi Delta Kappa/Gallup poll of the public's attitudes toward the public schools. *Phi Delta Kappan, 80,* 46–47.

Table 1.7: Public School Students' Ratings of Teachers and Teaching Skills, by Race/Ethnicity: 1996 (in percent)

	Total	School Location			Race/Ethnicity		
		Urban	Suburban	Rural	White	Black	Hispanic
Teacher quality							
Excellent	16	18	17	11	15	19	16
Pretty good	57	51	56	68	62	47	51
Only fair	20	23	20	16	17	25	24
Poor	5	7	5	5	5	6	5
Don't know	1	2	2	0	1	3	4
Teaching skills							
Understanding of subject	77	71	80	83	81	68	73
Helping students who are having trouble with studies	70	67	70	74	72	67	63
Treating students with respect	65	63	63	70	67	59	61
Keeping control and discipline	65	59	66	71	68	59	56
Caring about students' futures	62	60	65	62	63	62	61
Encouraging students' academic interests	58	51	64	59	61	49	47
Making learning interesting	39	41	38	38	38	42	44
Taking an interest in students' home and personal lives	27	26	25	31	26	31	28

Source: Louis Harris and Associates. (1996). *The Metropolitan Life survey of the American teacher part II: Students voice their opinion of their education, teachers and schools.* New York: Metropolitan Life Insurance Co.

nation as a whole, to the local schools, and to the local public school attended by the respondent's oldest child. As was true in every past poll, the more respondents know about the school, the more likely they are to give a higher rating: raters gave local public schools in their communities higher ratings than the schools nationally, and the schools attended by their children were likely to be rated higher than those in the entire community. In addition, parents with children in public schools rate these schools higher than parents with children in private schools rated the public schools.

When students in a national survey were asked to rate the teaching skills of their teachers, the results showed some interesting, and sometimes disturbing, similarities and dissimilarities across racial and ethnic groups. As the data in Table 1.7 indicate, overall, students in rural areas and white students tended to rate their teachers higher than those in urban and suburban areas or black and Hispanic students. The most disturbing finding was that across all groups, less than 40% of students surveyed gave teachers a grade of A or B for their efforts to "make learning interesting for everyone," and only one fourth gave them an above average grade for "taking an interest in students' home and personal lives" (Louis Harris and Associates, 1996).

Summary

There are as many definitions of *teacher* as there are reasons for becoming a teacher. It is important that those considering the profession evaluate their perceptions and expectations of teaching and their motives for considering teaching as their chosen profession.

After a period of serious criticism of the teaching profession and teacher preparation, the status of the profession appears to be improving. And a greater percentage of the practicing teaching force reports being satisfied with teaching as a career. There is still a shortage of minority teachers, but more and more bright and talented individuals are entering the teaching profession, either through traditional baccalaureate programs or through the growing number of alternative certification programs.

As the current demand for teachers intensifies, various proposals for differential compensation have been made in an effort to attract qualified individuals to teaching. The next chapter discusses other efforts to make teaching more attractive by increasing professionalization and reviews other professional opportunities available to teachers.

Key Terms

Alternative certification	Incentive pay
Board certified	Indirect compensation
Certification	Integrated studies
Emergency (temporary) certificate	Interstate reciprocity
Employee services	Single salary schedule

Discussion Questions

1. What is your perception of what a teacher is and does? How is your perception reflected in your responses to the questions following the opening vignette?

2. Was there any single event or experience that motivated you to choose teaching as a career?

3. What are the advantages and disadvantages of teaching as a career? Have you considered teaching as a career? If yes, what motivated you to prepare to become a teacher?

4. What strategies should be used to attract more top-quality students to teaching?

5. Should people be required to complete a teacher training program to become a teacher? Should there be any minimum requirements?

6. The public has increasingly expressed support for the competency testing of teachers. In your opinion, should prospective teachers be required to pass a competency test?

7. The public has also shown increasing support for merit pay for teachers. What are the pros and cons of merit pay? To what extent are financial incentives likely to improve job performance?

Internet Resources

1. See Appendix.

2. **www.nbpts.org**
   The home page for the National Board for Professional Teaching Standards provides information about the board, the standards, what states and local school districts are doing to encourage teachers to seek national certification, and a list of all nationally certified teachers.

3. **www.ets.org**
   The home page for the Educational Testing Service provides information about the Praxis II series as well as financial aid, job search, certification, and more.

4. **www.aacte.org**
   The home page for the American Association of Colleges of Teacher Educa-

tion provides information about AACTE projects and programs, as well as links to other sites related to teaching and teacher education.

5. **www.tc.edu/~teachcomm**
   The home page for the National Commission on Teaching & America's Future is a source of current information on teacher education, licensing, and national certification.

6. **www.cat.uc.edu/class/salisbwa/home.html**
   This is the home page for the High School for the Teaching Profession, an alternative high school in Cincinnati, Ohio.

References

American Association of Colleges of Teacher Education (AACTE). (1997). *Teacher education policy in the states: A 50-state survey of legislative and administrative actions.* Washington, DC: Author.

Barrett, J. (1998, May 27). Demand for teachers reaching crisis point. *Arizona Republic,* p. B3.

Bradshaw, L., & Hawk, P. (1996). *Teacher certification: Does it really make a difference in student achievement?* Greenville, NC: UNCARE.

Carnegie Forum on Education and the Economy. (1986). *A nation prepared: Teachers for the 21st century.* Washington, DC: Carnegie Forum.

Cruickshank, D. R., and Associates. (1996). *Preparing America's teachers.* Bloomington, IN: Phi Delta Kappa Educational Foundation.

Drummond, S. (1994, June 8). Outlook for new teachers in job market rosy. *Education Week,* p. 5.

Duhon-Haynes, G., Augustus, M., Duhon-Sells, R., & Duhon-Ross, A. (1996). Post baccalaureate teacher certification programs: Strategies for enhancement, improvement, and peaceful co-existence with traditional teacher certification programs. (ERIC Document Reproduction Service No. ED 404 334).

Educational Research Service. (1995). *Fringe benefits for teachers in public schools, 1994–95.* Arlington, VA: Author.

Eisner, E. W. (1994). *The educational imagination* (3rd ed.). New York: Macmillan.

Good, C. V. (Ed.). (1973). *The dictionary of education.* New York: McGraw-Hill.

Goodlad, J. I. (1994). *Education renewal: Better teachers, better schools.* San Francisco: Jossey-Bass.

Greene, J. E. (1971). *School personnel administration.* New York: Chilton Book Company.

Harris, L. & Associates, Inc. (1995). *The Metropolitan Life survey of the American teacher 1984–1995.* New York: Metropolitan Life Insurance Co.

Harris, L. & Associates, Inc. (1996). *The Metropolitan Life survey of the American teacher 1996, part II: Students voice their opinions on their education, teachers, and schools.* New York: Metropolitan Life Insurance Co.

Haselkorn, D., & Fideler, E. (1996). *Breaking the glass ceiling: Paraeducator pathways to teaching.* Belmont, MA: Recruiting New Teachers, Inc.

Holmes Group. (1986). *Tomorrow's teachers: A report of the Holmes Group.* East Lansing, MI: Holmes Group.

Kohl, H. R. (1976). *On teaching.* New York: Schocken Books.

Latham, A. S. (1998). Teacher satisfaction. *Educational Leadership, 55*(5), 82–83.

Mellander, G. A. (1997). Tomorrow's teachers. *Hispanic Outlook in Higher Education, 8*(5), 4.

Murnane, R. J. (1995). Supply of teachers. In L. W. Anderson (Ed.), *International encyclopedia of teaching and teacher education* (pp. 72–76). New York: Pergamon.

National Commission on Excellence in Teacher Education. (1985). *A call for change in teacher education.* Washington, DC: AACTE.

National Council for the Accreditation of Teacher Education (NCATE). (1995). *Standards, procedures, and policies for the accreditation of professional education units.* Washington, DC: NCATE.

National Education Association. (1998, May 13). *As teacher salaries fall behind in the United States, NEA expresses concern over ability to hire.* www.nea.org/nr980513.

Rose, L. C., & Gallup, A. M. (1998). The 30th annual Gallup poll of the public's attitudes toward the public schools. *Phi Delta Kappan, 72,* 41–56.

Shafritz, J. M., Koeppe, R. P., & Soper, E. E. (1988). *The facts on file dictionary of education.* New York: Facts on File.

Smith, B. O. (1987). Definitions of teaching. In M. J. Durkin (Ed.), *The international encyclopedia of teacher education.* New York: Pergamon Books.

State teachers by the numbers. (1997, November 21). *Education Week,* p. 19D.

Streisand, B., & Toch, T. (1998, September 14) Many millions of kids and too few teachers. *U.S. News & World Report,* 24–25.

Teaching quality. (1997, November 21). *Education Week,* p. 16D.

Tom, A. R. (1997). *Redesigning teacher education.* Albany: State University of New York Press.

U.S. Department of Education, National Center for Education Statistics. (1991). *The condition of education, 1991.* Washington, DC: U.S. Department of Education.

U.S. Department of Education, National Center for Education Statistics. (1996). *The condition of education, 1996.* Washington, DC: U.S. Department of Education.

U. S. Department of Education, National Center for Education Statistics. (1997a). *Digest of education statistics, 1997.* Washington, DC: U.S. Department of Education.

U.S. Department of Education, National Center for Education Statistics. (1997b). *Job satisfaction among America's teachers: Effects of workplace conditions, background characteristics, and teacher compensation.* Washington, DC: U.S. Department of Education.

U.S. Department of Education, National Center for Education Statistics. (1998). *Projections of education statistics to 2008.* Washington, DC: U.S. Department of Education.

Villegas, A. M., & Clewell, B. C. (1998). Increasing teacher diversity by tapping the paraprofessional pool. *Theory Into Practice, 37,* 121–125.

Zimpher, N. L. (1987). Certification and licensing of teachers. In M. J. Durkin (Ed.), *International encyclopedia of teaching and teacher education.* New York: Pergamon Books.

Chapter 2

A teacher who is attempting to teach without inspiring the child to learn is hammering on a cold iron.

Horace Mann (1796–1859)

Development of the Profession

➤ *Jenna, a new teacher, has been contacted about joining the local teachers' organization and its state and national affiliates. She has also been contacted about joining the local and national organization for her subject area or grade level. Jenna has limited funds and does not feel that she can afford membership in both groups. She is also concerned about the difference between being a "joiner" or being an active contributing member in the organization(s).*

What criteria should guide Jenna's decision about membership? What are the relative benefits of joining the local teachers' organization or the organization for one's subject area or grade level? What responsibilities do you assume when you join a professional organization?

Teaching is a complex and challenging occupation. In an analysis of the complexity of the work and knowledge required of over 60 jobs ranging from fast food worker to surgeon, Rowan (1994) reported that teaching is complex work that requires high levels of general education and specific preparation. These findings are consistent with the current interest in promoting the further professionalization of teaching. However, a *profession* is composed of its individual members, and the extent to which teaching becomes accepted among the professions will be determined by the cumulative commitment and activities of individual teachers. As you read and discuss this chapter and the related activities, consider the following outcome objectives and their impact on you as a potential teacher.

- Evaluate the duties of elementary and secondary school teachers in terms of the recognized criteria for a profession.
- Identify the factors that should be considered in teacher evaluations.
- Analyze the extent to which you feel competent on each of the principles relative to new teacher assessment.

- Identify the programs and services provided by the major teacher organizations in your state and local school districts.
- Describe the programs and services provided by the professional organization for your teaching field.

Teaching as a *Profession*

Is teaching a profession? Many references are made to the profession of teaching, but the actual status of teachers continues to be a matter of discussion and debate. Few would contend that teaching has attained the status of medicine or law, but some might argue that teaching as an occupation compares favorably with the ministry, accounting, engineering, and similar professions.

Elementary and secondary school teaching is one of the most challenging and stimulating occupations, but teachers encounter a wide range of expectations such as the following in their day-to-day work:

- planning activities
- guiding student learning in the classroom
- keeping records
- providing necessary reports
- maintaining adequate information about students
- communicating with parents

Within the past several years, various factors have contributed to an increase in the status of teachers. Some of them are:

1. Standards for teacher education programs have been raised.
2. State licensing requirements have been increased.
3. Additional use has been made of entry-level examinations for teachers.
4. Professional certification programs are being implemented.
5. Teaching has come to be viewed as a career rather than an interim occupation.

Changes like these have increased satisfaction with teaching as a career and have contributed to a growing recognition of teaching as a profession. Teachers today are more likely to be teaching in their field of preparation than they were 35 years ago. A 1996 survey reported that 82.6% of teachers were teaching in grades and subjects that matched their preparation, compared with 68.6% in 1961 (NEA Research, 1997)

What satisfactions do you think you will derive from being a teacher?

Teacher satisfaction with the profession is indicated by the percent in a recent survey who indicated that they would choose teaching again; as shown in Figure 2.1, 62.6% of the respondents indicated that they would choose teaching again. An additional 20% indicated that the chances were about even (NEA Research, 1997). In a recent study, teachers tended to give the nation's schools a higher rating than did teachers in previous studies and believed that the schools in which they were teaching were among the nation's best. They also contended that members of the teaching profession were one of public education's greatest assets and that their colleagues were doing a first-rate job in the classroom (Langdon, 1997).

Figure 2.1: Teacher Satisfaction With Teaching as Measured by Willingness to Teach Again

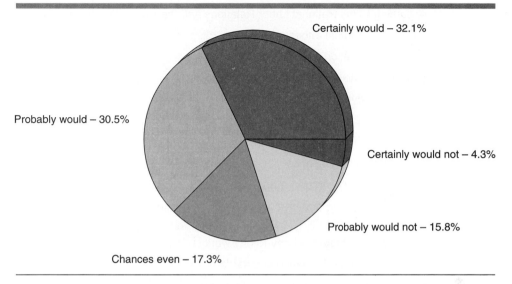

Certainly would – 32.1%

Certainly would not – 4.3%

Probably would not – 15.8%

Chances even – 17.3%

Probably would – 30.5%

Source: NEA Research. (1997). *NEA today: Status of the American public school teacher, 1995–96.* Washington, DC: National Education Association.

Requirements of a Profession

For years, there has been a continuing debate over whether teaching is or is not a profession. References to the teaching profession are heard from lay persons, politicians, and the media; however, those references are only a starting point in the analysis. The term *profession* refers to occupations requiring a high degree of knowledge and skill to perform social functions that are most central to the well-being of society (Hoyle, 1995).

Criteria for classifying an occupation as a profession are presented in Figure 2.2. The summary criteria discussed in this chapter include advanced knowledge and specialized preparation, provision of essential services to society, exercise of discretion, autonomy and freedom from direct supervision, standardized output and performance standards, code of professional standards, and professional organizations.

Advanced Knowledge and Specialized Preparation

Although teaching requires a period of specialized study, policy makers and members of the academic community do not agree on the course of study that produces a teacher or the order in which the courses should be taken. For instance, several education reform reports advocate that professional education courses be delayed until completion of general education and academic major

Figure 2.2: Criteria for Classifying an Occupation as a Profession

According to the National Labor Relations Act, the occupation must:

• Be an intellectual endeavor

• Involve discretion and judgment

• Have an output that cannot be standardized

• Require advanced knowledge

• Require a prolonged period of specialized study

In addition, the American Association of Colleges of Teacher Education calls for:

• Provision of essential services to society

• Decision making in providing services

• Organization into one or more professional societies for the purpose of socialization and promotion of the profession

• Autonomy in the actual day-to-day work

• Agreed-upon performance standards

• Relative freedom from direct supervision

requirements, or even until after completion of the baccalaureate degree. Other reports suggest that college graduates with no professional education courses should be permitted to serve as intern teachers, but with a higher level of supervision than that traditionally provided for beginning teachers.

Many teacher educators believe that a specific body of knowledge can be identified that is necessary and appropriate for the education of teachers. While acquisition of a comprehensive knowledge base is important, it does not provide complete guidance for professional practice. As is the case with other professions, teachers often confront unique problems or situations that do not lend themselves to "formulae" solutions. For this reason, teachers must cultivate the ability to cope with the unexpected and act wisely in the face of uncertainty (National Board of Professional Teaching Standards [NBPTS], 1998). The executive director of the National Commission on Teaching and America's Future has written that teachers need to know:

■ Their subject matter "deeply and flexibly" so that they can not only help students create cognitive maps, relate ideas to one another, and address misconceptions, but also see for themselves how ideas connect across fields and to everyday life.

■ Child and adolescent development and an understanding of how to support growth in various domains—cognitive, social, physical, and emotional.

■ Several kinds of knowledge about learning: what it means to learn different kinds of material for different purposes and how to decide which kinds of learning are most necessary in different contexts; how to use different teaching strategies; how to identify the strengths of different learners; how to work with students who have specific learning disabilities or needs; and how students acquire knowledge.

- About curriculum resources and technologies to connect their students with various sources of information and knowledge.
- How to structure collaboration/interaction among students, how to collaborate with other teachers, and how to work with parents to learn more about their children and to shape supportive experiences at school and at home.
- How to analyze and reflect in practice, to assess the effects of their teaching, and to refine and improve their instruction. (Darling-Hammond, 1998, pp. 7–8)

Provision of Essential Services to Society

There is little doubt concerning the public's perception that teachers provide an essential service to society. The importance of education in a democratic society has always been recognized: "If a nation expects to be ignorant and free in a state of civilization, it expects what never was and never will be." This often-quoted statement by Thomas Jefferson reinforces the importance of education to the preservation of the nation. Teachers play a critical role in the educational process.

Many practicing teachers have indicated that the importance of education was a reason for their selection of teaching as a career. Over two thirds (68.1%) of the respondents in a recent survey indicated that they had chosen teaching because of a desire to work with young people, and 41.8% indicated that they had chosen teaching because of the value of education in society (NEA Research, 1997).

The Exercise of Discretion

Given the relative isolation of individual classrooms and the variety of decisions that a teacher must make during the typical school day, teachers routinely exercise discretion and judgment in providing services to their students. However, teachers are not free agents. They function in an educational environment that is larger than an individual classroom, constrained by school policies and regulations, adopted curriculum guides, and state requirements. Such districtwide concerns as scope and sequence of instruction must be considered. The typical teacher has a group of students for a period of one year, but the educational experiences in that classroom during the year will influence the learning patterns of those students over a period of years. Thus, it would appear that teachers' decisions should be in harmony with the school district's overall plan and policies.

How do the expectations of teachers compare with the potential rewards?

Autonomy and Freedom From Direct Supervision

Teachers have a relatively high degree of autonomy in their actual day-to-day work, and the degree of direct supervision is rather limited. However, when compared with independent, fee-charging professionals, teachers have less autonomy and freedom. Teachers function in the social setting of a school with other teachers. The culture of the school requires a degree of structure and interaction

While much of the instructional role of the teacher is performed in the isolation of the individual classroom, teachers are required to work cooperatively with other educators on the numerous tasks necessary to the successful operation of the school.

among both teachers and students. In addition, parents and taxpayers have an interest in ensuring that teachers act like responsible professionals. Some degree of supervision is necessary to provide the desired assurances.

Standardized Output and Performance Standards

There appears to be near-universal acceptance of the concept of individual differences among students; however, some of the school reforms appeared to assume that the work of teachers can be standardized and uniformly measured and that incentive pay for teachers would improve student performance. The original school reforms in Kentucky and South Carolina included bonuses or rewards for individual teachers; however, these have been repealed because of unintended consequences such as unethical behavior of teachers and a divisive effect on morale in schools. Provisions for teacher bonuses were authorized in the Texas reforms, but were never funded (King & Mathers, 1996; Kohn, 1993).

Code of Professional Standards

An additional criterion that might be used in determining whether teaching meets the criteria of a profession is whether practicing teachers are to assume responsibility for policing their peers and enforcing a code of professional standards. The alternative is for teachers to be monitored or policed by a public agency, typically at the state level. Such bodies usually are referred to as professional practices boards or commissions. Their purpose is to take appropriate disciplinary action against teachers following a review of reports of questionable professional conduct. A number of states have these bodies, which review the professional performance of teachers on a referral basis.

Professional Organizations

Teaching appears to meet this criterion of a profession because of the two national organizations for teachers—the National Education Association and the American Federation of Teachers—and a full range of specialized subject matter organizations. These bodies serve the functions of socialization and promotion of the profession. Questions might be raised, however, about the extent to which these organizations have developed programs to enhance the profession and to transmit and enhance skills and knowledge throughout the teacher's career.

How would you rank teaching on the criteria of a profession?

Unresolved Questions

Previous observations suggest that some questions about the professional status of teachers remain unresolved. Consistent themes in the education reform reports include:

- increased preservice requirements
- higher standards for entrance and continued service
- greater emphasis on career advancements for teachers

Public school teaching differs from other professions in several ways. Typically, a recipient of a professional service may choose which person will provide the service. In contrast, parents or students often have little choice in the assignment of a teacher. An additional criterion is that many of the professions certify the competencies of their members. Teaching appears to be moving in this direction as evidenced by the growing number of teachers receiving national certification as well as the establishment of the Interstate New Teacher Assessment and Support Consortium discussed in Chapter 1. Currently, all states have licensing requirements that serve as minimum standards for teachers, and approximately one fourth of the states have established independent professional standards boards ("Teacher Quality," 1997). However, as discussed in Chapter 1, in all states, temporary or emergency licenses are still issued when teacher shortages develop.

From a different perspective and simply stated, discussions about the professionalism of teaching often center on pay, higher admission standards, quality preparation, continuing education, and good working conditions. Related concerns include adequate supplies and equipment, opportunities to interact with colleagues, and reasonable latitude in making decisions. These changes cannot be achieved immediately, but they can have a significant cumulative effect. Even though each of these is important, they do not define the profession, nor are they the primary motive for the interest in professionalizing teaching. Rather, the major reason for the professionalization of teaching is to increase the probability that students will be well educated (Brandt, 1993; Darling-Hammond & Wise, 1992).

The Professionalization of Teaching

Great strides in the professionalization of teachers have been made in the past several decades. In the first half of this century, many preparation programs for teachers provided initial licensing after successful completion of a few weeks of summer school following high school graduation. As discussed in Chapter 1, current programs typically involve intensive, structured four- and five-year preparation programs that conclude with the awarding of a bachelor's or a master's degree. Other evidence of the increased professionalization of teaching may be found in the increased interest in the development of professional standards, the quality versus quantity dilemma, increased opportunities for professional development, career development, mentoring, and increased interest in self-renewal programs.

Development of Professional Standards

The interest in and acceptance of national standards have been interesting outcomes of the school reform movement; however, each set of standards often is developed in isolation from other standards with limited attention being given to the interactive implications. The National Board for Professional Teaching Standards has developed standards for beginning and experienced teachers; the Interstate New Teacher Assessment and Support Consortium (INTASC) has developed standards for licensing beginning teachers; the National Council for the Accreditation of Teacher Education (NCATE) has developed standards for institutions; states have developed teacher education program approval standards; and content standards have been developed in a variety of disciplines taught in the elementary and secondary schools. The unfinished task is the alignment of the various standards in a meaningful way so that they can be integrated into teacher education programs. The American Association of Colleges of Teacher Education (AACTE), NCATE, and the Association of Teacher Educators (ATE) have taken the leadership in an effort to align standards in teacher education with the content standards and the standards for beginning and experienced teachers (Vaughn, 1998). Figure 2.3 lists the INTASC principles related to the professional expectations of teachers; the focus is on understandings and practices.

Figure 2.3: Interstate New Teacher Assessment and Support Consortium Principles Related to Professional Expectations of Teachers

Principle 1: The teacher understands the central concepts, tools of inquiry, and structures of the discipline(s) he or she teaches and can create learning experiences that make these aspects of subject matter meaningful for students.

Principle 2: The teacher understands how children learn and develop and can provide learning opportunities that support their intellectual, social, and personal development.

Principle 3: The teacher understands how students differ in their approaches to learning and creates instructional opportunities that are adapted to diverse learners.

Principle 4: The teacher understands and uses a variety of instructional strategies to encourage students' development of critical thinking, problem solving, and performance skills.

Principle 5: The teacher uses an understanding of individual and group motivation and behavior to create a learning environment that encourages positive social interaction, active engagement in learning, and self-motivation.

Principle 6: The teacher uses knowledge of effective verbal, nonverbal, and media communication techniques to foster active inquiry, collaboration, and supportive interaction in the classroom.

Principle 7: The teacher plans instruction based upon knowledge of subject matter, students, the community, and curriculum goals.

Principle 8: The teacher understands and uses formal and informal assessment strategies to evaluate and ensure the continuous intellectual and social development of the learner.

Principle 9: The teacher is a reflective practitioner who continually evaluates the effects of his/her choices and actions on others (students, parents, and other professionals in the learning community) and who actively seeks out opportunities to grow professionally.

Principle 10: The teacher fosters relationships with school colleagues, parents, and agencies in the larger community to support students' learning and well-being.

Source: Interstate New Teacher Assessment and Support Consortium. (1998). Interstate New Teacher and Support Consortium principles related to professional expectations of teachers. Washington, DC: American Association of Colleges of Teacher Education.

Quality versus Quantity

As discussed in Chapter 1, various observers of American education have raised questions about the quality and quantity of elementary and secondary school teachers. Issues of quality have been related to the abilities, competencies, and preparation of current and future teachers. Issues of quantity have been related to the relationship between the projected supply of teachers and the estimated vacancies in the schools.

Quality and quantity concerns interact because higher quality requirements, or increased standards for teachers, may affect the quantity of persons eligible to enter teaching or the willingness of current teachers to remain in teaching. One position is that higher standards will shrink the pool of aspirants; an opposite position is that higher standards will contribute to a higher level of prestige for teaching and result in more able college students pursuing teaching as a career.

The quantity concern is further complicated by the unknown effect of teacher stress and *burnout*. As expectations increase, teachers may exhibit some of the early effects of stress and burnout when they develop chronic feelings of emotional exhaustion, withdrawal from students, and a feeling that they are not accomplishing anything worthwhile in their work. As teachers are expected to correct societal ills, instill values, teach basic and higher order thinking skills, prepare students for a global marketplace, and participate in site-based management, stress likely will increase (Schwab, 1995).

Another concern about quality is the relative ability of practicing teachers. No one knows what effect the recent state and national interest in higher standards for schools will have on the continued quality of the teaching staff. The increased standards may contribute to a higher status for teaching, or higher standards may be viewed as an encroachment on the freedom of the teacher. If the former is the case, experienced quality teachers may be more likely to remain in teaching, and higher-quality students may be attracted to teaching. If the higher standards are difficult to attain, some experienced teachers may desert the classroom in favor of other occupations.

Changes in societal and individual perceptions of teaching as a career may also influence the career decisions of a major reservoir of teaching talent not currently in the teaching force. Many concerns about the staffing of schools would be alleviated if the pool of persons who are graduates of teacher education programs, but are not currently teaching, should decide to enter the field. Several factors, such as changes in the nation's economic conditions and employment market, school enrollment increases, and improved working conditions and financial rewards for teachers, could result in an increased demand for teachers and greater interest in teaching as a career (Fox, 1987; Leftwich, 1994).

What advancements in teaching as a profession would encourage you to make teaching a career?

Professional Development

Completion of the teacher preparation program does not mean that a person has mastered all that one needs to know in order to be an effective teacher. In fact, most observers recognize that teachers need to develop professionally by continuing to learn about the process of teaching and their subject areas as long as they are in the profession.

Teachers have an increasing number of avenues for personal and *professional development*. Many choose to join the professional organization most closely related to their teaching field. This membership provides access to professional materials, but the most critical benefit probably will be the contacts with other teachers, offering the possibilities for a professional peer support network. Other methods of growth might include the development of a personal professional library and an independent study program.

An alternative professional development program and a more structured approach is to enroll in an advanced degree program in a college or university. The challenge of this approach is to develop an individualized program and select components that will improve competencies as a teacher, as well as meet degree requirements.

Career Development

Traditional career opportunities in teaching probably were more accurately defined as career opportunities in education. Elementary and secondary school teaching was often viewed as a necessary entry-level experience before one became a school administrator or college professor in the humanities, sciences, or professional education. Changes in teacher salary schedules, teachers' roles, and retirement benefits have improved professional opportunities and rewards. As a result, persons are encouraged to consider elementary and secondary school teaching as a life career.

Career Ladders

Several of the early school reform proposals in the 1980s advocated the creation of a *career ladder* recognition and pay system to recognize the growth and development of beginning teachers into *master teachers*. The sequential series of steps leading to a master teacher status has not garnered broad-based support among either teachers or local school boards. This career ladder concept assumed differences in status titles, pay levels, and lengths of contract for teachers. The progression included beginning, or apprentice, teachers; a second-level professional teacher; a third-level senior teacher; and the fourth level of master teacher. The development of the national certification program offers a more economical and higher status process for recognizing outstanding teachers. In fact, a number of states and school districts are conferring master teacher, "lead teacher," or "mentor teacher" status on teachers certified by the NBPTS (NBPTS, 1998).

Even though support for the career ladder structure has been limited, school districts have involved experienced, outstanding teachers as mentors for beginning teachers and in leadership roles in curriculum development activities. These tasks can be personally and professionally rewarding as well as beneficial to the school and other teachers. Opportunities to participate in professional activities outside the classroom contribute to a sense of professional renewal and permit the school district to recognize the special competencies of these teachers.

Mentoring

The formal and informal relationships that an experienced teacher develops with beginning teachers provide one illustration of professionalization; these relationships often are referred to as peer socialization or *mentoring* (Little, 1993). Such

As a new teacher, what kinds of assistance would you like to receive from a mentor?

interactions can contribute to the growth of the experienced teacher and be invaluable sources of information and support for the beginning teacher. In contrast to other professions in which an entry-level employee often enters as a junior member of a team consisting of persons with a range of experience, the beginning teacher typically is assigned a classroom of students in an elementary school or a series of classes in a secondary school and is expected to assume the same responsibilities as an experienced teacher.

The concept of mentoring usually involves the development of a support relationship between a beginning and an experienced teacher. The mentor provides basic information about the operation of the school, as well as advice, counsel, and support that the beginner may seek when confronted with problems. The goal of such programs is to establish a relationship and an initial professional contact that will develop into a collegial relationship.

Rather than being in isolation, teachers are involved in helping each other, and they view this as a positive experience. When asked what had helped them most as teachers, the most frequent response was cooperative and competent colleagues (NEA Research, 1997). The key to school reform may well be the

Experienced and beginning teachers can work together in a mentoring relationship or a "buddy" system and share experiences to improve student and teacher performance.

development of programs to mentor the mentors. If mentors are to guide, assist, support, and nurture other teachers, they also need mentoring in both process and content (Eckmier & Bunyan, 1995).

Self-Renewal

The routine of teaching is tempered by the excitement of new students arriving each semester or school year. However, the continuing pressures of the classroom and the possibilities of teaching the same grade level or the same subject for several decades can have a depressing effect on even the most enthusiastic person. Traditionally, self-renewal has been viewed as the responsibility of the individual teacher; however, experience suggests that school districts can benefit from the development of joint self-renewal or professional renewal efforts with teachers (McLaughlin, Pfeifer, Swanson-Owens, & Yee, 1986).

Local school districts use a variety of approaches to address the teacher burnout problem. Among the renewal programs available in various school districts across the country are:

- sabbaticals for advanced study
- periodic change of school or teaching assignment
- attendance at workshops or professional conferences
- visitation programs

Another option involves providing teachers with alternative assignments in curriculum or staff development programs. The purpose of such programs is to recognize outstanding teachers by providing them with a break from the classroom while continuing to engage in professionally challenging experiences of benefit to the local school district.

Teacher Evaluation

Teachers are evaluated in a variety of ways. Students, parents, fellow teachers, and administrators have been evaluating teachers since the opening of the first school. Unfortunately, evaluation procedures often have been informal, unsystematic, and based on randomly gathered anecdotal information. For these reasons, considerable progress has been made in identifying the goals of the activity and developing formal teacher evaluation procedures.

The theoretical purpose of any local school district's formal teacher evaluation program is to improve the teaching and learning conditions by improving the overall performance of the teachers in the school district. The two most common evaluation procedures used to accomplish this are:

- systematic gathering and reporting of information about the performance of an individual teacher for the purpose of helping the teacher improve performance
- providing information that can be used in making decisions about retention or dismissal of the teacher

The optimal result of the teacher evaluation program is to help the practicing teacher improve classroom performance.

Any discussion of the evaluation of teachers eventually centers around a series of what, how, and who questions. As illustrated below, these questions vary in their complexity.

What to Evaluate?

Identifying *what* is to be evaluated is the most critical decision in the evaluation process. To the extent possible, this should be a collaborative decision. Common courtesy dictates that the person being evaluated be informed as to the evidence, or information, to be gathered in the evaluation process. Yet this may be the most difficult task in the evaluation process. The challenge is to identify the components of the evaluation and the behaviors and information that are to be observed, secured, and recorded during the evaluation process. A major difficulty is that the "what question" cannot be answered until the observable elements have been identified. The concept of teaching as a profession assumes more than the identification of behaviors or practices indicative of good teaching by school administrators or outside experts. There must also be development of some degree of consensus between the person being evaluated and that person's professional peers.

How to Conduct the Evaluation?

The second task is to ensure that the person being evaluated understands how the evaluation information is to be gathered, including the procedures and criteria to be used. This involves a determination of the types of information to be provided by the teacher, the number of classroom observations, the process for making the assessment, and the methods to be used in informing the teacher as to the relative level of performance.

Another concern in this second task is the process that will be used in making decisions about the content, design, and implementation of the evaluation program. The decision-making process will be influenced by both the strength of the local teachers' organization and the administrative philosophy of the school district. Involvement and participation suggest positive attributes that should contribute to an overall supportive and positive instructional climate in the school district. Confrontation and lack of involvement likely will be further evidenced in a lack of professional respect and communication between teachers and administrators.

Who Does the Evaluation?

The third task is to identify the person(s) *who* will conduct the evaluation. One facet of the "who" task is related to the role of the profession in evaluating its own members—teachers evaluating teachers. A second facet of the who task is the role of the immediate supervisor or building principal in visiting, observing, and communicating with teachers concerning the relative quality of their performance and the steps that should be taken to improve it. A third facet of the who task is the extent to which the evaluation team should include the school district's central office administrators and teachers from both inside and outside the school district.

Currently, the major interests are that evaluations be:

- conducted in a more systematic manner
- based on criteria related to acceptable levels of classroom performance as a teacher
- based on an adequate number of observations

Depending on the procedures, quality of communication, and human relations skills found in a school district, the evaluation system can contribute to either an increase or a decline in teacher morale and performance.

As a new teacher, what would you want to know about the school district's evaluation process?

Teachers as Leaders

Many school reform reports and the resulting school improvement models discussed in Chapter 15 project teachers into various leadership roles in school improvement efforts. The reports and the models call for teachers to assume a more active role in determining the direction of a school's program. There is general agreement that teachers should assume a leadership role in the classroom, but Peterson and Deal (1998) emphasize the important role of teachers as leaders of a school. In contrast to the managerial role of principals, teacher leadership in schools is more collegial and more oriented to how schools ought to be as contrasted to what they are (Urbanski & Nickolaou, 1997). This expanded role for teachers also is consistent with the positions of the major teacher organizations discussed in later portions of this chapter.

In addition to teaching students and providing leadership at the building level, some teachers assume leadership roles to advance their profession and to improve teacher and student learning. Some serve as mentors, peer evaluators, and interveners who assist fellow teachers who need support and coaching. Others work at the district or state level in curriculum development or professional development programs. Some write about teaching and learning and demonstrate innovative teaching practices. Because effective teacher leaders model what needs to be done in the schools, these teachers have a level of credibility that is rarely attained by practitioners (Urbanski & Nickolaou, 1997).

A critical element to the success of the school reform movement is for teachers to become lifelong learners. In this context, teachers should embrace questions, welcome the opportunity to try new ideas, be willing to take risks, and enjoy thinking about ways to improve the educational enterprise. As schools are confronted with conflicting demands for change, the contributions that teachers make as leaders will become more critical (Sipe, 1997). In their various roles, teachers have a variety of opportunities to advance the profession and improve education.

Professional Code of Ethics

Various professions have codes of ethics that serve as standards for behavior of members of the profession. Codes of ethics do not have the status of law, but indicate the aspirations of members of the profession and provide standards by which to judge conduct. In some instances, the professional organization monitors and enforces the *code of ethics* for its membership. In others, a public agency may assume the monitoring and enforcement role. Reporting of noncompliance can come from a variety of sources including professional peers, clients, supervisors, and the public at large.

The ethical considerations of teaching are different from other professions. As noted by the National Board for Professional Teaching Standards:

> Unique demands arise because a client's attendance is compulsory and, more importantly, because the clients are children. Thus, elementary, middle and high school teachers are obligated to meet a stringent ethical standard. Other ethical demands derive from the teacher's role as a model of an educated person. Teaching is a public activity; a teacher works daily in the gaze of his or her students, and the extended nature of their lives together in schools places special obligations on the teacher's behavior. Students learn early to draw and read lessons from their teacher's characters. Teachers, consequently, must conduct themselves in a manner students might emulate. Their failure to practice what they preach does not long elude students, parents or peers. Practicing with this additional dimension in mind calls for a special alertness to the consequences of manner and behavior. Standards for professional teaching ought, therefore, to emphasize its ethical nature. (NBPTS, 1998)

In what ways have societal expectations of teachers changed in recent years?

The NEA has adopted a code of ethics for the education profession. The NEA Code of Ethics, presented in detail in Figure 2.4, contains two sections: commitment to students and commitment to the profession. The student section notes the expectations of fair, equitable, and nondiscriminatory treatment of students. The section on commitment to the profession contains standards of personal conduct in the performance of professional duties and relationships to others.

In an earlier era, codes of conduct for teachers were adopted by local school boards. These codes often were related to personal as well as professional conduct, regulating such things as marital status, style of clothing, and places in the community that were "off limits" to teachers. In those days, failure to abide by the requirements was used as justification for dismissal or other punitive action against the teacher. The requirements of yesteryear are quite different from the current concept of codes of ethics that focus on professional conduct. Responsibility for enforcement now resides with the profession rather than with a local school district's governing body.

Figure 2.4: Code of Ethics of the Education Profession

Preamble

The educator, believing in the worth and dignity of each human being, recognizes the supreme importance of the pursuit of truth, devotion to excellence, and the nurture of democratic principles. Essential to these goals is the protection of freedom to learn and to teach and the guarantee of equal educational opportunity for all. The educator accepts the responsibility to adhere to the highest ethical standards.

The educator recognizes the magnitude of the responsibility inherent in the teaching process. The desire for the respect and confidence of one's colleagues, of students, of parents, and of the members of the community provides the incentive to attain and maintain the highest possible degree of ethical conduct. The *Code of Ethics of the Education Profession* indicates the aspiration of all educators and provides standards by which to judge conduct.

The remedies specified by the NEA and/or its affiliates for the violation of any provision of this *Code* shall be exclusive and no such provision shall be enforceable in any form other than one specifically designated by the NEA or its affiliates.

Principle I: Commitment to the Student

The educator strives to help each student realize his or her potential as a worthy and effective member of society. The educator therefore works to stimulate the spirit of inquiry, the acquisition of knowledge and understanding, and the thoughtful formulation of worthy goals.

In fulfillment of the obligation to the student, the educator–

1. Shall not unreasonably restrain the student from independent action in the pursuit of learning.

2. Shall not unreasonably deny the student access to various points of view.

3. Shall not deliberately suppress or distort subject matter relevant to the student's progress.

4. Shall make reasonable effort to protect the student from conditions harmful to learning or to health and safety.

5. Shall not intentionally expose the student to embarrassment or disparagement.

6. Shall not on the basis of race, color, creed, sex, national origin, marital status, political or religious beliefs, family, social or cultural background, or sexual orientation unfairly–

    a. Exclude any student from participation in any program

    b. Deny benefits to any student

    c. Grant any advantage to any student

7. Shall not use professional relationships with students for private advantages.

8. Shall not disclose information about students obtained in the course of professional service, unless disclosure serves a compelling purpose or is required by law.

Figure 2.4: Code of Ethics of the Education Profession *(continued)*

Principle II: Commitment to the Profession
The education profession is vested by the public with a trust and responsibility requiring the highest ideals of professional service.

In the belief that the quality of the services of the education profession directly influences the nation and its citizens, the educator shall exert every effort to raise professional standards, to promote a climate that encourages the exercise of professional judgement, to achieve conditions which attract persons worthy of the trust to careers in education, and to assist in preventing the practice of the profession by unqualified persons.

In fulfillment of the obligation to the profession, the educator—

1. Shall not in an application for a professional position deliberately make a false statement or fail to disclose a material fact related to competency and qualifications.

2. Shall not misrepresent his/her professional qualifications.

3. Shall not assist any entry into the profession of a person known to be unqualified in respect to character, education, or other relevant attribute.

4. Shall not knowingly make a false statement concerning the qualifications of a candidate for a professional position.

5. Shall not assist a noneducator in the unauthorized practice of teaching.

6. Shall not disclose information about colleagues obtained in the course of professional service unless disclosure serves a compelling professional purpose or is required by law.

7. Shall not knowingly make false or malicious statements about a colleague.

8. Shall not accept any gratuity, gift, or favor that might impair or appear to influence professional decisions or actions.

Source: NEA Handbook, Washington, DC: National Education Association, 1986–87.

Teachers' Organizations

One of the new teacher's initial decisions is the degree of commitment to teaching as a profession. Teachers often find themselves confronted with the choice of which and how many organizations to join. They may affiliate with one of the national teachers' organizations and also with organizations whose focus is on a particular subject or educational specialty. Affiliation is an indication of the commitment to teaching as a profession and as a career. In some districts, there may be only one active teacher organization; in others, the new teacher may have the opportunity to choose among two or more organizations. Not only will there likely be the opportunity to join a local organization, but the teacher will also have the opportunity to join a state and national organization. The dilemma does

Teachers gather at national meetings to share ideas and address national educational issues.

not end with the general organization; specialized local and national subject matter organizations related to the teaching area also exist.

The challenge is to choose carefully among the options and make the choices that will benefit you most as you begin your teaching career. An important consideration may be a person's level of commitment to the organization and its program or the extent to which the person intends to become involved in the organization's activities.

National Teachers' Organizations

In the summer of 1998, observers of the national teachers' organizations anticipated a possible merger of the National Education Association (NEA) and the American Federation of Teachers (AFT) into the United Organization; however, the merger proposal did not receive a simple majority of the NEA voting delegates, much less the two-thirds vote required for passage ("NEA Delegates," 1998). The national leadership of both organizations had prepared the merger proposal and supported the concept. Reasons for the merger proposal included presentation of a united front for teachers and elimination of the need for the human and fiscal resources currently used by the two organizations to compete

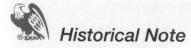

Historical Note

The Birth of Teachers' Unions

In 1857, teachers' organizations from 10 states joined to form the National Teachers Association (NTA). In 1870, the NTA merged with the American Normal School Association and the National Association of School Superintendents to form the National Education Association (NEA). Although the NEA was concerned with broad educational issues, at the beginning it was dominated primarily by college presidents and school superintendents and had no division for classroom teachers. The organization did not concern itself with teacher welfare. Further, the NEA leaders would not have thought that such action was professional. At this point, the NEA was in no sense a labor union.

The first teachers' labor union was the Chicago Teachers Federation (CTF), formed in 1897. In

1902, the CTF affiliated with the Chicago Federation of Labor. This action was condemned by the Chicago school board. The CTF eventually severed the tie when it lost a battle against the school board's arbitrary decision against union membership. Even with this setback, the CTF continued to grow. In New York City, another union, the Interborough Association of Women Teachers, claimed 12,000 members in the early 1900s. This was the largest local teachers' union in the country. Unions also were formed in many other cities as teachers sought to follow the lead of the growing labor union movement and improve their working conditions through organizational representation and membership.

for membership. In addition to the loss of organizational identity, opposition to the merger was based on the traditional linkages between the AFT and the general labor movement. Even though the national merger failed, some state organizations are considering merger, and a few local units are affiliated with both organizations. News reports indicated that the United Organization would have had about 3.2 million members, including the current teacher membership base as well as healthcare providers, education support personnel, and state and local government employees (Archer, 1998a; Archer, 1998b; & Bradley, 1998).

National leadership support in the two organizations for the merger was so strong that both the AFT and the NEA will need some time for reflection as they contemplate maintaining their separate existences. Rather than devoting their resources and energies to competition, the leaders have come to recognize that they must look beyond the immediate interest of their members, become advocates for teaching as a profession and for public education as an essential American institution, and focus on improving the quality of teacher and student performance (Kerchner, Koppich, & Weeres, 1998).

The National Education Association is the larger of the two national teachers' organizations. Formed in 1857 as a professional association, its members are found in all types of school districts. In contrast, the American Federation of Teachers has fewer total members, and its activities are concentrated in the nation's urban areas. The membership of both organizations includes professional educators other than classroom teachers, and some persons hold memberships in both organizations.

The NEA's membership is estimated to be about 2.4 million; the AFT's membership has been estimated at more than 500,000.

For almost 100 years, the NEA was the umbrella organization for higher as well as elementary and secondary educators. (See the Historical Note on p. 54 for a short history of the NEA.) Various teacher specialty and administrator organizations were under the NEA umbrella, and individuals held memberships in the specialty group and the overarching organization. Until the 1960s, leadership roles in the NEA and its state affiliates often were held by school superintendents and higher education personnel. Starting in the 1960s, elementary and secondary school classroom teachers have assumed the leadership roles. The organization's program now focuses more on services to teachers and state and local teacher organizations. The president of the NEA has recently advocated that the NEA press for improvement in teacher education programs, push for higher standards in teacher licensure, and assume greater control of the professional development of teachers (Chase, 1998).

In contrast, teachers always have provided the leadership for the AFT. Although the organization has included building principals among its members, central office administrators have been viewed as district management and considered to be in an adversarial relationship with teachers (Eaton, 1975).

Both the NEA and the AFT provide a variety of professional development activities and services for their members. Publications include national research reports, a journal for members—*Today's Education* (NEA) and *Changing Education* (AFT)—and a variety of handbooks and related documents. Most of these publications are oriented toward improving teacher performance and working conditions, or providing source information about the status of American education. Both organizations conduct annual conferences at the state and national levels and provide a variety of workshop training activities related to either professional or organizational development.

The president of the AFT has called for an increase in teacher effectiveness and has noted that the AFT has been active in efforts to improve teacher education and licensure, provide professional development, and provide peer assistance programs for teachers who are having trouble (Feldman, 1998). Representatives of both the NEA and the AFT served on several of the national school reform commissions. In their participation in the reform reports, the primary goals of both organizations have been to enhance the professional status and working conditions of teachers and create a more positive attitude toward teachers and education.

State Organizations for Teachers

In addition to their national headquarters and national programs, the NEA and the AFT both have units at the state level. The NEA has been more active at the state level; the organization has served as an advocate for teacher tenure and certification statutes, revisions in state school finance programs, federal aid for education, and related educational improvements. The AFT also supports many similar activities, but the general perception has been that the AFT's strength has been concentrated in the organizational units at the local school district level. The current school reform and accountability movements have placed additional stress on both organizations.

Local Organizations for Teachers

The benefits of local organizations are multiple. One benefit is the opportunity to interact with fellow professionals in professional and social activities. Other benefits are related to the collective representation of the teachers in discussions with the school board and administration.

At the school district level, the NEA and the AFT have both encouraged teachers to negotiate salaries and working conditions with local school district administrators and school boards. The AFT has been bargaining virtually since its creation; the NEA started major professional negotiations or collective bargaining initiatives in the 1960s. During the intervening years, in most of the states, teachers have become actively involved in formal and informal negotiations with school boards. In some states, the negotiations are voluntary; in others, school boards are required by state law to enter into a contract with the local teachers' organizations about salaries and working conditions. The result has been an increase in the control and input that teachers have over issues related to their pay and conditions of employment.

Subject Matter Organizations for Teachers

In addition to the general organizations for all teachers, professional organizations have been formed for each discipline. Professional development activities provided by the subject matter organizations typically include a publication program and conferences and workshops for members. These subject matter

Professional Reflections

"Do not teach in isolation. Find a mentor, a friend, or the teacher next door to your class to discuss daily occurrences, good and bad."

"After you have become an experienced teacher, always learn something new each year."

Ginger Brown, Teacher of the Year, California

". . . it is especially important for a teacher to be involved in the community. . . . Service clubs, community clubs, and church groups offer the teacher the opportunity to learn about their community, meet interesting citizens, and even work directly with students' parents. As the community gets to know the teacher, the teacher will find the community not only interested in what is happening in our schools, but also willing to get more involved."

Keith Robinson, Teacher of the Year, Iowa

organizations are independent of the U.S. Department of Education, state educational agencies, and local school districts. They are less prone to be politically active than the two national umbrella organizations for all teachers, but they do influence teachers' positions toward education reform proposals (Little, 1993).

Some specialized organizations such as the Council for Exceptional Children (CEC) include as their members parents and interested citizens as well as professional educators; others, such as the National Conference of Teachers of English (NCTE), the National Council for Teachers of Mathematics (NCTM), the National Council for the Social Studies (NCSS), and the National Science Teachers Association (NSTA), draw their members from teachers at all levels of education. These groups typically do not become involved in direct discussions with school officials about working conditions of teachers; however, they may adopt statements of principles or standards about total teaching load, textbook selection procedures, and selection and use of instructional materials. In this way, the specialized organizations do assume an advocacy role for changes in state or federal legislation related to their teaching area.

Examples of other organizations oriented to specific support roles in the schools include the American Library Association (ALA) and the American Association for Counseling and Development (AACD). A broader-based organization is the Association for Supervision and Curriculum Development (ASCD), which includes teachers, administrators, and college professors. Specialized organizations for school district central office personnel and building principals include the American Association of School Administrators (AASA), the National Association of Secondary School Principals (NASSP), and the National Association of Elementary School Principals (NAESP). With some exceptions, these groups tend to be stronger at the state and national levels. For example, both the National Association of Secondary School Principals and the American Association of School Administrators recently have initiated assessment programs to improve the personal and professional knowledge and skills of administrators.

Teachers' Organizations and Public Policy Issues

Both the NEA and the AFT assume an active role in promoting various federal education programs to improve elementary and secondary education. In addition, most of the subject matter organizations also have representatives who provide advice and counsel to Congress and the U.S. Department of Education on legislation, regulations, and administrative procedures.

The Council for Exceptional Children has had a continuing interest in the passage and implementation of both state and federal legislation related to education of students with disabilities. The National Science Teachers Association and the National Council for Teachers of Mathematics supported federal legislation to improve elementary and secondary school instruction in science and mathematics. Many educational interest groups also were involved in the recent reauthorization of federal elementary and secondary education programs for students with disabilities, educationally disadvantaged students, and at-risk youth.

Summary

One outcome of the school reform movement has been an increased focus on the professionalization of teachers. Professional expectations of teachers have been formulated. Advances also have been made in procedures for evaluating teachers, and local school districts are providing increased opportunities for professional development.

The effect of efforts to reform education on teacher quality and quantity is not known. Higher standards may drive out teachers or may attract more as the reputation of the profession increases. The tradition of teaching being viewed as a stepping stone to careers in administration and higher education is being replaced by teaching being seen as a career in itself. As job rewards and leadership opportunities have increased, other changes in working conditions have made teaching more attractive.

In Chapter 3, you will have the opportunity to reflect on the major philosophies. You will also see their influence on the educational process and profession of today.

Key Terms

Burnout
Career ladder
Code of ethics
Master teacher

Mentoring
Profession
Professional development

Discussion Questions

1. Which professional organization(s) do you plan to join as a new teacher?

2. In what ways does teaching differ from professions such as law, medicine, and accounting?

3. To what extent will you have the knowledge and skills expected of a teacher?

4. What are the provisions for collective bargaining for teachers in your state?

5. What responsibility does the beginning teacher have for continued professional development? What are the professional development requirements for teachers in school districts with which you are familiar?

6. What steps can you take to make your teacher evaluation a positive experience that will help you improve your performance?

7. What steps are taken to monitor the extent to which teachers comply with codes of ethics in school districts with which you are familiar?

8. What reasons might there be for not joining a professional organization?

Internet Resources

1. See Appendix.

2. **www.nea.org**
   The National Education Association home page not only provides detailed information about the NEA, its membership, and programs, but discussion about what's happening in American education and links to other sites where education issues are addressed.

3. **www.aft.org**
   The American Federation of Teachers home page, like the NEA home page, provides not only a range of information about the organization and its programs, but access to various reports and discussions about educational policy issues and links to related sites.

4. **www.nsdc.org**
   The National Staff Development Council home page provides information about NSDC membership, programs, and conferences, as well as links to online resources in staff development.

5. **www.k-12jobs.com**
   The site provides postings for teaching and administrative jobs in education, including salaries, and contract information, as well as links to state certification offices.

6. **www.jobtrack**
   The home page for Jobtrack, one of the largest and most popular career sites, lists job openings for teachers and other educational positions.

References

Archer, J. (1998a, June 24). AFL-CIO label is most ticklish of issues for NEA members deciding union's future. *Education Week,* pp. 16–17.

Archer, J. (1998b, June 24). NEA's Chase travels nation to lobby for a single union. *Education Week,* p. 18.

Bradley, A. (1998, June 24). NEA delegates down to final days to weigh merits of merger with AFT. *Education Week,* pp. 1, 16–19.

Brandt, R. (1993). What do you mean, professional? *Educational Leadership, 50*(6), 5.

Chase, B. (1998). NEA's role: Cultivating teacher professionalism. *Educational Leadership, 55*(5), 18, 20.

Darling-Hammond, L. (1998). Teacher licensing that supports learning. *Educational Leadership, 55*(5), 6–11.

Darling-Hammond, L., & Wise, A. (1992). Teacher professionalism. *Encyclopedia of Educational Research* (pp. 1359–1366). New York: Macmillan.

Eaton, W. E. (1975). *The American Federation of Teachers, 1916–61.* Carbondale, IL: Southern Illinois University Press.

Eckmier, J., & Bunyan, R. (1995). Mentor teachers: Key to educational renewal. *Educational Horizons, 13*(3), 124–129.

Feldman, S. (1998). AFT's role: Bringing vitality to teaching. *Educational Leadership, 55*(5), 19, 20.

Fox, J. N. (1987). The supply of U.S. teachers. In K. Alexander & D. H. Monk (Eds.), *Attracting and compensating America's teachers* (pp. 49–68). Cambridge, MA: Ballinger.

Hoyle, E. (1995). Teachers as professionals. In L. W. Anderson (Ed.), *International Encyclopedia of Teaching and Teacher Education* (pp. 11–15). New York: Pergamon.

Kerchner, C., Koppich, J., & Weeres, J. (1998). New and improved teacher unionism: But will it wash? *Educational Leadership, 55*(5), 21–24.

King, R. A., & Mathers, J. K. (1996). *The promise and rewards of school improvement.* Greeley, CO: University of Northern Colorado.

Kohn, A. (1993). *Punished by rewards: The trouble with gold stars, incentive plans, A's, praise, and other bribes.* Boston: Houghton Mifflin.

Langdon, C. (1997). *The fourth Phi Delta Kappa poll of teachers' attitudes toward the public schools.* Bloomington, IN: Phi Delta Kappa.

Leftwich, K. (1994). Job outlook 2005: Where to find the good jobs. *Vocational Education Journal, 69*(7), 27–29.

Little, J. W. (1993). Teachers' professional development and education reform. *Educational Evaluation and Policy Analysis, 15,* 129–151.

McLaughlin, M. W., Pfeifer, R. S., Swanson-Owens, D., & Yee, S. (1986). Why teachers won't teach. *Phi Delta Kappan, 67,* 420–426.

National Board of Professional Teaching Standards (NBPTS). (1998). http://www.nbpts.org.

NEA delegates vote not to adopt the principles of unity. (1998, July 10). httpl//www.nea.org.

NEA Research. (1997). *Status of the American public school teacher, 1995–96: Highlights.* Washington, DC: National Education Association.

Peterson, K., & Deal, T. (1998). How leaders influence the culture of schools. *Educational Leadership 56*(1), 28–30.

Rowan, B. (1994). Comparing teachers' work with work in other occupations: Notes on the professional status of teaching. *Educational Researcher, 23*(6), 4–17, 21.

Schwab, R. (1995). Teacher stress and burnout. In L. W. Anderson (Ed.), *International Encyclopedia of Teaching and Teacher Education* (pp. 52–57). New York: Pergamon.

Sipe, R. (1997). Meeting the professional development needs of reform leaders. *International Journal of Educational Reform, 6*(2), 147–154.

Teacher Quality (1997, January 22). Quality counts. Supplement to *Education Week,* 40–44.

Urbanski, A., & Nickolaou, M. (1997). Reflections on teachers as leaders. *Educational Policy, 11*(2), 243–254.

Vaughn, J. C. (1998). *Completing the circle of education reform: The need for standards, assessments, and support for teacher education.* Reston, VA: Association of Teacher Educators.

Part Two

Philosophy and Its Impact on the Schools

Chapter 3

The philosophy of the classroom is the philosophy of the government in the next generation.

Abraham Lincoln

The Major Philosophies

➤ *It is late Friday afternoon and classes have been dismissed at John F. Kennedy High School. A few students are left in the chemistry laboratory cleaning equipment and in the visual arts and industrial arts classrooms putting finishing touches on semester projects that are due Monday. The sound of a lonely basketball dribbling in the nearby gymnasium echoes down the corridor. The school seems rather eerie in its stark quietude—a far cry from the loud sounds and activities of an hour before.*

The faculty lounge also is empty except for a group of four teachers in a heated discussion. Ms. Jenkins, who has taught an introductory biology course for the past seven years, appears agitated over the school district's new policy concerning electives. She makes a passionate argument to the rest of her colleagues at the table, alleging that it is a mistake to allow students a choice in determining their own program of study. Her major thesis is that adolescents are not capable of making such choices and if left to their own whims will opt for the easiest, least demanding courses, and will avoid the mathematics, life science, and physical science courses that most colleges and universities require.

Mr. Rhodes, a soft-spoken and gentle individual who has taught courses in anthropology, sociology, and psychology for the past three years, attempts to argue an opposing viewpoint. He directs his comments to the entire group, but his attention is focused primarily on Ms. Jenkins. His counterargument is that adolescents, and even very young children, are capable of decision making. In fact, according to Mr. Rhodes, most individuals, if left on their own, will choose what is good for them and are capable of making quality educational decisions at a very early age.

Do you agree with Ms. Jenkins or Mr. Rhodes? What additional arguments might you give to support your position?

The opposing viewpoints of Ms. Jenkins and Mr. Rhodes are examples of basic philosophic issues. Their different points of view concerning choice reflect their different personal philosophies as well as their philosopies of education.

For many, philosophy connotes a certain type of abstract or theoretical thinking that seems far removed from the day-to-day life of the elementary or secondary classroom teacher. However, every teacher and every classroom reflects a set of assumptions about the world. Those principles or assumptions comprise one's personal philosophy as well as one's educational philosophy. In this chapter, we will outline some of the basic philosophic questions as well as review some of the major traditional (idealism, realism, and neo-Thomism) and contemporary (pragmatism and existentialism) philosophies. Last, we describe the analytic approach to the study of philosophy, along with its application to educational practice.

As you study the philosophies outlined in this chapter, you may begin to question your personal philosophy. To help you better understand the philosophies and where your personal philosophy fits within that framework, consider the following objectives:

- Explain the relationship between general philosophy and the philosophy of education.

- Discuss the three approaches to the study of philosophy.

- Describe the three branches of philosophy.
- Compare the metaphysics of idealism, realism, neo-Thomism, pragmatism, and existentialism.
- Compare the epistemology of idealism, realism, neo-Thomism, pragmatism, and existentialism.
- Compare the axiology of idealism, realism, neo-Thomism, pragmatism, and existentialism.
- Identify the philosophies that take an optimistic view of human nature and those that take a pessimistic view.

- Explain philosophic analysis in education.
- Contrast philosophic analysis with the descriptive study of philosophy.
- Discuss your philosophy of life and how it has changed over time.

What Is Philosophy?

One formal definition of philosophy as a discipline of inquiry states that philosophy is "the rational investigation of the truths and principles of being, knowledge, or conduct" (*Random House Dictionary,* 1986). Perhaps the most simple, yet comprehensive, definition is that philosophy is "love of wisdom and the search for it."

The formal study of philosophy enables us to better understand who we are, why we are here, and where we are going. Whereas our personal philosophy of life enables us to recognize the meaning of our personal existence, our *philosophy of education* enables us to recognize certain educational principles that define our views about the learner, the teacher, and the school. To teach without a firm understanding of one's personal philosophy and philosophy of education would be analogous to painting a portrait without the rudimentary knowledge and skills of basic design, perspective, or human anatomy. Although you may not have thought about your personal philosophy in a formal sense, you certainly have personal beliefs that have shaped your life. After you have studied and discussed this chapter, you should be able to better articulate your personal philosophy of life.

Approaches to the Study of Philosophy

According to Wingo (1974), there are three main approaches to the study of philosophy: (1) descriptive, (2) normative, and (3) analytic. The descriptive approach is concerned with learning about various schools of philosophic thought and how the philosophers associated with these schools created the thought or position. The normative approach is concerned with values. It is not interested in "what is" (which is the goal of descriptive philosophy) but rather, "what ought to be." Using this approach, the philosophic thought is explored and critiqued and determinations are made as to rightness and wrongness. The analytic approach is concerned with an analysis of language, concepts, and theories. The

Table 3.1: **Approaches to the Study of Philosophy**

Approach	Definition	Example
Descriptive	Learning about various schools of philosophic thought.	Idealism stresses the world of the mind and ideas. Realism stresses the world of physical things.
Normative	Learning about values or "what ought to be."	Should birth control information be dispensed in health classes on high school campuses?
Analytic	Learning how to analyze language, concepts, and theories.	Explain the concept of discipline and its application to your philosophy of education.

goal of analytic philosophy is to improve our understanding of education by clarifying our educational concepts, beliefs, arguments, and assumptions. For example, an analytic philosopher of education would attempt to understand questions such as these: What is experience? What is understanding? What is readiness? (See Table 3.1 for further descriptions of these approaches to the study of philosophy.)

Jonas Soltis (1978), a noted philosopher of education, suggested that the descriptive and normative approaches to the study of philosophy can be combined. To Soltis, these approaches represent the traditional view of philosophy as a discipline that seeks an understanding of human life, including the way the world is; the way it ought to be; and what is good, right, and suitable. Similar to Wingo, Soltis described the analytic approach to the study of philosophy as a more contemporary view that seeks a precise language by examining and questioning certain concepts. Also, according to Soltis, the various approaches to philosophy are not mutually exclusive and can be incorporated. The analytic philosopher professes to be "doing" philosophy as opposed to "studying" about philosophy from a descriptive perspective.

In this chapter and the one that follows we incorporate all three approaches to the study of philosophy. The descriptive and normative approaches are utilized in the presentation of the major philosophies in this chapter and the major educational theories in Chapter 4. The analytic approach, with its analysis of selected educational concepts, is also described in the last section of this chapter.

Branches of Philosophy

Although there is much debate and little agreement about which of the schools of philosophy are most accurate, relevant, or even complete, there is general agreement concerning the basic components or branches of philosophy: metaphysics, epistemology, and axiology. These branches are concerned with the answers to the following three basic questions that are important in describing any philosophy:

- What is the nature of reality?
- What is the nature of knowledge?
- What is the nature of values?

The framework these questions provide enables us to study the major schools of philosophy from a descriptive approach. These branches and questions are elaborated upon in the following section and summarized in Figure 3.1.

Metaphysics: What Is the Nature of Reality?

Of the three basic questions, What is the nature of reality? is perhaps the most difficult to answer because its elements are vague, abstract, and not easily identi-

Figure 3.1: Summary of Branches of Philosophy

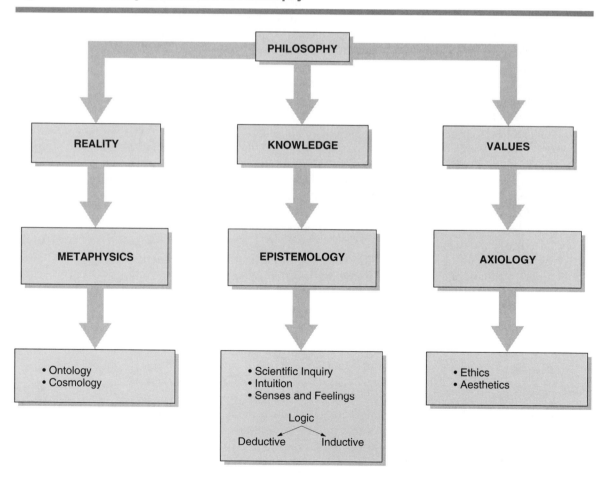

fiable. According to two recognized educational philosophers, Van Cleve Morris and Young Pai (1976),

> Some individuals . . . consider reality a kind of "given" quality or "ground" of the human situation. We are unable to discuss the nature and character of this ground because we can never truly know it; there is nothing against which we can see it.
>
> It is . . . basically irrational or a-rational, possibly even transitional, or beyond the reach of human mentality, and hence not subject to intelligent study. (p. 28)

In spite of its abstraction and vagueness, most philosophers would agree that the study of the nature of reality (meaning of existence) is one of the key concepts in understanding any philosophy.

The branch of philosophy that is concerned with the nature of reality and existence is known as *metaphysics*. Metaphysics is concerned with the question of the nature of the person or self. It addresses such questions as whether human nature is basically good, evil, spiritual, mental, or physical. Metaphysics can be subdivided into the areas of ontology and cosmology.

Ontology raises some fundamental questions about what we mean by the nature of existence and what it means for anything "to be." *Cosmology* raises questions about the origin and organization of the universe, or cosmos.

Should schools concern themselves with questions regarding the origin of the universe? Why or why not?

Epistemology: What Is the Nature of Knowledge?

The branch of philosophy that is concerned with the investigation of the nature of knowledge is known as *epistemology*. To explore the nature of knowledge is to raise questions about the limits of knowledge, the sources of knowledge, the validity of knowledge, the cognitive processes, and how we know. There are several "ways of knowing," including scientific inquiry, intuition, insight, experience, the senses, feelings, trial and error, research, and logic (Eisner, 1985). Logic is a key dimension in the traditional philosophies. Logic is primarily concerned with making inferences, reasoning, or arguing in a rational manner, and includes the subdivisions of deduction and induction. *Deductive logic* involves deducing a concrete application from a general principle. *Inductive logic,* on the other hand, begins with a combination of facts or true examples and from these facts a general principle or rule is formulated. Figure 3.2 further describes these two types of logic.

Axiology: What Is the Nature of Values?

Where epistemology explores the question of knowledge, *axiology,* the study of the nature of values, seeks to determine what is of value. To evaluate, to make a judgment, to value, literally means applying a set of norms or standards to human conduct or beauty. Axiology is divided into two spheres: ethics and aesthetics. *Ethics* is concerned with the study of human conduct and examines moral values—right, wrong, good, or bad. *Aesthetics* is concerned with values in beauty, nature, and the "aesthetic experience." The creative production of beauty is usually associated with music, painting, literature, dance, or the so-called "fine arts."

Figure 3.2: Types of Logic

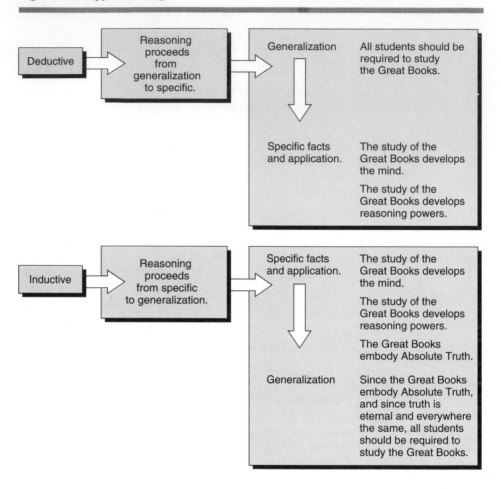

One of the current debates in education centers around the question of whether moral education, character education, ethics, or values education should be a responsibility of the school. The Controversial Issue on page 69 poses arguments for and against the place of moral education, character education, ethics, or values education in the classroom; the Ask Yourself box on page 70 lists a number of questions that are asked by the three branches of philosophy. The questions provide a framework for you to examine and perhaps articulate your own philosophy of life. Your answers to these questions also reflect some of the basic assumptions you hold, which will determine how you view your students and their capacity to learn; how you view the curriculum and its subject matter; how you view the evaluation process; and how you view the general classroom environment. Your philosophy of life and philosophy of education are interdependent and provide a basis for your view of life, as well as your view of teaching.

Controversial Issues

Should Moral Education, Character Education, Ethics, or Values Education Be a Responsibility of the School?

Although axiology or the study of values is a major component or branch of all philosophies, the question of whether moral education, character education, ethics, or values education should be taught in the school remains a controversial issue. The history of American education confirms that the didactic teaching of moral values, including religious values, was once a central feature of the school.

Today, some parents and educators are suggesting that ethical questions and moral dilemmas do indeed have a place in the educational enterprise. Others have expressed strong opinions against the school's role in moral or values education. The arguments, pro and con, concerning moral education, character education, ethics, or values education are:

Arguments For

1. The teaching of values is not a new phenomenon and follows the earlier works of Plato, Aristotle, Dewey, and Piaget who linked values to cognitive development, which has a place in the classroom.

2. A character education curriculum is a powerful tool for teaching basic American values.

3. The discussion of moral dilemmas integrates critical thinking and ethics, which develops moral reasoning skills.

4. The school is the best place for assisting learners to understand their own attitudes, preferences, and values. The role of the school is to help students sort through value confusion so they can live by their values.

5. Students should excel in their core academic subjects. They should also excel in the basic virtues or morals.

Arguments Against

1. The teaching of values is not the purview of the school, but that of the family and church.

2. Too many teachers lecture their students about the importance of certain "appropriate" values without demonstrating those values by their own actions or behaviors.

3. No individual is "valueless," thus all teachers, by the nature of their position, have the potential of imposing their values on their students.

4. The function of the school is to educate, not proselytize or indoctrinate; therefore, moral education, character education, and values education do not belong in the classroom.

What is your view of moral education, character education, or values education?

Idealism

Idealism is considered the oldest philosophy of Western culture, dating back to ancient Greece and the time of Plato. For the idealist, the world of the mind, ideas, and reason is primary.

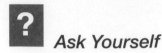

What Is My Philosophy of Life?

Philosophic Questions	Branches of Philosophy
1. Are human beings basically good or is the essential nature of the human being evil?	What is the nature of reality? (Metaphysics—ontology)
2. What causes certain events in the universe to happen?	What is the nature of reality? (Metaphysics—cosmology)
3. What is your relationship to the universe?	What is the nature of reality? (Metaphysics—cosmology)
4. What is your relationship to a higher being (God)?	What is the nature of reality? (Metaphysics—ontology)
5. To what extent is your life basically free?	What is the nature of reality? (Metaphysics—ontology)
6. How is reality determined?	What is the nature of reality? (Metaphysics—ontology)
7. What is your basic purpose in life?	What is the nature of reality? (Metaphysics—ontology)
8. How is knowledge determined?	What is the nature of knowledge? (Epistemology)
9. What is truth?	What is the nature of knowledge? (Epistemology)
10. What are the limits of knowledge?	What is the nature of knowledge? (Epistemology)
11. What is the relationship between cognition and knowledge?	What is the nature of knowledge? (Epistemology)
12. Are there certain moral or ethical values that are universal?	What is the nature of values? (Axiology—ethics)
13. How is beauty determined?	What is the nature of values? (Axiology—aesthetics)
14. What constitutes aesthetic value?	What is the nature of values? (Axiology—aesthetics)
15. Who determines what is right, just, or good?	What is the nature of values? (Axiology–ethics)

Metaphysics

Idealism stresses mind over matter. For the idealist, nothing exists or is real except for an idea in the mind of the person or the mind of God, the Universal Mind. The universe can be explained as a creative and spiritual reality that includes the notions of permanence, order, and certainty. Morris and Pai (1976) suggest that there are two major divisions of reality in the world: apparent reality and real reality.

Apparent reality is made up of day-to-day experiences. "This is the region of change, of coming and going, of being born, growing, aging, and dying; it is the realm of imperfection, irregularity, and disorder; finally, it is the world of troubles and suffering, evil and sin" (Morris & Pai, 1976, p. 47). *Real reality,* on the other hand, is the realm of ideas and is therefore the realm of eternal truths, perfect order, and absolute values. For the idealist, real reality reigns above apparent reality, since real reality embodies perfection and eternal ideas that do not change (Morris & Pai, 1976).

Wingo (1974) summarized how the mind and spirit constitute reality and the perfect order for the idealist.

> One part of the basic thesis of all idealism is that mind is prior; that when we seek what is ultimate in the world, when we push back behind the veil of immediate sense experience, we shall find that what is ultimate in the whole universe is of the nature of mind or spirit (the two words are interchangeable in most discussions of idealism)—just as it is mind that is ultimate in the inner world of personal experience. (p. 95)

If the mind is prior, in the sense that it is ultimate, then material things either do not exist (i.e., are not real), or if they do exist, their existence depends in some fashion on the mind. For example, an idealist would contend that there is no such thing as a chair, there is only the idea of a chair.

The idealist's concept of reality considers the self as one in mind, soul, and spirit. Such a nature is capable of emulating the Absolute or Supreme Mind.

Epistemology

Since idealism accepts a primarily mental explanation for its metaphysics or reality, it is not surprising that idealists also accept the premise that all knowledge includes a mental grasp of ideas and concepts. Inductive and deductive logic are heavily emphasized by idealism. Since the mind is the primary reality, it is important to master the science of logic. Logic provides the framework for unifying our thoughts. While reason, logic, or revelation are primary ways of "knowing" by idealists, especially traditional idealists, modern idealists also accept intuition as a dimension of knowing.

One of the most important considerations of knowledge to the idealist is its relationship to truth. Idealists accept the following propositions concerning knowledge and truth:

1. The universe is rational and orderly and therefore intelligible.
2. There is an objective body of truth that has its origin and existence in the Absolute Mind and that can be known, at least in part, by the human mind.
3. The art of knowing is essentially an act of reconstructing the data of awareness into intelligible ideas and systems of ideas.
4. The criterion for the truth of an idea is coherence; that is, an idea is true when it is consistent with the existing and accepted body of truth. (Wingo, 1974, p. 103)

If you were an idealist, what eternal ideas would you recommend be taught in the schools?

Some idealists believe that it is not necessarily truth that is important, but rather the search for truth that is the ultimate challenge. But they also believe that most of us resort to the lowest level (mere opinions about truth) and never reach what might be considered "Ultimate Truth." However, while we may never grasp all Truth, we have the potential to aspire to wisdom. We can improve on the quality of our ideas and move closer to the Ultimate Truth.

Axiology

Just as the idealists believe that order is an important element of reality, order is also considered a basic principle of values. Furthermore, values can be classified and ordered into a hierarchy or classification system. According to the educational philosopher Marler (1975), intuition is the means by which many idealists discover the presence of values and determine the hierarchy of those values.

Idealists believe that human behavior is intentional and not merely the response to external stimuli. Rather, within the human self is an inherent urge for self-realization, which provides the basic motivation for behavior. Since behavior is intentional, we cannot escape the need to value (or devalue) the things and events that we experience (Wingo, 1974).

To the idealist values are rooted in existence and are part of reality. "We enjoy values not only because our emotions and sentiments are appropriately aroused but because the things we value are realities that have existence themselves and are rooted in the very structure of the cosmos" (Butler, 1966, p. 74).

Values also are absolute. The good, the true, and the beautiful basically do not change from generation to generation, or from society to society. They are not created by man but are part of the very nature and being of the universe (Kneller, 1971). They are, in fact, reflections of the Absolute Good, the Absolute Truth, and the Absolute Beauty-God. Figure 3.3 provides an overview of idealism.

Leading Proponents

The Greek philosopher Plato (427–347 B.C.), the disciple of Socrates, is considered the father of idealism. In his famous "Allegory of the Cave," found in *The Republic* (1958), Plato inferred that each of us lives in a cave of shadows, doubts, and distortions about reality. However, through education and enlightenment, the real world of pure ideas can be substituted for those distorted shadows and doubts.

Judaism and Christianity were both influenced by the philosophy of idealism in different ways. Judeo-Christian teaching suggested that ultimate reality could be found in God through the soul. A prominent theologian of the fourth and fifth centuries, and one who applied a number of Plato's assumptions to Christian thought, was St. Augustine (354–430). Plato's assumptions, as applied by St. Augustine, provided the rationale for the religious idealism that influenced Western thought for centuries (Ozmon & Craver, 1990).

Idealist thought influenced the writings of a number of major philosophers, including René Descartes, Immanuel Kant, and Georg Wilhelm Friedrich Hegel.

Figure 3.3: Idealism at a Glance

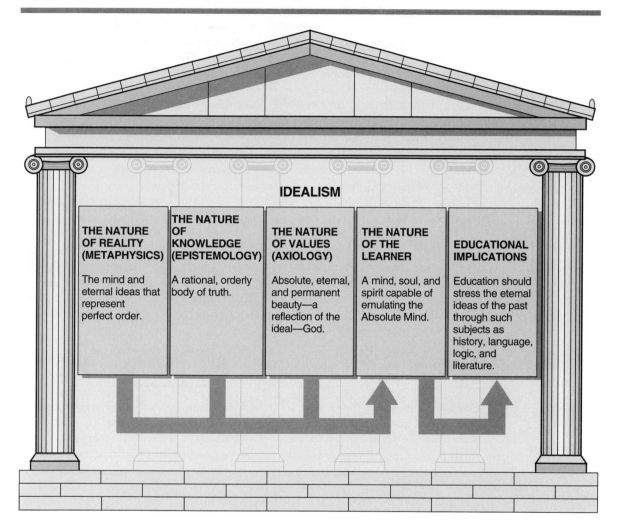

IDEALISM

THE NATURE OF REALITY (METAPHYSICS)

The mind and eternal ideas that represent perfect order.

THE NATURE OF KNOWLEDGE (EPISTEMOLOGY)

A rational, orderly body of truth.

THE NATURE OF VALUES (AXIOLOGY)

Absolute, eternal, and permanent beauty—a reflection of the ideal—God.

THE NATURE OF THE LEARNER

A mind, soul, and spirit capable of emulating the Absolute Mind.

EDUCATIONAL IMPLICATIONS

Education should stress the eternal ideas of the past through such subjects as history, language, logic, and literature.

The French philosopher Descartes (1596–1650), in his famous dictum, "*Cogito, ergo sum*—I think, therefore I am," declared that as humans we may doubt everything, but we cannot doubt our own existence. The concept of existence is further interpreted by Wingo (1974).

> I may succeed in doubting the existence of everything else, one thing is certain: every time I think, I exist. The primary and ultimate fact of my experience is mind and consciousness. It is not my physical body of members and organs that is necessarily real, for it is possible to believe that my body does not exist. The ultimate reality in my experience is my mind. It alone can be known to be real. (p. 95)

Descartes not only accepted the place of the finite mind and ideas as advanced by Plato, but determined that all ideas, save one, depend on other ideas.

The only idea that does not depend on any idea other than itself is the idea of Perfect Being or God. The process used by Descartes, later known as the *Cartesian method,* involved the derivation of axioms upon which theories could be based by the purposeful and progressive elimination of all interpretations of experience except those that are absolutely certain. This method came to influence a number of fields of inquiry, including the sciences (Ozmon & Craver, 1990).

Immanuel Kant (1724–1804), recognized as one of the world's greatest philosophers, also incorporated the major tenets of idealism into his thinking. Kant believed there were certain universal moral laws known as *categorical imperatives* that guide our actions or behaviors. One of Kant's categorical imperatives was "above all things, obedience is an essential feature in the character of a child." This moral maxim has become a primary basis for moral training or character development in education (Ozmon & Craver, 1990).

The German philosopher Hegel (1770–1831) was an idealist who approached reality as a "contest of opposites" such as life and death, love and hate, individual and society. For Hegel, each idea (thesis) had its own opposite (antithesis). The confrontation of the thesis (e.g., man is an end in himself) and antithesis (e.g., man cannot be merely an end to himself—he must also live for others) produces a resolution or synthesis (e.g., man fulfills his true end by serving others). This synthesis becomes a new thesis, which when crossed with a new antithesis forms a new synthesis, and so on (Morris & Pai, 1976).

Can you think of examples of categorical imperatives that might be espoused by Idealists and that would be relevant to education today?

Realism

Realism, like idealism, is one of the oldest philosophies of Western culture, dating back to ancient Greece and the time of Aristotle. Classical or Aristotelian realism is the antithesis of idealism. For the realist, the universe exists whether the human mind perceives it or not. Matter is primary and is considered an independent reality. The world of things is superior to the world of ideas.

Metaphysics

Realism stresses the world of nature or physical things and our experiences and perceptions of those things. Morris and Pai (1976) describe the role of human beings in relation to the world of nature.

> What are human beings, then, say the Realists, but tiny spectators of an enormous machine, the cosmos. They stand before it as fleas before an electronic computer, but with one advantage: intelligence. Gradually, piece by piece, they can come to a wider and fuller understanding of their world. And this is possible because this world, like any machine, is not a haphazard, fortuitous collection of atoms and molecules, but a structure built according to plan and endowed (as is the automobile engine) with predetermined and necessary movements. (p. 54)

For the realist, then, reality is composed of both matter (body) and form (mind). Matter can only "become" (be shaped or organized into being) by the mind. Moreover, the interaction of matter and form is governed not by God but by scientific, natural laws.

As to the nature of self, the realist considers the person a sensing and rational being capable of understanding the world of things. The person, like all matter and form, has evolved from and is subject to nature and its laws.

Epistemology

There are several methods of discovering knowledge that realists perceive to be important. For some realists, the objects of our knowledge are presented directly in consciousness with no intervening mental construct or mental state, and with none needed to account for our knowledge of the external world. That is, we know by direct sensing. For other realists, knowledge is established by the *scientific method,* that is, by the systematic reporting and analysis of what is observed, and the testing of hypotheses formulated from the observations. To these realists, the purpose of inquiry is to discover truth and follow the scientific laws that govern things and events (Wingo, 1974). In essence, a logical, systematic approach to the discovery of knowledge is fundamental to the realist.

Consider yourself a realist. To what extent might you use the scientific method as a basis of inquiry in a beginning music class? In a class of preschoolers?

Axiology

In the axiology of realism, values are derived from nature. In the area of ethics, natural law or moral law are the major determinants of what is good; that which is good is dependent on leading a virtuous life, one in keeping with these natural or moral laws.

Although realism does not adhere to any hard and fast set of rules, realists believe that deviating from moral truth will cause injury both to persons and to society. To protect the common good, certain codes of conduct or social laws have been written and must be followed (Power, 1982).

For the realist, aesthetics is the reflection of nature. What is valued is that which reflects the orderliness and rationality of nature. Figure 3.4 provides an overview of realism.

Leading Proponents

Aristotle (384–322 B.C.), a pupil of Plato, is considered the father of realism. Aristotle disagreed with Plato's premise that only ideas are real. For Aristotle, reality, knowledge, and value exist independent of the mind and their existence is not predicated by our ideas. According to Aristotle, material things have existed since the beginning of time, prior to our knowledge of their existence, and they will continue to exist after we depart (Power, 1982).

Two other representatives of realism were Francis Bacon (1561–1626) and John Locke (1632–1704). Bacon, both a philosopher and a politician, advanced a scientific form of realism that depended on the inductive method of inquiry. Following a similar path, Locke's advocacy of realism stemmed from his study of human knowledge. One of Locke's major notions, the *tabula rasa* concept, has gained wide acceptance. According to this concept there are no such things as innate ideas. We come into the world with a mind like a blank sheet of paper.

Figure 3.4: Realism at a Glance

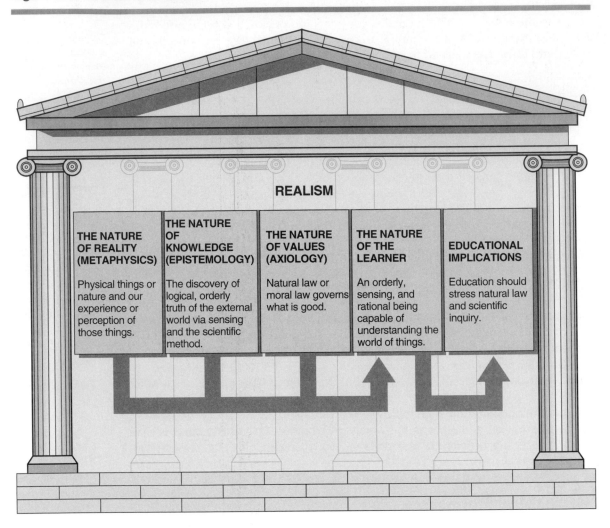

REALISM

THE NATURE OF REALITY (METAPHYSICS)	THE NATURE OF KNOWLEDGE (EPISTEMOLOGY)	THE NATURE OF VALUES (AXIOLOGY)	THE NATURE OF THE LEARNER	EDUCATIONAL IMPLICATIONS
Physical things or nature and our experience or perception of those things.	The discovery of logical, orderly truth of the external world via sensing and the scientific method.	Natural law or moral law governs what is good.	An orderly, sensing, and rational being capable of understanding the world of things.	Education should stress natural law and scientific inquiry.

Knowledge is acquired from sources independent of the mind as a result of sensation and reflection (Ozmon & Craver, 1990).

Other major philosophers who contributed to realism as a scientific inquiry include the English mathematicians and philosophers Alfred North Whitehead (1861–1947) and Bertrand Russell (1872–1970).

Neo-Thomism

The third of the traditional philosophies is *neo-Thomism*. Neo-Thomism, or its antecedent, Thomism, dates to the time of St. Thomas Aquinas (1225–1274) in the

Today's students follow the precepts of Aristotle by formulating, testing, and discovering knowledge through the scientific method.

thirteenth century. Aquinas attempted to bridge the dualism of idealism and realism that had separated philosophic thought up to his time. For the neo-Thomist, God exists and can be known by both faith and reason.

Metaphysics

Neo-Thomists believe that it is God who gives meaning and purpose to the universe. God is the Pure Being that represents the coming together of essence and existence. Things exist independently of ideas; however, both physical objects and human beings, including minds and ideas, are created by God. Thus, while both physical objects and God are real, God is preeminent. Neo-Thomists conceive of the essential nature of human beings as rational beings with souls, modeled after God, the Perfect Being.

Epistemology

Although some philosophers believe that one can come to know God only through faith or intuition, neo-Thomists believe that it is through both faith and our capacity to reason that we come to know God. Aquinas, like Aristotle, perceived that human beings were endowed with the powers of rationality and reason, which set them apart from other animals (Gutek, 1991).

Have you ever attended or known anyone who attended a parochial school? How did that experience compare with attendance at a public institution?

Figure 3.5: Neo-Thomism at a Glance

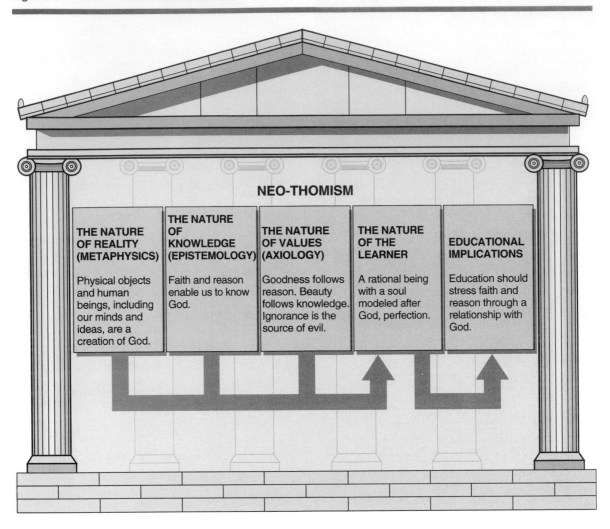

NEO-THOMISM

THE NATURE OF REALITY (METAPHYSICS)

Physical objects and human beings, including our minds and ideas, are a creation of God.

THE NATURE OF KNOWLEDGE (EPISTEMOLOGY)

Faith and reason enable us to know God.

THE NATURE OF VALUES (AXIOLOGY)

Goodness follows reason. Beauty follows knowledge. Ignorance is the source of evil.

THE NATURE OF THE LEARNER

A rational being with a soul modeled after God, perfection.

EDUCATIONAL IMPLICATIONS

Education should stress faith and reason through a relationship with God.

To the neo-Thomist there is a hierarchy of knowing. At the lowest level is scientific or synthetic knowing. At the second level there is analytic or intuitive knowing. And at the highest level there is mystical or revelatory knowing (Morris & Pai, 1976).

Axiology

For the neo-Thomist, ethically speaking, goodness follows reason. That is, values are unchanging moral laws established by God, which can be discerned by reason. As a corollary, ignorance is the source of evil. If people do not know what is right, they cannot be expected to do what is right. If, on the other hand, people do know what is right, they can be held morally responsible for what they do. In terms of aesthetics, the reason, or intellect, is also the perceiver of beauty. That which is valued as beautiful is also found pleasing to the intellect (Morris & Pai, 1976). Figure 3.5 provides an overview of neo-Thomism.

Leading Proponents

Thomas Aquinas, a theologian of the thirteenth century from whom neo-Thomism takes its name, is credited with interfacing the secular ideas of Aristotle and the Christian teachings of St. Augustine. Neo-Thomism is also called *religious realism* and *scholasticism*. Both Aristotle and Aquinas viewed reality via reason and sensation. Aquinas believed God created matter out of nothing and gave meaning and purpose to the universe. In his most noted work, *Summa Theologica,* he used the rational approach suggested by Aristotle to answer various questions regarding existence and Christianity. As a result, many of the supporting arguments of Christian beliefs rely on Thomas Aquinas, and Roman Catholicism considers Thomism its leading philosophy (Ozmon & Craver, 1990).

Pragmatism

Pragmatism, or *experimentalism,* as a philosophy, focuses on the things that work. Primarily viewed as a philosophy of the twentieth century developed by Americans such as John Dewey (see Chapter 7), pragmatism has its roots in British, European, and ancient Greek tradition (Ozmon & Craver, 1990). For the pragmatist, the world of experience is central.

Metaphysics

Unlike the classical or traditional philosophies, which view reality as a thing, metaphysics to the pragmatist is a process rather than a substantive "something." For the pragmatist, reality is an event, a process, a verb (Morris & Pai, 1976). As such, it is subject to constant change and lacks absolutes. Meaning is derived from experience, which is simply an interaction with one's environment (Garrison, 1994).

Epistemology

Since pragmatism's theory of knowledge accepts no truth as absolute, it advocates the idea that truth is determined by function or consequences. In fact, pragmatists shun the use of the word *truth* and at best speak of a "tentative truth" that will serve the purpose until experience evolves a new truth. Knowledge is arrived at by scientific inquiry, testing, questioning, and retesting—and is never conclusive.

Axiology

Where traditional philosophers concentrate primarily on metaphysics and epistemology, the pragmatist focuses primarily on axiology or values. As with truths, values to the pragmatist are only tentative. They are constructed from experience and are subject to testing, questioning, and retesting. For the pragmatist, that which is ethically

The teaching of Dewey is evident in classrooms where children actively participate in projects and social activities.

or morally good is that which works, that which leads to desirable consequences. The focus on consequences is not to imply that the pragmatist is only concerned with what works for the self. In fact, the pragmatist is concerned with social consequences. "What works" is what works for the larger community, not just the self.

Regarding aesthetic values, for pragmatists what is beautiful is not determined by some objective ideal but by what we experience when we see, feel, and touch. Art is a creative expression that reflects consensus. Figure 3.6 presents an overview of pragmatism.

An 80-year-old woman who is dying of cancer has requested assistance from her son, husband, physician, and the Hemlock Society to aid her in the design of her own suicide. How might a pragmatist deal with this ethical dilemma?

Leading Proponents

Although there are a number of British and European philosophers who support the pragmatist philosophy, such as Jean-Jacques Rousseau (see Chapter 5), Auguste Comte (1798–1857), and Charles Darwin (1809–1882), pragmatism has received its major impetus from American philosophers such as Charles Sanders Peirce (1839–1914), William James (1842–1910), and John Dewey (1859–1952).

Peirce believed that true knowledge depends on verification of ideas through experience. Ideas are merely hypotheses until tested by experience. Although Peirce's philosophy was very complicated and included the concepts of the nature of God, immortality, and the self, his premise of verification by experience was the major influence on pragmatism (Ozmon & Craver, 1990). William James

Figure 3.6: Pragmatism at a Glance

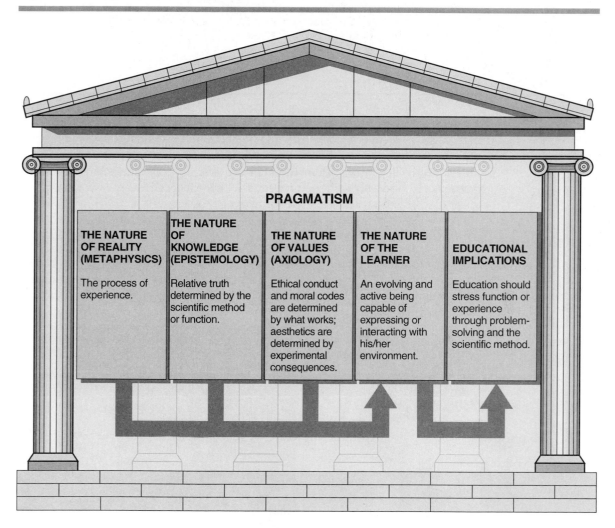

PRAGMATISM

THE NATURE OF REALITY (METAPHYSICS)	THE NATURE OF KNOWLEDGE (EPISTEMOLOGY)	THE NATURE OF VALUES (AXIOLOGY)	THE NATURE OF THE LEARNER	EDUCATIONAL IMPLICATIONS
The process of experience.	Relative truth determined by the scientific method or function.	Ethical conduct and moral codes are determined by what works; aesthetics are determined by experimental consequences.	An evolving and active being capable of expressing or interacting with his/her environment.	Education should stress function or experience through problem-solving and the scientific method.

incorporated his views of pragmatism in both philosophy and psychology. James also emphasized the centrality of experience. To James there were no absolutes, no universals, only an ever-changing universe.

It was James's contemporary, John Dewey, who had the greatest influence on American pragmatism. For Dewey, experience, thought, and consequence were interrelated.

> Thought or reflection, as we have already seen virtually if not explicitly, is the discernment of the relation between what we try to do and what happens in consequence. No experience having a meaning is possible without some element of thought. But we may contrast two types of experience according to the proportion of reflection found in them. All our experiences have a phase of "cut and try" in

them—what psychologists call the method of trial and error. We simply do something, and when it fails, we do something else, and keep on trying until we hit upon something which works, and then we adopt that method as a rule of thumb measure in subsequent procedures. (Dewey, 1916, pp. 169–170)

Existentialism

Existentialism appeared a century ago as a revolt against the mathematical, scientific, and objective philosophies that preceded it. Existentialism voiced disfavor with any effort toward social control or subjugation. Beginning with the work of the Danish philosopher Søren Kierkegaard (1813–1855), existentialism focused on personal and subjective existence. For the existentialist, the world of existence, choice, and responsibility is primary.

Metaphysics

Unlike the realists and neo-Thomists who believe that essence precedes existence, the existentialists believe that existence precedes essence. For the existentialist there is neither meaning nor purpose to the physical universe. We are born into the

The search for meaning, purpose in life, and individual existence continues to challenge contemporary youth as it challenged Kierkegaard in the nineteenth century.

universe by chance. Moreover, according to existentialism, since there is no world order or natural scheme of things into which we are born, we owe nothing to nature but our existence (Kneller, 1971). Existentialists believe that because we live in a world without purpose, we must create our own meaning (Gutek, 1988).

In addition to existence, the concept of choice is central to the metaphysics of existentialism. To decide who and what we are is to decide what reality is. Is it God? Reason? Nature? Science? By our choices we determine reality. According to a leading existentialist, Jean-Paul Sartre (1956), we cannot escape from the responsibility to choose, including the choice of how we view our past.

Epistemology

Similar to their position concerning reality, the existentialists believe that the way we come to know truth is by choice. The individual self must ultimately make the decision as to what is true and how we know. Whether we choose logic, intuition, scientific proof, or revelation is irrelevant; what matters is that we must eventually choose. The freedom to choose carries with it a tremendous burden of responsibility that we cannot escape. Because there are no absolutes, no authorities, and no single or correct way to the truth, the only authority is the authority of the self.

Axiology

For the existentialist, choice is imperative not only for determining reality and knowledge but also for determining value. Van Cleve Morris (1966) explains that concerning values, authenticity and choice are key.

> And who is the authentic? The individual whose example is perhaps beyond the reach of most of us; the individual who is free and who knows it, who knows that every deed and word is a choice and hence an act of value creation, and, finally and perhaps decisively, who knows that he is the author of his own life and must be held personally responsible for the values on behalf of which he has chosen to live it, and that these values can never be justified by referring to something or somebody outside himself. (p. 48)

Whether we are discussing ethics or aesthetics, we cannot escape our freedom to choose or our freedom to value. And here is the dilemma, say the existentialists. Since there are no norms, no standards, and no assurances that we have chosen correctly or rightly, choice is frustrating and exasperating at times. It is often much easier to be able to look to a standard or benchmark to determine what is right, just, or of value than to take responsibility for the choices we have made. Yet this is a very small price we pay for our free will. Figure 3.7 presents an overview of existentialism.

Leading Proponents

The leading proponent, indeed the "father of existentialism," was Søren Kierkegaard. Kierkegaard renounced scientific objectivity for subjectivity and personal choice. He was concerned with individual existence and attacked

Figure 3.7: Existentialism at a Glance

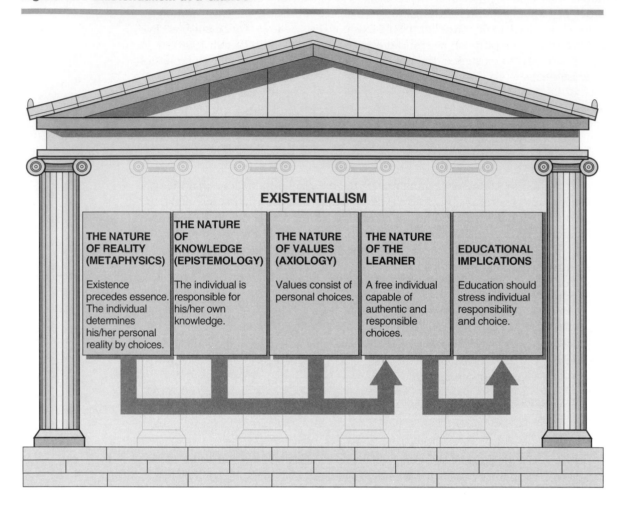

EXISTENTIALISM

THE NATURE OF REALITY (METAPHYSICS)	THE NATURE OF KNOWLEDGE (EPISTEMOLOGY)	THE NATURE OF VALUES (AXIOLOGY)	THE NATURE OF THE LEARNER	EDUCATIONAL IMPLICATIONS
Existence precedes essence. The individual determines his/her personal reality by choices.	The individual is responsible for his/her own knowledge.	Values consist of personal choices.	A free individual capable of authentic and responsible choices.	Education should stress individual responsibility and choice.

Hegelian philosophy on the grounds that it depersonalized the individual. He believed that we must understand our souls and destinies, and that we must take complete responsibility for the choices we make. He also believed in the reality of God (Ozmon & Craver, 1990).

Another nineteenth/twentieth-century expositor of existentialism was Martin Buber (1878–1965). Buber, a Jewish philosopher-theologian, advocated an "I-Thou" relationship whereby each individual recognizes the other's personal meaning and reality. Buber suggested that both the divine and human are related, and by one's personal relationship with the other, one can enhance one's spiritual life and relationship with God. Buber's humanistic existentialist views had a profound impact, not only on philosophy and theology but on psychology, psychiatry, literature, and education (Ozmon & Craver, 1990).

Influenced by the philosophy of Immanuel Kant and Edmund Husserl (1859–1938), who developed a philosophical method called *phenomenology,* or the study of phenomena, Martin Heidegger (1889–1976) expanded and revised phenomenology to another philosophical method known as *hermeneutics,* or the interpretation of lived experience (Ozmon & Craver, 1990). The major thesis of Heidegger's numerous writings was the search for meaning. For Heidegger, metaphysical reality had to include such emotional phenomena as dread, anguish, concern, and sensitivity.

Jean-Paul Sartre's (1905–1980) public appeal exceeded that of Kierkegaard and Heidegger, and many devotees of existentialism considered Sartre the spokesman for the human condition. Sartre claimed that free choice implies total responsibility for one's own existence. There are no antecedent principles or purposes that shape our destiny. Responsibility for our existence extends to situations of the gravest consequence, including the choice to commit suicide (Kneller, 1958). Sartre's major philosophic work, *Being and Nothingness* (1956), is considered one of the major philosophic treatises of the twentieth century. According to Sartre, since there is no God to give existence meaning, humanity exists without any meaning until we construct our own meaning and purpose.

Other proponents of existentialism include Friedrich Nietzsche, Karl Jaspers, and Franz Kafka. The French writers and philosophers Albert Camus (1913–1960), Gabriel Marcel (1889–1973), Maurice Merleau-Ponty (1908–1961); and the philosopher-theologian Paul Tillich (1886–1965); as well as a number of playwrights (e.g., Eugene Ionesco, Samuel Beckett, and Edward Albee) who are also considered spokespersons for the existentialist philosophy.

Analytic Philosophy

As we study the major philosophies and their corollary educational theories, it becomes evident that these descriptive schools of thought, or "isms" as they are often called, are very broad in their aims, are quite eclectic, and at times appear to lack clarity. Critics of the descriptive approach to philosophy point out that the philosophies of idealism, realism, neo-Thomism, and the like have major limitations in that they try to prescribe certain things and make normative judgments. Moreover, they render educational statements that are jargon-ridden and not verifiable. For these reasons a number of philosophers began to move away from traditional thinking about philosophy and theory as disciplines and began to focus their attention on analysis or clarification of the language, concepts, and methods that philosophers use (Ozmon & Craver, 1990; Partelli, 1987). The so-called "analytic movement" that resulted was less concerned with the underlying assumptions about reality, truth, and values addressed by descriptive philosophy than with clarification, definition, and the meaning of language.

One contemporary analytic philosopher is Jonas Soltis. Soltis (1978) pointed out the importance of philosophical analysis for teachers.

> We must be clear about its intent [language of education] and meaning and not be swayed by its imagery and poetry. The analytic temperament and techniques should prove very useful to all practicing educators in getting them to think through with care and precision just what it is they are buying from theorists, and

Professional Reflections

"Define your philosophy of education. Write down what you perceive it to be and then revisit it regularly."

Jacqueline Collier, Teacher of the Year, Ohio

"Everything you learn in college is ideas. Take the risks to go beyond the boundaries of a book. Explore your own ideas or ideas inspired by someone. Find out what does and doesn't work for you . . ."

Michael Soliday, Teacher of the Year, Nevada

more importantly, just what it is they're after and how best that might be achieved. (p. 88)

Analysis in philosophy began in the post–World War I era when a group of European natural scientists and social scientists formed what became known as the Vienna Circle. These scholars were particularly concerned about the alienation between philosophy and science that existed at that time. One of the major outcomes of the work of the Vienna Circle was that it clarified the joint roles of both science and philosophy. For example, it was determined that if the testing of hypotheses through experimentation and observation were to be the purview or charge of science, then the proper role of philosophy should be the analysis of the logical syntax of scientific language (Magee, 1971).

The concept of *logical positivism,* or *logical empiricism,* grew out of the thinking of the Vienna Circle. Logical positivism or logical empiricism suggests that the language of science consists of two types of expressions: logical and empirical. Eventually, the concept of logical positivism became associated with the "principle of verification." This principle asserts that no proposition should be accepted as meaningful unless it can be verified on formal grounds, logical or empirical (Magee, 1971).

One of the most important logical positivists was Ludwig Wittgenstein (1889–1951). Wittgenstein (1953) argued that the role of the sciences should be to discover true propositions and true facts while the role of philosophy should be to resolve confusion and clarify ideas.

The assumptions that were made by logical positivists became so rigid and restrictive that their popularity began to wane. Today, very few individuals identify themselves as logical positivists.

By the 1950s logical positivism shifted to linguistic analysis, or the analytic philosophy movement. A leading spokesperson for this paradigm shift was Israel Scheffler (b. 1923). In his first major work, *The Language of Education* (1960), Scheffler focused attention on how philosophical analysis can help teachers formulate their beliefs, arguments, and assumptions about topics that are particularly important to the teaching and learning process. Scheffler, and later Magee (1971), suggested that one of the best ways for teachers to do this is by answering the types of questions that analytic philosophers pose. Some of these questions might be:

1. What are teaching, learning, and education?
2. What is the meaning of authority in education?
3. What is the relationship between the concept of excellence and the concept of equality in a democratic educational system?
4. What is moral education? (Magee, 1971, p. 42)

How would you answer each of these questions?

Each prospective teacher should learn the art or science of *philosophical analysis*. One of the first steps in learning this process is to raise questions about the assumptions we make, the values we hold, the theories we propose, the procedures we use, and the methods we trust. In short, philosophical analysis confronts the language of education and forces the educator to translate his or her professional expression into parsimonious and meaningful terms. This clarification is important in resolving educational controversies and in explaining educational policies (Gutek, 1988).

Summary

The study of philosophy enables us to better understand our philosophy of life. One of the most effective methods of developing a philosophy of life is to respond to three basic questions: What is the nature of reality? What is the nature of knowledge? What is the nature of values? These three questions and their accompanying responses comprise the branches of philosophy.

The philosophies of idealism, realism, and neo-Thomism are considered the classical or traditional philosophies, while pragmatism and existentialism represent the contemporary or modern philosophies. The traditional philosophies are more concerned with the past, truths, and absolutes, while the contemporary philosophies are more concerned with the present or future and do not subscribe to the idea of "absolute truths."

While the study of descriptive philosophy provides a mechanism for translating basic philosophic tenets into educational practice, it is quite restrictive. Most philosophies are too broad in scope and lack precise meaning and clarity. Today, many philosophers and educators believe that a more effective way to study philosophy is by philosophical analysis, which is concerned with clarifying the language we use to describe our educational concepts and assumptions.

In the next chapter, we will see how these basic philosophic views have led to a number of theories of education. We will also see the impact of these theories on educational programs and practices.

Key Terms

Aesthetics

Apparent reality

Axiology

Cartesian method

Categorical imperatives

Cosmology

Deductive logic	Ontology
Epistemology	Phenomenology
Ethics	Philosophical analysis
Existentialism	Philosophy of education
Hermeneutics	Pragmatism
Idealism	Real reality
Inductive logic	Realism
Logical positivism (logical empiricism)	Religious realism
Metaphysics	Scientific method
Neo-Thomism	Scholasticism

Discussion Questions

1. Consider the vignette at the beginning of this chapter. Which philosophy would you ascribe to Ms. Jenkins? To Mr. Rhodes? Explain.

2. Which of the philosophies discussed in this chapter is most like your own? In what ways? Which is the most unlike your own? In what ways?

3. List all the ways of knowing. Does what is to be known (i.e., the subject matter) dictate the approach to knowing? Explain.

4. How would representatives of each of the philosophies discussed in this chapter respond to the following statement? "Concepts such as understanding, insight, appreciation, and interest have no place in the curriculum since they cannot be observed."

5. Construct an argument using deductive reasoning to explain the following statement: "Teaching does not imply education and education does not imply learning."

6. Which of the major philosophies would be most apt to use the following fundamental principles: justice, freedom, truthfulness, "should" or "ought," and honesty?

7. The metaphor "learning is essentially growing" depicts which philosophy? Name three other metaphors that depict three other major philosophies.

8. Choose three basic educational concepts that are important to most educators. Describe the process you would go through in analyzing the language used to ensure that the meanings of the concepts were clear, concise, and verifiable.

Internet Resources

1. **www.udel.edu/apa/**
   The home page for the American Philosophical Association provides information about the organization and its activities, as well as links to numerous sites dedicated to various philosophers, guides to philosophy, journals, and more.

2. **www.personal.monash.edu.au/~dey/phil**
   Philosophy in Cyberspace has links to literally hundreds of sites dealing with the various branches of philosophy and philosophers.

3. **www.ic.nanzan-u.ac.jp/~kaneko/**
   The Ancient Philosophy home page provides information and resources related to ancient Greek philosophy and related topics.

4. **members.aol.com/jmageema/ index.html**
   The Thomistic Philosophy Page provides an introduction to Thomism with links to articles and related sites.

5. **www3.shore.net/~vanegas/analytic**
   This site provides a forum for those interested in exploring analytic philosophy.

6. **wings.buffalo.edu/philosophy/ ontology**
   This site contains information on ontology and its history and applications.

7. **www.siu.edu/~dewwyctr/**
   The home page for the Center for Dewey Studies houses a wealth of source materials by and about Dewey. Hear Dewey read from his own work.

References

Butler, J. D. (1966). *Idealism in education.* New York: Harper & Row.

Dewey, J. (1916). *Democracy and education: An introduction to the philosophy of education.* New York: Macmillan.

Eisner, E. (Ed.). (1985). *Learning and teaching the ways of knowing: The eighty-fourth yearbook of the National Society for the Study of Education.* Chicago: The University of Chicago Press.

Garrison, J. (1994). Realism, Deweyan, pragmatism, and educational research. *Educational Researcher, 23*(1), 5–14.

Gutek, G. L. (1988). *Education and schooling in America.* Englewood Cliffs, NJ: Prentice-Hall.

Gutek, G. L. (1991). *Cultural foundations of education.* New York: Macmillan.

Kneller, G. F. (1958). *Existentialism and education.* New York: John Wiley & Sons.

Kneller, G. F. (1971). *Introduction to the philosophy of education.* New York: John Wiley & Sons.

Magee, J. B. (1971). *Philosophical analysis in education.* New York: Harper & Row.

Marler, C. D. (1975). *Philosophy and schooling.* Boston: Allyn and Bacon.

Morris, V. C. (1966). *Existentialism in education.* New York: Harper & Row.

Morris, V. C., & Pai, Y. (1976). *Philosophy and the American school.* Boston: Houghton Mifflin.

Ozmon, H. A., & Craver, S. M. (1990). *Philosophical foundations of education.* Columbus, OH: Merrill.

Partelli, J. P. (1987). Analytic philosophy of education: Development and misconceptions. *Journal of Educational Thought, 21*(1), 20–24.

Plato. (1958). *The Republic.* (F. Carnford, Trans.). New York: Oxford University Press.

Power, E. J. (1982). *Philosophy of education: Studies in philosophies, schooling and educational policies.* Englewood Cliffs, NJ: Prentice-Hall.

Sartre, J. P. (1956). *Being and nothingness.* (H. Barnes, Trans.). New York: Philosophical Library.

Scheffler, I. (1960). *The language of education.* Springfield, IL: Charles C. Thomas.

Soltis, J. F. (1978). *An introduction to the analysis of educational concepts.* Reading, MA: Addison-Wesley.

Wingo, G. M. (1974). *Philosophies of education: An introduction.* Lexington, MA: D. C. Heath.

Wittgenstein, L. (1953). *Philosophical investigations.* New York: Macmillan.

Chapter 4

The roots of education are bitter, but the fruit is sweet.

Aristotle, 4th century B.C.

The Impact of Educational Theories on Educational Practice

▶ *During a typical microteaching session in a methods class, six prospective teachers had just finished presenting a 20-minute lesson in their subject field using the instructional technique of their choice. What was surprising to the instructor was that no two students had used the same technique.*

Jim, a physical education major, had chosen demonstration as the major technique for his 20-minute session on chipping in golf. Beth, an art major, had used the group project as the technique for her lesson on basic design, and Sam, a history major, had used lecture as the principal instructional technique to teach about the Spanish-American War. During the class critique, all three students expressed how well prepared they felt they had been and how appropriate each of their instructional techniques had proven to be. The class

concurred with their self-assessments. Then, in a surprise move, Beth turned to Sam and added, "You know, even though I felt that your lesson on the Spanish-American War was excellent and your minilecture held my attention, I would not feel comfortable giving a lecture to an art class."

"What do you mean?" asked Sam, rather flabbergasted at her comment.

"Just what I said, Sam," Beth replied. "Maybe it's the subject matter of art or maybe it's just me. It just doesn't fit with basic design!"

Do you agree with Beth? What is the relationship between the preferred method or instructional technique used by the teacher and his or her philosophy of education?

Like Beth, many students enrolled in preprofessional teacher education programs do not recognize the relationship between the study of philosophy and educational practice. One explanation for this is that much of the subject matter of teacher education is taught in a fragmented fashion with little or no connection to its philosophic roots. As a result, the student or novice teacher is unable to discern how important educational concepts such as curriculum, teaching methods, classroom management, evaluation, and the role of the teacher are related to educational theory or philosophy of education.

In this chapter you will be introduced to six major educational theories and their impact on educational practice. Based on these theories and their application to practice, you will be encouraged to formulate your own philosophy of education. Information regarding the impact of the six major educational theories on curriculum, teaching methods, classroom management, evaluation, and the role of the teacher will be presented.

To help you study these important concepts, consider the following outcome objectives:

- Define an educational theory and explain its relationship to philosophy as a discipline.

- Identify the various underlying protests that led to the establishment of the theories of perennialism, progressivism, behaviorism, essentialism, existentialism, and social reconstructionism.

- Compare the curricula of perennialism, progressivism, behaviorism, essentialism, existentialism, and social reconstructionism, including neo-Marxism, critical theory, and postmodern constructivism.
- Compare the teaching methods that characterize perennialism, progressivism, behaviorism, essentialism, existentialism, and social reconstructionism.
- Compare the preferred classroom management of perennialism, progressivism, behaviorism,

essentialism, existentialism, and social reconstructionism.

- Compare the evaluation techniques of the perennialist, progressivist, behaviorist, essentialist, existentialist, and social reconstructionist.
- Describe the role of the teacher from a perennialist, progressivist, behaviorist, essentialist, existentialist, and social reconstructionist perspective.
- Formulate your philosophy of education.

Having examined the assumptions that underlie the major philosophies, it is now appropriate to examine how these basic assumptions translate to educational theories and practice. The major traditional and contemporary philosophies that were discussed in Chapter 3 each have a corollary educational theory. It is the combination of philosophy and theory that will enable us to frame our own philosophy of education.

Theories of Education

Theory may be defined in two ways. First, a theory is a hypothesis or set of hypotheses that have been verified by observation or experiment. Second, a theory is a general synonym for systematic thinking or a set of coherent thoughts. Thus a *theory of education* is a composite of systematic thinking or generalizations about schooling (Kneller, 1971).

A well-thought-out theory of education is important, for it helps to explain our orientation to teaching and allows us to defend our position with respect to how we manage learning. In short, a theory of education enables the teacher to explain what he or she is doing, and why. It provides academic accountability.

The major theories of education to be examined in this chapter include six schools of thought: perennialism, progressivism, behaviorism, essentialism, existentialism, and social reconstructionism, including neo-Marxism, critical theory, and postmodern constructivism. Each theory was developed as a protest against the prevailing social and educational climate of the time. For example, the protest culminating in perennialism was a protest against secularization and the excessive focus on science and technology, at the expense of reason, that dominated society and its educational institutions at the time.

As you review each educational theory, keep in mind the similarities and differences among the theories and the reason or rationale behind the protest that led to their development.

Perennialism

Eternal or perennial truths, permanence, order, certainty, rationality, and logic constitute the ideal for the perennialist. The philosophies of neo-Thomism and realism are embedded in the perennialist theory of education. Kneller (1971) described six basic principles of *perennialism:*

1. Despite differing environments, human nature remains the same everywhere; hence, education should be the same for everyone.
2. Since rationality is man's highest attribute, he must use it to direct his instinctual nature in accordance with deliberately chosen ends.
3. It is education's task to impart knowledge of eternal truth.
4. Education is not an imitation of life, but a preparation for it.
5. The student should be taught certain basic subjects that will acquaint him with the world's permanencies.
6. Students should study the great works of literature, philosophy, history, and science, in which men through the ages have revealed their greatest aspirations and achievements. (pp. 42–45)

The educational focus of perennialism is on the need to return to the past, namely, to universal truths and such absolutes as reason and faith. The views of Thomas Aquinas best personify this educational theory. (The Historical Note on page 94 gives a brief look at Aquinas's life.) Although perennialism has been associated historically with the teachings of the Roman Catholic Church, as a theory of education it has received widespread support from lay educators. Aristotle's views best represent this group of perennialists. Whether one is an ecclesiastical (Thomist) or a lay (neo-Thomist) perennialist, one would envision the purpose of schooling to be to cultivate the rational intellect and to search for the truth.

Curriculum

For the ecclesiastical perennialist, Christian doctrine is an important aspect of the curriculum. The holy scriptures, the catechism, and the teaching of Christian dogma play a significant role. Wherever possible, theistic works would take precedence over purely secular works (Morris & Pai, 1976).

Both ecclesiastical and lay perennialists emphasize a concern for subject matter. The cognitive subjects of philosophy; mathematics, especially algebra and geometry; history; languages; the fine arts; literature (in particular, the *Great Books*); and science occupy a central position in the perennialist curriculum. Mastery of these subjects is considered necessary for the training of the intellect.

Consider yourself a perennialist. Choose 10 Great Books that you believe best represent absolute truth. At what grade level would you introduce these Great Books?

Historical Note

St. Thomas Aquinas

St. Thomas Aquinas was born of a noble family in Roccasecca, Italy, in 1224. From 1239 to 1244 he attended the University of Naples, where he came in contact with the Dominican order. Against the violent opposition of his parents, Thomas became a Dominican friar in 1244. During the years 1245 to 1252, he studied philosophy and theology under the tutelage of the German theologian St. Albertus Magnus. From 1252 to 1259 and again from 1269 to 1272 he taught at the University of Paris where he was known as "The Angelic Doctor." In between he taught at the Papal Curia in Italy.

Aquinas' two most influential works were the *Summa Contra Gentiles,* which expressed the doctrine of scholasticism or Christian philosophy, and his most important work, *Summa Theologica.* In the latter work Thomas attempted to explain the truth of Christian theology and advanced the proposition that conflict need not exist between reason and faith.

Thomas believed that the government had a moral responsibility to assist the individual to lead a virtuous life. He further postulated that governments must not violate human rights, including the right to life, education, religion, and reproduction. Laws passed by human beings must be in concert with divine laws.

Thomas Aquinas died in 1274. In 1323, Pope John XXII canonized him and since then his philosophy has become the official doctrine of the Roman Catholic Church. In 1567, Pope St. Pius V proclaimed him a doctor of the Church. He has also been proclaimed the patron saint of all Catholic schools, colleges, and universities.

In addition, perennialists contend that character training and moral development have an appropriate place in the design of the curriculum.

Perennialists such as Mortimer Adler (1984) have placed less emphasis on subject matter. Rather, they view the curriculum as the context for developing intellectual skills, including reading, writing, speaking, listening, observing, computing, measuring, and estimating.

Teaching Methods

Perennialists maintain that education involves confronting the problems and questions that have challenged people over the centuries. Adler (1984) suggests three specific methods of instruction:

1. Didactic teaching by lectures or through textbook assignments;
2. Coaching that forms the habits through which all skills are possessed; and
3. Socratic teaching by questioning and by conducting discussions of the answers elicited. (pp. 8–9)

Prior to studying the great works of literature, philosophy, history, and science, students would be taught methods of critical thinking and questioning strategies to prepare them to engage in "dialogue" with the classical writers. For the ecclesiastical perennialists the highest goal of education is union with God.

For these perennialists any type of teaching method that brings the learner into direct contact with the Supreme Being would be encouraged.

Classroom Management

In addition to training the intellect, perennialists believe that the teacher has the obligation to discipline the student in order to train the will. They would consider the most appropriate classroom environment for training the will to be one that reinforces time on task, precision, and order. In addition to orderliness and structure, for the ecclesiastical perennialists the learning environment would also reflect an appreciation for prayer and contemplation.

Evaluation

The standardized, objective examination would be the favored evaluation tool of the perennialist. Because the study of the classical tradition of the Great Books promotes an exchange of ideas and insights, the essay examination would also be utilized.

The Perennialist Teacher

Perennialists view the teacher who is well educated in the liberal arts as the authority figure, the instrument that provides for the dissemination of truth. And if the teacher is the disseminator, then the student is the receptacle for learning. The metaphor "director of mental calisthenics" has been used to describe the perennialist teacher (Morris & Pai, 1976).

Another metaphor that describes the perennialist teacher is "intellectual coach" who can engage students in the Socratic dialogue. The perennialist teacher must be a model of intellectual and rational powers. He or she must be capable of logical analysis, comfortable with the scientific method, well versed in the classics, have a good memory, and be capable of the highest forms of mental reasoning. Kane (1950) describes the major qualifications of the perennialist teacher: "stability, that one may never deviate from the truth; clarity, that one may not teach with obscurity; and utility, that one may seek God's honor and glory and not his own" (p. 14).

Leading Educational Proponents

Jacques Maritain (1882–1973), a French Catholic philosopher who served as ambassador to the Holy See and who was a prominent figure in the United Nations Educational, Scientific and Cultural Organization (UNESCO), is perhaps the best spokesperson for the ecclesiastical perennialist position. According to Maritain (1941), intelligence alone is not sufficient to comprehend the universe fully. One's relationship to a Spiritual Being is necessary to understand the cosmos or universe. Robert M. Hutchins (1899–1977), former chancellor of the University of Chicago and founder of the Center on the Study of Democratic Institutions, was a noted spokesperson for the lay perennialist perspective. Hutchins (1936) argued that the ideal education is one that is designed to develop the mind. This can be done best by a curriculum that concentrates on the Great Books of Western civilization.

Both Robert Hutchins (left) and Mortimer Adler (right) advocated the Great Books and the enduring lessons from the past.

The work of Mortimer Adler in the 1980s represents a resurgence of perennialism. In *The Paideia Proposal: An Educational Manifesto* (1982), Adler advocated a curriculum that would be appropriate for all students. Adler, as well as Hutchins, opposed differential curricula (e.g., vocational vs. academic) and contended that all students in a democratic society should have access to the same high-quality education. This education is characterized by a curriculum that includes language, literature, mathematics, natural sciences, fine arts, history, geography, and social studies. Like Hutchins, Adler favored the Great Books tradition and maintained that by studying the great works of the past, one can learn enduring lessons about life that are relevant today. In 1993, Terry Roberts replaced Mortimer Adler and took over as director of the National Paideia Center at the University of North Carolina. Today the principles of the Paideia movement can be found in low income multicultural public schools as well as elite academies (Ruenzel, 1997).

E. D. Hirsch, Jr., Diane Ravitch, and Chester Finn all speak from the perennialist position with their emphasis on preserving a defined body of knowledge. According to Hirsch, Kett, and Trefil (1993), this common knowledge or collective memory is not only shared by literate Americans but is characteristic of a national culture and is known as *cultural literacy*. Hirsch (1996) suggests that students are doomed to failure if they have not been exposed to a rigorous curriculum based on this common body of knowledge. Allan Bloom, another

As a response to Allan Bloom's perceived "crisis in our civilization," what suggestions would you make for revamping the general studies curriculum at the university level?

perennialist, has referred to the crisis of liberal education, particularly in the university, as an intellectual crisis. In his book *The Closing of the American Mind* (1987), Bloom refers to "cultural illiteracy" as the crisis of our civilization. Like Hutchins and Adler, Bloom advocates teaching and learning about the Great Books, as they provide knowledge and information that have lasting significance.

The curriculum of St. John's College at Annapolis, Maryland, and Santa Fe, New Mexico, which emphasizes the importance of studying the Great Books tradition, is an excellent example of the perennialist curriculum. Figure 4.1 presents an overview of perennialism.

Figure 4.1: Perennialism at a Glance

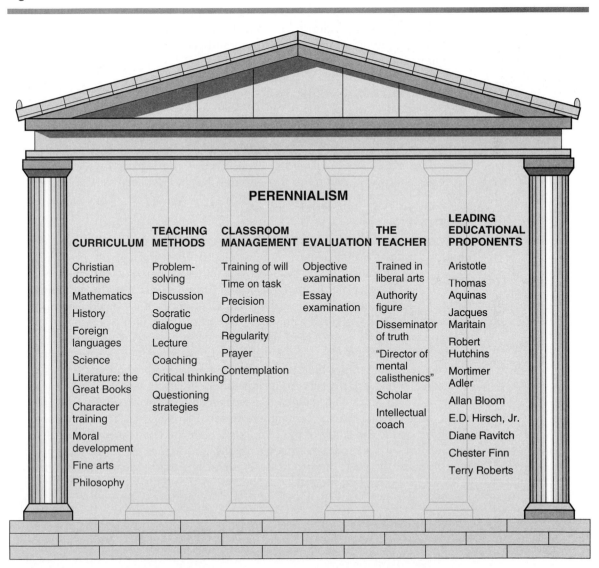

PERENNIALISM

CURRICULUM	TEACHING METHODS	CLASSROOM MANAGEMENT	EVALUATION	THE TEACHER	LEADING EDUCATIONAL PROPONENTS
Christian doctrine	Problem-solving	Training of will	Objective examination	Trained in liberal arts	Aristotle
Mathematics	Discussion	Time on task	Essay examination	Authority figure	Thomas Aquinas
History	Socratic dialogue	Precision		Disseminator of truth	Jacques Maritain
Foreign languages	Lecture	Orderliness		"Director of mental calisthenics"	Robert Hutchins
Science	Coaching	Regularity			Mortimer Adler
Literature: the Great Books	Critical thinking	Prayer		Scholar	Allan Bloom
Character training	Questioning strategies	Contemplation		Intellectual coach	E.D. Hirsch, Jr.
Moral development					Diane Ravitch
Fine arts					Chester Finn
Philosophy					Terry Roberts

Progressivism

There are a variety of opinions concerning whether it is most appropriate to describe the educational theory that follows as instrumentalism or *progressivism*. Regardless of the terminology used, what is common to any description of these terms is an educational theory that embraces the notion that the child is an experiencing organism who is capable of "learning by doing." The authors of this text believe that the term progressivism best describes this educational theory. The philosophy of pragmatism is embedded in the progressivist theory of education.

Kneller (1971) summarized six basic principles of the educational theory of progressivism.

1. Education should be life itself, not a preparation for living.
2. Learning should be directly related to the interests of the child.
3. Learning through problem-solving should take precedence over the inculcating of subject matter.
4. The teacher's role is not to direct but to advise.
5. The school should encourage cooperation rather than competition.
6. Only democracy permits—indeed encourages—the free interplay of ideas and personalities that is a necessary condition of true growth. (pp. 48–52)

This view of education is grounded in the scientific method of inductive reasoning. As an educational theory, it encourages the learner to seek out those processes that work, and to do those things that best achieve desirable ends.

Curriculum

The progressivist curriculum can be best described as experience-centered, relevant, and reflective. Such a curriculum would not consist of a given set of predetermined facts or truths to be mastered, but rather, a series of experiences to be gained. For Dewey (1963) "anything, which can be called a study, whether arithmetic, history, geography, or one of the natural sciences, must be derived from materials which at the onset fall within the scope of ordinary life-experiences" (p. 73).

The curriculum of progressivism would integrate several subjects but would not reflect universal truths, a particular body of knowledge, or a set of prescribed core courses. Rather, it would be responsive to the needs and experiences of the individual, which would vary from situation to situation. Lerner (1962) described such a curriculum as child centered, peer centered, growth centered, action centered, process and change centered, and equality centered. The progressivist is not interested in the study of the past, but is governed by the present. Unlike the perennialist or essentialist who advocate the importance of the cultural and historic roots of the past, the progressivist advocates that which is meaningful and relevant to the student today.

Teaching Methods

For the progressivist, since there is no rigid subject matter content and no absolute standard for what constitutes knowledge, the most appropriate teaching method is the project method. The experience-centered, problem-solving curriculum lends itself to cooperative group activities whereby students can learn to work together on units or projects that have relevance for their own lives. The indispensable instructional strategy that would be used along with the project method is the scientific method. However, unlike the perennialist or essentialist who view the scientific method as a means of verifying truth, the progressivist views scientific investigation as a means of verifying experience. What makes the outcome of certain hypotheses true for the progressivist is that they work and are related to the individual's experience.

Since the progressivist curriculum is not a static curriculum but rather an emerging one, any teaching method that would foster individual and group initiative, spontaneity of expression, and creative new ideas would be used. Classroom activities in critical thinking, problem solving, decision making, and cooperative learning are examples of some of the methods that would be incorporated in the curriculum. For the progressivist, "teaching is . . . exploratory rather than explanatory" (Bayles, 1966, p. 94).

Classroom Management

Progressivism views learning as educating "the whole child," including the physical, emotional, and social aspects of the individual. As a result of this holistic view of education, the environment is considered fundamental to the child's nature.

How can a subject-oriented secondary school teacher justify a holistic view of education?

The type of classroom management that would appeal to a progressivist would be an environment that stimulates or invites participation, involvement, and the democratic process. The atmosphere of the classroom would be active, experience directed, and self-directed (Dewey, 1956). Such an environment would not only be child centered or student centered, but would also be community centered. It would feature an open environment in which students would spend considerable time in direct contact with the community or cultural surroundings beyond the confines of the classroom or school. Students would experience the arts by frequenting museums and theaters. They would experience social studies by interacting with individuals from diverse social groups and social conditions. They would experience science by exploring their immediate physical world. All students would be involved in a "social" mode of learning (Westheimer & Kahne, 1993).

The progressivist teacher would foster a classroom environment that practices democracy. Students and parents would be encouraged to form their own councils and organizations within the school to address educational issues and advance social change. Teachers would advocate site-based management and democratic decision making with regard to the administration of the school.

Since students would decide on appropriate rules and content to be studied, the teacher would manage groups of students engaged in a variety of simultaneous classroom tasks. Being able to distinguish between instructional and disruptive noise, to cope with a number of distractions, and to plan for the problems that emerge from a student-centered classroom are a few of the daily challenges that confront the progressivist teacher.

Evaluation

What type of
process-oriented
evaluation would
you be most
comfortable
using in your
teaching?

Because progressivism supports the group process, cooperative learning, and democratic participation, its approach to evaluation differs from the more traditional approaches. For example, the progressivist would engage in *formative evaluation,* which is process oriented and concerned with ongoing feedback about the activity underway, rather than the measurement of outcomes. Monitoring what the students are doing, appraising what skills they still need to develop, and resolving unexpected problems as they occur would be typical examples of the type of evaluation used by the progressivist.

The Progressivist Teacher

The metaphor of the "teacher as facilitator" or "director of learning" might best describe the progressivist teacher. Such a teacher is not considered to be the authority, or disseminator of knowledge or truth, like the perennialist or essentialist teacher. Rather, he or she serves more as a guide or supervisor who facilitates learning by assisting the student to sample direct experience. The teacher's role is to help his or her pupils to acquire the values of the democratic system. Although the teacher is always interested in the individual development of each student, the progressivist instructor would envision his or her role as focusing beyond the individual. Progressivism by its very nature is socially oriented; thus the teacher would be a collaborative partner in making group decisions, keeping in mind their ultimate consequences for the students.

Leading Educational Proponents

Progressivism had its impetus in the first decades of the twentieth century at a time when many liberal thinkers alleged that American schools were out of touch with the advances that were being made in the physical and social sciences and technology (see Chapter 7). John Dewey, perhaps more than any other American educator, is credited with having advanced progressivism. Dewey's approach to progressivism differed from earlier progressive educators in that rather than emphasize the individual learner, Dewey emphasized the importance of the teacher/student interaction and the importance of education as a social function.

One of the most important principles of Dewey's educational theory was the connection between education and personal experience. For Dewey (1938), experience was the basis of education. However, he cautioned that not all experiences are equal.

> The belief that all genuine education comes about through experience does not mean that all experiences are genuinely or equally educative. Experience and education cannot be directly equated to each other. For some experiences are mis-educative. Any experience is mis-education that has the effect of arresting or distorting the growth of further experience. (p. 25)

John Dewey's establishment of the University Laboratory School at the University of Chicago provided the clinical testing ground for his educational theory. His leadership at the University of Chicago and his subsequent work at Teachers College, Columbia, left a legacy to American education. Although some educators would argue that progressivism in education is not relevant for the twenty-first century, its profound impact on American education through the 1960s and 1970s is without debate. In fact, its critics contend that progressivism was the major cause of the decline in student performance in the 1960s and 1970s. Vestiges of progressivism can be found in *nongraded schools, alternative schools,* the *whole-child movement,* and *humanistic education.* Figure 4.2 presents an overview of progressivism.

What do you see as the advantages and disadvantages of a nongraded school?

Figure 4.2: Progressivism at a Glance

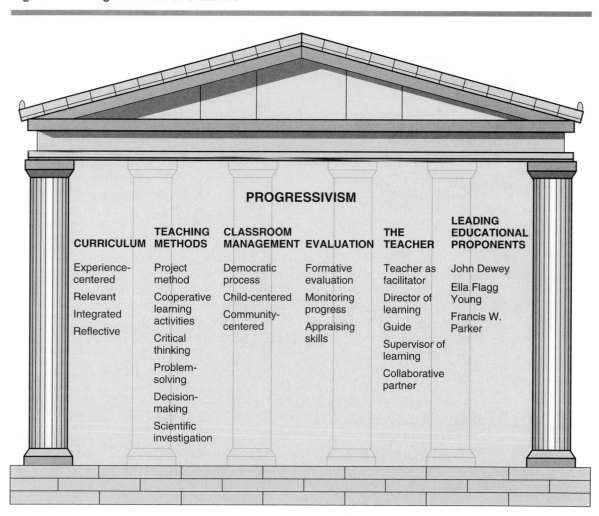

PROGRESSIVISM

CURRICULUM	TEACHING METHODS	CLASSROOM MANAGEMENT	EVALUATION	THE TEACHER	LEADING EDUCATIONAL PROPONENTS
Experience-centered	Project method	Democratic process	Formative evaluation	Teacher as facilitator	John Dewey
Relevant	Cooperative learning activities	Child-centered	Monitoring progress	Director of learning	Ella Flagg Young
Integrated		Community-centered	Appraising skills	Guide	Francis W. Parker
Reflective	Critical thinking			Supervisor of learning	
	Problem-solving			Collaborative partner	
	Decision-making				
	Scientific investigation				

Behaviorism

Behaviorism, or behavioral engineering, is an educational theory that is predicated on the belief that human behavior can be explained in terms of responses to external stimuli. The basic principle of behaviorism is that education can best be achieved by modifying or changing student behaviors in a socially acceptable manner through the arrangement of the conditions for learning. For the behaviorist, the predictability and control of human behavior are paramount concepts. The control is obtained not by manipulating the individual, but by manipulating the environment.

The basic principles of the theory of behaviorism are as follows:

1. All behaviors are both objective and observable.
2. All behaviors are caused.
3. As natural organisms we seek positive reinforcement and avoid punishment.
4. The teacher should arrange conditions under which learning can occur.
5. Technology makes it possible for teachers to teach beyond their knowledge of content or subject matter.
6. Students will learn best by the use of carefully planned schedules of reinforcement.

There are two major types of behaviorism: (1) *classical conditioning,* or stimulus substitution behaviorism, and (2) *operant conditioning,* or response reinforcement behaviorism (Phillips & Soltis, 1991). Classical conditioning, based on the work of the Russian physiologist Ivan Pavlov (1849–1936) and the American experimental psychologist John B. Watson (1878–1958), demonstrates that a natural stimulus that produces a certain type of response can be replaced by a conditioned stimulus. For example, Pavlov found that in laboratory experiments with dogs a natural stimulus such as food will produce a natural response such as salivation. However, when Pavlov paired the natural stimulus (food) with a conditioned stimulus (bell), he found that eventually the conditioned stimulus (bell) produced a conditioned response (salivation). Watson eventually used Pavlov's classical conditioning model to explain all human learning.

The operant conditioning model can best be described by the work of psychologists E. L. Thorndike (1874–1949) and B. F. Skinner (1904–1990). Both Thorndike and Skinner suggested that any response to any stimulus can be conditioned by immediate reinforcement or reward. Skinner later determined that an action or response does not have to be rewarded each time it occurs. In fact, Skinner found that random reward, or intermittent reinforcement, was a more effective method for learning than continuous reward. Skinner also discovered that behavior could be shaped by the appropriate use of rewards.

As a theory of education, behaviorism was a protest against the importance placed on mental processes that could not be observed (e.g., thinking or motivation). Today, behaviorism has taken a more moderate stance, and has adopted a cognitive-behavioral approach that attempts to change not only individuals' behaviors, but their thoughts and perceptions as well.

 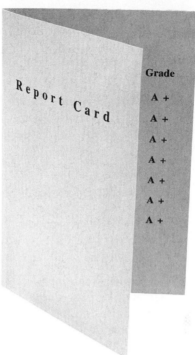

B.F. Skinner advocated reinforcement as a method of shaping behavior.

Curriculum

Unlike the curricula of perennialism and essentialism, which advocate a prescribed subject matter, the behaviorist curriculum is not interested in subject matter per se, but is interested in environmental variables such as teaching materials, teaching methods, and teacher-classroom behaviors, since they directly influence the learner's behavior (Wittrock, 1987). The behaviorist curriculum includes cognitive problem-solving activities whereby students learn about their belief systems, recognize their power to influence their environment, and employ critical-thinking skills.

As a teacher how could you help your students learn about their belief systems or values?

Teaching Methods

Behaviorist theory is primarily concerned with the process of providing contingencies of reinforcement as the basis for any strategy or method. If there are appropriate opportunities for the learner to respond, and appropriate reinforcers that are readily available, learning will take place, say the behaviorists. Skinner supported the use of the teaching machine, or *programmed instruction,* as an effective teaching method. Programmed instruction enables individual students to answer questions about a unit of study at their own rate, checking their own answers and advancing only after answering correctly. A chief advantage of the teaching machine, or programmed instruction, is the immediate reinforcement that it provides. Today, computers have replaced the teaching machine. A wide variety of computer-assisted instruction, including interactive multimedia, has become a favored teaching method of many educators, in particular the behaviorists.

Classroom Management

For the behaviorist, classroom management is an integral part of the process of learning. Emmer (1987) described two general principles that guide the behaviorist teacher in classroom management.

1. Identify expected student behavior. This implies that teachers must have a clear idea of what behaviors are appropriate and are not appropriate in advance of instruction.
2. Translate expectations into procedures and routines. Part of the process of translating expectations into procedures is to formulate some general rules governing conduct. (pp. 438–439)

Other components of good management include careful monitoring or observation of classroom events; prompt and appropriate handling of inappropriate behavior; using reward systems, penalties, and other consequences; establishing accountability for completion of assignments; and maintaining lesson or activity flow (Emmer, 1987). Behaviorism is widely used in special education and mainstream classroom environments.

Evaluation

Measurement and evaluation are central to the behaviorist. Specified *behavioral objectives* (e.g., the behaviors or knowledge that students are expected to demonstrate or learn) serve not only as guides to learning for the student, but as standards for evaluating the teaching-learning process. For the behaviorist, only those aspects of behavior that are observable, and preferably measurable, are of interest to the teacher. Advocates of behavioral objectives claim that if teachers know exactly what they want students to learn and how they want them to learn, using behavioral objectives can be an efficient method for gauging how much learning has occurred. Measurement and evaluation also provide a method for obtaining accountability from teachers since they are pivotal to the learning process. Two other types of evaluation used by the behaviorist teacher are performance contracting and teaching students to record their own progress.

The Behaviorist Teacher

Since education as behavioral engineering entails a variety of technical and observational skills, the behaviorist teacher must be skilled in a variety of these techniques. Moreover, since behavioral engineering depends on psychological principles, the teacher must be knowledgeable about psychology, in particular educational psychology that emphasizes learning. Also, since behaviorism focuses on empirical verification, the teacher must be well versed in the scientific method.

The behaviorist teacher is very concerned about the consequences of class-room behavior. Therefore, the teacher must be able to recognize which reinforcers are most appropriate. In addition, the behaviorist teacher must be skilled in using a variety of schedules of reinforcement that are effective and efficient in shaping and maintaining desired responses.

To establish the behaviors that will be most beneficial to the learner, behaviorist teachers are most concerned with the student achieving specific objectives or competencies. For this reason the teacher must be capable of planning and using behavioral objectives, designing and using programmed instruction, using computers, and utilizing performance contracting. Two of the most appropriate metaphors for describing the behaviorist teacher are "the controller of behavior" and "the arranger of contingencies."

What type of reinforcer would be most apt to motivate you to learn?

Leading Educational Proponents

As previously noted, classical conditioning had its beginnings with Pavlov and Watson. Both maintained that classical conditioning was the key mechanism underlying all human learning. The behaviorists Thorndike and Skinner are known for the concept of operant conditioning, which suggests that reinforcement of responses (operant behavior) underlies all types of learning. Another noted behaviorist, psychologist David Premack, determined that organisms often freely choose to engage in certain behaviors rather than other behaviors. Consequently, providing access to the preferred activities can serve as a reinforcement for not engaging in nonpreferred activities. To apply the *Premack principle* in the classroom, the teacher first must observe and carefully record the behavior that students more often freely choose to perform, and the relative frequency of competing behaviors (Bates, 1987). Figure 4.3 provides an overview of behaviorism.

Essentialism

Historically, there have been a variety of opinions concerning whether essentialism is a true educational theory. A number of scholars have suggested that *essentialism* is actually perennialism in disguise. If one were to choose an adjective that best describes essentialism, it would probably be "eclectic." The philosophies of idealism and realism are embedded in the essentialist theory of education. Essentialism began as a protest against the decline of intellectual and moral standards. Many essentialists based their criticisms on American education by comparisons with other countries such as Japan and Germany (Gutek, 1997).

Wingo (1974) described six basic tenets of essentialism:

1. Americans largely have lost sight of the true purpose of education, which is intellectual training. We tend to confuse education with all kinds of social, psychological, and vocational services that often are lumped together under the rubric "life adjustment."

Figure 4.3: Behaviorism at a Glance

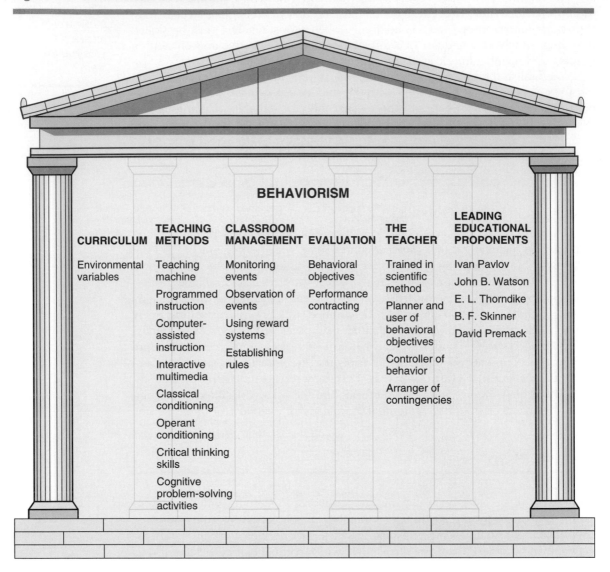

BEHAVIORISM

CURRICULUM	TEACHING METHODS	CLASSROOM MANAGEMENT	EVALUATION	THE TEACHER	LEADING EDUCATIONAL PROPONENTS
Environmental variables	Teaching machine	Monitoring events	Behavioral objectives	Trained in scientific method	Ivan Pavlov
	Programmed instruction	Observation of events	Performance contracting	Planner and user of behavioral objectives	John B. Watson
	Computer-assisted instruction	Using reward systems			E. L. Thorndike
	Interactive multimedia	Establishing rules		Controller of behavior	B. F. Skinner
	Classical conditioning			Arranger of contingencies	David Premack
	Operant conditioning				
	Critical thinking skills				
	Cognitive problem-solving activities				

2. The rigor of our educational programs and teaching methods has been declining steadily for several decades. This is true in some measure of every level of the school system from the kindergarten to the university, but the condition is particularly acute in the elementary and secondary schools.

3. We have failed to provide for the education of our brightest children because instruction has been pitched at the level of the mediocre student, and the ablest have been systematically deprived in the name of "equality" and "democracy."

4. The curricula of our schools have been diluted by the introduction of courses consisting largely of "life adjustment" trivia, and these worthless substitutes have crowded out the historic disciplines that are the core of the true education.

5. Intellectual achievement has declined steadily among American students.

6. The schools are failing to meet their obligations to American youth and to American society. They are not only failing in the intellectual task, they also are failing in their responsibility to transmit those values that are the basis of the American tradition. (pp. 51–52)

Like the perennialists, essentialists believe that the best preparation for life is learning the culture and traditions of the past.

Curriculum

The curriculum of the essentialist school is a basic education that includes instruction in the "essentials," including reading, writing, and computing at the primary grades, and history, geography, natural sciences, and foreign languages at the upper elementary grades. At the secondary level, the curriculum would place a major emphasis on the common core that all students should complete. Such a core would normally include four years of English, three or four years of social studies, a course in American government, and a year of natural science and general mathematics or algebra (Conant, 1959). Such a common core represents the comprehensive high school that was most popular during the 1950s. Some essentialists believe that the educational curriculum should not be limited only to the academic disciplines. They suggest that the physical and emotional well-being of the child is important (Wingo, 1974). Overall, essentialists maintain that the educational program should not permit any "frivolous" subjects, but rather should adhere strictly to sound academic standards. Probably more than any other educational theory, essentialism deplores the lack of educational standards or the so-called "soft pedagogy."

What subjects might be construed as "frivolous" by an essentialist?

Teaching Methods

If the basic disciplines, or basic subjects, are at the heart of the school curriculum, then the methods of instruction that are to support such a curriculum include the more traditional instructional strategies such as lecture, recitation, discussion, and the Socratic dialogue. Written and oral communication occupy a prominent place in the instructional milieu of the essentialist school. Like perennialists, essentialists view books as an appropriate medium for instruction.

Generally, essentialist educators have found educational technology to be congruent with their educational theory. They prefer instructional materials that are paced and sequenced in such a way that students know what they are expected to master. Detailed syllabi, lesson plans, learning by objectives, competency-based instruction, computer-assisted instruction, and audio-tutorial laboratory methods are other examples of teaching strategies that would be acceptable to the modern-day essentialist.

Classroom Management

Like the perennialists, who advocate intellectual discipline as well as moral discipline, the essentialists maintain that character training deserves an important place in the school. William Bennett (1993), former secretary of education, has strongly endorsed essentialism since it advocates moral literacy. Bennett proposes the use of stories, poems, essays, and other works to help children achieve moral literacy and learn to possess the traits of character that society most admires. For the essentialist, students attend school to learn how to participate in society, not to manage the course of their own instruction. They prepare for life by being exposed to essential truths and values, as well as by exercising discipline. Thus, the essentialist teacher would take great pains in designing and controlling a classroom environment that creates an aura of certainty, an emphasis on regularity and uniformity, and a reverence for what is morally right.

Evaluation

Of all the theories of education, essentialism is perhaps most comfortable with testing. In fact, the entire essentialist curriculum reflects the influence of the testing movement. Extensive use of IQ tests, standardized achievement tests, diagnostic tests, and performance-based competency tests are examples of the widespread application of measurement techniques. Competency, accountability, mastery learning (see Chapter 15), and performance-based instruction have gained increasing acceptance by many educators as a result of the essentialists' influence on educational practice.

The Essentialist Teacher

The essentialist teacher, like the perennialist teacher, is an educator who has faith in the accumulated wisdom of the past. Rather than having majored in educational pedagogy, the essentialist teacher would have majored in a subject matter discipline, preferably in the liberal arts, sciences, or the humanities. The essentialist educator is viewed as either a link to the so-called "literary intellectual inheritance" (idealism), or a demonstrator of the world model (realism). To be an essentialist teacher is to be well versed in the liberal arts and sciences, to be a respected member of the intellectual community, to be technically skilled in all forms of communication, and to be equipped with superior pedagogical skills to ensure competent instruction. One of the most important roles of the teacher is to set the character of the environment in which learning takes place (Butler, 1966).

Contemporary essentialists such as Delattre (1984) have been critical of the preprofessional training of teachers, since they believe that their training falls short of what is demanded of teachers today.

> Many have been subjected to too many textbooks and not enough original books: some have never read basic and profound works on learning, knowing, and teaching—have never been exposed to Deuteronomy, works by Plato, Aristotle, Loyola, Milton, Agassiz, Hadas, or Highet, not to mention Augustine and

the intellectual predecessors of Dewey. That is, some cannot teach themselves in any systematic program of study because they do not know enough to design one, and their own teachers are not always qualified to do so for them. (p. 159)

Leading Educational Proponents

Although essentialism can be traced to Plato and Aristotle, its greatest popularity has emerged in the twentieth century. As noted in Chapter 7, in the 1930s and 1940s William C. Bagley, Arthur E. Bestor, and Herman H. Horne (1874–1946) led the essentialist criticism of the progressivism of Dewey and his followers. They formed the Essentialist Committee for the Advancement of American Education. In the 1950s, Admiral Hyman G. Rickover (1900–1986) became the spokesperson for the essentialists. According to Rickover (1963), the quality of American education declined considerably as a result of "watered-down" courses and "fads and frills." He called for a return to the basics, with particular emphasis on mathematics and science.

A major revival of essentialism has been evidenced by the *back-to-basics movement* that gained support in the 1970s and was echoed in the education reform reports of the 1980s. For example, *A Nation at Risk* (National Commission on Excellence in Education, 1983), the premier of these reports, recommended a core of *new basics:* English, mathematics, science, social studies, and computer sciences, and for the college-bound, a foreign language. Many of the other reports not only proposed similar cores, but also called for improvement in their content and increased rigor in their standards. The success of the essentialist position is evidenced by the steps taken in a number of states to mandate curricula, strengthen graduation requirements, and increase student testing and evaluation. Essentialism is the dominant philosophy in our schools today. Figure 4.4 presents an overview of essentialism.

Existentialism

Freedom, responsibility, choice, anxiety, authenticity, alienation, paradox, and human subjectivity are the hallmarks of existentialism. Existentialist philosophy represents a protest against the earlier efforts of Western philosophy to reduce the human being to an essence or universal—to an abstraction (Wingo, 1974). For the existentialist, to reduce human life to such an abstraction is to deny the individual his or her existence. The philosophy of existentialism is embedded in the existentialist theory of education. Kneller (1971) described some of the basic principles of the educational theory of existentialism.

1. Students should be urged to take responsibility for, and to deal with, the results of their actions.
2. Teachers should not simply impose discipline on their students but rather should demonstrate the value of discipline.
3. Students should be helped to discover that true freedom implies communion, not self-interest.

Figure 4.4: Essentialism at a Glance

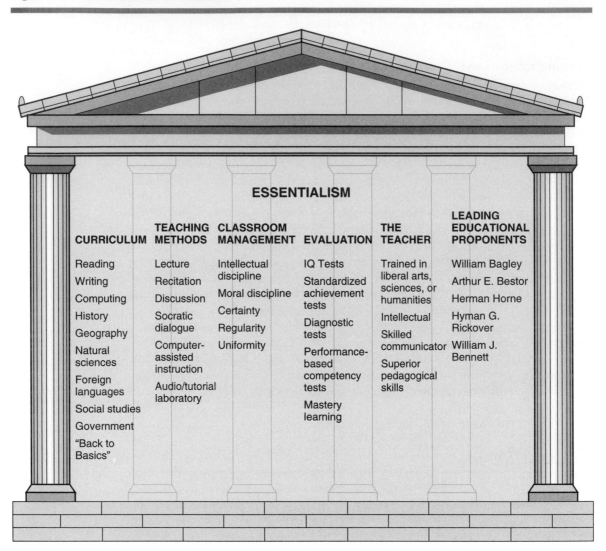

ESSENTIALISM

CURRICULUM	TEACHING METHODS	CLASSROOM MANAGEMENT	EVALUATION	THE TEACHER	LEADING EDUCATIONAL PROPONENTS
Reading	Lecture	Intellectual discipline	IQ Tests	Trained in liberal arts, sciences, or humanities	William Bagley
Writing	Recitation	Moral discipline	Standardized achievement tests		Arthur E. Bestor
Computing	Discussion	Certainty			Herman Horne
History	Socratic dialogue	Regularity	Diagnostic tests	Intellectual	Hyman G. Rickover
Geography		Uniformity	Performance-based competency tests	Skilled communicator	
Natural sciences	Computer-assisted instruction			Superior pedagogical skills	William J. Bennett
Foreign languages	Audio/tutorial laboratory		Mastery learning		
Social studies					
Government					
"Back to Basics"					

For the existentialist, the child or student has a "right to live the extreme choice, the right to change, and the right to spontaneous self-realization" (Barnes, 1968, p. 296). The purpose of education is to foster self-discovery and consciousness of the freedom of choice, as well as the responsibility for making choices.

Curriculum

Like that of progressivism, the curriculum of the existentialist school evolves around the student's needs and interests. However, unlike progressivism, which emphasizes group learning, existentialism emphasizes the individual and views learning as a private and personal matter. It is a student-centered curriculum of individual choice. The main objective of such a curriculum is to immerse the student in a variety of existential situations that authenticate his or her own experience.

Although there are no universals in such a curriculum, there is a favored subject matter: the humanities. For the existentialist, the humanities offer visible evidence of the suffering that accompanies the human condition.

> Above all, it is the spiritual power of the humanities and the essential urge for affirmation inherent in all forms of art that attract the existentialist. To read and see how men in history have struggled with their conscience, labored with fate, rebelled against existing orders and absolutes, and poured life-blood into their creations becomes a source of inspiration for the existentialist in his approach to learning. (Kneller, 1958, p. 125)

The essence of the curriculum is to stress the awareness of "being" and the awareness of "nothingness." The assumption made by the existentialist is that by dwelling on the unpleasant idea of meaninglessness or nothingness and its accompanying anxiety and absurdity, we ultimately create an affirmation of self and find a purpose in life. The curriculum, then, awakens a fundamental awareness in the learner. Such a subjective awareness has been called "the existential moment" (Marler, 1975; Morris, 1966) which marks the beginning of taking responsibility for assigning meaning to one's own life. Unlike the curriculum of perennialism and essentialism, which seeks Absolute Truth, the existentialist seeks "personal truth."

Have you ever experienced "the existential moment"? Describe the experience.

Teaching Methods

Since existentialists view the greatest obstacles to authenticity to be fear and conformity (Kneller, 1984), the teaching methods they would use would not reinforce fear or conformity, but would value "existential anxiety," which is the anxiety associated with the freedom to choose. Existential anxiety is a prerequisite to growth, and as such is considered to be probably the most powerful experience that a student can have. It breaks down defenses, questions values and beliefs, and reveals the person as he or she really is. The best methods for encouraging and nourishing a certain amount of existential anxiety are those that teach decision making, or choosing among alternatives.

The so-called "affective" approaches to values education, which engage students in cognitive discussions along with affective experiences, would be a favored teaching method of the existentialist teacher. In addition, the Socratic method, which includes asking questions, refining answers, and asking further questions until a conclusion is reached, would be another important instructional strategy because it produces self-knowledge. Nel Noddings (1993), a contemporary existential philosopher, describes some of the teaching strategies that are consistent with the existential pedagogy.

> In the discussion of religious, metaphysical, and existential questions, teachers and students are both seekers. Teachers tell stories, guide the logic of discussion,

point to further readings, model both critical thinking and kindness, and show by their openness what it means to seek intelligent belief or unbelief. (p. 135)

Furthermore, the existentialist teacher would provide time for self-reflection and privacy because the questions of human existence are best addressed in the quietude of private time and space.

Classroom Management

The most appropriate metaphor for the classroom environment of an existential school is an *open classroom* (i.e., an open instructional space or "classroom without walls") where students enjoy the freedom to move about. Within such an environment, learning is dedicated to self-discovery and individual choice. Such a classroom invites participatory decision making and does not view the teacher as the authority figure. Rather, the teacher is considered a mediator who permits students to exercise freedom within a nonpunitive, democratic community.

Evaluation

Because authenticity and authentic teaching reflect the uniqueness of the individual teacher, the existential teacher spurns the use of standardized tests, rejects the notion of accountability, and stresses a more subjective form of appraisal or evaluation. The school is viewed as a place for experiencing life and making meaning out of nonmeaning, a place where students come to grips with their own values. The source of those values is inconsequential. What matters most is that there is a personal endorsement for valuing and choosing. Within this paradigm of choice, the teacher is not viewed as an evaluator, monitor, or critic, but rather as a subjective or reflective artist who is committed to helping students fulfill their personal goals.

The Existentialist Teacher

With the overriding concern for the individual as the ultimate chooser, the existentialist teacher would model valuing, decision making, and choosing. Such a teacher would pose moral and ethical, as well as intellectual, questions to his or her students. The teacher's job would be to awaken students to the ultimate responsibility that they must bear for the decisions that they make. The teacher who would be most comfortable with the tenets of existentialism is typically one who is flexible, nondirective, and impervious to the type of noise and disorder that often accompanies an informal, open class atmosphere (Kneller, 1984). The teacher's role is to help the individual achieve his or her potential and to strive for self-actualization (Greene, 1967).

The existentialist teacher attempts to become an excellent example of authenticity for students. By incorporating a humanistic approach to teaching, the existentialist educator would encourage a more personal and interactive teacher-student relationship. The whole child or student would be viewed as primary, and the existentialist would be concerned with the cognitive as well as affective components of the student's development. Furthermore, since the thrust of existentialism is the search for meaning and purpose, the teacher would be an individual who is comfortable with being introspective and reflective. Imagination and insight are important criteria for the existentialist teacher.

Last, the existentialist teacher is an advocate for self-education and academic freedom. The teacher would encourage students to take responsibility for their own learning and education. Teaching, says the existentialist, is neither a science nor a technology, but an art.

Leading Educational Proponents

Perhaps the most well-known educational existentialists are A. S. Neill (1883–1973), Carl Rogers (1902–1987), and John Holt (1923–1985), as well as contemporary writers Charles Silberman and Jonathan Kozol. Neill, who founded Summerhill School outside London shortly after World War I, offered an educational experience built on the principle of learning by discovery in an atmosphere of unrestrained freedom. He contended that learning will evolve from the student's interest. According to Neill (1960), regardless of their age or maturity level, students are capable of self-discipline and can be responsible for their own learning. A similar institution established in 1968 and still in operation today in Framingham, Massachusetts, is Sudbury Valley School, which operates on the existential principles that foster individual choice, democracy, and personal responsibility. Long and Ihle (1988) described the basic components of the school.

> Sudbury Valley operates on the principle that children's natural tendencies toward wanting to grow up, to be competent, to model older children and adults, and to fantasize, should be the foundation for education. Consequently,

Individual choice, democracy, and personal responsibility are key ingredients of Sudbury Valley School.

the school has set no curriculum and no activity takes place unless a student asks for it. Instead, the school offers a wide variety of educational options, including instruction in standard subjects in both group and tutorial formats; field trips to Boston, New York, and the nearby mountains, and seacoast; and facilities that include a laboratory, a woodworking shop, a computer room, a kitchen, a darkroom, an art room, and a number of music rooms. (p. 449)

Carl Rogers (1969), in his *Freedom to Learn,* asserted that the only things that one person can teach another person are those that are relatively inconsequential and of little or no significance. Only learning that is self-discovered and self-appropriated through experience can significantly influence behavior.

John Holt (1981), Charles Silberman (1970), and Jonathan Kozol (1972; 1991) were supporters of open schools, free schools, or alternative schools that flourished during the mid-1960s. Similar to Summerhill or Sudbury Valley, these nontraditional schools emphasized a permissive, or humanistic education that abhorred any type of rigidity or structure. In spite of the appeal of the humanistic education movement, its heyday was very short-lived, and it was eventually replaced by the back-to-basics movement of the 1970s.

Two current spokespersons for the existentialist theory of education are Maxine Greene and Nel Noddings. Noddings, a former teacher of mathematics

Nel Noddings (left) and Maxine Greene (right) advocate for the existential principles of choice, responsibility, and personal meaning.

and currently a leading philosopher of education, suggests an alternative educational model that stresses the *challenge to care*.

> We must consider Heidegger's deepest sense of care. As human beings, we care what happens to us. We wonder whether there is a life after death, whether there is a deity who cares about us, whether we are loved by those we love, whether we belong anywhere; we wonder what we will become, who we are, how much control we have over our own fate. For adolescents these are among the most pressing questions: Who am I? Who will love me? How do others see me? Yet schools spend more time on the quadratic formula than on any of these existential questions. (1992, p. 20)

Figure 4.5 presents an overview of existentialism.

Figure 4.5: Existentialism at a Glance

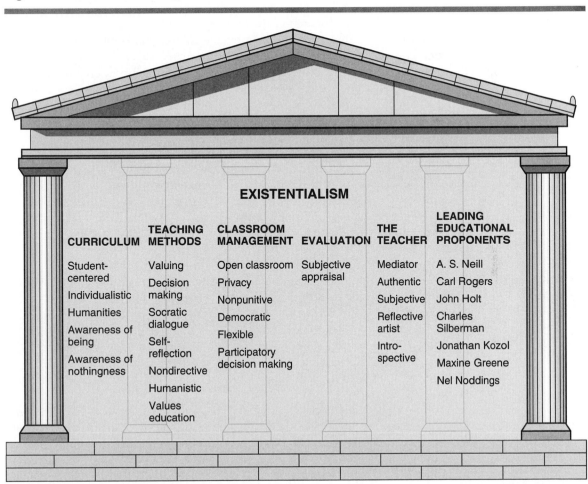

		EXISTENTIALISM			
CURRICULUM	TEACHING METHODS	CLASSROOM MANAGEMENT	EVALUATION	THE TEACHER	LEADING EDUCATIONAL PROPONENTS
Student-centered	Valuing	Open classroom	Subjective appraisal	Mediator	A. S. Neill
Individualistic	Decision making	Privacy		Authentic	Carl Rogers
Humanities	Socratic dialogue	Nonpunitive		Subjective	John Holt
Awareness of being	Self-reflection	Democratic		Reflective artist	Charles Silberman
Awareness of nothingness	Nondirective	Flexible		Intro-spective	Jonathan Kozol
	Humanistic	Participatory decision making			Maxine Greene
	Values education				Nel Noddings

Social Reconstructionism, Critical Theory, and Postmodern Constructivism

Social reconstructionism can be traced to the philosophies of both pragmatism and existentialism (Jacobsen, 1999). Throughout history there have been social reconstructionists who have aspired to improve, change, or reform society, including its educational institutions. Certainly Plato, who advocated a design for a future state in the *Republic,* could be considered a social reconstructionist, as could the Christian philosopher Augustine, who sought to create an ideal Christian state. Likewise, Karl Marx (1818–1883), who envisioned a reconstructed world based on international communism, is considered a social reconstructionist (Ozmon & Craver, 1990). Each of these individuals advocated far-reaching changes that anticipated radical social and educational reforms.

The educational theory of social reconstructionism has two predominant themes: (1) society is in need of change or reconstruction, and (2) education must take the lead in the reconstruction of society. It was John Dewey who suggested the term *reconstructionism* by the title of his book, *Reconstruction in Philosophy* (1920). Shortly thereafter, in the early 1930s, a group known as the "Frontier Thinkers" looked to the schools for leadership in creating a "new" and "more equitable" society (Kneller, 1971). These educational reformers advocated changes beyond what Dewey envisioned in his theory of progressivism. His emphasis was on the democratic social experience, theirs was on social reform.

Modern social reconstructionism had its beginnings in Marxist philosophy. According to Marx, capitalism and its emphasis on competition and the control of property in the hands of a few led to an alienated workforce who found little meaning or purpose in their work. Marx's later writings recommended a total social revolution against the ruling class by the working class. Several major revolutionary figures were greatly influenced by the philosophy of Marx. Two such figures were Fredrich Engels (1820–1895) and Vladimir Ilich Lenin (1870–1924), both of whom proposed violent revolution by the working class.

Following the impact and influence of Marxism-Leninism in the East, Marxist thought spread to the West and became known as the "Frankfurt School." Eventually the term *critical theory* was applied to the Frankfurt School and included the melding of the philosophies and theories of Kant, Hegel, Freud, and Marx. At the heart of the Frankfurt School was analysis, scrutiny, and the critique of all ideologies. Some of the leading proponents of the Frankfurt School included Max Horkheimer (1895–1971), Theodor Adorno (1903–1969), and Herbert Marcuse (1898–1979) (Ozmon & Craver, 1990).

Today, critical theorists have moved beyond Marxism and have become spokespersons for liberation theology, feminism, racial equality, the ecology movement, and other forms of social reconstruction. One of the major contributions of critical theory has been to make known the political nature of education, including social control and power and its relationship to schooling. Stanley Aronowitz and Henry A. Giroux (1985), both leading contemporary proponents of critical theory, look to the classroom teacher for a more activist role in bringing about change.

> If radical educators are going to take seriously the need to develop workable alternatives to the current forms of schooling, . . . they will . . . have to investigate how the teaching field has evolved under conditions where race, gender, and class-specific practices have become part and parcel of the teaching profession. This suggests that teachers be prepared not only to produce oppositional forms of knowledge and social practice, but that they also be prepared to struggle and to take risks in fighting against injustices . . . (p.161)

More recently, some critical theorists have identified with a philosophical movement called *postmodern constructivism*. Postmodern constructivism represents a combination of existentialism, pragmatism, and the critical theory of Marxism (Pulliam & Van Patten, 1995). Similar to other social reconstructionists, postmodern constructivists emphasize innovation, change, and diversity, but differ in their view of metaphysics or how reality is constructed and perceived. They believe that individuals construct their own meaning from personal experience. They also suggest that history itself is a social construction (Newman, 1998).

Give several examples of how students might construct their own knowledge and meaning in your subject area.

According to contemporary critical theorists, modern reconstructionists must help create communities of "responsible defiance and action" (Giroux, 1988). Modern reconstructionism has been called a "theory of education-as-politics," a "theory of transformation," and "a theory of social reform." For the social reconstructionist, the school should be an agency of social change, a participant in the construction of a society free of all forms of discrimination, and an institution that is concerned with issues of global welfare.

Curriculum

Since the majority of social reconstructionists believe in the importance of democracy and the proposition that the school is the fundamental institution in modern society, the curriculum of the social reconstructionist school would reflect those democratic ideals. The emphasis of the curriculum would be on literacy, not cultural literacy, but *critical literacy*. Such a curriculum would denounce any form of the politics of exclusion, including elevating Eurocentrism as the model for cultural literacy. Rather, it would challenge all unequal power relationships and focus on power as applied to class, gender, sexuality, race, and nationalism. Critical theorists would focus on an analysis of language as well as an exploration of the students' own autobiographical histories, languages, and cultures.

Students would be challenged to think about the world in critical terms, to examine the hidden values of knowledge (Kincheloe, 1993), and to acquire and critically question moral beliefs (Liston & Zeichner, 1988). As postmodern constructivists, students would be encouraged to construct new ideas, concepts, and meanings based on their past knowledge and experience. (See Chapter 14 for a more detailed description of the constructivist curriculum). Cultural pluralism,

Social reconstructionists aspire to improve, change, or reform society.

human relations, group dynamics, problem detecting, problem solving, and the politics of change would be highlighted. Rather than concentrate on separate subjects, students would consider societal problems such as the place of biomedical ethics in improving the quality of life, the need to conserve our natural resources, and the issues of foreign policy and nationalism.

Teaching Methods

Teaching methods associated with social reconstructionism would encourage students to become involved in the social problems that confront the community and society. Rather than merely reading and studying about the problems of the poor or the disenfranchised, the students would spend time in the community becoming acquainted with and immersed in their problems and their possible solutions. They would interview community members to learn about the realities of their lives, including the constraints and obstacles they face in trying to change their situation; they would analyze, research, and link the underlying issues to institutions and structures in the community and larger society. Last, they would take some action or responsibility in planning for change.

The teaching strategies of computer simulation, role-playing, cooperative learning, internships, and work-study experiences would be compatible with social reconstruction. Students would work closely with older peers and adults on various aspects of problem detection and problem solving to enlarge their range of experience. Social reconstructionists, in particular, critical theorists, draw heavily on the use of the metaphor and the narrative as a teaching method since it is essential to all scientific and creative thinking and involves the mix of different ideas in unforseen ways (Kincheloe, 1993).

Classroom Management

The classroom environment of the social reconstructionist would be a climate of inquiry that questions the assumptions of the status quo and examines societal issues and future trends. The social reconstructionist would strive to organize his or her classroom in a classless, nonsexist, and nonracist manner. Social reconstructionists have a penchant for utopian thinking and alternative solutions. Therefore, the environment of the classroom might take on a "think tank" or problem-solving atmosphere in which students would be encouraged to take on new roles and experiment with the ideal world. There would be less emphasis on management and control, and more focus on community building in the classroom. Individualized instruction based on the students' varied cultures, experiences, and needs would be important.

An atmosphere that promotes analysis, criticism, and action research would best describe this type of classroom environment. Conflict resolution and differences in world views would be encouraged and reinforced.

Evaluation

Social reconstructionists and critical theorists oppose standardized testing including teacher competency testing. For a social reconstructionist, the foundation for evaluation would evolve around the ability to think in critical terms and to expose underlying assumptions and practices. The type of evaluation that would be appropriate for both the student and the teacher in a social reconstructionist school would be *authentic assessment* including formative evaluation, which would entail a cooperative effort between student and teacher, student and student, teacher and administrator or supervisor, and community and teacher. Information would be shared regularly during periodic formal and informal conferences, and the student or teacher being evaluated would be an active participant in the process. Although the social reconstructionist educator would consider the needs of the individual as well as the needs of the organization, conflict would not be viewed as failure, nor would the lack of consensus be considered problematic.

The Social Reconstructionist Teacher

The metaphors "shaper of a new society," "transformational leader," and "change agent" aptly describe the social reconstructionist teacher. George S. Counts (1933) described the teacher and his or her responsibilities for reform in the following way:

> To teach the ideal in its historic form, without the illumination that comes from an effort to apply it to contemporary society, is an extreme evidence of intellec-

Ivan Illich (left) and Paulo Freire (right) found new approaches to education that revolutionized schooling.

tual dishonesty. It constitutes an attempt to educate the youth for life in a world that does not exist. Teachers, therefore, cannot evade the responsibility of participating actively in the task of reconstituting the democratic tradition and of thus working positively toward a new society. (p. 19)

Social reconstructionist teachers must also be willing to engage in ongoing renewal of their personal and professional lives. They must be willing to critique and evaluate the conditions under which they work, and extend their educative role outside the domains of the classroom and school. They must have a high tolerance for ambiguity, be comfortable with constant change, and be willing to think about their own thinking and the cultural and psychosocial forces that have shaped it. As an educational reformer, such a teacher detests the status quo and views the school as a particular culture in evolution. Moreover, he or she views the larger society as an experiment that will always be unfinished and in flux. Such a teacher must be willing to engage in, and form, alliances with community groups, neighborhood organizations, social movements, and parents to critique and question the practice of school democracy and school policy.

The social reconstructionist teacher should have excellent interpersonal communication skills and have command of languages. He or she should have a background in the sociology of education, the politics of education, conflict management, organizational theory, and organizational development. The teacher must be open to diversity and view education from a global perspective. He or she must be widely read and be able to make available alternative materials and literature that reflect the amassed cultural experiences of marginal groups. According to Giroux (1993), the role of the teacher is "to engage popular culture, to question and unlearn the benefits of privilege, and to allow those who have generally not been allowed to speak to narrate themselves, to speak from the specificity of their own voices" (p. 54).

Leading Educational Proponents

George S. Counts, Theodore Brameld (1904–1987), Harold Rugg, John Childs, and W. H. Kilpatrick were perhaps the best known of the American social reconstructionists who, in the early part of this century, attempted to bring about major educational reform. Each of these individuals advocated the transformation of society and envisioned an ideal and more equitable world. Two contemporary spokespersons for the social reconstructionist theory of education are Ivan Illich (1926–) and Paulo Freire (1921–1997).

Illich (1974), in his *Deschooling Society,* maintained that since schools have corrupted society, one can create a better society only by abolishing schools altogether and finding new approaches to education. Illich called for a total political and educational revolution. Freire, who was born, was educated, and taught in Latin America, proposed that education be drawn from the everyday life experiences of the learners. From his students, the illiterate and oppressed peasants of Brazil and Chile, he drew his theory of educational reconstructionism. In his *Pedagogy of the Oppressed* (1973), Freire maintained that students should not be manipulated or controlled but should be involved in their own learning. According to Freire, by exchanging and examining their experiences with peers and mentors, students who are socially, economically, and politically disadvantaged can plan, initiate, and take action for their own lives. As with any learners, the key to working with these disadvantaged individuals is a teacher who respects and cares about his or her students.

During the past two decades, several leading proponents of critical theory, or critical pedagogy, have gained prominence in the literature and have made a major impact on curriculum reform in almost all disciplines. Critical theorists do not view the major philosophical works as "truths," but constructed works that dominant groups have used at various points in history to secure a sense of legitimacy and power (Gutek, 1997). They also question the legitimacy of knowledge and who controls "how and what we know." Unlike idealists, realists, perennialists, and essentialists, who do not question who controls the social and economic goals of education, critical theorists do. Some of the major proponents of critical theory include Michael W. Apple, Stanley Aronowitz, Sam Bowles, Cleo Cherryholmes, Herbert Gintis, Henry A. Giroux, Joe L. Kincheloe, Colin Lankshear, Peter L. McLaren, Jane Roland Martin, William B. Stanley, and Robert E. Young.

Michael Apple is one of the leading spokespersons of critical theory who has questioned, "Who controls the social economic purposes of education?"

Some of the leading proponents of postmodern constructivism include Jean-Francois Lyotard, Jacques Derrida, Michael Foucault, and Richard Rorty (Beck, 1994). Figure 4.6 presents an overview of social reconstructionism including the role of critical theory and the postmodern constructivist movement.

Identifying Your Philosophy of Education

Educational philosophies and educational theories do not remain static, but constantly change depending on the social, economic, and political climate at the time. Upon visiting any school, it quickly becomes evident that a variety of philosophies and theories of education can coexist in the same school, or perhaps in the same classroom. Few teachers operate from a single philosophical or theoretical perspective. Most educators are eclectic and sample a variety of ideas, propositions, principles, or axioms that represent a smorgasbord of views.

Identifying and developing your philosophy of education may appear to be a formidable task. Yet, it is one of the most important tasks that you will probably be asked to perform as a prospective teacher. It is not uncommon to be asked to articulate your philosophy of education on job applications or in job inter-

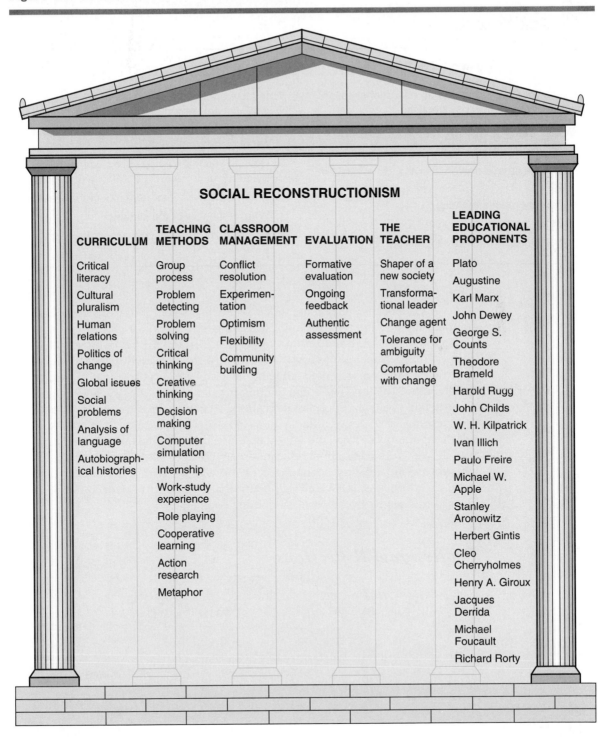

SOCIAL RECONSTRUCTIONISM

CURRICULUM	TEACHING METHODS	CLASSROOM MANAGEMENT	EVALUATION	THE TEACHER	LEADING EDUCATIONAL PROPONENTS
Critical literacy	Group process	Conflict resolution	Formative evaluation	Shaper of a new society	Plato
Cultural pluralism	Problem detecting	Experimentation	Ongoing feedback	Transformational leader	Augustine
Human relations	Problem solving	Optimism	Authentic assessment	Change agent	Karl Marx
Politics of change	Critical thinking	Flexibility		Tolerance for ambiguity	John Dewey
Global issues	Creative thinking	Community building		Comfortable with change	George S. Counts
Social problems	Decision making				Theodore Brameld
Analysis of language	Computer simulation				Harold Rugg
Autobiographical histories	Internship				John Childs
	Work-study experience				W. H. Kilpatrick
	Role playing				Ivan Illich
	Cooperative learning				Paulo Freire
	Action research				Michael W. Apple
	Metaphor				Stanley Aronowitz
					Herbert Gintis
					Cleo Cherryholmes
					Henry A. Giroux
					Jacques Derrida
					Michael Foucault
					Richard Rorty

Ask Yourself

What Is My Philosophy of Education?

To assess your preference for an educational philosophy, answer the following questions.

1. Are students intrinsically motivated to learn?
2. Should education be the same for everyone?
3. Are there certain universal truths that should be taught?
4. What determines morality?
5. What is the ideal curriculum?
6. What is the purpose of schooling?
7. If you were to choose one method or instructional strategy, what would it be?
8. What type of classroom environment is most conducive to learning?
9. How do you know when your students have learned?
10. What is the most important role of the teacher?
11. What is the role of the student?
12. How should prospective teachers be prepared?

views. School districts may require that you express your philosophical ideas and compare them to the philosophy or mission of the school district.

In Chapter 3 you were asked to respond to a series of questions that reflected your personal philosophy of life. You were also advised that the answers to those questions represented some of the assumptions you hold about teaching and learning. The time has come to combine philosophy, theory, and practice in constructing your philosophy of education. Your responses to the basic theoretical questions listed above reflect your philosophy of education. As you ask yourself these questions, recall the importance of clarity and meaning in the language you choose. Your ideas about education may change before you enter the teaching profession, and may change one or more times during the course of your career. Nevertheless, it is vitally important that you begin to conceptualize those ideas at this stage of your professional development.

Professional Reflections

"Teachers must believe that all students are capable of learning, then create a learning environment that propels students to success."

Carol Banaszynski, Teacher of the Year, Wisconsin

"Teachers must realize that all students do not start at the same point or with the same agendas. Sometimes, just developing a classroom climate that is conducive to learning is a major obstacle."

Linda S. Bates, Teacher of the Year, New Mexico

Summary

There are six major theories of education: perennialism, progressivism, behaviorism, essentialism, existentialism, and social reconstructionism. Educational theories influence educational practice by their impact on curriculum, teaching methods, classroom management, evaluation, and the role of the teacher. Each theory developed from a particular philosophy or philosophies. Most theories were formulated as a protest against the prevailing social and cultural forces at the time. The educational theories of perennialism and essentialism have much in common in that they underscore the importance of a liberal education and the wisdom of the past. Behaviorism differs from the other educational theories in that behaviorists believe all behaviors are both objective and observable, while the other theories do not.

Progressivism, existentialism, and social reconstructionism share a common theme in that each of them is more concerned with the study of the present and future than the past. Unlike the perennialist or essentialist who emphasize the important cultural and historic roots of the past, the progressivist, existentialist, and social reconstructionist stress that which is meaningful and relevant to the student today.

In the next chapter, you will explore the historical origins of Western education. You will also examine the beginnings of American education as it evolved in the thirteen original colonies.

Key Terms

Alternative schools

Authentic assessment

Back-to-basics movement

Behavioral objectives

Behaviorism

Classical conditioning

Critical literacy

Critical theory

Cultural literacy

Essentialism

Formative evaluation

Great Books

Humanistic education

New basics

Nongraded schools

Open classroom

Operant conditioning

Perennialism

Postmodern constructivism

Premack principle

Programmed instruction

Progressivism

Social reconstructionism

Theory

Theory of education

Whole-child movement

Discussion Questions

1. Reflect on the vignette at the beginning of this chapter. Which theory of education would you ascribe to Jim? To Beth? To Sam? Explain.

2. Describe the relationship among philosophy of life, educational theory, and philosophy of education.

3. Which of the theories of education presented in this chapter is most similar to your theory of education? In what ways is it similar?

4. B. F. Skinner and other advocates of operant conditioning have been criticized for their emphasis on control. Are freedom and control incompatible concepts in the classroom? Explain.

5. As a social reconstructionist, list five major changes that you would propose for education and schooling in the twenty-first century. Should teachers and students be involved in promoting these changes? Why? Why not?

6. Compare and contrast the teaching methods advocated by the essentialist and the existentialist.

7. Describe the classroom management strategies advocated by the perennialist. How do they differ from those of the behaviorist?

8. Choose a leading educational proponent of essentialism and, using his or her theory, construct a letter to the editor of a newspaper suggesting how the training of teachers today should be reformed.

Internet Resources

1. **www.udel.edu/apa/**
   The home page for the American Philosophical Association provides information about the organization and its activities, as well as links to numerous sites dedicated to various philosophers, guides to philosophy, journals, and more.

2. **www.personal.monash.edu.au/ ~dey/phil**
   Philosophy in Cyberspace has links to literally hundreds of sites dealing with the various branches of philosophy, philosophers, organizations, journals, conferences, forums, and more.

3. **www.earlham.edu/suber/ philinks.htm**
   Guide to Philosophy on the Internet provides links to a host of guides, dic-

tionaries, quotations, biographies, and mailing lists—almost any topic of interest to the student of philosophy.

4. **plato.stanford.edu**
   Stanford Encyclopedia of Philosophy is a "dynamic" (i.e., continually updated), searchable encyclopedia of philosophy.

5. **ftp.tuwlen.ac.at/faqs/newsfaqs/ alt.postmodern/alt.postmodern-FAQ**
   This is a frequently asked questions (FAQ) archive that provides a host of general information on postmodernism.

6. **www.cudenver.edu/~mryder/ ite-data/postmodern.html**
   This comprehensive site houses a collection of resources on critical and postmodern theories.

References

Adler, M. (1982). *The Paideia proposal: An educational manifesto.* New York: Macmillan.

Adler, M. (1984). *The Paideia program.* New York: Macmillan.

Aronowitz, S. A., & Giroux, H. A. (1985). *Education under siege: The conservative, liberal and radical debate over schooling*. MA: Gergin & Garvey.

Barnes, H. E. (1968). *An existentialist ethics*. New York: Alfred A. Knopf.

Bates, J. A. (1987). Reinforcement. In M. J. Dunkin (Ed.), *The international encyclopedia of teaching and teacher education* (pp. 349–358). New York: Pergamon Books.

Bayles, E. E. (1966). *Pragmatism in education*. New York: Harper & Row.

Beck, C. (1994). Postmodernism, pedagogy, and philosophy of education. *Philosophy of education: Proceedings of the forty-ninth annual meeting of the Philosophy of Education Society*. Urbana, IL: Philosophy of Education Society, University of Illinois.

Bennett, W. J. (1993). *The book of virtues: A treasury of great moral stories*. New York: Simon & Schuster.

Bloom, A. (1987). *The closing of the American mind*. New York: Simon and Schuster.

Butler, J. D. (1966). *Idealism in education*. New York: Harper & Row.

Conant, J. B. (1959). *The American high school today*. New York: McGraw-Hill.

Counts, G. S. (1933). *A call to the teachers of America*. New York: John Day.

Delattre, E. J. (1984). The intellectual lives of teachers. In C. E. Finn, D. Ravitch, & R. T. Fancher (Eds.), *Against mediocrity* (pp. 154–171). New York: Holmes & Meier.

Dewey, J. (1920). *Reconstruction in philosophy*. New York: H. Holt.

Dewey, J. (1938). *Experience and education*. New York: Macmillan.

Dewey, J. (1956). *The child and the curriculum and the school and society*. Chicago: University of Chicago Press.

Dewey, J. (1963). *Experience and education*. New York: Collier.

Emmer, E. T. (1987). Classroom management. In M. J. Dunkin (Ed.), *The international encyclopedia of teaching and teacher education* (pp. 437–446). New York: Pergamon Books.

Freire, P. (1973). *Pedagogy of the oppressed*. New York: Seabury Press.

Giroux, H. A. (1988). *Schooling and the struggle for public life: Critical pedagogy in the modern age*. Minneapolis, MN: University of Minnesota Press.

Giroux, H. A. (1993). *Living dangerously: Multiculturalism and the politics of difference*. New York: Peter Lang.

Greene, M. (1967). *Existential encounters for teachers*. New York: Random House.

Gutek, G. (1997). *Philosophical and ideological perspectives on education*. Boston: Allyn and Bacon.

Hirsch, E. D., Jr., Kett, J. F., & Trefil, J. (1993). *The dictionary of cultural literacy*. Boston: Houghton Mifflin.

Hirsch, E. D., Jr. (1996). *The schools we need and why we don't have them*. New York: Doubleday.

Holt, J. (1981). *Teach your own*. New York: Delacorte/Seymour Laurence.

Hutchins, R. M. (1936). *The higher learning in America*. New Haven, CT: Yale University Press.

Illich, I. (1974). *Deschooling society*. New York: Harper & Row.

Jacobsen, D. A. (1999). *Philosophy in classroom teaching*. Upper Saddle River, NJ: Prentice Hall.

Kane, T. (1950). Noblest teacher of teachers. *Dominicans, 35,* 14.

Kincheloe, J. L. (1993). *Toward a critical politics of teacher thinking: Mapping the postmodern*. Westport, CT: Bergin & Garvey.

Kneller, G. F. (1958). *Existentialism and education*. New York: John Wiley & Sons.

Kneller, G. F. (1971). *Introduction to the philosophy of education*. New York: John Wiley & Sons.

Kneller, G. F. (1984). *Movements of thought in modern education*. New York: John Wiley & Sons.

Kozol, J. (1972). *Free schools*. Boston: Houghton Mifflin.

Kozol, J. (1991). *Savage inequalities*. New York: Crown.

Lerner, M. (1962). *Education and radical humanism*. Columbus, OH: Ohio State University Press.

Liston, D., & Zeichner, K. (1988). *Critical*. Paper presented to the American Educational Research Association, New Orleans, LA.

Long, L., & Ihle, E. (1988). Philosophy of education. In M. P. Sadker & D. M. Sadker,

Teachers, schools, and society (pp. 422–459). New York: Random House.

Maritain, J. (1941). *Scholasticism and politics.* New York: Macmillan.

Marler, C. D. (1975). *Philosophy and schooling.* Boston: Allyn and Bacon.

Morris, V. C. (1966). *Existentialism in education.* New York: Harper & Row.

Morris, V. C., & Pai, Y. (1976). *Philosophy in the American school.* Boston: Houghton Mifflin.

National Commission on Excellence in Education. (1983). *A nation at risk: The imperative for educational reform.* Washington, DC: U.S. Government Printing Office.

Neill, A. S. (1960). *Summerhill: A radical approach to child rearing.* New York: Hart.

Newman, J. W. (1998). *America's teachers.* New York: Longman.

Noddings, N. (1992). *The challenge to care in schools: An alternative approach to education.* New York: Teachers College Press.

Noddings, N. (1993). *Educating for intelligent belief or unbelief.* New York: Teachers College Press.

Ozmon, H. A., & Craver, S. M. (1990). *Philosophical foundations of education.* Columbus, OH: Merrill.

Phillips, D. C., & Soltis, J. F. (1991). *Perspectives on learning.* New York: Teachers College Press.

Pulliam, J. D., & Van Patten, J. (1995). *History of education in America* (6th ed.). Columbus, OH: Merrill.

Rickover, H. G. (1963). *Education and freedom.* New York: New American Library.

Rogers, C. R. (1969). *Freedom to learn.* Columbus, OH: Merrill.

Ruenzel, D. (1997, May/June). Look who's talking. *Teacher Magazine, 8,* 26–31.

Silberman, C. (1970). *Crisis in the classroom.* New York: Random House.

Westheimer, J., & Kahne, J. (1993). Building school communities: An experience-based model. *Phi Delta Kappan, 75* (4), 324–328.

Wingo, G. M. (1974). *Philosophies of education: An introduction.* Lexington, MA: D.C. Heath.

Wittrock, M. C. (1987). Models of heuristic teaching. In M. J. Dunkin (Ed.), *The international encyclopedia of teaching and teacher education* (pp. 68–76). New York: Pergamon Books.

Part Three

Historical Foundations of Education

Chapter 5

Only the educated are free.

Plato

American Education: European Heritage and Colonial Experience

➤ In his tenth Annual Report, the great American educator Horace Mann said, "I believe in the existence of a great, immutable principle of natural law . . . which proves the absolute right of every human being that comes into the world to an education; and which, of course, proves the correlative duty of every government to see that the means of that education are provided for all."

The United States Supreme Court, in Brown v. Topeka (1954), stated: "Today education is perhaps the most important function of state and local governments. Compulsory school attendance laws and the great expenditures for education both demonstrate our recognition of the importance of education to our democratic society. It is required in the performance of our most basic public responsibilities, even service in the armed forces. It is the very foundation of good citizenship. . . . Such an opportunity [of an education], where the state has undertaken to provide it, is a right which must be made available to all on equal terms." Yet, since the Constitution makes no mention of education, the question of whether it should be considered one of the fundamental rights implicitly guaranteed has been one of continued debate.

In your opinion, is the right to an education one of those inalienable rights that should be guaranteed by the government? Why? What are the implications of your decision?

When the courts consider cases that involve interpretation of the Constitution or specific laws, they often review historical records and consider the context of the time to try to determine the intent of the lawmakers. Similarly, studying the history of education helps educators to understand the development of educational thought and practice and to evaluate present educational institutions, theories, and practices in the light of past successes and failures. To help you develop insights into the European and colonial background of American education presented in this chapter, keep the following learning objectives in mind:

- Contrast Spartan and Athenian education.
- Compare Aristotle's and Plato's educational philosophies.
- Explain the contribution of Quintilian to the development of European educational thought and practice.
- Describe the influence of Arab scholars on Western education.
- Discuss the impact of the Reformation on the provision of education.

- Identify the contributions of Bacon, Comenius, Locke, Rousseau, Pestalozzi, Herbart, and Froebel to current educational practice.
- Describe the curriculum in colonial elementary and secondary schools and the forces that shaped it.
- Compare education in the New England, Middle Atlantic, and Southern colonies.

European Background of American Education

Education in Ancient Societies

The oldest known schools were those of Sumer, an area lying between the Tigris and Euphrates rivers in Mesopotamia. They date from the third millennium B.C. Most of these schools were connected with a temple and taught writing and some calculations. The Sumerian language was not alphabetic, but consisted of 600 or more characters. Writing was done on clay tablets called cuneiform tablets, so a school was called the Tablet House or *edubba*.

Temple schools were also operated in ancient Egypt. Attended almost exclusively by the children of the upper class, their purpose was to prepare the educated bureaucracy needed to administer the vast Egyptian empire and to further the technologies needed to build the architectural monuments for which Egypt is so well known. The curriculum of the Egyptian school at the lower level emphasized writing, music, religion, astronomy, and mathematics. After six to ten years a limited number of students went on to advanced studies in religion, medicine, and architecture. Students were taught using an elaborate system of pictographic script known as hieroglyphics. While lower-level students used clay tablets, students at the upper level used papyrus, a form of paper made from reeds that was invented by the Egyptians.

Although the Sumarians and Egyptians did operate schools, the Greeks are considered the first real educators in the Western world, "for they were the first western peoples to think seriously and profoundly about educating the young, the first to ask what education is, what it is for, and how children and men should be educated" (Castle, 1967, p. 11). However, while the Greeks were interested in education, they were not all in agreement as to what form it should take. For example, as described next, the content and approach to education in the two principal city-states, Sparta and Athens, were quite different.

Education in Sparta

Sparta was predominantly a military state, and education reflected Spartan life. The maintenance of military strength was the most important goal of the government. The welfare of the individual came second to the welfare of the state, life was regimented by the state, and severe limits were placed on individual freedoms. Creative or strictly intellectual pursuits were discouraged. The aim of the educational system was to inculcate patriotism and the ideal of the sacrifice of the individual to the state, as well as to develop and train physically fit and courageous warriors.

At the age of seven, boys were enrolled in state military companies where they lived in public barracks and ate at common tables. Training was concerned with cultivating the four great virtues: prudence, temperance, fortitude, and obedience. A system of exercise and games, becoming more military as the boys got older, was designed to make them obey commands, endure hardships, and be successful in battle. Dance and music were taught, but they too involved military and moral themes. Only minimal attention was given to reading and writing.

Girls in Sparta received no formal education. They were trained at home by their mothers in the ideals of the state and housewifery. They were also organized by troops and engaged in competitive sports. Their physical training was so that they might produce strong sons for the state.

Education in Athens

Where Sparta was renowned for its military preeminence, Athens was a democracy that held the individual in the highest regard. There was no compulsory education in Athens, except for two years beginning at age 18 when military training was required of all males. Schools in Athens were private and were restricted to those who could afford the fees.

Education in Athens prior to 479 B.C. (the defeat of Sparta), referred to as "the old education," consisted of sending boys aged 7 to 14 to several schools: the *didascaleum* or music school; the home or building of the *grammatistes* for the study of reading, writing, and arithmetic; and the *palestra* for physical education. After age 14 formal education stopped, although some youth continued their education at the *gymnasia* where they received more severe physical training, somewhat military in nature. From age 18 to 20 a program involving military, public, and religious service was required of all young men; upon completion full citizenship was granted. The aim of educating males in the Athenian state was to prepare a cultivated, well-mannered, physically fit, and agile individual ready for participation in Athenian citizenship.

What aspects of the educational systems of Sparta and Athens do you find appropriate for today's students?

The traditional view of the education of girls in Athens is that they only received instruction at home. Yet archaeological evidence seems to point to a different conclusion. Various pottery and statues depict girls going to school (e.g., a girl holding a tablet in one hand and a purse containing her astragals in the other), as well as reading, writing, and engaging in sports. However, it is uncertain how widespread these practices were (Beck, 1964).

Sophists. The "new Greek education" (post–479 B.C.) continued much the same at the elementary level. At the secondary level, however, a new element was introduced—the Sophists, traveling teachers who charged admission to their popular lectures. In the absence of a legal profession, some Sophists developed the practice of logography, the writing of speeches that their clients could deliver in courts of law. Sets of speeches and handbooks on rhetoric were sold. Schools of rhetoric grew in size and number. Two of the more famous Sophists were Gorgras, a renowned orator who in his seventies was still enthralling the audience at the Olympic Games of 407 B.C., and Protagoras. The latter was considered to be so brilliant that he could charge a student as much as $10,000. Even Plato esteemed Protagoras as a man of sterling quality. Protagoras is considered the father of European grammar and philosophy (Meyer, 1972).

Socrates (469–399 B.C.). In contrast to the Sophists, Socrates did not commercialize his teaching and accepted no fees. He also disagreed with the use of knowledge merely to achieve success or gain power, but believed that knowledge was ethically and morally important to all men. According to Socrates, knowledge was a virtue that was both eternal and universal.

To Socrates the purpose of education was not to perfect the art of rhetoric, but to develop in the individual his inherent knowledge and to perfect the ability to reason. Socrates believed that education and society were inextricably related: society was only as good as its schools. If education was successful in producing good citizens, then society would be strong and good.

Can you recall an example of the application of the Socratic Method in your own educational experience?

Socratic Method. Socrates employed a dialectical teaching method that has come to be known as the *Socratic Method* and is similar to the inquiry method practiced today. Using this method Socrates would first demolish false or shaky opinions or assumptions held by the student while disclaiming any knowledge himself. Then, through a questioning process based on the student's experiences and analyzing the consequences of responses, he led the student to a better understanding of the problem. Finally, he brought the student to a discovery of general ideas or concepts that could be applied to new problems.

> "What is courage?" he would casually ask a soldier.
> "Courage is holding your ground when things get rough."
> "But supposing strategy required that you give way?"
> "Well, in that case you wouldn't hold—that would be silly."
> "Then you agree that courage is neither holding or giving way."
> "I guess so. I don't know."
> "Well, I don't know either. Maybe it might be just using your head. What do you say to that?"
> "Yes—that's it; using your head, that's what it is."
> "Then shall we say, at least tentatively, that courage is presence of mind—sound judgment in time of stress?"
> "Yes." (Meyer, 1972, p. 26)

Plato. Socrates' most famous pupil was Plato. Plato founded the *Academy,* a school of higher learning that admitted both males and females. Fees were not charged, but donations were accepted. As a teacher Plato practiced a variety of methods. Sometimes he employed the Socratic Method. At other times he assigned individual exercises and problems. Sometimes he lectured, though according to Meyer (1972), he was too technical and lecturing was not his best performance. Plato's theory of education is most clearly put forward in *The Republic* and the *Law.* In *The Republic* Plato begins by accepting Socrates' premise that "knowledge is virtue." He then expounds on the nature of knowledge and lays out the framework for both a political and social system, including an educational system. Plato believed that the state should operate the educational system. The aim of the schools was to discover and develop the abilities of the individual, to aid the individual in discovering the knowledge of truth that is within each of us, and to prepare the individual for his or her role in society. The curriculum was to include reading, especially the classics, writing, mathematics, and logic. Plato also emphasized the physical aspects of education. However, games and sports, as well as music, were important not for the purpose of entertainment but to improve the soul and achieve moral excellence.

Although Plato advocated universal education, he presumed that few possessed the capacity to reach its final stages. Those who passed the successive selection tests and reached the highest levels of wisdom and devotion to the state were to rule the state—the philosopher was to be king (Good & Teller, 1969). Education, then, is the means by which one arrives at the ultimate good. In the process it promotes the happiness and fulfillment of the individual (because he is sorted into the social office to which he is most fitted), as well as the good of the state. Plato's belief in leadership by the most intelligent has been espoused by countless since, including some of the founders of our nation. His belief in unchanging ideas and absolute truths has earned him the title of "the Father of Idealism."

Aristotle. Aristotle was Plato's most famous student. For 20 years he studied and taught at the Academy. However, as the picture at the beginning of this chapter aptly reminds us, and as discussed in Chapter 3, they differed in some important respects. In the picture Plato is shown pointing heavenward as Aristotle points earthward. And that, metaphorically, was the main difference between them: Plato was the idealist, the lover of the metaphysical; Aristotle was a realist, the more scientific of the two (Winn & Jacks, 1967).

It is probably fair to say that Aristotle has had more of an impact on education than either Socrates or Plato, perhaps because he gave the most systematic attention to it. Aristotle is credited with the introduction of the scientific method of inquiry. He systematically classified all branches of existing knowledge and was the first to teach logic as a formal discipline. He believed that reality was to be found in an objective order.

Like Plato, Aristotle believed in the importance of education to the functioning of society and that education should be provided by the state; unlike Plato, he did not believe in educating girls. The aim of education, he felt, is the achievement of the highest possible happiness of the individual by the development of the intellect through the cultivating of habits and the specific use of inductive and deductive reasoning (Bowen, 1972). An additional aim is to produce the good person and good citizen. "The good person should have goodness of intellect which may be achieved by instruction, and goodness of character attained through conditioning of the control of habits" (Gillett, 1966, p. 36).

Last, Aristotle believed that there was a common core of knowledge that was basic to education, which included reading, writing, music, and physical education. This belief in a "core" of knowledge has prevailed through the centuries and is the basis for the core course requirement in American schools and colleges today.

Education in Rome

The Roman conquest of Greece in the second century B.C. brought thousands of Greek slaves to Rome and brought Romans into contact with Greece and its culture. The educational theories of the Greeks had a great impact on the

Romans, and by the end of the first century they dominated Roman education. The formal Roman school system that evolved (and that influenced education throughout Europe for centuries) was composed of the elementary school, known as the *ludus,* and the secondary school or grammar school. At the ludus children aged 7 to 12 were taught reading, writing, and accounting. Girls could attend the ludus, but usually that was as far as their education extended. *Grammar schools* were attended by upper class boys aged 12 to 16 who learned grammar (either Greek or Latin) and literature. From age 16 to 20 boys attended the school of rhetoric where they were instructed in grammar, rhetoric, dialectic, music, arithmetic, geometry, and astronomy. Universities were founded during the early years of the Roman Empire. Philosophy, law, mathematics, medicine, architecture, and rhetoric were the principal subjects taught.

Quintilian (35–95 A.D.). The most noteworthy Roman educator was Quintilian, tutor to the emperor's grandsons. His influence on Roman schooling has had a subsequent impact on education through the centuries. Quintilian was so respected that he was made a senator and was the first known state-supported teacher (Wilkins, 1914). His *Institutio Oratoria (Education of the Orator)* is considered to be "the most thorough, systematic and scientific treatment of education to be found in classical literature, whether Greek or Roman" (Monroe, 1939, p. 450).

Quintilian believed education should be concerned with a person's whole intellectual and moral nature, and should have as its goal the production of the effective moral man in practical life (Monroe, 1939). Accordingly, in addition to instruction in grammar and rhetoric, Quintilian recommended a broad literary education that included music, astronomy, geometry, and philosophy. Such an education was to take place in the schools, preferably the public schools, not at home with private tutors as had been the earlier practice in Rome. Public (i.e., group) education, he maintained, provided the opportunity for emulation, friendships, and learning from the successes and failures of others. Progressive for his time, Quintilian (cited in Monroe, 1939) disapproved of corporal punishment.

> first because it is a disgrace . . . and in reality . . . an affront; secondly, because if a boy's disposition be so abject as not to be amended by reproof, he will be hardened . . . (by) stripes. Besides, after you have coerced a boy with stripes, how will you treat him when he becomes a young man, to whom such terror cannot be held out? (pp. 466–467)

The Ask Yourself on page 137 will help you examine your position on corporal punishment in today's schools.

In many other respects Quintilian's views seem remarkably modern. Recognizing that "study depends on the good will of the student, a quality that cannot be secured by compulsion," Quintilian supported holidays because "relaxation brings greater energy to study, and also games because it is the nature of young things to play" (Castle, 1967, p. 138). He believed in the importance of early training to child development. Of the proper methods of early instruction Quintilian said: "Let his instruction be an amusement to him; let him be questioned

Should Quintilian be required for teacher education students? Why or why not?

? Ask Yourself

Does Corporal Punishment Have a Place in the Schools?

Quintilian vehemently opposed corporal punishment. The U.S. Supreme Court has said that corporal punishment does not violate the Constitution. Still, a number of states have abolished corporal punishment in the schools. In others, the decision to administer corporal punishment and the procedure to be followed in its administration have been delegated to local school districts. What is your position on corporal punishment? Ask yourself the following questions:

1. Does corporal punishment serve as a deterrent to undesirable behavior?

2. If it is practiced, for what infraction should it be reserved?

3. Who should administer it?

4. Should a teacher or administrator who administers excessive corporal punishment be held liable to prosecution under child abuse statutes?

5. Would you administer corporal punishment if required by the district? (If, for example, district policy stated that after three unexcused tardies to any one class, the student is to be given three swats by the teacher of the class.)

6. If struck by a student, how would you respond?

and praised; and let him never feel pleased that he does not know a thing . . . let his powers be called forth by rewards, such as that age prizes" (cited in Monroe, 1939, p. 455). He also maintained that children should not be introduced to specific subject matter until they are mature enough to master it. Last, Quintilian emphasized the importance of recognizing individual differences when prescribing the curriculum. He charged the teacher to "ascertain first of all, when a boy is entrusted to him, his ability and disposition . . . when a tutor has observed these indications, let him consider how the mind of his pupil is to be managed" (cited in Monroe, 1939, p. 465).

The Roman system of education spread throughout Western Europe. The schools of medieval Europe retained the standard curriculum of the Roman schools: grammar, rhetoric, logic, mathematics, geometry, music, and astronomy. And, Latin remained the language of the scholar until recent times. Figure 5.1 provides an overview of education in Sparta, Athens, and Rome.

Education in the Middle Ages

The period between the end of the Roman Empire (476 A.D.) and the fourteenth century is known as the Middle Ages. The Germanic tribes that conquered the Romans appropriated not only their land but much of their culture and their Catholic religion. The Roman Catholic Church became the dominant force in

Figure 5.1: Education in Ancient Societies

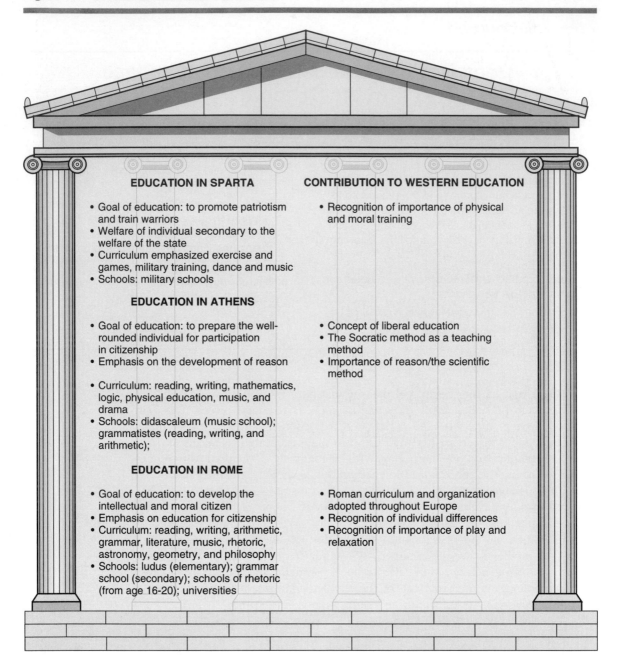

EDUCATION IN SPARTA

- Goal of education: to promote patriotism and train warriors
- Welfare of individual secondary to the welfare of the state
- Curriculum emphasized exercise and games, military training, dance and music
- Schools: military schools

EDUCATION IN ATHENS

- Goal of education: to prepare the well-rounded individual for participation in citizenship
- Emphasis on the development of reason

- Curriculum: reading, writing, mathematics, logic, physical education, music, and drama
- Schools: didascaleum (music school); grammatistes (reading, writing, and arithmetic);

EDUCATION IN ROME

- Goal of education: to develop the intellectual and moral citizen
- Emphasis on education for citizenship
- Curriculum: reading, writing, arithmetic, grammar, literature, music, rhetoric, astronomy, geometry, and philosophy
- Schools: ludus (elementary); grammar school (secondary); schools of rhetoric (from age 16-20); universities

CONTRIBUTION TO WESTERN EDUCATION

- Recognition of importance of physical and moral training

- Concept of liberal education
- The Socratic method as a teaching method
- Importance of reason/the scientific method

- Roman curriculum and organization adopted throughout Europe
- Recognition of individual differences
- Recognition of importance of play and relaxation

society and in education. By the end of the sixth century public education had all but disappeared, and what remained took place under the auspices of the church. At the secondary level, monastic schools, originally established to train the clergy, educated boys in the established disciplines of the Roman schools. Theology was studied by those preparing for the priesthood. One important function of the monastic schools was preserving and copying manuscripts. Had it not been for the monastic schools, many of the ancient manuscripts we have today would have been lost.

Alcuin and the Palace School

Another type of school, the palace school, was established by the Emperor Charlemagne (742–814). Charlemagne brought one of the most revered scholars and teachers of his age, Alcuin of York (England), to his court to establish a school. Through Alcuin's efforts, the school became an important force in education in Europe. Charlemagne and all the members of his family studied at the school, and many future teachers, writers, and scholars were trained there.

During this time the curriculum consisted of what was called the *seven liberal arts,* which included the *trivium* (grammar, rhetoric, and logic) and the *quadrivium* (arithmetic, geometry, music, and astronomy). The term "liberal arts," if not the exact subjects, is still used today to describe that portion of the college curriculum that is not concerned with technical or professional studies.

Thomas Aquinas

The most important scholar and philosopher of the Middle Ages was the Dominican monk St. Thomas Aquinas. As discussed in Chapter 3, his philosophy, called *scholasticism* or *Neo-Thomism,* is the foundation of Roman Catholic education. Aquinas was able to reconcile religion with the rationalism of Aristotle. He believed that human beings possess both a spiritual nature, the soul, and a physical nature, the body. He also maintained that man is a rational being and that through the deductive process of rational analysis man can arrive at truth. When reason fails, man must rely on faith. Thus reason supports what man knows by faith: reason and faith are complementary sources of truth. In accordance with this philosophy, the schools were to teach both the principles of the faith and rational philosophy. The curriculum was to contain both theology and the liberal arts.

The Medieval Universities

During the later Middle Ages, as the Crusades opened Europe to other parts of the world and as many of the Greek masterpieces that had disappeared from Europe but had been preserved by Arab scholars were rediscovered, there was an intellectual revival that manifested itself not only in scholasticism but in the establishment of several of the world's great universities. The University of Salerno, established in 1050 A.D., specialized in medicine; the University of Bologna (1113 A.D.) in law; the University of Paris (1160 A.D.) in theology; and Oxford University (1349 A.D.) in liberal arts and theology. By the end of the Middle Ages some 80 universities were in existence (Meyer, 1972). Some, such as the University of Paris, grew out of a cathedral school, in this case Notre Dame. Others evolved from associations called *universitas,* which were chartered corporations of teachers and students, organized for their protection against interference from secular or religious authorities.

At first most universities did not have buildings of their own but occupied rented space. The curriculum at the undergraduate level followed the seven liberal arts. Classes started soon after sunrise. The mode of instruction was lecture in Latin, with the teacher usually reading from a text he had written. Student guilds or unions, commonplace at the time, ventured to tell the professors how fast to speak. At Bologna the students wanted to get full value for their fees and required the professors to speak very fast. By contrast, the Parisian students insisted on a leisurely pace, and when the authorities ordered some acceleration, the students not only "howled and clamored" but threatened to go on strike (Meyer, 1972). More exciting than the lectures were the *disputations* at which students presented and debated opposing intellectual positions. The disputations also served to prepare students for the much dreaded day when they would defend their theses. The Historical Note below provides a brief glimpse of the life of the university student in medieval times. Note the differences and similarities with today.

Of all the institutions that have survived from medieval times to the present, with the exception of the Catholic Church, the university bears the closest resemblance to its ancient ancestors. As it was then, it is still an organization of students and professors dedicated to the pursuit of knowledge. It still grants the

If the student guild or union were in effect today, what changes might it recommend for undergraduate education?

 Historical Note

Life of the Medieval University Student

Although academic life was rigorous, students had many privileges. They were exempt from military service and from paying taxes. A student who shaved his head and assumed a few other burdens became one of the clerical class and was allowed some of the benefits associated with it. For example, if he broke what would be considered civil law, he was tried under church law, not civil law. However, in keeping with his clerical status the student was required to be celibate. If he did stray, he could continue with his studies, but lost his privileges and could receive no degree.

Medieval students were not without vices. Taverns often surrounded the universities and at the taverns were women and gambling. More seriously, students at Oxford were said to roam the streets at night, assaulting all who passed. In Rome the students went from tavern to tavern committing assault and robbery. At Leipzig they were fined for throwing stones at professors, and at Paris they were excommunicated for shooting dice on the altars of Notre-Dame.

Although these acts were the exceptions rather than the rule, such actions, as well as the attitude of the students, who held townspeople in low regard, were sufficient to lead to open hostilities between "town" and "gown." Some separation exists between town and gown in many university communities today, perhaps a legacy from our medieval ancestors.

Source: Based on accounts in Meyer, A. E. (1972). *An educational history of the western world.* New York: McGraw-Hill.

Even before the Middle Ages, Arab universities had been established in Spain and the Middle East.

medieval degrees: the bachelor's, the master's, and the doctor's. In most universities students are still required to study a given curriculum, and if they seek the doctorate are required to write a thesis or dissertation and to defend it publicly. The gowns worn at academic ceremonies today are patterned after those worn by our medieval ancestors. And deans, rectors, and chancellors still exist, though their duties have changed (Meyer, 1972).

Influence of Arab Scholars

While it is true that "without the Arabs much of the Greek philosophical tradition would have been lost to the world" (Ulich, 1971, p. 193), their contribution to Western education goes beyond that. Motivated in part by a desire to spread their Islamic faith, Arab scholars carried both their religious and their intellectual ideas and scientific advancements throughout northern Africa, as far as India and as far west as Spain. Libraries were established in all their principal towns (the library of one Arab ruler was so large that the catalog alone was said to fill 40 volumes), and to each mosque was attached a public school (Draper, 1970). The scholars in these schools and the Arab universities produced copious dictionaries, lexicons, pharmacopoeias, and encyclopedias, as well as all forms of literature and treatises on topics ranging from algebra (an Arab word) and astronomy to commerce and agronomy (Draper, 1970).

The Arab contribution to the advancement of medicine and medical education is particularly noteworthy. Not only did the Arabs establish hospitals throughout their far-flung empire, but also, as early as the beginning of the tenth century, Arab physicians were required to pass an examination and possess a license (Totah, 1926). The most famous and influential Arab philosopher-scientist of the tenth and eleventh century, Avicenna (Ibn Sīnā) (980–1037), wrote over 100 treaties on Aristotelian philosophy and medicine. Of his two most famous works the *Encyclopedia Britannica* declares the *Kitāb ash-Shitā,* which covers logic, metaphysics, and the natural science, to be the "largest work of its kind ever written by one man," and *The Canon of Medicine* to be "the most famous single book in the history of medicine both East and West" ("Avicenna," 1997, p. 740). The latter "served as the guide for medical education throughout Europe and was still in use as late as 1650" (Totah, 1926, p. 7).

Numerous other advances in mathematics and science made by Arab scholars were adopted by Western educators and European culture. One of the most enduring examples is the adoption of the Arabic numbering system to replace the cumbersome Roman numbering system which used Latin letters. Last, it should be noted that the institutions of higher education established by the Arabs throughout Spain, in Egypt, and in the Middle East provided the model for those that were established in Europe during the Middle Ages (Ulich, 1971).

Education During the Renaissance

The Renaissance began in the fourteenth century and reached its high point in the fifteenth century. It is so called because it represented a *renaissance* or rebirth of interest in the humanist aspects of Greek and Latin thought. When Constantinople fell to the Muslims in 1453, many Byzantine scholars came to Italy, bringing with them the works of classical antiquity that had been forgotten in the West, most notably Quintilian's *Education of the Orator.* The influence of this treatise, great as it had been in imperial Rome, was even greater in the Renaissance (Woodward, 1906). Quintilian was viewed as the prime authority on Roman educational ideals. It is symbolic of the respect given Quintilian that Erasmus, the most noted educator of the Renaissance, should apologize for touching on the aims or methods of teaching "seeing that Quintilian has said in effect the last word on the matter" (Woodward, 1906, p. 10).

During the Middle Ages the Catholic Church was dominant and emphasis was on the hereafter. In the fourteenth and fifteenth centuries the increase in trade and commerce, the increase in science and technology, the growth of the Italian city-states, and the rise of a new aristocracy whose wealth came from trade and banking brought an end to the old social, economic, and political order and in so doing brought a greater concern for the here than the hereafter.

Humanism

The dominant philosophy of the Renaissance was *humanism*. Rejecting scholasticism and the model of the cleric as the educated man, the humanists considered the educated man to be the man of learning described in the classics. The first products of the Renaissance in education can be seen in the famous *court schools.* Like the school of Alcuin in the ninth century, they were connected to the courts of reigning families. Like many modern preparatory boarding schools, they housed boys aged 8 or 10 to age 20. They emphasized what Woodward (1906) called the "doctrine of courtesy"—the manners, grace, and dignity of the antique culture. At the court schools a humanist curriculum was taught that included not only the seven liberal arts, but reading, writing, and speaking in Latin, study of the Greek classics, and, for the first time, the study of history. Following the teachings of Quintilian, games and play were also emphasized, individual differences were recognized, and punishment was discouraged. The goal was to produce the well-rounded, liberally educated *courtier*—the ideal personality of the Renaissance.

Erasmus (1466–1536)

The foremost humanist of the Renaissance was Desiderius Erasmus of the Netherlands. Although Erasmus was not a prolific writer, what he wrote was full of charm and wit, and as a result was widely read. His *Colloquies,* textbooks on Latin style, also contained instruction in religion and morals and were among the most important textbooks of his time. In *Upon the Method of Right Instruction* he proposed the systematic training of teachers. His views on pedagogy are found in his treatise *Of the First Liberal Education of Children.* It contained much that had been advanced by Quintilian: the abolition of corporal punishment, the value of play and games, and the necessity of understanding the student's individual needs and abilities.

The educational program of Erasmus was characteristic of the humanist school, which can be described as:

> return to the ancients; classical tongues to be studied in the sources, and no longer in barbarous manuals; rhetorical exercises to be substituted for useless and obscure dialectic; the study of nature to animate and vivify literary studies; the largest possible diffusion of human knowledge without distinction of age or sex. (Laurie, 1968, p. 55)

Education During the Reformation

The period of history known as the Reformation formally began in 1517 when an Augustinian monk and professor of religion named Martin Luther nailed his *Ninety-five Theses,* questioning the authority of the Catholic Church, to the door of the court church in Wittenberg, Germany. In the years that followed a religious revolution swept the European continent, resulting in a century of war and reformation of the Church. Those who protested the authority (and abuses) of the Church came to be known as Protestants. The invention of the printing press enabled their doctrine to be spread rapidly.

Speculate on the impact of the invention of the printing press on education.

Vernacular Schools

In disavowing the authority of the Church, the Protestant reformers stressed the authority of the Bible over that of the Church. They also stressed the responsibility of each person for his own salvation. Therefore it was necessary that each person be able to read the Scriptures and, as a corollary, to be educated. The initial product of this belief was the establishment of *vernacular schools*—primary or elementary schools that offered instruction in the mother tongue or "vernacular" and a basic curriculum of reading, writing, mathematics, and religion.

Vernacular schools were established throughout Germany by Philip Melanchthon and Johann Bugenhagen following Luther's teachings. Melanchthon in particular is noted for his advocacy of universal elementary education and has been called the "Schoolmaster of Germany." Elementary schools also began to appear in other Protestant strongholds, especially those that followed the teachings of John Calvin, such as in the Netherlands, in Scotland, and in the canton of Geneva (Switzerland) where Calvin established a theocratic dictatorship.

Luther (1483–1546)

Martin Luther believed that every child should have a free and compulsory elementary education. Education should be supported by the state and the state should have the authority and responsibility to control the curriculum, the textbooks, and the instruction in the schools. His *Letters to the Mayors and Aldermen of All Cities of Germany in Behalf of Christian Schools* stressed the spiritual, economic, and political benefits of education. The curriculum was to include classical languages, which were to be learned by practice. Grammar, mathematics, science, history, physical education, music, and didactics were all considered important. Theology was taught and study of Protestant doctrines was accomplished through the catechism (a question and answer drill).

Although formal schooling was important to the establishment of a "priesthood of believers," Luther thought such public instruction should occupy only part of the day. At least one or two hours a day should be spent at home in vocational training, preparing for an occupation through an apprenticeship. Secondary schools, designed primarily as preparatory schools for the clergy, taught Hebrew as well as the classical languages, rhetoric, dialectic, history, mathematics, science, music, and gymnastics. A university education, whose purpose was seen as providing training for higher service in the government or the Church, was available only to those young men who demonstrated exceptional intellectual abilities.

Calvin (1509–1564)

John Calvin's views on education were very similar to those of Luther. He too stressed the necessity of a universal, compulsory, state-supported education that would not only enable all individuals to read the Bible themselves and thereby attain salvation, but would profit the state through the contributions of an educated citizenry. The school was also seen as a place for religious indoctrination. Calvin also supported a two-track educational system consisting of common schools for the masses and secondary schools teaching the classical, humanist curriculum for the preparation of the leaders of church and state. Calvin's influence was widespread, especially in the colonies of the New World.

The Reformation in England

In contrast to what was taking place on the continent, the Protestant Reformation in England did not lead to an increase in the number of schools, but to a decrease.

When Henry VIII broke with the Catholic Church and closed the Catholic monasteries, the monastic schools were also closed. Under Elizabeth I such schools as existed were placed under the regulation of the Anglican Church. The few secondary (Latin grammar) schools that continued to exist were established by a town council or by an individual benefactor and were narrow and sectarian in nature. Uniform textbooks were required throughout the country, the curriculum was rigid, and discipline was severe.

Calvinism spread to England. The English Calvinists, called Puritans, aspired to reform or purify the Anglican Church, which had maintained much of the structure of the Catholic Church. Persecuted for their efforts and seeking religious freedom, the Puritans were important in the settlement of the American colonies.

The Jesuits

While the Reformation was taking place outside the Catholic Church, a Counter-Reformation in the Church resulted in the formation of the Society of Jesus, or Jesuits, by Ignatius of Loyola (1491–1556). The Jesuits became a teaching order and were instrumental in the establishment of a number of secondary schools and universities throughout Europe. Their major contribution to education was in the training of teachers. They established, perhaps for the first time in history, a specific plan for the selection, training, and supervision of teachers.

Which of the major colleges and universities in the United States were founded and are operated by the Jesuits?

Later European Educational Thought

The Reformation opened the door not only to the questioning of superstition and religious dogma, but also to investigation of the laws of nature. The Reformation gave way to the Age of Enlightenment or Reason, so called because of the great reliance placed on reason and scientific inquiry. Philosophers and scholars believed that observation and scientific inquiry were the avenues to the discovery of the "natural laws" that dictated the orderly operation of the universe.

Bacon

The English philosopher Francis Bacon mentioned in Chapter 3 was central to this movement. He was also important to education because of the emphasis he placed on scientific inquiry rather than on accepting previously derived hypotheses. He emphasized the need for education to develop what today is termed "critical thinking skills." The Utopia described in his *The New Atlantis* envisioned a research university not inconsistent with modern ideas.

Comenius (1592–1670)

Bacon had a major influence on Jan Amos Comenius, a Moravian bishop. Like Bacon he was a proponent of what is termed *sense realism,* which is the belief that learning must come through the senses through observational experience. Accordingly, education must allow children to observe for themselves and experience by doing. The notion of sensory learning was later expanded by Locke, Rousseau, and Pestalozzi.

Comenius also shared Bacon's belief in the scientific method and an ordered universe that could be discovered through reason and experience. Comenius attempted to identify the developmental stages of children and is said to be the first educator to propose a theory of child growth and development. He proposed a set of teaching methods that incorporated both the deductive method and whatever instructional method was most appropriate for the specific developmental stage of the child.

Comenius proposed that teaching be straightforward and simple and proceed from concrete examples to abstract ideas, that it deal with things before symbols, and that it have practical application. He affirmed Quintilian's beliefs in regard to individual differences, motivation, and corporal punishment. Finally, he believed in a general learning, *paideia,* which should be possessed by all educated persons.

Comenius was perhaps the first educator to propose universal public education. He had a profound effect on Western education through his influence on the thinking of such educational leaders as Johann Pestalozzi, Horace Mann, John Dewey, and Mortimer Adler. Mortimer Adler's dedication to *The Paideia Program: An Educational Syllabus* (1984) reads:

> To
> John Amos Comenius
> Who, more than 300 years ago
> envisaged the educational ideal that
> *The Paideia Program* aims to realize
> before the end of this century.

Locke

Although the English philosopher John Locke is best known for his political theories, which served as the basis for the American and French constitutions, he also had a profound influence on education. As discussed in Chapter 3, Locke taught the *tabula rasa* concept of the human mind, which says that we come into the world with our minds a blank slate. We then learn through sensation. "A sound mind in a sound body is a short but full description of a happy state in the world" are his first words in *Some Thoughts Concerning Education* (Axtell, 1968, p. 114). The sound body needs fresh air, recreation, exercise, and good hygiene. The sound mind, like the sound body, needs exercise and discipline. The curriculum he recommended included, beyond the three Rs, history, geography, ethics, philosophy, science, and conversational foreign languages, especially French. Mathematics was also emphasized, not to make the scholar a mathematician, but to make him a reasonable man. Locke believed the goal of education was to create the moral, practical individual who could participate effectively in the governing process.

Rousseau (1712–1778)

In the later eighteenth century an educational movement called *naturalism* developed. Its emphasis on freedom and the individual formed the basis for modern educational theory and practice. The forerunner of the movement was Jean-Jacques Rousseau. Like Locke, Rousseau is perhaps best remembered for his political theories. His book *Social Contract* had a strong influence on the thinking of those involved in both the French and American revolutions. Although he was never an educator, Rousseau expounded a theory and philosophy of education that influenced many educators, including John Dewey and other progressive educators. Rousseau has also been called the "father of modern child psychology" (Mayer, 1973).

Like Comenius, Rousseau believed in stages of children's growth and development and in the educational necessity of adapting instruction to the various stages. His major thoughts on education are contained in his novel *Émile,* which puts forward the ideal education for a youth named Émile. He contended that the child is inherently good and that it is society that corrupts the natural goodness of man. Like Locke he was concerned with the physical growth and health of the child. The education of Émile was to be child centered, concerned with developing his natural abilities. He was to learn by his senses through direct experience and was not to be punished. Émile's education was to progress as he was ready and as his interests motivated him. Finally, he was taught a trade in order to prepare him for an occupation in life.

How do can you, as an educator, reconcile a belief in the inherent goodness of the child with the doctrine of original sin?

Pestalozzi (1746–1827)

Johann Heinrich Pestalozzi was a Swiss educator who put Rousseau's ideas into practice. Pestalozzi has had a profound impact on education throughout much of the Western world. The Prussian government sent teachers to be instructed by him, and educators came from all over the world, including the United States, to observe and study his methods. He was made a citizen of the French Republic and knighted by the czar of Russia. Horace Mann and Henry Barnard came under his influence. Edward A. Sheldon, superintendent of schools in Oswego, New York, established a teacher training school at Oswego in 1861 that followed Pestalozzi's methods.

Pestalozzi's philosophy of education incorporated the child-centered, sensory experience principles of Rousseau. He believed with Rousseau in the natural goodness of human nature and the corrupting influence of society. He also supported Rousseau's idea of individual differences and "readiness" to learn. His belief in the development of the total child to his or her maximum potential has been given its greatest recognition during the second half of the twentieth century in the movement for the education of the disadvantaged.

Perhaps more than Rousseau, Pestalozzi recognized the importance of human emotions in the learning process. It was important, he believed, that the child be given feelings of self-respect and emotional security. It also was important that the teacher treat students with love. In fact, it can be said that the ideal of love governs Pestalozzi's educational philosophy. Pestalozzi was especially fond of poor children and recognized the need to provide them with a school environment that addressed their physical and emotional needs.

Like Comenius, Pestalozzi believed that instruction must begin with the concrete and proceed to the abstract. Materials should be presented slowly, in developmental order from simple to complex, from known to unknown. The *object lesson* centers on concrete materials within the child's experience, involves discussion and oral presentation, and replaces rote learning (Gillett, 1966).

Herbart (1776–1841)

One of the Prussian educators who studied under Pestalozzi was Johann Friedrich Herbart. Herbart believed that the aim of education should be the development of moral character. His pedagogical theory included three key concepts: *interest, apperception,* and *correlation*. Instruction can only be successful if it arouses interest. Interests are derived from both nature and society, and thus the curriculum should include both the natural and social sciences. All new material presented to the child is interpreted in terms of past experiences by the process of apperception. Additionally, ideas are reinforced and organized in the mind by the process of correlation (Gillett, 1966).

Herbart maintained that any suitable material could be learned if presented systematically. The five steps in the Herbartian methodology included:

1. *Preparation*—preparing the student to receive the new material by arousing interest or recalling past material or experiences
2. *Presentation*—presenting the new material
3. *Association*—helping students see the relationship between old and new ideas
4. *Generalization*—formulating general ideas or principles
5. *Application*—applying the ideas or principles to new situations

Herbart's ideas had a significant influence on American education. The National Herbartian Society, founded in 1892, became the National Society of the Scientific Study of Education. Herbart made the study of educational psychology of paramount importance. He demonstrated the significance of methodology in instruction and careful lesson planning. But, perhaps most important, two hundred years later his theories of learning have been incorporated into constructivism and validated by what the emerging brain research has revealed about how we learn (see discussion in Chapter 14).

Froebel (1782–1852)

Friedrich Froebel was the third member of what Gillett (1966) called the nineteenth century's "famous pedagogical triumvirate" that broke with subject-centered instruction and created a new concern for the child. Froebel is known for the establishment of the first kindergarten (1837) and for providing the theoretical basis for early childhood education. Although Froebel accepted many of Pestalozzi's ideas associated with child-centeredness, Froebel was more concerned with activity than Pestalozzi, but less concerned with observation. According to Froebel, the primary aim of the school should be self-development through self-expression. Self-expression took place through games, singing, or any number of creative and spontaneous activities, which were to be part of an *activity curriculum*. Froebel was also concerned with the development of creativity in children. He viewed the classroom as a miniature society in which children learned social cooperation.

Froebel developed highly stylized materials that were mass produced and used throughout the world. They were designed to aid self-expression and bring out the "divine effluence" (the fundamental unity of all nature with God) within

Recall your own experience in the primary grades. To what extent was your educational experience similar to Frobel's activity curriculum?

The learning of social cooperation and playing creatively with objects are important in early childhood education according to Froebel.

each child. Materials referred to as *gifts* and *occupations* were used. The gifts were objects that did not change their form (e.g., wooden spheres or cubes), symbols of the fundamentals of nature. The occupations were materials used in creative construction or design whose shape changed in use (e.g., clay or paper). Used together they were said to ensure the progressive self-development of the child.

One of Froebel's pupils, Margaretha Schurz, opened the first kindergarten in the United States in Watertown, Wisconsin. John Dewey adopted many of Froebel's principles and used them in his famous laboratory school at the University of Chicago. Today, the kindergarten is recognized for its importance in the educational process and as a socializing force. It is the cornerstone of our educational system.

Table 5.1 gives an overview of the educational theories we have discussed and their influence on Western education.

Education in Colonial America

The English, the predominant settlers of the American colonies, had the greatest influence on the educational system that emerged in the colonies, but the French

Table 5.1: Western European Educational Thought, 1200 A.D.–1850 A.D.

Theorist	Educational Theories	Influence on Western Education
Aquinas (1225–1274)	Human beings possess both a spiritual and a physical nature. Man is a rational being. Faith and reasons are complementary sources of truth.	Provided basis for Roman Catholic education.
Erasmus (1466–1536)	The liberally educated man is one educated in the seven liberal arts, steeped in the classics and in rhetoric. Systematic training of teachers is needed. Follower of Quintilian.	Advanced the need for the systematic training of teachers and a humanistic pedagogy. Promoted the importance of politeness in education.
Luther (1483–1546)	Education is necessary for religious instruction, the preparation of religious leaders, and the economic well-being of the state. Education should include vocational training.	Provided support for concept of free and compulsory elementary education. Promoted concept of universal literacy.
Calvin (1509–1564)	Education serves both the religious and political establishment: elementary schools for the masses where they could learn to read the Bible and and thereby attain salvation; secondary schools to prepare the leaders of church and state.	Concept of two-track system and emphasis on literacy influenced education in New England and ultimately the entire nation.
Bacon (1561–1626)	Education should advance scientific inquiry. Understanding of an ordered universe comes through reason.	Provided major rationale for the development of critical thinking skills. Proposed the concept of a research university.
Comenius (1592–1670)	Learning must come through the senses. Education must allow the child to reason by doing. There is a general body of knowledge *(paideia)* that should be possessed by all.	Provided theory of child growth and development. Concept of *paideia* profoundly influenced numerous Western educational leaders.
Locke (1632–1704)	Children enter the world with their minds like a blank slate *(tabula rasa)*. The goal of education is to promote the development of reason and morality.	Provided support for the concept of the reasonable man and the ability and necessity for the reasonable man to participate in the governing process.

and Spanish also played a role. The French empire spread from Canada to Louisiana. French priests, particularly the Jesuits, followed explorers and fur traders into the wilderness to convert and educate the Native Americans. The Catholic influence on education, which can still be seen today in cities as far apart as Quebec and New Orleans, can be traced to the Jesuits and to orders of teaching nuns.

Table 5.1: *continued*

Theorist	Educational Theories	Influence on Western Education
Rousseau (1712–1778)	Major proponent of naturalism, which emphasized individual freedom. The child is inherently good. Children's growth and development goes through stages, which necessitates adaptation of instruction. Education should be concerned with the development of the child's natural abilities.	Naturalism provided basis for modern educational theory and practice. Father of modern child psychology.
Pestalozzi (1746–1827)	Education should be child centered and based on sensory experience. The individual differences of each child must be considered in assessing readiness to learn. Each child should be developed to his or her maximum potential. Ideal of love emphasized the importance of emotion in the learning process. Instruction should begin with the concrete and proceed to the abstract.	Concept of maximum development of each child provided support for education of the disadvantaged. Pestalozzian methods exported throughout Europe and to the United States. One of the earliest theories of instruction formally taught to teachers.
Herbart (1776–1841)	The aim of education should be the development of moral character. Any material can be learned if presented systematically: preparation, presentation, association, generalization, and application. Instruction must arouse interest to be successful. Education is a science.	Elevated the study of educational psychology. Demonstrated the significance of methodology in instruction. Advanced the concept that education is a science and can be studied scientifically.
Froebel (1782–1852)	The aim of education should be to ensure self-development through self-expression. Self-expression takes place through an activity curriculum. The school should promote creativity and bring out "divine effluence" within each child.	Established first kindergarten. Provided theoretical basis for early childhood education.

The Spanish empire was no less vast, containing at various times the entire Southwest, Florida, and California. Spanish Catholic priests, especially the Franciscans, also followed the explorers and sought to convert and educate the Native Americans. On the heels of the priests came Spanish settlers migrating north from Mexico. By 1800 almost 25,000 Spanish-speaking people were living in the Southwest. What little formal education most children of these settlers received took place at one of the missions established by the priests. These missions also often taught Native Americans not only the Spanish language but agricultural and vocational skills. Children of more affluent settlers were schooled at home by tutors or were sent to schools in Mexico or Spain.

English Settlement

The first English settlement in North America was at Jamestown (Virginia) in 1607. In 1620, the Pilgrims, a group of Separatist Puritans (Protestants who wanted not only to purify but to separate from the Church of England), settled at Plymouth (Massachusetts). Ten years later a group of nonseparatist Puritans founded the Massachusetts Bay Colony. This colony became a focal point of migration, and other New England colonies (Rhode Island, New Haven [Connecticut], New Hampshire, Maine) developed from this base (Cohen, 1974). Many of the colonists who came to the New World were filled with a sense of religious commitment, largely Protestant, which shaped their views on life and education. However, the settlers in different regions did not all share the same views on religion, society, or education. These variations are explored in the following sections.

Education in the New England Colonies

According to Cubberley (1934), the Puritans who settled New England "contributed most that was of value for our future educational development" (p. 14). The New England colonists sustained a vigorous emphasis on education even in the hostile new environment. In fact, by 1700 the New England colonies could boast of literary rates that were often superior to those in England (Cohen, 1974).

Initially, the Puritans attempted to follow English practice regarding the establishment and support of schools by relying on private benefactors and limiting the role of the state. However, the general absence of wealthy Puritan migrants soon led to the abandonment of this practice and, because of fears that parents were neglecting the education of their children, to a more direct role for the state (Cohen, 1974).

First Education Laws

How do the basic purposes of education in Colonial America compare with those of today?

The Massachusetts Law of 1642 ordered the selectmen of each town to ascertain whether parents and masters (of apprentices) were, in fact, providing for the education of their children. The selectmen were also to determine what the child was being taught. The child of any parent or master failing to meet his obligation could be apprenticed to a new master who would be required to fulfill the law. Although the law neither specified schools nor required attendance, it is said to have established the principle of compulsory education. Five years later, the Education Law of 1647 ordered every township of 50 households to provide a teacher to teach reading and writing, and all townships of 100 or more households to establish a grammar school. Although there was no uniform compliance nor administration of these laws, they show how important education was to the Puritans and demonstrate their belief in the necessity of a literate citizenry for the functioning of political society. The laws also served as models for other colonies and are considered the first education laws in America.

Religious Influence

In New England, as in the other colonies, the institutions of secular government, including education, were closely aligned with the dominant religious group. The Puritans brought with them many of the educational views of the Reformation, namely that education was necessary for religious instruction and salvation, as well as for good citizenship. As the Massachusetts Law of 1642 explained, there was a need to ensure the ability of children "to read and understand the principles of religion and the capital laws of this country." This purpose is also evidenced by the first words of the Massachusetts Education Law of 1647, also called the "old Deluder Satan Law": "It being one chief project of that old deluder, Satan, to keep men from knowledge of the Scriptures." The founding of Harvard College in 1636 was also based on religious motives—to ensure that there would be an educated ministry for the colony. Fearful that there would be no replacements for the ministers who first came with them, the colonists dreaded "to leave an illiterate Ministry to the churches, when our present Ministers should lie in the Dust" (Cubberley, 1934, p. 13).

Elementary School

The New England colonists not only shared Calvin's view of the aim of education, but they also adopted the two-track system advocated by Calvin and other scholars of the Reformation. Town schools and *dame schools* were established to educate the children of the common folk in elementary reading, writing, and mathematics. The dame schools were held in the kitchen or living room of a neighborhood woman, often a widow, usually a person with minimal education herself, who received a modest fee for her efforts. Girls were allowed to attend the dame schools, and some did attend the town schools, but most received only a minimal education. So-called "writing" or "reading schools" were concerned with the teaching of these disciplines and operated on a fee basis. *Charity* or *pauper schools* were operated for the children of the poor who could not afford to attend other schools.

Education was also made available as a result of the apprenticeship system whereby a child was apprenticed to a master to learn a trade. In addition, the master was required by the terms of the indenture to ensure that the apprentice received a basic education. For some children this was the avenue by which they learned what little reading and writing they knew.

Instruction in the schools was primarily religious and authoritarian. Students learned their basic lessons from the *hornbook,* so called because the material was written on a sheet of parchment, placed on a wooden board, and covered with a thin sheath of cow's horn for protection. The board was shaped like a paddle and had a handle with a hole in it so it could be strung around the child's neck.

The New England Primer

The *New England Primer* was used with slightly older children. The primer is an excellent example of the interrelationship between education and religion. Although different editions of the primer varied somewhat in the 150 years of its publication, which began in 1690, it usually featured an alphabet and spelling

The dame school provided the only education many colonial children received.

guide, followed by one of the things that made the primer famous—24 little pictures with alphabetical rhymes as illustrated in Figure 5.2.

The primer also included the Lord's Prayer, the Creed, the Ten Commandments, a listing of the books of the Bible, and a list of numbers from 1 to 100, using both Arabic and Roman numerals. Another prominent feature of the primer was a poem, the exhortation of John Rogers to his children, from John Foxe's *Book of Martyrs,* with a picture of the martyr burning at the stake as his wife and children look on. The primer ended with a shortened version of the Puritan catechism (Ford, 1962).

Secondary Grammar Schools

Secondary grammar schools existed for the further education of the male children of the well-to-do. They also served as preparatory schools for the university where the leaders of the church and political affairs were to be trained and which required proficiency in Latin and Greek for admission. The Boston Latin School, established in 1635, became the model for similar schools throughout New England.

Figure 5.2: An Alphabet Including Both Religious and Secular Jingles

A   In *Adam's* Fall
We Sinned all.

B   Thy Life to Mend
This *Book* Attend.

C   The *Cat* doth play
And after flay.

D   A *Dog* will bite
A Thief at night.

E   An *Eagles* flight
Is out of fight.

F   The Idle *Fool*
Is whipt at School.

G   As runs the *Glafs*
Mans life doth pafs.

H   My *Book* and *Heart*
Shall never part.

J   *Job* feels the Rod
Yet bleffes GOD.

K   Our *K I N G* the
good
No man of blood.

L   The *Lion* bold
The *Lamb* doth hold.

M   The *Moon* gives light
In time of night.

N   *Nightingales* fing
In Time of Spring.

O   The *Royal Oak*
it was the Tree
That fav'd His
Royal Majeftie.

P   *Peter* denies
His Lord and cries

Q   Queen *Efther* comes
in Royal State
To Save the JEWS
from difmal Fate

R   *Rachel* doth mour,
For her firft born.

S   *Samuel* anoints
Whom God appoint:

T   *Time* cuts down all
Both great and fmall.

U   *Uriah's* beauteous Wife
Made *David* feek his
Life.

W   *Whales* in the Sea
God's Voice obey.

X   *Xerxes* the great did
die,
And fo muft you & I,

Y   *Youth* forward flips
Death foonest nips,

Z   *Zacheus* he
Did climb the Tree
His Lord to fee,

Source: Ford, P. L. (Ed.). (1962). *The New England Primer.* New York: Teachers College Press.

Education at the grammar school was quite different from that at the dame or town school. The emphasis was on Latin, with some Greek and occasionally Hebrew. Other disciplines included those necessary for the education of the Renaissance concept of the educated man. The course of study in the grammar school lasted fairly intensively for six to seven years, although students "tended to withdraw and return, depending on familial need and circumstances; and since school was conducted on a year-round basis and instruction organized around particular texts, it was fairly simple for a student to resume study after a period of absence" (Cremin, 1970, p. 186).

University Education

Education in the university in the early colonial period was also based on the classically oriented curriculum of English universities. As Cohen (1974) described it:

> The undergraduate courses revolved around the traditional Trivium and Quadrivium but without musical studies, the Three Philosophies (Metaphysics, Ethics, Natural Science), and Greek, Hebrew, and a chronological study of ancient history. As in English universities logic and rhetoric were the basic subjects in the curriculum. . . . Compositions, orations, and disputations were given the same careful scrutiny as at English universities. (p. 66)

Education in New England During the Later Colonial Period

Social and Economic Changes. The Age of the Enlightenment or Age of Reason that swept the Western world in the seventeenth century had found its way to the shores of the American colonies by the eighteenth century. As in Europe it brought greater concern for independent rationality, a repudiation of supernatural explanations of phenomena, and a greater questioning of traditional dogma. At the same time that the Enlightenment was sweeping the colonies, the population of the colonies increased rapidly and their economy outgrew their localized base of farming and fishing. Trade and commerce increased and a new mercantile gentry emerged (Cohen, 1974). The mercantile activities of the new middle class called for a freer environment and increased religious toleration.

Birth of the Academy. It was inevitable that the educational system would change to meet the needs of the intellectual, economic, and social order. The writing and dame schools began to give way to town schools. The curriculum at the elementary level, while still dominated by reading and writing, placed greater importance on arithmetic than before. Greater concern was also shown for practical and vocational training at both the elementary and secondary levels.

Many grammar schools, however, refused to change their classical curricula. As a result, numerous academies and private venture schools sprang up in the larger towns, teaching subjects useful in trade and commerce. If the prestigious Boston Latin School would not teach mathematics, others would. Advertisements for these schools filled the newspapers of the time. One such 1723 advertisement appearing in New York City read:

> There is a school in New York, in the Broad Street, near the Exchange, where Mr. John Walton, late of Yale College, Teacheth Reading, Writing, Arethmatick, whole

Numbers and Fractions, Vulgar and Decimal, The Mariners Art, Plain and Merca-
tors Way; Also Geometry, Surveying, the Latin Tongue, the Greek and Hebrew
Grammers, Ethicks, Rhetorick, Logick, Natural Philosophy and Metaphysicks, all
or any of them for a Reasonable Price. The School from the first of October till
the first of March will be tended in the Evening. If any Gentlemen in the Country
are disposed to send their Sons to the said School, if they apply themselves to
the Master he will immediately procure suitable Entertainment for them, very
Cheap. Also if any Young Gentlemen of the City will please to come in the
Evening and make some Tryal of the Liberal Arts, they may have the opportunity
of Learning the same things which are commonly Taught in Colledges. (Seybolt,
cited in Rippa, 1997, pp. 61–62)

Which would you prefer to attend the Boston Latin School or Mr. Walton's school? Why?

Growth of Colleges. During this period several colleges were founded in the New
England colonies: Collegiate School, now Yale University, in 1701; the College of
Rhode Island, now Brown University, in 1764; and Dartmouth College in 1769. The
colleges of this era also reflected the growing secularism of the society. This was
evidenced in a broadened curriculum. In 1722 Harvard established its first profes-
sorship in secular subjects—mathematics and natural philosophy. By 1760 the scientific subjects accounted for 20% of the student's time. Another manifestation of
the growing secularism was the change in graduates' careers. Theology remained
the most popular career, but an increasing number of graduates were turning to
law, medicine, trade, or commerce as the New England colleges became centers of
independence, stimulation, and social usefulness (Cohen, 1974).

Education in the Middle Colonies

The New England colonies had been settled primarily by English colonists who
shared the same language, traditions, and religion. The settlers of the middle
colonies (New York, New Jersey, Pennsylvania, Delaware) came from a variety of
national and religious backgrounds. Most had fled Europe because of religious
persecution and were generally more distrusting of secular authority than the
New England colonists. Thus, while the schools in the middle colonies were as
religious in character as those in New England, because of the diverse religious
backgrounds it was not possible for the government in any colony to agree on
the establishment of any one system of state-supported schools. Thus it fell to
each denomination to establish its own schools. The consequence of this pattern
was the absence of any basis for the establishment of a system of public schools
or for state support or regulation of the schools.

New York

The colony of New Netherlands was established in 1621 by the Dutch. Initially,
New Netherlands was similar to the New England colonies. Schools were supported by the Dutch West India Company and were operated by the Dutch Reformed Church. After the colony was seized by the British and became the royal
colony of New York (1674), state responsibility and support was withdrawn, and
except for a few towns that maintained their own schools, formal schooling
became a private concern. Education at the elementary level was by private

tutors for the upper class, private venture schools for the middle class, and denominational schools for the lower class.

Most notable of the denominational schools were those operated by a missionary society of the Church of England, the Society for the Propagation of the Gospel in Foreign Parts (SPG). The apprenticeship system also was very strong in New York and provided the means by which some children gained an education. However, since few towns established their own schools and the provision of education was principally left to the will or ability of parents to send their children to private or denominational schools, illiteracy rates were high (Cohen, 1974).

Education at the secondary level was even more exclusively private or parochial. The private venture secondary schools were few in number and questionable in quality.

Higher education was absent for any but the few who could afford to leave the colony. It was not until 1754 that the first institution of higher education, Kings College, now Columbia University, opened in the colony.

New Jersey

As in New York, education in New Jersey was primarily private and denominational. The religious diversification was great and each of the sects—Dutch Reformed, Puritan, Quaker, German Lutheran, Baptist, Scotch-Irish Presbyterian—established its own schools. The SPG also operated schools for the poor. A few towns, mainly those in the eastern region settled by the Puritans, established town schools. Secondary education was limited. Because of the primarily rural, agrarian economy, the private venture secondary schools found in the other middle colonies were lacking. However, the proximity to New York and Philadelphia did provide access to their secondary institutions for those who could afford it (Cohen, 1974).

It is in the realm of higher education that the colony of New Jersey most distinguished itself. Prior to the Revolution in it were founded more colleges than in any other colony: the College of New Jersey, now Princeton University, in 1746, and Queens College, now Rutgers University, in 1766.

Pennsylvania

The Pennsylvania colony was founded in 1681 by a Quaker, William Penn. The Quakers, or Society of Friends, were very tolerant of other religions; consequently, a number of different religious groups or sects settled in Pennsylvania. William Penn advocated free public education, and the Pennsylvania Assembly enacted a law in 1683 providing that all children be instructed in reading and writing and be taught "some useful trade or skill." Yet the colony did not develop a system of free public education, primarily because of the great diversity among the settlers. A few community-supported schools were established, but as in the other middle colonies, formal education was primarily a private or denominational affair.

However, the major difference between this Middle Atlantic colony and the others was that the various denominations did, in fact, establish a fairly widespread system of schools in Pennsylvania. The SPG founded a number of charity schools, including a school for black children in Philadelphia. The Moravians also established a number of elementary schools, including the first nursery school in the colonies, and were active in efforts to Christianize and educate the Native Americans. They devised a script for several Native American languages and translated the Bible and other religious materials into these languages. In their pedagogical practices they were influenced by Comenius, who was a Moravian bishop (Gutek, 1991).

The Quakers were the most significant denomination in terms of educational endeavors. Their belief that all were created equal under God led not only to the education of both sexes and to the free admission of the poor, but also to the education of blacks and Native Americans. A school for black children was established in Philadelphia as early as 1700.

Schools were also established at the secondary level by various denominations. The Moravians established a boarding school for girls at Bethlehem, one of the first in the colonies. Since the Quakers do not have a ministry, they were not as interested in the establishment of secondary schools leading to that vocation. In their secondary schools they emphasized practical knowledge rather than the classical curriculum studied at most secondary schools at that time.

A number of private secondary schools were opened during the later colonial period, many offering such practical subjects as navigation, gauging, accounting, geometry, trigonometry, surveying, French, and Spanish. Among them was Benjamin Franklin's Philadelphia Academy, opened in 1751.

Benjamin Franklin (1706–1790)

Franklin was strongly influenced by the writings of John Locke and was a proponent of practical education. In his *Proposals Relating to the Education of Youth in Pennsylvania* he laid out the plan for a school in which English was to be the medium of instruction rather than Latin. This break with tradition was important, for in effect it proposed that vernacular English could be the language of the educated person. Franklin also proposed that students be taught "those Things that are likely to be most useful and most ornamental. Regard being had to the several Professions which they are intended" (Gillett, 1969, p. 138).

From this statement of principle Franklin went on to detail the specific subject matter:

> All should be taught "to write a fair hand" and "something of drawing"; arithmetic, accounts, geometry, and astronomy; English grammar out of Tillotson, Addison, Pope, Sidney, Trenchard, and Gordon; the writing of essays and letters; rhetoric, history, geography, and ethics; natural history and gardening; and the history of commerce and principles of mechanics. Instruction should include visits to neighboring farms, opportunities for natural observations, experiments with scientific apparatus, and physical exercise. And the whole should be suffused with a quest for benignity of mind, which Franklin saw as the foundation of good breeding and a spirit of service, which he regarded as "the great aim and end of all learning." (Cremin, 1970, p. 376)

To what extent do you agree with Franklin on what should be the "great aim and end all of all learning"?

As time passed Franklin's academy gave less emphasis to the practical studies and came to more closely resemble the Latin grammar school. Before he died Franklin declared the academy a failure as measured against his initial intent (Cremin, 1970).

Founding of the University of Pennsylvania. Franklin was also instrumental in the founding in 1753 of the College of Philadelphia, now the University of Pennsylvania. Unlike its sister institutions, the College of Philadelphia was nonsectarian in origin (although it later came under Anglican control). The curriculum of the college was perhaps more progressive than those at other institutions. Students were allowed a voice in the election of courses, and the curriculum emphasized not only the classics but also mathematics, philosophy, and the natural and social sciences. A medical school was established in connection with the college. The college appointed as the first professor of chemistry in the colonies Dr. Benjamin Rush (Cohen, 1974), one of the signers of the Declaration of Independence, a noted physician and the father of American psychiatry.

Delaware

Delaware, founded in 1638 as a Swedish colony, New Sweden, fell under Dutch control in 1655, then under the rule of the English with their conquest of New Netherlands. Education in Delaware was greatly influenced by Pennsylvania. Pennsylvania's general abandonment of the responsibility for the provision of education to private or denominational groups after 1683 was followed in Delaware. Although a number of elementary schools were established in the colony, the level of literacy remained low. During the colonial period formal secondary education was available on a very limited basis, and no institution of higher education was established in Delaware (Cohen, 1974).

Education in the Southern Colonies

Social and Economic Systems

The Southern colonies (Maryland, Virginia, the Carolinas, and Georgia) differed in significant ways from the New England and Middle Atlantic colonies. The Southern colonies were royal colonies administered by governors responsible directly to the king. The prevailing view was that it was the responsibility of parents to educate their children, not the government. Consequently, local governments were not required to establish or support schools. And, where religious dissatisfaction was the principal motivation for the settling of New England, the reasons for settlement of the Southern colonies, where the Church of England was the established church, were primarily economic.

Rather than small farms and commerce, the economy of the Southern colonies was based on the plantation and slave system. The plantation system created distinct classes dominated by the aristocratic plantation owners. The relatively small population of the Southern colonies was widely dispersed. This factor limited the growth of any public or universal system of education.

Elementary and Secondary Education

As a result of the social and economic structure of the Southern colonies, educational opportunities were largely determined by social position. The children of the plantation owners and the wealthy commercial classes in the Tidewater cities

Professional Reflections

"An educator's primary function is not to present facts, but to enlighten. Cherish that role in your mind and in your heart and you will be a successful educator."

Carol Banaszynski, Teacher of the Year, Wisconsin

"Always teach to the whole child; socially, physically, emotionally, and academically."

Sheba Brown, Teacher of the Year, Mississippi

received their education from private tutors or at private Latin grammar schools before being sent to a university. In the early colonial period it was common for the children of the plantation aristocracy to be sent to England to receive their secondary or, more often, their university education. However, this practice was on the decline by the later colonial period (Cohen, 1974; Gutek, 1991).

For the majority in the other classes the only education available was at the elementary level, informally through the apprenticeship system, or formally at endowed (free) schools, charity schools, denominational schools, "old field schools," or private venture schools. Virginia was the most active of the Southern colonies in attempting to ensure the education of apprenticed children, especially orphaned children. Often this education took place in so-called "workhouse" schools.

The endowed or free schools were few in number and actually were not free except to a small number of poor boys. The charity schools were primarily those operated by the SPG. The influence of the SPG in the Southern colonies was significant and represented "the nearest approach to a public school organization found in the South before the Revolution" (Cohen, 1974, p. 129). Schools operated by other denominations were also established in the Southern colonies. In some rural areas where other schooling was not available, several small planters or farmers might build a schoolhouse on an abandoned tobacco field. These "old field schools" generally charged a fee and offered only the most basic education. Private venture elementary schools were found in some of the largest cities.

At the secondary level, except for the private venture schools, only a very small number of schools existed. And even the number of private venture schools was limited. As a result of the public neglect of education, overall the educational level of the Southern colonies was below that of most of the Northern colonies, especially those in New England.

Higher Education: The College of William and Mary

The only institution of higher education established in the South prior to the Revolutionary War was the College of William and Mary, established in 1693 to train ministers for the Church of England. Like Harvard, the only older institution of higher education in the colonies, it also originally offered the traditional curriculum. However, by the first quarter of the eighteenth century it began to broaden

Figure 5.3: Education in Colonial America

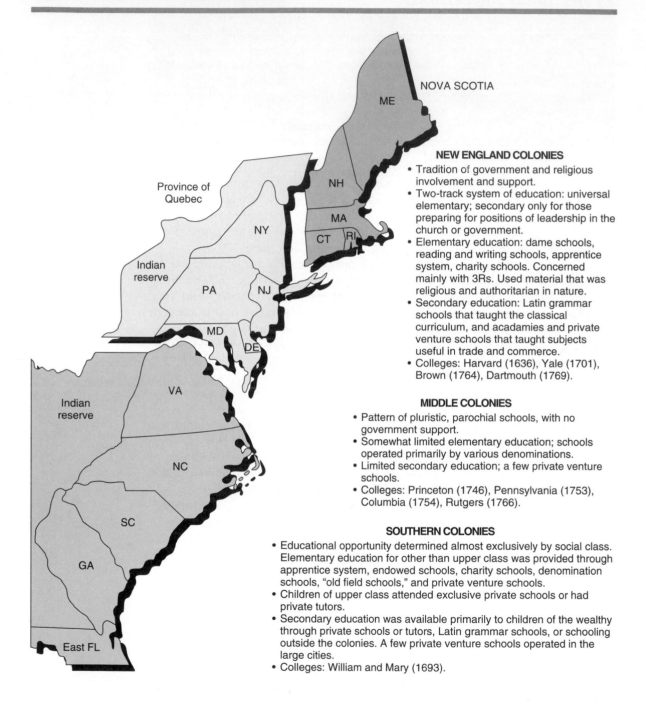

NOVA SCOTIA

ME

Province of Quebec

NH

MA

NY

CT RI

Indian reserve

PA

NJ

MD

DE

VA

Indian reserve

NC

SC

GA

East FL

NEW ENGLAND COLONIES

- Tradition of government and religious involvement and support.
- Two-track system of education: universal elementary; secondary only for those preparing for positions of leadership in the church or government.
- Elementary education: dame schools, reading and writing schools, apprentice system, charity schools. Concerned mainly with 3Rs. Used material that was religious and authoritarian in nature.
- Secondary education: Latin grammar schools that taught the classical curriculum, and acadamies and private venture schools that taught subjects useful in trade and commerce.
- Colleges: Harvard (1636), Yale (1701), Brown (1764), Dartmouth (1769).

MIDDLE COLONIES

- Pattern of pluristic, parochial schools, with no government support.
- Somewhat limited elementary education; schools operated primarily by various denominations.
- Limited secondary education; a few private venture schools.
- Colleges: Princeton (1746), Pennsylvania (1753), Columbia (1754), Rutgers (1766).

SOUTHERN COLONIES

- Educational opportunity determined almost exclusively by social class. Elementary education for other than upper class was provided through apprentice system, endowed schools, charity schools, denomination schools, "old field schools," and private venture schools.
- Children of upper class attended exclusive private schools or had private tutors.
- Secondary education was available primarily to children of the wealthy through private schools or tutors, Latin grammar schools, or schooling outside the colonies. A few private venture schools operated in the large cities.
- Colleges: William and Mary (1693).

its curriculum. In fact, one educational historian states that by 1779 its curriculum was probably the most advanced in the United States (Cohen, 1974).

Figure 5.3 presents an overview of education in colonial America.

Summary

The schools of the United States can trace their ancestry to those of ancient Greece and Rome. Educational idealism is based on the philosophy of Plato. The scientific method popularized in the twentieth century is rooted in the philosophy of realism espoused by Aristotle. And a number of the more progressive educational positions of this century were advanced by the Roman educator Quintilian: opposition to corporal punishment, advancement of the concept of readiness learning, and support for the recognition of individual differences in learners.

The concept of universal public education that we enjoy today was a product of the Reformation. It was brought to New England by the Puritans who held the view that education was necessary for religious instruction and salvation, as well as for good citizenship. However, the earliest American educational systems were not free, were limited at the secondary levels, and, in ways that would be prohibited today, were dominated by the religious establishment. In the next chapter we will continue to trace the evolution of the American educational system from the Revolution to the twentieth century.

Key Terms

Activity curriculum
Charity (pauper) school
Dame schools
Grammar school
Hornbook
Humanism
Naturalism

Object lesson
Paideia
Sense realism
Seven liberal arts
Socratic method
Tabula rasa
Vernacular schools

Discussion Questions

1. How would Aristotle and Plato answer the question posed at the beginning of this chapter: Should the right to an education be guaranteed by the government?

2. What impact did the Reformation have on the education of common people?

3. What ideas of Pestalozzi and Froebel are in practice in the schools of your community?

4. Describe the status of higher education in colonial America.

5. Contrast education in the New England, Middle Atlantic, and Southern colonies. Do any legacies of these differences remain today?

6. What was the contribution of the apprenticeship system to education in the colonies?

Internet Resources

1. **grid.let.rug.nl/ahc/hist.html**
   WWW Services for Historians provides links to "general" historical sites as well as to the History of Education site.

2. **www.socsci.kun.nl/ped/whp/histeduc/**
   The History of Education site is an international archive of links and source materials about the history of education and the history of childhood.

3. **www.webcom.com/shownet/medea/grklink.html**
   The Ancient Greek site on the Web provides a range of links to Ancient Greek resources online.

4. **www.hartford-hwp.com/gateway/index.html**
   This site provides a comprehensive index to history on the web, including an extensive list of search engines to locate Internet resources.

5. **www.yahoo.com/arts/humanities/history/**
   This is the Yahoo search engine's list of history resources by region, subject, or time period (ancient, Middle Ages, Renaissance, etc.).

6. **www.entrex.org**
   This site provides biographies of early colonists and descriptions of their daily lives.

7. **www.chatpress.com/uae-5html**
   This site hosts a lengthy discussion of the influence of culture, politics, religion, and so on on education in the northern, middle, and southern colonies.

References

Adler, M. J. (1984). *The Paideia program: An educational syllabus*. New York: Macmillan.

Avicenna. (1997). In *The new encyclopedia Britannica* (Vol. 1, pp. 739–40). Chicago: Encyclopedia Britannica.

Axtell, J. L. (Ed.). (1968). *The educational writings of John Locke*. Cambridge, England: Cambridge University Press.

Beck, A. G. (1964). *Greek education 450–350 B.C.* London: Methuen & Co.

Bowen, J. (1972). *A history of Western education*, 1. London: Methuen & Co.

Castle, E. B. (1967). *Ancient education and today*. Baltimore, MD: Penguin Books.

Cohen, S. S. (1974). *A history of colonial education, 1607–1776*. New York: John Wiley & Sons.

Cremin, L. A. (1970). *American education: The colonial experience, 1607–1783*. New York: Harper & Row.

Cubberley, E. P. (1934). *Readings in public education*. Cambridge, MA: Riverside Press.

Draper, J. W. (1970). Cultural developments in Spain. In H. J. Siceluff (Ed.), *Readings in the history of education* (pp. 47–51). Berkeley, CA: McCutchan.

Ford, P. L. (Ed.). (1962). *The New England primer*. New York: Columbia University Teachers College.

Gillett, M. (1966). *A history of education: Thought and practice*. Toronto: McGraw-Hill.

Gillett, M. (Ed.). (1969). *Readings in the history of education*. Toronto: McGraw-Hill.

Good, H. G., & Teller, J. D. (1969). *A history of Western education*. Toronto: Collier-Macmillan.

Gutek, G. L. (1991). *Education in the United States: An historical perspective*. Englewood Cliffs, NJ: Prentice-Hall.

Laurie, S. S. (1968). *Studies in the history of educational opinion from the Renaissance*. London: Frank Cass & Co.

Mayer, F. (1973). *A history of educational thought*. Columbus, OH: Merrill.

Meyer, A. E. (1972). *An educational history of the Western world*. New York: McGraw-Hill.

Monroe, P. (1939). *Source book of the history of education for the Greek and Roman period*. New York: Macmillan.

Rippa, S. A. (1997). *Education in a free society: An American history* (8th ed.). New York: Longman.

Totah, K. A. (1926). *The contribution of the Arabs to education*. New York: Bureau of Publications, Teachers College, Columbia University.

Ulich, R. (Ed.). (1971). *Three thousand years of educational wisdom* (2nd ed.). Cambridge, MA: Harvard University Press.

Wilkins, A. S. (1914). *Roman education*. Cambridge, England: Cambridge University Press.

Winn, C., & Jacks, M. (1967). *Aristotle*. London: Methuen & Co.

Woodward, W. H. (1906). *Studies in education during the age of the Renaissance, 1400–1600*. Cambridge, England: Cambridge University Press.

Chapter 6

Those who cannot remember the past are condemned to repeat it.

Santayana

American Education: From Revolution to the Twentieth Century

➤ The Boston Examiner   *Thursday, July 13, 1867*
New U.S. Commissioner of Education Deplores Training of Teachers

In an address last evening to the National Education Association meeting in New York, Mr. Henry Barnard, the newly appointed United States Commissioner of Education, commented on the inadequate training possessed by the vast majority of teachers who teach our young. According to Commissioner Barnard: "Too many of those we have entrusted to guide and guard our nation's youth have little knowledge beyond that which they are attempting to impart. Indeed, we might well question whether their knowledge is superior to that of many of their fellow tradesmen. Not only is the depth and breadth of their knowledge of the curriculum matter a subject of concern, but where knowledge is possessed, there exists most often an absence of any training in pedagogy." The commissioner went on to say that "teachers will not be elevated to that place in society and receive that compensation they so richly deserve until they are required to undertake a special course of study and training to qualify them for their office."

Do these comments sound familiar? Which of the concerns expressed by Barnard remain concerns today? Which are no longer concerns?

At the time Henry Barnard made these remarks, the nation was less than 100 years old but had already more than tripled in size and increased tenfold in population. Before the century was over, the population would double again. The educational system grew with the nation, sometimes responding to, sometimes leading social and economic changes.

As you study the history of American education from the birth of the nation to the beginning of the twentieth century, think about the following objectives:

- Describe the impact of Thomas Jefferson and Noah Webster on American education in the early nineteenth century.
- Identify the contributions that monitorial schools, Sunday schools, infant schools, and free school societies made to the expansion of educational opportunities in the early national period.
- Compare the curriculum and purposes of the academy with that of the grammar school and the high school.
- Discuss the development of common schools in the United States and the roles that Horace Mann, Henry Barnard, Emma Willard, and Catherine Beecher played in that development.
- Outline the development of secondary education in the United States.
- Discuss the factors leading to the growth of higher education in nineteenth-century America.
- Compare the educational opportunities provided to Native Americans, Hispanic Americans, Asian Americans, and black Americans in the nineteenth century.
- Trace the development of teacher education in the United States.

Education in the Revolutionary and Early National Period

On July 4, 1776, the 13 colonies declared their independence from England. Education was one of the casualties of the war that followed. Pulliam and Van Patten (1995) described the state of education during the war years:

> Illiteracy increased because rural schools had to close their doors and even the larger town Latin grammar schools were crippled. British occupation of New York caused schools to be abandoned there. New England schools continued to operate but they suffered from a lack of funds and teachers.
>
> Higher education was restricted in part because many talented teachers were Loyalists. Books were scarce since they came from England and colonial printers could not maintain their presses without outside supplies. Yale College was broken up into groups centered in different towns, while Harvard's buildings and those of the College of Rhode Island housed provincial troops. Dartmouth had neither money nor books, and classes had to be discontinued at the College of Philadelphia. The College of New Jersey and William and Mary also suffered but were not closed.
>
> British support, as in the case of the Anglican SPG, was cut off and never revived. Lack of money and the interruption of the normal economic process made the operation of educational institutions almost impossible. Teachers and scholars joined the fighting forces while school buildings were converted into barracks. Tory or Loyalist teachers were turned out of their schools. Sometimes the schools were burned and libraries scattered or destroyed. (pp. 47–48)

What would be the impact of a major war on colleges and universities today?

Articles of Confederation and the Constitution

After the war the leaders of the new nation set about the business of devising a government that would encompass the ideas for which they had fought. The first attempt at self-governance under the Articles of Confederation provided little authority to the central government and established no executive or judicial branches. When this government proved inadequate, delegates from each state met in the summer of 1787 and drafted the Constitution, which after ratification in 1789 launched the new republic. Perhaps because of the former colonists' suspicion of a strong central government, or perhaps because of the association of education with theology, neither the Articles of Confederation nor the Constitution mentioned education.

Northwest Land Ordinances

Despite the fact that neither the Articles of Confederation nor the U.S. Constitution mentioned education, there can be no doubt that the nation's founders recognized the importance of education to a country in which the quality of representation depended on citizens' ability to make informed choices at the ballot box. Their concern is made clear by both the legislation they enacted and congressional testimonies.

Even before the adoption of the Constitution, Congress enacted two ordinances that contained articles supportive of education. The Land Ordinance of 1785, which provided for a survey of the Northwest Territory, set aside the 16th section of land in each township for the support of education. Article Three of the Northwest Ordinance of 1787, which incorporated the Northwest Territory, proclaimed "Religion, morality, and knowledge being necessary to good government and the happiness of mankind, schools and the means of education shall be forever encouraged."

The Founding Fathers and Education

George Washington devoted a major portion of his first address to Congress to the importance of education: "There is nothing which can better deserve your patronage than the promotion of science and literature. Knowledge is in every country the surest basis of public happiness" (Madsen, 1974, p. 66).

The replies from the Senate and House expressed lawmakers' agreement. From the Senate: "Literature and Science are essential to the preservation of a free constitution; the measures of government should therefore be calculated to strengthen the confidence that is due to that important truth." And from the House: "The promotion of science and literature will contribute to the security of free government" (Madsen, 1974, p. 66).

The Founding Fathers were aware that changing their form of government was only the beginning of the revolution. As Benjamin Rush, a proponent of a national university and universal education, remarked: "We have changed our form of government, but it remains to effect a revolution of our principles, opinions, and manners, so as to accommodate them to the forms of government we have adopted" (Cremin, 1982, p. 1). Rush and his compatriots worked untiringly at devising endless versions of political and educational arrangements. Although they differed on many details, there were at least four beliefs common to their discussions: (1) that the laws of education must be relative to the form of government, hence a republic needs an educational system that motivates citizens to choose public over private interest; (2) that what was needed was a truly American education purged of all vestiges of older, monarchical forms and dedicated to the creation of a cohesive and independent citizenry; (3) that education should be genuinely practical, aimed at the improvement of the human condition, with the new sciences at its heart; and (4) that American education should be exemplary and a means through which America could teach the world the glories of liberty and learning (Cremin, 1982).

Is there a place in today's educational system for a system of federally operated national universities as proposed by Dr. Rush?

Thomas Jefferson

While many of the Founding Fathers expressed their views on the importance of education, perhaps none is so well known for his educational views as Thomas Jefferson (1743–1826). Jefferson, who was strongly influenced by the philosophy of Locke, believed that government must be by the consent of the governed and that men were entitled to certain rights that could not be abridged by the government. Jefferson was one of the chief proponents of the addition of a Bill of

Rights to the Constitution. As Rippa (1997) noted, "Few statesmen in American history have so vigorously strived for an ideal [liberty]; perhaps none has so consistently viewed education as the indispensable cornerstone of freedom" (p. 55).

Plan for a State Education System. Jefferson's *Bill for the More General Diffusion of Knowledge,* introduced in the Virginia legislature in 1779, provided for the establishment of a system of public schools that would provide the masses with the basic education necessary to ensure good government, public safety, and happiness. Under the bill each county would be subdivided into parts called *hundreds;* each hundred was to provide an elementary school, supported by taxes. Attendance would be free for all white children, male and female, for three years. The curriculum would be reading, writing, arithmetic, and history. The bill also proposed that the state be divided into 20 districts with a public boarding grammar school built in each district. Those attending would be not only those boys whose families could afford the tuition, but also the brightest of the poorer students from the elementary schools whose tuition would be paid by the state. The curriculum of the grammar school was to include Latin, Greek, geography, English, grammar, and higher mathematics. Finally, upon completion of grammar school, ten of the scholarship students would receive three years' study at the College of William and Mary at state expense. The remaining scholarship students, according to Jefferson, would most likely become masters in the grammar schools.

Although this plan, viewed in today's light, appears strikingly elitist, in Jefferson's day it was considered excessively liberal and philanthropic. In fact, it was defeated by the Virginia legislature, no doubt in large part because of the unwillingness of the wealthy to pay for the education of the poor. Nonetheless, the plan is considered important because it removed the stigma of pauperism from elementary education (Rippa, 1997) and because it proposed a system of universal, free public education, if only for three years.

Founding the University of Virginia. Jefferson's interest in education also extended to establishing the University of Virginia. After leaving the presidency in 1809, he devoted much of his energies to that effort. Sometimes called "Mr. Jefferson's University," no college or university ever bore so completely the mark of one person. He created the project in every detail: he designed the buildings and landscape (even bought the bricks and picked out the trees to be used as lumber), chose the library books, designed the curriculum, and selected the students and faculty. The university opened in 1825, a year before Jefferson's death on July 4, 1826, exactly 50 years after the adoption of the immortal document he wrote—the Declaration of Independence (Rippa, 1997).

Noah Webster

It was a teacher, Noah Webster (1758–1843), who had the most influence on education in the new republic. Where the nation's founders had sought political independence from England, Webster sought cultural independence (Gutek, 1991). Webster believed that the primary purpose of education should be the inculcation of patriotism, and that what was needed was a truly American education rid of

The buildings, landscape, and curriculum of the University of Virginia were designed by Thomas Jefferson.

European influence (Madsen, 1974). These goals could best be accomplished, he believed, by creating a distinctive national language and curriculum. To this end Webster prepared a number of spelling, grammar, and reading books to replace the English texts then in use; an American version of the Bible; and what became the world-famous *American Dictionary of the English Language.*

Of his textbooks, the most important was the *Elementary Spelling Book,* published in 1783, often referred to as the "blue-back speller" because of the color of the binding. By 1875, 75 million copies of the speller had been sold (Spring, 1997), many of which were used again and again. The book included both a federal catechism with political and patriotic content, and a moral catechism whose content was related to respect for honest work and property rights, the value of money, the virtues of industry and thrift, the danger of drink, and contentment with one's economic status (Rippa, 1997; Spring, 1997). According to the noted historian Henry S. Commager, "No other secular book had ever spread so wide, penetrated so deep, lasted so long" (cited in Rippa, 1997, p. 60).

Webster supported the concept of free schools in which all American children could learn the necessary patriotic and moral precepts. As a member of the Massachusetts legislature he worked for the establishment of a state system of education and is credited by some as initiating the common school movement, which culminated in Horace Mann's work in the 1830s (Spring, 1997). He also supported the

What textbook in your elementary or secondary education had the greatest influence on you? Why?

education of women, as they would be the mothers of future citizens and the teachers of youth. However, he envisioned a rather limited and "female" education for them and counseled parents against sending their daughters to "demoralizing" boarding schools. A staunch patriot whose proposals sometimes bordered on the fanatic (e.g., the proposal that the first word a child learned should be "Washington"), Webster has been called the "Schoolmaster of the Republic."

Educational Innovations

Although Webster and others promoted the establishment of a uniquely American education, some of the major innovations in American education in the first quarter of the nineteenth century were of European origin. Among these were the monitorial school, the Sunday school, and the infant school. The period also witnessed the efforts of the free school societies and, more important, the rise of the academies. Each of these made a contribution, but the primary pattern of schooling that developed in the first half of the nineteenth century emerged from the common school movement, which is discussed in the next section. However, a review of these alternatives illustrates how the country, in the absence of established state systems, was searching for a suitable educational pattern for the new and developing nation (Gutek, 1991).

Monitorial Schools

Monitorial schools originated in England and were brought to America by a Quaker, Joseph Lancaster. In the Lancasterian monitorial system, one paid teacher instructed hundreds of pupils through the use of student teachers or monitors who were chosen for their academic abilities. Monitorial education was concerned with teaching only the basics of reading, writing, and arithmetic. The first monitorial school in the United States was opened in New York City in 1806, and the system spread rapidly throughout the states. One such school in Pennsylvania was designed to accommodate 450 students.

> The teacher sits at the head of the room on a raised platform. Beneath and in front of the teacher are three rows of monitors' desks placed directly in front of the pupils' desks. The pupils' desks are divided into three sections . . . and each section is in line with one of the rows of monitors' desks . . . a group of pupils would march to the front of the room and stand around the monitors' desks, where they would receive instruction from the monitors. When they finished, they would march to the rear part of their particular section and recite or receive further instruction from another monitor. While this group was marching to the rear, another group would be marching up to the front to take their places around the monitors. When finished, the pupils would march to the rear, and the group in the rear would move forward to the second part of their section to receive instruction from yet another monitor. Because each of the three sections had a group in front, one in the rear, and one in the middle working on different things, a total of nine different recitations could be carried on at one time. (Spring, 1997, p. 65)

The monitorial system was attractive not only because it provided an inexpensive system for educating poor children, but because submission to the system was supposed to instill the virtues of orderliness, obedience, and industriousness. As already noted, the system gained wide appeal. However, in time the system declined. It appeared to be suited only for large cities with large numbers of students rather than small towns and rural areas. It was also criticized because it only afforded the most basic education. Yet, instead of being an educational dead end, as depicted by many educational historians, Lancasterian monitorialism may have been the model for the factory-like urban schools that emerged in the United States in the late nineteenth century (Gutek, 1991).

Free School Societies: Charity Schools

The Lancasterian system was considered ideal for the schools operated by the various free school societies. These societies operated charity schools for the children of the poor in urban areas. In some instances, as in New York City, they received public support. Overall they were not a major factor in the history of education; nonetheless, for a period they did provide the only education some children received. For example, by 1820 the Free School Society of New York City (renamed the Public School Society in 1826 and placed under the city department of education in 1853) was teaching more than 2,000 children (Cremin, 1982).

Sunday Schools

Another educational plan introduced to America was the *Sunday school,* begun by Robert Raikes in 1780 in England. The first Sunday school in America opened in 1786 in Virginia. Its purpose was to offer the rudiments of reading and writing to children who worked during the week, primarily in the factories of the larger cities, and to provide them with an alternative to roaming the streets on Sunday. Although the Bible was commonly its textbook, originally the Sunday school was not seen as an adjunct of the church and was not intended to promote conversion. By 1830, however, their initial practical purpose had been superseded by religious interests and they had become primarily religious institutions operated by Sunday school societies with an evangelical mission. They grew in number, reaching out to the frontier and becoming available to children from homes of all sorts. In new communities they often paved the way for the common school (Cremin, 1982).

Infant Schools

The *infant school* was originated in England by Robert Owen, who also established one of the first infant schools in the United States at his would-be Utopia, a collective at New Harmony, Indiana. Established primarily in the eastern cities, these schools were taught by women and were designed for children aged four to seven who, because they would go to work in a factory at a very early age, probably would not receive any other schooling. The primary schools designed along this model did not survive long. However, in a few cities the primary schools had been designed as preparatory to entry into the elementary school and often became part of the town school system. In the 1850s the followers of Froebel revived the idea behind this form of infant school in the form of the kindergarten.

The Growth of the Academy

More significant in foreshadowing the coming changes in patterns of formal schooling was the growth of the academy. Although today the term *academy* brings to mind an exclusive private institution with a college-preparatory curriculum, or perhaps military training, in the late eighteenth and early nineteenth centuries the term was more broadly applied. As we have seen, Franklin's academy and similar institutions were interested in providing an alternative to the traditional curriculum of the Latin grammar schools by providing a "practical" education.

The real growth of the academy occurred after the Revolutionary War. The variations among academies were great. Some were indeed prestigious and exclusive. Others were nothing more than log cabins. Stimulated by the founding of the United States Military Academy at West Point in 1802 and the Naval Academy at Annapolis in 1848, many were established as military schools. Admission to some was open to all comers, others catered to special clients. Some were boarding schools, some were day schools. Some were teacher owned, others were organized by groups of parents or individuals, and yet others by denominations or various societies. Their curriculum usually depended, at least in part, on the students who were enrolled, but most offered an education beyond the three Rs. In the larger academies Latin and Greek were offered along with English grammar, geography, arithmetic, and other studies deemed "practical" or in demand. The academies are also noted for the importance placed on science in the curriculum. By the end of the early national period, some of the larger academies were also offering courses designed to provide preparation for teaching in the common schools (Cremin, 1982; Madsen, 1974).

Academies for Women

A number of the academies were established for women and are important for the role they played in providing females the opportunity for an education beyond the elementary school. Some bore the name "seminaries" and were important in the training of female teachers, teaching being about the only profession open to women at the time. In 1821 the Troy Female Seminary in New York was opened by Emma Willard, a lifelong activist for women's rights. Opposed to the finishing school curriculum of the female boarding schools, Willard proposed a curriculum that was "solid and useful." Mount Holyoke Female Seminary in Massachusetts, founded in 1837 by Mary Lyon, provided a demanding curriculum that included philosophy, mathematics, and science.

Do you support recent efforts to end publicly supported all male or all female schools?

Catherine Beecher, the sister of Harriet Beecher Stowe, founded both the Hartford Female Seminary (1828) and the Western Institute for Women (1832), both important institutions in the training of female teachers. Following the path forged by the female seminaries in New England, seminaries sprang up in other regions of the country, being especially popular in the South.

By the mid-nineteenth century there were more than 6,000 academies in the United States enrolling 263,000 students. The academy is considered by most educational historians as the forerunner of the American high school. Its broad range of curricular offerings responded to the demands of the growing middle class and demonstrated that there was an important place in the educational

Figure 6.1: Nineteenth-Century Educational Innovations and Their Twentieth-Century Descendants

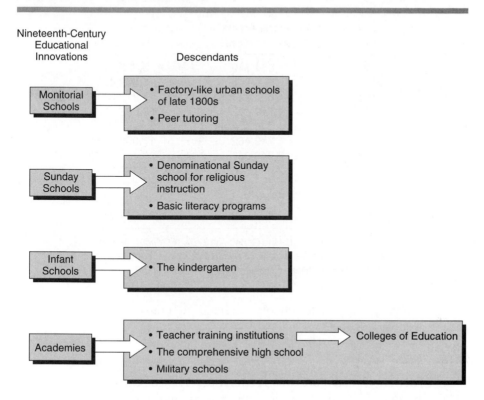

system for a secondary educational institution for non-college-bound as well as college-bound youth. The broadened curriculum, combined with the more liberal entrance requirements, allowed the entrance of people of various religious and social backgrounds and were major steps in democratizing American secondary education (Rippa, 1997).

Figure 6.1 gives an overview of the nineteenth-century educational institutions we have discussed.

Education in the Nineteenth and Early Twentieth Centuries

The Common School Movement

The period 1830–1865 has been designated the age of the common school movement in American educational history. It is during this period that the American educational system as we know it today began to take form. Instead of sporadic state legislation and abdication of responsibility, state systems of education were established. State control as well as direct taxation for the support of the *common*

Table 6.1: Area and Population of the United States, 1790–1890

Year	Land Area (square miles)	Population
1790	864,746	3,929,214
1800	864,746	5,308,483
1810	1,681,824	7,239,881
1820	1,749,462	9,638,453
1830	1,749,462	12,865,020
1840	1,749,462	17,069,453
1850	2,940,042	23,191,876
1860	2,969,640	31,443,321
1870	2,969,640	39,818,449
1880	2,969,640	50,155,783
1890	2,969,640	62,947,714

Source: U.S. Bureau of the Census. (1975). *Historical statistics of the United States, colonial times to 1970* (p. 8). Washington, DC: U.S. Government Printing Office.

schools—publicly supported schools attended in common by all children—became accepted practices.

Moving Forces

Demands of a Larger and More Urban Population. The common school movement was the product of a variety of economic, social, and political factors. Between 1830 and 1860, over a million square miles of territory were added to the United States. During the same period the population exploded from 13 million to 32 million (see Table 6.1). Of this growth, 4 million came from immigration.

Not only was there an increase in immigration, but the national origins of the immigrants were different. Whereas before this era the majority of immigrants had come from Northern Europe and shared much the same cultural and religious backgrounds as the inhabitants of their new homeland, beginning in the 1830s and 1840s larger numbers came from Ireland, Germany, and Southern Europe and were often Roman Catholic. At the same time, the United States was rapidly changing from a predominantly rural nation to one that was scattered with cities. In 1820 there were only 12 cities in the then 23 states with a population of over 10,000; by 1860 the number had increased to 101 and 8 had a population of over 100,000 (Binder, 1974).

The growth in the cities was a result of the growth in industrialization. For example, in 1807 only 15 cotton mills were in operation in the United States; by 1831 there were 801 mills employing 70,000 workers (Rippa, 1997). These changing economic and social patterns gave rise to an increasing urban population, which included concentrations of children who needed schooling, a more industrialized economy that required a trained workforce, and in certain areas a Roman Catholic population that challenged Protestant domination.

Demands of the Working Class. In this context the common schools were seen by the working class, who could not afford to educate their children at private expense, as avenues for upward social and economic mobility. Critical of pauper or charity schools, the newly emerging workingmen's organizations were open in their support of tax-supported common schools. The common schools were seen as providing the education necessary for protection against the tyranny of the upper class and for equal participation in a democracy. The leaders of business and industry also supported common schools. They saw them as a means of ensuring a supply of literate and trained workers.

Social Control. The dominant English-speaking, upper-class Protestants saw a different merit in the common schools. This group viewed the common schools as agencies of social control over the lower socioeconomic classes. According to Gutek (1991), social control in this context meant

> imposing by institutionalized education the language, beliefs, and values of the dominant group on outsiders, especially on the non-English speaking immigrants. Common schools were expected to create such conformity in American life by imposing the language and ideological outlook of the dominant group. For example, by using English as the medium of instruction, the common schools were expected to create an English-speaking citizenry; by cultivating a general value orientation based on Protestant Christianity, the schools were expected to create a general American ethic. (pp. 87–88)

Most social groups also saw the common schools as a means of controlling crime and social unrest. Knowledge was seen as "the great remedy for intemperance: for in proportion as we elevate men in the scale of existence . . . so do we reclaim them from all temptation of degrading vice and ruinous crimes" (Binder, 1974, p. 32).

Needs of the Frontier. Interest in the establishment of common schools was not limited to the industrialized regions of the East. As the frontier moved steadily westward, the one-room schoolhouse, often the only public building in a community, became the symbol of civilization and the center of efforts to keep literacy, citizenship, and civilization alive in the wilderness (Gutek, 1991).

Extended Suffrage. On the political front, the age of the common school coincided with the age of the common man. In the early years of the republic the right to vote in many states was limited to those who owned property. Gradually this began to change and many states, especially those on the frontier, extended suffrage to all white males. The result of the extension of suffrage was not only increased office-holding by the common man, but increased pressure for direct taxation to support common schools.

Education Journals and Organizations. The movement for common schools began in the Northeast. To some extent the public had been introduced to the basic ideas of the common school movement through the writings of individuals like Webster and Rush, and through the arguments for social and moral reform made by the leaders of the charity school movement and the Lancasterian monitorial system. However, perhaps the two most important mechanisms for spreading the ideology of the common school were educational periodicals and educational organizations.

Between 1825 and 1850 more than 60 educational journals came into existence (Spring, 1997). These journals served not only to popularize education, but also to keep teachers informed of educational innovations and ideas from home and abroad. Among the most important were the Massachusetts *Common School Journal,* founded and edited by Horace Mann; the *Connecticut Common School,* edited for several years by Henry Barnard; and the prestigious *American Journal of Education,* also edited from 1855 to 1881 by Henry Barnard. Among their other material, these journals printed part or all of several reports (e.g., the Cousin Report and the Stowe Report) describing the Pestalozzian reforms of Prussian education (Rippa, 1997).

Of the educational organizations, the most noteworthy were the American Institute of Instruction, the Western Literary Institute and College of Professional Teachers, and on a more national scale, the American Lyceum. The American Lyceum was founded in 1826 by a Connecticut farmer, Josiah Holbrook, as an organization devoted to advancing the education of children and adults. By 1839 there were 4,000–5,000 local *lyceums* in the United States actively presenting programs, demonstrations, mutual instruction, and informative lectures in favor of school reforms. Cremin (1982) credits educational organizations with spearheading the common school movement, "articulating its ideals, publicizing its goals, and instructing one another in its political techniques; indeed, in the absence of a national ministry of education, it was their articulating, publicizing, and mutual instruction in politics that accounted for the spread of public education across the country" (p. 176).

Horace Mann

If any one person were to be given the title "Father of American Education," that person would be Horace Mann (1796–1859). Elected to the Massachusetts legislature in 1827, Mann, a brilliant orator, soon became the spokesperson for the common school movement. He led a campaign to organize the schools in Massachusetts into a state system and to establish a state board of education.

Upon the creation of the state board of education in 1837 Mann gave up his political career and a chance at the governorship to become the board's first secretary and the chief state school officer. He served in this position for 12 years and used it as a platform for proclaiming the ideology of the common school movement, as well as other educational ideals. In addition to his numerous lectures, editorships, and other writings, each year Mann wrote a report to the legislature reciting current educational practice and conditions and making recommendations for improvement. These reports were distributed in other states and abroad, and were significant in influencing educational legislation and practice throughout the country.

In his own state, Mann campaigned vigorously to increase public support for education and public awareness of the problems facing education in the form of

Do you subscribe to any educational journals? How valuable has it been to your professional development?

dilapidated, unsanitary facilities and substandard materials, as well as the short-comings of the local school committees. Mann was also critical of the status of the teaching profession and the training of teachers. As a result of his efforts, state appropriations to education were doubled, 50 new secondary schools were built, textbooks and equipment were improved, and teachers' salaries in Massachusetts were raised more than 50%. Mann also fought for the professional training of teachers and established three normal schools (teacher training institutions), the first such schools in America. The first of these normal schools was established in 1839 at Lexington, Massachusetts.

In his Tenth Annual Report (1846) Mann asserted that education was the right of every child and that it was the state's responsibility to ensure that every child was provided an education. Although Mann himself did not promote compulsory attendance but rather *regular* attendance, this report was instrumental in the adoption by the Massachusetts legislature of the nation's first compulsory attendance law in 1852.

Like several prominent educators of his time, Mann had visited the Prussian schools and observed the Pestalozzian methods. His Seventh Report (1843) gave a positive account of his observations. He was particularly impressed with the love and rapport shared by the teachers and students involved in these schools. He also shared Pestalozzi's and Catherine Beecher's belief that women were the better teachers for the common schools.

The view Mann expounded on the role of the common school in promoting social harmony and ensuring the republic would be guided by an intelligent, moral citizenry was not original or unique. But at a time when the common school movement was spreading across the nation, when it came to defining its basic principles and articles of faith, he was unquestionably the chief spokesperson (Binder, 1974).

Henry Barnard

Another major leader of the common school movement was Henry Barnard (1811–1900). Like Mann he served in the state (Connecticut) legislature, worked to establish a state board of education, and then became the board's first secretary (1838–1842). He then served in a similar capacity in Rhode Island (1845–1849) and later became the first U.S. commissioner of education.

Much of Barnard's influence on educational theory and practice came through his numerous lectures and writings and, more important, through his editorship of the *American Journal of Education*. Barnard is also credited with initiating the *teachers' institute* movement discussed later in this chapter. Barnard's greatest successes lay in his democratic philosophy, "schools good enough for the best and cheap enough for the poorest," and as a disseminator of information about better schools. He is sometimes called the "Father of American School Administration" (Pulliam & Van Patten, 1995).

Catherine Beecher

Catherine Beecher (1800–1878), the founder of the Hartford Female Seminary and the Western Institute for Women, was a strong supporter of the common school and saw her task as focusing the attention of the nation on the need for a corps of female teachers to staff the common schools. She set forth a plan for a nationwide system of teacher training seminaries. Although the plan was not adopted, her efforts on behalf of the common school were a force in its acceptance, and her work on behalf of women pointed to a new American consensus concerning female roles (Cremin, 1982).

State Support

How does the practice of some districts charging fees for participation in extracurricular activities affect the participation of the children of the poor?

The idea of having universal common schools was one thing, but paying for them through direct taxation of the general public was another. Until the 1820s or 1830s, the only really free education was that provided by the charity schools, or in certain other schools if the parents were willing to declare themselves paupers. Often local or county taxes levied on specific activities, for example liquor licenses or marriage fees, provided partial support for the schools, but the remainder of the expenses were charged to the parents in the form of a *rate bill*. The rate bill was, in effect, a tuition fee based on the number of children. Even though the fee might be small, poor parents often could not afford it, so their children either did not attend school or took turns attending.

State support for the schools was very limited. One emphasis of the common school movement was greater state support. Beginning in the first quarter of the nineteenth century several states began to provide aid for public schools. Funds came from either the permanent school fund (derived largely from the sale of public lands), direct taxation, or appropriations from the general fund. Conditions were usually placed on the receipt of funds; for example, that local support must equal or exceed state support, or that the schools must be kept open a minimum length of time.

By 1865 systems of common schools had been established throughout the northern, midwestern, and western states, and more than 50% of the nation's children were enrolled in public schools. The lowest enrollments were in the South, where the common school movement had made little progress.

As the common school movement progressed, the pressure to make these schools completely tax supported increased. In 1827 Massachusetts became the first state to do away with the rate bill. Pennsylvania's Free School Act of 1834 was a model for eliminating the pauper school concept. Although other states soon followed these examples and by constitutional or legislative enactment adopted the concept of public support for public schools open to all children, it was not until 1871 that the last state (New Jersey) abolished the rate bill, making the schools truly free.

State Control

Creation of State Superintendents of Education. As is usually the case, increased support is accompanied by increased efforts to control. The effort to establish some control or supervision was marked by the creation of an office of state superintendent, or commissioner of education, and a state board of education. In 1812 New York became the first state to appoint a state superintendent, Gideon

Hawley. His tenure in office was filled with such controversy that in 1821 he was removed from office and the position was abolished and not recreated until 1854. Nonetheless, by the outbreak of the Civil War, 28 of the 34 states had established state boards of education and chief state school officers. By and large these officers and boards were vested with more supervisory power than real control. Initially their major responsibilities involved the distribution of the permanent school funds and the organization of a state system of common schools.

Creation of Local School Districts and Superintendents. The creation of a state system of common schools paralleled the establishment of school districts and the establishment of local and county superintendents. The New England states instituted the district system in the early years of the nineteenth century and it spread westward during the next three decades. Local supervision was provided by the district or county superintendent, whose primary duty was to supervise instruction. The development of the position of county superintendent of schools helped bring about some degree of standardization and uniformity in areas that had numerous small, rural school districts (Gutek, 1991). The evolution of the office of city school superintendent quickly followed that of the district and county office. The first city superintendent was appointed in Buffalo in 1837, and was soon followed in Louisville, St. Louis, Providence, Springfield, Cleveland, Rochester, and New Orleans. One of the major responsibilities of the early city superintendents was to develop a uniform course of study. This development was concurrent with the establishment of graded schools (Spring, 1997).

Organization and Curriculum

The common schools varied in terms of size, organization, and curriculum, depending on their location. In rural areas the one- or two-room school was dominant; progress was not marked by movement from one grade to another, but by completing one text and beginning another. In larger cities and towns, grading had been introduced. On the frontier, where there remained some distrust of too much education, the curriculum was often limited to the three Rs; in larger cities it tended to be broader. A great variety of textbooks appeared and their authors began to practice the more modern educational teachings. For example, the extremely popular *McGuffey Readers* continued to teach "the lessons of morality and patriotism, but the stern, direct preachments of earlier schoolbooks were replaced or supplemented by stories and essays designed to appeal to youthful interest" (Cremin, 1982, p. 96). Rote learning, drill, and practice did not disappear from the classroom, but a more Pestalozzian approach that placed a value on the sensitivities and individuality of the child was making some inroads.

What would be the advantages and disadvantages of attending a one- or two-room rural school over a large, urban school?

Secondary School Movement

Public *secondary schools* offering education beyond the elementary school did not become a firmly established part of the American educational scene until the last quarter of the nineteenth century. However, the beginnings of the movement occurred well before the Civil War. Perhaps not unexpectedly, the lead was taken by

The one-room schoolhouse was the symbol of free, public education in rural and frontier America.

those states that had been first to establish systems of common schools. Boston inaugurated the high school movement in 1821 with the opening of the English Classical School, renamed the Boston English High School in 1824. The school was open to boys only and was intended to be an alternative to the Latin grammar school and to provide "an education that shall fit him (the child) for active life, and shall serve as a foundation for eminence in his profession, whether Mercantile or Mechanical" (Binder, 1974, p. 107). Such an education, as we have seen, could otherwise be obtained only by sending the child to a private academy.

Ten years later, in 1831, the first American *comprehensive* (and coeducational) *high school,* offering both English and classical courses of study, was opened in Lowell, Massachusetts. In 1838 Philadelphia opened a coeducational high school with three tracks: a four-year classical curriculum, a four-year modern language curriculum, and a two-year English curriculum.

Slow Beginnings

In the years before the Civil War the high school movement expanded slowly. By 1860 there were only 300 high schools in the nation compared to more than 6,000 academies. Of the 300, more than 100 were located in Massachusetts. Mass-

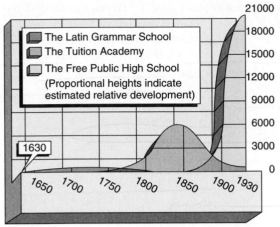

Figure 6.2: The Development of Secondary Schools in the United States, 1630–1930

Source: Cubberley, E.P. (1948). *The history of education* (p. 699). Cambridge, MA: Riverside Press.

achusetts was unique in requiring communities of 50 families or more to provide secondary level education (Binder, 1974).

The slow growth of the high school can be partially explained by the fact that, unlike the common school, the high school was not being overwhelmingly demanded by the masses. It appeared to be more a reformer's response to urbanization and industrialization. Middle or upper class reformers, adopting the philosophy and rhetoric of the common school advocates, viewed their efforts as democratizing secondary education, providing a means of maintaining social values, and promoting economic progress. As a result, prior to the Civil War most high schools were located in urban areas; it was there that a sufficient number of students and tax support were most often found.

The Movement Grows as Industry and the Economy Grow

The years after the Civil War were marked by rapid industrial growth and technological change. These trends intensified the demand for skilled workers. A great tide of immigration brought people who needed not only skills but also knowledge of American values and ideals. The mood of the masses changed, and a high school education was increasingly seen as necessary to the full realization of one's social and economic goals. Economic growth also created a larger tax base that could be used to support an expanded educational system. Consequently, the number of public high schools increased. During the 1880s the number of high schools surpassed the number of academies (see Figure 6.2), and by 1890 there were 2,526 public high schools enrolling 202,063 students, compared to the 1,632 private academies with their 94,391 students (Gutek, 1991).

Tax Support, Compulsory Attendance, and the Decline of Illiteracy

The public secondary school movement was given further impetus by the finding of the Michigan Supreme Court in the famous *Kalamazoo* case (*Stuart et al. v.*

School District No. 1 of the Village of Kalamazoo, 1874). By its ruling that the legislature could tax for the support of both elementary and secondary schools the court provided the precedent for public support of secondary education. By the end of the century the publicly supported high school had replaced the academy in most communities and had become an established part of the common school system in every state.

The *Kalamazoo* decision having quashed the argument that public funds could not be used for secondary education, compulsory attendance laws soon followed. The passage of child labor laws and the increasing demand for an educated workforce were also instrumental in driving the adoption of compulsory attendance laws. By 1918 all states had enacted laws requiring full-time attendance until the child reached a certain age or completed a certain grade. One result of this increase in school attendance was the declining illiteracy rate from 20% of all persons over 10 years of age in 1870 to 7.7% in 1910 (Graham, 1974).

Illiteracy rates varied by segment of the population. As a result of the pre–Civil War prohibition on teaching blacks in most southern states and inadequate education after the war, blacks had the highest illiteracy rate, 30.4% in 1910. The illiteracy rate was also high among the older population, which had not been the beneficiary of universal, compulsory education. Whites who were the children of a foreign-born parent had the lowest illiteracy rate, 1.1%. Literacy rates also varied by region. The South, which not only had the most blacks but also had been the slowest in developing systems of common schools, had the highest illiteracy rate (Graham, 1974).

The Committee of Ten

As previously noted, in its origins the high school had been viewed as a provider of a more practical education. The need to assimilate the children of the new immigrants, and the more technical demands of industry, placed additional pressures on the schools to include a curriculum that could be immediately useful and that included vocational training (Graham, 1974). However, there were educators who did not share this esteem for the "practical curriculum." In 1892, in an effort to standardize the curriculum, the National Education Association established the Committee of Ten. The committee was chaired by Charles Eliot, the president of Harvard University, and was largely composed of representatives of higher education. The committee recommended an early introduction to the basic subjects and uniform subject matter and instruction for both college-bound and terminal students, with few electives. And, while four curricula were recommended (classical, Latin-scientific, modern language, and English), the entire curriculum was dominated by college-preparatory courses. Using the psychology of mental discipline as a theoretical rationale, the Committee claimed that the recommended subjects would be used profitably by both college-bound and terminal students because they trained the powers of observation, memory, expression, and reasoning (Gutek, 1991). The committee also recommended that each course meet four or five times weekly for one year, for which the student would receive a *Carnegie Unit.*

The Seven Cardinal Principles of Secondary Education

The view of the Committee of Ten was immediately challenged by many educators and within 25 years there was little support for its position. In 1918 the National Education Association appointed another committee, the Commission on the Reorganization of Secondary Education, to review the curriculum and organization of secondary education in light of the many changes that had swept American society. The commission issued its seven *Cardinal Principles of Secondary Education,* which identified what should be the objectives of the high school curriculum: (1) health, (2) command of fundamental academic skills, (3) worthy home membership, (4) vocational preparation, (5) citizenship, (6) worthwhile use of leisure time, and (7) ethical character.

As compared to the recommendations of the Committee of Ten, only one of these principles, command of fundamental processes, was concerned with college preparation. Instead, the commission viewed the high school as a much more comprehensive institution in terms of both integration of the various ethnic, religious, and socioeconomic groups, and accommodation of the various educational goals of students.

Patterns of Curricular Organization

By the mid-1920s the essential shape of the American comprehensive high school was apparent. It was an institution that offered a range of curricula to students of differing abilities and interests. Four basic patterns of curricular organization were in evidence: (1) the college preparatory program, which included courses in English language and literature, foreign languages, mathematics, the natural and physical sciences, and history and social sciences; (2) the commercial or business program, which offered courses in bookkeeping, shorthand, and typing; (3) the industrial, vocational, home economics, and agricultural programs; and (4) a modified academic program for students who planned to terminate their formal education upon high school completion. The typical high school program was four years and was attended by students aged 14 to 18. Exceptions were the six-year combined junior-senior high schools (Gutek, 1991).

The Junior High School

The two-year and three-year *junior high schools* that began to appear in some urban districts, offering grades 6 and 7, or 6, 7, and 8, were an outgrowth of the Committee of Ten's recommendation that academic work begin earlier and that elementary schooling be reduced from eight to six years. Their growth was also encouraged by the work of G. Stanley Hall, who wrote the first book on adolescent development and emphasized the developmental differences between childhood and preadolescence that would justify a reorganization of the eight–four system. Others felt greater opportunity for industrial and commercial training should be given before high school. As a result of these and other proposals, in 1909 junior high schools were established in Columbus, Ohio, and Berkeley, California. Other cities soon followed, and the junior high school became commonplace in the United States after 1930 (Pulliam & Van Patten, 1995).

Did you attend a junior high school? If so, what educational experiences do you recall that reinforce the positive value of the junior high school over other organizational plans?

Higher Education

As was discussed in the preceding chapter, nine colleges were founded during the colonial period. In the period after the Revolution and before the Civil War, the number increased dramatically. Compared to a tenfold increase in the population, there was a twentyfold increase in the number of colleges during this period (Madsen, 1974). This increase was a result of both people moving westward who wanted colleges close at hand, and some denominations choosing to establish their own colleges rather than have their members educated at colleges operated by other denominations. Thus, of the colleges founded before 1860, less than 10% were state institutions.

By and large the colleges were very small. For example, it was not until after the Civil War that Harvard had a graduating class of 100. During the late colonial and early national periods the curriculum of the colleges became more "liberal," but it retained its heavy classical overlay and its emphasis on religion.

In 1816 the New Hampshire legislature, dominated by the more liberal Jeffersonian Republicans and concerned by what appeared to be the antiliberal sentiments of the board of trustees, enacted legislation to convert Dartmouth College from a private to a state institution. In the Dartmouth College case (*Trustees of Dartmouth College v. Woodward,* 1819), the U.S. Supreme Court upheld the original contract from the king of England which had given private status to the college. The effect of the case was not only to establish the principle that the state could not impair contracts, but also to provide a secure foundation for the system of private colleges we have today.

Patterned after the English universities of Oxford and Cambridge, American colleges offered professional studies in theology, medicine, and eventually in law. Lecture and recitation remained the most common modes of instruction. Discipline was strict and the entire atmosphere authoritarian. As a result, student riots sometimes occurred: in 1807 over half the student body of Princeton was suspended; in 1830 Yale experienced the "bread and butter rebellion"; and on one occasion over half the senior class at Harvard was expelled. Intercollegiate athletics being unheard of, literary and debating societies provided some outlet for student enthusiasm (Madsen, 1974).

Growth of Public Institutions

The first state institutions of higher education were established in the South: the University of Georgia in 1785, the University of North Carolina in 1789, the University of Tennessee in 1794, and the University of South Carolina in 1801. In the second quarter of the nineteenth century the same nationalistic, democratic spirit that gave rise to the common school also produced an increase in public institutions of higher education. These appeared largely in the Midwest: Indiana University in 1820, the University of Michigan in 1837, and the University of Wisconsin in 1848.

State institutions, unlike denominational institutions, were publicly supported and controlled. In contrast to an emphasis on classical languages and philosophy, their curricula tended to emphasize the sciences and modern languages. The growth of public institutions was also enhanced by a federal land-grant policy, which granted two townships of land to each state when it entered the union for the support of institutions of higher education.

The Morrill Acts and the Establishment of Land-Grant Institutions

By the mid-nineteenth century there was growing recognition among farmers and laborers that equality of opportunity required an education that would contribute to an improved economic condition. Finding the majority of existing colleges unresponsive and irrelevant to their needs, they urged the establishment of a new institution, the industrial college. In response, the first Morrill Act was passed by Congress and signed by President Lincoln in 1862. The act granted 30,000 acres of land to each state for each senator and representative it had in Congress based on the 1860 census. The income from the land was to be used to support at least one college that would "teach such branches of learning as are related to agriculture and mechanical arts, . . . in order to promote the liberal and practical education of the industrial classes in the several pursuits and professions of life."

The Second Morrill Act of 1890 provided for direct annual grants of $15,000 (increasing annually to $25,000) to each state to support land-grant colleges. The bill also provided that no grant would be given to any state that denied admission to its land-grant colleges because of race without providing "separate but equal" institutions.

As a result of the Morrill Acts, 65 new land-grant colleges were established. Among the first of the new institutions of higher education were the universities of Maine (1865), Illinois and West Virginia (1867), California (1868), Purdue and Nebraska (1869), Ohio State (1870), and Arkansas and Texas A & M (1871). Seventeen states, mostly in the South, also established separate land-grant colleges for blacks under the provisions of the Second Morrill Act. Together the Morrill Acts provided both the foundation for a new type of curriculum at government expense and powerful incentives for greatly expanded state systems of higher education (Rippa, 1997).

Higher Education for Women

Significant developments were also being made in the higher education of women during this period. As discussed earlier, a number of women's seminaries or colleges had been opened prior to the Civil War. A few coeducational colleges also existed before the Civil War (e.g., Oberlin, 1833; Antioch, 1853; and the State University of Iowa, 1858). However, it was not until after the Civil War that women's higher education really began to flourish. Several women's colleges (e.g., Vassar, 1865; Wellesley, 1875; Smith, 1875; Radcliffe, 1879; and Bryn Mawr, 1880) were established that offered programs comparable to those found in the colleges for men. In addition, with the impact of the Civil War casualties on enrollments, and in financial distress, an increasing number of formerly all-male institutions began admitting women, albeit selectively. By 1880 about half the colleges and universities admitted women (Pulliam & Van Patten, 1995). However, while a wide curriculum was open to women, severe restrictions were placed on their access to facilities, libraries, and lectures. And, in the end, teaching remained the most accessible and socially acceptable option for women.

The Emergence of the Modern University

In the last decades of the nineteenth century and the first decades of the twentieth century, two other institutions made their appearance on the higher educational scene in America: the university and the *junior college*. In contrast to the small, single-purpose, largely undergraduate colleges, the emerging universities were large and multipurpose. Influenced by the German universities where many of them had studied, American professors and college presidents worked to establish graduate programs and emphasize research. By the end of the nineteenth century, the American university had come to look much as we know it today with an undergraduate college of liberal arts and sciences, a graduate college, and various professional colleges.

Founding of Junior Colleges

Have you ever attended a junior or community college? Would you support the movement toward having all lower division education take place at these institutions?

The initiative for the establishment of junior colleges came in the late nineteenth century from a number of university presidents who viewed the first two years of higher education as more appropriate to secondary education. They wanted to free their faculty from what they considered secondary education responsibilities so that they could devote themselves more to research and graduate education. In 1901 the first public junior college was established, the Joliet (Illinois) Junior College. Although initially established to offer courses that would transfer to four-year institutions, it soon began to offer terminal and vocational programs as well (Gutek, 1991). In 1907 California passed a law giving school boards the authority to offer high school graduates courses comparable to those required during the first two years of college (Rippa, 1997). By the early 1920s the concept of the junior college was well established. During the late 1920s, encouraged by the Smith-Hughes Act, which provided federal aid to vocational education, junior colleges developed more extensive vocational and technical education programs. In subsequent decades they not only expanded rapidly, but as their goal was expanded to include serving the broad-based needs of the community, they became transformed into today's community colleges (Gutek, 1991).

Education of Minorities

The progress of education in the United States has not been uniform across all regions, socioeconomic classes, or races. To many the schoolhouse door was closed and the promise of equal educational opportunity an unrealized dream. Native Americans, Hispanic Americans, Asian Americans, and African Americans in particular have had to struggle to realize the promise of an equal education.

Education of Native Americans

The formal education of Native Americans was initiated by missionaries who equated education with Christianity and the virtues of civilized life. The Society for the Propagation of the Gospel and the Moravians were among the more active of the missionary groups. Just as education for the white colonists was primarily for the purpose of training for the ministry, so too it was hoped that education would equip Native Americans to become missionaries to their people.

However, the efforts of missionary or philanthropic groups were limited, and the town and grammar schools enrolled few Native Americans. Efforts to provide any higher education were even more limited. In 1653 a college was founded at Harvard to instruct Native American students in the same classical education received by whites. Dartmouth College was originally established for the education of Native Americans, but was soon dominated by the children of the white colonists.

The initial response to the formal, traditional education offered by the colonists was distrust and rejection. Benjamin Franklin quoted one Native American leader as saying:

> Several of our young people were formerly brought up at the colleges of the Northern Provinces; they were instructed in all your Sciences; but, when they came back to us, they were bad Runners, ignorant of every means of living in the Woods, unable to bear either Cold or Hunger, knew neither how to build a Cabin, take a Deer, or kill an Enemy, spoke our Language imperfectly, were therefore neither fit for Hunters, Warriors, nor Counsellors; they were totally good for nothing. (cited in Kidwell & Swift, 1976, p. 335)

Treaties and Mission Schools. During the first century of the new republic much of the education of the Native Americans came about as a result of federal legislation or negotiated treaties. According to the terms of the treaties, 389 of which were signed with various tribes between 1778 and 1871, in return for relinquishing their land, the Native Americans were given money payments, guarantees of the integrity of the land they retained, and promises of educational services (Kidwell & Swift, 1976). The predominant means by which the federal government met its obligation to provide educational services was through support of mission schools operated on the reservation by religious groups. These schools concentrated on teaching English, the three Rs, some vocational and agricultural training, and, of course, religion. Instruction was given primarily in the native tongue, as this was viewed as the best way to lead Native Americans to conversion. In 1917 this arrangement, which in effect constituted government support of sectarian education, ended (Butts, 1978).

Boarding Schools. The decline of the mission schools was accompanied by the establishment of three other forms of Native American education: (1) the off-reservation boarding school, (2) the reservation day school, and (3) public schools. The off-reservation boarding school was a product of the *assimilation* approach that became popular after the Civil War. As discussed in Chapter 8, this approach advocated the immersion of Native Americans into the predominant white culture, and was established on the belief that the most lasting and efficient way this assimilation could take place was to remove children from their tribal setting and subject them, in a strict disciplinary setting, to an infusion of American values, language, and customs.

The first major boarding school was established in 1879 at Carlisle, Pennsylvania, by General Richard Pratt. Vocational and industrial training was emphasized at this and other off-reservation boarding schools. By the turn of the

Class at Carlisle Indian boarding school, circa 1900.

century, 25 off-reservation boarding schools had been established (Szasz, 1977). However, they were subject to much criticism. The physical and living conditions were often inadequate. The dropout rate was high. Students often returned to the reservation rather than enter white society, and upon return to the reservation found they were either unable to apply the training they had received, or that it was irrelevant.

Reservation Day Schools and Public Schools. The reservation day schools offered several advantages over the off-reservation boarding school; not only were they less expensive, but also they were more acceptable to parents. Consequently, day schools increased in number after the turn of the twentieth century.

Although Native Americans in the eastern United States who were not under the jurisdiction of the federal government had already been attending off-reservation public schools, a newer phenomenon was the public school located on the reservation. These schools initially had been built to accommodate the white people who rented land on the reservation. The on-reservation public schools tended to encourage not only assimilation, but learning. As one Indian agent wrote, "Indian children progress much faster when thrown in contact with white children than they do when they are all kept together with whites excluded" (Szasz, 1977, p. 11).

The Meriam Report. In 1924 Congress granted U.S. Citizenship to all Native Americans. At the same time, the appalling living conditions and reprehensible treatment of Native Americans were brought to public view by a number of reformers determined to improve their plight. In response the Bureau of Indian Affairs (BIA) commissioned the Brookings Institution for an independent study of Native American life in the United States. The report, issued in 1928 and called the Meriam Report, documented the intolerable conditions of Native American life and pointed out that much of their poverty was caused by their loss of land. It also criticized the BIA educational program, exposing the inadequate industrial training, overcrowded dormitories, inadequate diet, and physical punishment in the boarding schools. The report discouraged the practice of boarding schools and encouraged the construction of day schools that could also serve as community centers. It accused the reservation system of creating isolation and concluded that the best way to improve the living standards of Native Americans was to educate them so they could be assimilated into white society (Kidwell & Swift, 1976).

How successful have been efforts to assimilate Native Americans into mainstream society?

The Meriam Report marked the beginning of a change in BIA policy. After 1928, BIA appropriations for education increased dramatically, efforts were made to deal with conditions in government schools, and curriculum reform was initiated. Soon a major share of the BIA's budget was allocated to education, with the goal of assimilating Native Americans into mainstream society.

Education of Hispanics

The story of the involvement of the United States in the education of Hispanics is largely to be told in relation to the Spanish-speaking peoples of the southwestern United States and begins with the acquisition of this territory from Mexico in 1848 at the end of the Mexican-American War. For the Mexicans who chose to remain in the territory after the U.S. takeover, or for those who fled across the border in the years that followed, life became marked by discrimination, prejudice, and segregation. Although segregation was not imposed by law *(de jure)* as it was for blacks in the South, it nonetheless existed by practice *(de facto):* separate schools and/or classes, poorer facilities, fewer well-trained teachers, and smaller budgets. English was used for instruction, whether understood or not, and the use of Spanish in the classroom or playground was often forbidden (Butts, 1978).

Any improvement in the educational condition of Mexican American children was hampered by the attitudes of many of their parents who failed to see the value of an education that was aimed at undermining their traditional beliefs and culture. It was also hampered by the articulated views of the larger society, including many educators, that Mexican Americans were mentally inferior. Many Mexican American children also suffered the additional handicap of migrancy. Often those who traveled from place to place working in the fields did not attend school at all. Few attended beyond the primary years, and their failures were viewed as natural by educators and the Anglo society in general. Such schooling as they did receive emphasized learning English, vocational and manual arts training, health and hygiene, and the adoption of such American core values as cleanliness, thrift, and punctuality (Carter & Sequra, 1979).

During the Depression years many rural Mexican Americans moved to the cities, bringing their problems to a wider consciousness. Also during the 1930s and 1940s greater attention was given to the concerns of Mexican Americans in some states, especially California and New Mexico (Carter & Sequra, 1979). However, it would not be until a quarter century later that any marked progress was made as the "consciousness and conscience of the nation began to stir under the proddings of a new generation of Anglo liberals and especially new Chicano leadership" (Butts, 1978, p. 251).

Education of Asian Americans

Asian immigration to the United States did not occur in any significant numbers until the mid-1850s when Chinese workers were recruited as cheap labor to work in the mines and railroads of the West. Throughout the nineteenth century and well into the twentieth century Asian Americans experienced much of the discrimination in the schools and the larger society as did other minorities. For example, from 1871 to 1885, by their deliberate exclusion by state school law, Chinese children were excluded from the public schools in California. When the decision of the state supreme court in *Tape v. Hurley* (1885) forced a change in the law, most school boards responded by providing segregated, so-called "Oriental schools." Typically, these facilities were inferior to the facilities attended by white students.

Sometimes Asian Americans were allowed to attend white schools but were segregated in different rooms or on a different floor. In the classroom the special language needs of these students were largely ignored as school systems attempted to force mastery of the English language and were reluctant to employ Asian American teachers or staff. The result was that many Asian American children experienced grave academic difficulties (Weinburg, 1997).

Legally *(de jure)* segregated schools for Chinese American children were the norm, not the exception, until the 1940s. However, many other Asian American children attended nonsegregated schools, or at the least were not subjected to *de jure* segregation. However, *de facto* school segregation continued to be a familiar feature of Asian American education well into the second half of the twentieth century, perpetuated in large part by the residential concentration of Asian American families (Weinburg, 1997). However, this segregation has been uneven, and as Asian Americans began to move out of their all-Asian communities, white schools were forced to open their doors to these students (Spring, 1998).

Education of Blacks

Although blacks came to America before the Puritans, 20 having been sold to the colonists at the Jamestown colony in 1619, their educational history was anything but similar. The majority of blacks living in the United States during the first 300 years of its history lived in the South and, until after the Civil War, as slaves. On the eve of the Civil War there were about 4 million black slaves and one-half million free blacks, out of a total U.S. population of 31 million.

Education of Slaves. For the majority of slaves, education was virtually nonexistent. A few slave owners educated their slaves, and some missionary or philanthropic groups provided limited and sporadic schooling. However, by the third decade of the nineteenth century the rise of militant abolitionism and the fear of slave revolts had led to the enactment of the so-called "Black Codes," which, among other things, prohibited the education of slaves. As Pifer (1973) described the pre–Civil War status of education for the slave:

> Education was thought to give the slave too high an opinion of himself and access to such pernicious ideas as those expressed in our Declaration of Independence, namely, that all men are created equal and have certain inalienable rights. In short, education was dangerous. Nevertheless, some slaves and some whites, at great personal risk, defied these harsh laws and engaged in clandestine learning and teachings, but the sum total of education for slaves, all the same, was meager. (p. 8)

Education of Free Blacks Prior to the Civil War. The education of free blacks was also very limited. In the decades preceding the Civil War, as common school systems were developed in the North, blacks more often than not found themselves in segregated schools. An important legal support for this segregation (and also the legal basis for segregation for the remainder of the century) was provided by the Massachusetts Supreme Court decision in *Roberts v. City of Boston* (1850), which said that separate but equal schools did not violate the rights of the black child.

Despite the difficulties, some free blacks did obtain an education. In some communities the children of free slaves attended public schools or the private schools established by various religious, philanthropic, or abolitionist societies. The SPG was one of the most active groups in these efforts. The outbreak of the Civil War in 1861 found about 4,000 blacks in schools in the slave states and 23,000 in the free states (West, 1972). A few blacks even obtained a higher education. A small number went abroad to England or Scotland, a few attended the limited number of American colleges that admitted blacks, notably Oberlin in Ohio and Berea in Kentucky, and others attended the three black colleges established before 1860: Cheyney State College (1839) and Lincoln University (1854) in Pennsylvania and Wilberforce University (1856) in Ohio.

Many of the free blacks who gained a higher education prior to 1860 did so under the auspices of the American Colonization Society, which was established in 1817 to send free blacks to the colony of Liberia in Africa, founded by the society in 1822. The education of the free blacks was undertaken to provide the doctors, lawyers, teachers, clergy, and civil servants needed by the colony. Although not all those educated by the Society went to the colony, or if they went did not remain, enough did so as to provide the colony and the Republic of Liberia, which it became in 1847, with its leadership elite (Pifer, 1973).

Reconstruction. The period of Reconstruction (1865–1877) following the Civil War brought new factors to bear on education in the South in general and the education of blacks in particular. One such force was the hundreds of teachers

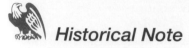

Historical Note

Zeal for Learning Among Freedmen, 1868

Dear Brethren and Sisters;

Since I last wrote I have commenced my school and have now been teaching just four weeks. Everything was finally arranged so that on Monday Nov. 30th I opened school with twenty-five scholars. Since then the number has been steadily increasing and now it numbers forty-two with a prospect of large additions after their great holiday Christmas week is past.

From all the accounts of Freedmen's schools which I had heard and read previous to coming here I expected to find them anxious to learn but after all, I confess I was unprepared for the amount of zeal manifested by most of them for an education. I can say as one did of old, "The half had not been told me." I am surprised each day by some new proof of their anxiety to learn. Nearly all ages, colors, conditions and capacities are represented in my school. Ages ranging from five to sixty-five; Colors from jet-black with tight curling hair to pale brunette with waving brown hair.

Some, a few of them could read quite readily in a second reader and many more knew the alphabet and were trying patiently to spell out short easy words, while by far the greater number could not distinguish a letter. I have had as many as nineteen in my alphabet class at one time but it is now reduced to four.

One old woman over sixty, after spending three weeks on the alphabet and finally conquering it, said she wanted to learn to spell Jesus first before spelling easy words for said she, "Pears like I can learn the rest easier if I get that blessed name learned first." So now she looks through the Bible for that name and has learned to distinguish it at sight from other words. The older members of the school are as quiet and orderly as I could desire but the children are not so very different from other children. They love mischief and play and the prevailing vice among them is deceit. But education has all the charm of novelty to them and they learn with astonishing rapidity. They come to school as well provided with books as children usually do.

Your Sister in Christ,
Pamelia A. Hand

Source: Reprinted by permission of Macmillan Publishing Company from *The Black American and Education* (pp. 73–74) by Earle H. West. Copyright © 1972 by Merrill Publishing Company.

---

who, supported by various northern churches and missionary societies, moved to the South to educate those who had been liberated. Another factor was the emergence of charitable *educational foundations,* philanthropy in a new form. The first of these, established in 1867, was the Peabody Fund for the Advancement of Negro Education in the South. It later merged with the Slater Fund to support industrial education and teacher preparation. Among the others, the largest was the General Education Board set up by John D. Rockefeller in 1902 (Pifer, 1973; West, 1972).

Another major force affecting the education of blacks in the South during this period was the Freedmen's Bureau. The bureau was responsible for the establishment of some 3,000 schools, and by 1869 some 114,000 students were in attendance in these schools (the Historical Note above gives the account of one teacher in a freedmen's school). These schools followed the New England common school model in terms of their curriculum (reading, writing, grammar, geography, arithmetic, and music) and moral outlook (the importance of certain values and the responsibility of citizenship), but added a new dimension—industrial training. In the view of northern educators, industrial training would prepare blacks for the occupations they were most suited to perform in the South (Gutek, 1991).

The Hampton Institute. Agricultural and industrial education were emphasized by the Hampton Institute, founded in 1868 by a representative of the Freedmen's Bureau, General Samuel Chapman Armstrong. Armstrong intended that the institution provide blacks with a "practical learning" that would prepare them for a productive life. It is also significant to note that the Hampton Institute played an important role in the training of black teachers. In fact, as one historian reminds us, the traditional attention given to Hampton as an agricultural and industrial school has obscured the fact that Hampton was founded and maintained primarily to train black teachers for the South. Indeed, between 1872 and 1890, 604 of Hampton's 723 graduates became teachers (Anderson, 1978).

Booker T. Washington. Booker T. Washington (1856–1915) was perhaps the most famous graduate of the Hampton Institute. It was there he developed the educational ideas that led to the establishment of his Tuskegee Institute in 1880. Some black leaders, such as W. E. B. DuBois, who in 1907 cofounded the National Association for the Advancement of Colored People, argued against what they viewed as a position of accommodation or compromise and protested that it was wrong for blacks to be given only one educational direction (industrial) and whites several. However, to Washington and others who supported industrial education, this approach appeared the most immediate and practical way for blacks to improve their economic and social position.

Do you consider Booker T. Washington a realist or an accommodationist?

Washington's efforts were successful: 10 years after its founding, Tuskegee had a faculty of 88 and a student body of 1,200, making it one of the largest institutions of higher education in the South. And, Tuskegee, even more so than Hampton, was important in the training of teachers. Washington headed the Tuskegee Institute until his death in 1915.

Black Colleges and Universities. In addition to Hampton and Tuskegee, several other distinguished black colleges and universities were established in the immediate post–Civil War years. These include Atlanta University, founded in 1865 by the American Baptist Mission Society; Howard University, chartered in 1868 by the Congregationalists; Fisk University, established in 1866 by the American Missionary Association; and Mehary Medical College, originally Walton College, founded in 1865 by the Methodist Episcopal Church. Somewhat later, as a result of the Second Morrill Act of 1890, black land-grant colleges were established in each of the southern and border states—17 in all (Pifer, 1973).

Segregated Public Schools. Yet another factor changing the face of education in the South during the Reconstruction period was legislation leading to the establishment of tax-supported public or common school systems. Many freedmen recently elected to state legislatures were a force in this movement. Many of these black legislators as well as some white legislators advocated integration in the newly established schools. In fact, many of the state statutes or constitutional provisions established the schools without making reference to either integration or segregation. However, none of the southern states actually instituted an integrated system, and what began as custom became law in all the southern states. Yet the efforts of the various groups and agencies did result in a dramatic reversal of the educational status of black Americans from a literacy rate estimated at 5% or 10% at the outbreak of the Civil War to one of 70% by 1910.

From the end of Reconstruction through the turn of the century a system of racial segregation was established in the South that remained in effect until the desegregation movement of the 1950s and 1960s. The practice of segregation was sanctioned by the 1896 U.S. Supreme Court decision in *Plessy v. Ferguson,* which said that separate railroad cars did not violate the Constitution. But the "separate but equal" doctrine, while always producing separate, rarely produced equal. Nonetheless, after the 1870s the federal government effectively withdrew from the promotion of the civil and educational rights of blacks.

During this same period, ever-increasing numbers of white children from immigrant and lower socioeconomic families were entering the enlarged public school system; between 1880 and 1895 white enrollment in the public schools increased 106% compared to 59% for black enrollment (Frazer, cited in Hare & Swift, 1976). The "rise of the poor whites" placed increased financial demands on public revenues and often resulted in funds being diverted from black schools to improve other schools (Gutek, 1991). To this was added the disenfranchisement of blacks by many southern states and the delegation of authority to local school boards to divide state education funds as they saw fit. From the court approval of segregation, the loss of political power, and the decreased financial support emerged the "separate but inferior" system that marked so much of the South until well after the mid-twentieth century.

Teacher Education

The formal training of teachers in the United States did not begin until the nineteenth century. In colonial America teachers at the elementary level were often young men who taught for only a short time before studying for the ministry or law. Given the strong relationship between church and education, more often than not they were chosen more for their religious orthodoxy than their educational qualifications. In fact, they were often viewed as assistant pastors and in addition to their teaching they were expected to perform various duties related to the functioning of the church. In many small communities the minister himself was the schoolmaster.

Unfortunately, too often the "career teachers" were individuals who had been unsuccessful at other occupations or those whose personal character and civil conduct left something to be desired. It was also not uncommon in colonial America to find teachers who were indentured servants—persons who had sold their services for a period of years in exchange for passage to the New World.

Perhaps the closest to any teacher preparation was that received by those individuals who entered teaching after serving as apprentices to schoolmasters. In fact, some historians refer to the apprenticeship training received by Quaker teachers as the first teacher education in America (Pulliam & Van Patten, 1995).

A distinction was made between teachers at the elementary level and those at the secondary level, not in the teacher training they received, but in the higher status the secondary teachers held in society and the higher education they possessed. Teachers in the Latin grammar schools and academies were normally graduates of secondary schools, and, not uncommonly, had received some college education, while those at the elementary level very often had little more than an elementary education themselves.

Although most histories of education identify the Colombian School at Concord, Vermont, established by the Reverend Samuel Hall in 1823, as the first formal teacher training institution, a good argument can be made that the first such institution was actually the previously mentioned Troy Female Seminary opened by Emma Willard in 1821 (Spring, 1997).

Willard established the seminary to train female teachers in both the subject areas and pedagogy. She also wrote a textbook on pedagogy, as did Catherine Beecher, the head of Mount Holyoke. Each graduate of the Troy Female Seminary received a signed certificate confirming her qualifications to teach. Long before the first state-supported normal schools in Massachusetts were opened by Horace Mann, the Troy Seminary had prepared 200 teachers for the common schools (Rippa, 1997). In fact, this and other academies were responsible not only for expanding educational opportunities for women, but also for preparing a large number of individuals for the teaching profession and were thus strongly supported by Horace Mann.

Establishment of Normal Schools

The greatest force, however, in increasing the professional training of teachers was the establishment of *normal schools*. As we have seen, Horace Mann, Henry Barnard, Catherine Beecher, and others who worked for the establishment of common school systems recognized that the success of such systems was dependent upon the preparation of a sufficient quantity of adequately trained teachers. This in turn demanded the establishment of institutions for the specific training of teachers, that is, normal schools. These educational leaders also believed that the teaching force for the common schools should be female, not only because women supposedly made better teachers at the elementary level, but because they were less expensive to hire. The fact that at least the latter was true is shown in Table 6.2, which compares the salaries of men and women teachers from the years 1841–1864, as well as the salaries of teachers in rural areas with those in cities.

The growing enrollments in the common schools also created a growing demand for teachers. The response in one state after another was the establishment of normal schools. The New York State Normal School at Albany, the next established (1844) after those in Massachusetts, was headed by David P. Page. His book, *Theory and Practice of Teaching or the Motives and Methods of Good*

Table 6.2: Average Weekly Salaries of Teachers, 1841–1864

| Year | Rural | | City | |
	Men	Women	Men	Women
1841	$4.15	$2.51	$11.93	$4.44
1845	3.87	2.48	12.21	4.09
1850	4.25	2.89	13.37	4.71
1855	5.77	3.65	16.80	5.79
1860	6.28	4.12	18.56	6.99
1864	7.86	4.92	20.78	7.67

Source: From *The American School, 1642–1985: Varieties of Historical Interpretation of the Foundations and Development of American Education* by Joel Spring. Copyright © 1986 by Longman Publishing Group. Reprinted with permission from Longman Publishing Group.

School Keeping, published in 1847, became the standard text in teacher education. By 1875 at least 70 normal schools were receiving some state support, and by 1900 there were a reported 345 normal schools in the United States (Pulliam & Van Patten, 1995).

Admission to the normal school required only an elementary education. The course of study lasted one or two years and included a review of material to be taught in the elementary school, instruction in methods of teaching, "mental philosophy" (i.e., educational psychology), and classroom management. Overriding the curriculum was a concern for the development of moral character. A prominent feature of these normal schools was the model school, the forerunner of the laboratory school, where students could practice teaching.

Teacher Institutes

Despite the spread of normal schools, as late as 1900 only a bare majority of teachers had attended normal schools. Before this time, the most important institution in the training of teachers was the teacher institute. A common practice of school districts was to hire individuals with no formal training, with the condition that their continued employment depended on attendance at a teacher institute. The typical institute met once or twice a year, from several days to four weeks, usually in the summer months. In less populous areas the institutes were often conducted by the county superintendent of schools. Some were offered in connection with institutions of higher education. The primary purpose of many institutes was to provide a brief course in the theory and practice of teaching with great emphasis placed on elevating the moral character of the teacher (Spring, 1997). At others teachers were inspired by noted educators, instructed in new techniques, and informed of the most modern material (Binder, 1974).

Are you attending or have you ever attended a college or university that began as a normal school? What influence has this history had on the institutional climate?

Normal School Curriculum and Standards Strengthened

Toward the end of the nineteenth century the character of the normal school began to change. Not only did the burgeoning population create an increased

Normal schools were the primary institutions for the training of teachers in common schools.

demand for elementary or common school teachers, but the secondary school movement created a concomitant demand for secondary school teachers. To meet this demand normal schools began to broaden their curriculum to include the training of secondary school teachers. At the same time, they began to require high school completion for admission. The passage of teacher certification statutes that specified the amount and type of training required of teachers contributed to the expansion of the normal school program from two to three years, and eventually, during the 1920s, to four years. By this time normal schools were beginning to call themselves state teachers' colleges. In time, with the broadening of the curriculum to embrace many of the liberal arts, the "teacher" designation was dropped and most became simply "state colleges." Some of these former normal schools have become the largest and most respected universities in the United States.

Universities Enter Teacher Training

During the late nineteenth century the universities became increasingly involved in teacher education. Teacher training at the college or university level had been offered at a limited number of institutions as early as the 1830s, but it was not until toward the end of the nineteenth century that universities entered the field of teacher preparation to any measurable extent (Pulliam & Van Patten, 1995). Their involvement stemmed in part from the increased demand for secondary

Professional Reflections

"Teachers are not those to whom they erect statues in city parks. They will never get rich . . . their greatest wealth is to give a child the competence to complete a task and the courage to try more."

Maureen Spraight, Teacher of the Year, Rhode Island

"Never stop learning. Teaching and learning are synonymous."

Joyce G. Valenti, Teacher of the Year, New York

school teachers. The universities had always been institutions for the education of those who taught in the grammar schools, academies, and high schools. However, they did not prepare these students as teachers *per se*, but as individuals who had advanced knowledge of certain subject matter. The increased demand for secondary school teachers, the late entrance of the normal schools into the training of secondary school teachers, and the growing recognition that the professionalization of teaching demanded study of its theory and practice led to the increased involvement of universities in teacher education. The University of Iowa established the first chair of education in 1873, other midwestern universities followed, and in 1892 the New York College for the Training of Teachers (Teachers College) became a part of Columbia University. After the turn of the century teacher training departments became commonplace in most universities.

Summary

The Founding Fathers recognized the importance of education to the development of the new nation. As the nation marched through the nineteenth century and became an industrial giant, the demand for skilled workers and the demand of the working class who saw education as a path to success combined to expand the offering of publicly supported education through the secondary school. The growth of higher education can also be attributed to these forces. Indeed, today it is the recognition of education's importance to our national prominence and its vital role in assuring our continued economic prosperity that has served as the motivation for much of the current activity to reform our nation's schools.

Unfortunately, while the educational opportunities afforded much of the population were greatly expanded in the nineteenth century, the history of the education of minorities was basically one of neglect and segregation. It would not be until the third quarter of the twentieth century that any marked progress would be made in improving the education of Native Americans, Mexican Americans, Asian Americans, and blacks. In the next chapter many of these efforts will be detailed, as well as efforts to reform every aspect of the educational system.

Key Terms

Academy
Assimilation
Carnegie unit
Charity School
Common school
Comprehensive high school
De facto segregation
De jure segregation
Educational foundations
Infant school

Junior college
Junior high school
Lyceum
Monitorial school
Normal school
Rate bill
Secondary school
Sunday school
Teachers' institute

Discussion Questions

1. In what ways do Henry Barnard's concerns in the opening of the chapter echo the concerns regarding teacher education expressed in the newspapers today?

2. In what ways were Thomas Jefferson's plans for an educational system elitist? Egalitarian?

3. What was the significance of each of the following to expanding educational opportunities in the United States?
   a. monitorial schools
   b. Sunday schools
   c. infant schools
   d. free school societies

4. Describe the contributions of Horace Mann, Catherine Beecher, and Henry Barnard to the common school movement.

5. What influence did Prussian education have on American education in the early nineteenth century?

6. Describe the impact of the Second Morrill Act on the provision of education to minorities in the United States.

7. What impact has the historical neglect of the education of minorities had on their education and on the educational system today?

8. What was the contribution of Emma Willard to women's education? To teacher education?

9. Compare the role of the university with that of the normal school in the education of teachers.

Internet Resources

1. **www.the history net.com**
   This comprehensive history site is cosponsored by the National Historical Society.

2. **www.socsci.kun.nl/ped/whp/ histeduc/**
   The History of Education Site is an international archive of links and source materials about the history of education and the history of childhood.

3. **www.si.edu**

   The home page for the Smithsonian Institute provides a guide to all its museums.

4. **www.niu.edu/acad/leps/ blackwell.html**

   The Blackwell History of Education Museum and research collection has an extensive collection of materials about the history of education.

5. **sun1.iusb.edu/eduweb01/**

   The History of American Education Web Project broadly covers the history of education and educators in the United States with pictures that link to additional texts.

6. **www.duke.edu/~ehsl/education/ index.html**

   This site provides primary sources as well as links to sites concerned with the history of Native American education.

7. **www.cobleskill.edu/schools/mcs/ csbest/school.htm**

   An illustrated discussion of rural education in the late 1800s provides a basic impression of school practices in America's one-room schools.

References

Anderson, J. D. (1978). The Hampton model of normal school industrial education, 1868–1900. In V. P. Franklin & J. D. Anderson (Eds.), *New perspectives on black educational history.* Boston: G. K. Hall.

Binder, F. M. (1974). *The age of the common school, 1830–1865.* New York: John Wiley & Sons.

Butts, R. F. (1978). *Public education in the United States.* New York: Holt, Rinehart and Winston.

Carter, T. P., & Sequra, R. D. (1979). *Mexican Americans in school: A decade of change.* New York: College Entrance Examination Board.

Cremin, L. A. (1982). *American education: The national experience, 1783–1876.* New York: Harper and Row.

Graham, P. A. (1974). *Community & class in American education.* New York: John Wiley & Sons.

Gutek, G. L. (1991). *Education in the United States: An historical perspective.* Englewood Cliffs, NJ: Prentice-Hall.

Hare, N., & Swift, D. W. (1976). Black education. In D. W. Swift (Ed.), *American education: A sociological view.* Boston: Houghton Mifflin.

Kidwell, C. S., & Swift, D. W. (1976). Indian education. In D. W. Swift (Ed.), *American education: A sociological view.* Boston: Houghton Mifflin.

Madsen, D. L. (1974). *Early national education, 1776–1830.* New York: John Wiley & Sons.

Pifer, A. (1973). *The higher education of blacks in the United States.* New York: Carnegie Corporation.

Plessy v. Ferguson, 163 U.S. 537, 16 S. Ct. 1138 (1896).

Pulliam, J. D., & Van Patten, J. (1995). *History of education in America* (6th ed.). New York: Merrill.

Rippa, S. A. (1997). *Education in a free society: An American history* (8th ed.). New York: Longman.

Roberts v. City of Boston, 59 Mass. (5 Cush.) 198 (1850).

Spring, J. (1997). *The American school 1642–1996* (4th ed.). New York: Longman.

Spring, J. (1998). *American education* (8th ed.). Boston: McGraw-Hill.

Stuart et al. v. School District No. 1 of the Village of Kalamazoo, 30 Michigan 69 (1874).

Szasz, M. C. (1977). *Education and the American Indian.* Albuquerque, NM: University of New Mexico Press.

Trustees of Dartmouth College v. Woodward, 17 U.S. (4 Wheat) 518 (1819).

Weinberg, M. (1997). *Asian-American education: Historical backgrounds and current realities.* Mahwah, NJ: Lawrence Erlbaum Associates.

West, E. (1972). *The black American and education.* Columbus, OH: Merrill.

Chapter 7

Human history becomes more and more a race between education and catastrophe.

H. G. Wells, *The Outline of History* (1920)

Modern American Education: From the Progressive Movement to the Present

➤ *In the 1930s, faculty and students at Oglethorpe University created a "time room" where artifacts from the history of civilization were preserved in their original form, on film and paper. Film footage was also included that presented a verbal and visual condensed version of significant events in the history of the world up to that time.*

Suppose you and your classmates were requested to create a time room on the history of American education. What artifacts would you include in your room? If you made a video chronicle of education, what would it include?

As you may have discovered in answering the above questions, capturing the most noteworthy happenings from a period of time, whether in a capsule, a room, or a chapter is a challenge. The challenge becomes greater the more rapidly changing the times and the more diverse the areas to be included.

In this chapter the history of American education begun in Chapters 5 and 6 is brought to the present. Although covering a relatively short period of time from a historical perspective, this period has witnessed the most rapid expansion of education in our nation's history and some of the most marked changes. So much has taken place that we could not focus in detail on every contributing personality or intervening variable. Consider the following objectives as you study this chapter:

- Identify the major economic, political, and social forces affecting education in the twentieth century.
- Describe the progressive education movement in the United States.
- Compare the impact of the Great Depression, World War II, and the Cold War on education.
- Evaluate the progress of the civil rights movement and the War on Poverty.
- Outline the developments in education during the 1970s, 1980s, and 1990s.
- Trace the fluctuation of federal support for education in the twentieth century.

The Twentieth Century Unfolds

The People and Nation Grow

The twentieth century brought marked changes in American social, economic, political, and educational life. Population growth continued at a staggering rate: from 50 million in 1880 to 76 million in 1900 and 106 million in 1920. Although birthrates declined, improvements in medicine and sanitation led to lower infant mortality and the overall death rate. A significant portion of the population growth was the result of immigration. In the two decades before the turn of the century, an average of almost 500,000 immigrants per year arrived in this country. The numbers grew to more than 1 million per year in 1905–07, 1910, and 1913–14 (U.S. Bureau of the Census, 1975).

At the same time that the population was experiencing rapid growth, it was becoming increasingly urban. According to the 1920 census, for the first time in our nation's history, the number of those living in towns of 2,500 (54.2 million) exceeded those living in rural areas (51.6 million). Although the westward movement continued throughout the late nineteenth and early twentieth centuries, by 1890 the frontier was closed; that is, the Bureau of Census could not draw a line of demarcation beyond which the population was less than two persons per square mile.

America experienced growth not only at home, but also on the international scene. In the last years of the nineteenth century and the beginning of the twentieth century the United States acquired Guam, the Philippines, Puerto Rico, the Hawaiian Islands, the Virgin Islands, and the Panama Canal Zone. The nation also engaged in a war with Spain; landed troops in Mexico, Nicaragua, and Haiti; helped put down a revolt in China; and in 1917 entered the fight to make the world safe for democracy.

Economic Growth

The economic growth of the United States during this period was even more profound than the population growth. Whereas the population increased less than fourfold in the post–Civil War to pre–World War I period, production increased tenfold (Gray & Peterson, 1974). This was a period of rapid growth for the railroads and other transportation and communication industries. The expansion of the railroads brought an end to the frontier and linked all parts of the nation, as did an ever-expanding network of telephone lines. At the same time, the transatlantic cable and transworld shipping linked this nation with others. The expansion in the transportation industry opened up new markets for the growing agricultural and manufacturing industries. By 1920 the United States had become the largest manufacturing nation in the world.

Paradoxically, this period of stellar economic growth is also regarded as a dark chapter in American history because of the abuses in industry (Gray & Peterson, 1974). The business leaders who helped bring about the growth and contributed to the abuses have been referred to as "robber barons," and the business and political corruption of the era touched every aspect of American life. The plight of workers (including children) in factories, the unsafe and unsanitary working conditions, the horrors of industrial accidents, and descriptions of life in the poverty-ridden slums filled the tabloids and stirred political and social reforms.

Politics and Reform

Antitrust legislation was enacted in an attempt to control monopolies and their unfair business practices. The progressive movement that emerged at the turn of the century was responsible for a flood of labor legislation addressed at regulating the labor of women and children, wages and hours, and health and safety conditions. Workers also sought to improve their plight through labor unions. Increased union activity met with harsh resistance and persecution; violence and loss of life were not uncommon. Yet by 1920 one fifth of all nonagricultural workers in the nation were organized; in view of employer hostility, this was a considerable achievement (Kirkland, 1969).

In the political arena the progressive movement gained momentum in the years after 1900. Decrying the excesses of big business, the progressives challenged the cherished ideal of limited government and urged the government to protect consumers against unfair monopolistic practices, workers (particularly women and children) against exploitation, and the less fortunate against any form of social injustice. Reform became the "order of the day" on the local, state, and national levels as progressives sought to wrest control of government from the business community and use it to bring about social change.

Forces in Education

Significant changes in the educational arena accompanied those in the social, economic, and political arenas. The urbanization of the population and the popularity of the automobile made possible the building of larger schools and contributed to the consolidation of rural school districts. The number of school districts in the United States gradually decreased from over 130,000 at the turn of the century to approximately 15,500 in 1990. State control of education increased in a number of areas: certification of teachers, requirements for teacher education programs, curricular requirements for the schools, standards for school facilities, and provisions for financial support.

At the same time, the size of the school population increased more rapidly than the overall population. In the three decades between 1890 and 1920 the school-age population increased 49% and school enrollments 70%. The growth in the student population was accompanied by an 80% growth in the number of teachers and other nonsupervisory personnel. During the same period the average length of the school term increased by 27 days. More teachers and longer terms translated into significant increases in expenditures (see Table 7.1).

For a number of years the average length of the school term has been 180 days. Do you support current efforts to extend the school year? Why or why not?

Table 7.1: Historical Summary of U.S. Public Elementary and Secondary School Statistics, 1870–1930 (all dollars unadjusted)

	1870	1880	1890	1900	1910	1920	1930
Enrollments							
Total school age (5–17 yrs.) population (thous.)	12,055	15,066	18,543	21,573	24,009	27,556	31,417
Total enrollment in elementary and secondary schools (thous.)	6,872	9,867	12,723	15,503	17,814	21,578	25,678
Percent of population aged 5–17 enrolled in public schools	57.0	65.5	68.6	71.9	74.2	78.3	81.7
(in private schools)	(NA)	(NA)	(9.5)	(6.4)	(5.2)	(4.9)	(7.8)
Attendance							
Average daily attendance (thous.)	4,077	6,144	8,154	10,633	12,827	16,150	21,265
Average length of school terms (in days)	132.2	130.3	134.7	144.3	157.5	161.9	172.7
Average number of days attended per pupil enrolled	78.4	81.1	86.3	99.0	113.0	121.2	143.0
Instructional staff							
Total classroom teachers/ nonsupervisory staff (thous.)	201	287	364	423	523	657	843
Men	78	123	126	127	110	93	140
Women	123	164	238	296	413	565	703
Average annual salary of instructional staff	$189	$195	$252	$325	$485	$871	$1,420
Finance							
Total revenue receipts (thous.)	(NA)	(NA)	$143,195	$219,766	$433,064	$970,120	$2,088,557
Percent of revenue receipts from:							
Federal government	(NA)	(NA)	(NA)	(NA)	(NA)	.3	.4
State government			18.2	17.3	15.0	16.5	16.9
Local government			67.8	67.7	72.1	83.5	82.7
Total expenditures per pupil in ADA	$16	$13	$17	$20	$33	$64	$108

Source: U.S. Department of Education, National Center for Education Statistics. (1997). *Digest of education statistics. 1997* (Table 39). Washington, DC: U.S. Government Printing Office.

The Progressive Era in American Education

The Beginnings of Progressive Education

The progressive reform movement, which had such a widespread impact on political, social, and economic life, also found expression in education. Progressive education traces its intellectual roots to Rousseau and its beginnings in this country to Francis W. Parker, superintendent of schools in Quincy, Massachusetts, and later head of the Cook County Normal School in Chicago. Parker studied in Europe and became familiar with the work of Pestalozzi and Froebel. He shared their belief that learning should emanate from the interests and needs of the child and that the most appropriate curriculum was an activity-based one that encouraged children to express themselves freely and creatively.

The practice school of Cook County Normal School was organized as a model democratic community. Art was an integral part of the curriculum, as were nature studies, field trips, and social activities. Rather than deal with multiple, discrete subject matter, the curriculum attempted to integrate subjects in a way that made it more meaningful to the learner. In all things Parker's aim was to make the child the center of the educational process.

Dewey

Among the parents of children at Parker's school in Chicago was John Dewey, professor of philosophy and pedagogy at the University of Chicago. Dewey was impressed with the philosophy and methods of the school and in 1896 established his own laboratory school at the University of Chicago. Through his many writings and articulation of his philosophy, Dewey provided the intellectual foundation for progressive education. In fact, Dewey was said to be "the real spokesman for intellectual America in the Progressive Era" (Bonner, 1963, p. 44).

Dewey's progressivist educational theories are discussed in Chapter 4. He rejected the old, rigid, *subject-centered curriculum* in favor of the *child-centered curriculum* in which learning came through experience, not rote memorization. Problem-solving method was the preferred approach, and motivation was at the center of the learning process. The goal of education was to promote individual growth and to prepare the child for full participation in our democratic society.

Dewey maintained that the child should be viewed as a total organism and that education is most effective when it considers not only the intellectual but also the social, emotional, and physical needs of the child. He thought that education was a lifelong process and that the school should be an integral part of community life, a concept that gave support to the development of the community school. Dewey wrote some 500 articles and 40 books. His influence was felt not only in philosophy and education, but also in law, political theory, and social reform. He left an imprint on American education that has been unparalleled in this century. His classic *Democracy and Education* (1916) provided perhaps the

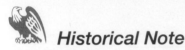

Historical Note

Ella Flagg Young, Pioneer School Administrator

Ella Flagg Young served as a teacher, principal, and area superintendent of schools before receiving her doctorate from the University of Chicago. From 1899 to 1904, she was a professor of pedagogy at the University of Chicago and a colleague of John Dewey with whom she collaborated on several published works. She also served as supervisor of instruction at Dewey's laboratory school at the university. Dewey regarded Ella Flagg Young as the "wisest person on school matters" with whom he had ever come in contact.

In 1905, Ella Flagg Young became principal of Chicago Normal School, and from 1907 to 1915 served as the superintendent of schools for Chicago, the first woman to head a large city school system. In 1910, she was elected president of the National Education Association, the first woman to hold this office.

Throughout her career, Ella Flagg Young sought to improve the training and condition of teachers.

She espoused democratic administration and organized teachers' councils to provide teachers with a greater voice in decision making. She worked for higher teachers' salaries and once resigned as a superintendent because of the Board of Education's policies regarding teachers' organizations and salaries. At the outbreak of World War I, she became chairman of the Women's Liberty Loan Committee and, although over 70 years old, traveled throughout the country on its behalf. While on one trip, she became ill and died on October 18, 1918.

Ella Flagg Young's capable administration of both the National Education Association and Chicago's schools was a victory for all women educators. She inspired many women to seek positions of leadership and led many men (and women) to reconsider the capabilities of women for administration.

---

strongest statement of his educational theories and provided the rationale for a generation of educators who were part of what was to be known as the progressive education movement.

Ella Flagg Young

Ella Flagg Young, who is featured in the Historical Note above, was an important figure in the progressive education movement, both in her own right and through her influence on John Dewey. Dewey acknowledged that he was constantly getting ideas from her: "More times than I could say I didn't see the meaning or force of some favorite conception of my own until Mrs. Young had given it back to me . . . it was from her that I learned that freedom and respect for freedom mean regard for the inquiring and reflective processes of individuals" (McManis, 1916, p. 121). Like Dewey, Young proposed that teaching methods give fullest expression to the individual interests of the child, that education recognize the total experiences the child brings to the school, and that "the curriculum must provide the child with experience that builds on his or her natural interests and tendencies" (Webb & McCarthy, 1998, p. 231).

From her positions as principal of the Chicago Normal School, superintendent of Chicago schools, and president of the National Education Association, as well as through her numerous presentations and publications, Young was able to play a visible and important role in education in the years leading up to the first World War. She strove to bring greater democracy to education by providing teachers a greater voice and by encouraging the extension of the principles of democracy to the classroom.

Progressive Education Association

The formation of the Progressive Education Association (PEA) in 1919 gave what previously had been a "rather loosely joined revolt against pedagogical formalism" a vigorous organizational voice (Cremin, 1962). The association adopted seven guiding principles.

1. The child should be given the freedom to develop naturally.
2. Interest provides the motivation for all work.
3. The teacher should be a guide in the learning process, not the task-master.
4. The scientific study of pupil development should be promoted by the refocusing of information to be included on school records.
5. Greater attention should be given to everything that affects the child's physical development.
6. The school and home should cooperate to meet the natural interests and activities of the child.
7. The Progressive School should be a leader in educational movements. (*Progressive Education*, 1924, pp. 1–2)

The Progressive Education Association published a journal, *Progressive Education,* from 1924 to 1955. In its early years *Progressive Education* devoted considerable space to the concept of "creative self-expression." According to Harold Rugg, professor at Teachers College, Columbia University, and a leading spokesperson for the PEA, creative self-expression was the essence of the progressive education movement (Cremin, 1962).

Another well-known spokesperson for progressive education, William H. Kilpatrick, was also on the faculty at Teachers College. Kilpatrick translated Dewey's philosophy into a practical methodology, the *project method.* The project method was an attempt to make education as "lifelike" as possible. At the heart of the educative process was to be "wholehearted purposeful activity," activity consistent with the child's own goals. Kilpatrick, while sharing Dewey's belief in the importance of problem solving, went beyond Dewey in his child-centered emphasis and in his rejection of any organized subject matter (Cremin, 1962).

During the 1930s (1932–1940) the PEA conducted a study of almost 3,000 students from progressive and nonprogressive high schools regarding the schools' effectiveness in preparing graduates for college. The results of the study, *The Eight Year Study,* showed that students from progressive high schools not only achieved higher than students from traditional high schools, but also were better adjusted socially.

What activity in your educational experience was the best example of creative self-expression? Was it intended as such by the teacher, or did it take place by accident?

Higher Education

The influence of the progressive education movement was also felt in higher education. The great model of progressive higher education was the University of Wisconsin. The Wisconsin model was based on the idea that "the obligation of the university was to undertake leadership in the application of science to the improvement of the life of the citizenry in every domain" (Cremin, 1988, p. 246). This was accomplished through faculty research and service, the training of experts, and extended education.

College and university enrollments rose steadily during the pre–World War I years and then surged after the war, partly as a result of those who had come to higher education as part of the Student's Army Training Corps and then stayed after the war ended. Enrollments rose from almost 600,000 in 1919–20 to 1.1 million in 1929–30.

Most of these students were seeking a professional or technical education, primarily in education, business, and engineering, and enrolled not in the universities but in the growing number of junior colleges and the teacher education institutions. The number of junior colleges increased from 52 in 1920 to 277 in 1930, and to 456 in 1940 (U.S. Bureau of the Census, 1975); the number of colleges for teachers grew from 45 in 1920 to four times that number by 1940 (Pulliam & Van Patten, 1995). The normal schools across the country were as typical of the progressive service orientation in higher education as the state universities: "they presumed to prepare scientifically trained experts; they extended their learning to all comers; and they prided themselves on their sensitivity to popular need" (Cremin, 1988, p. 248).

The Child Study Movement

During the first two decades of the twentieth century, as the progressive movement was gaining momentum, two related movements were taking place that would have far-reaching consequences—the child study and measurement movements. The child study movement began with the pioneering work of G. Stanley Hall. Hall established a center for applied psychology at Johns Hopkins University in 1884, the year Dewey graduated from the same institution. Later, as president of Clark University, he brought together the first group of scholars interested in the scientific study of the child through the careful observation of children at various stages of development (Pulliam & Van Patten, 1995).

Hall and his colleagues recognized that emotional growth and personality development were just as important as cognitive development in understanding the child. They saw the child as an evolving organism and believed that once educators understood how the child developed, they would be better able to foster that development (Perkinson, 1977). These early efforts were important in laying the foundation for educational psychology and for the recognition and inclusion of this discipline in teacher education. Child study, the stage theory of learning propounded by theorists such as Jean Piaget, the specialties of child and adolescent psychology, as well as developmental psychology and the study of exceptional children, all owe their beginnings to Hall's work (Pulliam & Van Patten, 1995).

The Measurement Movement

Another cornerstone of educational psychology was laid by Lewis M. Terman, Edward L. Thorndike, and other psychologists involved in the development of the measurement movement. Although intelligence and aptitude tests had been in use for some time, the real breakthrough came when the French psychologists Alfred Binet and Theodore Simon developed an instrument based on an intelligence scale that allowed comparison of individual intelligence to a norm. Of the many adaptations of the Binet-Simon scale the most important for education was the so-called Stanford revision by Lewis Terman of Stanford University. It was also Terman who developed the *intelligence quotient (IQ),* a number indicating the level of an individual's mental development. Meanwhile, Thorndike and his students at Columbia developed scales for measuring achievement in arithmetic, spelling, reading, language, and other areas (Cremin, 1962).

World War I was a major factor in the growth of the measuring movement. The military needed a massive mobilization of manpower. It also needed a way to determine which men were suited for service and for what type of service. Out of this need a number of group intelligence tests were developed and ultimately were administered to hundreds of thousands of recruits. One unexpected result of this massive testing was the discovery of a large number of young men with educational (as well as physical) deficiencies: approximately one quarter of all recruits were judged illiterate. Deficiencies were particularly high among rural youth.

Within a decade of the end of the war, the measurement movement had become a permanent part of American education. According to Heffernan (1968), the "apparent objectivity of the test results had a fascination for school administrators and teachers. Certainty seemed somehow to attach to these mathematically expressed comparisons of pupil achievement" (p. 229). Throughout the country students were classified, assigned, and compared on the basis of tests. Often the tests were used wisely to diagnose learning difficulties and assess individual differences. Unfortunately, they were also used to make comparisons without consideration of differences in school populations, to make judgments about the quality of teaching, and most distressing, to make subjective judgments about students' potential (Heffernan, 1968). Regrettably, these misuses of tests continue today.

Have you ever taken a test that you felt was biased in terms of race, ethnicity, or gender? What positive benefits, if any, have you gained from taking national standardized tests?

Education During the Great Depression

The crash of the stock market in October 1929 ushered in the greatest depression our nation has ever experienced. The period was marked by the failure of banks and businesses, the closing of factories, mass unemployment, bread lines, soup kitchens, and tent cities. Unemployment was particularly high among minorities and young people. As many as 6 million young people were out of school and unemployed in 1933–1935. Many had no occupational training or experience. In a labor market overrun with experienced workers, they had few opportunities for employment (National Policies Commission, 1941).

The Depression also had a serious impact on the operation of schools. In many states, especially in the hard-pressed South and Southwest, schools were

The Civilian Conservation Corps offered youth both employment and educational opportunities.

closed or the school year shortened. In school districts throughout the land the local school boards were unable to pay their teachers and issued them promissory notes agreeing to pay them when revenues were collected. And in almost every school district the number of teachers was reduced, class size increased, and the number of courses in the high school curriculum cut (Gutek, 1991).

What effects can pronounced economic upswings and downswings have on the public schools and colleges and universities?

Until the Great Depression the relationship of the federal government to education was clear: Education was viewed as a function of the states and local school districts. These entities were responsible for operating educational programs. Beginning in 1933, with the creation of the Civilian Conservation Corps (CCC) and later the National Youth Administration (NYA), this established relationship changed markedly. The CCC and the NYA were two of the federal emergency agencies created under President Roosevelt's New Deal to provide "work relief" for the unemployed. The CCC provided temporary work for over 2 million people 18–25 years of age on various conservation projects. The NYA administered two programs, a work relief and employment program for needy, out-of-school youth aged 16–25, and a program that provided part-time employment to needy high school and college students to help them continue their education. At its peak in 1939–40 approximately 750,000 students in 1,750 colleges and 28,000 secondary schools participated in NYA programs.

When it became clear to officials of both the CCC and the NYA that many participants lacked not only vocational skills but basic skills in reading, writing, and arithmetic, they moved to meet these needs by means of educational activities operated and controlled by the agencies themselves. In time Congress changed the authorizing language of each agency to include an educational function. Although both these measures were terminated as the war economy stimulated employment, the fact that the federal government actually operated and controlled educational activities that could have been offered by state or local educational systems marked a departure from the past that was of concern to many educators, including the National Education Association (National Policies Commission, 1941).

Other New Deal programs provided relief to the financially depressed schools. The Public Works Administration (PWA) provided assistance for the building of numerous public buildings, including almost 13,000 schools. The Works Projects Administration (WPA) provided employment for teachers in adult education, art education, and nursery schools. And, under a program that became the forerunner of the National School Lunch Program, the Department of Agriculture distributed surplus foods to the schools.

Indian New Deal

Several New Deal measures were directed at improving the plight of Native Americans and became known as the Indian New Deal. The Indian New Deal was an attempt to remedy the conditions described by the Meriam Report. Among the actions taken was the cessation of the sale of allotted Indian land, the organization of tribal councils as legal bodies, the investment of the Bureau of Indian Affairs with the right to contract with states for educational services, and the ending of the boarding school system (although because of distance constraints several off-reservation boarding schools still exist). The Johnson-O'Malley Act of 1934 provided supplemental funds to public schools to provide for the special costs associated with transportation, school lunches, or activities such as graduation (Kidwell & Swift, 1976).

Native American education was also the beneficiary of other programs of Roosevelt's New Deal—the Works Projects Administration, the Public Works Administration, and the Civilian Conservation Corps—as they provided job training, income, and improvements on the reservations, including construction of schools and roads and conservation of land, water, and timber. The total result of the New Deal was "the most dynamic program of Indian education in the history of the Indian Service" with a "curriculum more suited to the needs of the child; . . . community day schools and a decreased emphasis on boarding schools; and a better qualified faculty and staff" (Szasz, 1977, p. 48).

George C. Counts and the John Dewey Society

The experience of the Depression had a significant impact on many progressive educators who came to believe that the schools had a responsibility to redress social injustices. At the 1932 convention of the Progressive Education Association, in an address entitled "Dare Progressive Education Be Progressive," George C. Counts challenged the child-centered doctrine and urged educators to focus less on the child and more on society, to "face squarely and courageously every social issue, come to grips with life in all its stark reality . . . develop a realistic and comprehensive theory of welfare, fashion a compelling and challenging vision of human destiny . . ." (Perkinson, 1977). In effect, Counts asked the schools to take the lead in planning for an intelligent reconstruction of society. Although the *social reconstructionism* movement never gained much of a foothold in American education, it served to associate progressive education in the minds of many people with "an economic radicalism that smacked of social-ism and communism" and ultimately contributed to its growing unpopularity in the postwar years (Spring, 1976).

Counts was joined in his deep concern about socioeconomic conditions in America and his belief that educators should do something to address them by liberal progressive educators such as William H. Kilpatrick and Harold Rugg. In 1935 these individuals joined with other social reformers to form the John Dewey Society for the Study of Education and Culture, and began publishing a journal, *The Social Frontier,* which became the focus of educational extremism during the 1930s. The position of Counts and his contemporaries was sharply criticized by many conservative progressives and was responsible for a deepening schism within the Progressive Education Association.

Turning Tides

Although progressive education and innovations such as the community school and the project method were popular, protests against the child-centered ideal and its lack of emphasis on fundamentals gained momentum under another pro-fessor of education at Teachers College, William Bagley, and other educators as-sociated with the educational theory of *essentialism* discussed in Chapter 4 (Pulliam & Van Patten, 1995). Like Arthur Bestor in the 1950s and the reform reports in the 1980s, Bagley looked at American education and judged it weak, lacking in rigor, full of "frills," and inadequate in preparing youth for productive participation in society. The essentialists were also critical of the social recon-structionists and argued that instead of attempting to reconstruct society, educa-tors would serve society better by preparing citizens who possessed the knowl-edge of the fundamental skills and subjects that provide a basis for understanding, and for the collective thought and judgment essential to the op-eration of our democratic institutions (Bagley, 1938).

The Influence of War

As the war with Nazi Germany spread in Europe and American factories increas-ingly were called on to supply the Allied war effort, the American economy began to recover from the Depression. Once this country entered the war, every institution, including the schools, was dominated by the war effort (see Figure 7.1). According to a statement made by the National Education Association shortly after the attack on Pearl Harbor:

> When the schools closed on Friday, December 5, they had many purposes, and
> they followed many roads to achieve those purposes. When the schools opened

Figure 7.1: A War Policy for American Schools, A Statement of the Educational Policies Commission of the National Educational Association

The responsibilities of organized education for the successful outcome of the war involve at least the following activities:

- Training workers for war industries and services.

- Producing goods and services needed for the war.

- Conserving materials by prudent consumption and salvage.

- Helping to raise funds to finance the war.

- Increasing effective manpower by correcting educational deficiencies.

- Promoting health and physical efficiency.

- Protecting school children and property against attack.

- Protecting the ideals of democracy against war hazards.

- Teaching the issues, aims, and progress of war and the peace.

- Sustaining the morale of children and adults.

- Maintaining intelligent loyalty to American democracy.

Source: Educational Policies Commission. (1942). *A war policy for American schools.* Washington, DC: National Education Association.

on Monday, December 8, they had but one dominant purpose—complete, intelligent, and enthusiastic cooperation in the war effort. (Education Policies Commission, 1942, p. 3)

Impact on Schools

The war had a heavy impact on the schools. Not only did large numbers of teachers leave the classroom for the battlefield, but also enrollment dropped significantly as youth chose not to return to school or to go to work. High school enrollments declined from 6.7 million in 1941 to 5.5 million in 1944 (Knight, 1952). In addition, financial support, already low because of the Depression, was further reduced as funds were diverted from education to the war effort. Some assistance was provided by the Lanham Act of 1941 to school districts overburdened by an influx of children from families employed in defense industries or on military bases. The so-called "impact aid" continues today under the provisions of Public Laws 815 and 874.

Colleges and universities were also affected by the war. Enrollments declined sharply; the enrollment of civilian students was cut almost in half between 1940 and 1944. There was also a severe reduction in instructional staff and revenues. Institutional income in 1944 and 1945 was 67% of what it had been in 1940 (Knight, 1952). Income would have been reduced even more dramatically had it not been for the large research projects commissioned by the federal government. These

Table 7.2: Institutions of Higher Education, Faculty, and Enrollments, 1919–20 to 1994–95

	Total institutions	Total faculty	Total enrollment
1919–20	1,041	48,615	597,880
1929–30	1,409	82,386	1,110,737
1939–40	1,708	146,929	1,494,203
1949–50	1,851	245,722	2,659,021
1959–60	2,008	380,554	3,639,847
1969–70	2,525	450,000	8,004,660
1979–80	3,152	675,000	11,569,899
1989–90	3,535	824,220	13,538,560
1994–95	3,688	915,000	14,278,790

Source: U.S. Department of Education, National Center for Education Statistics. (1997). *Digest of education statistics 1997* (Table 168). Washington, DC: U.S. Government Printing Office.

vast research enterprises transformed many universities into what Clark Kerr (1963) has termed "federal grant universities."

Colleges and universities also played a vital role in preparing men for military service, for war industries, and for essential civilian activities. By the end of 1943, 380,000 men were involved in specialized training in 489 colleges and universities, many as part of the Army Specialized Training Program or the Navy College Training Program (Knight, 1952).

What is your position in the current debate about the appropriateness of ROTC on college and university campuses?

The Postwar Years

Toward the end of the war, in an effort to assist veterans whose schooling had been interrupted by military service, the Servicemen's Readjustment Act of 1944 was passed. The G.I. Bill of Rights, as it became known, provided benefits to 7.8 million veterans of World War II to help them further their education. The benefits subsequently were extended to veterans of the Korean, "Cold," and Vietnam wars; eventually almost 15 million veterans were involved. The G.I. Bill also initiated a great postwar popularization of higher education. More men and women representing a greater age range and varied social, economic, cultural, and racial groups attended colleges and universities than ever before (Cremin, 1988) (see Table 7.2).

In addition, while returning servicemen filled college and university classrooms, within a decade the postwar "baby boom" hit the public schools. Between 1946 and 1956 kindergarten and elementary school enrollments increased 37%, from 17.7 million to 24.3 million (U.S. Bureau of the Census, 1975).

The Critics and the Decline of Progressive Education

One of the foremost critics of progressive education in the postwar years was Arthur Bestor. In his most famous critical study, *Educational Wastelands,* Bestor deplored the anti-intellectual quality of American schools, which he argued had been caused by progressive education. Bestor advocated a rigorous curriculum of well-defined subject matter disciplines and the development of the intellect as the primary goal of education. Bestor later became one of the founders of the Council on Basic Education, an organization dedicated to the promotion of a basic academic curriculum. Two other leading critics of the contemporary educational scene were former Harvard president James Conant and Admiral Hyman Rickover. Their criticisms foreshadowed the back to basics movement of the 1970s.

Progressive education was also hurt by its identification with an educational program known as *life adjustment education.* Focusing on the majority of youth who do not attend college, life adjustment education stressed functional objectives, such as vocation and health, and rejected traditional academic studies. Critics of progressive education found in life adjustment education a perfect target: "it continued an abundance of slogans, jargon, and various anti-intellectualism; it carried the utilitarianism and group conformism of latter-day progressivism to its ultimate trivialization" (Ravitch, 1983, p. 70).

However, in the end it was not its critics that killed progressive education. It died because it was no longer relevant to the time. The great debate about American education continued until 1957 when the Soviet Union launched Sputnik, the first space satellite. Then, in a nation suddenly concerned with intelligence and the need for increased science and mathematics skills, progressive education seemed out of step. By the time it disappeared in the mid-1950s it had strayed far from the "humane, pragmatic, open-minded" approach proposed by Dewey (Ravitch, 1983).

The Montessori Movement

Concerns about academic standards also contributed to a revival of an approach to early childhood education developed by the Italian physician and educator, Maria Montessori. Although Montessori's approach had been introduced in this country before World War I, it was not until the 1950s that a second and more widespread interest led to the establishment of hundreds of Montessori schools. Its resurgence in the 1950s was fueled in part by parents searching for more academically oriented early childhood programs than those found in most public schools. Its movement gained further attention in the 1960s as many Head Start programs adopted the Montessori approach (Gutek, 1997).

Although they were different in many ways, Montessori shared with Froebel a belief that "children possessed an interior spiritual force that stimulated their self-activity" (Gutek, 1997, p. 344). In keeping with this belief, the Montessori method emphasizes sensory training and the use of didactic materials, learning episodes, and physical exercises in a structured environment. Interest and motivation are at the heart of the method. Materials are intended to arouse the student's interest, and interest provides the motivation for learning. Instruction is highly individualized and is designed to develop self-discipline and self-confidence. The role of the Montessori teacher is to be aware of the child's readiness to learn, to make sure the child has the materials to learn, and to guide the child through experiences.

From Sputnik to the New Federalism

Few times in history has a single event had such an impact on education as the launching of Sputnik in October 1957. The event seemed to confirm the growing fear that the United States was losing in the Cold War technological and military races with the Soviet Union because of a shortage of trained teachers, engineers, and students.

Curriculum Reforms

Reacting to public pressures, in 1958 the federal government passed the National Defense Education Act (NDEA). By directing significant federal funding to specific curricular areas, particularly mathematics, science, and modern foreign languages, the federal government for the first time attempted to influence the curriculum in general elementary and secondary education. The NDEA sponsored the efforts of academic specialists to revise the curriculum according to the latest theories and methods. Soon the "new math," "new chemistry," "new grammar," and other "new" revisions were being developed and introduced in the schools. Summer institutes were held to train teachers in the use of the new materials and methods. The NDEA also provided funding for science, mathematics, and foreign language laboratories; media and other instructional material; and improvement of guidance, counseling, and testing programs, especially those efforts directed at identification and encouragement of more capable students. Student loans and graduate fellowships were also funded under the NDEA.

The curriculum reforms initiated by the NDEA of 1958 and an expanded version of that act in 1964 were further stimulated by James Conant's widely publicized study of secondary education, *The American High School Today* (1959), which recommended increased rigor and an academic core of English, mathematics, science, and the social sciences. Underlying these curricular reforms was the learning theory of Jerome Bruner, which stressed the teaching of the structure of the disciplines (i.e., the major concepts and methods of inquiry of the discipline) and the stage concept of child development formulated by Jean Piaget. According to Bruner, some form of the structure of a discipline could be taught to students at each stage of their cognitive development. These theories gave credence to the *spiral curriculum* sequencing pattern whereby subject matter is presented over a number of grades with increasing complexity and abstraction.

If a major federal initiative such as the NDEA were being considered to fund programs to meet today's educational demands, what specific programs would you recommend be funded?

The NDEA set the stage for the federal government's increased involvement in education. In the decade that followed, the federal government waged another war in which it became, for perhaps the first time in our nation's history, a major force in the educational arena. This war was the War on Poverty.

Education and the War on Poverty

In the early 1960s large numbers of Americans became aware that at least one quarter of the population had been bypassed by the postwar prosperity and lived in dire poverty. The results were rising crime rates, a decline in qualified

Presidents Johnson and Kennedy declared a war on poverty, using education as a major weapon in the fight.

manpower for military service, and a number of other social and economic problems. Books, reports, and high-impact media coverage such as Edward R. Murrow's documentary on migrant farm workers, "Harvest of Shame," brought a flood of interest in the elimination of poverty. As a result, the Democratic administrations of John F. Kennedy in 1963 and Lyndon B. Johnson in 1964 declared a War on Poverty. In an effort to win the war, federal legislation was passed to subsidize low income housing, improve health care, expand welfare services, provide job retraining, undertake regional planning in depressed areas such as Appalachia, and improve inner-city schools (Church & Sedlak, 1976).

Education was viewed as a major factor in the elimination of poverty. Poor children as well as those of certain minority groups, it was noted, consistently failed to achieve. In the optimistic view of many politicians, social scientists, and educators, the "cultural deprivation" (i.e., lack of middle-class attitudes and incomes) of the poor was attributable to a lack of education, and if the poor were provided the skills and education for employment, they could achieve middle class economic and social status and break the "cycle of poverty" (Zigler & Valentine, 1979).

Federal Education Legislation

The War on Poverty on the education front was waged by a number of initiatives. The Vocational Education Act of 1963 more than quadrupled federal funds for vocational education. The purpose of the act was to enhance occupational training opportunities for persons of all ages by providing financial assistance to vocational and technical programs in high schools and nonbaccalaureate postsecondary institutions. The Manpower Development and Training Act, enacted the same year, was directed at providing retraining for unemployed adults.

The Economic Opportunity Act (EOA) of 1964 established the Job Corps to train youth between 16 and 21 in basic literacy skills and for employment, and also established a type of domestic Peace Corps, Volunteers in Service to America (VISTA). Perhaps the most popular and controversial component of the EOA was Project Head Start, a program aimed at disadvantaged children three to five years old who would not normally attend preschool or kindergarten. President Johnson called Head Start a "landmark," not only in education but in "the maturity of our democracy." Head Start, he foretold, would "strike at the basic cause of poverty" by addressing it at its beginnings—the disadvantaged preschool child. As the name suggests, the intent of the program was to give disadvantaged children a head start in the educational race so that once in school they might be on equal terms with children from nondisadvantaged homes. The Head Start Program, while perhaps not living up to all of President Johnson's expectations, has proved to be the most successful of the compensatory education programs.

The major piece of educational legislation enacted as part of the War on Poverty was the Elementary and Secondary Education Act of 1965 (ESEA). The most far-reaching piece of federal education legislation to date, the ESEA provided over $1 billion in federal funds to education. Although it was directed at specific programs, populations, and purposes, it represented more general aid than previous federal aid programs.

The ESEA included five major sections or titles. The largest, receiving about 80% of the funds, was Title I, which provided assistance to local school districts for the education of children from low income families. The compensatory education programs funded through Title I were intended to maintain the educational progress begun in Head Start. Title I was to become the major education component of the War on Poverty (Spring, 1976). Other sections of the ESEA provided funds for library resources, textbooks, and instructional materials; supplemental education centers; educational research and training; and strengthening state departments of education. The act was expanded in 1966 and 1967 to include programs for Native American children, children of migrant workers, the handicapped (Title VI), and children with limited English-speaking ability (Title VII).

In the same year that the ESEA was passed, Congress passed the Higher Education Act, which provided direct assistance to institutes of higher education for facility construction and library and instructional improvement, as well as loans and scholarships to students. The year 1965 also saw the establishment of the

National Foundation of the Arts and the Humanities to promote and encourage production, dissemination, and scholarship in the arts and humanities.

In 1967 the Educational Professions Development Act was signed into law by President Johnson. In 1968, the last year of Johnson's Great Society, the Vocational Education Act was expanded and its funding authorization doubled. In addition, the Higher Education Act was amended to consolidate previous legislation involving higher education and a number of new program initiatives.

Between the years 1963 and 1969 Congress passed more than two dozen major pieces of legislation affecting education. These laws dramatically increased federal involvement in education and provided vast sums of money for elementary and secondary schools, vocational schools, colleges, and universities. In 1963–1964 federal funds for elementary and secondary schools totaled almost $900 million. By 1968–1969 this had rocketed to $3 billion, and the federal government's share of the financing of education had risen from 4.4% to 8.8%. Perhaps equally as important as the increased funding was the shift in emphasis from identifying the gifted, which had marked the 1950s, to a concern for the disadvantaged.

Have you been a beneficiary of any federally sponsored educational program? What educational benefits did you receive from this participation?

The Civil Rights Movement

The Brown Decision

The schools not only were given a major role in the War on Poverty, but they also became a stage for much of the drama of the civil rights movement. The *Brown v. Board of Education of Topeka* decision of 1954, which ordered an end to legalized segregation in education, stated that segregated educational facilities are inherently unequal and generate a feeling of inferiority that affects the child's motivation to learn. However, instead of being the climax of the struggle for racial equality in education, *Brown* marked the beginning of the civil rights revolution. Although the civil rights movement began with blacks, perhaps because the basic vision of what was wrong was most visible in the history of blacks in America, the general principles of the movement were later applied to advancing the rights of women, racial and ethnic groups, the aged, and the handicapped (Sowell, 1984).

The *Brown* decision met with massive nationwide resistance in the form of legal maneuvers and violence, resulting in countless confrontations between federal authorities who sought to enforce the law and local police or citizens who sought to obstruct it. The most dramatic physical confrontations occurred

> in 1957 when President Eisenhower sent federal troops to Little Rock to insure that black students were safely enrolled, over the objections of the state's governor, in Central High School; in 1962 when large numbers of federal marshals were required to force James Meredith's enrollment at the University of Mississippi over the objections of the state authorities, an incident in which two lives were lost; and in 1963 when President Kennedy nationalized the Alabama National Guard to enforce the integration at the state university. (Church & Sedlak, 1976, p. 446)

At the same time that school desegregation was making limited progress (see Chapter 9 for a discussion of desegregation), the civil rights movement was gaining momentum on other fronts. Freedom rides, sit-ins, boycotts, and other forms of nonviolent protest both appealed to the national conscience and focused national attention on a movement that would not be denied. President John F. Kennedy pressed for the passage of a federal civil rights statute that would end segregation in public facilities, attack discrimination in employment, and require nondiscriminatory practices in programs and institutions receiving federal funds. Five days after his assassination, his successor, Lyndon B. Johnson, appeared before Congress and sought its passage, declaring it the most fitting honor of his memory. The Civil Rights Act of 1964, when passed, became one of the most significant pieces of social legislation in the United States in this century (Spring, 1976).

The Civil Rights Act and Desegregation

To what do you attribute the increase in the number of incidences of racial violence in the schools and on colleges and universities campuses?

The Civil Rights Act of 1964 further involved the federal government in the activities of the schools. Title VI of the act prohibits discrimination against students on the basis of race, color, or national origin in all institutions receiving federal funds. Title VII forbids discrimination in employment based on race, religion, national origin, or—as of 1972—sex. The act authorized the withholding of federal funds from any institution or agency violating the law. It also authorized the U.S. attorney general to take legal action to achieve school desegregation and provided federal financial assistance to school districts attempting to desegregate.

The passage of the Civil Rights Act of 1964 and the education acts of 1965 combined with the growing intolerance of the Supreme Court to the resistance to the *Brown* decision to create a "carrot-and-stick" mechanism that dramatically increased the pace of school desegregation. Federal expenditures for education, including higher education, increased from $4.5 billion in 1966, to $8.8 billion in 1970, to $13.4 billion in 1974—"thus the carrot; and the Supreme Court continued to strike down devices for evading school desegregation—thus the stick" (Cremin, 1988, p. 264). As detailed in Chapter 9, in a series of decisions between 1968 and 1972 the Supreme Court struck down *de jure* segregation in the South and *de facto* segregation in the North.

Further Advances

The civil rights movement in education also made advances on other fronts. Previously, instruction in most schools was given only in English. In the 1960s, however, attention was turned to the growing Hispanic population of the large cities and states outside the Southwest. In 1968 the Bilingual Education Act was passed, giving federal funds to school districts to provide bilingual education to low income students with limited English proficiency. Additional support for bilingual education was provided by the 1974 *Lau v. Nichols* decision by the Supreme Court, which said that schools must provide special language programs for non-English-speaking children. In response, Congress passed the Bilingual Education Act of 1974, which provided for bilingual education for all children with limited English ability as a means of promoting educational equity (Cremin,

1988). At the same time, the Indian Education Act of 1972 and the Indian Self-Determination and Education Assistance Act of 1975 expanded the rights of Native Americans in regard to the education of their youth, and sought to ensure increased educational opportunity for those youth.

Title IX of the 1972 Education Amendments, which prohibited sex discrimination against employees and students in educational programs receiving federal funds, was a major victory in the extension of the civil rights movement to women. And in 1975, the landmark Education for All Handicapped Children Act established the right of all handicapped children to a free and appropriate education. Each of these topics is covered in greater detail in later chapters.

Social Unrest

The late 1960s and early 1970s also saw a series of urban riots and the sometimes passive, sometimes violent student rights and anti–Vietnam War movements, which began with protests on college campuses but often spilled into the streets. Both movements tended to have a negative impact on the civil rights movement through a subliminal process of guilt by association. Many members of academia

College campuses became the scene for many civil rights and antiwar demonstrations of the 1960s and 1970s.

as well as the larger society became disenchanted with the civil rights movement, "not because they disagreed with or were unsympathetic to its legitimate claim, but because the Student Rights Movement, which they strongly opposed, got its impetus, simulation, and example from the Civil Rights Movement" (Tollett, 1983, p. 57). A campaign against demonstrations and riots and for the restoration of law and order helped put Richard Nixon in the White House in 1969 and reelect him in 1972.

During the 1980s the civil rights movement was slowed considerably by the actions of both the courts (see Chapters 9 and 12) and the Reagan administration. The budget of the Office of Civil Rights was cut, investigations were "cursory," and enforcement and compliance were loosened. The Department of Justice not only seemed uninterested in enforcing civil rights plans, it attempted to block efforts to broaden the scope of civil rights and to strengthen affirmative action. The current status of the various civil rights interests (e.g., desegregation, discrimination, education of minority and special populations) is discussed elsewhere in this text.

The 1970s: Retreat and Retrenchment

During the Nixon administration (1969–1974) support for many of the initiatives begun during the Kennedy and Johnson administrations was reduced. The Nixon administration represented a conservative reaction to student demonstrations and the demands of the civil rights movement. "The conservative reaction included a retreat from the programs of the War on Poverty . . . a renewed emphasis on the power of the educational expert, the spread of the concept of accountability in education, increased emphasis on testing, and the use of behavioral psychology in the classroom" (Spring, 1997, p. 388). At the same time, the 1970s witnessed increased attention to the needs of handicapped persons. The Vocational Rehabilitation Act of 1973 sought to increase the physical access of handicapped persons to educational institutions, vocational training, and employment. During the Ford administration (1974–1977) the Education for All Handicapped Children Act of 1975 (now the Individuals with Disabilities Education Act) discussed in Chapter 9 was enacted.

Under the Carter administration (1977–1981) the federal education budget was increased, from 8.8% of the total elementary and secondary revenues in 1977 to 9.8% in 1980 (see Table 7.3). Under his administration a Department of Education was established. Keeping his campaign promise to the National Education Association, Carter overcame congressional opposition and in 1979 legislation was passed to elevate the Office of Education to department status, making its secretary a member of the president's cabinet. Carter appointed Shirley Hufstadler, a federal appeals court judge, as the first secretary of education. The appointment of a federal judge was indicative of the Carter administration's commitment to enforcing legislation directed at protecting civil rights and promoting equality of educational opportunity (Ravitch, 1983).

The decade of the 1970s was a time of uncertainty for the schools. Not only were schools faced with spiraling operating costs, but teachers hurt by inflation were becoming more strident in their salary demands. At the same time, revenues for the schools were actually declining. The decline in revenues was a result of two forces: (1) the "revolt" of taxpayers against rising taxes, especially property taxes, which are the major source of tax revenues for the schools, and (2) a decline in enrollments, which brought with it a reduction in state revenues, since most states, to a large extent, base their aid to local school districts on enrollment. In 1971, for the first time since World War II, the total number of elementary and secondary students enrolled in the public schools declined (see Figure 7.2).

Revenues and enrollments weren't the only things in education declining during the 1970s; test scores and public confidence in the schools were also declining. The decline in Scholastic Aptitude Test (SAT) scores witnessed in the 1960s continued into the 1970s: SAT scores fell almost 60 points from 1970 to 1980. Concern about the lower academic achievement of students led many parents and politicians to call for a "back to basics" and to seek greater accountability from the schools. And, parents in poor schools began to look to the courts to remedy the inequalities that were reflected in inferior schools and reduced educational opportunity. In 1973 the Supreme Court of California handed down a decision in *Serrano v. Priest,* which has been followed by the courts in over a dozen states in the quarter century that followed. In *Serrano,* the court held that the quality of a child's education could not depend on the wealth of the district. Similarly, the concern for student achievement, the push

Figure 7.2: Elementary and Secondary School Enrollment

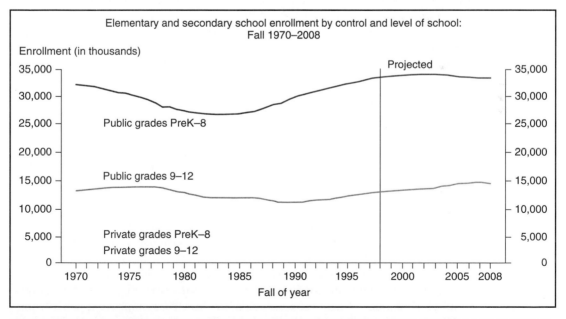

Source: U.S. Department of Education, National Center for Education Statistics. (1998). *Projections of education statistics to 2008.* (Figure 7). Washington, DC: U.S. Department of Education.

for a back to basics, and the demand for greater accountability have continued unabated to the present.

The 1980s: Renewed Conservatism and Reform

The election of Ronald Reagan in 1980 brought a resurgence of conservatism in both politics and education. Reagan's New Federalism called for reduced federal spending for social programs, including education, and encouraged a greater role for state and local governments, as well as a greater involvement of the business community in both supporting schools and setting goals and standards. The National Education Consolidation and Improvement Act of 1981 sought to consolidate the massive array of federal aid programs into several large block programs. However, Reagan's proposal for the entire block was less than what formerly had been spent for the ESEA alone. In fact, in every budget request made while he was in office, President Reagan proposed reductions in federal spending for education, and from fiscal years 1980 to 1989, federal funds for elementary and secondary education declined by 17%, and for higher education by 27% (U.S. Department of Education, 1989). Reagan's conservative education agenda included not only a reduced federal role, but also the elimination of the Department of Education, the removal of objectionable materials and methods from the classroom, a return to the basics, support for home schooling, and a return of prayer to the classroom.

Much of the conservative agenda regarding federal aid to education stemmed from the fact that many conservatives blamed the schools for the social unrest of the 1960s and early 1970s and for many of the social problems that were seen as undermining the very moral fabric of the country. The conservative response to the presumed educational excesses of the 1960s and 1970s led to a continuation of the public debate about the condition of education. While Sputnik and technological competition with the Russians had focused attention on the educational system in the 1950s, in the 1980s it was economic competition with the Japanese that brought the educational system into the forefront of public debate. In response to the growing belief that the decline in the quality of the educational system was a major factor in the nation's declining economic and intellectual competitiveness, President Reagan appointed a National Commission on Excellence in Education. Its report, *A Nation at Risk: The Imperative for Educational Reform,* in strong and stirring language described a "rising tide of mediocrity" and declared that it would have been seen as "an act of war" if any unfriendly power had imposed our educational system on us.

A Nation at Risk was followed throughout the 1980s by various other reports on the status of education. Collectively they are responsible for what has been referred to as the "Educational Reform Movement of the 1980s." This reform movement has been characterized as having two waves. The first wave responded to the recommendations of *A Nation at Risk* and similar reports and sought to bring about reform by state actions directed at improving achievement and accountability. States enacted higher graduation requirements, standardized curriculum mandates, increased the testing of both teachers and students, and

Table 7.3: Public Elementary and Secondary School Revenues, by Source, 1940–1997 (in thousands of dollars)

School Year Ending	Federal Amount	Federal Percent of Total	State Amount	State Percent of Total	Local Amount	Local Percent of Total	Total
1940	39,810	1.8	684,354	30.3	1,536,363	68.0	2,260,527
1950	155,848	2.9	2,165,689	39.8	3,115,507	57.3	5.437,044
1952	227,711	3.5	2,478,596	38.6	3,717,507	57.9	6,423,816
1954	355,237	4.5	2,944,103	37.4	4,567,512	58.1	7,866,852
1956	441,442	4.6	3,828,886	39.5	5,416,350	55.9	9,686,677
1958	486,484	4.0	4,800,368	39.4	6,894,661	58.6	12,181,513
1960	651,639	4.4	5,768,047	39.1	8,326,932	56.5	14,746,618
1962	760,975	4.3	6,789,190	38.7	9,977,542	56.9	17,527,707
1964	896,956	4.4	8,078,014	39.3	11,569,213	56.3	20,544,182
1966	1,996,954	7.9	9,920,219	39.1	13,439,886	53.0	25,356,858
1968	2,806,469	8.8	12,275,536	38.5	16,821,063	52.7	31,903,064
1970	3,219,557	8.0	16,062,776	39.9	20,984,589	52.1	40,266,923
1972	4,467,969	8.9	19,133,256	38.3	26,402,420	52.8	50,003,645
1974	4,930,351	8.5	24,113,409	41.4	29,187,132	50.1	58,230,892
1976	6,318,345	8.9	31,776,101	44.6	33,111,627	48.5	71,206,073
1978	7,694,194	9.4	35,013,266	43.0	38,735,700	47.6	81,443,160
1980	9,503,537	9.8	45,348,814	46.8	42,028,813	43.4	96,881,165
1982	8,186,466	7.4	52,436,435	49.7	49,568,346	45.0	110,191,257
1984	8,567,547	6.8	60,232,981	47.8	57,245,892	45.4	126,055,419
1986	9,975,622	6.7 6.4	73,619,575	49.4	65,532,582	43.9	149,127,779
1988	10,716,687	6.3	84,004,415	49.5	74,840,873	44.1	169,561,974
1989	11,902,001	6.2	91,768,911	47.8	88,345,462	46.0	192,016,374
1990	12,700,784	6.1	98,238,633	47.3	97,608,157	46.6	208,547,573
1992	15,493,330	6.6	108,783,449	46.4	110,304,605	47.0	234,581,384
1994	18,581,511	6.8	127,719,673	46.8	126,836,715	46.4	273,137,899
1996	19,959,187	7.0	137,697,045	48.1	128,755,175	44.9	286,411,407
1997	20,613,840	6.9	146,679,858	48.9	132,702,752	44.2	299,995,450

Source: U.S. Department of Education, National Center for Education Statistics. (1997). *Digest of education statistics,* 1997 (Table 158). Washington, DC: U.S. Government Printing Office; National Education Association. (1997). *Estimates of school statistics.* Washington, DC: Author.

raised certification requirements for teachers. School districts throughout the nation increased their emphasis on computer literacy, homework, and basic skills; established minimum standards for participation in athletics; and lengthened the school day and the school year.

The second wave of reform, beginning in 1986, focused not at the state level, on state mandates and centralization of authority, but at the local level and at the structure and processes of the schools themselves. The second wave of reform also sought to balance the concern over the impact of education on the economy and the push for excellence of the first wave with a concern for equity and the disadvantaged students who might become further disadvantaged by the "new standards of excellence." The recommendations from the second wave of reform, coming from such noted educators as John Goodlad, Theodore Sizer, and Ernest Boyer, called for change from the bottom up, not from the top down and dealt with such issues as decentralization, site-based management, teacher empowerment, parental involvement, and school choice. *Restructuring,* a buzzword of the second wave of reform, was associated with a number of prescriptions: year-round schools, longer school days and years, recast modes of governance, alternative funding patterns, all-out commitments to technology, and various combinations of these and other proposals (Kaplan, 1990). The reform of teacher education discussed in Chapter 1 to a significant degree also grew out of the second wave of reform. Other state and local responses to the second wave of reform continued into the 1990s and are discussed in the chapters that follow.

The 1990s: National Goals, National Standards, and Choice

The 1990s began with an unprecedented event—for the first time in our nation's history, state and national leaders joined in setting goals for the schools. The National Governors' Association and the Bush administration in early 1990 approved six national education goals to be accomplished by the year 2000. President Bush was unable to gain Congressional support for his strategy for implementing the goals, a plan called America 2000, largely because of the controversy surrounding a key feature of the plan—vouchers to promote school choice.

The 1990s also saw education assume a place of prominence on the political agenda that it has never before held. As observed by Terrel H. Bell, Secretary of Education under President Reagan:

> George Bush proclaimed himself to be the "Education President" during his successful 1988 campaign. President Bill Clinton brought the less-than-spectacular Bush record in education to the attention of the voters during the campaign of 1992 and promised to be a more effective "Education President." This has never happened in the nation's history. Education is now a major, high priority national concern, as well as a state and local responsibility. (1993, p. 595)

How would you describe an "Education President"?

The Clinton administration did, in fact, attempt to keep its commitment to education. The first two years of the Clinton administration have been said to be the most productive in terms of major education legislation since 1965–66. The Clinton plan to implement the national goals was called the Goals 2000: Educate America Act. Goals 2000 adopted the six goals articulated by the National Governors' Association and added two new goals related to parent participation and teacher education and professional development (see Figure 7.3). The act not only formalized the national education goals, but it also formalized the develop-

President Clinton showed his commitment to education by signing the Goals 2000: Educate America Act.

ment of national standards and new assessment systems and established a "new federal partnership to reform the nation's educational system" (U.S. Department of Education, 1994).

The Goals 2000 Act established a National Education Standards and Improvement Council (NESIC) to develop model standards for all major academic areas. This included curriculum content standards, student performance standards, and "opportunity-to-learn" standards. As discussed in Chapter 15, curriculum standards and performance standards have been developed by a number of professional organizations such as the National Council of Teachers of Mathematics and the National Council for the Social Studies. Curriculum standards have also been developed by all states and most have linked performance standards to the content standards.

The opportunity-to-learn standards refer to the conditions and resources necessary to provide all students the opportunity to achieve the content and performance standards. According to many, the opportunity-to-learn standards represent "the most contentious and ultimately the most far-reaching provision of the Goals

Figure 7.3: The National Education Goals

1. *School Readiness.* By the year 2000, all children in America will start school ready to learn.

2. *High School Completion.* By the year 2000, the high school graduation rate will increase to at least 90 percent.

3. *Student Achievement and Citizenship.* By the year 2000, all students will leave grades 4, 8, and 12 having demonstrated competency over challenging subject matter including English, mathematics, science, foreign languages, civics and government, economics, arts, history, and geography, and every school in the United States will ensure that all students learn to use their minds well, so they may be prepared for responsible citizenship, future learning, and productive employment in our Nation's modern economy.

4. *Teacher Education and Professional Development.* By the year 2000, the Nation's teaching force will have access to programs for the continued improvement of their professional skills and the opportunity to acquire the knowledge and skills needed to instruct and prepare all American students for the next century.

5. *Mathematics and Science.* By the year 2000, United States students will be first in the world in mathematics and science achievement.

6. *Adult Literacy and Lifelong Learning.* By the year 2000, every adult American will be literate and will possess the knowledge and skills necessary to compete in a global economy and exercise the rights and responsibilities of citizenship.

7. *Safe, Disciplined, and Alcohol- and Drug-Free Schools.* By the year 2000, every school in the United States will be free of drugs, violence, and the unauthorized presence of firearms and alcohol, and will offer a disciplined environment conducive to learning.

8. *Parental Participation.* By the year 2000, every school will promote partnerships that will increase parental involvement and participation in promoting the social, emotional, and academic growth in children.

Source: H. R. 1804 Goals 2000 Educate America Act, Sec. 101. (1994).

2000 legislation" because they shift the focus from equal access to "whether these services are actually delivered to all children" (Lewis, 1994, p. 601). At issue regarding the opportunity to learn standards is what level of opportunity is satisfactory and how it will be funded.

Goals 2000 was seen as providing the framework for relating and reinforcing other major education initiatives. These included a reform of the student loan program which allowed students to bypass banks and get loans directly from the educational institutions and provided for a variety of repayment options; the establishment of a National Service Trust to provide education grants in return for community service; a reauthorization and expansion of the Head Start program; and a Schools to Work Opportunity Act which encouraged the development of school-to-work programs to train non-college-bound youth for careers in high-skill occupations.

Perhaps the most important program under the Goals 2000 umbrella was the Improving America's Schools Act, which reauthorized the Elementary and Secondary Act, for five years and supported and encouraged comprehensive reform at the state and local levels to meet the national goals. A major provision of the act required states (with the input of local school districts) to develop school improvement plans that establish high content and performance standards in order to become eligible to receive Title I funds. This provision forced Title I schools to participate in the Goals 2000 Act.

School Choice, Charter Schools, and Privatization

The Republican takeover of the U.S. Congress and many state legislatures in the 1994 elections put Goals 2000 in conflict with a renewed conservative agenda and signaled an escalation of what historian Joel Spring (1997) has called the "cultural wars," and what many educators considered an attack on the public schools by the most conservative religious and political groups. Opposition to Goals 2000 became "part of a wider debate over the movement to establish national subject matter curriculum standards" (Walsh, 1995, p. 4). Although some indicators, such as SAT scores, improved throughout the 1980s in the wake of the reform movements, large numbers of parents continued to be dissatisfied with a school system that "valued diversity over diction and affirmative action over arithmetic" and were demanding the right to send their children to the school of their choice funded at public expense. They also demanded the end of multicultural and bilingual education and affirmative action, and greater control over curriculum content and materials (see Chapter 12).

A key feature of the 1994 Republican "Contract With America" was support for choice and privatization in education. Indeed, support for school choice came from parents across the ideological spectrum, and a growing number of states and school districts moved to allow choice among public schools. Their hope was that competition would do what regulation had failed to do (Hertert, 1998). Another old idea found renewed interest when several states considered voucher proposals. Only two states, Wisconsin and Ohio, ultimately adopted voucher proposals. The plans in both cases would allow low income children to attend private schools. Both programs were immediately challenged in the courts.

Another avenue for increasing parental choice was *charter schools*. In 1972 California became the first state to pass a charter school law. As discussed in Chapter 13, charter schools are publically supported schools established upon the issuance of a charter from the state, local school board, or other designated entity. They are intended to give greater autonomy to the school and greater choice in educational programs to parents and students. The Republican takeover of many state legislatures in 1994 lent support to the movement, and by 1998 over 800 charter schools were in operation in 26 states (Nathan, 1998). The federal government lent its support to the charter school movement in 1997 when President Clinton pledged $100 million to help create 3,000 more charter schools by the year 2,000 (Hardy, 1997).

The fall of 1996 saw not only the reelection of President Bill Clinton but also record enrollments in the public schools. The impact of the "baby boom echo"— the children of the 76 million baby boomers born between the end of World War II

Would you be willing to teach in a charter school? Are there any sponsors you would be reluctant to work for?

Controversial Issues

Parental Public School Choice

One of the most popular proposals of the emerging restructuring movement is the proposal to let parents choose the public school their children will attend. According to the Gallup Poll, 60% of Americans favor public school choice. However, a number of educational groups, as well as many in the lay public, oppose choice plans. The reasons stated by proponents of each side include the following:

Arguments For

1. Breaks the monopoly of the public schools and makes them more responsible to the forces of the marketplace.
2. Competition will promote efficiency and excellence in operation.
3. Encourages diversity in programs.
4. Students achieve better in schools they have chosen to attend.
5. Parents are more satisfied with and committed to the schools when they have a choice.
6. Teacher satisfaction and morale is higher in schools of choice.

Arguments Against

1. Will lead to ethnic, racial, and socioeconomic segregation.
2. Conditions will worsen in poorest districts as students leave and take their per-pupil state aid with them.
3. Transportation costs will be dramatically increased.
4. Potential for fluctuations in enrollments make planning for staffing and budgeting difficult.
5. Most parents would not be able to make an informed choice among the alternative schools.

What, if any, support for parental choice is there in your state? How has it been evidenced? What is your position on parental public school choice?

and 1964—was strengthened by continued immigration, pushing school enrollments beyond the record 1971 baby boom enrollment of 51.3 million. Enrollments in the fall of 1996 reached 51.7 million and were projected to reach 54.3 million by the year 2008 (see Figure 7.2) with the greatest increases in California and Texas. The growing enrollments combined with growing teacher retirements and reform initiatives such as reducing class size to worsen the teacher shortages already happening in many districts and discussed in Chapter 1.

Growing enrollments and criticisms of the operation of the public schools opened the door even wider for the privatization movement which gained momentum in the mid-1990s. A number of school districts, experimented with various forms of privatization, often over the objections of teacher groups. Some districts contracted with for-profit firms such as Educational Alternatives or the Edison Project to operate one or more schools on a for-profit basis. Other districts contracted with various providers for leadership or instructional services.

Professional Reflections

"Education is more than a set of abstract principles or objectives. Education is a human relationship that has long range and important consequences. What we do and what we don't do impacts the lives of people in ways that we can never fully anticipate."

Mark Mavrogianes, Teacher of the Year, Colorado

"The lessons we learn best we teach ourselves. Teachers should be the guides to students on a journey of self-discovery."

Cathy Pittman, Teacher of the Year, Georgia

While some districts were voluntarily giving over the operation of schools to private contractors, other districts were basically taken over, not by private contractors, but by the state. Beginning in late 1996, several local school districts saw their local control stripped away as power was shifted from the school board to a designated administrator (e.g., in New York City and Washington, D.C.), or to a panel of appointed trustees (Hartford, Connecticut). Numerous other districts found themselves in similar peril at the time this book was being written (Hertert, 1998).

During President Clinton's second term debate at the federal level continued over whether there should be a federal Department of Education, voluntary national testing, and private school choice. Many were concerned that the proposed tests would not only represent "dumbed-down standards," but were a step toward a national curriculum (Hardy, 1997). Faced with a larger Republican majority in Congress, and weakened by personal scandals and threats of impeachment, Clinton was able to hold off any significant reductions in federal spending for education, but was unable to advance any of his major education proposals.

Some historians have interpreted the events of the 1990s—increased choice, charter schools, privatization, and the abandonment of support for education as a source of equal educational opportunity—as a spelling of the end of the common school (Spring, 1997). Others take a less pessimistic view, but like the authors of this text share a concern over what appears to be the unrelenting criticism of the public schools as they face the daunting task of educating an increasingly multicultural and multiracial/multiethnic society, meeting the needs of at-risk students, implementing the most effective curriculum designs and instructional strategies, and responding to a myriad of legal challenges. Each of these issues and challenged are discussed in the chapters that follow.

Summary

Much of the history of education in this century can be seen in terms of a swing from one view of education to another. The progressive education movement, which began at the turn of the century and continued to gain popularity through the 1930s, gave way in the post–World War II years to a more conservative view of the purpose of education, which was a response to a perceived decline in the nation's technological supremacy. In the 1960s the tide turned again in favor of a more liberal and child-centered approach and schools became a vital weapon in the War on Poverty. The schools were also placed center stage in the civil rights struggles of the 1960s and 1970s.

The late 1970s and 1980s once again saw a renewed interest in basics and a national cry for reform of the entire educational system. At the beginning of the 1990s education assumed an unprecedented place on the political agenda and played a major role in the election of the "Education President" Bill Clinton in 1992. Education remained on the political agenda but took a different direction with the Republican takeover of Congress in the mid-1990s, which led to renewed efforts at the federal level, as well as at the state level, to advance a conservative education agenda that includes support for deregulation, increased choice, vouchers, privatization, and school prayer. These efforts continued throughout the 1990s. Some predictions of what lies ahead for education in the United States are discussed in Chapter 16.

Key Terms

Charter schools
Child-centered curriculum
Essentialism
Intelligence quotient
Life adjustment education

Project method
Restructuring
Spiral curriculum
Subject-centered curriculum

Discussion Questions

1. What criteria did you use in deciding what artifacts to include in your "time room" or video on the history of education?

2. Compare the high school curricula of 1930, 1960, 1990, and 2000.

3. Describe the impact of the two world wars on American higher education.

4. To what extent have the schools either changed society or adapted to changes in society in this century?

5. Trace the changing involvement of the federal government in education in the twentieth century. What has been the impact of declining federal financial support?

6. What is your response to Joel Spring's assertion that the end of the common school is at hand?

7. What have been the most significant positive and negative changes in education during your lifetime? What changes/reforms do you think need to be made?

Internet Resources

1. See Appendix.

2. **grid.let.rug.nc/ahc/hist.html**
   WWW Services for Historians provides links to "general" historical sites as well as to a History of Education site.

3. **www.socsci.kun.nl/ped/whp/ histeduc/**
   The History of Education Site is an international archive of links and source materials about the history of education and history of childhood.

4. **gopher.ed.gov:10000/ll/publications/ majorpub/120yr**
   This site hosts a compilation of statistical data on American education collected by the U.S. Department of Education beginning in 1870.

5. **www.si.edu**
   The home page for the Smithsonian Institute provides a guide to all its museums.

6. **www.wmich.edu/politics/mlk**
   This site gives a time line of the American Civil Rights movement beginning with 1954 and *Brown v. Topeka.*

7. **www.schoolchoices.org**
   Billed as the "Citizens' Guide to Education Reform," this site provides information and links to the various school choice proposals.

References

Bagley, W. C. (1938). An essentialist platform for the advancement of American education. *Educational Administration and Supervision, 24,* 241–56.

Bell, T. H. (1993). Reflections one decade after A Nation at Risk. *Phi Delta Kappan, 74,* 592–597.

Bonner, T. N. (1963). *Our recent past: American civilization in the twentieth century.* Englewood Cliffs, NJ: Prentice-Hall.

Brown v. Board of Education, 347 U.S. 483 (1954).

Church, R. L., & Sedlak, M. W. (1976). *Education in the United States.* New York: The Face Press.

Conant, J. B. (1959). *The American high school today.* New York: McGraw-Hill.

Cremin, L. A. (1962). *The transformation of the school.* New York: Alfred A. Knopf.

Cremin, L. A. (1988). *American education: The metropolitan experience, 1876–1980.* New York: Harper & Row.

Education Policies Commission. (1942). *A war policy for American schools.* Washington, DC: National Education Association.

Gray, R., & Peterson, J. M. (1974). *Economic development of the United States.* Homewood, IL: Richard D. Irwin.

Gutek, G. L. (1991). *Education in the United States: An historical perspective.* Englewood Cliffs, NJ: Prentice-Hall.

Gutek, G. L. (1997). *Historical and philosophical foundations of education* (2nd ed.). Columbus, OH: Merrill.

Hardy, L. (1997). Main events. *Educational Vital Signs,* a supplement to the *American School Board Journal, 184*(12), A4–A8.

Heffernan, H. (1968). The school curriculum in American education. In *Education in the states: Nationwide development.* Washington, DC: Council of Chief State School Officials.

Hertert, L. G. (1998). What the governors propose for 1998. *School Business Affairs, 64*(7), 28–32.

Kaplan, G. (1990). Pushing and shoving in videoland U.S.A.: TV's version of education (and what to do about it). *Phi Delta Kappan, 71,* K11–K12.

Kidwell, C. S., & Swift, D. W. (1976). Indian education. In D. W. Swift (Ed.), *American education: A sociological view.* Boston: Houghton Miffin.

Kirkland, E. C. (1969). *A history of American economic life* (4th ed.). New York: Appleton-Century-Crofts.

Knight, E. W. (1952). *Fifty years of American education.* New York: The Ronald Press.

Lau v. Nichols, 414 U.S. 563 (1974).

Lewis, A. C. (1994). Goals 2000 is not more of the same. *Phi Delta Kappan, 75,* 660–601.

McManis, J. T. (1916). *Ella Flagg Young and a half century of the Chicago public schools.* Chicago: A. C. McClurg.

Nathan, J. (1998). Heat and light in a charter school movement. *Phi Delta Kappan, 79,* 499–505.

National Policies Commission. (1941). *The Civilian Conservation Corps, the National Youth Administration, and the public schools.* Washington, DC: National Education Association.

Perkinson, H. J. (1977). *The imperfect panacea: American faith in education, 1965–1976* (2d ed.). New York: Random House.

Progressive Education. (1924). 1, 2.

Pulliam, J. D., & Van Patten, J. (1995). *History of education in America* (6th ed.). Columbus, OH: Merrill.

Ravitch, D. (1983). *The troubled crusade—American education, 1945–1980.* New York: Basic Books.

Serrano v. Priest, 487 P. 2d 1241 (1971).

Sowell, T. (1984). *Civil rights: Rhetoric or reality.* New York: William Morrow.

Spring, J. (1976). *The sorting machine: National educational policy since 1945.* New York: David McKay.

Spring, J. (1997). *The American school, 1642–1996* (4th ed.). New York: McGraw-Hill.

Szasz, M. C. (1977). *Education and the American Indian.* Albuquerque, NM: University of New Mexico Press.

Tollett, K. S. (1983). *The right to education: Reaganism, Reaganomics, or human capital?* Washington, DC: Institute for the Study of Educational Policy, Howard University, 47.

U.S. Bureau of the Census. (1975). *Historical statistics of the United States, colonial times to 1970.* Washington, DC: U.S. Government Printing Office, Series H 316–326.

U.S. Department of Education, National Center for Education Statistics. (1989). *Condition of education 1989.* Washington, DC: U.S. Government Printing Office.

U.S. Department of Education, National Center for Education Statistics. (1994). *Condition of education 1994.* Washington, DC: U.S. Government Printing Office.

Walsh, M. (1996). Main events. *Educational Vital Signs,* a supplement to *The American School Board Journal, 183*(12), A4–A6.

Webb, L. D., & McCarthy, M. M. (1998). Ella Flagg Young: Pioneer of democratic school administration. *Educational Administration Quarterly, 34,* 224–242.

Zigler, E., & Valentine, J. (Eds.). (1979). *Project Head Start: A legacy of the War on Poverty.* New York: The Face Press.

Part Four

The Schools and Society

Chapter 8

In teaching there should be no class distinctions.

Confucius (551–478 B.C.)

School and Society

➤ *It was almost midnight and Ms. Cohen had one more term paper to read before retiring. It was an exhausting time before finals. Each semester she vowed that she would not assign a 20-page term paper to her senior social studies honors class. But, each semester she made the same assignment. And each semester she was glad that she did.*

This semester she seemed to have an exceptionally gifted class. Of her 25 honors students, at least 75% had received admission and scholarships to more than one college or university. She glanced at her grade book and noticed some of the titles of the students' term papers. They read like a list of college theses, she thought, as she picked up the last term paper. It was David Marshall's paper and she smiled as she read his title: "Equal Educational Opportunity and the American Dream: You've Got to Be Kidding!"

As she turned to his introduction, Ms. Cohen was struck by the thoughtful perceptions and insights of this 17-year-old. His introduction read as follows:

To assume that the school as an institution can rectify the problems and concerns of the poor is either naivete or sheer ignorance. The truth of the matter is that schools not only reflect the classes within the society, but they do everything they can to reinforce those divisions. Until we recognize that the basic concept of society must be reconceptualized and that social classes must be eliminated, the goal of equal educational opportunity will continue to be, at best, a fantasy or myth.

If David Marshall had written such an introduction to a term paper for your class, how might you respond? To what extent do you agree or disagree with David's assumptions about equal educational opportunity? About social class? Why or why not?

The issues that David Marshall has raised are central to any discussion of the relationship between the school and society. In this chapter various dimensions of the relationship between the school and society are explored. First, the concepts of culture, subculture, society, socialization, acculturation, and enculturation are examined. Then the purposes and expectations of schooling are described, and education and inequality are discussed. Last, educational achievement and attainment in relation to social class, ethnicity, race, and gender are examined. As you study this material, keep in mind the following objectives:

- Define the basic concepts of culture, subculture, society, socialization, acculturation, and enculturation.
- Explain how the family, the peer group, and the mass media socialize children and youth.
- Describe the intellectual, economic, and social purposes of schooling.

- Compare the social selection and social mobility purposes of education.
- Identify the major issues related to the inequality of educational opportunity.
- Describe the social class system in the United States.

- Compare the educational achievement and attainment of social class groups, ethnic and racial groups, and males and females.

- Evaluate the causes of differences in educational achievement and attainment among social class groups, ethnic and racial groups, and between males and females.

Some Basic Concepts

Before we can fully comprehend the relationship between the school and society, it is important to understand the concepts of culture and subculture. *Culture* may be defined as the behavioral patterns, ideas, values, attitudes, norms, religious and moral beliefs, customs, laws, language, institutions, art, artifacts, and symbols characteristic of a given people at a given period of time. Every culture passes on, or transmits, its patterns and products of learned behavior to the young.

Complex societies such as the United States include a variety of subcultures. A *subculture* is a group of people distinguished by its ethnic, racial, religious, geographic, social, economic, or lifestyle traits. Most of us are members of a variety of subcultures.

Describe the cultures, subcultures, and societies to which you currently belong.

In addition to understanding the concepts of culture and subculture, it is also important to understand the concept of society. A *society* refers to a group of persons who share a common culture, government, institutions, land, or a set of social relationships. A person may be a member of several societies at the same time: a religious society, a professional society, and a social society. Each of these societies also will have its own culture or subculture. *Socialization* is the process by which persons are conditioned to the customs or norms of a particular culture. *Acculturation* is the adoption of the cultural patterns of the dominant group by the oppressed group (Gollnick & Chinn, 1994). We learn about our culture through *enculturation*. We learn about other cultures through *acculturation*.

Agents of Socialization

The concept of education is very similar to the concept of socialization, since both aim to preserve and transmit the intellectual, moral, and aesthetic values of the society. In addition, both socialization and education take place not only in school, but also through a variety of institutions and media outside the school (see Figure 8.1). Of these, the family, the peer group, and the mass media seem particularly important and are examined in the sections that follow.

The Family

Although the organization of the family varies from culture to culture and from one period of history to the next, there are certain basic functions that all families

Figure 8.1: Socializing Agents That Transmit Culture

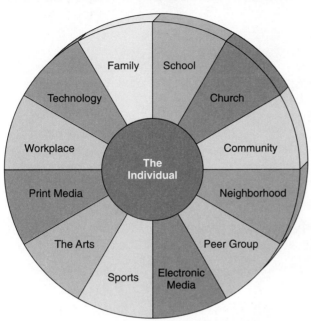

Source: Cushner, K., McClelland, A., & Safford, P. (1996). *Human diversity in education: An integrative approach.* New York: McGraw-Hill, 66.

serve. One of those is the socialization function. Children are born into families and, for a significant period in their lives, in particular their early years, the family is the only world that the children know. Thus the family is the major socializing agent for the young. It is the family that first introduces the child to the world at large, and it is the family that transmits the culture's values to the young. Parents pass on their perceptions, values, beliefs, attitudes, experiences, and understandings to their children. These primary impressions are long-lasting and very difficult to modify or change. They also have significant impact on children's later educational development and success in school. The home and family environment, including parent/child interactions, the use of language in the home, child-rearing practices, and how sex roles are perceived in the home are a few of the many influences that are associated with the child's later educational achievement or attainment (Webb & Sherman, 1989).

Although traditionally the family has been the major instrument of socialization for the young, in the last quarter-century more and more of the responsibility for socialization has been transferred to the school or other institutions. The major reason schools and other institutions have taken on a greater role as socializing agents is the change in the structure of the family.

What were the child-rearing practices in your home during your formative years? How were sex roles perceived?

Extended families in many cultures play a major role in the socialization of children.

The Changing Family

How has your family configuration changed over the past two decades?

Since World War II, the family configuration has changed dramatically. In fact, change is the one constant that has been identified with the family (Wallis, 1992). Demographic, economic, and cultural changes have altered the very definition of "family" as we perceive it today. The "traditional" or nuclear family of two or more school-age children, with a father who works and a mother who stays home to care for the children, is no longer the norm. Only 20% of children live in such families today (Annie E. Casey Foundation, 1998). Dual-career families, single-parent families, ethnically and linguistically different families, and blended families with previously divorced fathers and mothers living together with children from previous marriages and the present marriage have become the norm rather than the exception.

The following highlights describe the families and households of today:

- The average household size is 2.64 (U.S. Bureau of the Census, 1997a).
- Twenty-eight percent of families with children under the age of 18 are maintained by a single parent. The population of children living in single-parent families more than doubled since 1990 (U.S. Bureau of the Census, 1997a).
- Seventeen percent of the single-parent families are headed by the father; 41% are headed by the mother who never married (U.S. Bureau of the Census, 1997a).
- More than 50% of families with children under the age of 13 (including dual-career and single-parent families) regularly require some nonparental childcare assistance (Annie E. Casey Foundation, 1998).
- Approximately 3.5 million children under the age of 13 spend time alone at home (Annie E. Casey Foundation, 1998).
- The number of children in working-poor families increased from 4.3 million to 5.7 million from 1989 to 1996 (Annie E. Casey Foundation, 1998).

Socialization Responsibility Shifts

Today's families spend less time together than they did in the past. When they do spend time together, it is often spent watching television. Little interaction occurs and less time is given to teaching children acceptable values and behaviors. As a result, the school has taken on the function of teaching certain subjects that were once considered the purview of the family. For example, sex education and values education, domains that were traditionally considered the responsibility of the family and church, have been transferred to the school.

The schools also have become involved in other functions that historically were considered family responsibilities. For example, schools provide breakfast and lunch for needy children, offer counseling and mental health services, make referrals for medical and psychological needs, and offer parent education in after-school programs. These changes have left the family with fewer social roles and have diminished the family's socialization function.

The Peer Group

The peer group is one of the most significant institutions for socializing the child or adolescent. Each peer group has its own set of rules and regulations, its own social organization, its own customs, and in some cases, its own rituals and language. Children develop friendship patterns at a very early age. By the age of 11, these friendship groups are fairly well established. Although the peer group relationship may be transitory in nature, its influence can be profound. Unlike the family influence, which tends to lessen with time, the peer group becomes more influential with the advancing age of the child or adolescent (Levine & Levine, 1996).

As a socializing agency, the peer group reflects and reinforces the values of the adult society (e.g., competition, cooperation, honesty, and responsibility). The peer group communicates what constitutes appropriate sex roles and appropriate social behavior in the culture. It also legitimizes and prioritizes the value of information received from a variety of sources. The peer group serves as a reference group for the young. That is, the child or adolescent learns to judge himself

Describe the peer groups in your early life that served as an agent of socialization for you.

or herself against the attitudes, values, and aspirations of his or her peers, and learns to act in accordance with those values (Levine & Levine, 1996).

In addition to peer groups within the school, peer groups outside the school serve as agents of socialization for children and adolescents. These peer groups consist of a variety of youth-serving agencies such as the Boy Scouts, Girl Scouts, YMCA, YWCA, and Little League, as well as male and female friendship cliques, and social and antisocial gangs. Like the peer groups within the school, these social groups offer opportunities for learning rules and rites of passage, as well as peer bonding.

The Mass Media

The mass media is a term commonly used to refer to the television, popular music, movie, music video, radio, newspaper, and magazine industries. Of these, the one that has perhaps the most influence on children and adolescents is television. In fact, increasingly it is acknowledged that the socialization effect of television is almost as strong as the home, school, and neighborhood in influencing children's development and behavior. Because of its strong impact, the mass media are often referred to as "the other curriculum" or "parallel school system" (Davies, 1993).

Time Watching Television

According to a recent report, while leisure reading has declined, television viewing has increased. For example, in 1996, 36% of 9-year-olds, 48% of 13-year-olds, and 39% of 17-year-olds reported watching television three or more hours per day. On the other hand, regardless of age, fewer children indicated that they read for enjoyment daily (U.S. Department of Education, 1997a). African American children watch more television (six or more hours per day) than their white or Hispanic counterparts (four or more hours per day). It has been suggested that the difference in television viewing may be more of a factor of poverty than race or ethnicity ("Glued to Their TV Sets," 1996). Whatever the reason, given that by the time the average child graduates from high school, he or she will have spent more time being entertained by the media than any other activity except sleeping (Davies, 1993), the potential effects of the exposure are significant.

Effects of Television Viewing

Although the positive effects of television in broadening our experiences and shrinking our world have been tremendous, in recent years increasing concerns have been raised regarding the negative effects of television. Of these, perhaps the greatest concern is the negative effect of television violence on children. It is estimated that the average child is exposed to at least 13,000 violent deaths on television. A recent National Television Violence Study revealed that 75% of violent scenes on TV contained no remorse, criticism, or penalties for violence. The study also found that few programs showed the long-term consequences of physical aggression (Seppa, 1997).

While it is not possible to establish a direct cause and effect relationship, there is compelling evidence to link exposure to television acts of aggression with subsequent aggressive acts on the part of viewers (Feldman & Coats, 1993; Thoman, 1995). As a result of the potential harmful effects of television violence on children, the American Academy of Child and Adolescent Psychiatry (1995) has suggested that children and adolescents may become "immune" to the horror of violence; may gradually accept violence as a way to solve problems; may imitate the violence they observe; and may identify with certain characters, victims, and/or victimizers.

Television and School Achievement

The relationship between television viewing and school achievement is also a matter of concern. Except for limited evidence that television viewing may increase vocabulary, most studies that have examined the relationship between television viewing and school achievement have found a negative correlation between the amount of viewing and the level of achievement, especially at the higher levels of viewing (Anderson & Collins, 1988; Beentjes & Van der Voort, 1988). Overall, as the number of hours of television increases, the average proficiency in reading, mathematics, geography, and history decreases (U.S. Department of Education, 1994). Many teachers also complain that increased television viewing shortens attention spans, interferes with homework, and creates in children an expectation that they must be entertained.

Since television is here to stay and its impact on children is so profound, the challenge for parents and educators is to find ways to make it a positive educational tool and to mitigate against its negative influence. This can be done by reinforcing the positive messages and values communicated through television. Research has shown that the influence of television is greatest when its messages are confirmed by other social agents or when the influence of other institutions is declining. Thus, if the schools can combine the positive messages of television with other prosocial teachings, the television message may be kept in perspective.

The Purposes and Expectations of Schooling

Just as there are a variety of theories of education that influence how we view the teaching and learning process, there are also a variety of theories or perspectives that influence what we perceive to be the primary purposes of schooling. However, regardless of one's theoretical orientation, most would agree that schools serve an intellectual, economic, and social purpose.

Intellectual Purpose: To Acquire Knowledge and Skills

To acquire cognitive knowledge and skills has been lauded as one of the most desired goals and purposes of schooling. Although they may disagree on what body of knowledge and which skills are the most important, philosophers and educational theorists, teachers, parents, and individuals across the economic, social, and political structure have underscored this purpose. The school has traditionally been viewed as the institution where students can acquire the necessary knowledge and skills to become responsible and productive citizens. That same theme has been reiterated down through the centuries.

Economic Purpose: To Compete in a Global Economy

One of the most important purposes of education is to provide students with the necessary knowledge and skills to compete in a global economy. Education also contributes to economic growth and development primarily through its effect on productivity, influencing productivity by upgrading the skills of the labor force. In addition, research has shown that more educated workers (1) are less likely to lose time because of unemployment and illness; (2) are more likely to innovate and be aware of, and receptive to, new ideas and knowledge; (3) produce better goods and render services with greater skill; and (4) produce more goods and services in a given period of time because of their skill, dexterity, and knowledge (Webb, McCarthy, & Thomas, 1988). In addition, schooling prepares children to support the economic system by enhancing the development of personal attributes compatible with the industrial workplace; it provides them with the credentials required for the practice of various occupations and careers. This purpose of schooling aimed at training students as future workers has also been referred to as its social efficiency goal (Labaree, 1994). Additionally, the school socializes the future worker for industry through the "hidden curriculum" (see Chapter 14), which emphasizes the need for planning, particularly punctuality, time on task, cooperation, independence, and following the rules.

A recognition of the importance of education to the economic survival of our nation served as the major impetus for the reappraisal of education by the reform reports of the 1980s. The importance placed on education in terms of our nation's global standing is attested to by the attention given to, and the debate over, the achievement of American students compared to those of other countries on such international comparisons as the Third International Mathematics and Science Study (TIMSS).

Social Selection or Social Mobility

To acknowledge education's role in advancing economic growth and development raises an important and controversial question. Should the schools promote social selection or social mobility in American education? One of the primary positions on this issue is the one shared by Marxists, neo-Marxists, and critical theorists, which states that the schools serve a *social selection* purpose. According to this group, the schools essentially serve the wealthy and powerful at the expense of the poor. The schools, they contend, serve the upper classes by socializing the multitudes to conform to the values and beliefs that are necessary to maintain the existing social order. Critical theorists argue that the classroom, with its extrinsic reward system and hierarchical relationship between teacher and student, is like a miniature factory system. Through the hidden curriculum, students are taught the goals and ideology of the capitalist system. They further contend that the real purpose of schooling, which they point out is controlled by the elite, is to train the workers needed for business and industry, not to promote the movement of disadvantaged, lower class youth into the upper classes (Spring, 1998).

An opposing point of view is that one of the purposes of the school is to advance *social mobility*. This position, often called the meritocratic position, recognizes that a class system does exist, but also recognizes that such a class system is not rigid; that school achievement and years of schooling attained, as well as other evidence of individual merit (ability and effort), significantly contribute to an improvement in social status. Those who espouse the meritocratic position maintain that social class and a class society do not prevent individuals from improving their social status. Rather, they argue that individuals fail to improve their social class or social prestige because of numerous factors, including genetic inferiority, the organizational structure of the school, the attitudes and values of the educational staff, individual aspirations, and family environment (Selakovich, 1984).

Social Purpose: To Transmit Cultural Values

One of the major purposes of schooling is to socialize the young in the norms and values of society. The school trains children for responsible citizenship and socializes them for their future adult roles. In short, the school trains the individual for life. Through the curriculum, classroom rules, and interactions with teachers and other adults, children learn the symbols and rituals of patriotism and the values of our democratic society. They also learn the behaviors that are supported and valued by the system. They come to understand that to be a "good boy" or a "good girl" means to obey and to succeed. To be bad is to disobey or to fail. Competition is valued, as is "working well together," "cooperating nicely," or "being a team player."

Within the culture of the school, teachers exercise significant control over how the culture is transmitted to the young. It is the teacher who ultimately determines what subject matter will be taught and the manner in which the subject matter will be conveyed. As a result of that control, teachers are one of the central figures in the socialization process. The teacher is the symbol of authority to the child. Within the social system and reward structure created by teachers in their classrooms, children learn the beliefs, values, and expectations of the larger society.

Think back to your elementary school experience. Which teacher(s) had the most impact on you? Why?

The schools also play an important role in promoting a sense of moral responsibility (Bennett & LeCompte, 1990). This was an explicit expectation of the schools throughout much of America's history. The textbooks and curriculum of the school were directed toward the development of character and moral behavior. Teachers were expected not only to exhibit high ethical and moral principles, but also to teach those principles to their students. Although the continued push for separation of church and state has greatly eliminated the religious involvement that was the vehicle for much of this training, the emphasis on moral development continues to be one of the important expectations of schooling. And, as the family has relinquished more and more of its role in transmitting moral responsibility, the school has, in part, taken on this function.

In fulfilling its socialization role, the school is constantly challenged to assume a major role in either (1) inculcating or reinforcing the past or present values of the social order or (2) encouraging the adoption of new and emerging values for the culture. Often, the school is called on to reinforce and transmit the common values of the past and, at the same time, to implement social change. However, despite challenges in fulfilling its socialization role "schools must ultimately take the responsibility for socializing our youth if their families fail to socialize them. It is better that schools take the responsibility for socializing children while they are still in their formative years than for our society to rehabilitate them after they have become destructive or dysfunctional" (Friedman, 1993, p. 178).

The Inequality of Educational Opportunity

Notwithstanding the popular rhetoric that schools advance economic growth, economic productivity, and social mobility, the goal of equal educational opportunity for all has never been fully achieved in the United States. This is graphically evidenced by the *Savage Inequalities* discussed by Kozol (1991). Disparities in per-pupil expenditures that ranged from $3,000 in poor districts compared to $25,000 in affluent districts were marked by lower salaries, poor working conditions, antiquated classroom equipment, higher rates of teacher absenteeism, and significantly more safety problems.

Some of the basic elements that traditionally have been considered in the concept of equal educational opportunity are:

- Providing a free education up to the level that constitutes the principal entry point to the labor force.
- Providing a common curriculum for all children, regardless of background.
- Providing for children from diverse backgrounds to attend the same school.
- Providing equality of financial expenditures within a given locality (Coleman et al., 1966).

However, according to James S. Coleman, noted researcher and professor of sociology and education and one of the most widely published critics of the myth of equal educational opportunity, providing the above elements, although meritorious, does not ensure equal educational opportunity. For example, providing a free education up to a certain level does not mean that children will stay in school to take advantage of it. Moreover, providing the education really only means exposure to a given curriculum; it does not ensure equality of achievement. Neither does a common curriculum assume equal educational opportunity. In fact, the change in the secondary school curriculum in the early twentieth century, from a classical curriculum appropriate for the college-bound to a nonclassical curriculum more fitting for those adolescents seeking a terminal education, created a form of tracking that defined a certain expectation for the child's future. As the child is matched with the curriculum path (vocational vs. higher education), certain decisions and explicit assumptions are made about the child's future attainment and career goals.

The idea that equal educational opportunity will be accomplished if children from diverse backgrounds are allowed to attend the same school also was challenged by Coleman (1966; 1990). The fact that children of different races and backgrounds attend the same schools does not ensure equality of various intangibles (e.g., that they bring the same interest in learning, arouse the same expectations from teachers) nor equality of results.

Last, providing equality of expenditures within a given locality via local taxes does not lead automatically to equal educational opportunity. Here Coleman referred to his own research as well as to that of others, which demonstrated that expenditures had very little impact on educational attainment when compared to family characteristics and home environment.

How far we are from equal educational opportunity is evident particularly when one examines certain subgroups in the society and their educational achievement and attainment. In the following section the educational achievement and attainment of the following subgroups will be examined: social class, ethnic, racial, and gender.

Social Class Differences and School Achievement and Attainment

When asked to which social class they belong, the majority of Americans identify themselves as being middle class. Sociologists maintain that a number of social classes exist within most societies, distinguishable by great differences in wealth, prestige, and power. (See the Historical Note on page 252 for a review of the concept of social class.) One's social class or *socioeconomic status* (SES) is determined by a number of variables including income, level of formal education, occupation, housing, organizational membership, race, ethnicity, and gender (Rich, 1992).

Social Classes in the United States

The *social class* system in the United States has traditionally been represented by a hierarchy of five classes or groups: upper class, upper middle class, lower middle class, upper working class, and lower working class. The proportion of individuals in each class is determined by community size and economic factors (Levine & Levine, 1996). Over the years, differences between certain classes have disappeared. For example, blue-collar workers of the working class have enjoyed greater gains in income during the past 30 years than lower middle class white-collar workers, thereby eliminating some of the earlier distinctions between the two groups. At the same time that some class distinctions are becoming more arbitrary, there is some indication that due to technological advancement and other economic reasons, the high income and high status upper class is growing at the same time that the low income, low status lower class is also increasing (Levine & Levine, 1996).

Historical Note

The Concept of Social Class

The concept of social class and social stratification can be found as early as the time of Plato (427–347 B.C.) and Aristotle (384–322 B.C.). Although Plato and Aristotle did not attempt to advance any particular theory to explain the causes and consequences of such stratification, they did recognize the different classes that existed in their social structures. Both Plato and Aristotle discussed social class distinctions in the ideal society. Plato envisioned a utopian society that was divided into three social classes— guardians, auxiliaries, and workers. According to Plato, the guardians would be a disinterested ruling elite. Aristotle acknowledged three social classes including the very wealthy, the very poor, and the middle class. According to Aristotle, in the ideal political system the middle class would be the dominant or ruling class.

By the seventeenth and eighteenth centuries, the concept of social class was an important subject for discussion. During this period, John Locke (1632–1704) developed a theory of social class that identified two separate classes: property owners and laborers. In 1755 the French philosopher Jean-Jacques Rousseau recognized the existence of social classes by describing what he referred to as natural inequalities and those inequities that resulted from the social order.

Perhaps more than any other political philosopher, Karl Marx (1818–1883) was able to demonstrate the relationship between social class and the political economy. For Marx, what distinguishes one type of society from another is the mode of production (i.e., technology and the division of labor). Marx hypothesized that each mode of production creates a particular class system whereby one class controls the process of production and the other class or classes become the producers or service providers for the dominant/ruling class. Marx was primarily concerned with modern capitalist society. He envisioned a successful working class revolution and the birth of a new classless society.

While recognizing the changes occurring among the different classes, the five-class structure still remains a viable and convenient method of differentiating one group from another. The *upper class,* which comprises only 3% of American society, includes those individuals who control great wealth, power, and influence. Members of the *upper middle class,* which includes 22% of society, do not have the family background of the upper class. They are generally leading professionals, high-level managers, or corporate executives who are well educated and financially well off. The *lower middle class,* 34% of the population, consists of middle income business people; white-collar clerical and salespersons; skilled workers such as factory foremen; farm owners; and some building, electrical, and plumbing contractors. The *upper working class* is made up largely of blue-collar workers in skilled and semiskilled jobs and represents 28% of the population. The *lower working class* consists of that 13% of society who are often referred to as the *underclass* and are composed of individuals with incomes at or below the poverty level who are usually poorly educated and often unemployed. According to Rose (1992), underclass usually includes the hardcore unemployed who have lived in poverty for a lengthy period of time, such as 8 out of the last 10 years, and excludes those individuals who are temporarily poor due to loss of a job or other unfortunate circumstances.

The socioeconomic distinctions among the social classes affect not only lifestyles, patterns of association, and friendships, but patterns of school achievement and attainment. In fact, the preponderance of evidence from all over the world suggests that socioeconomic status affects school achievement and attainment more than any other variable, including race (Brody, 1989).

Social Class and School Achievement

One of the first and best known studies in the United States to address the relationship between achievement and socioeconomic variables was that conducted by Coleman and his associates, who analyzed data from more than 645,000 students and about 4,000 schools (Coleman et al., 1966). Their report, *Equality of Educational Opportunity,* documented the relationship between test scores, ethnic and racial status, various socioeconomic characteristics of the student's family and peers, and various teacher and school characteristics (e.g., facilities, expenditures per pupil, number of library books, and class size). The findings showed that the single most important variable accounting for differences in test scores was the educational and social class background of the family. The second most important variable was the educational and social class background of the other children in the school. The Coleman report generated considerable discussion regarding whether and to what extent schools do make a difference. Although the methodology was subject to criticism, reanalysis of this data by other researchers (Jencks et al., 1972; Mosteller & Moynihan, 1972), as well as numerous other studies since, have resulted in the same conclusion: Socioeconomic status is the major determinant of school success.

A number of indicators of school success have been linked to various indicators of socioeconomic status. The *National Assessment of Educational Progress (NAEP),* by congressional mandate, periodically tests a national representative sample of students in public and private schools in certain subject and skill areas such as reading, mathematics, and science. The NAEP studies have revealed that in general, achievement is related to parental education, an indicator of socioeconomic status: NAEP proficiency scores at each age level consistently increase as level of parental education increases. For example, in 1996, NAEP mathematics scores for children of college graduates were 20 points higher than those of children of high school dropouts at grade 4, 13 points higher at the 8th grade, and 16 points higher at the 12th grade (U.S. Department of Education, 1998). Similar findings by the College Entrance Examination Board indicate that students from families with the lowest parental education and income levels receive the lowest scores overall on the Scholastic Aptitude Test (SAT), the test most frequently taken by college-bound seniors (see Figure 8.2).

Social Class and Educational Attainment

The relationship between social class and educational attainment is evidenced by differences in dropout rates and continuation beyond high school. The educational and occupational levels of parents have been found to be the most

Identify your social class and indicate what impact your socioeconomic status has had on your educational achievement and attainment.

Figure 8.2: Scholastic Aptitude Test (SAT) Scores and Parental Education

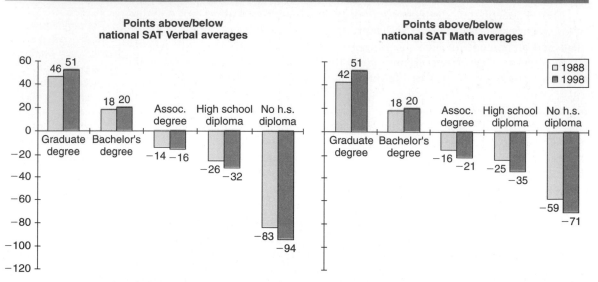

Source: News from the College Board, College Board Online, http://www.collegeboard.org/press/senior98/html/satcll.html

significant predictors for dropping out of school. Regardless of race or ethnicity, students from low income or underclass families were more likely to repeat a grade and to drop out than those from middle or upper class families. In 1996, young people from families in the lowest 20% of family income were five times more likely to drop out of school than those from the highest 20% of income (U.S. Department of Education, 1997b).

Social class, in particular the educational and occupational levels of parents, is also a good predictor of education beyond high school and college completion. For example, 31% of high school graduates from the highest socioeconomic strata go on to complete college compared to only 5% from the bottom socioeconomic strata (Levine & Levine, 1996).

Contributing Factors

The condition of poverty seems to be the major socioeconomic indicator affecting educational achievement and attainment. In 1995, nearly 36.4 million people, or 14% of the population, lived in families below the poverty level. Children under the age of 18 continue to represent a significant segment of the poor (40%), even though they comprise only 25% of the total population. Children under the age of six are especially at risk for poverty. In 1995, the overall poverty rate for children under the age of six was 23.7% (U.S. Bureau of the Census, 1997a). More than half (58.8%) of the children under the age of six who live in a single-parent home headed by a female live in poverty compared to 11.5% of such children in married-couple families (Lamison-White, 1997).

Over 40 million people of all ages live in families with income below the poverty level.

The effects of poverty are seen early in the child's development and academic career. Poverty's adverse effects on achievement are visible as early as the first grade, and the differences appear to become greater as the child progresses through school. In addition, it is estimated that 11% of children end up in special education classes because of cognitive and developmental problems, many of which could have been prevented if even the simplest and most inexpensive prenatal health care had been available to their mothers (Haverman & Wolfe, 1994; Reed & Sautter, 1990).

Ethnic Differences and School Achievement and Attainment

Ethnic groups are subgroups of the population that are distinguished by having a common cultural heritage (language, customs, history, etc.). Significant differences in educational achievement and attainment are found among different ethnic groups in this country. The Hispanic population (28 million) is the second largest and fastest-growing minority group in this country, representing 11% of the entire population. Hispanics are a diverse group made up of Mexican Americans, Puerto Ricans, Cubans, and "Other," which includes persons from Spain,

Central and South America, the Caribbean, and those who identify themselves as Latino, Hispano, Spanish American, etc. In 1996, 14% of the children in the United States were Hispanic. It is anticipated that by the year 2020, more than one in five American children will be Hispanic (U.S. Bureau of the Census, 1996).

Hispanics are geographically concentrated in a small number of states. One in three Hispanics resides in California. Texas is home for approximately one in every five Hispanics. Other large numbers of Hispanics reside in the Northeast in New York, New Jersey, and Massachusetts; Florida in the South; Illinois in the Midwest; and Arizona, New Mexico, and Colorado in the Southwest (U.S. Bureau of the Census, 1993).

Hispanics and School Achievement

Hispanics continue to be one of the most undereducated groups in America. They exhibit overall low academic achievement compared to their Anglo counterparts. However, while they have made some gains, the most recent National Assessment of Educational Progress (NAEP) results indicate that Hispanic children's reading scores at ages 9, 13, and 17 continue to be substantially lower than those of their white peers. And, as shown in Figure 8.3, the NAEP reading scores for Hispanics at age 9 are higher than those of their African American peers (U.S. Department of Education, 1997a).

Figure 8.3: Trends in Average NAEP Reading Proficiency by Race/Ethnicity: 1971–1996

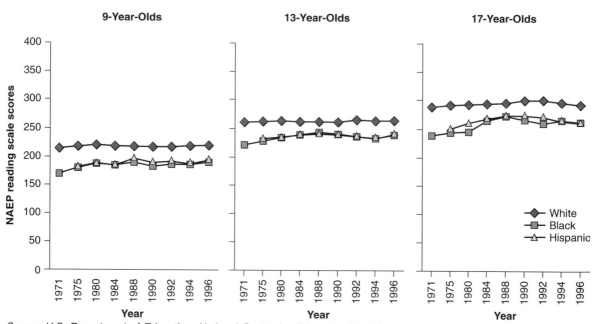

Source: U.S. Department of Education, National Center for Education Statistics. (1997). *NAEP 1996 trends in academic progress. Assessment of Educational Progress.* Washington, DC: U.S. Government Printing Office.

Between 1978 and 1996, average NAEP mathematics scores for white students at ages 13 and 17, while remaining higher than those for Hispanic and African American students, increased at a slower rate than those of Hispanic, closing the gap between these two groups. Figure 8.4 depicts the NAEP trends in mathematics by race and ethnicity for the period 1973 to 1996, while Table 8.1 provides trend data for another common measure of academic achievement, SAT scores. As seen, the only racial or ethnic group experiencing a decline in SAT scores over the 10-year period, 1988–1998 were Mexican Americans and Hispanics/Latinos.

Hispanics and Educational Attainment

Ethnic differences have also been shown to be related to educational attainment. Hispanics have one of the highest dropout rates of all ethnic and racial groups. By the time Hispanics reach high school age, approximately 25% are two or more years overage for their grade level, a condition that places them at risk for dropping out. Nationally, approximately 29% of all Hispanics aged 16–24 have dropped out of high school compared to 13% of African Americans, 7% of whites, and 5% of Asian Americans (U.S. Department of Education, 1998). Most of the dropouts occur before the 10th grade. The dropout rate for Hispanics has not changed significantly since 1982. What has changed is the increased dropout rate for recent Hispanic immigrants. In 1996, the dropout rate for Hispanics aged

Figure 8.4: Trends in Average NAEP Mathematics Proficiency by Race/Ethnicity: 1973–1996

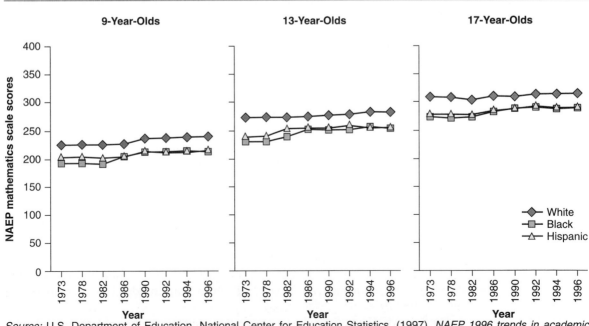

Source: U.S. Department of Education, National Center for Education Statistics. (1997). *NAEP 1996 trends in academic progress. Assessment of Educational Progress.* Washington, DC: U.S. Government Printing Office.

Table 8.1: Ten-Year Trends in Average Scholastic Aptitude Test (SAT) Scores by Racial/Ethnic Groups

| | Verbal | | | | | Mathematics | | | | |
| | | | | Difference | | | | | Difference | |
	1988	1997	1998	1-yr.	10-yr.	1988	1997	1998	1-yr.	10-yr.
American Indian, Alaskan Native	471	475	480	5	9	466	475	483	8	17
Asian, Asian American, Pacific Islander	482	496	498	2	16	541	560	562	2	21
African American/Black	429	434	434	0	5	418	423	426	3	8
Mexican American	459	451	453	2	(6)	460	458	460	2	0
Puerto Rican	431	454	452	(2)	21	434	447	447	0	13
Hispanic/Latino	463	466	461	(5)	(2)	463	468	466	(2)	3
White	522	526	526	0	4	514	526	528	2	14
Other	485	512	511	(1)	26	487	514	514	0	27
All College-Bound Seniors	505	505	505	0	0	501	511	512	1	11

Source: News from the College Board, College Board Online, http://www.collegeboard.org/press/senior98/html/satt3.html

16–24 years born outside the United States was 44% compared to 17% for first-generation Hispanics and 22% for later-generation Hispanics. Hispanic immigrants were seven times more apt to drop out than non-Hispanic immigrants (U.S. Department of Education, 1997b).

In the attainment of postsecondary education, Hispanics also lag behind the non-Hispanic population. Approximately 29% of Hispanics 25 years and over have completed some college and 10% have completed a bachelor's degree or more. Figure 8.5 presents the differences in educational attainment by race, ethnicity, and age.

Contributing Factors

The low educational achievement and attainment of many Hispanic youth is no doubt associated with socioeconomic status. In 1996, the poverty rate for Hispanics was 29.4% compared to 11.2% for non-Hispanic whites (Lamison-White, 1997). The same year, the median income of Hispanic-origin households was $24,906, 67% of the median income of white households (U.S. Bureau of the Census, 1997b).

Nationally, Hispanic children are also underrepresented in preprimary education, which may explain their lack of readiness to participate in elementary

Figure 8.5: Differences in Educational Attainment by Race and Hispanic Origin, Aged 25 Years and Older: 1997

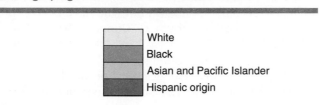

White
Black
Asian and Pacific Islander
Hispanic origin

High school degree or more

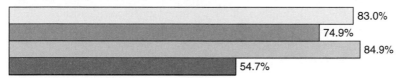

83.0%
74.9%
84.9%
54.7%

Some college or more

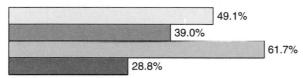

49.1%
39.0%
61.7%
28.8%

Bachelor's degree or more

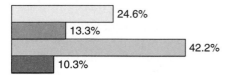

24.6%
13.3%
42.2%
10.3%

Source: U.S. Bureau of the Census, (1997). *Current Population Survey,* Washington, DC: U.S. Government Printing Office.

school. Another explanation for the poorer performance of Hispanic children is their linguistic minority background. The term *linguistic minority* is used to refer to those who are native speakers of English but who have been exposed to some other language in the home since birth (O'Conner, 1989). Hispanic children whose primary language is not English have experienced many more academic difficulties than have their English-speaking peers.

Other contributing factors that may account for the differences in both low achievement and low attainment of Hispanic students include the inferior and segregated schools they attend which are often understaffed, poorly equipped, poorly funded, and staffed by mostly non-Hispanic teachers. Low parental schooling levels and the high English illiteracy among Hispanic adults, which makes it difficult for Hispanic parents to effectively participate in their children's education, also contribute to the underachievement of Hispanic youth (Orum & Navarrete, 1991; Valdez, 1992).

How do you explain why it has become increasingly difficult to convince legislators that we either pay now or pay later for programs aimed at the disadvantaged?

Racial Differences and School Achievement and Attainment

African Americans

The 34 million African Americans in the United States make up 13% of the total population (U.S. Bureau of the Census, 1997c). Approximately two million are immigrants who were born in Africa, Central or South America, the Caribbean, or other geographic areas outside the United States (Levine & Levine, 1996). In 1996, African Americans comprised the largest minority population group including 16 percent of the total child population (U.S. Bureau of the Census, 1997c).

African Americans and School Achievement. Like Hispanic students, African American students have shown overall improvement in achievement during the past two decades. However, in spite of the gain, African American students still perform below the level of white and Hispanic students. For example, as shown in Figures 8.3 and 8.4, the African American students' reading and mathematics proficiency scores on the 1996 National Assessment for Educational Progress at ages 9, 13, and 17 were below those of white and Hispanic students. Reading scores for African Americans in all age groups did increase between 1977 and 1996, but have now begun to flatten. However, African American students aged 9 and 17 did demonstrate increases in their mathematics scores over the period 1990–1996 and as a result have narrowed the performance gap between white and African American students.

Racial and ethnic differences also are found in the results of other standardized tests. For example, several groups experienced gains on either the verbal or mathematics portion of the Scholastic Aptitude Test over the past year. The American Indian/Alaskan Native students demonstrated the greatest gains (see Table 8.1).

African Americans and Educational Attainment. Another indicator of racial differences can be found in high school completion rates. In 1996, the high school completion rates for African Americans who were 25 years of age or older was 74% compared to 83% for whites. African Americans also tend to complete high school at an older age than whites, reflecting the fact that African Americans are more likely than whites to fail and repeat one or more grades.

As shown in Figure 8.5, the attainment of higher education also differs by race. For example, in 1997 approximately 39% of African Americans 25 years of age or older completed some college compared to 49% of whites. For the same age cohort, 13% of African Americans completed a bachelor's degree or more compared to approximately 25% of whites.

Contributing Factors. As in the case of Hispanics, explanations for achievement and attainment differences between African Americans and whites are to be found in the lower socioeconomic status and the social milieu of African American families. In 1996, the poverty rate for African Americans was 28%, not significantly different from that of Hispanics, which was 29% (Lamison-White, 1997). The median family income for African Americans was $23,482 or 63% of the family income of white households (U.S. Bureau of the Census, 1997b).

African American children continue to be at an educational disadvantage relative to whites because of lower average levels of parental education and the greater likelihood of living in a single-parent household that is living below the poverty level. They are also less likely to be enrolled in preprimary education and are more likely to be below grade level for their respective age. African American adolescents are also more likely than whites to be either threatened or injured with a weapon in school (U.S. Department of Education, 1994).

During the past decade it has become more apparent that one of the major reasons African American children do not achieve as well as white children is that the public schools are not meeting the needs of poor children in general. Also, it is suggested that many African American children may bring to school skills, attitudes, and achievement orientations that differ from those of their white, middle class peers. Too often, these differences are perceived as fixed deficits by teachers, counselors, and administrators who, rather than provide for these differences, often relegate African American children to a permanently inferior position in the school, and the self-fulfilling prophecy continues (Bock & Moore, 1986).

Asian Americans

Asian Americans are defined as those Americans whose ancestry can be traced to such Asian countries as Cambodia, China, India, Japan, Korea, Laos, the Philippines, Thailand, and Vietnam. The Bureau of the Census combines Asian Americans with Pacific Islanders for reporting purposes. Pacific Islanders include Polynesians, Micronesians, or Melanesians, Samoans, Guamanians, native Hawaiians, Tahitians, Northern Mariana Islanders, Palauans, and Fijians. Approximately 60% of the total Asian American and Pacific Islander population live in the western part of the United States (Parkay & Stanford, 1992). While these subgroups share different cultures, values, and customs, they also share a common goal, namely the respect for an education (Wong, 1992).

The Asian and Pacific Islanders in the United States are the fastest growing racial group in America.

Although their percentage of the U.S. population is relatively small (4%), the 10 million Asian Americans and Pacific Islanders in the United States are the fastest growing racial group in America. It is anticipated that by the year 2020, the Asian American population will increase from 4% to 6% (U.S. Bureau of the Census, 1997d).

Asian Americans and School Achievement. Research on the achievement of Asian Americans has been limited, a condition that has been justified by the fact that their achievement is generally greater than that of other racial and ethnic groups. For example, Asian American college-bound seniors have consistently outscored whites and all other racial/ethnic groups on the mathematics component of the Scholastic Aptitude Test (see Table 8.1). Other examples of the high achievement of Asian Americans can be found in the incidence of significant numbers of finalists and winners in the National Merit Scholarship Program, Truman Scholars, and high school valedictorians.

Asian Americans and Educational Attainment. In 1997, 85% of all Asian Americans 25 years or older had completed high school or its equivalency (see Figure 8.5).

Moreover, Asian Americans have the lowest percentage of dropouts among all racial and ethnic groups.

Regarding postsecondary education, in 1997 approximately 42% of Asian Americans who were 25 years of age and older had completed a bachelor's degree compared to 25% of whites. Among the 25–29 year old cohort, the difference between Asian American attainment and white attainment is much greater; 29% of whites compared to 51% of Asian Americans completed a bachelor's degree (U. S. Bureau of the Census, 1998).

Contributing Factors. Much of the research that has been done on Asian American students' achievement has concentrated on the factors contributing to their success. Cultural factors have been found to be among the most important variables. Among the cultural variables noted are high expectations of parents and teachers, a supportive home learning environment that reinforces academic success, and a high value placed on education for self-improvement and family honor (Weinberg, 1997). Morrow (1991) explained that Southeast Asian children are taught from an early age to develop a sense of moral obligation and loyalty to the family that demands unquestioning loyalty and obedience not only to parents, but also to all authority figures including teachers and other school personnel. When Asian American students do have educational problems, their problems often go unnoticed because of the stereotype of the "model minority student" (Strouse, 1997).

To what do you attribute the proportional overrepresentation of Asian-Americans in the sciences as opposed to fields such as education or social work?

One other possible explanation for the academic success of Asian Americans has been their advantaged socioeconomic standing (SES): the 1995 median household income for Asian Americans was $46,360 compared to $37,161 for whites (U.S. Bureau of the Census, 1997d). As previously noted, the relationship between SES and attainment has been documented by research.

Native Americans

Native Americans are a diverse population of more than 554 different tribes, each with its own culture, and 250 surviving languages. Approximately 2.3 million Native Americans make up only a little over one half of 1% of the population. Sixty percent of the population are under the age of 25. The Native American population is projected to reach 3.1 million by 2020 and almost double its present size by 2080. Approximately 900,000 Native Americans live on or near Indian reservations (U.S. Bureau of the Census, 1997a; U.S. Bureau of Indian Affairs, 1998).

Native Americans and School Achievement. Even more limited than the research on the achievement of Asian Americans is the research on the achievement and attainment of Native Americans. The annual National Education Goals Report on reading achievement at grade 4 indicated that the disparity between American Indian/Alaskan Native and white students was 19 percentage points, at grade 8, 16 points, and at grade 12, 23 points. Similarly, there was a gap in mathematics performance in grades 4, 8, and 12. In 1996, at grade 4, the disparity between American Indian/Alaskan Native and white students in mathematics achievement was 20 percentage points, at grade 8, 18 points, and at grade 12, 17 points (National Education Goals Panel, 1997).

Native Americans and Educational Attainment. The dropout rate for Native Americans continues to be the highest for all racial and ethnic groups. The latest data for postsecondary attainment of Native Americans showed that 66% had completed high school and some college, 9% had attained a bachelor's degree, and 3% had a graduate or professional degree (U.S. Bureau of the Census, 1995).

Contributing Factors. There are a number of explanations for the lower levels of educational achievement and attainment of Native American/Alaskan Native students. Many Native American children come from disadvantaged homes in which parents have lower levels of educational attainment and lower socioeconomic status. The unemployment on Indian reservations averages about 37% (U. S. Bureau of Indian Affairs, 1998). The limited English proficiency of many Native American parents, coupled with the English-only instruction in many schools, also may have exacerbated the problems of Native American students and prevented their parents from becoming involved in their children's educational experience.

Other possible explanations for the academic deficiencies include the pronounced use of cultural referents that are foreign to the native cultures, language differences, the poor quality of prior education, and inadequate preparation for national testing (Tippeconnic & Swisher, 1992). Some studies have pointed out that the cultural values of Native American students promote a learning style that inhibits interaction with adults or in new situations, and creates a reluctance to volunteer to ask or answer questions (Baratz-Snowden, Rock, Pollack, & Wilder, 1988).

Several studies have been conducted to determine the reasons for the high dropout rates of Native American/Alaskan Natives. The causes and reasons given for dropping out tend to differ based on the perceptions of students, educational staff, or parents. Students report that the major reasons for not staying in school are expulsions, lack of interest, pregnancy, inability to adjust to school, lack of parental support, problems at home, feelings of mistrust, alienation, and the importance of family responsibilities (Dehyle, 1992; Swisher & Hoisch, 1992). Staff perceptions of why students drop out include lack of parental skills to encourage and monitor school attendance, extra family responsibilities taken on by students that interfere with schooling, both student and parental substance abuse, poor study skills, and distrust of the Bureau of Indian Affairs school system (Swisher & Hoisch, 1992).

Ledlow (1992) cautions educators not to conclude that there is a single cause or explanation for the disproportionate high rate of dropouts among Native American children and youth. According to Ledlow, the dropout rates vary from school to school, year to year, tribe to tribe, male to female, BIA to public school, etc. There is, however, overwhelming evidence that both economic and social issues are very significant in explaining the high dropout rate, and those same economic and social issues may also explain the lack of retention among other minority groups. Callahan and McIntire (1994) recommend that while it is important to recognize how the Native American/Alaskan Native student might differ from students of the dominant culture, it is equally as important to recognize the diversity among students within tribal groups. For example, the family's attitudes toward traditionalism, whether the student is from a multitribal home, the degree of monolingualism or bilingualism in the family, and the parents' educational background all impact educational outcomes.

Gender Differences and School Achievement and Attainment

Educational Achievement

Research over the past two decades has demonstrated that gender differences in educational achievement do not appear all at once, but rather develop gradually over a long period of time and are particularly evident by the seventh grade (Grossman & Grossman 1994; Schmuck & Schmuck, 1994). Conclusions from multiple studies suggest that females on the average score higher than males on cognitive tests and tasks that measure verbal fluency, knowledge areas such as literature and foreign languages, reading comprehension, writing, fine motor tasks, perceptual speed, and speech articulation. They also receive higher grades in all or most school subjects. Males, on the other hand, excel on cognitive tests and tasks that require transformations in visual/spatial relationships; tasks that involve moving objects; motor skills; and proportional, mechanical, and scientific reasoning. They also excel at geography and abstract mathematics and scientific reasoning (Halpern, 1997).

On the 1996 NAEP assessment of reading proficiency (see Figure 8.6), females continue a trend that has been evidenced for 20 years to outscore males in each age group (9, 13, and 17). The opposite occurred in mathematics proficiency. In 1996 males received higher mathematics scores than females in each age category. In science, male students also outperformed female students at ages 13 and 17 on the NAEP assessment, but there were no significant differences found between the sexes at age 9 (U.S. Department of Education, 1997a).

The comparative achievement of males and females on the Scholastic Aptitude Test demonstrates a clear pattern of gender differences. For the past 16 years, males have outscored females on the verbal section of the SAT (see Figure 8.7). Males also consistently score higher than females on the mathematics section of the SAT. However, while males outscored females on the mathematics section of the SAT by 35 points in 1998, as seen in Figure 8.7, the 496 score of females represents a noticeable improvement in the scores of females over the past decade. One explanation for the improvement is that more females are completing higher-level mathematics courses such as calculus, as well as chemistry and physics.

The differential in the scores of males and females continues at the postsecondary level. Data indicate that males score higher than females on the Graduate Record Examination (GRE), Medical College Admission Test (MCAT), Law School Admission Test (LSAT), and the Graduate Management Admission Test (GMAT) (Sadker, 1996).

Figure 8.6a: Trends in the Reading Proficiency Scores for 9-, 13-, and 17-Year-Olds by Gender, 1971–1996

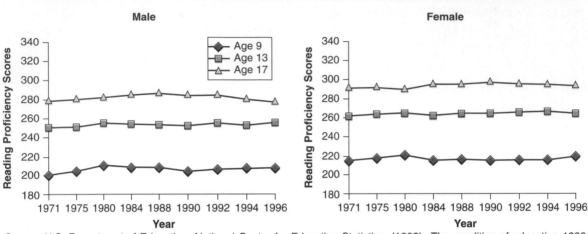

Source: U.S. Department of Education, National Center for Education Statistics. (1998). *The condition of education 1998.* Washington, DC: U.S. Government Printing Office.

Figure 8.6b: Trends in the Mathematics Proficiency Scores for 9-, 13-, and 17-Year-Olds by Gender, 1973–1996

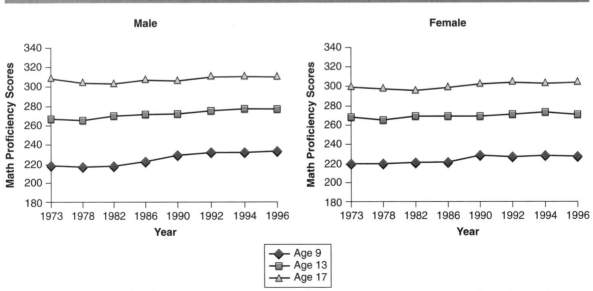

Source: U.S. Department of Education, National Center for Education Statistics. (1998). *The condition of education 1998.* Washington, DC: U.S. Government Printing Office.

Figure 8.7a: Average SAT Scores of College-Bound Seniors by Gender, 1967–1998

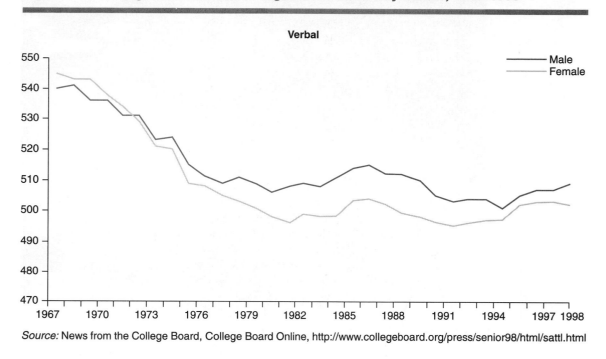

Source: News from the College Board, College Board Online, http://www.collegeboard.org/press/senior98/html/sattl.html

Figure 8.7b: Average SAT Scores of College-Bound Seniors by Gender, 1967–1998

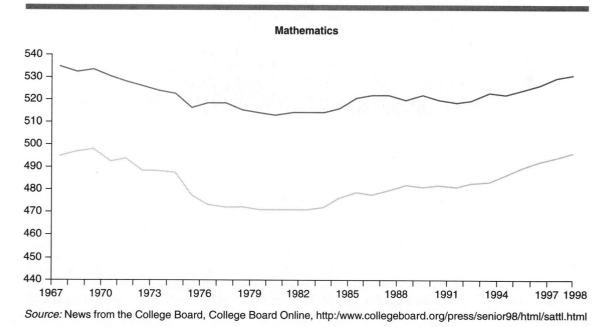

Source: News from the College Board, College Board Online, http://www.collegeboard.org/press/senior98/html/sattl.html

Gender differences in mathematics continue to decline.

Gender Differences and Educational Attainment

Sex differences are also evident in educational attainment. In terms of high school completion, there are no statistical differences between high school completion rates for males and females who are 25 years of age or older. The completion rate for both males and females is approximately 82%. However, for the most part, at the postsecondary level, the attainment rates of males is higher than that of females. Approximately 56% of males 25 years old or older compared to 47% of females had completed some college or more in 1997. And, 26% of males attained a bachelor's degree compared to 22% of females (U.S. Bureau of the Census, 1998).

Contributing Factors

A number of hypotheses have been offered to explain why males and females achieve differently. The most common explanation is that the differences can be largely attributed to the sex-role socialization they receive from parents and the sex-role stereotyping and sexism they experience in the school and the larger society. Myra and David Sadker (1994), noted researchers on gender differences and sex roles, suggest the following ways that our school systems may cheat girls:

> Girls and women learn to speak softly or not at all; to submerge honest feelings, withhold opinions, and defer to boys; to avoid math and science as male

Have you ever taken either the ACT or the SAT? To what extent do you feel that your score was affected by your race/ethnicity, gender, or social class?

Professional Reflections

"Teaching is political. Teachers need to be proactive politically. We need to tell the public what's really happening in schools, what students really can do, and how schools have improved over the last 20 years."

Denise Bryan, Teacher of the Year, South Dakota

domains; to value neatness and quiet more than assertiveness and creativity; to emphasize appearance and hide intelligence. Through this curriculum in sexism they are turned into educational spectators instead of players. (p. 13)

Another possible contributing factor that might explain, at least in part, why females score lower than males on the majority of achievement tests is that females also tend to score lowest on measures of self-esteem. This difference is particularly evident from elementary school to high school (Spring, 1998). The reasons for the decline in self-esteem coupled with the decline in academic achievement are not always obvious by research findings. However, there is ample evidence that indicates "compared to boys, adolescent girls experience greater stress, are twice as likely to be depressed, and attempt suicide four or five times as often as males" (Debold, 1995).

Summary

In this chapter the definitions of culture, subculture, society, socialization, acculturation, and enculturation were presented. The family, the peer group, and the mass media were examined as agents of socialization. Of these institutions, the family has undergone the most significant changes since World War II. As a result of those changes, many of the earlier functions of the family have now been transferred to the school. At the same time, as children spend more time viewing television, its influence on their behavior and school achievement has increased. Schools have various purposes and serve an intellectual, political, and social function. Of these, the debate as to whether the schools promote social selection or social mobility remains controversial in American education.

Many would agree that there are numerous opportunities for education, but most believe that equal educational opportunity is more a myth than a fact in the American educational system. The myth of equal educational opportunity is particularly evident as one examines differences in the educational achievement and attainment of social class groups, ethnic groups, racial groups, and between males and females. In the next chapter, we will look at some of the strategies that have been employed to increase equality of educational opportunity and ameliorate against the effects of economic and cultural discrimination.

Key Terms

Acculturation

Cultural pluralism

Culture

Enculturation

Ethnic group

Linguistic minority

Mass media

National Assessment of Educational
    Progress (NAEP)

Social class

Social mobility

Social selection

Socialization

Society

Socioeconomic status

Subculture

Discussion Questions

1. In response to the opening vignette which describes David Marshall's paper, what are some of the possible ways he might reconceptualize the basic concept of society?

2. Describe some of the ways that the structure of your family has changed over time. To what extent have those changes been positive? To what extent have they been negative?

3. How could you, as a teacher, attempt to mitigate against the negative influence of television on children's aggressive behavior? What suggestions would you make to parents?

4. Reflect on the high school from which you graduated. To what extent did it promote upward social mobility? In what ways did it resemble a miniature factory system?

5. Discuss what is meant by the cycle of poverty. What can the schools do to break this cycle?

6. Discuss the impact of differing cultural values on school achievement and attainment. Give specific examples.

7. Discuss the common factors contributing to the underachievement of Hispanics, African Americans, and Native Americans.

8. What are the levels of educational attainment of the females in your family? The males? What factors account for any differences that may exist between the two groups? To what extent are the factors evident today?

Internet Resources

1. See Appendix

2. **nces.ed.gov**
   The National Center for Education Statistics is a repository for information on the National Assessment of Educational Progress.

3. **www.ets.org**
   The home page for the Educational Testing Service provides access to SAT and GRE test data, career information, and research reports dealing with various issues in assessment and instruction.

4. **www.yahoo.com/society_and_culture**
   From Yahoo's home page click on "Society and Culture." From there you will be led to a vast network of sites dealing with such chapter-related topics as Culture and Groups, Families, Gender, Diversity, Poverty, and much, much more.

5. **www.ssc.wisc.edu/irp**
   The Institute for Research on Poverty at the University of Wisconsin provides on-line publications and a large number of links to poverty-related statistics and information.

6. **www.wsu.edu:800/vcwsu/commons/topics/culture/culture-index.html**
   This site provides definitions and discussion of the concept of culture.

References

American Academy of Child and Adolescent Psychiatry. (1995). *Children & TV violence.* http://www.aacap.org/web/aacap/factsfam/violence.htm.

Anderson, D. R., & Collins, P. A. (1988). *The impact of children's education: Television's influence on cognitive development.* Washington, DC: U.S. Department of Education, Office of Educational Research and Improvement.

Baratz-Snowden, J., Rock, D., Pollack, J., & Wilder, G. (1988). *The educational progress of language minority children: Funding from the NAEP 1985–86 special study.* Princeton, NJ: National Assessment of Educational Progress/Educational Testing Service.

Beentjes, J. W., & Van der Voort, T. H. (1988). Television's impact on children's reading skills: A review of research. *Reading Research Quarterly, 23,* 389–413.

Bennett, K. P., & LeCompte, M. D. (1990). *How schools work: A sociological analysis of education.* New York: Longman.

Bock, R. D., & Moore, E. G. (1986). *Advantage and disadvantage: A profile of America's youth.* Hillsdale, NJ: Lawrence Erlbaum Associates.

Brody, J. (1989). Minority achievement. *Executive Educator, 11,* A9.

Callahan, C. M., & McIntire, J. A. (1994). *Identifying outstanding talent in American Indian and Alaska Native students.* Washington, DC: U.S. Department of Education, Office of Educational Research and Improvement.

Annie E. Casey Foundation. (1998). *Kids count data book: State profiles of child well-being.* Baltimore, MD: Author.

Coleman, J. S. (1990). *Equality and achievement in education.* Boulder, CO: Westview.

Coleman, J. S., Campbell, E. Q., Hobson, C. J., McPartland, J., Mood, A. M., Weinfield, F. D., & York, R. L. (1966). *Equality of educational opportunity.* Washington, DC: U.S. Government Printing Office.

Davies, J. (1993). The impact of the mass media upon the health of early adolescents. *Journal of Health Education, 24* (6), 528–535.

Debold, E. (1995). Helping girls survive the middle grades. *Principal, 74,* 22–24.

Dehyle, D. (1992). Constructing failure and maintaining cultural identity: Navajo and the school leavers. *Journal of American Indian Education, 31,* 24–47.

Feldman, R. S., & Coats, E. (1993). *Socialization processes in encoding and decoding: Learning effective nonverbal behavior.* A symposium paper presented at the annual meeting of the Society for Research in Child Development, New Orleans, LA.

Friedman, M. I. (1993). *Taking control: Vitalizing education.* Westport, CN: Praeger.

Glued to their TV sets: The viewing habits of black children may be more of a factor of poverty than of race. (1996, July 1–7). *The Washington Post National Weekly Edition,* 31.

Gollnick, D. M., & Chinn, P. C. (1994). *Multicultural education in a pluralistic society.* Columbus, OH: Merrill.

Grossman, H., & Grossman, S. (1994). *Gender issues in education.* Boston: Allyn and Bacon.

Halpern, D. F. (1997). Sex differences in intelligence. *American Psychologist, 52*(10), 1091–1102.

Haverman, R. H., & Wolfe, B. (1994). *Succeeding-generations: On the effects of investments in children.* New York: Russell Sage Foundation.

Jencks, C., Smith, M., Arland, H., Bane, M. J., Cohen, D., Gintis, H., Heyns, B., & Michelson, S. (1972). *Inequality: A reassessment of the effect of family and schooling in America.* New York: Basic Books.

Kozol, J. (1991). *Savage inequalities: Children in America's schools.* New York: Crown.

Labaree, D. F. (1994). An unlovely legacy: The disabling impact of the market on American teacher education. *Phi Delta Kappan, 75*(8), 591–595.

Lamison-White, L. (1997). U.S. Bureau of the Census. (Current Population Reports, Series P60-198). *Poverty in the United States: 1996.* Washington, DC: U.S. Government Printing Office.:

Ledlow, S. (1992). Is cultural discontinuity an adequate explanation for dropping out? *Journal of American Indian Education, 31*(3), 21–36.

Levine, D. U., & Levine, R. F. (1996). *Society and education.* Boston: Allyn and Bacon.

Morrow, R. D. (1991). The challenges of Southeast-Asian parental involvement. *Principal, 70,* 20–22.

Mosteller, F., & Moynihan, D. P. (Eds.). (1972). *On equality of educational opportunity: Papers deriving from the Harvard University faculty seminar on the Coleman report.* New York: Random House.

National Education Goals Panel. (1997). *The national education goals report: Building a nation of learners.* Washington, DC: U.S. Government Printing Office.

O'Conner, M. C. (1989). Aspects of differential performance by minorities on standardized tests: Linguistic and sociocultural factors. In B. R. Gifford (Ed.), *Test policy and test performance: Education, language, and culture* (pp. 129–181). Boston: Kleewer.

Orum, L., & Navarrete, L. (1991). Project EXCEL. *Community Education Journal, 18*(4), 9–19.

Parkay, F. W., & Stanford, B. H. (1992). *Becoming a teacher: Accepting the challenge of a profession.* Boston: Allyn and Bacon.

Reed, S., & Sautter, R. C. (1990). Children of poverty: The status of 12 million young Americans. *Phi Delta Kappan, 71,* K1–K12.

Rich, J. M. (1992). *Foundations of education: Perspectives on American education.* New York: Merrill.

Rose, S. J. (1992). *Social stratification in the United States.* New York: New Press.

Sadker, D. (1996, September). Where the girls are. *Education Week,* 49–50.

Sadker, M., & Sadker, D. (1994). *Failing at fairness.* New York: Charles Scribner's Sons.

Schmuck, P. A., & Schmuck, R. A. (1994). Gender equity: A critical democratic component of America's high schools. *NASSP Bulletin, 78,* 22–31.

Selakovich, D. (1984). *Schooling in America: Social foundations of education.* New York: Longman.

Seppa, N. (1997, June). Children's TV remains steeped in violence. *APA Monitor,* 36.

Spring, J. (1998). *American education* (8th ed.). Boston: McGraw-Hill.

Strouse, J. (1997). *Exploring themes of social justice in education.* Upper Saddle River, NJ: Prentice Hall.

Swisher, K., & Hoisch, M. (1992). Dropping out among American Indians and Alaska Natives: A review of studies. *Journal of American Indian Education, 31*(2), 3–23.

Thoman, E. (1995). Media violence: The search for solutions. *Momentum, XXVI*(1), 47–49.

Tippeconnic, J. W., III, & Swisher, K. (1992). American Indian education. In M. C. Alkin (Ed.), *Encyclopedia of Educational Research* (pp. 75–77). New York: Macmillan.

U.S. Bureau of the Census. (1993). (Current Population Reports, Series P 23, No. 183). *Hispanic Americans today.* Washington, DC: U.S. Government Printing Office.

U.S. Bureau of the Census. (1995). *How we're changing: Demographic state of the nation:*

1995. Washington, DC: U.S. Government Printing Office.

U.S. Bureau of the Census. (1996). (Current Population Reports, P 25-1130). *Population projections of the United States by age, race, and hispanic origin: 1995 to 2050*. Washington, DC: U.S. Government Printing Office.

U.S. Bureau of the Census (1997d). (Current Population Reports, P20-503). *The Asian and Pacific Islander population in the United States: March 1996*. Washington, DC: U.S. Government Printing Office.

U.S. Bureau of the Census (1997c). (Current Population Reports, P20-498). *The black population in the United States: March 1996 (update)*. Washington, DC: U.S. Government Printing Office.

U.S. Bureau of the Census. (1997a). *How we're changing: Demographic state of the nation: 1997*. Washington, DC: U S Government Printing Office.

U.S. Bureau of the Census (1997b). (Current Population Reports, P60-197). *Money income in the United States: 1996*. Washington, DC: U.S. Government Printing Office.

U.S. Bureau of the Census (1998). (Current Population Reports, P20-505). *Educational attainment in the United States: March 1997*. Washington, DC: U.S. Government Printing Office.

U.S. Bureau of Indian Affairs. (1998). *American Indian today*. http://www.doi.gov/bia/aitoday/aitoday.html.

U.S. Department of Education, National Center for Education Statistics. (1994). *The condition of education 1994*. Washington, DC: U.S. Government Printing Office.

U.S. Department of Education, National Center for Education Statistics. (1997b). *Dropout rates in the United States: 1996*. Washington, DC: U.S. Government Printing Office.

U.S. Department of Education, National Center for Education Statistics. (1997a). *The condition of education 1997*. Washington, DC: U.S. Government Printing Office.

U.S. Department of Education, National Center for Education Statistics. (1998). *The condition of education 1998*. Washington, DC: U.S. Government Printing Office.

Valdez, C. (1992). Education of Hispanic-Americans. In M.C. Alkin (Ed.), *Encyclopedia of Educational Research* (pp. 592–597). New York: Macmillan.

Wallis, C. (1992). The nuclear family goes boom! *Time, 140*(27), 42–44.

Webb, L. D., McCarthy, M. M., & Thomas, S. (1988). *Financing elementary and secondary education*. Columbus, OH: Merrill.

Webb, R. B., & Sherman, R. R. (1989). *Schooling and society*. New York: Macmillan.

Weinberg, M. (1997). *Asian-American education*. Mahwah, NJ: Lawrence Erlbaum Associates.

Wong, L. Y. S. (1992). Education of Asian-Americans. In M. C. Alkin (Ed.), *Encyclopedia of Educational Research* (pp. 95–96). New York: Macmillan.

Chapter 9

As a son of a tenant farmer, I know that education is the only valid passport from poverty. As a former teacher—and I hope a future one—I have great expectations of what this law will mean for all of our young people . . . I believe deeply no law I have signed or will ever sign means more to the future of America.

President Lyndon Johnson upon signing the Elementary and
Secondary Education Bill, April 1, 1965

Responding to a Diverse and Multicultural Society

➤ *At the end of the second week of school a student, Linda Wilson, comes to the counseling office with a problem. She complains that she has been the subject of harassment by the teacher and students in the auto mechanics class. According to Linda, the boys refuse to work with her on small group projects, ignore her when she talks to them, and on various occasions have hidden her tools or put grease in her book. One day when she went to her car she found all the air let out of her tires with a note on the windshield saying, "Do it yourself if you're such a red-hot mechanic!" She says she knows Mr. Thompson, the teacher, is aware of the students' behavior but just ignores it. According to Linda, Mr. Thompson acts as if she's stupid when she asks a question, always refers to the class as "You men," and when discussing employment opportunities makes it clear that auto mechanics is for men only. Linda says she's really interested in auto mechanics, but under the circumstances wants to drop the course.*

Do you agree with Linda that she should drop the course? Why or why not? What other options would you suggest to Linda? What evidence is there of sexism, sex role stereotyping, or sex discrimination?

As we have seen in previous chapters of this text, a variety of circumstances have combined in society and the schools to restrict the educational opportunities of many students, including students such as Linda Wilson. This chapter presents a number of strategies for responding to a diverse and multicultural society while combating inequity and inequality in education. As you review these strategies, consider the following learning objectives:

- Differentiate the concepts of cultural pluralism, multiculturalism, and multicultural education.
- List the major court decisions concerning segregation and discuss their impact on local school districts.
- Discuss the possible effects of desegregation on the academic achievement and self-esteem of racial and ethnic minority students and on community integration.
- Describe current issues in the education of Native Americans/Alaska Natives.

- Discuss the variety of types of bilingual education and the controversy surrounding the education of linguistic minority children.
- Describe the major compensatory education programs and their current status.
- Outline the principles inherent in the Individuals With Disabilities Education Act and their impact on American education.
- Discuss the progress of gender equity in education and the process for its attainment.

Beginning in the 1960s with the civil rights movement and the federal government's War on Poverty, numerous federal programs were initiated to promote educational opportunity. In addition to the federal initiatives, state governments, professional organizations, and the private sector have introduced strategies to combat inequality in education. In this chapter the following strategies are discussed: multicultural education, desegregation, Native American/Alaskan Native education, education of migrant and immigrant students, bilingual education, compensatory education, education of students with disabilities, and the promotion of gender equity.

From Assimilation to Multiculturalism

In spite of the fact that we have always been a pluralistic nation, the attention to cultural diversity is a relatively new phenomenon in the United States. Multiculturalism is the latest in the progression of educational responses to diversity. *Multiculturalism* is defined as the inclusion of all cultures regardless of race, ethnicity, religion, social class, gender, age, exceptionality, and sexual orientation. The initial response, assimilation, attempted to make it possible for everyone to be "melted" into a homogeneous whole (Cushner, McClelland, & Safford, 1996). Assimilation dates from the colonial period and was particularly favored during the period from 1880 to 1945 when countless numbers of immigrants came to America from eastern and southern European nations. During this period, "military-style" assimilation was advocated, meaning the rapid assimilation of immigrant children, by force if necessary. Military-style assimilation encouraged English-only classrooms, the Anglicization of immigrants' names and of the school community, and no use of the native language, even outside the school environment. Since the Anglocentric curriculum was considered standard, any other culture was viewed substandard (Stein, 1986).

Did you or any of your ancestors come to America as immigrants? What was your or their assimilation experience?

From 1945 to 1968, assimilation continued not as "military-style," but as "missionary-style." This type of assimilation reflected the cultural deprivation theory, an environmentalist theory that blamed poor school achievement on deficiencies in the minority culture rather than on inheritance of low intelligence. It also reflected the amalgamation theory, which contended that not to assimilate would be to preordain the immigrants to poverty and exclude them from the mainstream. The solution adopted by many school districts during this period was to attempt to replace parental and community values with the values of the Anglo middle class (Stein, 1986).

In spite of the rhetoric concerning the importance of uniformity, patriotism, and the Anglo-Saxon tradition, by the 1960s it was clear that the assimilation approach had many shortcomings. African Americans, Hispanics, Native Americans, and other racial and ethnic groups continued to experience discrimination, and attempts to increase upward mobility of children from poor families were generally unsuccessful. Thus, during the 1960s, concurrent with the civil rights movement, the concept of cultural pluralism replaced the assimilation concept.

Multiculturalism includes all cultures including race, ethnicity, religion, social class, age, exceptionality, and sexual orientation.

Cultural pluralism is defined as "a state in which people of diverse ethnic, racial, religious, and social groups maintain autonomous participation within a common civilization" (McNergney & Herbert, 1998, p. 297). The philosophy of pragmatism is embedded in the concept of cultural pluralism, which can be traced to the early writings of William James, John Dewey, and their contemporaries such as Horace Kallen, Alain Locke, and Randolph Bourne. Kallen's essay, *Democracy Versus the Melting Pot* (1915), is often credited with being the founding document of cultural pluralism (Menand, 1997). Kallen used the term *cultural pluralism* to describe "a new kind of polity and a new kind of public education, in which a variety of cultures besides that of England and English-influenced America would receive a significant place in American public education" (Glazer, 1997, pp. 85–86). Unlike assimilation, which disregards differences and requires one group to conform to the culture of another, cultural pluralism gives prominence to being dissimilar and celebrates the uniqueness of a variety of cultures and subcultures.

While cultural pluralism envisioned the universe as multiple and recognized the importance of separate identities, many believed that, like assimilation, it too was restrictive in its view of inclusion. That is, while references to race and ethnicity are explicit in the concept of cultural pluralism, multiculturalists argue that

Figure 9.1: Themes in a Eurocentric, Patriarchal Curriculum

The United States is the land of wealth and opportunity; it is open to all who try; anyone can get what he works for.

American history flowed from Europe to the East Coast of North America; from there it flowed westward.

American culture is of European origin; Europe is the main source of worthwhile cultural achievements.

National ideals are (and should) consist of individual advancement, private accumulation, rule by majority as well as by market demand, loyalty to U.S. government, in addition to freedom of speech.

Some social problems existed in the past, but they have been solved.

Most problems society faces have technical solutions, for which science and math offer the best keys.

Americans share consensus about most things; differences are individual and can be talked out (usually in one story).

Other places in the world may have poverty and problems, but the U.S. does not; we tend to solve other nations' problems.

America is basically white, middle class, and heterosexual; white wealthy men are the world's best thinkers and problem-solvers and usually act in the best interests of everyone.

Source: Sleeter, C. E. (1996). *Multicultural education as social activism.* Albany: State University of New York Press, p. 93.

pluralism encompasses more than race and ethnicity. Multiculturalism, they argue, also includes social class, religion, age, exceptionality, gender, and sexual orientation.

Multicultural Education

The concept of muliculturalism provides the theoretical basis for multicultural education. Students from varied backgrounds often find their school culture to be alien to their home environment. In recent years, research has suggested that when students' acculturation prepares them for a social context that differs from the social context of the school, alienation may result. *Multicultural education* is a strategy for addressing this alienation by recognizing, accepting, and affirming a broad view of human differences and similarities. Multicultural education has been defined as a concept, idea, and philosophy (Gay, 1995). It has also been viewed as a reform movement, field of study, and an emerging discipline (Banks & Banks, 1995; McNergney & Herbert, 1998). As a reform movement it questions the Eurocentric and patriarchal world view that has dominated the educational curriculum. Figure 9.1 presents an overview of the themes that reflect the Eurocentric patriarchal curriculum.

James Banks (1993), a leading proponent of multicultural education, describes multicultural education as having five dimensions.

- The *content integration* dimension, which deals with the extent to which teachers use examples, data, and other information from a variety of cultures and groups to illustrate the key concepts, principles, generalizations, and theories in the subject or discipline.
- The *knowledge construction* dimension, which includes discussion of the ways in which the implicit cultural assumptions, frames of reference, perspectives, and biases within a discipline influence the construction of knowledge.
- The *prejudice reduction* dimension, which focuses on the characteristics of children's racial attitudes and on strategies that can be used to help students develop more positive racial and ethnic attitudes.
- The *equity pedagogy* dimension, which exists when teachers use techniques and teaching methods that facilitate the academic achievement of students from diverse racial and ethnic groups and from all social classes.
- The *empowering school culture and social structure* dimension, which would require the restructuring of the culture and organization of the school so that students from diverse racial, ethnic, and social-class groups will experience equality and a sense of empowerment. (pp. 25, 27)

To accomplish the goals inherent in these dimensions, multicultural education employs a variety of curricular, instructional, and other educational practices. Banks (1997) suggests that these practices may be visualized as a hierarchy that reflects the degree of multicultural reform. As depicted in Figure 9.2, the lowest level in the hierarchy is represented by the "Contributions Approach" and the highest level by the "Action Approach."

While still on the margins rather than at the center of the curriculum, multicultural education has made significant progress in the last two decades. Multicultural content is increasingly becoming part of core courses at all levels of education. The majority of teacher training programs as well as the National Council for Accreditation of Teacher Education have endorsed the study of multicultural education for all prospective teachers.

However, despite the progress being made in integrating the principles of multicultural education into the curriculum, multicultural education continues to be attacked by critics who view it as a costly and unnecessary entitlement program for minorities. Glazer (1997) highlights some of the critics' other major fears: "An emphasis on multiculturalism will teach our children untruths; It will threaten national unity; It will undermine civic harmony; It will do nothing to raise the achievement of the groups expected to benefit from it" (p. 34). Individuals such as Diane Ravitch, Arthur Schlesinger, Jr., William Bennett, and E. D. Hirsch argue that while the teaching of other cultures may be valuable, educators should not lose sight of our European tradition which has served as the centerpiece for our government and its institutions (Howe, 1997; Spring, 1998).

Multicultural Influences on Student Learning

One way that school districts have endorsed multicultural education is by recognizing differences in learning or cognitive styles that stem from a combination of biological, psychological, cultural, and social factors and accommodating these

How would you describe your learning and cognitive style?

Figure 9.2: Continuum of Multicultural Curriculum Integration

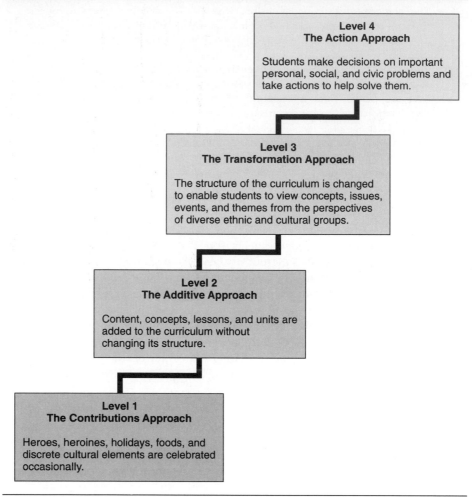

Level 4
The Action Approach

Students make decisions on important personal, social, and civic problems and take actions to help solve them.

Level 3
The Transformation Approach

The structure of the curriculum is changed to enable students to view concepts, issues, events, and themes from the perspectives of diverse ethnic and cultural groups.

Level 2
The Additive Approach

Content, concepts, lessons, and units are added to the curriculum without changing its structure.

Level 1
The Contributions Approach

Heroes, heroines, holidays, foods, and discrete cultural elements are celebrated occasionally.

Source: Banks, J. A. (1997). Approaches to multicultural curriculum reform. In J. A. Banks & C. A. Banks (Eds.), *Multicultural issues and perspectives*. Boston: Allyn and Bacon, p. 233.

differences by using a variety of instructional approaches. Differences in cognitive styles may be found between those who are characterized as field-independent analytic thinkers and those who are characterized as field-dependent descriptive thinkers. An individual with a field-independent style will tend to organize his or her environment and approach tasks on a step-by-step sequence, while an individual with a field-dependent style will be more likely to attend to global aspects of the curriculum and prefer multiple activities. Field-independent learners function well in competitive environments and prefer to work independently, while field-dependent learners prefer cooperative activities.

Teachers need to recognize the variety of learning styles related to ethnic and social differences.

Research has shown that differences in learning and cognitive styles may be related to cultural factors as well as socioeconomic factors. For example, there is some evidence that members of the dominant cultural group in the United States tend to be more field-independent, while many members of the oppressed groups tend to be more field-dependent. Teachers need to be aware of their own style of learning in addition to their students' preferred learning styles. Teachers need to be sensitive to the importance of a variety of cultural factors on learning and to adapt and modify their instruction accordingly (Cushner, McClelland, & Safford, 1996; Gollnick & Chinn, 1998; Salend, 1998).

Another dimension of learning styles has to do with the learner's preferred sensory mode of learning. That is, while "all six senses (sight, sound, smell, touch, taste, and movement) are normally open to learning stimuli, some individuals tend to learn most easily and efficiently through one of the sensory modes" (Cushner, McClelland, & Safford, 1996, p. 125).

Still other variations in learning styles are related to social preferences. For example, some students respond better to learning environments that encourage cooperative learning activities; others may be more comfortable with an independent learning approach; and others may be more successful in an environment that stresses competitive learning. A final dimension, the cognitive-psychological dimension, refers to the disposition of the learner to be a global or analytic learner, to be right brain or left brain dominant, or to be reflective or impulsive (Cushner, McClelland, & Safford, 1996).

Creating Equal Educational Opportunities for Racial and Ethnic Minorities

Desegregation

School *desegregation* is a complex and controversial issue. It is multidimensional in that it has personal, political, social, legal, and educational aspects. Historically, children and youth in the United States generally have attended socially segregated schools, a reflection of a segregated society. They also have attended socioeconomically segregated schools. This is particularly true for African American children, but it is also true for other social and ethnic minority groups. School segregation also extends to teachers. African American teachers typically are concentrated in schools that primarily serve African American students, while white teachers tend to be concentrated in schools that primarily serve white students.

The First Phase

Desegregation is a strategy for realizing constitutional protection and equality of educational opportunity. Desegregation became a major issue in American education with the landmark Supreme Court case of *Brown v. Board of Education* (1954). This case involved elementary school students in Topeka, Kansas, who filed suit challenging a Kansas law that sanctioned racially separate schools. The Court ruled that segregation has a detrimental effect and concluded that the doctrine of "separate but equal" has no place in public education. Recognizing the importance of any order they might make and the uniqueness of each community, the Court ordered that schools must desegregate "with all deliberate speed." Local school districts were charged with the responsibility of creating desegregation plans under the supervision of the closest federal district court.

In the early years of school desegregation, attention was focused on the *de jure* segregated districts in the southern states. Initially, districts attempted to accomplish desegregation by adopting freedom of choice plans. In most instances, these plans had little impact on the level of segregation, and a decade after *Brown,* little progress toward integration had been made. In *Green v. County School Board of New Kent County* (1968), the Supreme Court ruled that if freedom of choice plans were not working, other means must be used. These means could include forced busing (*Swann v. Charlotte-Mecklenburg Board of Education,* 1971). Throughout the 1970s the courts exercised broad powers in ordering remedies, and substantial desegregation was attained in southern school districts (McCarthy, Cambron-McCabe, & Thomas, 1998). Table 9.1 lists some important Supreme Court desegregation cases related to the public schools.

The Second Phase

The second phase of desegregation moved beyond the *de jure* segregation in the South to the *de facto* segregation that existed in many communities outside the South. In these communities, state law did not explicitly mandate segregation,

Busing as a strategy to achieve school desegregation has met with mixed results.

but local zoning ordinances, housing restrictions, attendance zones, *gerrymandering,* or other deliberate official actions were designed to segregate African Americans. And, the resolve of the Supreme Court to end *de facto* segregation seemed to equal its resolve to end *de jure* segregation. In a case involving Denver, Colorado, *Keyes v. School District No. 1* (1973), the Supreme Court held that when official actions had a segregative intent, they were just as illegal as *de jure* segregation. In subsequent cases, the Court ruled that "if school officials are unable to refute that intentional school segregation existed when *Brown I* was rendered, their post-1954 acts must be assessed in light of their *continuing affirmative duty* to eliminate the effects of such segregation" (McCarthy, Cambron-McCabe, & Thomas, 1998, pp. 487).

Table 9.1: Selected U.S. Supreme Court Desegregation Cases Related to the Public Schools

Case	Decision
Brown v. Board of Education of Topeka (1954)	The doctrine of separate but equal in education is a violation of the Fourteenth Amendment.
Green v. County School Board of New Kent County (1968)	Local school boards should immediately take whatever steps are necessary to achieve a unitary system.
Swann v. Charlotte-Mecklenburg Board of Education (1971)	Transportation of students to opposite-race school is permissible to achieve desegregation.
Keyes v. School District No. 1 (Denver) (1973)	Proof of intent to segregate in one part of a district is sufficient to find the district to be segregated and to warrant a dis-trictwide remedy. For purposes of defin-ing a segregated school, blacks and Hispanics may be considered together.
Milliken v. Bradley (1974)	In devising judicial remedies for desegre-gation, the scope of the desegregation remedy cannot exceed the scope of the violation.
Dayton Board of Education v. Brinkman (1977)	Judicially mandated desegregation plans cannot exceed the impact of the segre-gatory practices.
Board of Education of Oklahoma City Public Schools v. Dowell (1991)	Desegregation decrees are not intended to operate in perpetuity, and can be dissolved when a district has made good faith effort to comply and to the extent practical has eliminated the vestiges of past discrimination.
Freeman v. Pitts (1992)	Lower courts can relinquish supervision of a school district under desegregation decree in incremental stages before full compliance has been achieved in every area of school operations.
Missouri v. Jenkins (1995)	Once the effects of legally imposed segregation have been eliminated, the goal of desegregation plans need not be to maintain racial balance but to return control to state and local authorities. Any resegregation of neighborhood schools that may result is not unconstitutional.

During the 1980s, although the Reagan administration did little to pursue de-segregation cases, numerous school districts continued to be involved in deseg-regation struggles. And, magnet schools became a popular strategy to achieve desegregation and to reduce "white flight." *Magnet schools,* which attempted to attract white students to predominantly minority schools, were one of the favored strategies of the Reagan administration in out-of-court settlements of desegrega-tion cases, and by the 1990s were incorporated into the concept of choice in ed-ucation (Spring, 1998). Magnet school plans are also a response to the substantial opposition to transferring pupils for desegregation purposes and the growing minority population in urban areas that works against achieving desired levels of integration.

New Directions in the 1990s: Resegregation

In the decades after *Brown* numerous districts across the country came under court decree to end segregation. Many of these tried in good faith for years to im-plement the court's decree but were frustrated in their efforts by changing eco-nomic and community demographics that have resulted in many urban areas be-coming increasingly minority. As a result, in some instances school districts that had become integrated experienced *resegregation.*

In a series of decisions in the 1990s, a more conservative Supreme Court re-sponded to the plight of these districts. In 1991, in *Board of Education of Okla-homa City Public Schools v. Dowell,* the Supreme Court ruled that a court order desegregation decree can be terminated or dissolved when the school board has in *good faith* made efforts to comply with the decree and has *to the extent prac-tical,* given past history and current conditions, eliminated the vestiges of past discrimination. The next year, in *Freeman v. Pitts,* the Supreme Court continued down the course charted by *Dowell* and ruled that federal judges can exercise "incremental withdrawal" of their supervision of desegregation orders and sug-gested that a specific time limit be placed on a district's efforts to desegregate, es-pecially if the district is one experiencing rapid demographic changes. The effect of these two decisions was not only to bring an end to the judicial oversight of desegregation plans for a number of school districts, but also to provide these districts the opportunity to fashion new remedies that appear more likely to be successful given the current circumstances of the district.

In a landmark case in 1995, *Missouri v. Jenkins,* the Supreme Court addressed what must be done and how much must be invested in attempting to desegre-gate. In this case, the Kansas City school system and the state of Missouri had re-portedly spent $1.7 billion between 1986 and 1995 on a massive desegregation plan that involved renovation and building of facilities, an expensive program of magnet schools, and remedial instruction to bring minority students to national norms on achievement as ordered by a lower federal court (Kunen, 1996). The Supreme Court, in its ruling, held that desegregation efforts should be limited in time and scope and that the goal of desegregation plans need not be to achieve racial balance but to restore control to state and local authorities as expeditiously as possible. The court ruled that once the district has eliminated the effects of legally imposed segregation, the schools can revert to their "natural" pattern of

To what extent are you familiar with examples of both segregation and resegrega-tion?

segregation. As explained by the *Jenkins* court: "The Constitution does not prevent individuals from chosing to live together, to work together, or to send their children to school together, so long as the state does not interfer with their choices on the basis of race" (p. 2063).

The decisions in *Dowell, Pitts,* and *Jenkins* were viewed by some as necessary corrections to judicial excesses. Many others viewed them as the court turning its back on *Brown*. Without question, the decisions were part of a pattern of reversals of civil rights policies in the 1990s, which included decisions against affirmative action and voting rights (Orfield, 1997a). The effect of these decisions has been to encourage school districts to bring to an end busing and other desegregation strategies in favor of neighborhood schools. That resegregation is occurring is already evident in a number of communities. Within a matter of weeks of the *Jenkins* decision a federal district court approved the resegregation of Denver. Challenges to other desegregation orders abound.

The movement toward resegregation is troublesome for many parents and educators. It is true that some desegregation policies have been flawed and that attempts at forced desegregation in some of the largest cities with limited minority populations have seemed futile, if not irrelevant. However, a return to the myth that separate can be equal has serious consequences for our nation. As Harvard sociologist Gary Orfield (1997b) warns:

What positive strategies might you suggest to prepare for the major demographic shift that will occur by 2050 as described by Gary Orfield?

> When we celebrate the Tricentennial of American Independence, there will be a huge non-white majority in our country if well-established demographic trends continue. The leaders of what seem likely to be the last generations of a predominantly European-origin America need to consider not only what the current majority prefers but also what will produce a viable society for their children to live in when their descendants will be worried about minority rights for whites.
>
> What we do now, in either discarding or building upon the possibilities of Brown will do much to shape how we proceed through the vast demographic transition that the Census Bureau predicts will make our school age population less than two-fifths white by 2050. It would be much better if we enter that transition with multiracial public schools that offer equal opportunity, strong protection for minority rights, and training to live in a profoundly multiracial society. (p. 361)

Native American/Alaska Native Education

The education of Native American and Alaska Native children has a unique history in this country because the federal government was obligated by various treaties to provide for the education of Native American children. The course of this federal involvement, which was detailed in earlier chapters, was largely one of dictating educational policy and practice. It was not until the self-determination movement gained strength in the late 1960s that a serious commitment was made in federal policy to increase the involvement of Native Americans in the management of their own affairs, including education.

The Self-Determination Movement

Three important legislative mandates have increased participation and decision making by Native Americans: the Indian Education Act of 1972; its successor, the

More Native American parents than ever before are actively involved in the education of their children.

Indian Self-Determination and Education Assistance Act of 1975; and the Indian Education Amendments of 1988. Since the passage of these legislative mandates, a number of tribes have opted to operate schools under contract with the federal government, rather than leave their operation to the Bureau of Indian Affairs (BIA). Funding has been provided by the BIA, but the schools have elected Native American school boards. More Native American parents than ever before are actively involved in the education of their children, serve on school boards or special committees, or are otherwise involved in providing direction to the schools serving Native American children and youth.

The 1990s witnessed a revived interest in the education of Native Americans. This was evidenced by the Native American Languages Act of 1990 directed at the survival of Native American language and the activities of the Indian Nations at Risk Task Force (INATF). And, in 1992 a White House Conference on Indian Education was held to develop recommendations for the improvement of educational programs and make these programs more relevant to the needs of the Native American communities.

Many Native Americans have looked to the Indian Nations at Risk Task Force for the impetus for change. The task force commissioned papers from experts in Native American education, conducted site visits and interviews, and held hearings. The task force issued a final report (1991) and a number of recommendations, part of which included a set of 10 educational goals for all federal, tribal, private, and public schools that educate Native American children. These goals, patterned after the national education goals, are presented in Figure 9.3.

Federal Support

Of the 80,893 public schools in the United States, 1,244 have a Native American/Alaska Native student enrollment of at least 25 percent (U.S. Department of Education, 1997). Public schools enrolling Native American students receive federal assistance under several programs. Public school districts that include federal, nontaxable Indian reservations receive federal impact aid as a substitute for lost tax revenues. Funds are provided under the Johnson O'Malley Act for supplemental programs in public schools that benefit Native American children and have been approved by a Native American education committee. Examples include home-school coordinators, remedial tutoring, field trips, and cultural programs. Funds are also provided under the Indian Education Act for supplemental instructional activities for Native American students in public schools. To ensure that Native Americans have a voice in the development and delivery of these programs, parental and community participation is required.

The federal government also supports the construction, operation, and maintenance of approximately 170 Bureau of Indian Affairs (BIA) schools located primarily in the rural communities of the Southwest, Northern Plains, South Central region, and Alaska. BIA schools include day schools, boarding schools, schools operated under contract with tribal governments, and schools operated cooperatively with public schools. In addition, Native American students in both BIA-supported and public schools receive special services if they are disadvantaged, have no or limited English proficiency, have a disability, or are enrolled in vocational education.

The School Experience: Barriers to Success

Despite the many changes and improvements in Native American education, the investigations of the Indian Nations at Risk Task Force and the work of the White House Conference on Indian Education revealed that many Native American children attend schools with an unfriendly climate "that fails to promote appropriate academic, social, cultural, and spiritual development," and where the curriculum is presented "from a purely Western (European) perspective, ignoring all that the historical perspective of American Indians and Alaska Natives has to contribute," by teachers "with inadequate skills and training to teach Native children effectively," and "with few Native educators as role models." In such an environment, Native students tend to lose their native language abilities and find themselves relegated to lower ability tracks (INATF, 1991). And, in far too many public schools, "perfunctory parent committees funded by meagerly funded federal projects" is the only involvement Native Americans have in the administration of the education of their children (Charleston, 1994).

Figure 9.3: National Education Goals for Native Americans and Alaska Natives

Goal 1: Readiness for School
By the year 2000 all Native children will have access to early childhood education programs that provide the language, social, physical, spiritual, and cultural foundations they need to succeed in school and to reach their full potential as adults.

Goal 2: Maintain Native Languages and Cultures
By the year 2000 all schools will offer Native students the opportunity to maintain and develop their tribal languages and will create a multicultural environment that enhances the many cultures represented in the school.

Goal 3: Literacy
By the year 2000 all Native children in school will be literate in the language skills appropriate for their individual levels of development. They will be competent in their English oral, reading, listening, and writing skills.

Goal 4: Student Academic Achievement
By the year 2000 every Native student will demonstrate mastery of English, mathematics, science, history, geography, and other challenging academic skills necessary for an educated citizenry.

Goal 5: High School Graduation
By the year 2000 all Native students capable of completing high school will graduate. They will demonstrate civic, social, creative, and critical thinking skills necessary for ethical, moral, and responsible citizenship and important in modern tribal, national, and world societies.

Goal 6: High-Quality Native and non-Native School Personnel
By the year 2000 the numbers of Native educators will double, and the colleges and universities that train the nation's teachers will develop a curriculum that prepares teachers to work effectively with the variety of cultures, including the Native cultures, that are served by schools.

Goal 7: Safe and Alcohol-Free and Drug-Free Schools
By the year 2000 every school responsible for educating Native students will be free of alcohol and drugs and will provide safe facilities and an environment conducive to learning.

Goal 8: Adult Education and Lifelong Learning
By the year 2000 every Native adult will have the opportunity to be literate and to obtain the necessary academic, vocational, and technical skills and knowledge needed to gain meaningful employment and to exercise the rights and responsibilities of tribal and national citizenship.

Goal 9: Restructuring Schools
By the year 2000 schools serving Native children will be restructured to effectively meet the academic, cultural, spiritual, and social needs of students for developing strong, healthy, self-sufficient communities.

Goal 10: Parental, Community, and Tribal Partnerships
By the year 2000 every school responsible for educating Native students will provide opportunities for Native parents and tribal leaders to help plan and evaluate the governance, operation, and performance of their educational programs.

Source: U.S. Department of Education (1991). *Indian nations at risk: An educational strategy for action, final report of the Indian Nations at Risk Task Force.* Washington, DC: U.S. Department of Education.

While there are many excellent schools serving Native American/Alaska Native children, the above description would not be an uncommon one. Some of the disastrous results have been described elsewhere in this text: the highest dropout rate of any racial or ethnic group, lower levels of educational attainment, and the lowest rate of postsecondary participation of any group. Absenteeism also runs high among Native American students. And, tragically, Native American students have a suicide rate for adolescents that is 10 times that of their Anglo peers (Webb & Metha, 1996).

Responding to the Challenge

To address these conditions, the Indian Nations at Risk Task Force declared four national priorities for Native American/Alaska Native education.

- Developing parent-based and culturally, linguistically, and developmentally appropriate early childhood education;
- making the promotion of students' tribal language and culture a responsibility of the school;
- training more Native teachers; and
- strengthening tribal and Bureau of Indian Affairs colleges. (Reyhner, 1994, p. 35)

Recommendations of the White House Conference on Indian Education were similar. In particular, heavy emphasis was placed on tribal involvement and control of education at all levels as a necessary step to reforming Native American education. One of the most hopeful signs of change has been the education reform efforts being conducted at Bureau of Indian Affairs schools. Using the major objectives of the 10 educational goals, the BIA has initiated a comprehensive school improvement plan that includes the adoption of educational standards, staff retraining, program consolidation, parental involvement, integrated curriculum (native language and culture are critical features), authentic assessment, school-to-work planning, and increased classroom technology (St. Germaine, 1995a).

Many of the problems of Native American education are a result of problems in the larger society, including racism and poverty, and until these problems are solved Native American education will continue to reflect them (White House Conference on Indian Education, 1992). Nonetheless, there is much that can be done, and is being done, to improve Native American education. Native American/Alaska Native communities have become increasingly aware of the fact that they must take responsibility for the educational systems to whom they entrust their youth. Fortunately, these communities are willing and anxious to assume this responsibility as are the educational communities. The challenge is onerous.

> If schools are to succeed in their mission, there are numerous barriers for Indian children to overcome. Half-hearted efforts and sporadic innovations will not do. What is needed is systemic change—teacher by teacher, subject by subject, classroom by classroom, school by school, and administration by administration. The mission of education is too complex for simplistic remedies. (St. Germain, 1995b, p. 36)

Creating Equal Educational Opportunities for Migrant Students

For decades, much of the economic health of our nation has depended on migratory farm workers who are often viewed as the "invisible" and most disadvantaged of all minority groups (Velazquez, 1994/95). In the United States, there are more than 780,000 children who along with their families move from one geographic region to the next to harvest crops. Many migrant families move in and out of school districts as often as 10 or more times in a given year. Approximately 90% of these children reside in households whose family members do not speak English (Kindler, 1995). Their nomadic existence, coupled with low hourly wages, no benefits, inadequate housing in crowded surroundings, poor sanitation, poor nutrition, and a lack of adequate health care can be summarized in a single word—poverty. The majority of migrant farmworkers are Hispanic (94%), with 80% born in Mexico. Six to 10 percent of the migrants are white or African Americans (Martin, 1994).

The irregular school attendance of migrant students along with linguistic barriers and cultural differences often lead to community isolation, alienation, and powerlessness. The eventual outcome is dropping out of school. During the harvest season it is not uncommon for the migrant child or youth to be employed 16 to 18 hours per week. By the time migrant children reach age 12, they often lag behind their school-age peers in both educational achievement and grade level (Bell, Roach, & Sheets, 1994). Across all grade levels, twice as many migrant students are retained for at least one year compared to their peers. And, students who have been retained in grade level are most vulnerable for dropping out of school (Trotter, 1992).

Migrant students are often underidentified and underserved in special education classes and programs. The federal government supports migrant programs for all students through the states. It also provides funding for migrant students with special needs. The Migrant Education Program (MEP), which was reauthorized in the Improving America's School Act (IASA) of 1994, became more restrictive in terms of eligibility and made a number of changes in priority for services and school aid programs. However, in spite of these changes, many migrant students continue to be eligible for a variety of local, state, and federal assistance including other Chapter 1 programs.

Given the special needs of migrant students, migrant educators perform multiple roles including individual instruction; educational support such as serving as interpreters for parents; ensuring that students obtain the necessary medical, dental, and health-related services; providing transportation for families; and training in English as a Second Language (ESL) (Salend, 1990). Beck, Kratzer, and Isken (1997) point out that serving transient or migratory students places a tremendous burden on school districts in terms of clerical time, testing materials for new students, and textbooks. Schools are often not compensated with additional district or state funds for the financial burden they bear when serving large numbers of migrant students. In spite of the numerous challenges and insur-mountable obstacles faced by migrant students and their families, many of these students have been able to achieve educational success. That success is due in no small part to the exemplary staff and programs that are committed to serving the migrant population.

Meeting the Educational Needs of Immigrant Students

The majority of legal immigrants who have migrated to the United States come from the following countries: Mexico, Mainland China, the Philippines, Vietnam, the former Soviet Union, the Dominican Republic, India, Poland, El Salvador, and the United Kingdom. Immigrant children make up about 5% of the student body of schools and colleges in the United States. Once they are enrolled in school, immigrant students are more likely than native-born students to make academic choices early in their school careers to attend college, and they complete high school within the same time period as their native-born peers. However, the age at immigration does appear to be an important factor in determining high school completion. For example, Hispanics who enter the United States after the age of 15 are less likely to complete high school than those who immigrate at a younger age (Schwartz, 1996).

The problems encountered by immigrant students are enormous given the number of obstacles and barriers they must overcome such as learning a new language, adjusting to a new culture, lacking school records, etc. Immigrant stu-dents who are refugees and who escaped a variety of forms of repression are more likely to be at risk for problems than immigrants who did not have to con-front such hardships (Salend, 1998).

While many immigrant children become quickly acclimated to American schooling and achieve at levels equal to or greater than native-born students, many others need assistance to succeed. For these students the programs in bilin-gual and multicultural education discussed elsewhere in this chapter can provide important interventions. Other strategies for teaching immigrant students are pre-sented in Figure 9.4.

Creating Equal Educational Opportunities for Linguistic Minority Students

Approximately three million limited-English elementary and secondary students attend U.S. public schools. In California, one out of every four students, or 1.4 million, is a limited-English-speaking student. More than 70% of these students

Figure 9.4: Teaching Students Who Are Immigrants

Educators can facilitate the education of students who are immigrants by considering the following suggestions:

- Allow students to tell their story through narratives, role playing, and bibliotherapy.
- Offer language enrichment programs.
- Encourage students to do projects using materials in their native language.
- Be sensitive to the problems individuals face in learning a second language.
- Understand the cultural, economic, and historical factors that have had a significant impact on students.
- Teach students about their new culture.
- Use nonverbal forms of expression including music, dance, and art.
- Use peers and community members as a resource.
- Employ media in the students' native languages.
- Offer culturally sensitive in-school and extracurricular activities and encourage students to participate in these activities.

- Provide students with access to peer discussion and support groups that are relevant to their interests and experiences.
- Involve parents, extended family members, and knowledgeable community members in the student's educational program.
- Provide students and their families with native language materials dealing with school-related information and information about their rights.
- Contact the Clearinghouse for Immigration Education (800-441-7192), the National Center for Immigrant Students (617-357-8507), or the National Coalition of Advocates for Students (617-357-8507), organizations that disseminate information about model school programs and organizations, teacher-made materials, relevant research, and resource lists addressing the needs of immigrant students and their families.

Source: Harris (1991); Nahme Huang (1989) as cited in Salend, S. J. (1998). *Effective Mainstreaming: Creating inclusive classrooms* (3rd ed.). Columbus, OH: Merrill, p. 45.

speak Spanish at home while the remainder speak one of 327 other languages. The majority of limited-English students reside in either California, Florida, Illinois, New Jersey, New York, or Texas (Portner, 1998).

Bilingual Education

Bilingual education is an instructional program designed to provide an effective education to students in their native language while they are learning English. Bilingual education, like multicultural education, is a vehicle for promoting cultural pluralism. In practice, bilingual education includes a broad range of programs and provides instruction for limited-English-proficient as well as non-English-proficient students.

Federal Involvement in Bilingual Education

Federal support for bilingual education programs began in 1968 through an amendment to the Elementary and Secondary Education Act of 1965 entitled the Title VII Bilingual Education Program, also referred to as the Bilingual Education Act (BEA). However, while the BEA prompted school districts to design and implement programs for language minority students, it was the Supreme Court decision in *Lau v. Nichols* (1974) that provided the major impetus for federal involvement in the education of children with English language deficiencies and raised public awareness of the need for bilingual education. In *Lau* the Court ruled that "there is no equality of treatment merely by providing students with the same facilities, textbooks, teachers, and curriculum; for students who do not understand English are effectively foreclosed from any meaningful education" (p. 566). The Court in *Lau* relied on Title VI of the Civil Rights Act of 1964 to conclude that school districts are obligated to provide for all children with English language deficiencies.

Although the Court mandated that the schools provide assistance for children with English language deficiencies, it did not require a specific type of instructional model for language minority education. That is, the Court did not specify whether Title VII requires bilingual education, English as a Second Language, or any nonbilingual educational approach. As a result, each state and territory has defined its own approach to the education of language minority students. State legislative provisions may also mandate the criteria for program eligibility and for the type of program to be offered. However, in most states school districts are allowed a great deal of latitude in determining the manner in which they incorporate the native language of the student. In the end, such local factors as languages spoken, resources available, and geographic dispersion will play major roles in defining the programs (Sevilla, 1992).

Support for bilingual education grew throughout the 1970s. However, in the 1980s bilingual education became a politically controversial issue when the Reagan administration opposed bilingual education and supported English immersion programs that had been used with earlier immigrant groups. Then Republican Senator S. I. Hayakawa headed an organization called U.S. English that sought to make English the official language of the nation, and in numerous states "English-only" promoters sought the passage of legislation to declare English to be the official language of the state and the only language to be used in conducting public affairs.

In 1988, major amendments to the Bilingual Education Act were made. These amendments provided additional funding for English-only instructional programs and decreased funding for bilingual programs. They also specified that a percentage of the funds be distributed for certain types of educational programs, special alternative instruction programs, developmental bilingual education programs, programs of academic excellence, family English literacy programs, and programs for special populations. The act also limited student participation in bilingual programs to three years.

By the mid-1990s public opposition to native-language teaching programs was being voiced by a significant number of individuals including immigrant parents. Their concerns focused on the fact that children routinely remained segregated in bilingual programs for three years or more, and in some cases in excess of six years. Nowhere has the opposition been more heated than in California, where in 1998 voters approved a referendum, Proposition 227, the so-called "English for the Children" initiative. This referendum mandated that students with limited proficiency in English be taught in a special English immersion program for no more than one year before being mainstreamed into the regular English classrooms. Similar initiatives are underway in several other states ("Bilingual education," 1998).

Bilingual Education Program Options

While all bilingual education programs incorporate instruction in two languages, the amount of emphasis placed on each language is determined by the program option selected. The following types of bilingual education program options have been used:

- *Structural immersion.* Students are taught their academic subjects by teachers who are fluent in the student's native language. While the student is allowed to speak in their first language, the instructor responds in English. If necessary, structural immersion may be combined with *English as a Second Language (ESL)* instruction, which is also taught in English but includes both non-English-speaking and limited-English-speaking students.
- *Bilingual maintenance.* Students are instructed in both the native language and English. The goal is for students to function effectively in both languages; neither language is given priority status. Another goal is to maintain the ability to speak, read, and write in the student's first language while developing English.
- *Transitional bilingual.* The student's primary language is used to make the transition to total use of English. Academic instruction is usually devoted to a half day of each language. The goal is to transfer to English as quickly as possible rather than to become literate in two languages.
- *Two-way bilingual immersion.* Beginning in the early elementary years, while following a regular curriculum, all subjects are taught in two languages. In most two-way bilingual immersion programs, half the students tend to be native Spanish speakers while the other half are native English speakers. The advantage is that non-English speakers gain proficiency in English while developing their first language. Two-way bilingual immersion programs have become increasingly popular over the past two decades and have been formally endorsed in California (Crandall, 1998).

The question of which bilingual program option is most effective for students whose primary language is not English will continue to be debated well into the next millennium.

Improving African American Language Skills: The Black English Debate

Black English or *ebonics* is a dialect spoken primarily by urban African Americans (Cushner, McClelland, & Safford, 1996). Since Black English has been a basic form of speech communication for many working-class African American children who have experienced difficulties with reading and other academic subjects, it has been argued that the most effective strategy for helping such students is to teach them in their primary language, Black English. The goal being that once they are able to master reading in Black English they can transition to standard English. Several large urban school districts in California and New York

What are your views regarding the place of Black English or ebonics in the curriculum?

have explored a variety of teaching strategies to help speakers of Black English acquire competence in standard English (Levine & Levine, 1996). For example, in 1996 the Oakland, California, school board recognized Black English as the primary language of many African American students and suggested that not only should teachers be trained in Black English, but $2 million should be spent over the next five years to ensure that African American students become fluent in standard English (Hardy, 1997).

Issues in Dealing With Linguistic Minority Students

Teachers need to be aware of the multitude of problems that face linguistic minority students. The characteristics of linguistic minority students are often confused with the characteristics of students who display learning disabilities. Table 9.2 compares the characteristics of linguistic minority students with those of students with learning disabilities. Unfortunately, due to these similarities, linguistic minority students are often overreferred or inappropriately placed in special education classes (Salend, 1998).

Table 9.2: Comparison of Characteristics of Students With Learning Disabilities With Characteristics of Second Language Learners

Characteristics of Students With Learning Disabilities	Characteristics of Second Language Learners
Significant difference between the student's performance on verbal and nonverbal tasks and test items	May have more success in completing nonverbal tasks than verbal tasks.
Difficulty mastering academic material	May experience difficulty learning academic material that is decontextualized and abstract.
Language difficulties	May exhibit language difficulties that are a normal aspect of second language acquisition, such as poor comprehension, limited vocabulary, articulation problems, and grammatical and syntactical errors.
Perceptual difficulties	May exhibit perceptual difficulties related to learning a new language and adjusting to a new culture.
Social, behavioral, and emotional difficulties	May experience social, behavioral, and emotional difficulties as part of the frustration of learning a new language and adjusting to a new culture.
Attention and memory difficulties	May exhibit attention and memory problems because it is difficult to concentrate for extended periods of time when instruction is delivered in a new language.

Source: Fradd & Weismantel (1989); Mercer (1987) as cited in Salend, S. J. (1998). *Effective mainstreaming: Creating inclusive classrooms* (3rd ed.). Columbus, OH: Merrill, p. 97.

Compensatory Education for Disadvantaged Students

Compensatory education programs designed to overcome the deficiencies associated with educational and socioeconomic disadvantages have been an important part of federal educational policy and funding since the Elementary and Secondary Education Act was passed in 1965. As discussed in Chapter 7, Title I of that act was the centerpiece of President Lyndon Johnson's Great Society education program and was viewed as an important weapon in the War on Poverty. The intent of Title I was to "enhance the education of disadvantaged children, improve their achievement, and hence redistribute economic and social opportunities in society" (Durbin, 1989, p. 27). Federal funds were allocated to states to be reallocated to local school districts based on the number of low income families, which was viewed as an indicator of student educational need. At the local level, services were provided to eligible students and to entire schools with high concentrations of disadvantaged students. Both disadvantaged public and nonpublic schools could receive services. The enactment of Title I stimulated a number of states to initiate their own compensatory education programs, not only because of the political popularity of social issues at the time, but also because of the growing concern for issues of equity. By the 1990s, compensatory education programs were in place in over half the states (Thompson, Wood, & Honeyman, 1994).

In 1981 Title I was converted into Chapter 1 of the Education Consolidation and Improvement Act. Chapter 1 retained essentially the same features as Title I, the major change being a reduction in federal regulations, placing greater responsibility for monitoring local programs on the states. In 1994, when Chapter 1 was reauthorized as part of the Elementary and Secondary Education Act, its label was changed back to Title I. More important than its name change, however, was the fact that changes in the formula for distribution of funds favored states with the highest percentage of poor children. Also, a new initiative, Early Head Start, was authorized to provide child development and family support services to pregnant women and low income households with children under the age of three. In addition, as pointed out in Chapter 7, in order to remain eligible for Title I funds, states are required to develop school improvement plans that establish high content and performance standards, thereby linking Title I with the reform initiative laid out by the Goals 2000: Educate America Act. In 1998, approximately $7.5 billion in federal funds was appropriated for the Title I compensatory education program.

Types of Programs

Compensatory education programs encompass a variety of educational services delivered primarily in program-eligible schools during school hours. The most common types of programs are:

1. Programs under Early Head Start, which provide infant education and family support services.
2. Early childhood readiness programs such as Head Start, which prepare children between the ages of three and five for school. Head Start is a comprehensive program that combines educational programs, medical and nutritional benefits, parent involvement, and social services.
3. Programs for primary students such as Transition Head Start, which continues Head Start services into the second grade.
4. Programs for secondary education students such as Upward Bound are directed at dropout prevention and at increasing the preparation and participation of disadvantaged youth for postsecondary education through tutoring, instruction in basic skills, and counseling services.
5. Enrichment programs in subject areas. Almost all Title I districts offer programs in reading (e.g., Success for All). Most also offer programs in mathematics, and a lesser percentage (25%) offer programs in language arts.
6. Programs for handicapped students. Almost three fourths of the Title I districts provide services to mentally handicapped students. In most districts, these students must be eligible for Title I to receive services.
7. Bilingual education and English as a Second Language (ESL). Both options of instruction are offered to students with limited English proficiency. Again, normally the students must be eligible for Title I to receive services.
8. Programs for migrant students. Most migrant programs are usually found in larger school districts.
9. Psychological and social services for disadvantaged students.

What are the advantages and disadvantages of pulling students out of the regular class to receive compensatory instruction?

Most Title I instruction is provided through the "pullout" method, in which eligible students are removed from the regular classroom to receive additional instruction, usually in reading, mathematics, and language arts. Instruction lasts about 30 minutes and is delivered in smaller classes by separately hired "Title I teachers," often with the assistance of aides and often with more equipment and materials than are available in the regular classroom. Even though there is some criticism of pullout models, they are popular with school districts because they are the safest way of meeting the requirement that Title I funds be spent only on students eligible for Title I. However, in the last decade changes in Title I regulations have made it easier for a growing number of districts to replace pullout programs with programs that allow in-class assistance.

The Effectiveness of Title I Programs

Research findings on the effectiveness of Title I programs have been mixed. For example, several studies of Head Start found that children who participated in Head Start programs improved substantially in social competence. However, their gains in cognitive development (as measured by IQ scores or academic achievement tests) were not sustained by second grade. Subsequent longitudinal research has shown that there may be a "sleeper effect" operating, in that the gains from the preschool participation may not be obvious until several years after participation in the program has been terminated. And, there is promising research that suggests that low status students who participate in a preschool compensatory program demonstrate higher IQ scores, are more likely to find and hold a job, are more apt to continue their education to the postsecondary level, and are less likely to be arrested or on welfare in later years compared to their peers who did not participate in compensatory education. Overall, the evidence suggests that marginal students benefit the most from participation in programs for the disadvantaged (Levine & Levine, 1996).

Currently Title I serves only about half the students eligible to receive services. Services are especially limited at the secondary level. Although it would require a considerable increase in funding to extend and expand Title I programs, thoughtful policy makers and educators realize that this is what is required if President Johnson's dream of breaking the cycle of poverty is to be realized. It is also what is required if the very first national educational goal, "All American children will start school ready to learn," is to be met.

Creating Equal Educational Opportunities for Students With Disabilities

Students with mental and physical disabilities who are receiving services in federally supported programs make up approximately 12% of the students in public schools for grades K–12 (U.S. Department of Education, 1998). Special education for these children was not routinely provided by most state and local school systems until the third quarter of this century. In fact, prior to the 1970s most state laws allowed the expulsion or absolute exclusion from school of children who were deemed uneducable, untrainable, or otherwise unable to benefit from the regular education program. It was not until two important federal court decisions in the early 1970s (*Pennsylvania Association of Retarded Citizens v. Commonwealth of Pennsylvania,* 1972, and *Mills v. Board of Education,* 1972) that the right of children with disabilities to an education was recognized by most states and school districts.

Individuals With Disabilities Education Act and Section 504

These decisions, combined with intense lobbying by special education professionals, interest groups, and parents of children with disabilities, led Congress in 1975 to pass the Education for All Handicapped Children Act (EHA) (Public Law 94–142). The EHA, often referred to as the Bill of Rights for Handicapped Children, and its successors have served not only to guarantee the rights of children with disabilities but also to expand the rights of all children. By 1986, the EHA was amended (Public Law 99–457) to extend the right to a free and appropriate education to all children with disabilities from birth to age five and early intervention programs for infants and toddlers with disabilities. In 1990, legislation reauthorized the EHA and renamed it the Individuals With Disabilities Education Act (IDEA) (Public Law 101-476). The IDEA expanded the categories of disabilities to include autism and traumatic brain injury. It also included transition services, early intervention programs for children who are exposed to maternal substance abuse, and a commitment to the needs of linguistically and ethnically diverse youth with disabilities (Salend, 1998).

Certain disabled students who do not qualify for special education services under the IDEA may qualify for service under Section 504 of the Rehabilitation Act (Public Law 93–112) approved by Congress in 1973. Section 504 is based on a more comprehensive definition of disability than the IDEA. As a result, students with attention deficit disorder, temporary and chronic health conditions, communicable diseases, eating disorders, and to a certain extent substance abuse disorders are entitled to special education services under Section 504 (Salend, 1998).

The EHA introduced a number of principles that have had a great impact on American education. These principles, expanded through the IDEA and subsequent legislation and litigation, are summarized in the sections that follow.

Right to a Free and Appropriate Education

Perhaps the most fundamental and important principle of the IDEA is that *all* children aged 3 to 18 years with disabilities must have available to them a free appropriate education and related services designed to meet their unique needs. This provision of the law means that no children, regardless of the nature or severity of their disability, can be denied a public education. In addition, P.L. 99–457 offers financial and technical assistance to school districts in developing programs for disabled children from birth to age three.

The IDEA does not specify what programs and services must be provided to satisfy the guarantee of appropriate education. Rather, this must be decided on a case-by-case basis and in many instances has been the subject of considerable controversy and litigation. Some guidance was provided by the U.S. Supreme Court in *Board of Education v. Rowley* (1982) in which the Court stated that a free appropriate public education did not mean "an opportunity to achieve full potential commensurate with the opportunity provided to other children," but rather, "*access* to specialized instruction and related services which are designed to provide educational benefit to the handicapped child." Since *Rowley,* while the courts have continued to support parents in their attempts to expand services to their disabled children, they do tend to accept the most *reasonable* program rather than require the best possible program.

Nondiscriminatory Evaluation

This provision requires that each child must receive a comprehensive evaluation before being placed in any special education program. Placement cannot be made on the basis of a single test, but on multiple measures and procedures. Additionally, whatever evaluation mechanisms are used must be nondiscriminatory in terms of culture, race, and language, and must be designed for assessment with specific handicaps (e.g., tests for non-English speakers or tests for the visually impaired).

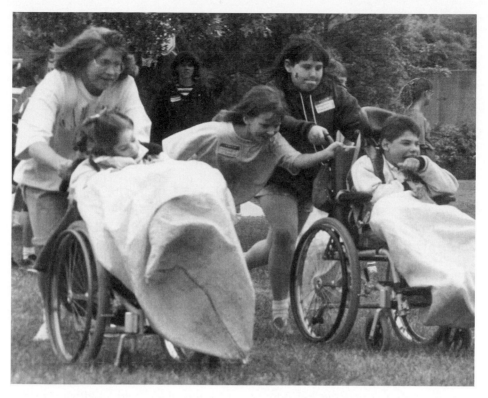

The right to a free and appropriate education is fundamental to the principle of IDEA.

Individualized Educational Program

The IDEA requires that an *individualized education program* (IEP) be prepared for each child who is to receive special education services. Designed to meet the unique needs of the child for whom it is developed, the IEP is prepared by a team of educators, parents, and, if appropriate, the student. The IEP includes a description of present performance; a statement of annual goals, including short-term objectives; a statement of services to be provided and their duration; and evaluation criteria and procedures to determine if the objectives are being achieved. IEPs are reviewed annually and provide the means for ensuring parent involvement in the educational decisions affecting their children, the means for accountability, the delivery of services, and a record of progress. Recent amendments to the IDEA now recommend that transition services and, if needed, assistive technology be added to the IEP.

Least Restrictive Environment

The IDEA mandates that children with disabilities are to be educated in the *least restrictive environment* possible. This requirement has encouraged the practice of *mainstreaming* children with disabilities, to the maximum extent possible, into the regular classroom where they have contact with nondisabled children.

The concept of the IEP has met with success for special education needs. How might the IEP be used with all students?

The courts have interpreted this provision to mean that children with disabilities should not be removed from the regular educational setting unless the nature or severity of the disability is such that education in the regular classroom, even with the use of supplemental aids and services, cannot be achieved satisfactorily. In every case, a disabled child cannot be moved from the regular classroom without a due process hearing, and schools have been required to provide supplemental services in the regular classroom before moving the disabled child to a more restrictive environment.

The least restrictive environment principle does not require mainstreaming; in fact, the IDEA does not mention mainstreaming. What the principle does call for is the careful consideration of all possible placement alternatives for each disabled child before a final placement is made. In the end it may be necessary to place the child in a segregated setting in order to provide him or her with the most appropriate education, or in order to prevent the disruption of the educational process for other students. Students may also be placed in private schools at public expense if the district is not able to provide an appropriate placement. See Figure 9.5 for the continuum of special education placements.

Due Process

The extensive procedural requirements of the IDEA are designed to ensure the rights of children with disabilities to receive a free appropriate education and to protect them from improper evaluation, classification, and placement. Parents have the right to obtain an individual evaluation of their child in addition to that conducted by the school district, and to be involved in every stage of the evaluation, placement, and educational process. Parents must be informed of the IEP conference and encouraged to attend. In addition, the school district must inform parents in writing or in a format understandable by them before it initiates, changes, or refuses to initiate or change the identification, evaluation, or educational placement of the child. Parents also have the right to a due process hearing to challenge the district's decision on any of these matters and to examine all records pertaining to their children.

Current Enrollments

Since the EHA was implemented in 1978, the number of children enrolled in federally supported education programs has risen steadily (see Table 9.3). This is due primarily to the growth in the numbers of students classified as having a learning disability, that is, having a disorder or delayed development in one or more of the processes of thinking, speaking, reading, writing, listening, or doing arithmetic operations. The percentage of students with disabilities classified as learning disabled rose from 22% to 45% between 1978 and 1996. As shown in Table 9.3, in 1996 the second largest category of enrollment for students with disabilities was speech or language impairment, followed by mental retardation.

Figure 9.5: Continuum of Special Education Placements

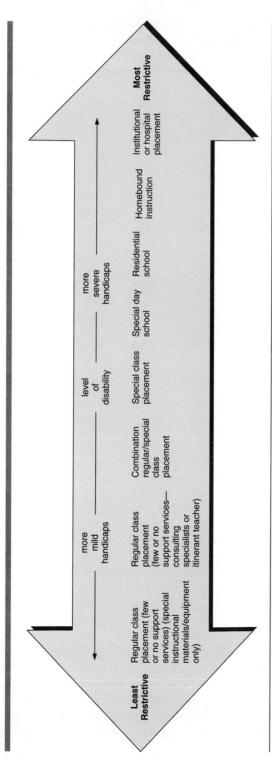

Source: Peterson, N. L. (1988). *Early intervention for handicapped and at-risk children* (p. 337). Denver, CO: Love Publishing Company, Reprinted with permission.

Table 9.3: Number of Elementary and Secondary Students Served in Federally Supported Education Programs for the Disabled and Number as a Percentage of Total K–12 Enrollment, by Type of Disability, School Year Ending 1978, 1996, 1998 (number served in thousands)

Type of Disability	1978		1988		1996	
	Number Served	Percent of Total	Number Served	Percent of Total	Number Served	Percent of Total
Specific learning disabilities	964	2.21	1,928	4.82	2.579	5.75
Speech or language impairments	1,223	2.81	953	2.38	1022	2.28
Mental retardation	933	2.14	582	1.45	570	1.27
Serious emotional disturbance	288	.66	373	.93	438	.98
Hearing impairments	85	.20	56	.14	67	.15
Orthopedic impairments	87	.20	47	.12	63	.14
Other health impairments	135	.31	45	.11	133	.30
Visual impairments	35	.08	22	.06	25	.06
Multiple disabilities	—	—	77	.19	93	.21
Deaf-blindness	—	—	1	<.005	1	<.005
Preschool disabled	—	—	363	.91	544	1.21
Total	3,751	8.61	4,446	11.10	5,573	12.43

Source: U.S. Department of Education, National Center for Education Statistics. (1997). *Digest of education statistics 1997* (Table 52). Washington, DC: U.S. Department of Education.

The Least Restrictive Environment and Inclusion Debate

Just as the IDEA does not define what is meant by an appropriate education but leaves the issue to be decided on a case-by-case basis, so too it does not define what is meant by the "least restrictive environment" but leaves this to be decided one child at a time. The least restrictive environment issue has been central to expanded efforts to increase the number of students with disabilities who are included in regular classroom settings.

The terms *mainstreaming* and *inclusion* are often used interchangeably and thus cause confusion. *Mainstreaming* has been used to refer to either partial or full-time programs designed to educate students with disabilities by placing them in the same general education setting with their nondisabled peers (Salend, 1998). *Inclusion* consists of serving students with a variety of abilities and disabilities in the regular classroom along with the appropriate support services. It is usually viewed as a full-time placement (Roach, 1995).

The inclusion movement is driven by a respect for diversity and by a strong commitment to the rights of students with disabilities to be part of the schools and communities they share with nondisabled students (McLaughlin & Warren, 1994). Those who support inclusion argue that inclusion not only contributes to the academic and social progress of children with disabilities, but also creates greater tolerance on the part of students who are not disabled and better prepares them to live in an integrated society.

? *Ask Yourself*

Inclusion Checklist

The following checklist for practicing (or prospective) teachers reflects an inclusion philosophy. The more "yes" answers, the more positive toward responsible inclusion is the respondent.

1. Are you (would you be) willing to have age-appropriate students with disabilities in your class?

2. Do (would) you modify your curriculum, instructional methods, and materials to meet the diverse needs of students in your class?

3. Are you (would you be) open to suggestions and modifications in your teaching and classroom management?

4. Are you (would you be) willing to share your teaching responsibilities with other professionals?

5. Do you expect disabled students to be as successful in meeting their own goals as nondisabled students are in meeting theirs?

6. Do (would) you call on students with disabilities as much as you call on other students in your class?

7. Do (would) you use heterogeneous grouping?

8. Do (would) you use peer tutoring?

9. Do (would) you use adaptive technology and customized software?

10. Have you attended training sessions about responsible inclusion?

Source: Lombardi, T. P. (1994). *Responsible inclusion of students with disabilities.* Bloomington, IN: Phi Delta Kappa Educational Foundation.

As a result of the inclusion movement, inclusion has become the norm, not the exception, for students with disabilities, and for the first time these students are spending more of their time in a regular classroom than in any other school setting. However, the inclusion movement has generated some concern over the extent to which students are being integrated without the support necessary to make the transition successful. Many educators and parents are also concerned that inclusion is being used to save money at the expense of providing needed services to students with disabilities, and that it may have a detrimental effect on the learning of nondisabled students.

To assess your support for the concept of inclusion, complete the checklist above.

How prepared are you for having a student with a severe physical disability mainstreamed into your class-room?

Promoting Gender Equity

Despite the gains that have been made since the 1972 passage of Title IX prohibiting *sex discrimination* in education, females still confront a number of barriers to achieving equal educational opportunity. Numerous studies—perhaps the most recognized being those of the American Association of University Women (AAUW)—have documented these barriers and the various forms of sexism encountered by females in the schools. The AAUW (1991) report, *Shortchanging Girls, Shortchanging America,* documented the results of a survey of 3,000 school children and described the dramatic loss of self-esteem among adolescent girls and linked it to their experiences in schools. Not surprisingly, since self-esteem affects aspirations, the study also found that as girls mature, they become less confident in their academic abilities and express more limited career aspirations. The report also found that teachers initiate more communication with males than females; praise males more often for the intellectual content and quality of their work and praise girls more often for neatness and form; and that when teachers criticize boys, they often suggest it is because boys are not trying hard enough, but when they criticize girls there is no suggestion that effort would improve the results.

The second AAUW report, *How Schools Shortchange Girls* (1992), represented a comprehensive compilation of more than 1,300 research studies on the experience of girls in schools. The research reviewed documented differential treatment of girls across a number of dimensions in the classroom and the curriculum, and that this differential treatment is consistent across grades, subjects, districts, and the gender or experience of the teacher. Among the findings were that boys receive more teacher attention of all kinds, that girls remain underrepresented in curriculum materials, and that the instructional activities that are used appeal more to boys' interests than girls' and are presented in formats in which boys excel. A third AAUW report, *Hostile Hallways* (1993) found that approximately 75% of female students are victims of *student-to-student sexual harassment.*

In their fourth report, *Growing Smart: What's Working for Girls in School* (1995), data compiled by AAUW researchers confirmed that schools contribute to subtle (and not-so-subtle) forms of *sex bias.* For example, it was more common than not to find teachers still giving girls less attention, praise, feedback, and detailed instruction than they gave to boys. In addition, girls were often channeled away from subjects that lead to high-paying jobs such as science and technology (DeFazio, 1996). These results confirm similar findings of sex bias in the classroom reported by Sadker and Sadker (1994) in their book, *Failing at Fairness: How America's Schools Cheat Girls.*

The latest AAUW research reports, *Girls in the Middle: Working to Succeed in School* (1996), *Separated by Sex: A Critical Look at Single-Sex Education for Girls* (1998), and *Gender Gaps: Where Schools Still Fail Our Children* (1998), suggest that public schools continue to fail to meet the needs of girls and recommend strategies and educational reform that can help foster a more equitable academic climate.

Another recent study, *The Girl's Report: What We Know and Need to Know About Growing Up Female* (1998), commissioned by the National Council for Research on Women and written by Lynn Phillips, is based on a comprehensive compilation of more than 200 research studies on the experiences of female adolescents. The report presents a mixed picture that shows that while most

Give personal examples of differential treatment of both males and females in the elementary school, high school, and college/university level.

girls are competent and resilient, they face numerous social, economic, psychological, and health barriers and are often denied the chance to fulfill their potential. On the one hand, girls continue to perform well in reading and language arts and their mathematics achievement almost matches that of boys. On the other hand, they have unequal access to sports programs, are almost twice as likely to be depressed as boys, are more likely to consider and attempt suicide, and are often the victims of violence in and out of the school (Phillips, 1998).

In contrast, *The Metropolitan Life Survey of the American Teacher: Examining Gender Issues in Public Schools* (1997), presents a more optimistic picture of the experiences of girls at school.

- Girls are no less interested and motivated than boys to get a good education. Girls are as likely as boys to aim high, to expect to have opportunities to succeed in life equal to those of boys as a group, and are perceived to be as competitive in school as boys. In addition, they are just as confident as boys that they will achieve their future goals.
- Compared to boys, girls appear more definite about going to college and more focused on education as one of their top goals. They are also more likely than boys to receive encouragement from their teachers and friends and to feel their teachers are good role models for them to learn from and emulate.
- Minority girls are the most optimistic of all groups. They are the group most likely to choose getting a good education as their top goal. They are also more likely to hold the view that they will have the same opportunities to succeed in life as others. Furthermore, they are more likely than other groups to pride themselves on their ability to succeed.
- Teachers consistently express a more optimistic view of girls than of boys. They believe girls are more likely than boys to graduate from college, to set higher goals for themselves and to exhibit more inner confidence in their ability to pursue their goals. (Louis Harris and Associates, 1997, pp. 3–4)

Strategies for Achieving Gender Equity

The attainment of *gender equity* requires the elimination of various forms of *sexism*. Sexism can be exhibited in a number of ways. Lee, Marks, and Byrd, (1994) examined sexism in single-sex and coeducational classrooms and found the following examples:

- *Gender reinforcement* (perpetuation of conventional behaviors typically associated with being male or female, such as telling girls to "be ladylike").
- *Embedded discrimination* (sexism in language, historical records, literary texts, or visual displays, such as bulletin boards, reflecting quotations from only male authors).
- *Sex role stereotyping* (characterization of individuals according to traditional social roles or definitions such as depicting women only as nurses, teachers, or homemakers).
- *Gender domination* (prerogatives exercised by males in relation to females, such as allowing boys to dominate computer use).
- *Explicit sexuality* (treatment of females as sex objects).

Advocates of single-sex education purport that all-girl schools or classrooms can remedy sexism.

Lee, Mark, and Byrd, (1994) have proposed the following six proactive strategies to achieve gender equity:

- *Amelioration of inequitable practices* (encouraging girls to take calculus and other advanced mathematics courses to correct limited access in the past).
- *Resistance to sex-role stereotyping* (inviting males and females in nontraditional roles as guest speakers).
- *Compensatory recognition of female achievement* (monitoring the curriculum to ensure that women authors and women scientists are represented).
- *Sensitization to gender issues* (providing for the discussion of sexism, gender stratification, and the feminization of poverty).
- *Gender-neutral affirmation of skills and abilities* (praising a female student for her good problem-solving ability and reinforcing a male student for his sensitivity to others).
- *Positive instructional strategies* (making a concerted effort to reinforce gender equity in the classroom and playground).

Another proactive strategy that has been suggested to remedy the problem of sexism is single-sex education. Advocates of single-sex education purport that in an all-girls school or classroom, female students can achieve the type of educational opportunity that has traditionally been missing in some coed classrooms. They point to the success of graduates of women's colleges to support their argument (Spring, 1998). Others argue that while there are no cognitive reasons to uphold sex-segregated education, there may be social reasons (Kleinfeld & Yerian, 1995).

Professional Reflections

"Take off the blinders that hide the fact that our student populations are changing. Remove the compulsion to teach the same way we were taught. Keep the standards, maintain the same knowledge base, 'teach the basics,'—but deliver it in a different way."

Peggy J. Woods, Teacher of the Year, Arizona

"To succeed as a teacher . . . make sure that students feel successful in learning . . . Make them buy into the idea of learning . . . never make the assumption that all students come to class eager for academics . . . Find a way to make students care, to make them want to learn."

Shawn Eric DeNight, Teacher of the Year, Florida

Still another proactive strategy that has been proposed to remedy a deficiency that many female students experience (i.e., poor spatial reasoning) is to offer remedial instruction to improve girls' spatial reasoning skills. Proponents of this recommendation point to the multitude of remedial programs in the schools that have benefited males (i.e., special programs for learning disabilities, in particular reading, programs for attention deficit disorder, etc.). Virtually no remedial programs in the schools address the particular learning needs of females (Halpern, 1997).

The attainment of gender equity should be one of the primary goals of all educational institutions. As our citizens attempt to remain competitive in the twenty-first century world markets, Plato's words of 2,500 years ago seem remarkably relevant: "Nothing can be more absurd than the practice . . . of men and women not following the same pursuits with all of their strength and with one mind, for thus the state . . . is reduced to a half " (Laws, VII, 805).

Summary

Desegregation is one of many strategies for realizing equality of educational opportunity. It is also a strategy based on constitutionally guaranteed protections. Educating children with disabilities and language minority students, and ensuring gender equity, are other strategies similarly based. Although the financial support afforded these programs is not guaranteed, unless the Supreme Court reverses current law and decisions, their existence is. Other strategies—compensatory education and the education of Native Americans and Alaska Natives—are solely creations of statute and rely entirely on state and federal statutes for their existence.

The presence of each of these strategies in the American educational system has served to expand not only the educational opportunities of the targeted populations, but of all students. It is largely through the efforts of those asserting their rights under the constitutionally based programs that the rights of all students have been expanded. The success of our educational system and, indeed, our economic and social structure depends on the full participation of all children. This chapter focused attention on strategies for increasing equality of educational opportunity. The next chapter turns to strategies directed at specific populations of "at-risk" youth.

Key Terms

Bilingual education
Cognitive styles
Compensatory education
Desegregation
Ebonics
English as a Second Language (ESL)
Gender Equity
Inclusion
Individualized education program (IEP)
Learning disability

Least restrictive environment
Magnet schools
Mainstreaming
Multicultural education
Sex bias
Sex discrimination
Sexism
Sex role stereotyping
Student-to-student sexual harassment
"white flight"

Discussion Questions

1. Have you ever personally experienced sexism, sex role stereotyping, or sex discrimination in either an academic or work-related situation? Explain.

2. Today, many youth feel alienated from the school and find little identification and meaning in the educational process. As a teacher, what can you do to reach these students?

3. What do you see as the major obstacles to racial and ethnic integration in the schools?

4. Discuss ways in which the Individuals With Disabilities Education Act has benefited all children.

5. What economic benefits can the nation hope to gain from significantly increased funding of compensatory education?

6. Describe the bilingual education program in a school district with which you are familiar. What evidence exists that it has improved the academic performance of its participants? Is it viewed as helping or hindering progress toward racial or ethnic integration?

7. Compare the treatment of males and females in the schools with their treatment in other institutions.

8. How do the missions of bilingual education, special education, and gender equity in education complement each other?

Internet Resources

1. **www.cal.org**

   This is the home page for Center for Applied Linguistics, a nonprofit organization dedicated to applied research about language and culture in the classroom. It provides information about bilingual education, dialects (Ebonics), immersion education, immigrant education, and English as a Second Language (ESL).

2. **www.ced.sped.org**

   This is the site for the Council for Exceptional Children (CEC), one of the largest international organizations dedicated to helping improve educational outcomes for individuals with exceptionalities, students with disabilities, and/or the gifted.

3. **www.aauw.org**

   This is the home page for the American Association of University Women (AAUW), an organization devoted to the pursuit of gender equity. For the past few years the AAUW has published numerous reports on the current status of Title IX, gender equity resources for K–12 teachers, and lessons learned about what type of educational strategies work for females.

4. **nces.ed.gov**

   The National Center for Education Statistics (NCES) is the primary federal agency for collecting and analyzing data relative to education in the United States and other nations. The Website is a storehouse of valuable information on the National Assessment of Educational Progress (NAEP) data by race, ethnicity, and gender, and online discussion about educational topics such as women in mathematics and science, the social context of education, educational progress of minorities, and the indicators of school crime and safety.

5. **yahoo.com/society_and_culture**

   This search engine provides a vast amount of online information on such topics as culture and groups, disabilities, families, gender, Civil Rights, diversity, minorities, poverty, and race relations.

6. **mdac.educ.ksu.edu**

   The Midwest Desegregation Assistance Center is a federal organization funded by the U.S. Department of Education. It provides technical assistance, professional development, and dissemination of information on race equity, gender equity, and national origin equity to public school districts.

7. **php.indiana.edu/~aisri**

   The American Indian Studies Research Institute at Indiana University is an interdisciplinary center providing access to American Indian-related research products and links.

References

American Association of University Women (AAUW). (1991). *Shortchanging girls, shortchanging America.* Washington, DC: AAUW Educational Foundation.

American Association of University Women (AAUW). (1992). *How schools shortchange girls: A study of major findings on girls and education.* Washington, DC: AAUW Educational Foundation and the National Education Association.

American Association of University Women (AAUW). (1993). *Hostile hallways: The AAUW survey on sexual harassment in America's schools.* Washington, DC: AAUW Educational Foundation.

American Association of University Women (AAUW). (1995). *Growing smart: What's working for girls in school.* Washington, DC: AAUW Educational Foundation.

American Association of University Women (AAUW). (1996). *Girls in the middle: Working to succeed in school.* Washington, DC: AAUW Educational Foundation.

American Association of University Women (AAUW). (1998). *Separated by sex: A critical look at single-sex education for girls.* Washington, DC: AAUW Educational Foundation.

American Association of University Women (AAUW). (1998). *Gender gaps: Where schools still fail our children.* Washington, DC: AAUW Educational Foundation.

Banks, J. A. (1997). Approaches to Multicultural curriculum reform. In J.A. Banks, & C. A. Banks (Eds.), Multicultural issues and perspectives. Boston: Allyn and Bacon.

Banks, J. A. (1993). *Multicultural education: Development, dimensions, and challenges.* Phi Delta Kappan, *1,* 22–28.

Banks, J. A., & Banks, C. A. (Eds.). (1995). *Handbook of research on multicultural education.* New York: Macmillan.

Beck, L. G., Kratzer, C., & Isken, J. (1997). Caring for transient students in one urban elementary school. *Journal for Just and Caring Education, 3*(3), 343–369.

Bell, D., Roach, P., & Sheets, G. (1994). The nation's invisible families: Living in the stream. *Rural Educator, 15*(3), 27–30.

Bilingual education. (1998). *Education week on the web.* http://www.edweek.org/contex/topics/biling.htm.

Board of Education of Oklahoma City Schools v. Dowell, 111 S.Ct. 630 (1991).

Board of Education v. Rowley, 458 U.S. 175 (1982).

Brown v. Board of Education, 347 U.S. 483 (1954).

Charleston, G. M. (1994). Toward true native education: A treaty of 1992. *Journal of American Indian Education, 33*(2), 12–56.

Crandall, M. (1998). Two-way talk. *The American School Board Journal, 185*(1), 23–25.

Cushner, K., McClelland, A., & Safford, P. (1996). *Human diversity in education.* New York: McGraw-Hill.

DeFazio, J. (1996). What do girls want from their schools? *The School Adminstrator, 53*(2), 44.

Durbin, J. (1989). *Assessment of the vertical equity of state supported compensatory education programs in Arizona.* Unpublished doctoral dissertation, Arizona State University.

Freeman v. Pitts, 112 S.Ct. 1430 (1992).

Gay, G. (1995). Curriculum theory and multicultural education. In J. A. Banks, & C.A. Banks (Eds.), *Handbook of research on multicultural education* (pp. 25–43). New York: Macmillan.

Glazer, N. (1997). *We are all multiculturalists now.* Cambridge, MA: Harvard University Press.

Gollnick, D. M., & Chinn, P. C. (1998). *Multicultural education in a pluralistic society.* Columbis, OH: Merrill.

Green v. County School Board of New Kent County, 391 U.S. 430 (1968).

Halpern, D. F. (1997). Sex differences in intelligence: Implications for education. *American Psychologist, 52*(10), 1091–1102.

Hardy, L. (1997, December). Main events: Debates over control of education took center stage this year. *Education Vital Signs,* A4–A8.

Louis Harris and Associates. (1997). *The Metropolitan Life survey of the American Teacher: Examining gender issues in public schools.* New York: Author.

Howe, K. (1997). *Understanding equal educational opportunity.* New York: Teachers College Press.

Indian Nations at Risk Task Force. (1991). *Indian nations at risk: An educational strategy for action.* Final report. Washington, DC: U.S. Department of Education.

Keyes v. School District No. 1, 413 U.S. 189 (1973).

Kindler, A. L. (1995). *Education of migrant children in the United States.* Washington, DC: National Clearinghouse for Bilingual Education at George Washington University.

Kleinfeld, J. S., & Yerian, S. (Eds.). (1995). *Gender tales: Tensions in the schools.* New York: St. Martin's Press.

Kunen, J. S. (1996). The end of integration. *Time, 147*(18), 39–45.

Lau v. Nichols, 414 U.S. 563 (1974).

Lee, V. E., Marks, H. M., & Byrd, T. (1998). Sexism in single-sex and coeducational independent secondary school classrooms. *Sociology of Education, 67*(2), 92–120.

Levine, D. U., & Levine, R. (1996). *Society and education.* Boston: Allyn and Bacon.

Martin, P. (1994). *Migrant farmworkers and their children.* Charleston, WV: ERIC Clearinghouse on Rural Education and Small Schools (ED 376 997).

McCarthy, M. M., Cambron-McCabe, N. H., & Thomas, S. T. (1998). *Public school law* (4th ed.). Boston: Allyn and Bacon.

McLaughlin, M. J., & Warren, S. H. (1994). The costs of inclusion. *The School Administrator, 51*(10), 8–19.

McNergney, R., & Herbert, J. (1998). *Foundations of education.* Boston: Allyn and Bacon.

Menand, L. (1997). The return of pragmatism. *American Heritage, 48*(6), 48–63.

Mills v. Board of Education of the District of Columbia, 348 F. Supp. 866 D.D.C. (1972).

Missouri v. Jenkins, 115 S.Ct. 2038 (1995).

Orfield, G. (1997b). Toward an integrated future. In G. Orfield & S. E. Eaton and the Harvard Project on School Desegregation, *Dismantling Desegregation* (pp. 331–351). New York: The New Press.

Orfield, G. (1997a). Turning back to segregation. In G. Orfield & S. E. Eaton and the Harvard Project on School Desegregation, *Dismantling Desegregation* (pp. 1–22). New York: The New Press.

Pennsylvania Association of Retarded Citizens v. Commonwealth of Pennsylvania, 343 R. Supp. 279 (E. D. Pa. 1972).

Phillips, L. (1998). *The girl's report: What we know and need to know about growing up female.* Washington, DC: The National Council for Research on Women. http://www.ncrw.org/research/grptpres.htm.

Portner, R. (1998). The case against bilingual education. *The Atlantic Monthly, 281*(5), 29–30, 38–39, 42–43.

Reyhner, J. (1994). *American Indian/Alaska Native education.* Bloomington, IN: Phi Delta Kappa Foundation.

Roach, V. (1995). Supporting inclusion: Beyond the rhetoric. *Phi Delta Kappan, 77*(4), 295–299.

Sadker, M., & Sadker, D. (1994). *Failing at fairness: How America's schools cheat girls.* New York: Charles Scribner's Sons.

Salend, S. J. (1990). A migrant education guide for special educators. *Teaching Exceptional Children, 22*(2), 18–21.

Salend, S. J. (1998). *Effective mainstreaming: Creating inclusive classrooms.* Columbus, OH: Merrill.

Schwartz, W. (1996). *Immigrants and their educational attainment: Some facts and findings.* New York: ERIC Clearinghouse on Urban Education. (ERIC Document Reproduction Service No. ED 402398).

Sevilla, J. (1992). Bilingual education: The last 25 years. In P. Anthony & S. L. Jacobson (Eds.), *Helping at-risk students: What are the educational and financial costs?* (pp. 38–63). Newbury Park, CA: Corwin Press.

Spring, J. (1998). *American education.* Boston: McGraw-Hill.

Stein, C. B., Jr. (1986). *Sink or swim: The politics of bilingual education.* New York: Praeger.

St. Germaine, R. (1995a). BIA schools complete first step of reform effort. *Journal of American Indian Education, 35,* 30–38.

St. Germaine, R. (1995b). Bureau schools adopt Goals 2000. *Journal of American Indian Education, 35,* 39–43.

Swann v. Charlotte-Mecklenburg Board of Education, 402 U.S. 1 (1971).

Thompson, D. C., Wood, R. C., & Honeyman, D. S. (1994). *Fiscal leadership for schools: Concepts and practices.* New York: Longman.

Trotter, A. (1992). Harvest of dreams. *American School Board Journal, 179*(8), 14–18.

U.S. Department of Education, National Center for Education Statistics. (1997). *Characteristics of American Indian and Alaskan Native education*. Washington DC:http://nces.ed.gov/pubs97/9745.html.

U.S. Department of Education, National Center for Education Statistics. (1998). *Condition of education*. Washington, DC: U.S. Government Printing Office.

Velazquez, L. C. (1994/95). Addressing migrant farmworkers' perceptions of school-ing, learning, and education. *Rural Educator, 16*(2), 32–36.

Webb, L. D., & Metha, A. (1996). Suicide among American Indian youth: The role of the schools in prevention. *Journal of American Indian Education, 56,* 22–32.

White House Conference on Indian Education. (1992). *The final report of the White House Conference on Indian Education: Executive Summary*. Washington, DC: White House Conference on Indian Education.

Chapter 10

Child abuse casts a shadow the length of a lifetime.

Herbert Ward, 1985

Students at Risk

> *It was twilight when Tom Wright finished packing the last box in his apartment. The movers had already taken the furniture. All that remained were a few boxes. As Tom lifted one of the boxes, an old photograph fell to the floor. He picked it up and smiled as he recognized his eighth grade graduating class.*
>
> *Twelve years had passed since that photo was taken. It seemed more like an eternity. He studied the photo for a long time. He immediately identified one of his best boyhood friends. Whatever happened to Jake Nash? He and Jake began kindergarten together and were like brothers for the entire eight years of elementary school. The last time he saw Jake was the summer after the photo was taken. Tom went on to Springview High School, but Jake moved away. It was so sudden, Tom remembered. He and Jake had planned for high school*
>
> *together. But that summer Jake's life was turned upside down. Jake's mother and father divorced and shortly afterward his younger sister, Karen, attempted suicide. In August Jake, his mother, and his sister moved to Michigan to be near his grandparents. He and Tom promised that they would see each other often. But that never happened. They exchanged a few letters and phone calls for a year or so, then grew apart. Tom was horrified and shocked when he later learned from Jake's former neighbor that Jake had dropped out of high school in his senior year and had been indicted on drug trafficking charges on his twenty-first birthday.*
>
> *What, if any, clues indicated that Jake was at risk for dropping out of school? For substance abuse? For suicide?*

Jake is typical of millions of youth in and out of our schools whose life experiences and situations place them at risk for educational, emotional, and physical problems. In this chapter at-risk children and youth are described. In addition, the methods of identifying a number of at-risk conditions and behaviors are suggested, and prevention and intervention strategies that are used successfully in the schools are presented. The following objectives should guide you in your study of at-risk populations:

- Discuss the relationship between risk, resiliency, and protective factors.
- Identify the predictors of being at risk.
- Describe the conditions or behaviors associated with substance abuse.
- Discuss prevention and intervention strategies aimed at reducing the occurrence of substance use and abuse among youth.
- Identify the suicidal child or adolescent.
- Review strategies for suicide prevention and intervention.

- Explain the incidence and consequence of dropping out of school.
- Describe successful teen pregnancy prevention and intervention programs.
- Suggest reasons why certain adolescents are at high risk for AIDS and STDs
- Name the common signs or indicators of sexual abuse.
- Describe the extent of the problem of violence in the schools.
- Explain why gay, lesbian, and bisexual youth are at risk for a variety of self-destructive behaviors.

At-Risk Children and Youth

A variety of terms are used to describe children and adolescents who are in need of special treatment or special services. Often, they are referred to as being *at risk*. The main characteristic of this group of youngsters is that they are already achieving below grade level or are likely to experience educational problems in the future. The term *at risk* is also used to describe children and youth who are already experiencing or are likely to experience physical and mental health problems.

Children and adolescents can be at risk for a variety of reasons. A child whose parents are in the process of finalizing a divorce and who is failing in school is definitely at risk. So is a seven-year-old whose older sister just committed suicide, or a preschooler whose mother is an alcoholic and whose father has been cited for sexually abusing his teenage daughter. All of these youngsters are at risk for academic underachievement, social maladjustment, and possible mental health problems.

Identifying the At-Risk Student

Early identification is the key to developing and implementing effective educational programs for at-risk students. Among the most prominent behaviors or factors that identify the at-risk student are underachievement; retention in grade; social maladjustment; discipline problems; dropping out of school; low parental support; physical problems; using and abusing drugs or alcohol; engaging in premature, unprotected sexual activity; being a victim or perpetrator of violence; and contemplating or attempting suicide. Other researchers have reported additional risk factors: being born to, or raised by, a mentally ill parent; suffering from the loss of a significant other; having experienced prenatal trauma or poor health status at birth; being from a poor family; and living in an abject environment such as being homeless (Gersten & Shamis, 1988; Jessor, 1993).

The research also indicates that a disproportionate number of ethnic/minority children, in particular African American, Hispanic, and Native American children; non-English-speaking children; children of single-parent families; and gay, lesbian, and bisexual youth, are represented among the at-risk population. Certain individuals in these groups have a high incidence of at-risk behavior, including low achievement, dropping out of school, teen pregnancy, and suicide.

Risk, Resiliency, and Protective Factors

Which protective factors might have contributed to your resiliency and success.

During the past decade a number of researchers focused their attention on at-risk youth who have been able to succeed despite their overwhelming hardships, obstacles, and major life events. They discovered that these youngsters were resilient and had developed the necessary coping mechanisms and characteristics for success. Furthermore, they found that the absence of a risk factor is often associated with the presence of a *protective factor* that accounts for a positive outcome or a lower than expected incidence of maladaptive behavior or illness (Pellegrini, 1990). The protective factors that appear to be associated with *resiliency* include:

- *Personal attributes.* Personal attributes include positive temperament, above average intelligence, social competence such as academic achievement, participation and competence in activities both in and out of school, high self-esteem, self-discipline, self-efficacy (individual's perception of competence in various situations), and problem-solving skills (Garmezy, 1985; Rae-Grant, Thomas, Offord, & Boyle, 1989).
- *Family factors.* Family factors include supportive and nurturing parents, family stability and cohesiveness, adequate income, appropriate rules, and high expectations for children (Rak & Patterson, 1996).

The model suggests several points where adults—in particular, school personnel—can facilitate and influence resiliency. McMillan and Reed (1994) suggest teachers should identify achievement reference points, aid students in establishing long-range goals, and continually relate success to effort and ability. Teachers, administrators, and counselors need to be trained to provide classroom environments that stress high academic achievement while building positive self-esteem. Such an environment should emphasize time-on-task, student interaction and success, and positive reinforcement for desired classroom behaviors. Figure 10.1 describes several factors that influence resilient at-risk students.

The remainder of this chapter describes a number of at-risk conditions or behaviors and discusses how they might be identified. In addition, for each at-risk condition or behavior, prevention and intervention strategies are explored. The conditions or behaviors to be discussed include drug and alcohol abuse; suicide; dropping out of school; teenage pregnancy; AIDS and other sexually transmitted diseases; child abuse, including sexual abuse and neglect; and violence. The conditions that place gay, lesbian, and bisexual youth at risk for a variety of self-destructive behaviors are also discussed.

Figure 10.1: Conceptual Model of Factors Influencing Resilient At-Risk Students

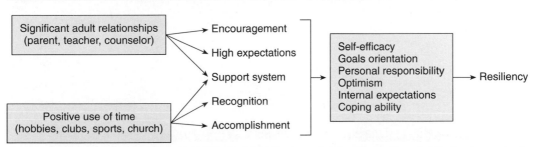

Source: McMillan, J. H., & Reed, D. F. (1994). At-risk students and resiliency: Factors contributing to academic success. *Clearing House, 67,* 140. Reprinted with permission of the Helen Dwight Reid Educational Foundation. Published by Heldref Publications, 1319 Eighteenth St., N.W., Washington, DC 20036-1802. Copyright 1994.

Tobacco, Drug, and Alcohol Use and Abuse

In spite of the health risks associated with tobacco, its use among U.S. adolescents in grades 9–12 increased by one third between 1991 and 1997 (from 27% to 36%). As the data in Table 10.1 indicate, use of tobacco products is highest among white students. Rates for minorities, while lower than those for whites, have been increasing at a rate faster than those for whites, reversing a declining trend that began in the early 1980s. Cigarette smoking is especially on the rise among younger teens. In 1997, 33% of ninth graders had smoked cigarettes during the past month and another 10% reported using smokeless tobacco (Centers for Disease Control, 1998).

Early prevention efforts are a key to combating this serious problem that affects adolescents of all cultures and socioeconomic classes.

Table 10.1: Percentage of High School Students Who Use Cigarettes, Alcohol, Cocaine, and Marijuana by Sex, Race/Ethnicity, and Grade—United States, 1997

	Cigarette Use			Alcohol Use			Marijuana Use			Cocaine Use		
Category	Female	Male	Total	Female	Male	Total	Female	Male	Total	Female	Male	Total
					Race/Ethnicity							
White	39.9	39.6	**39.7**	51.6	56.0	**54.0**	21.2	28.0	**25.0**	2.3	3.7	**3.1**
Black	17.4	28.2	**22.7**	34.9	39.2	**36.9**	21.4	35.6	**28.2**	0.2	1.2	**0.7**
Hispanic	32.3	35.5	**34.0**	50.7	56.7	**53.9**	23.3	33.1	**28.6**	5.3	6.9	**6.2**
					Grade							
9	32.6	34.2	**33.4**	43.7	44.7	**44.2**	20.1	26.8	**23.6**	3.6	4.1	**3.9**
10	35.1	35.6	**35.3**	45.3	48.7	**47.2**	20.9	28.5	**25.0**	1.5	3.6	**2.6**
11	31.7	40.7	**36.6**	47.8	57.8	**53.2**	22.9	34.7	**29.3**	2.2	3.7	**3.1**
12	38.8	40.0	**39.6**	53.7	60.2	**57.3**	21.9	30.3	**26.6**	2.2	4.5	**3.5**
Total	**34.7**	**37.7**	**36.4**	**47.8**	**53.3**	**50.8**	**21.4**	**30.2**	**26.2**	**2.4**	**4.0**	**3.3**

Source: Centers for Disease Control and Prevention. (1998). Youth risk behavior surveillance—United States, 1997. *MMWR,* 47 (No. 55-3).

Alcohol use among youth and adolescents is a major problem facing the schools and the larger society. In a national survey by the Centers for Disease Control and Prevention (CDC), an alarming 47% of 10th graders and 57% of 12th graders reporting having drunk one or more drinks in the past month. Perhaps more disturbing, 30% of 10th graders and 39% of 12th graders reported episodic heaving drinking (consuming five or more drinks in a row on one or more occasions in the past month) (CDC, 1998).

Equally disturbing is the fact that over one half of high school students reported that they had used an illicit drug by the time they reached their senior year. As disturbing as these data are, the real picture may be even more severe. Most of the research on youth substance use has been limited to students who remain in school. If dropouts were included in the studies, the magnitude of the problem would far exceed the current estimates (Eggert & Herting, 1991). Current patterns of drug use among American high school students are presented in Table 10.1.

The Effects of Drug and Alcohol Abuse

Drug and alcohol abuse are related to a variety of at-risk behaviors including unintentional injury (automobile accidents), school failure, unintended pregnancy, AIDS and other sexually transmitted diseases, violent and abusive behavior, and other psychological and social problems (National Institute on Drug Abuse, 1997c). On an individual level, drug and alcohol abuse interfere with cognitive development and academic achievement. On a societal level, neighborhoods near schools often become the target of drug dealers, many of whom are students themselves. Additionally, crimes of violence often are associated with substance abuse, particularly among teenage gang members. Research also suggests that teenage drug abuse is a contributing factor to personal, social, and occupational maladjustment in later young adulthood. For example, it has been found that habitual use of marijuana and hard drugs as a teen are predictive of later job instability, emotional turmoil, and early divorce. It has also been found that use of hard drugs (hypnotics, stimulants, cocaine, inhalants, and narcotics) as a teenager can contribute to deterioration in social relationships, increased loneliness, and suicidal ideation as an adult (Guy, Smith, & Bentler, 1994).

The prevention of drug use and abuse is not only a moral imperative, but it also represents a cost savings to society. Data from the National Institute on Drug Abuse (NIDA) (1997b), suggest that for every dollar spent on drug use prevention, communities can save four to five dollars in costs for drug abuse treatment and counseling. The research also suggests that youth who do not use illicit drugs, alcohol, and tobacco prior to the age of 18 are likely to avoid chemical-dependency problems over their lifetime (National Clearinghouse for Alcohol and Drug Information, 1998b).

Identifying Alcohol and Drug Use

Parents, teachers, counselors, and administrators are better prepared to provide early intervention when they recognize the difference between normal childhood and adolescent behavior and behavior that may indicate substance use or abuse. Psychological and interpersonal factors that place certain children and adolescents at risk for alcohol and drug use include low self-esteem, unassertive behavior, antisocial and aggressive behavior, lack of commitment to the school, and poor school achievement. The strongest risk predictors are attitudes toward drug use and association with peers. Family factors such as substance abuse by parents or siblings coupled with environmental factors such as poverty and violence make certain youngsters more vulnerable than others (U.S. Department of Education, 1993). Family victimization such as sexual molestation is also believed to be a contributing factor to drug and alcohol abuse (Watts & Ellis, 1993).

The differences between so-called normal behavior and behavior that may reflect substance use or abuse often are a matter of degree. For example, it is normal for a child or adolescent to spend time alone. However, it is usually not normal to exhibit sudden, almost complete withdrawal from family or peers. Overall, the best predictor of possible substance abuse is a pattern of changes, not any single behavioral change.

Prevention Strategies

Prevention strategies include those programs, activities, and services that help reduce the occurrence of substance use and abuse in children and adolescents. The Drug Free Schools and Communities Act (as amended) assists states in establishing new drug prevention programs or supplementing existing programs. With the assistance provided by federal funds under this act, a number of states have developed substance-abuse prevention programs and have provided training for educators. In addition, mental health agencies have collaborated with school districts to develop and implement substance-abuse prevention curricula that emphasize problem solving, life skills training, assertion training, peer resistance training, decision making, affective education, self-esteem building, and health-wellness. Research has demonstrated that successful substance-abuse prevention programs teach resistance skills while correcting erroneous perceptions about the prevalence and acceptability of drug use among peers (U.S. Department of Education, 1993).

A number of youth-oriented prevention initiatives have been introduced to reduce risk factors and strengthen protective factors that are associated with drug use. One such initiative is through legislation such as the Synar Amendment that requires states to develop laws that bar the distribution of tobacco products to minors. It emphasizes consistent enforcement, monitoring of retail outlets' compliance, and research regarding the amendment's effectiveness on rate of tobacco sales to youth, rate at which youth begin smoking, and amount of tobacco products used. States that fail to comply with the Synar Amendment risk losing a percentage of federal block grant funds allocated for substance abuse prevention and treatment programs (National Clearinghouse for Alcohol and Drug Information, 1998a).

Another possible means of reducing youth smoking is through policies restricting smoking in certain locations. Policies restricting smoking in public places and in schools have been found to be associated with fewer youth who smoke and lower average cigarette consumption by smokers.

Other examples of prevention strategies that target alcohol and drug abuse include the National Youth Anti-Drug Media Campaign, a multidimensional communications campaign that involves parents, mass media, the business community, and antidrug coalitions. The campaign's purpose is to counteract media messages and images designed to glamorize, legitimize, normalize, and condone drug use. More than four thousand community-based organizations are involved in combating and preventing the illegal use of drugs. (National Clearinghouse for Alcohol and Drug Information, 1998b).

Which substance abuse prevention programs are you familiar with in your school or school district? How successful have these programs been?

Drug use prevention has shifted from a simplistic approach to a more comprehensive approach that takes into consideration the multitude of factors that make children vulnerable to drug use. Regardless of the thrust of the prevention program, it is important that parental involvement be a component of the substance-abuse prevention curriculum.

Intervention Strategies

School-sponsored *intervention programs* are aimed at providing assistance to those children and adolescents who are already using or abusing drugs or alcohol. Among the more widely used intervention strategies are referral to mental health agencies and psychiatric out-patient treatment; peer counseling programs aimed at teens helping teens; school-based individual and group counseling; mental health consultation whereby community health agencies offer psychological services to school districts; and community practitioners, educators, and former substance abusers who monitor and treat children and teens who have drug and alcohol problems (Salzman & Salzman, 1989).

Chemical dependency has serious implications for the schools. Practically every teacher at all grade levels from middle school on will be confronted by a sizeable number of students who are engaging in regular use of drugs and/or alcohol. Beginning teachers need to become familiar with the educational prevention programs offered by their district and their school. They also need to become acquainted with the treatment programs available in the community for children, adolescents, and their families. The school counselor, social worker, psychologist, or school nurse will be an invaluable resource to the beginning teacher who may feel unprepared to deal with this particular type of at-risk behavior.

Suicide

What suicide messages are there in rock music? To what extent do they influence children and adolescents?

Suicide is the third leading cause of death among youth 15 to 24 years of age; only accidents and homicides rank higher. For the 15- to 19-year-old, suicide ranks as the second leading cause of death. In the last 40 years, the suicide rate for 15- to 19-year-olds has quadrupled (Anderson, Kochanek, & Murphy, 1997). Annually there are approximately 14 suicides for every 100,000 adolescents. Whereas suicides account for 1.4% of all deaths in the United States annually, they comprise 14% of all deaths among 15- to 24-year-olds. Since 1980, the suicide rate for 15- to 19-year-olds has increased 28% and for 10- to 14-year-olds, 120%. On self-report surveys, 14% of all adolescents report that they have attempted suicide. This means that within a typical high school classroom, it is probable that three students (one boy and two girls) have attempted suicide during the past year. Since many suicide attempts go undetected or unreported, these data probably do not reflect the true magnitude of the problem. Approximately 60% of high school youth report having suicidal ideation (American Association of Suicidology, 1997).

Males are more apt to *complete* or commit suicide while females are more likely to *attempt* suicide. African American males (ages 15–19) have shown the largest increase in suicide rates among adolescents (165% increase since 1980). Native American youth are disproportionately overrepresented among suicidal youth. Gay, lesbian, and bisexual youth have also been found to be disproportionately overrepresented among suicidal youth (Edwards, 1997). Regardless of gender, race, or ethnicity, firearms are the most commonly selected suicide method among youth and account for two of every three completed suicides. (American Association of Suicidology, 1997).

What recommendations would you suggest as a means of restricting access to firearms by children and adolescents?

Identifying the Suicidal Child or Adolescent

Many of the symptoms of suicidal thoughts or actions are similar to the symptoms of depression. Parents, teachers, and counselors should be aware of the warning signs or indications that a child or adolescent may be suicidal. Table 10.2

Table 10.2: Indicators of Childhood or Adolescent Suicide

Psychosocial	Familial	Psychiatric	Situational
1. Poor self-esteem and feelings of inadequacy 2. Hypersensitivity and suggestibility 3. Perfectionism 4. Sudden change in social behavior 5. Academic deterioration 6. Underachievement and learning disabilities	1. Disintegrating family relationships 2. Economic difficulties and family stresses 3. Child and adolescent abuse 4. Ambivalence concerning dependence v. independence 5. Running away 6. Family history of suicide	1. Prior suicide attempt 2. Verbalization of suicide or talk of self-harm 3. Preoccupation with death 4. Repeated suicide ideation 5. Daredevil or self-abusive behavior 6. Mental illness such as delusions or hallucinations in schizophrenia 7. Overwhelming sense of guilt 8. Obsessional self-doubt 9. Phobic anxiety 10. Clinical depression 11. Substance abuse	1. Stressful life events 2. Firearms in the home 3. Exposure to suicide

Source: Adapted from Metha, A., & Dunham, H. J. (1988). Behavioral indicators. In Capuzzi, D., & Golden., L. *Preventing adolescent suicide* (pp. 49–86). Muncie, IN: Accelerated Development Inc. Reprinted with permission.

presents some of the major indicators of childhood or adolescent suicidal behavior. Of these indicators, a previous suicide attempt, a family history of suicide, major depression, substance abuse, stressful life events, sexual identity issues, and accessibility to firearms deserve mention because of their particular importance in predicting self-destructive behavior. In addition, children who tend to be preoccupied with death or who know a teenager who has attempted or completed suicide have also been found to be at risk for suicidal behavior.

The research suggests that substance abuse is linked closely to suicide and that drugs or alcohol may temper the fear of death (Garrison, McKeown, Valois, & Vincent, 1993). Similarly, the child or adolescent who experiences a significant number of stressful life events such as death of a parent, separation or divorce of parents, family turmoil or conflict, school failure, sexual or physical assault, or interpersonal conflict with a boyfriend or girlfriend may also be at risk, particularly if those stressors occur in combination with alcohol and drug use and the availability of firearms.

Signs of Depression

A strong relationship exists between major depression and suicide. The clinically depressed child or youth is likely to exhibit signs of hopelessness, a change in eating and sleeping habits, withdrawal from family and friends, substance abuse, persistent boredom, loss of interest in pleasurable activities, neglect of personal appearance, and frequent complaints about physical symptoms. In early adolescence, the depression is often masked by acting out or delinquent behavior. Older adolescents are more apt to resort to violence, drugs, alcohol, and sex rather than face their emotional pain.

All children and youth may experience some depression with its highs and lows, but the youngster who experiences a major depression is suffering from a serious mood disorder, with persistent symptoms that typically last for at least two or more weeks. These youngsters are most at risk for suicide during the period when the depression appears to subside. During this period they are most vulnerable because it is the time when they have the psychic energy to become acutely suicidal. Most children and youth who are suicidal will exhibit a number of verbal and nonverbal warning signs and clues. It behooves every parent and educator to be sensitive to any one of the signs or clues, since it may be the youngster's last desperate plea for understanding or help. If one or more of these signs is observed, the parent or educator should talk to the child about his or her concerns and seek professional help if those concerns or problems persist.

Prevention Strategies

While all school personnel should be trained in identifying suicidal youth, students also need training. The majority of suicide prevention programs for students emphasize a curriculum on decision making, problem solving, and general life skills training. Many of these prevention programs also include information about recognizing the signs and symptoms of depression and suicidal behavior and how to access help from the school and community (Kalafat & Elias, 1994). Such programs are often incorporated into the health curriculum. Some educators as well as some parents have concerns that exposure to such programs may have a negative effect on students who are already at risk for suicide, in particular students who may have made an earlier suicide attempt. There is no evidence in the research literature that exposure to such a curriculum has caused a suicide or suicide attempt. However, the research has recommended that for students who are already at risk for suicide, a prevention curriculum is not appropriate. Instead, such students need to be identified and immediately referred for treatment intervention and follow-up (Eggert, Thompson, Randell, & McCauley, 1995; Shaffer, Garland, Underwood, & Whittle, 1987).

The impetus for developing a suicide prevention and intervention program in the schools has also come from the courts. The courts in several cases ruled that school personnel can be held liable in the suicide death of a student for their failure to inform parents and the appropriate school officials of the student's suicide potential (Bjorklun, 1996). In the Controversial Issue on page 327 are arguments for and against the school's taking an active role in suicide prevention.

Controversial Issues

The School's Role in Suicide Prevention

The extent to which the schools should assume a role in suicide prevention is debated by educators, school boards, and parents. The reasons often given in favor of or against suicide prevention in the school are:

Arguments For

1. Suicide prevention programs can help students cope with the various stresses they experience in their school and personal lives.

2. Suicide prevention programs usually include a curriculum that teaches coping, problem-solving, and survival skills that are valuable life skills for all students.

3. Suicide prevention programs help teachers and students recognize the warning signs of the suicidal child or adolescent, enabling them to make a timely referral if necessary.

4. Suicide prevention programs offer training in peer counseling, which has been an invaluable strategy for identifying the suicidal child or adolescent.

5. The alarming statistics concerning suicide among children and adolescents require that schools take a proactive step in addressing the problem.

Arguments Against

1. School counselors, teachers, and other professional staff do not have the time or training to deal effectively with the suicidal youngster.

2. There is little research evidence that confirms that suicide prevention programs lessen suicidal behavior.

3. The liability of the school is unclear concerning suicide prevention programming.

4. Recent research on imitative and modeling behavior raises serious questions about offering suicide prevention programs in the schools, i.e., teaching about suicide will trigger a suicide, since children and youth are so suggestible.

What is your view of suicide prevention in the school? What types of program(s) exist in a school with which you are familiar?

Intervention Strategies

The most common suicide intervention program is the *crisis intervention team* approach. The crisis intervention team is composed of teachers, counselors, administrators, social workers, school nurses, and school psychologists trained to respond to a variety of crisis situations, including suicide. The members of the team meet regularly and participate in training workshops directed at crisis management. In regard to suicide, the role of crisis team members is to network with each other and identify the youngster who appears to be depressed, overwhelmed by stress, or displaying a *suicide gesture* or *suicide threat*. Problems are usually solved at the team level; however, the crisis team may refer a student to a community mental health agency or hospital for emergency care. Other intervention strategies include individual and group counseling, peer counseling, and referral to a suicide hotline for students who are in crisis when school is not in session. School personnel should not handle the suicidal person alone, they should notify parents if they suspect that a child or adolescent is suicidal, and they should hold the student in protective custody until the parents arrive.

Postvention Strategies

In addition to prevention and intervention strategies, a *postvention program* also is important for the school. The purpose of a postvention program is to help the school return to normal in the aftermath of a suicide and to prevent *cluster suicides*. Grief counseling, support groups, guidelines for interacting with the media, and follow-up care are examples of postvention strategies facilitated by the crisis intervention team.

Schools are in the best position to respond to suicidal concerns if they have prevention, intervention, and postvention policies and procedures in place. Such policies and procedures not only help ensure the safety of all students but also help to protect the staff and school from litigation. The worst time to plan for a crisis such as suicide or attempted suicide is during a crisis.

Today, no school is immune to the loss of a child or adolescent by suicide. Parents and teachers are often the last to recognize that the child or adolescent is at risk for taking his or her own life. The peer group will probably be the first to know that the child is in need of immediate help. Teachers need to be able to establish a trusting relationship with students so that they will come forward to seek the help they need to respond to a suicidal friend. Many beginning teachers feel very inadequate and fearful of handling a suicidal student for fear that their actions may precipitate an actual suicide or suicide attempt. The truth is that talking about suicidal tendencies will not exacerbate a suicide or suicide attempt. Most youngsters at risk for suicide are relieved to be able to articulate their fears and concerns to an adult who will listen. The worst response is no response.

Dropping Out of School

The majority of states and school districts define the *dropout* as a student who leaves school for any reason before graduation or completion of a program of study without transferring to another school or institution. Although the dropout rate has steadily declined since *A Nation at Risk,* the dropout rate in the United States continues to be a major problem. In 1996, 11% of young adults ages 15 through 24 years had dropped out of school. Dropout rates were approximately equal for males and females. However, the dropout rate for Hispanic youth (29%) was more than four times that of whites (7%), and twice that of African American youth (13%). Moreover, youth from families in the bottom 20% of all family incomes were eight times as likely to drop out of school as those in the top 20% of family incomes (U.S. Department of Education, 1997). Figure 10.2 depicts the trend in dropout rates for persons aged 16–24 over the period 1980–1996.

Figure 10.2: Percent of 16- to 24-Year-olds Who are Dropouts, by Race/Ethnicity: 1980–96

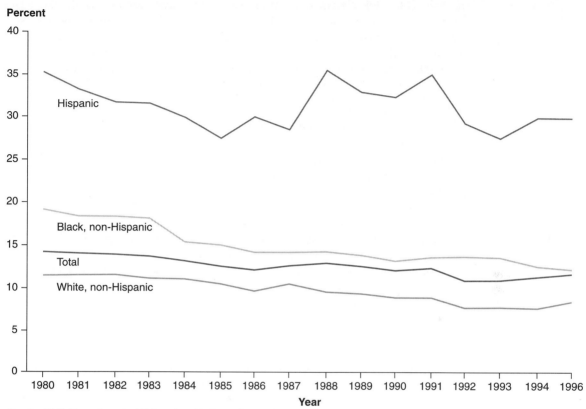

Source: U.S. Department of Education, National Center for Education Statistics. *Dropout rates in the United States: 1996.* Washington, DC: U.S. Department of Education.

Economic Consequences

The dropout problem has significant economic consequences for this nation. The projected lifetime earnings of a high school graduate is $260,000 more than a dropout. It has been estimated that billions of dollars in local, state, and federal tax revenues are lost each year from the reduced earnings of dropouts. If the costs associated with unemployment, welfare, and other social services provided to dropouts and their families are considered, the combined economic costs to society are significant. According to the U.S. Census, nearly half the heads of households on welfare were dropouts, and half of the U.S. prison population is composed of high school dropouts (Foster, 1996).

Identifying the Potential Dropout

Research has identified a number of factors to be associated with dropping out of school. Among those most commonly mentioned are poor academic performance;

having been retained in at least one grade; lack of basic skills, in particular, reading; problems at home; a history of school transfers and family moves; having a parent or older sibling who is a dropout; dislike for school; low socioeconomic status; lack of parental involvement in the school; limited English proficiency; and low self-esteem. In addition, dropouts are often individuals who have undiagnosed learning disabilities or emotional problems and who abuse drugs or alcohol. For female adolescents, pregnancy is the principal reason for dropping out of school.

Prevention Strategies

As with other at-risk behaviors, early identification of the potential dropout is critical. The earlier the identification, the more likely the dropout efforts will be successful. And, since the research indicates that the effects of dropping out are more devastating for females than males in terms of academic and economic implications, prevention programs should be especially sensitive to the needs of females. Unfortunately, some current school practices often contribute to the problem rather than prevent it. For example, while research has suggested that tracking or ability grouping, remediation, and sometimes suspension do not necessarily benefit students, the practices still continue (Quinn, 1991).

Why might dropping out of school have a more deleterious effect on females than on males?

Fortunately, a number of strategies have been found to be effective in preventing dropping out. They include placing at-risk students in alternative programs that differ from the traditional high school setting; individualized counseling; reducing the student–teacher ratio; more emphasis on vocational education, job skills training, and practical work experience; peer tutoring; English as a Second Language instruction; prenatal/pregnancy counseling; and day care (Quinn, 1991). In addition, since punitive school and classroom environments have been cited as important contributors to a lack of attendance, schools can combat dropping out by making every effort to make the school climate more positive (Mayer, et al., 1993).

Schools can also work to prevent dropping out by promoting so-called "engagement behaviors." Research has found that positive engagement behaviors such as coming to class and school on time, being prepared for and participating in class work, expending the effort needed to complete academic assignments, and not being disruptive in class can counteract negative influences and curb dropping out of school (American Psychological Association, 1997).

Intervention Strategies

Do you advocate the "dropouts don't drive law" as an intervention strategy? Why or Why not?

Of all the intervention strategies, mandatory suspension of a driver's license is probably the most controversial. Known as the "dropouts don't drive law," this strategy is intended to keep teens in school by revoking their driver's licenses if they drop out of school, are truant, or if they are not progressing toward graduation. Sixteen states have passed legislation that links driving privileges to school attendance (National Conference on State Legislatures, 1998).

All teachers have an obligation to try to prevent students from dropping out of school. School districts must improve their efforts at identifying the potential dropout and must find effective methods of working with the families of students who are at risk, in particular, non-English-speaking families.

Teenage Pregnancy

According to the National Center for Health Statistics nearly a half-million American teens give birth annually. In 1996, one out of every 20 girls aged 15 to 19 years gave birth, a decline of 12% from five years earlier (Meckler, 1998). Yet, despite the overall decrease, teen birthrates among minorities remain more than double the rate for white teens. In 1996, approximately 4% of non-Hispanic white teens had given birth compared to 11% of Hispanics and 9% of African American teenage girls. While the birthrate still remains high, the birthrate for African Americans is the lowest in recorded history (Meckler, 1998; Portner, 1998b).

There are several myths surrounding the teenage pregnancy problem. One myth is that teen pregnancy is an adolescent problem. According to a detailed two-year study of American teens by the Alan Guttmacher Institute, only 25% of the fathers of babies born to mothers age 17 and younger are also in their teens. In nearly one third of births to 15-year-olds, the father was at least six years older than the mother (Vobejda, 1994).

A second myth is that American adolescents who have had sexual intercourse have done so voluntarily. In truth, the majority have reported that they had done so involuntarily. Nearly 75% of young women who had sexual intercourse before the

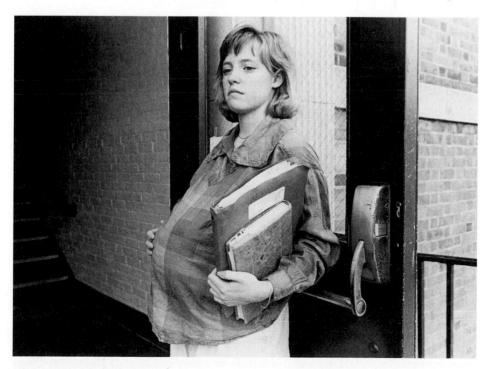

Pregnant teens are at high risk for dropping out of school.

age of 14 report that at some point they had been forced to have sex against their will (Vobejda, 1994). And it has been suggested that at least 5% of all births to teenage mothers are the result of rape (Boyer & Fine, 1992).

Consequences of Adolescent Pregnancy

Adolescent parenthood has profound implications for health care and social services, for poverty and crime, for family relationships, and for the institution of the school. Since so many teenage parents often lack sufficient health care insurance and the necessary funds for the delivery, they must resort to outside subsidies to meet their financial commitments. In addition, they often lack proper prenatal care, one of the major prerequisites for a healthy delivery. This, coupled with inadequate diet, has resulted in a significant number of premature deliveries with accompanying low birth weight. Unfortunately, premature infants often are at risk for a host of serious health problems at a later date. The mortality rate for teenage mothers also is higher than for any age group. Because teen mothers experience so many health problems before and after the birth, they place heavy demands on the accompanying social service agencies, which accentuates the costs for the teen, her family, and society. Many of the children of teen mothers become at risk educationally and psychologically and often are overrepresented in classes for the learning disabled and emotionally disturbed (Bonjean & Rittenmeyer, 1987). These "children of children" often become adolescent parents themselves, repeating the cycle and worsening the problem.

Teenage pregnancy has several major economic consequences. Many pregnant adolescents fail to complete the eighth grade or do not graduate from high school. As a result, their earning potential is seriously hampered and many become caught in the web of being poor, on welfare, and out of the labor force (Haveman & Wolfe, 1994). And, there is strong evidence that the transfer of poverty from the mother to her offspring may create a continued cycle of poverty for generations to come (Caldas, 1994).

Prevention Strategies

Because school district policies and practices vary widely regarding teen pregnancy prevention programs, it is important that teachers be aware of the policies in their district regarding this issue. The major aim of pregnancy prevention programs is to keep teens from conceiving. The majority of prevention programs in the schools encourage adolescents to abstain from sexual activity, others provide birth control information, and a few provide contraceptive devices. Typical school-based prevention strategies include a health curriculum that focuses on how to resist peer pressure and early sexual involvement, information about contraception, basic information about health and human sexuality, self-esteem enhancement, family planning, decision making, and communication skills. More recently, school-based health clinics have provided contraceptive counseling and related health services to adolescents in addition to providing counseling, physical examinations, immunization, and referrals to other community agencies. Pregnancy prevention programs that target the needs of Hispanic/Latino adolescent girls—in particular, Mexican American teens—are especially needed. The decline in birthrates can be attributed, at least in part, to school-based pregnancy prevention programs, the resultant decrease in sexual activity among youth, and increased use of contraceptives (Portner, 1998a).

In addition to the school, approximately 30% of communities across the country sponsor some type of teen pregnancy prevention program (U.S. Department of Health and Human Services, 1998a). Some examples of community-based programs include: the Children's Aid Society's program aimed at assisting youth in avoiding unintended pregnancy and making responsible sexual decisions; Life Options, a program that seeks to prevent early pregnancy and encourages school achievement, sponsored by the Association of Junior Leagues and the American Association of School Administrators; and the Postponing Sexual Involvement Curriculum developed by the Emory University School of Medicine and Grady Memorial Hospital Teen Services Program, aimed at providing youth with basic factual information and decision-making skills relative to reproductive health (U.S. Department of Health and Human Services, 1998b).

To what extent should the school bear the cost and responsibility for providing a pregnancy prevention and intervention program?

Intervention Strategies

The major goals of most intervention strategies are to provide prenatal care, parenting skills, and vocational and personal counseling to adolescent mothers in an effort to reduce the cycle of repeated pregnancies and welfare dependency. Parent resource centers, which are usually coordinated with school health clinics, have proven to be a promising intervention strategy. Such parent resource centers provide pregnant and parenting students with a wide range of health, educational, and social services including day-care nurseries. The students who are referred to such resource centers typically work with a case management team that includes a social worker, teacher, and nurse who interact with the students' parents and closely monitor the academic progress, attendance, and health of each girl and her baby.

One community-based program, Second Chance Homes, is targeted toward providing teen parents with the necessary skills for parenting, child development, family budgeting, health and nutrition, and the avoidance of repeat pregnancies (U.S. Department of Health and Human Services, 1998b). Public policy at the national level has also been directed at encouraging teenage parents to continue their education. A revision of federal welfare legislation passed in 1996 made a condition of eligibility for public assistance the requirement that unmarried minor parents stay in school and live at home or in an adult-supervised setting.

AIDS and Other Sexually Transmitted Diseases

Acquired immune deficiency syndrome (AIDS) is a serious disease caused by *human immunodeficiency virus (HIV),* which destroys the immune system and leaves the body susceptible to infection. Two diseases identified in AIDS patients are *Pneumocystis carinii* pneumonia, an infection of the lungs, and a rare form of cancer, Kaposi's sarcoma, both of which can cause death.

According to the Centers for Disease Control and Prevention, in 1996, for the first time in the history of the HIV/AIDS epidemic, the number of Americans diagnosed with AIDS declined. The positive impact of combination drug therapies, including the use of protease inhibitors, has helped to delay the progression from HIV infection to AIDS as well as AIDS deaths. However, of great concern is the fact that while the incidence of new diagnoses of AIDS has declined among white gay and bisexual males, the incidence among heterosexuals continues to rise by 11% for males and 7% for females (CDC, 1997a).

Also of concern is the fact that the number of 13- to 19-year-olds with AIDS more than quadrupled between 1990 (530 cases) and 1996 (2,754 cases). By the end of 1996, nearly 8,000 youth (ages 15 to 24) died of AIDS. Since the time from infection to symptoms may take as long as 8 to 12 years, the adolescent may be infected with HIV for a decade or longer before the AIDS symptoms appear (NIDA, 1997a).

The rates of other *sexually transmitted diseases (STDs),* are also high among adolescents. In fact, the highest rate of gonorrhea is found among 15- to 19-year-old females. The prevalence of *chlamydia infections,* and *human papillomavirus infections* (HPV) are also highest among adolescents. Teens who are particularly high risk for STDs are male homosexuals, sexually active heterosexuals, and intravenous drug users (CDC, 1997b).

Youth are particularly vulnerable for AIDS and other STDs because of their at-risk sexual behavior. The Centers for Disease Control and Prevention's (1998) Youth Risk Behavior Survey of high school students reported that 48% had sexual intercourse during their lifetime, and 35% were currently sexually active (having had intercourse during the preceding three months). African American students were significantly more likely than Hispanic or white adolescents to report using condoms as a protective measure. Fifty-seven percent of teens reported using a condom during their last sexual encounter. The significant number of sexually active teens increases their risk of exposure to the AIDS virus and other sexually transmitted diseases. Research has demonstrated that there is a strong relationship between drug and alcohol use and sexual activity. It has also shown that teens who engage in sex after using drugs or drinking alcohol are less apt to use condoms for protection (NIDA, 1997a).

Identifying AIDS

The following are some of the more common early symptoms of the HIV infection: fevers or night sweats; low energy, generalized weakness, or extreme fatigue; swollen lymph nodes; persistent diarrhea; thrush; and weight loss. Other symptoms include persistent cough; depression and/or anxiety; lack of concentration or forgetfulness; and headache, nausea, and vomiting. For females, one of the major symptoms is chronic pelvic inflammation.

Prevention Strategies

Since AIDS and other sexually transmitted diseases have far-reaching implications for our society, the schools have an obligation to offer prevention or educational strategies that address this problem. However, there is considerable controversy among school officials, health educators, and governmental officials regarding the most effective approach to AIDS and STDs education. While a number of vocal community and religious groups have argued that sexual abstinence should be the only prevention method emphasized, a number of school and health officials concerned about the spread of AIDS and STDs among youth have suggested that the educational curriculum should also include information on such topics as condom use and restricting sex to monogamous relationships.

Popham (1993) recommends that the following elements be included in all AIDS and STDs prevention curriculum: "(1) basic knowledge about how HIV and STDs are transmitted and how to reduce the risk of becoming infected; (2) interpersonal skills to be able to avoid, refuse, escape, or protect oneself in a risk situation, such as a situation where there is a likelihood of unprotected sexual intercourse or needle sharing by intravenous drug users; and, (3) suggestions for motivation to use the HIV and STDs relevant knowledge and skills" (p. 561).

Most communities do support AIDS and STDs education in the schools. However, a number of communities have requested that parental consent be obtained before any student participates in such an educational program.

To what extent should the schools be responsible for dispensing condoms to prevent AIDS and STDs?

Intervention Strategies

Over a decade ago, the Centers for Disease Control and Prevention issued guidelines to assist schools in developing policies and procedures for individuals with AIDS in the school environment. These guidelines recommend that students who have developed AIDS or are infected with the AIDS virus should not be excluded from school attendance except under certain circumstances (see discussion in Chapter 12). Nonjudgmental counseling for students with AIDS or STDs is one of the most important intervention strategies. In addition, schools must recognize the importance of confidentiality in working with adolescents who have developed AIDS, are infected with the AIDS virus, or have some form of sexually transmitted disease.

Teachers cannot ignore the reality of AIDS or other STDs. With the increasing number of adolescents who are sexually active, most teachers will probably encounter a student with the AIDS virus at some time in their careers and surely will encounter students with STDs.

Child Abuse and Neglect

The Child Abuse Prevention and Treatment Act (CAPTA), as amended and reauthorized in 1996 (Public Law 104–235, Section 111; 42 U.S.C. 510g), defines *child abuse* and *child neglect* as at a minimum, any recent act or failure to act resulting in imminent risk of serious harm, death, serious physical or emotional harm, sexual abuse, or exploitation of a child (under the age of 18, unless the child protection law of the State in which the child resides specifies a younger age for cases not involving sexual abuse) by a parent or caretaker (including any employee of a residential facility or staff person providing out-of-home care) who is responsible for the child's welfare. (p. 1)

Sexual abuse is further defined as

employment, use, persuasion, inducement, enticement, or coercion of any child to engage in, or assist any other person to engage in, any sexually explicit conduct or any simulation of such conduct for the purpose of producing any visual depiction of such conduct; or rape, and in cases of caretaker or interfamilial relationships, statutory rape, molestation, prostitution, or other form of sexual exploitation for children, or incest with children. (National Clearinghouse on Child Abuse and Neglect Information, 1998, p. 1)

Definitions of child abuse and neglect are also determined by state civil or criminal statutes.

The major types of child abuse include physical abuse, child neglect, sexual abuse, and emotional abuse. These can occur separately or in some form of combination. *Emotional abuse* is almost always present with other forms of maltreatment. In 1995, more than one million children were found to be victims of child abuse and neglect. More than half of the victims were seven years of age or younger with approximately 26% younger than four years old. Both boys (47%) and girls (52%) suffer from child abuse or neglect. Child fatalities constitute the most drastic form of child abuse and neglect. According to the child protective services, approximately 996 children died as a result of abuse or neglect in 1995 (U.S. Department of Health and Human Services, 1997a).

Physical Abuse

According to the National Committee for the Prevention of Child Abuse, approximately 25% of the child abuse cases each year are the result of *physical abuse* (U. S. Department of Health and Human Services, 1997b). Punching, beating, kicking, biting, burning, and shaking are examples of harming a child by physical abuse. Of those who have been physically abused, one out of eight reports having sustained an injury. And, in 1 out of 100 cases, the injury was severe enough to warrant medical attention. More girls than boys are physically abused, and most of the assaults are committed by acquaintances (72%) and juveniles (42%) ("Youths Report Cases of Abuse," 1994).

Child Neglect

Failure to provide for a child's needs is considered to be a form of *child neglect.* Such neglect can include *physical neglect, educational neglect,* and *emotional neglect.* Abandonment, expulsion from home, refusal to allow a runaway to return home, inadequate supervision, and the refusal to provide health care in a timely manner characterize a form of physical neglect. Failure to attend to a child's special educational needs, failure to enroll a child in school, and the tolerance of chronic truancy all constitute a form of educational neglect. Last, emotional neglect includes the failure to provide for the psychological well-being of the child, being inattentive to a child's needs for affection, and parental permission to use and abuse drugs or alcohol (National Clearinghouse on Child Abuse and Neglect Information, 1998). Neglect accounts for more than half of the cases of child abuse in the United States (U.S. Department of Health and Human Services, 1997b).

Sexual Abuse

Sexual abuse includes fondling a child's genitals, intercourse, incest, rape, sodomy, exhibitionism, sexual contact with a minor under the age of 16, and exploitation through prostitution or pornography. Sexual abuse involves coercion and deceit and is considered to be the most underreported form of child maltreatment due to its secrecy and code of silence. Approximately 13% of the cases of child abuse reported are due to sexual abuse (U.S. Department of Health and Human Services, 1997b).

One half of all rape victims are children and adolescents between the ages of 10 and 19, with 50% of those under the age of 16 (Greydanus & Shearin, 1990). Children and adolescents with disabilities are also at risk for both physical and sexual abuse (American Psychological Association, 1993).

Emotional Abuse

Emotional abuse includes such nonphysical abusive behaviors as blaming, disparaging, or rejecting the child; habitual scapegoating, belittling, and intimidating; treating siblings unequally; deliberately enforcing isolation; and continually withholding security and affection. Emotional abuse includes those acts or omissions by either parents or caregivers that have caused or could cause serious behavioral, cognitive, emotional, or mental disorders. Emotional abuse is almost always present when physical abuse, child neglect, or sexual abuse are identified (National Clearinghouse on Child Abuse and Neglect Information, 1998).

Identifying Child Abuse

Some of the common signs or indicators of child physical abuse include unexplained injuries, fractures, bruises, bite marks, and welts. A pattern of accidents may also be a common indicator. Children who have been subject to any form of abuse often exhibit a variety of behavior changes including aggressive or withdrawn behavior, neglected appearance, attention-seeking behavior, anxiety, or fear. They may engage in self-destructive behaviors and exhibit low self-esteem, depression, and severe emotional problems. They may be socially isolated, have poor relationships with parents, repeatedly run away, and have a history of frequent tardiness or absence from school. Some of the physical and behavioral indicators of possible neglect and abuse that teachers should be on the alert for are listed in Table 10.3.

Table 10.3: Physical and Behavioral Indicators of Possible Neglect and Abuse

Physical Indicators	*Behavioral Indicators*
Emotional Abuse and Neglect	
• Height and weight significantly below age level • Inappropriate clothing for weather • Scaly skin • Poor hygiene, lice, body odor. • Child left unsupervised or abandoned • Lack of a safe and sanitary shelter • Unattended medical or dental needs • Developmental lags • Habit disorders	• Begging or stealing food • Constant fatigue • Poor school attendance • Chronic hunger • Dull, apathetic appearance • Running away from home • Child reports that no one cares/looks after him/her • Sudden onset of behavioral extremes (conduct problems, depression)
Physical Abuse	
• Frequent injuries such as cuts, bruises, or burns • Wearing long sleeves in warm weather • Pain despite lack of evident injury • Inability to perform fine motor skills because of injured hands • Difficulty walking or sitting	• Poor school attendance • Refusing to change clothes for physical education • Finding reasons to stay at school and not go home • Frequent complaints of harsh treatments by parents • Fear of adults
Sexual Abuse	
• Bedwetting or soiling • Stained or bloody underclothing • Venereal disease • Blood or purulent discharge from genital or anal area • Difficulty walking or sitting	• Excessive fears, clinging • Unusual, sophisticated sexual behavior/knowledge • Sudden onset of behavioral extremes • Poor school attendance • Finding reasons to stay at school and not go home

Source: Cates, D. L., Markell, M. A., & Bettenhausen, S. (1995). At risk for abuse: A teacher's guide for recognizing and reporting child neglect and abuse. *Preventing School Failure,* 39 (2), 6.

What are the procedures for reporting child abuse in your state?

As discussed in Chapter 12, state child abuse statutes require that child abuse be reported by school counselors, school psychologists, social workers, teachers, nurses, or administrators to the local child protective agency, department of welfare, or law enforcement agency. It is important that teachers be familiar with the applicable state statues and the local school district's policies on reporting child abuse and neglect.

Prevention Strategies

A number of school-based prevention programs have been introduced to address a variety of forms of child abuse, in particular, sexual abuse. The major objectives of these programs are to increase the child's and adolescent's awareness of the risk of sexual abuse or exploitation, and to identify youngsters who are in abusive situations. The key elements of such prevention programs typically include (1) an awareness of body parts and how to distinguish between "good touch," "bad touch," and "confusing touch"; (2) the development of assertiveness or refusal skills; and (3) a discussion of how and where to obtain help (Minard, 1993). Many school districts have incorporated the prevention program content into the health education curriculum in order to keep it outside the controversial sex education domain. Curriculum units on life skills such as assertiveness training, coping with stress, decision making, problem solving, and locating community resources are also helpful in providing youngsters with the tools to address sexual abuse.

The use of humor and entertainment have also been used with all grade levels to transmit information about sexual abuse through theater performances, art, role playing, play therapy, puppets, coloring books, *bibliotherapy,* and so forth. Bibliotherapy includes the use of selected reading materials as a therapeutic prevention technique. Obtaining parental permission to participate in such a program is recommended.

Since child abuse is prevalent in all socioeconomic classes and ethnic and racial groups, it is likely that all teachers will be confronted with this problem at some point during their teaching careers. When this happens, it is important to remember not only one's legal obligation but one's obligation to the students. Although these are normally delicate and emotionally charged situations, avoidance is not the appropriate response. It is always better to err on the side of the child's welfare.

Intervention Strategies

The school can take a proactive role in supporting the child or adolescent who has been victimized by abuse. The teacher's attitude is critical. He or she is in a unique position to create a classroom environment that is safe, nurturing, and responsive to the needs of the abused youngster. The teacher can help an abused child set healthy boundaries and know that he or she will be respected. An important part of setting healthy boundaries is confidentiality. If a student chooses to confide in classmates and teachers, the information must be handled with utmost care to protect the child. Teachers need to set reasonable goals, but they also need to provide the support necessary for youngsters to feel confident and successful. Since abused children often feel powerless to control their environment, teachers can help them gain back a personal sense of control in a positive manner. And, since abused children have little self-esteem, a caring and sensitive teacher can help them learn that they have many strengths and that they are valued and accepted. To facilitate a sense of belonging, teachers should make a conscious effort to include these children in classroom activities. A structured and consistent daily schedule with clear expectations can also be an important first step in assisting the child or adolescent to regain a sense of control over his or her environment (Bear, Schenk, & Buckner, 1993; Lowenthal, 1996).

School Violence

Every day over 100,000 children bring a weapon to school, and every day 40 are killed or wounded at school with these weapons. One fifth of students are afraid to use school bathrooms. And, students aren't the only ones who are afraid at school. Every year more than 6,000 teachers are threatened by students (Lumsden, 1998).

A recent study of school violence found that over one half of the public elementary, middle, and secondary schools surveyed had experienced one or more incidents of crime/violence that was serious enough to report to law enforcement officials, 37% reported from one to five crimes, and 20% reported six or more crimes. Moreover, 10% had experienced one or more "serious" violent crimes such as murder, rape, suicide, physical attack or fight with a weapon, or robbery. The results of the study also showed a strong relationship between crime and the size, location, and minority enrollment of the school. Crime was more likely in larger schools, city schools (as opposed to town or rural schools), and schools

Crime and violence continue to plague public elementary, middle, and secondary schools.

with higher proportions of minority enrollments (U.S. Department of Education, 1998b).

Much of the violence in schools is gang related. There are estimated to be 23,000 youth gangs in the United States with 665,000 members (Wendel, 1997). Between 1989 and 1995 the number of gangs rose from 25% to 41% in central cities, from 14% to 26% in suburbs, and from 8% to 20% in nonmetropolitan areas (Sniffen, 1998). While youth gangs vary in composition and activities, most form an allegiance to a common purpose. The majority of gangs include juvenile and young adults who associate together for violent and criminal behavior. Asian, African American, Hispanic, white, interracial, white supremacist, or *skinhead* groups form gangs that range in size from a few members to thousands. Today it is not uncommon to find gang members as young as age seven or eight who are recruited to act as "drug or gun couriers." The majority of gang members are male; however, there has been an emergence of female gangs during the past decade.

Some youth gang activities are limited to wearing of so-called "gang attire" or "gang colors," "gang graffiti," minor fights, or acts of intimidation. However, a sizeable number of gang activities are associated with serious crimes such as gangbanging, drive-by shootings, aggravated assaults, and homicides (Kwok & Hermann, 1993). It is estimated that 80% to 90% of gang members have access to illegal weapons or firearms.

What gangs are active in your community? To what extent have they been associated with youth violence?

Prevention Strategies

The majority of public schools have initiated some type of formal school violence prevention and/or violence reduction program. Most of these programs attempt to reach students through a variety of in- and out-of-school activities, including teaching prosocial, problem-solving, conflict-resolution, and peer leadership and peer mediation skills; training in anger management, impulse control, self-esteem development, and stress management and reduction; instituting a peer mentoring program; offering drug and gang prevention programs; providing after-school activities; and providing incentives for good behavior, such as recognition and rewards for good school citizenship (Prothrow-Stith, 1994; Schwartz, 1998).

Other important components of a violence prevention program include: (1) a safe school environment and a positive school climate, where students, staff, and parents feel a sense of identity with the school; (2) strong leadership on the part of the principal; (3) a discipline code of conduct with clearly identified school rules and acceptable student behaviors; (4) ongoing staff development and in-service training; (5) increased surveillance of the school; (6) consistent student monitoring and discipline; (7) zero tolerance policies for various offenses (i.e., firearms, alcohol and drugs, violence); (8) community partnerships for violence prevention; (9) cultivating parental support; and (10) controlling campus access (Southeastern Regional Vision for Education & Florida Department of Education, 1996). Another prevention strategy increasing in use, in part due to federal funding under the Safe Schools Act, is placing law enforcement personnel, called school resource officers (SROs) on campus. Currently 6% of public

Figure 10.3: Early Warning Signs of Potentially Violent Youth

- Social withdrawal
- Excessive feelings of isolation and being alone
- Excessive feelings of rejection
- Being a victim of violence
- Feelings of being picked on and persecuted
- Low school interest and poor academic performance
- Expression of violence in writings and drawings
- Uncontrolled anger
- Patterns of impulsive and chronic hitting, intimidating, and bullying behaviors

- History of discipline problems
- Past history of violent and aggressive behavior
- Intolerance for differences and prejudicial attitudes
- Drug and alcohol use
- Affiliation with gangs
- Inappropriate access to, possession of, and use of firearms
- Serious threats of violence

Source: Dwyer, K., Osher, D., & Warger, C. (1998). *Early warning, timely response: A guide to safe schools.* Washington, DC: U.S. Department of Education.

schools have SROs or other law enforcement representatives on duty for 30 hours or more at the school (U.S. Department of Education, 1998b).

While having such prevention strategies as school resource officers and metal detectors on campus may be important, the most important action schools can take to prevent violence is to recognize the early warning signs that relate to violence and to get help for troubled youth. While it is not possible to predict violent behavior, research and experience have shown that for some youth and in some situations there are combinations of behaviors, emotions, and events that may lead to violence toward self or others. These "early warning signs" are presented in Figure 10.3. It is important to note that these warning signs be viewed as potential indicators, *not* predictors of violence. It would be inappropriate "and potentially harmful to use the early warning signs as a checklist against which to match individual children. Rather, the early warning signs are offered only as an aid in identifying and referring children who may need help" (Dwyer, Osher, & Warger, 1998, p. 8).

Intervention Strategies

While violence prevention programs can be effective in reducing the frequency and intensity of school violence, they cannot eliminate the problem. Some 5 to 10% of students will need more intense interventions to reduce their at-risk behaviors. These youth may require special education or mental health services, family service agencies, law enforcement, and the juvenile justice systems (Dwer, Osher, & Warger, 1998). Other services may include after-school activities, gang and drug prevention program components, and teaching of peer leadership and peer mediation skills (Prothrow-Stith, 1994).

Because most schools will experience some episode of violence, the violence prevention program should be linked to a crisis response plan, and the entire school staff, including full-time and part-time employees, should be trained in the procedures and responsibilities outlined in the plan. Such a plan will typically call for the establishment of a crisis response team and describe what to do both when a crisis occurs and in its aftermath. The purpose of such a team is to ensure the implementation of the plan and to minimize the effects of a crisis and prevent it from escalating. For example, members of a crisis team might be responsible for evacuating students to a safe area in the case of a violent act on campus, a bomb threat, or a natural disaster such as an earthquake; debriefing and leading a discussion or support group following the death or loss of one of the members of the school; and monitoring and supporting friends of a suicide or homicide victim (Poland, 1994).

The crisis response plan will necessarily involve community collaboration. Community collaboration is a key element for keeping situations from reaching the crisis stage and assisting students at risk of violent behavior. Coalitions between school personnel, law enforcement officials, juvenile justice authorities, family support systems, faith communities, hospital health officials, and business leaders can collectively reduce the incidents of violence in their schools and communities. Finally, it is important in responding to violence or threats of violence that schools look to federal, state, and local governments, not only to ensure that they are abiding by applicable laws and policies, but also as resources in violence prevention and intervention. Many state and local governments have developed crisis intervention manuals that are available to the local schools. Some offer training on school safety to school personnel.

At the national level, in response to the rising tide of school violence, in 1994 Congress passed the Gun Free Schools Act, which requires states, as a condition of receiving federal funding for elementary and secondary education, to put in place laws whereby students who bring guns to school are expelled for at least one year. All states are currently in compliance with the Gun Free Schools Act. As a result, in 1997 approximately 6,093 students were expelled for bringing firearms to school (Portner, 1998c).

Gay, Lesbian, and Bisexual Youth

It has been estimated that from 5 to 15% of teens are gay, lesbian, or bisexual (Walling, 1993). Gay, lesbian, and bisexual adolescents are at risk for a variety of problems that have been discussed in this chapter: alienation from family and peer group, violence, sexual abuse, school failure, sexually transmitted diseases, substance use and abuse, depression, and suicide. Studies indicate that 26% of gay and lesbian youth are forced to leave home because of their sexual orientation; 68% of gay teens and 83% of young lesbians use alcohol and other drugs on a regular basis; 41% of gay and lesbian youth experience violence from peers, family, or strangers; and 30% of youth suicides are completed by gay and lesbian youth (Edwards, 1997).

To be cast out of one's home; to be expelled from one's peer group; to be subjected to verbal, physical, and sexual abuse; or to question one's sexual identity can be traumatic emotional experiences for any individual. Yet, many gay, lesbian, and bisexual students must resort to confronting these issues alone. Unfortunately, in the two places where a child should feel safe and supported—the home and the school—gay and lesbian youth are routinely criticized (Anderson, 1997). In most school districts little is being done to address the concerns of gay, lesbian, or bisexual students. Some schools have published antiharassment policies to protect students; however, they have failed to enforce them. For example, in one case, *Nabozny v. Podlesny* (1996), a gay student had been subjected to years of taunts and threats at school that ultimately ended in violence. He was spat upon, urinated upon, subjected to a mock rape in a class of 20 students, and beaten and kicked until he had internal injuries. School administrators had repeatedly failed to act to stop the harassment, telling him he would expect such treatment if he was going to be gay and that "boys will be boys." The court found that the district had a responsibility to protect the student and had failed to do so. The district was required to pay almost one million dollars in damages.

In its *Guide to Sexual Harassment* discussed in Chapter 12, the Office of Civil Rights provided examples of anti-gay harassment that are prohibited by Title IX. These guidelines have significant implications for all schools since schools that fail to follow the guidelines in responding to this and other forms of sexual harassment are at risk for losing federal funding.

Improving the School Climate

Students respond to the fear, rejection, guilt, and alienation they feel by withdrawing from friends and family, abstaining or withdrawing from school, failing to concentrate, developing low self-esteem, and in the most serious cases, developing *major depression* or attempting suicide. Teachers and parents need to be alert to these signs and symptoms and take positive steps to ensure that all students feel safe and supported in school and are able to learn. Educators must address the larger, albeit sometimes difficult and controversial, issues of society (Gevelinger & Zimmerman, 1997).

Among the strategies that have been recommended to improve the school climate for gay, lesbian, and bisexual students are the following:

What strategies have been used in your school or school district to improve the school climate for gay, lesbian, and bisexual students?

- Staff development for school personnel should be provided, which includes a review of psychological and social research on homosexuality, encourages an examination of beliefs and attitudes toward homosexuality, and teaches staff how to help students that approach them with issues of sexual identity.
- Nondiscrimination policies that protect gay and lesbian employees and students from harassment, violence, and discrimination should be developed by the school district and should be included in student and employee handbooks; and, all other policies that deal with the health and welfare of students should be communicated to all those who are in contact with the students. And, since a policy that is not enforced is worthless, the policy should be enforced. When violations occur, teachers, counselors, and administrators should challenge anti-gay epithets and should speak out against any form of harassment (Anderson, 1994; Walling, 1993).

■ Issues of sexuality should be addressed in the health curriculum. In addition, the curriculum of all subjects should be an inclusive experience for all students. For example, sex equity could be discussed in a unit on civil rights in a social studies class and gay and lesbian writers could be highlighted in an English class (Anderson, 1997).

Intervention Strategies

School counselors are in a unique position to assist gay, lesbian, and bisexual students to cope with the psychological, social, and educational barriers they often face. They can also provide help for adolescents who are struggling with the confusion and fear associated with issues of adolescent sexuality. If a counselor has several self-identified homosexual students, he or she may wish to consider providing a support group for these youngsters (Robinson, 1994). However, before being referred to the group, a student should be required to meet with a trained staff member who can address more serious issues that might not be appropriate for a group setting (Gevelinger & Zimmerman, 1997). In addition, counselors, teachers, and administrators should be aware of the resources in the community that can be helpful to gay, lesbian, and bisexual youth. Among the resources that can be helpful include telephone hotlines and such organizations as Parents and Friends of Lesbians and Gays (P-FLAG) and Sex Information and Education Council of the United States (SIECUS).

While most school districts have not developed any unified strategy for dealing with the educational and emotional needs of gay and lesbian youth, there are many positive examples of those who have. One school district in Stratford, Connecticut, has taken great strides to ameliorate the educational opportunity for gay and lesbian students. Workshops and forums that address sexuality issues are provided by staff, school psychologists, nurses, and social workers who also provide support to students. Library resources and exhibits are inclusive of gay and lesbian materials as are many courses (Anderson, 1997). Similarly, the Archdiocese of St. Paul and Minneapolis formed a Study Group in Pastoral Care and Sexual Identity, which has been instrumental in providing training for

Professional Reflections

"Start with providing a fair, consistent, and safe environment. An effective classroom management plan is vital for establishing that type of ambiance. Next, a teacher must demonstrate *love in action.* This is accomplished by taking a personal interest in a student's life outside the classroom."

Kay A. Long, Teacher of the Year, Oklahoma

". . . When you become a teacher you become so much more. You become a child psychologist, a child advocate, activist, social worker, guidance counselor, advisor, confessor, builder of dreams, molder of futures, inventor, cheerleader, and educator."

T. Tracey Fallon, Teacher of the Year, New Jersey

administrators, teachers, and counselors; encouraging students to be tolerant and respectful of their gay and lesbian peers, while making sure they understand that behaviors that hurt others will not be tolerated; and encouraging the establishment of student support groups in each high school in the archdiocese (Gevelinger & Zimmerman, 1997). At the state level, several states publish resource guides on how to address homosexuality in school policies, services, and instruction. The Minnesota Department of Education's *Alone No More: Developing a School Support System for Gay, Lesbian, and Bisexual Youth* is one example. And, at least one state, Massachusetts, requires all teacher certification programs to include sensitivity training on homosexuality.

Summary

At-risk children and youth are a particular challenge for school personnel and mental health professionals. Because of their association with students, teachers and counselors play a vital role in identifying at-risk students. Prevention and intervention programs for a variety of at-risk behaviors have become the combined responsibility of schools, social service agencies, churches, parent groups, and law enforcement agencies. Although for each at-risk behavior a number of prevention and intervention strategies have been devised, growing evidence supports the primacy of early identification and treatment. Creating classrooms that foster resilience and strengthen protective factors is also most important. In Chapter 12 we will expand our discussion of the responsibilities of teachers. We will also consider their legal rights, as well as those of their students. But first we will explore the legal basis for public education and the legal issues surrounding the church-state relationship in education in Chapter 11.

Key Terms

Acquired immune deficiency syndrome (AIDS)

At risk

Bibliotherapy

Child abuse

Child neglect

Cluster suicides

Chlamydia infection

Crisis intervention team

Dropout

Emotional abuse

Human immunodeficiency virus (HIV)

Intervention programs

Major depression

Postvention programs

Prevention strategies

Protective factors

Resiliency

Sexual abuse

Sexually transmitted diseases (STDs)

Skinheads

Suicide gesture

Suicidal ideation

Suicide threat

Discussion Questions

1. If you were confronted with a suicidal child in your classroom, what steps might you take to ensure his or her safety? What type of information and experiences do prospective teachers need to better prepare them to work effectively with children who are at risk for suicidal behavior?

2. What role do schools play in promoting educational resilience? What specific resilience-promoting strategies might you use in your classroom?

3. How can the school help in combating teen pregnancy? AIDS? STDs? How comfortable would you be in discussing "safe sex" with your students?

4. How does peer pressure contribute to adolescent substance abuse and youth violence? How can teachers use the power of peer influence to combat these same problems?

5. How can the school and society more effectively address the problem of violence in the schools? Since the majority of youth die from homicide or suicide by gunshot wounds, what can and should be done to restrict the use of firearms by minors?

Internet Resources

1. **www.cdc.gov**
   The Website of the Centers for Disease Control and Prevention (CDC) provides a wealth of information including data and statistics on the health of adolescents with specific information on teen pregnancy, AIDS and other sexually transmitted diseases, risk behavior data, substance abuse, and suicide.

2. **www.nida.nih.gov**
   The Website of the National Institute on Drug Abuse (NIDA) provides up-to-date information on drug abuse as well as prevention research.

3. **www.childrendefense.org**
   The Children's Defense Fund is an excellent resource for information relative to the particular needs of poor, minority children and those with disabilities.

4. **www.urban.org**
   The Urban Institute, Washington, DC, provides profiles of pregnancy prevention programs that have successfully involved males.

5. **Eric-web.tc.columbia.edu/ administration/safety**
   The Website of the Eric Clearinghouse for Urban Education: School Safety includes a wide array of resources and links to school violence prevention.

6. **www.childabuse.org**
   The National Committee to Prevent Child Abuse (NCPA) makes available child abuse facts and statistics, as well as information on the prevention, intervention, and treatment of child abuse and neglect.

7. **www.ncrel.org**

North Central Regional Educational Laboratory (NCREL) provides easy to find, concise, and research-based information on topics such as at-risk children and youth, parent and family involvement, student diversity, resiliency, and safe and drug-free schools.

8. **www.pavnet.org**

Pavnet Online (Partners Against Violence Network) is a "vital library" of information on violence and youth-at-risk including programs, curricula, and technical information.

References

American Association of Suicidology. (1997). *Youth suicide fact sheet.* Washington, DC: Author.

American Psychological Association. (1993). *Violence & youth.* Washington, DC: Author.

American Psychological Association (1997, May). What leads high-risk students to success? *The APA Monitor, 8,* 11.

Anderson, J. (1994). School climate for gay and lesbian students and staff members. *Phi Delta Kappan, 76,* 151–154.

Anderson, J. D. (1997). Supporting the invisible minority. *Educational Leadership, 54*(7), 65–68.

Anderson, R. N., Kochanek, K. D., & Murphy, S. L. (1997). Advance report of final mortality statistics, 1995. *Monthly vital statistics report, 45* (11, Suppl. 2) (DHHS Publication No. (PHS) 97-1120). Hyattsville, MD: National Center for Health Statistics.

Bear, T., Schenk, S., & Buckner, L. (1993). Supporting victims of child abuse. *Educational Leadership, 50,* 42–47.

Bjorklun, E. (1996). School liability for student suicides. 106 *Education Law Reporter,* 21–32.

Bonjean, L. M., & Rittenmeyer, D. C. (1987). *Teenage parenthood: The school's response.* Bloomington, IN: Phi Delta Kappa Educational Foundation.

Boyer, D., & Fine, D. (1992). Sexual abuse as a factor in adolescent childbearing and child maltreatment. *Family Planning Perspectives, 24,* 4–11, 19.

Caldas, S. (1994). Teen pregnancy: Why it remains a social, economic, and educational problem in the U.S. *Phi Delta Kappan, 75,* 402–406.

Centers for Disease Control and Prevention. (1997a). CDC reports first-ever decline in AIDS diagnoses. http://www.cdc.gov/press/press919.htm.

Centers for Disease Control and Prevention. (1997b). Sexually transmitted disease surveillance 1996. http://wonder.cdc.gov/wonder/STD/STDD016.PCW.html.

Centers for Disease Control and Prevention. (1998). Youth risk behavior surveillance—United States, 1997. *MMWR, 47* (No. SS-3).

Dwyer, K., Osher, D., & Warger, C. (1998). *Early warning, timely response: A guide to safe schools.* Washington, DC: U.S. Department of Education.

Edwards, A. T. (1997). Let's stop ignoring our gay and lesbian youth. *Educational Leadership, 54* (7), 68–70.

Eggert, L. L., & Herting, J. R. (1991). Preventing teenage drug abuse: Exploratory effects of network and social support. *Youth and Society, 22,* 482–524.

Eggert, L. L., Thompson, E. A., Randell, B. P., & McCauley, E. (1995). *Youth suicide prevention plan for Washington state.* Olympia, WA: Washington State Department of Health.

Foster, S. (1996, November). High school dropout rate the lowest in two decades, yet rate for Hispanics remains high. *Counseling Today,* 52–53.

Garmezy, N. (1985). Stress-resistant children: The search for protective factors. In

Stevenson, J. E. (Ed.), *Recent research in developmental psychopathology. Journal of Child Psychology and Psychiatry.* Book supplement No. 4 (pp. 213–233). Oxford, England: Pergamon.

Garrison, C. Z., McKeown, R. E., Valois, R. F., & Vincent, M. L. (1993). Aggression, substance use, and suicidal behaviors in high school students. *American Journal of Public Health, 82,* 179–184.

Gersten, J. C. , & Shamis, S. (1988). Review of risk factors for children's mental health problems. *Children at risk.* Tempe, AZ: Arizona State University, 1–96.

Gevelinger, M. E. & Zimmerman, L. (1997). How Catholic schools are creating a safe climate for gay and lesbian students. *Educational Leadership, 55* (2), 66–68.

Greydanus, D. E., & Shearin, R. B. (1990). *Adolescent sexuality and gynecology.* Philadelphia: Lea & Febiger.

Guy, S. M., Smith, G. M., & Bentler, P. M. (1994). Consequences of adolescent drug use and personality factors on adult drug use. *Journal of Drug Education, 24,* 109–132.

Haveman, P., & Wolfe, B. (1994). *Succeeding generations: On the effects of investments in children.* New York: Russell Sage Foundation.

Jessor, R. (1993). Successful adolescent development among youth in high-risk settings. *American Psychologist, 48,* 117–126.

Kalafat, J., & Elias, M. (1994). An evaluation of a school-based suicide awareness intervention. *Suicide and Life-Threatening Behavior, 24,* 224–233.

Kwok, A., & Hermann, W. (1993, May 23). Gangs' killing fields. *The Arizona Republic,* A1.

Lowenthal, B. (1996). Educational implications of child abuse. *Intervention in School and Clinic, 32,* 21–25.

Lumsden, L. (1998). Trends and issues: School safety and violence prevention. ERIC Clearinghouse on Educational Management. http://www.eric.uoregon.edu/issues/safety/01.html

Mayer, G. R., Mitchell, L. K., Clementi, T., Clement-Robertson, E., Myatt, R., &

Bullara, D. T. (1993). A dropout prevention program for at-risk high school students: Emphasizing consulting to promote positive classroom climates. *Education and Treatment of Children, 16,* 135–146.

McMillan, J. H., & Reed, D. F. (1994). At-risk students and resiliency: Factors contributing to academic success. *Clearing House, 67,* 137–140.

Meckler, L. (1998, May 1). Birthrates for teens fall across U.S. *The Arizona Republic,* A1, A22.

Minard, S. (1993). The school counselor's role in confronting child abuse. *The School Counselor, 41,* 9–15.

Nabozny v. Podlesny, 92 F.3d 446 (7th Cir.1996).

National Clearinghouse for Alcohol and Drug Information (1998a). Limiting youth access to tobacco with the Synar amendment. http://www.health.org/pubs/qdocs/prevalert/15.html.

National Clearinghouse for Alcohol and Drug Information. (1998b). Youth oriented prevention initiatives. http://www.health.org/ndcs98/iv-.html.

National Clearinghouse on Child Abuse and Neglect Information. (1998). What is child maltreatment? http://www.calib.com/nccanch/pubs/whatis.htm.

National Conference on State Legislatures. (1998). *Linking driving privileges to school attendance 1998.* Denver, CO: Author.

National Institute on Drug Abuse. (1997c). Substance abuse: Alcohol and other drugs. http://odphp9.osophs.dhhs.gov/tours/subabuse.htm

National Institute on Drug Abuse. (1997b). Preventing drug use among children and adolescents: A research-based guide (NIH Publication No. 97-4212). Washington, DC: U.S. Department of Health and Human Services.

National Institute on Drug Abuse. (1997a). Facts supporting NIDA's drug abuse and AIDS prevention campaign for teens. Capsule series (C-90-01). http://www.nida.nih.gov/NIDA Capsules: NCFactsTeens. html.

Pellegrini, D. S. (1990). Psychosocial risk and protective factors in childhood. *Develop-*

mental and Behavioral Pediatrics, 11, 201–209.

Poland, S. (1994). The role of school crisis intervention teams to prevent and reduce school violence and trauma. *School Psychology Review, 23,* 175–189.

Popham, W. J. (1993). Wanted AIDS education that works. *Phi Delta Kappan, 74,* 559–562.

Portner, J. (1998a, May 13). Educators call birthrate drop payoff for sex ed. programs. *Education Week,* 6.

Portner, J. (1998b, February 25). Hispanic teenagers top black, white birthrate. *Education Week,* 5.

Portner, J. (1998c, May 20). Officials call gun report proof of crackdown. *Education Week,* 3.

Prothrow-Stith, D. (1994). Building violence prevention into the curriculum. *The School Administrator, 51,* 8–12.

Quinn, T. (1991). The influence of school policies and practices on dropout rates. *NASSP Bulletin, 75*(538), 73–83.

Rae-Grant, N., Thomas, H., Offord, D., & Boyle, M. (1989). Risk, protective factors, and the prevalence of behavioral and emotional disorders in children and adolescents. *Journal of the American Academy of Child Adolescent Psychiatry, 28,* 262–268.

Rak, C. F., & Patterson, L. E. (1996). Promoting resilience in at-risk children. *Journal of Counseling & Development, 74,* 368–373.

Robinson, K. E. (1994). Addressing the needs of gay and lesbian students: The school counselor's role. *The School Counselor, 41,* 326–332.

Salzman, K. P., & Salzman, S. A. (1989). *Characteristics of adolescents at risk for psychological dysfunction and school failure.* Paper presented at the Annual Convention of the American Educational Research Association, San Francisco, CA.

Schwartz, W. (1998). An overview of strategies to reduce school violence. *ERIC Digest.* New York: Teachers College, ERIC Clearinghouse on Urban Education.

Shaffer, D., Garland, A., Underwood, M., & Whittle, B. (1987). *An evaluation of three youth prevention programs in New Jersey.* Report prepared for the New Jersey State Department of Health & Human Services.

Sniffen, M. (1998, April 13). School crime up 25%: More teens report gangs. *The Arizona Republic,* A1–A2.

Southeastern Regional Vision for Education & Florida Department of Education. (1996). *Reducing school violence: Building a framework for school safety.* Greensboro, NC: University of North Carolina, School of Education, Author.

U.S. Department of Education, National Center for Education Statistics. (1993). *Reaching the goals: Safe, disciplined, and drug-free schools.* Washington, DC: U.S. Government Printing Office.

U.S. Department of Education, National Center for Education Statistics. (1997). *Dropout rates in the United States.* Washington, DC: U.S. Government Printing Office.

U.S. Department of Education, National Center for Education Statistics. (1998). Violence and discipline problems in U.S. public schools: 1996–97. http://nces.ed.gov/pubs98/violence/98030001.html.

U.S. Department of Health and Human Services. (1997a). Answers to frequently asked questions on child abuse and neglect. http://www.calib.com/nccanch/pubs/infact.htm.

U.S. Department of Health and Human Services. (1997b). National child abuse and neglect statistical fact sheet. http://www.calib.com/nccanch/pubs/stats.htm.

U.S. Department of Health and Human Services. (1998a). A national strategy to prevent teen pregnancy. http://aspe.os.dhhs.gov/hsp/teenp/strategy.htm.

U.S. Department of Health and Human Services. (1998b). Promising strategies. http://aspe.os.dhhs.gov/hsp/teenp/examples.htm.

Vobejda, B. (1994, June 7). Teens' use birth control up, study says. *The Arizona Republic,* A1.

Walling, S. R. (1993). Gay teens at risk. Bloomington, IN: Phi Delta Kappa Educational Foundation.

Watts, W. D., & Ellis, A. M. (1993). Sexual abuse and drinking and drug use: Implications for prevention. *Journal of Drug Education, 23,* 183–200.

Wendel, P. (1997, June). Counselors' role in youth gangs prevention and intervention. *Counseling Today,* 1, 10–11, 16–17.

Youths report cases of abuse, assault in survey. (1994, October 26). *Education Week, 10.*

Part Five

Legal and Political Control and Financial Support

Chapter 11

The law is the true embodiment
Of everything that is excellent.

W. S. Gilbert (1836–1911)

Legal Framework
for the Public Schools

> Like many schools, Oceanview High School has found it difficult to find qualified teachers to fill vacancies left by "baby boomer" retirees. In particular, Oceanview has had difficulty finding teachers for its advanced placement science courses. For this reason, Mr. Kindrick, principal of Oceanview, was particulary pleased when Jean Collins applied for an open science position. Mrs. Collins had recently moved to Oceanview with her family when her husband's company transferred him there. She had previously taught science at a private denomination high school.

> After an interview and following the district's hiring process, Mrs. Collins began teaching at Oceanview. Toward the middle of the fall semester Mr. Kindrick visited Mrs. Collins's class to conduct a scheduled performance evaluation. He found her to be an exceptionally gifted teacher who clearly cared about her students. On that occasion he did notice that Mrs. Collins was wearing a very large cross, approximately five to six inches long. A few days later he saw her at a faculty meeting and she was wearing the same cross. Within two weeks he received a call from Larry Kruz, the father of one of Mrs. Collins's students, complaining about the fact that, according to the student, Mrs. Collins wore the cross every day and that it was a distraction and seemed to get in the way as she wrote on the board and leaned over students' desks, exacerbated by the fact that she seemed to always be handling it. According to the father, he and the student, who were not Christians, were offended by Mrs. Collins's oversized cross and by what they considered her attempt to bring attention to it. They asked that Mr. Kindrick direct Mrs. Collins to stop wearing the cross.

> What action should Mr. Kindrick take? What additional information might be important to his decision? What constitutional issues are involved? What, if any, action should Mr. Kindrick have taken prior to Mr. Kruz's complaint?

The U.S. Constitution protects Mrs. Collins's right to freedom of religious expression as well as students' rights not to be subjected to state actions that further the establishment of religion. It is within the rules of action or conduct provided by federal and state constitutional provisions, federal and state statutory law, regulations and decisions of administrative agencies, and court decisions that the framework is established for the operation of the public schools. Before going into the specifics of the law as they affect students' and teachers' rights, this chapter provides a brief overview of the major sources of school law, the federal and state court systems, and their interrelationship in forming the legal basis for public education. After reading this chapter you should be able to:

- Identify federal constitutional provisions affecting education.
- Discuss the importance of state constitutional provisions affecting education.
- Compare statutory law, common law, and administrative law.

- Describe the levels of the federal court system and those of a typical state court system.
- Explain how challenges under the establishment clause are evaluated.

- Give the current posture of the courts in regard to prayer and Bible reading, student devotional activities, compulsory attendance, and private and home schooling.

- Distinguish between permissible and impermissible state aid to nonpublic education.

Federal Constitutional Provisions Affecting Education

Written contracts for the establishment of governments, known as *constitutions,* are uniquely American (Collins, 1969). Constitutions are the highest level of law. They are the fundamental laws of the people of a state or nation, establishing the very character and concept of their government, its organization and officers, its sovereign powers, and the limitations of its power. Constitutions are written broadly so as to endure changing times and circumstances. While constitutions can be changed by amendment, the process is normally difficult and is seldom utilized. The Constitution of the United States, written over 200 years ago, has served the needs of a fledgling nation and a world power, with only 26 amendments.

Education, though, is not mentioned in the U.S. Constitution. It is therefore considered to be one of the powers reserved to the states by the Tenth Amendment, which states, "The powers not delegated to the United States by the Constitution, nor prohibited by it to the States, are reserved to the States respectively, or to the people." Although the provision of education is considered one of the powers of the state, the supremacy clause of the Constitution (Article VI, Section 2) declares that the Constitution and the laws enacted by the U.S. Congress are the supreme law of the land. Thus the states, in exercising their authority, may not enact any laws that violate any provisions of the federal Constitution.

Several important sections of the federal Constitution have an impact on the schools (see Figure 11.1). Among these are Article I, Section 8; Article I, Section 10; and the First, Fourth, Fifth, Eighth, Ninth, Tenth, and Fourteenth Amendments. These constitutional provisions serve as the basis for education-related cases being brought to federal courts.

General Welfare Clause

In what ways does federal support of education contribute to the "common defense" of the United States?

Article I, Section 8, known as the general welfare clause, gives Congress the power to tax and to "provide for the common defense and general welfare of the United States." Over the years, the Supreme Court has interpreted the general welfare clause as authorizing Congress to tax and spend money for a variety of activities, education among them, that were construed as being in the general welfare. However, the general welfare clause does not give Congress the authority to do anything it pleases to provide for the general welfare, only to tax for that purpose. In regard to education, this means that while Congress may levy taxes to provide support for education, it may not legislate control of education.

Figure 11.1: Laws Affecting the Schools

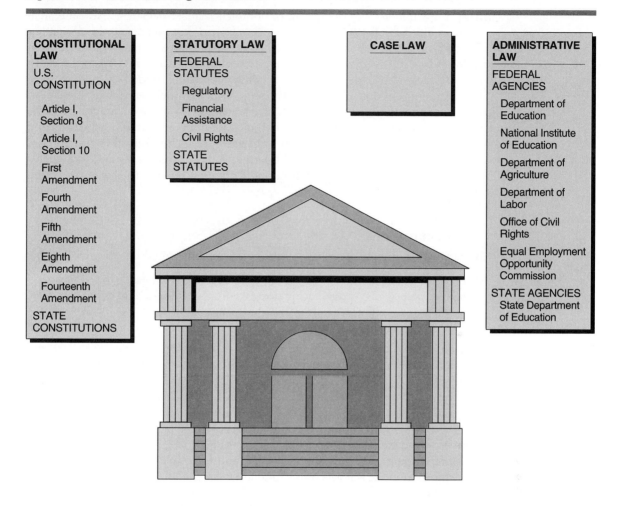

However, in recent years the Supreme Court has ruled that the federal government can attach conditions to the use of federal funds which, if not complied with, may result in the denial or withdrawal of the funds.

Exercising its authority under the general welfare clause, Congress has enacted a massive body of legislation that has provided direct federal support for a variety of instructional programs, as well as providing services and programs for identified special needs students and financial assistance to prospective teachers. Article I, Section 8 has also served as the authority for the federal government to establish the U.S. military academies; operate overseas schools for dependents of military and civilian personnel; and establish schools on Indian reservations, in the U.S. territories, and in the District of Columbia. In addition, Congress may operate libraries, such as the Library of Congress, and conduct a variety of other activities and operations deemed educational in nature.

Obligation of Contracts Clause

Article I, Section 10, the obligation of contracts clause, declares: "No state shall . . . pass any Bill of Attainder, *ex post facto* law, or law impairing the obligation of Contracts." This provision of the Constitution prohibits a state legislature from passing a law relative to teacher tenure or retirement that would be to the detriment of teachers who had acquired a contractive status under existing statutes. The obligation of contracts clause also protects school personnel who have contracts from arbitrary dismissals. That is, a teacher who has a contract cannot be dismissed during the term of that contract without a showing of cause and without due process (see discussion in Chapter 12). The obligation of contracts clause also protects both the school board and those businesses and individuals with whom it does business from nonperformance relative to the terms of the contract.

First Amendment

The First Amendment addresses several basic personal freedoms. It provides that

> Congress shall make no law respecting an establishment of religion, or prohibiting the free exercise thereof; or abridging the freedom of speech or of the press; or of the right of the people peaceably to assemble, and to petition the Government for a redress of grievances.

Increasingly, the first clause of the First Amendment, the establishment and free exercise of religion clause, has become the focus of litigation in education. The schools have become a battleground for some of the most volatile disputes over the appropriate governmental relationship vis-à-vis religion (McCarthy, Cambron-McCabe, & Thomas, 1998). As discussed later in this chapter, these cases have dealt with numerous issues surrounding (1) school practices objected to on the basis of promoting or inhibiting religion (e.g., released time, prayer, and Bible reading), (2) curriculum content, and (3) public funds used to provide support to nonpublic schools or to students or parents of students attending nonpublic schools.

The second clause of the First Amendment, that dealing with the freedom of speech and press, has also been the subject of a growing number of education cases in recent years. Both teachers and students have increasingly protested abridgements of their rights to express themselves—from wearing of long hair to publicly criticizing school board practices. Teachers have also become more concerned with what they consider attempts to infringe upon their academic freedom to select textbooks and other teaching materials and to practice certain teaching methodologies.

The third clause of the First Amendment, which deals with the rights of citizens to assemble, has also been called into question in a number of education cases concerning the freedom of association. Both students and teachers have become more assertive of their right to belong to various organizations, including those that may have goals contrary to that of the school system. The question of freedom of association has also been at issue in a number of cases dealing with

Students and their lockers are increasingly subject to search.

teachers' associations or unions. Questions of non-school-sponsored student assemblies are usually not addressed under this clause but under the freedom of religion (if that is their purpose) or freedom of expression clauses.

Fourth Amendment

The Fourth Amendment provides that the right of the people to be "secure in their persons, houses, papers, and effects, against unreasonable searches and seizures, shall not be violated and no warrants shall issue, but upon probable cause." The growing problem of student possession of drugs and other contraband has led to an increasing number of student searches. As we will see in the next chapter, the Fourth Amendment has served as the basis for a number of student challenges to warrantless searches of their automobiles, lockers, or persons by school officials and others. A few cases involving searches of teachers' desks or other personal belongings have also been heard.

Fifth Amendment

According to the provisions of the Fifth Amendment, no person shall be "compelled in any criminal case to be a witness against himself, nor be deprived of life, liberty, or property, without due process of law; nor shall private property be taken for public use, without just compensation." The first clause of the Fifth Amendment, the self-incrimination clause, has been invoked by teachers in refusing to answer questions about their affiliations and activities outside the school. However, the courts have ruled that teachers may not use the Fifth Amendment to avoid answering questions about their activities outside the classroom that relate to their qualifications or fitness to teach (*Beilan v. Board of Public Education,* 1958).

The second clause, the due process clause, is not usually involved in education cases. Rather, the due process clause of the Fourteenth Amendment is used because it relates directly to the states.

The last clause of the Fifth Amendment is relevant in those few cases where the state or school system is seeking to obtain private property for school purposes in the exercise of the government's right of *eminent domain,* the right to take private property for public use. Thus a school district attempting to gain property to enlarge a school may find it necessary to exercise its power of eminent domain (if such power has been given it by the state) if it has not been able to negotiate a voluntary purchase of the needed property. Whenever the power of eminent domain is exercised, just compensation must be given to the owners of the property that is taken.

Eighth Amendment

How have society's views regarding corporal punishment in the schools changed since you began school?

The Eighth Amendment, in part, provides protection against "cruel and unusual punishments." This amendment on occasion has been involved in challenging the practice or use of corporal punishment in schools. The Supreme Court has held, however, that disciplinary corporal punishment *per se* is not cruel and unusual punishment as anticipated by the Eighth Amendment (*Ingraham v. Wright,* 1977). This does not mean, however, that corporal punishment may not be prohibited by state or school district regulations or that punishment can be excessive. In fact, if the punishment causes physical harm, it may be grounds for a civil action for assault and battery.

Fourteenth Amendment

The Fourteenth Amendment is the federal constitutional provision most often involved in education-related cases because it pertains specifically to state actions and, as previously stated, education is a state function. The Fourteenth Amendment states:

> No State shall make or enforce any law which shall abridge the privileges or immunities of citizens of the United States; nor shall any State deprive any person of life, liberty, or property, without due process of law; nor deny to any person within its jurisdiction the equal protection of the laws.

The due process clause of the Fourteenth Amendment has proved to be of great importance to students in disciplinary actions and to teachers in negative personnel actions, and has been invoked in a wide array of issues involving student and teacher rights. As discussed in the next chapter, the equal protection clause has served as the basis for numerous cases involving discrimination on the basis of race, sex, handicapping condition, or other classifications used in the schools.

State Constitutional Provisions Affecting Education

Like the federal Constitution, state constitutions have provided the foundation for the enactment of subsequent innumerable statutes that govern the activities of the state and its citizens. However, unlike the federal Constitution, which contains no reference to education, every state constitution includes a provision for education, and all but one expressly provides for the establishment of a system of public schools. These provisions range from very general to very specific, but their overall intent is to ensure that schools and education be encouraged and that a uniform system of schools be established. For example, Article X, Section 3 (as amended, April 1972) of the Wisconsin constitution provides:

> The Legislature shall provide by law for the establishment of district schools, which shall be as nearly uniform as practical; and such schools shall be free and without charge for tuition to all children between the ages of 4 and 20 years.

The constitutions of 30 states expressly prohibit the use of public funds for the support of religious schools, and the constitution of every state except Maine and North Carolina contains a provision prohibiting religious instruction in the public schools.

The wording of the state constitutional provision for education has proved to be very important to the courts in determining whether particular legislative enactments were constitutionally permissible or required. For example, in a number of school finance cases the state courts have ruled that phrases in the constitution such as "a thorough and efficient system of education" required that the state provide a finance system that did not make the quality of a child's education dependent on the wealth of the school district.

Regardless of the particular provisions related to education contained in a state's constitution, the state constitution does not grant unlimited power to the state legislature in providing for the public schools. Rather, it establishes the boundaries within which the legislature may operate. The legislature may not then enact legislation exceeding these parameters or violate any provisions of the federal Constitution, which is the supreme law of the land.

Statutory Law

Statutory law is that body of law consisting of the written enactments of a legislative body. These written enactments, called statutes, constitute the second highest level of law, following constitutions. Where constitutions provide broad statements of policy, statutes establish the specifics of operation. Both the U.S.

Congress and state legislatures have enacted innumerable statutes affecting the provision of education in this country. These statutes are continually reviewed and often revised or supplemented by successive legislatures. They are also subject to review by the courts to determine their intent and to determine if they are in violation of the constitution.

Federal Statutes

Despite the federal constitutional silence on education, during each session the U.S. Congress enacts or renews numerous statutes that affect the public schools. Some of these, such as the Occupational Safety and Health Act (OSHA), which requires employers to furnish a safe working environment, although not directed specifically at school districts, do affect their operation. Many of the statutes enacted by Congress are related to the provision of financial assistance to the schools for a variety of special instructional programs, research, or programs for needy children. Still other federal statutes, federal civil rights statutes, also have had a considerable impact on educational programs and personnel. An overview of the major civil rights statutes affecting schools is provided in Table 11.1. They are discussed in more detail in relevant sections of this text.

State Statutes

What laws or statutes have recently been enacted in your state that affect certification?

Most of the statutory laws affecting the public schools are enacted by state legislatures. The power of the state legislature is *plenary,* or absolute; it may enact any legislation that is not contrary to federal and state constitutions. Although the principle is challenged every year by local school districts, the courts have clearly established that education is a function of the state, not an inherent function of the local school district, and that the local district has only those powers delegated to it by the state legislature. The courts have also affirmed the authority of the state to regulate such matters as certification, powers of school boards, accreditation, curriculum, the school calendar, graduation requirements, facilities construction and operation, and raising and spending of monies. In fact, the courts have made it clear that school districts have no inherent right to exist; they exist only at the will of the legislature and can be created, reorganized, or abolished by legislative prerogative.

Although the state legislature has in fact delegated the actual operation of the majority of the schools to the local school districts, the legislature still must pass legislation to administer the system as a whole and to provide for its financing and operation. Consequently, numerous education statutes exist in every state, and in every legislative session new statutes will be enacted that affect education.

Case Law

Distinct from statutes, regulations, or other sources of law is that body of law originating with historical usages and customs, including court decisions. This body of law is referred to as case law, or common law. Case law is based on the

Table 11.1: Summary of Major Civil Rights Statutes Affecting Education

Statute	Major Provision
Civil Rights Act of 1866, 1870 42 U.S.C. §1981	Provides all citizens equal rights under the law regardless of race
Civil Rights Act of 1871 42 U.S.C. §1983	Any person who deprives another of his/her rights may be held liable to the injured party
Civil Rights Act of 1871 42 U.S.C. §1985 and 1986	Persons conspiring to deprive another of his/her rights, or any person having knowledge of any such conspiracy, are subject to any action to recover damages
Civil Rights Act of 1866, 1870 (as amended) 42 U.S.C. §1988	Courts may award reasonable attorney fees to the prevailing party in any action arising out of the above acts and Title VI of the Civil Rights of 1964
Civil Rights Act of 1964, Title VI 42 U.S.C. §2000(d)	Prohibits discrimination on the basis of race, color, or national origin
Equal Pay Act of 1963 29 U.S.C. §206(D)	Prohibits sex discrimination in pay
Civil Rights Act of 1964, Title VII 42 U.S.C. §2000(e)	Prohibits discrimination in employment on the basis of race, color, religion, sex, or national origin
Age Discrimination in Employment Act of 1967 29 U.S.C. §621	Prohibits discrimination against any individual with respect to employment unless age is a bona fide occupational qualification
Education Amendments of 1972, Title IX 20 U.S.C. §1681	Prohibits sex discrimination in any education program or activity receiving federal financial assistance
Rehabilitation Act of 1973 (as amended) 29 U.S.C. §791	Prohibits discrimination against any "otherwise qualified handicapped individual"
Equal Educational Opportunities Act of 1974 20 U.S.C. §1703	Prohibits any state from denying equal educational opportunities to any individual based on his/her race, color, sex, or national origin
Americans with Disabilities Act of 1990 42 U.S.C. §12112	Prohibits discrimination against persons with disabilities
Individuals with Disabilities Education Act of 1990 20 U.S.C. §1400–1485	Individuals with disabilities must be guaranteed a free appropriate education by programs receiving federal financial assistance
Civil Rights Restoration Act of 1991 42 U.S.C. §1981 et seq.	Amends the Civil Rights Act of 1964, the Age Discrimination in Employment Act of 1967, and the Americans with Disabilities Act of 1990 with regard to employment discrimination

doctrine of *stare decisis,* which means "let the decision stand." The doctrine requires that once a court has laid down a principle of law as applicable to a certain set of facts, it will apply it to all future cases where the facts are substantially the same, and other courts of equal or lesser rank will similarly apply the principle (Black, 1990). However, adherence to the doctrine of *stare decisis* does not mean that all previous decisions may never be challenged or overturned. On numerous occasions a higher or subsequent court has rejected the reasoning of a lower or earlier court, or constitutional or statutory changes, in effect, have overturned the previous decision.

Administrative Law

Administrative law consists of the formal regulations and decisions of those state or federal agencies that are authorized by law to regulate public functions. These regulations carry the force of law, are subject to judicial review, and will stand as law unless found to be in conflict with federal or state constitutional provisions, statutes, or court decisions.

The U.S. Department of Education is the federal agency most directly concerned with education. The secretary of education is appointed by the president. The regulations issued by the Office of Civil Rights of the Department of Education in regard to the implementation of Title IX are a prime example of the profound impact that administrative law can have on the operations of the schools.

Among the other federal agencies that have significant interaction with schools are the Department of Agriculture, which administers the National School Lunch Act; the Department of the Health and Human Services, which administers Head Start; and the Department of Labor, which administers the Occupational Safety and Health Act. In addition, both the Office of Civil Rights of the Department of Education and another federal agency, the Equal Employment Opportunity Commission, are charged with enforcement of civil rights and nondiscrimination legislation.

The state agency that has the most direct control over and responsibility for education is the state department of education. A large body of administrative law is generated by this agency as a result of the promulgation of numerous rules and regulations relating to such areas as certification of teachers, accreditation of schools, adoption of textbooks, courses of study, minimum standards for specified areas, and distribution of state funds.

Powers and Organization of the Courts

According to our system of government a separation of power exists between the executive, legislative, and judicial branches. In school-related matters, the courts have generally taken the position that they will not intervene in a dispute unless all internal appeals have been exhausted. For example, where school board policy provides teachers with the right of direct appeal to the board, this avenue of appeal must be exhausted before the courts will hear the appeal. The exceptions to this provision are cases involving an alleged violation of a constitutionally protected right.

Courts cannot become involved in education cases of their own initiative. A case must be brought to the court for resolution. The most common type of school case brought to the court is one that requires the court to interpret laws within its jurisdiction. Another common type of school case requires the court to determine the constitutionality of legislative or administrative enactments.

Federal courts generally are involved in only two kinds of issues: those involving questions of interpretations of the federal Constitution or federal statutes, and those involving parties of different states. Sometimes a case will involve questions of both federal and state law. When this occurs, the federal court can decide on the state issue, but it must do so according to the rules governing the courts of that state. Most education cases that come to federal courts involve alleged violations of constitutionally protected rights or interpretations of federal statutes.

The Federal Court System

The federal court system consists of three levels of courts of general jurisdiction: a supreme court, district courts, and courts of appeals. In addition, the federal court system includes courts of special jurisdiction, such as the Customs Court or the Tax Court. These courts would normally not be involved in education cases (see Figure 11.2).

The lowest level federal courts are district courts. There are about 92 district courts: at least one in each state, and in the more populated states, such as California, New York, and Texas, as many as four. Federal district courts are given names reflective of the geographic area they serve; for example, S.D. Ohio indicates the Southern District of Ohio. District courts are the courts of initiation or original jurisdiction for most cases filed in the federal court system, including most education cases. They are trial courts, meaning that a jury hears the case. The decisions of federal district courts have an automatic right of appeal to the next level of federal courts—U.S. Circuit Courts of Appeals.

There are 13 circuit courts of appeals in the federal system. Twelve of the circuit courts have jurisdiction over a specific geographic area (see Figure 11.3). A thirteenth, the Federal Circuit, has jurisdiction to hear appeals in specific areas of federal law (e.g., customs, copyright, international trade). A circuit court hears appeals from the decisions of district courts and certain federal administrative agencies. It hears arguments from attorneys, but it does not retry the case. There is no jury. A panel of judges, usually three, hears the case and can affirm, reverse, or modify the decision of the lower court, or remand the case back to the lower court for modifications or retrial.

The decision of a federal circuit court is binding only on federal district courts within its geographic jurisdiction. Circuit courts have no power over state courts and do not hear appeals from them, nor does the decision of one circuit court bind other circuit courts or the district courts in other circuits. Thus it is

Figure 11.2: Federal Court System

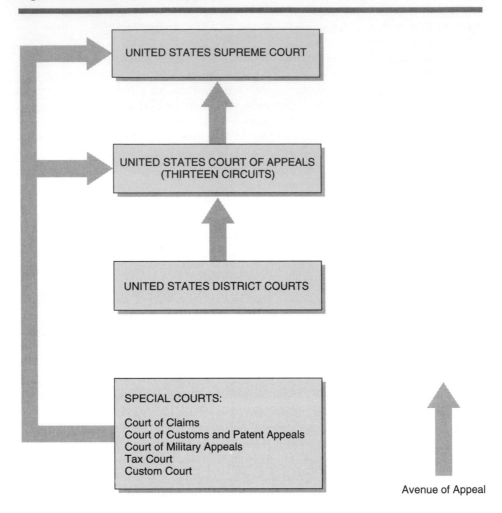

possible, and indeed it happens quite often, that one circuit court will rule one way, while another circuit court will rule in the reverse.

 The highest federal appeals court, indeed the highest court in the land, is the U.S. Supreme Court. Decisions of the Supreme Court are absolute: there is no appeal. If Congress or citizens do not agree with a decision of the Supreme Court, the only ways they can mediate against the effect of the decision are to pass a law or to get the Court to reconsider the issue in a later case. A notable example in education of the Supreme Court reversing itself on reconsideration is the case of *Brown v. Board of Education of Topeka* (1954). In *Plessey v. Ferguson* (1896), the Supreme Court had said "separate but equal" public facilities for blacks and whites were constitutionally permissible. But in 1954, in the *Brown* decision, the Court reversed this position and ruled that separate educational facilities for blacks and whites were inherently unequal.

Figure 11.3: The Thirteen Federal Judicial Circuits

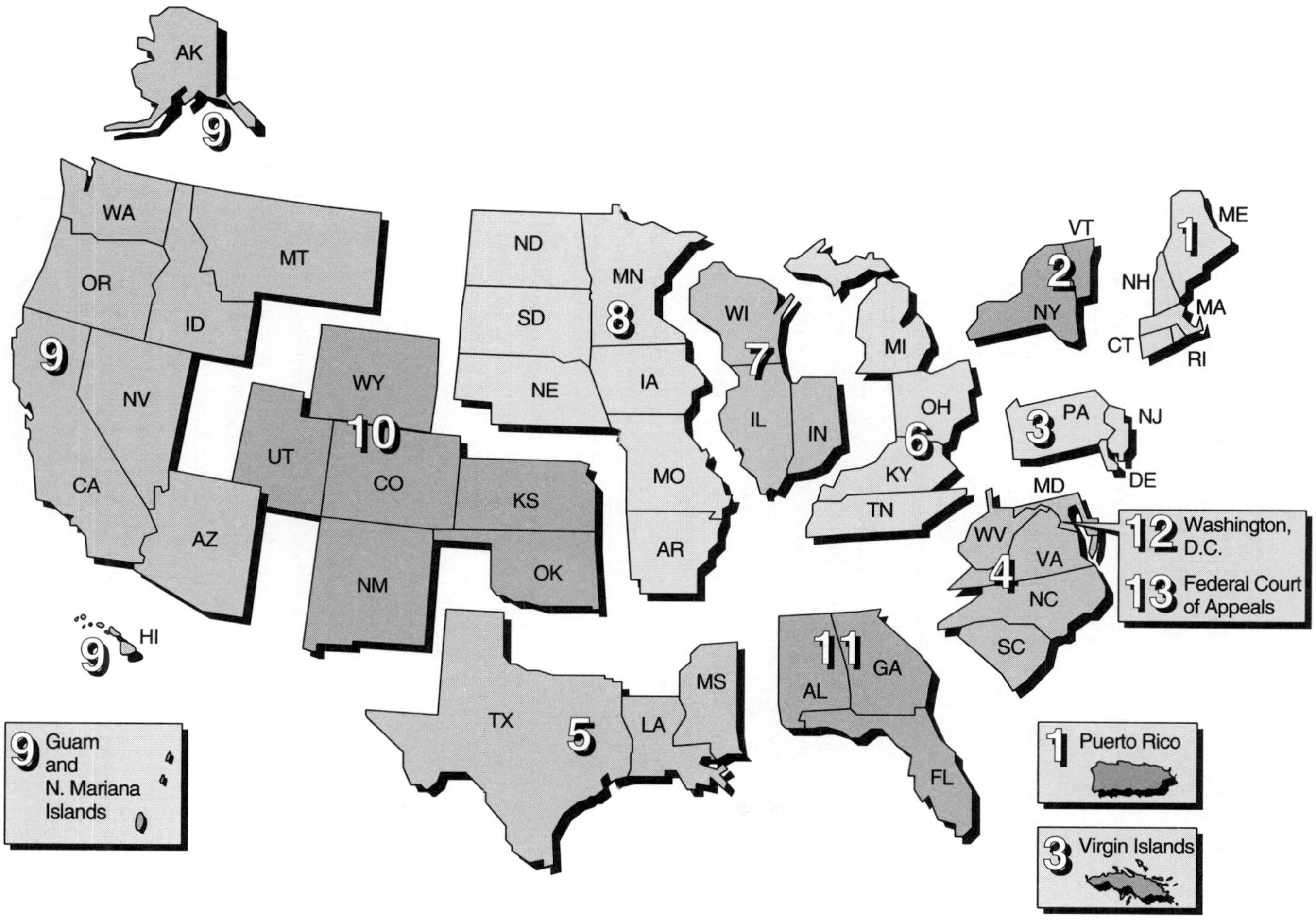

Historical Note

Thurgood Marshall: Breaking the Color Barrier on the U.S. Supreme Court

Thurgood Marshall was born July 2, 1908, in Baltimore. He graduated from Lincoln University in Pennsylvania (1903) and first in his class from Howard University Law School. After graduation he entered private practice while volunteering his services to the National Association of Colored People (NAACP). In 1936 he went to work for the NAACP and in 1940 became the chief of the organization's Legal Defense and Education Fund.

Marshall played a major role in the NASSP's efforts to end racial segregation. He won 29 of the 32 cases he argued before the Supreme Court, including the historic *Brown v. Board of Education* (1954), which opened the door for the integration of the nation's public schools, and *Sweatt v. Painter* (1950), which declared unconstitutional "separate but equal" facilities in higher education.

Marshall's reputation as the architect of the civil rights movement legal strategy led President John F. Kennedy to nominate him to the United States Court of Appeals for the Second Circuit in 1961. Opposition by southern senators delayed his confirmation for several months. In 1965 President Lyndon B. Johnson appointed him U.S. Solicitor General, and two years later nominated him to the United States Supreme Court. Marshall became the first black member of the Supreme Court. He was a steadfast liberal throughout his tenure on the court and "was the principal architect of a flexible definition of equality that gave black Americans the full rights of citizenship" (Holland, 1995, p. 367). By the time he retired in 1991, he had become part of the minority dissenting from a conservative majority. He died at the age of 84 (January 24, 1993) at Bethesda, Maryland.

The Supreme Court hears cases on appeal from lower federal courts or from state supreme courts if the state case involves questions of federal law. While thousands of cases are appealed to the Supreme Court each year, only a small number are heard. However, in recent years the number of education cases being appealed to the Supreme Court and heard by it has increased.

The State Court Systems

Since most education cases do not involve the federal Constitution or federal statutes, they are handled by state courts rather than federal courts. Like the federal court system, the state court system is created by the state constitution and subsequent legislative enactments. Although the specific structure of the court system and the names given to courts vary from state to state, in most respects state court systems resemble the federal court system in terms of having courts of limited and special jurisdiction and courts of appeal.

Most states have courts that are designated as courts of limited or special jurisdiction. The limitation may be related to the types of cases they may handle (e.g., probate courts or juvenile courts) or the amount in controversy (e.g., small claims courts or traffic courts). Generally, state court systems do not permit appeal of the decisions of courts of limited jurisdiction.

Thurgood Marshall argued the historic Brown v. Board of Education *before the Supreme Court. Throughout his career he played a major role in efforts to end segregation.*

All states have courts of general jurisdiction. Courts of general jurisdiction are generally trial courts, and as such hear witnesses, admit evidence, and, when appropriate, conduct jury trials. Depending on the state, courts of general jurisdiction may be referred to as district courts, county courts, circuit courts, superior courts, or supreme courts (in New York State). Appeals from the decisions of courts of general jurisdiction are made to state appellate courts, often referred to as courts of appeals. Like the federal appellate courts, state appellate courts do not retry cases but sit as a panel of judges to review the record of the trial court and hear attorneys' arguments.

The final appeal in state court systems is to the state supreme court, the final authority on questions related to the state constitution or state law. If the case involves federal issues, however, appeal may be taken from the state supreme court to the U.S. Supreme Court.

Religion and Education

The issue of the appropriate relationship between religion and the state has been one of the most controversial in American legal history. The establishment and free exercise clauses of the First Amendment state that "Congress shall make no law respecting an establishment of religion or prohibiting the free exercise thereof." The experience of the nation's founders with state control of education prompted a desire to erect what Jefferson called "a wall of separation between Church and State." Although the clauses make reference only to actions of the federal government (Congress), they are made applicable to the states by the Fourteenth Amendment, which prohibits state actions that violate the constitutional rights of citizens.

Do you recall being involved in any religious activities in a public school situation? Would it pass the Lemon *test?*

Maintaining the wall of separation without being "hostile to religion" has been the challenge faced by policy makers at every level of government, as well as by public school teachers and administrators. Often they find their actions challenged in the courts, and a number of cases have reached the U.S. Supreme Court (see Table 11.2). Since 1971 the courts have used a tripartite test to evaluate claims under the establishment clause. The test, often called the *Lemon* test (from the case in which it was developed, *Lemon v. Kurtzman,* 1971), asks three questions, all of which must be answered in the negative if the policy or action is to be judged constitutional (1) Does the policy or action have a primarily religious purpose? (2) Does the policy or action have the primary effect of advancing or inhibiting religion? (3) Does the policy or action foster an excessive entanglement between the state and religion? The issues most often contested can be categorized into three broad areas: religious activities, curriculum bias, and public support for nonpublic schools. Other areas of importance, if not as litigious, involve compulsory attendance and private and home schooling. Each of these are discussed in the sections that follow.

Religious Activities

Released Time for Religions Instruction
Traditionally, a not uncommon practice in American public schools was the releasing of children during the school day for religious instruction. In the first case to reach the Supreme Court, *McCollum v. Board of Education* (1948), students had been excused from regular classes to attend private religious instruction in another part of the building. The court ruled that the program violated the establishment clause of the First Amendment. Four years later the Court upheld a program in which, with parental request, children were permitted to leave the public school to receive religious instruction (*Zorach v. Clauson,* 1952). The distinction made by the court between *Zorach* and *McCollum* was that public school facilities were not involved in *Zorach.*

The case law that has evolved since *Zorach* has clarified that the schools "have the discretion to dismiss students to off campus premises for religious instruction, provided that schools do not encourage or discourage participation . . . (but) schools may not allow religious instruction by outsiders on school premises during the school day" (Walsh, 1995, p. 23).

Flag Salute, Bible Reading, and Prayer
Two of the most controversial rulings ever made by the U.S. Supreme Court involved compulsory flag salute and prayer in the public schools. In *West Virginia State Board of Education v. Barnette* (1943), the Court ruled that the compulsory

Table 11.2: Overview of Selected U.S. Supreme Court Cases Affecting Church-School Relations

Case	Decision
Pierce v. Society of Sisters (1925)	Parents have the right to educate their children in private schools.
Cochran v. Louisiana State Board of Education (1930)	States may provide secular textbooks to children attending sectarian schools.
West Virginia State Board of Education v. Barnette (1943)	Public schools may not require the salute to the flag.
Everson v. Board of Education (1947)	States may use public funds to provide for transportation of children to and from private, sectarian schools where state constitution permits it.
Illinois ex rel. McCollum v. Board of Education (1948)	Released time program whereby instruction is provided during school hours on school grounds is unconstitutional.
Zorach v. Clauson (1952)	Released time program whereby students are released to go off campus to receive instruction and where no state support is provided is constitutional.
Engel v. Vitale (1962)	Public schools may not require the recitation of prayers.
School District of Abington Township v. Schempp (1963)	State may not promote Bible readings and prayers, even when participation is not compulsory.
Epperson v. Arkansas (1968)	State law forbidding the teaching of evolution is unconstitutional.
Lemon v. Kurtzman (1971)	State support to nonpublic schools, their personnel, and their students is unconstitutional if it (1) has a primarily religious purpose, (2) either advances or inhibits religion, or (3) creates an excessive entanglement between church and state.
Muller v. Allen (1983)	State may provide income tax deduction for educational expenses of nonpublic school parents if also available to public school parents.
Wallace v. Jaffree (1985)	State laws authorizing classroom periods of silent meditation or prayer are unconstitutional.
Edwards v. Aguillard (1987)	Public schools may not be required to teach creationism.
Board of Education of Westside Community Schools v. Mergens (1990)	Schools must provide access to student-sponsored religious groups if access is provided to other student groups not directly related to the school's curriculum.
Lee v. Weisman (1992)	School-sponsored prayers at graduation exercises are unconstitutional.
Zobrest v. Catalina Foothills School District (1993)	School district provision of the services of a sign language interpreter to a student attending a sectarian school is constitutional.
Agostini v. Felton (1997)	State aid allocated to nonpublic schools on the basis of neutral, nonsectarian criteria is not unconstitutional.

flag salute violated the religious freedom of Jehovah's Witnesses. Following *Bar-nette,* the position of the courts has been that schools may lead the pledge of allegiance so long as student participation is voluntary. For example, in *Sherman v. Consolidated School District 21 of Wheeling Township* (1992) the Seventh Circuit Court of Appeals upheld an Illinois statute that provided for a voluntary pledge of allegiance. The court ruled that the statute did not violate the free exercise clause of the First Amendment because participation was voluntary and did not violate the establishment clause because the pledge, despite its reference to God, is not a religious exercise.

The issue of school prayer has been one of ongoing, and heated, dispute. In *Engel v. Vitale* (1962), parents challenged the use of a prayer composed by the New York Board of Regents as part of morning exercises. The denominationally neutral prayer read: "Almighty God, we acknowledge our dependence upon thee, and we beg thy blessings upon us, our parents, our teachers, and our country." The Supreme Court held that "it is no part of the business of government to impose official prayers for any group of American people" and to do so constituted a violation of the establishment clause.

The following year, the Supreme Court rendered another significant decision affecting both school prayer and Bible reading. In *School District of Abington Township v. Schempp* (1963), the Court declared unconstitutional Pennsylvania and Maryland statutes that required daily Bible reading and, in Maryland, recitation of the Lord's Prayer. Although children could be exempted from participation in the Maryland case upon request by their parents, the Court held that such activities, held in public school buildings under the supervision of public school personnel, served to advance religion in violation of the establishment clause of the First Amendment. While prohibiting Bible readings as a religious exercise, the Court in *Schempp* specifically noted that its opinion did not prevent studying the Bible as literature and studying *about* religion (e.g., the history of religion, comparative religion, and the role of religion in society).

Not only are state-imposed prayers and Bible readings constitutionally impermissible, so too are voluntary prayers and Bible readings in the classroom, whether given by teachers or students, or even if requested by students. The courts have found little to distinguish these from state-imposed prayers in that both are sanctioned by the school (*Jaffree v. Wallace,* 1985). Likewise, the courts in recent years have shown a reluctance to accept the stated nonsectarian purpose of periods of silent meditation (or silent prayer). In the lead U.S. Supreme Court decision, *Wallace v. Jaffree* (1985), the Court concluded that the intent of a 1981 Alabama statute providing for a period of silent meditation or prayer was clearly to encourage and/or accommodate prayer and thus violated the establishment clause. However, the Court did indicate that statutes providing for periods of silence that did not demonstrate legislative *intent* to encourage prayers would probably be upheld (see, e.g. *Bown v. Gwinett County School District,* 1997). Currently, "moment of silence" laws are in effect in about half the states, and the legality of each is subject to determination on a state-by-state basis.

One of the most frequently litigated areas relative to prayers has been prayers at graduation ceremonies. In the years following *Engel* and *Schempp*

The issue of prayer in the public schools has become the subject of increasing legal and political debate.

some courts ruled against such practices, while others found no establishment clause violation, judging them to be more ceremonial in nature with no intent to indoctrinate. The issue was at last addressed by the U.S. Supreme Court in 1992 in *Lee v. Weisman.* The case involved the practice of the Providence, Rhode Island, school system of allowing principals to select clergy to deliver prayers at graduation ceremonies. Although the clergy were instructed that the prayers were to be nonsectarian and were given a copy of "Guidelines for Civic Occasions" prepared by the National Conference of Christians and Jews, the Supreme Court, in a 5 to 4 decision, ruled that the school's policy violated the establishment clause. The Court focused on the fact that the school selected the clergy to deliver the prayers and gave directions to them. The Court did not apply the *Lemon* test, but employed what has since been referred to as the "coercion test." In the opinion of the Court, the "psychological coercion" placed on student dissenters to attend graduation ceremonies had the effect of government coercion of students to attend religious exercises. In the words of the Court:

> high school graduation is one of life's most significant occasions . . . a student is not free to absent herself from the graduation exercise in any real sense of the term, "voluntary," for absence would require forfeiture of those intangible

benefits which have motivated the student through youth and all her high school years . . . [t]he Constitution forbids the State to exact religious conformity from a student as the price of attending her own high school graduation. (pp. 2659–2660)

Lee v. Weisman left unanswered the question of the constitutionality of graduation prayers that are delivered by students. However, soon after *Lee,* the Fifth Circuit addressed this question in *Jones v. Clear Creek Independent School District* (1992). Here the court applied *Lee's* coercion test for the first time in review of a school district policy that allowed prayers offered by student volunteers selected by the graduating seniors. The court ruled that the practice was not an unconstitutional endorsement of religion because it was the decision of the seniors whether or not to have the prayer, not school officials. It also found that the practice did not coerce participation by objectors. According to the court, since the graduating class selected the presenter, students knew that the prayers "represent the will of their peers who are less able to coerce participation than an authority figure from the state or clergy" (p. 971).

Are you in favor of a constitutional amendment to authorize prayers and Bible reading in the schools?

Following the Supreme Court's refusal to review the decision in *Jones,* the *Jones* rationale has been applied by courts in other jurisdictions in upholding student-initiated and student-led prayer at commencement exercises. However, the courts have continued to object to prayers at other school sponsored events and activities, even if student-initiated, voluntary, and nonsectarian (see, e.g., *Ingebretsen v. Jackson,* 1996). In response, a number of states, as well as the U.S. Congress, have introduced legislation to introduce voluntary or student-led prayer into the public schools. Various amendments to the Constitution to authorize prayers or Bible reading in the schools have also been proposed. While such efforts have not yet succeeded at the national level, prayer supporters have been successful in including a school prayer provision into the Goals 2000: Educate America Act (P.L. 103–227) that prohibits state and local education agencies from using funds appropriated under the act to adopt policies that prevent voluntary school prayer.

Religious Displays and Observances

Every year courts around the country are faced with deciding whether specific actions of school districts, teachers, or students constitute either an unconstitutional advancement or prohibition of religion. The application of the *Lemon* test led the Supreme Court to overturn a Kentucky statute that required the posting of the Ten Commandments (purchased at private expense) in every classroom in the state (*Stone v. Graham,* 1980). A similar ruling by a Michigan court found that a picture of Jesus Christ prominently displayed outside the principal's office violated the First Amendment's establishment clause (*Washegesic v. Bloomingdale Public Schools,* 1994). On the other hand, the Supreme Court declined to review an Eighth Circuit decision upholding a school board policy that allowed the use of religious symbols if used temporarily in an unobjectionable manner and as an example of the cultural and religious heritage of the particular holiday (*Florey v. Sioux Falls School District 49-5,* 1980).

The *Lemon* test has also been applied to challenges of religious observances in the public schools. The courts have upheld holiday displays, programs, or songs that have some religious element but whose primary purpose and effect is secular. In fact, in *Doe v. Duncanville Independent School District* (1995) the Fifth Circuit Court stated that to prohibit the singing of certain songs that might be religious in origin, but were sung because of their recognized musical value, would be showing hostility to religion.

In deciding whether teachers and students can be absent from school for religious holidays, while the courts have generally recognized the right of school districts to place limits on the number of such absences, they have also required that reasonable accommodation be made for the exercise of staff and student religious beliefs. For example, while the courts have held that it is within the discretion of school districts to limit the number of paid leaves that are provided employees for religious leave, they have also held that to allow employees to take unpaid leave is a reasonable accommodation for the employee's religious beliefs. And, while scheduling public school holidays for periods that coincide with certain Christian religious holidays does not violate the establishment clause (*Koenick v. Felton,* 1997), designating Good Friday as a state-mandated school holidays does (*Metzl v. Leininger,* 1995). Last, schools are not obliged to schedule athletic events or other student activities such as graduation so as not to conflict with the religious holidays.

Religious Access to School Buildings

Partially in response to public sentiment that prayer and other devotional activities should not be banned from the school grounds, in 1984 Congress passed the Equal Access Act (EAA) (20 U.S.C., sections 4071–73). The act specified that if a federally assisted public secondary school provides a *limited open forum* to non-curriculum-related student groups to meet on school premises during the lunch hour, before or after school, or during other noninstructional time, "equal access" to that forum cannot be denied because of the "religious, political, philosophical, or other content of the speech at such meetings." While the EEA did not define a noncurriculum-related group, in 1990 the U.S. Supreme Court in *Board of Education of Westside Community Schools v. Mergens* defined a noncurriculum-related student group as

> any student group that does not directly relate to the body of courses offered by the school . . . [and] a student group directly relates to a school's curriculum if the subject matter of the group is actually taught, or will soon be taught, in a regularly offered course; if the subject matter of the group concerns the body of courses as a whole; if participation in the group is required for a particular course; or if participation in the group results in academic credit. (p. 239)

The Court went on to say that the direct relation to the curriculum does not mean "anything related to abstract educational goals" and that schools cannot evade the intent of the Act by "strategically describing existing groups" (*Mergens,* 1990, p. 244).

Use of school facilities by community groups, where there is no school sponsorship or supervision, while very different from use by student-initiated groups under the EAA, has also been the subject of ongoing controversy. Following *Mergens,* access to school facilities was expanded even further by the U.S. Supreme Court in *Lamb's Chapel v. Center Moriches School District* (1993), which said that school districts that allow community groups to use school facilities for civic or social purposes have created a limited open forum and cannot, therefore, bar religious groups from using the facilities on the same terms.

Challenges to the Curriculum

First Amendment challenges to the curriculum generally have been brought by parents attempting to eliminate specific courses, activities, or materials thought to be advancing religion. Increasingly, in recent years some parents have contended that certain courses, materials, and practices in the curriculum promote nontheistic or antitheistic beliefs, referred to as *secular humanism* or New Age theology and defined by their critics as faiths that deny God, deify man, and glorify reason. These parents demand that the influences of these "religions" be removed from the curriculum or that Christian doctrine be inserted in the curriculum to bring balance.

In the cases to date, the courts have rejected the argument that the challenged courses or materials advanced any nontheistic or antitheistic creed and have reaffirmed the position taken by the Supreme Court in 1968 in *Epperson v. Arkansas*. In this case, the Court struck down an Arkansas law forbidding instruction in evolution, stating: "The state has no legitimate interest in protecting any or all religions from views distasteful to them." For example, the courts have not been convinced that the teaching of sex education promotes an antitheistic faith. The courts consistently have found that sex education courses present public health information that promotes legitimate educational objectives, and that the establishment clause prevents the state from barring such instruction merely to suit the religious beliefs of some parents (McCarthy, Cambron-McCabe, & Thomas, 1998).

The courts generally are satisfied in these and other areas where statutes or policies allow the student to be exempted from the challenged course or exposure to the objectionable content. However, there are numerous instances in which schools have refused the exemption and have been upheld by the courts. For example, in *Ware v. Valley Stream High School District* (1989), the Court ruled that a New York regulation that required that all primary and secondary students receive instruction regarding AIDS prevention and alcohol and drug abuse did not violate the First Amendment rights of parents who believed that such education was "evil." The Court held that the state had a compelling interest in educating children regarding the dangers of drug and alcohol abuse and AIDS transmission.

The teaching of evolution is another area that has been targeted as advancing secular humanism. Following the ruling in *Epperson* that evolution is a science, not a secular religion, and that states cannot restrict student access to such information to satisfy religious preferences, attempts were made in several states to secure "balanced treatment" or "equal time" for the teaching of creationism. However, these statutes have also been invalidated. In *Edwards v. Aguillard*

(1987), the U.S. Supreme Court ruled that creation science is a religious doctrine and to require it be taught would violate the establishment clause. Similarly, school districts have been successful in requiring teachers to follow the prescribed curriculum, which includes teaching evolution, and to stop teaching creationism as if it were also a legitimate scientific theory (*Peloza v. Capistrano Unified School District,* 1994).

In addition to challenges to curricular programs, another set of challenges has focused on the use of specific curriculum materials or methods, the wearing of particular clothing in physical education classes, and coeducational dancing in physical education classes. Most of these challenges have involved challenges brought under the free exercise clause. In deciding these cases the courts applied the same analysis used in considering religious objections to secular courses and have said that the particular method or material does not violate the establishment clause, but that the free exercise clause may give the students the right to be excused from exposure to the objectionable material or practice (Sendor, 1997). Parents in Tennessee brought suit against a school district claiming that the required use of a specific Holt, Rinehart, and Winston basic reading series violated their rights by exposing their children to beliefs that were offensive to their religious beliefs. The parents maintained that after reading the series, a child might adopt the views of "a feminist, a humanist, a pacifist, an anti-Christian, a vegetarian, or an advocate of the 'one-world government.'" On appeal, the Sixth Circuit Court of Appeals concluded that exposure to concepts does not constitute promotion of the concepts, and that no evidence existed that students were asked to affirm or deny any religious beliefs, to engage in activity forbidden by their religious beliefs, or to refrain from engaging in any action required by their religious beliefs. Accordingly, no constitutional violations were found (*Mozert v. Hawkins County Public Schools,* 1987).

Many of the curriculum materials being objected to have been used for 25 years or more with limited objection (e.g., Huckleberry Finn, Catcher in the Rye, Of Mice and Men). To what do you attribute the recent objections to such materials?

Another reading series, the *Impressions* series published by Harcourt Brace and Jovanovich, has also been the focus of a number of challenges in recent years. The series uses the whole language approach to teach reading and among its readings are selections dealing with the supernatural and witchcraft. Both the Seventh and Ninth Circuit Courts have held that mere reading about these practices, or even creating poetic chants, did not constitute the practice or advancement of these practices (*Fleischfresser v. Directors of School District 200,* 1994; *Brown v. Woodland Joint Unified School District,* 1994). In fact, echoing what seems to be the sentiment of most courts in reviewing this type of case, the court quoted from the U.S. Supreme Court's 1948 decision in *McCollum:* "If we are to eliminate everything that is objectionable to any [religious group] or inconsistent with any of their doctrines, we will leave public education in shreds" (p. 235).

Few areas of the curriculum have not been challenged as advancing secular humanism or "New Age theology." One popular target has been the Quest drug prevention curriculum. Another that has received considerable media attention is outcomes-based education. Yet another, multicultural education, is faulted for threatening traditional values and cultural heritage. Global education, psychology, sociology, and instruction pertaining to values clarification and self-esteem are also vulnerable to attack (McCarthy, 1994). This vast body of litigation has not resulted in a concrete list of what can be included and what must be excluded from the school curriculum. However, some conclusions can be drawn.

> On the one hand, schools may not tailor their programs in accordance with religious beliefs, other religious instruction or theistic moral training, or endorse the Bible as the only true source of knowledge. On the other hand, schools may not systematically purge the curriculum of all mention of religion or ideas that are consistent with religious belief, endorse atheism, or declare that science is the only source of knowledge or that the Bible is not true. (Imber & Van Geel, 1993, p. 125)

Public Support for Nonpublic Schools

In recognition of the financial burden placed on parents who pay property taxes to support the public schools as well as tuition at nonpublic schools, legislatures have regularly attempted to provide some type of public support to the schools these parents' children attend. The legal issue involved in these attempts is whether the assistance violates the First Amendment prohibition against governmental actions that promote the establishment of religion.

While most state constitutions forbid state aid to religious schools, the courts have relied on the *child benefit theory* to provide several types of assistance whose primarily benefit is to the child rather than the private school itself. This theory was first articulated by the U.S. Supreme Court in *Cochran v. Louisiana State Board of Education* (1930). In that case, the Court upheld a Louisiana law that provided for the loan of textbooks to children attending nonpublic schools. The same rationale was applied in another Supreme Court decision, *Everson v. Board of Education* (1947), which supported a New Jersey law reimbursing parents for the cost of bus transportation for children attending both public and nonpublic schools. However, the fact that the U.S. Supreme Court has said that transportation, textbooks, or the provision of other services is permissible under the federal Constitution does not mean that the states are required to provide this assistance, or that such assistance may not be prohibited by state laws or constitutions. As previously stated, the constitutions of 30 states expressly forbid the use of public funds for the support of religious schools.

Since 1970 the courts have applied the *Lemon* test in determining the constitutionality of various state aid programs. Because no two cases present the same set of facts, and because the answers to such questions as What amount of government oversight creates an "excessive entanglement"? or Under what circumstances is the "primary effect" considered aid to religion as opposed to aid to education or aid to the student? vary depending on the facts, the decisions of the courts have taken different turns for different forms of government aid (Valente, 1998).

In *Wolman v. Walter* (1977), the U.S. Supreme Court ruled on an Ohio statute that sought to provide broad support for nonpublic schools. The Court found the following aid to be constitutional:

1. The purchase or loan of secular textbooks
2. The provision and scoring of such standardized tests as are available in the public schools of the state

The courts have shown increasing favor toward state aid programs directed to parochial school students, as opposed to the schools they attend.

3. Speech, hearing, and psychological diagnostic services provided at the nonpublic schools by employees of the public schools
4. Therapeutic and remedial services provided by employees of the public schools so long as they are off the premises of the nonpublic school

Ruled unconstitutional were:

1. The purchase or loan of instructional materials and audiovisual equipment (science kits, maps, globes, and charts)
2. Providing funds for field trips

In other decisions, the Court has approved support for the cost of testing and record-keeping required by the state (*Committee for Public Education and Religious Liberty v. Regan,* 1980), but disallowed support for teacher-prepared tests (*Levitt v. Committee for Public Education and Religious Liberty,* 1973). Also disallowed have been the maintenance and repair of school facilities (*Committee for*

Public Education and Religious Liberty v. Nyquist, 1973), salary reimbursement or supplements for parochial school teachers (*Lemon v. Kurtzman,* 1971), as well as offering community education programs after school hours in sectarian schools, taught by sectarian school teachers (*School District of City of Grand Rapids v. Ball,* 1985).

In recent years, the courts have shown a greater receptivity to various types of aid directed at providing services to students. For example, in *Zobrest v. Catalina Foothills School District* (1993), the Court did not rely on the *Lemon* test but more on the child benefit theory, or neutrality principle, in ruling in favor of a deaf student's request that the school district provide him with a sign language interpreter in the Catholic school he attended. The Court stated that

> When the government offers a neutral service on the premises of a sectarian school as part of a general program that is in no way skewed towards religion, it follows . . . that provision of service does not offend the Establishment Clause. (p. 2462)

Adopting this reasoning in an even more far-reaching decision in 1997, *Agostini v. Felton,* the U.S. Supreme Court overturned two of its earlier decisions and ruled that public school employees could provide Title I remedial services in the parochial school. According to the Court, while they will continue to ask if the purpose of the aid is to advance or inhibit religion, they have changed their stand on the criteria used to assess whether the aid has an impermissible effect. Rather than acting on the presumption that the mere presence of public school employees in parochial schools created an impermissible "symbolic link" between government and religion, they held that aid that is allocated on the basis of neutral, nonsectarian criteria is not invalid under the establishment clause.

While the courts seem to be taking a more permissive stance on public support of nonpublic school students, the body of law in this area has not provided comprehensive guidance distinguishing permissible from impermissible aid. As a result, states will undoubtedly continue to attempt to provide various forms of aid, and challenges to these attempts will be resolved on a case-by-case basis.

Vouchers

Vouchers are seen as a means of providing all parents greater choice in the school their child attends. In particular, vouchers are seen as a way to extend private school options to parents in urban areas. The last decade has seen increasing support for the voucher concept. President Bush included two kinds of federal vouchers as part of his failed America 2000 plan, and Senator Robert Dole proposed "opportunity scholarships" as part of his unsuccessful 1996 presidential campaign. To date, all attempts to provide vouchers for students to attend parochial schools have been overturned by the courts. However, the decisions by the Supreme Court in *Zobrest* and *Agostinti* suggest that it is possible that the courts might consider voucher plans that provide support to the student's family to be used at *any* private or public school to be religiously neutral. In any case, there appears to be no doubt that efforts to fashion voucher plans that will pass judicial muster will continue.

Tax Relief

Various tax deduction and tax credit proposals have been introduced in the U.S. Congress, as well as in almost every state legislature. They have invariably invoked challenges on establishment clause grounds. Two have reached the U.S. Supreme Court. In *Committee for Public Education and Religious Liberty v. Nyquist* (1973), the Court overturned a New York statute that allowed state income tax credits for parents of nonpublic school students. Although the plan aided parents rather than the schools, the court said it was nonetheless an aid to religion in violation of the establishment clause.

In the decade after *Nyquist,* various other tax relief measures were struck down by the courts. Then, in *Mueller v. Allen* (1983), the Supreme Court upheld a Minnesota statute that permitted a state income tax deduction to parents of both public and nonpublic school students for expenses for tuition, books, and transportation. The Court distinguished this case from *Nyquist* in that the New York statute provided the *tax benefits* only to parents of nonpublic school students. Here, the Court said, a secular purpose was served in providing financial assistance to a "broad spectrum" of the state's citizens. Following *Mueller,* a number of states considered similar tax benefit packages, but only five states have passed legislation providing tax benefits to parents of nonpublic students (Markwood, 1995). However, advocates undoubtedly will continue to lobby for their passage.

If income tax collections are reduced as a result of providing tax benefits, how should replacement tax revenues be generated?

Compulsory Attendance

Each of the 50 states has legislation requiring school attendance—at a public, private, or parochial school—by children of a certain age range residing within the state. The age range is normally from 6 to 16 years. However, while attendance is compulsory, attendance in a specific district or at a particular school within the district may legally be restricted to those residing within the district or within a certain attendance zone. It may be constrained by voluntary or court-ordered desegregation remedies.

The residency requirement is not the same as a citizenship requirement. The U.S. Supreme Court, in *Plyler v. Doe* (1982), upheld the right of children of illegal aliens to attend school in the district of their residence. According to the Court, the state's interest in deterring illegal entry was insufficient to justify the creation and perpetuation of a subclass of illiterates within our borders. On a similar note, the courts have ruled that school districts also must educate homeless youth who have no address but are living within their boundaries.

Although it is clearly established that compulsory attendance laws are not unconstitutional, the courts have placed some limits on the right of the state to compel school attendance. In 1972, in *Wisconsin v. Yoder,* the U.S. Supreme Court recognized the interests of the Amish people in preserving their 200-year-old established way of life from the teaching of the values and worldly knowledge found in the public high schools. Within the Amish community, children are given continued education beyond elementary education through vocational training. The U.S. Supreme Court, examining the successful existence of the

Professional Reflections

"Make sure each class knows the first day what you expect of them in their behavior, respect for each other and you, the quality and timeliness of work, and the consequences if they fall short."

Charles Rossetti, Teacher of the Year, Arkansas

"Focus on what you can do something about, otherwise you will get discouraged and overwhelmed."

Ginger Brown, Teacher of the Year, California

Amish way of life, found it to be, in effect, an alternative to formal secondary education that did fulfill the state's stated goals in compelling school attendance—to prepare children to be productive and contributing members of society.

The exception given to the Amish has not been extended to others espousing religious or philosophical objections. In such cases, unlike in *Yoder,* not only have plaintiffs not shown that separation from modern society is a tenet of their faith, but the courts have ruled that the state's interest in requiring a minimum education of its youth outweighed the objection given (see, e.g., *State v. Riviera,* 1993; *Battles v. Anne Arundel County Board of Education,* 1995).

Private and Home Schooling

The states' right to mandate school attendance does not extend to requiring that schooling takes place in the public schools. In 1925, in *Pierce v. Society of Sisters,* the Supreme Court recognized the right of parents to educate their children in private schools. However, the decision also recognized the right of the state to regulate private schools, including requiring that their teachers be certified and that their curricula comply with established state guidelines.

Home schooling as a form of private schooling is another alternative to attendance in the public schools. The interest in home schooling has increased dramatically in the last decade as more and more parents have become concerned about instruction or safety in the public schools. The number of home schoolers increased from 300,000 in 1992 to more than one million in 1998 (Guterson, 1998). A number of state and national associations support the efforts of home schoolers, and a vast array of commercial curriculum materials are directed at the home schooling market. In some states and school districts home-schooled children can enroll in independent study programs through a public school or participate in some form of part-time school attendance. In other areas teachers stay in touch with the children through the phone, mail, or home visits, while in still others the public school district provides resources or various forms of instructional support to home schooling families (Lines, 1995).

Should home schools be approved by the state? Should they receive state aid?

All states allow home schooling and 35 have adopted home school statutes or regulations (Klicka, 1996). These range from those that are very strict to those that

The number of home schoolers has increased in the past decade.

require no more than that the parents notify the local school board that they are educating their child at home (Lufler, 1994). More commonly, state statutes or regulations will require that (1) instruction be essentially equivalent to that taught in the public schools and include the subjects required by state law, (2) the parent or other adult providing the instruction be qualified (not necessarily certified) to teach, (3) some systematic reporting be made to local school authorities, and (4) a minimum number of hours of instruction per day be provided. In 15 states and the District of Columbia, home schools must be approved by the local school board (Richardson, 1989). And in about two thirds of the states, students in home schools must be tested to ensure that they are mastering basic skills. In fact, a federal court has upheld a state statute making ineligible for home schooling those students whose scores fall below the 40th percentile and do not improve after home remediation (*Null v. Board of Education,* 1993). However, where states have attempted to impose requirements on home schools that were not required of the public schools, or were unreasonable, the courts have overturned the requirements (e.g., *Clonlara, Inc. v. State Board of Education,* 1993, 180-day minimum school year requirement for home schools but not for public schools).

Summary

The legal foundation of education derives from state and federal constitutional provisions, the laws of state and federal legislatures, the enactments of state and federal agencies, and court decisions. Every state constitution includes a provision for education, and the wording of the provision has proved important in determining the obligation of the state in providing for education and the constitutionality of legislative action. Although the federal Constitution does not mention education, a number of its provisions affect education and afford protection to school personnel, pupils, and patrons.

The interaction of the institutions of religion and education has become the source of increasing legal controversy in recent years. A tension exists between the efforts of the schools to accommodate religion and yet maintain the wall of separation between church and state required by the First Amendment. Thus far the courts generally have been consistent in their decisions keeping religious practices and proselytizing efforts out of the schools. However, the decisions of the U.S. Supreme Court in *Mergens* and *Zobrest* represent not only a potential crack in the wall of separation between church and state, but also the growing conservative thrust of the Court. In the next chapter other constitutional rights of teachers and students are explored.

Key Terms

Administrative law

Child benefit theory

Constitution

Eminent domain

Ex post facto law

Home schooling

Lemon test

Limited open forum

Plenary

Secular humanism

Stare decisis

Statutory law

Tax benefits

Voucher

Discussion Questions

1. Given the situation described in the vignette at the beginning of this chapter, how might Mr. Kindrick accommodate Mrs. Collins's desire to wear the cross and students' desires not to be exposed to this symbol of Christianity?

2. What are the provisions of your state constitution regarding education?

3. Describe the levels and types of state courts in your state.

4. What is your school (or school system) policy on silent meditation? Is there support for prayer or Bible reading? On what grounds?

5. What is meant by the *Lemon* test? How effective has it been in distinguishing permissible and impermissible aid to nonpublic school students?

6. How does the child benefit theory serve to justify educational vouchers? How

385

does it operate in the school systems in your area? Are textbooks provided? Is bus transportation provided?

7. What First Amendment issues are currently being debated in the schools in your area?

Internet Resources

1. **www.uscourts.gov**
The Federal Judiciary Home Page provides information about the organization and operation of the federal courts as well as links to each of the federal circuit and district courts.

2. **www.lcweb.loc.gov/catalogue**
The home page for the Library of Congress On-line Catalogue provides access to the full text of all education laws.

3. **oyez.at.nwu.edu/oyez.html**
The site for the Oyez project at Northwestern University is dedicated to the U.S. Supreme Court with an index of cases, oral arguments for most cases argued before the Court since 1991, a virtual tour of the Court, and biographies of all justices, past and present.

4. **www.lawsource.com/also**
American Law Sources On-line provides links to all on-line sources of American law that are available without charge.

5. **www.findlaw.com**
Find Law provides links to law firms, cases and codes, the federal court, as well as its "Law Crawler" search engine.

6. **gsul.gsu.edu/metaindex/**
Meta-index for Legal Research provides links to judicial opinions, legislation, federal regulations, people in law, and other legal sources.

7. **web.lexisnexis.com/universe**
Lexis Nexis Academic Universe provides links to a wide range of legal reference information.

8. **www.ilrg.com**
The Internet Legal Resources Guide provides links to 4,000 web sites, including law journals, law outlines, law schools, and selected U.S. and state courts.

9. **www.lawcrawler.com**
Law Runner: A Legal Research Tool, a search engine powered by Alta Vista, facilitates a more efficient search of Alta Vista by searching only law sites.

References

Agostini v. Felton, 521 U.S. 203 (1997).
Aguilar v. Felton, 105 S. Ct. 3232 (1985).
Battles v. Anne Arundel County Board of Education, 904 F.Supp. 471 (D. Md. 1995).
Beilan v. Board of Public Education of Philadelphia, 357 U.S. 399 (1958).
Black, H. C. (1990). *Black's law dictionary.* St. Paul, MN: West Publishing Co.

Board of Education of Westside Community Schools v. Mergens, 58 L.W. 4720 (1990).
Bown v. Gwinett County School District, 112 F.3d 1464 (11th Cir. 1997).
Brown v. Board of Education of Topeka, 347 U.S. 483 (1954).
Brown v. Woodland Joint Unified School District, 27 F.3d 1373 (9th Cir. 1994).

Clonlara, Inc. v. State Board of Education, 501 NW.2d 88 (Mich. 1993).

Cochran v. Louisiana State Board of Education, 281 U.S. 370 (1930).

Collins, G. J. (1969). Constitutional and legal basis for state action. In L. S. Fuller & J. B. Pearson (Eds.), *Education in the states: Nationwide development since 1900.* Washington, DC: National Education Association.

Committee for Public Education and Religious Liberty v. Nyquist, 413 U.S. 756 (1973).

Committee for Public Education and Religious Liberty v. Regan, 444 U.S. 646 (1980).

Doe v. Duncanville Independent School District, 70 F.3d 402 (5th Cir. 1995).

Edwards v. Aguillard, 107 S. Ct. 2573 (1987).

Engel v. Vitale, 370 U.S. 421 (1962).

Epperson v. Arkansas, 393 U.S. 97 (1968).

Everson v. Board of Education, 330 U.S. 1 (1947).

Fleischfresser v. Directors of School District 200, 15 F.3d 680 (7th Cir. 1994).

Florey v. Sioux Falls School District 49-5, 619 F.2d 1311 (8th Cir. 1980), *cert. denied,* 449 U.S. 987 (1980).

Guterson, D. (1998, October 5). No longer a fringe movement. *Newsweek,* 71.

Holland, H. M. (1995). Thurgood Marshall. *Encyclopedia Americana* (Vol. 18, p. 367). Danbury, CT: Grolier.

Imber, M., & Van Geel, T. (1993). *Education law.* New York: McGraw-Hill.

Ingebretsen v. Jackson Public School District, 88 F.3d 274 (5th Cir. 1996).

Ingraham v. Wright, 430 U.S. 651 (1977).

Jaffree v. Wallace, 472 U.S. 38 (1985).

Jones v. Clear Creek Independent School District, 977 F.2d 963 (5th Cir. 1992).

Klicka, C. J. (1996). *Home schooling in the United States: A legal analysis.* Paeonian Springs, VA: Home School Legal Defense Association.

Koenick v. Felton, 973 F.Supp. 522 (D. Md. 1997).

Lamb's Chapel v. Center Moriches School District, 959 F. 2d 381 (2d Cir. 1992), rev'd, 113 S. Ct. 2141 (1993).

Lee v. Weisman, 505 U.S. 577 (1992).

Lemon v. Kurtzman, 93 S. Ct. 1463 (1971).

Levitt v. Committee for Public Education and Religious Liberty, 413 U.S. 472 (1973).

Lines, P. (1995). Home schooling. *ERIC Digest,* Number 95. Eugene, OR: Clearinghouse on Educational Management.

Lufler, H. S., Jr. (1994). Pupils. In S. B. Thomas (Ed.), *The yearbook of education law 1994* (pp. 59–87). Topeka, KS: National Organization on Legal Problems of Education.

Markwood, M. L. (1995). State constitutions and state aid to sectarian education. *Religion and Education, 22,* 31–45.

McCarthy, M. M. (1994). *External challenges to public education: Values in conflict.* Paper presented at the annual meeting of the American Educational Research Association, New Orleans, April, 1994.

McCarthy, M. M., Cambron-McCabe, N. B., & Thomas, S. B. (1998). *Public school law: Teachers and students rights* (4th ed.). Boston: Allyn and Bacon.

McCollum v. Board of Education of School District No. 71, 333 U.S. 203 (1948).

Metzl v. Leininger, 850 F.Supp. 740 (Ill. 1995).

Mozert v. Hawkins County Public Schools, 827 F. 2d 1058 (6th Cir. 1987).

Mueller v. Allen, 103 S. Ct. 3062 (1983).

Null v. Board of Education of the County of Jackson, 815 F.Supp. 937 (S. D. W. Va. 1993).

Peloza v. Capistrano Unified School District, 37 F.3d 517 (9th Cir. 1994), *cert. denied,* 115 S. Ct. 2640 (1995).

Pierce v. Society of Sisters, 268 U.S. 510 (1925).

Plessey v. Ferguson, 16 S. Ct. 1138 (1896).

Plyler v. Doe, 457 U.S. 202 (1982).

Richardson, S. N. (1989). Home schooling. *NOLPE Notes, 24*(6), 6.

School District of Abington Township v. Schempp, 374 U.S. 203 (1963).

School District of City of Grand Rapids v. Ball, 718 F. 2d 1389 (6th Cir. 1983), *aff'd,* 473 U. S. 373 (1985).

Sendor, B. B. (1997). *A legal guide to religion and public education* (2nd ed.). Dayton, OH: Education Law Association.

Sherman v. Consolidated District 21 of Wheeling Township, 980 F.2d 437 (7th Cir. 1992), *cert. denied,* 508 U.S. 950 (1993).

State v. Riviera, 497 N.W.2d 878 (Iowa 1993).

Steele v. Van Buren Public School District, 845 F. 2d 1492 (8th Cir. 1988).

Stone v. Graham, 449 U.S. 39 (1980).

Valente, W. D. (1998). *Law in the schools* (4th ed.). New York: Macmillian.

Wallace v. Jaffree, 105 S. Ct. 2479 (1985).

Walsh, M. (1995, August 2). President offers guidance on religion in schools. *Education Week,* pp. 23, 30.

Ware v. Valley Stream High School District, 545 N.Y.S. 2d 316 (N.Y. App. Div.), appeal denied, 545 N.Y.S. 2d 539 (N.Y. 1989).

Washegesie v. Bloomington Public Schools, 33 F.3d 679 (6th Cir. 1994), *cert. denied* 115S.Ct. 1822 (1995).

West Virginia State Board of Education v. Barnette, 319 U.S. 624 (1943).

Wisconsin v. Yoder, 406 U.S. 205 (1972).

Wolman v. Walter, 433 U.S. 229 (1977).

Zobrest v. Catalina Foothills School District, 113 S. Ct. 2462 (1993).

Zorach v. Clauson, 72 S. Ct. 679 (1952).

Chapter 12

If there is any principle of the Constitution that more imperatively calls for attachment than any other it is the principle of free thought—not free thought for those who agree with us, but freedom for the thought that we hate.

Justice Oliver Wendell Holmes, Jr. (1841–1935)

Teachers, Students, and the Law

➤ *Ms. Przanowski is a third grade teacher. It is the first day of the school year. After giving a writing assignment, she walks around the room. The children are bent over their desks busily writing "What I Did on My Summer Vacation." Stopping at Johnny Avery's desk, she notices deep scratch marks on his neck. When asked how he got the marks, Johnny says his cat scratched him. After school, however, Marty Robinson, who was sitting near Johnny when Ms. Przanowski asked the question and heard Johnny's reply, comes to her and volunteers that "Johnny has marks all over his back. I saw them during gym."*

The next day Ms. Przanowski asks Johnny about the marks and also asks him if he has any marks on his back and if she can see them. Johnny continues to say that the marks came from his cat, but refues to let Ms. Przanowski see his back.

What should Ms. Przanowski do now? What are the consequences for the teacher if she fails to report the incident and subsequent child abuse occurs and is confirmed? What are the consequences if she reports her suspicions and subsequent examination proves no further injury?

Like Ms. Przanowski, teachers must make decisions every day that affect the rights of students, their own rights, and their professional lives. Therefore, it is imperative that teachers be knowledgeable about applicable state and federal legislation, school board policies, and court decisions. After completing this chapter, you will be able to:

- Identify the personal and professional requirements for employment of prospective teachers.
- Describe teachers' employment rights as derived from the employment contract and tenure status.
- Discuss the teacher's responsibility in reporting child abuse and using copyrighted materials.
- Outline the legal requirements for dismissing a teacher.
- Provide an overview of teachers' rights, inside and outside the classroom.
- Define the elements of negligence.
- Compare equal opportunity and affirmative action.

- Contrast the procedural requirements for suspension, expulsion, and corporal punishment.
- Trace the development of student rights in the area of search and seizure.
- Explain the restraints that may be placed on student expression and personal appearance.
- Distinguish between *quid pro quo* and hostile environment harassment as the concepts apply to employees and students.
- Summarize the response of the courts and school districts to school attendance by AIDS victims.
- Discuss how the Buckley Amendment has expanded parental and student rights.

Teacher Rights and Responsibilities

Although school personnel are not expected to be legal experts, it is imperative that they understand their rights and obligations under the law and that these rights and obligations be translated into everyday practices in the schools. In this chapter the basic concepts of law are presented as they relate to terms and conditions of employment; teacher dismissal; teacher rights inside and outside the classroom; tort liability; discrimination, equal opportunity, and affirmative action; and certain legal responsibilities of teachers. Although there is some variation in the application of these legal concepts from one state or locality to another, certain topics and issues are of sufficient importance and similarity to warrant consideration. Some of these topics are also discussed in other chapters of this text. Here, attention is given to the legal considerations of these topics.

Terms and Conditions of Employment

As emphasized in the previous chapter, within the framework provided by state and federal constitutional and statutory protections, the state has complete power to conduct and regulate public education. Through its legislature, state board of education, state department of education, and local school boards, the state promulgates the rules and regulations for the operation of the schools. Among these rules and regulations are those establishing the terms and conditions of employment. The areas most often covered by state statutory and regulatory provisions are those dealing with certification, citizenship and residency requirements, health and physical requirements, contracts, and tenure.

Certification

As noted in Chapter 1, to qualify for most professional teaching, administrative, and other positions in the public schools, an individual must acquire a valid certificate or license. The certificate does not constitute a contract or guarantee of employment; it only makes the holder eligible for employment.

Does certification ensure a quality teaching force? How might they be improved in the state in which you plan to teach?

All states have established certification requirements for prospective teachers. These requirements may include a college degree with minimum credit hours in specific curricular areas, evidence of specific job experience, "good moral character," a specified age, U.S. citizenship, the signing of a loyalty oath, good health, and a minimum score on a job-related exam. Where specified certification requirements exist, failure to meet the requirements can result in dismissal of the employee.

Citizenship and Residency Requirements

The courts have upheld both citizenship and residency requirements for certification and/or as a condition of employment. With regard to the citizenship requirement, the U.S. Supreme Court has held that education is among those governmental functions that is "so bound up with the operation of the state as a governmental entity as to permit the exclusion from those functions of all persons who have not become part of the process of self-government" (*Ambach v. Norwick,* 1979, pp. 73–74).

Requirements that teachers reside within the district where they are employed have been upheld if it can be shown that there is a rational basis for the requirements. For example, the Arkansas Supreme Court determined that a school district requirement that teachers reside within the district or within 10 miles of town was "rationally related to community involvement and district identity as it related to tax base in support of district tax levies, and [the] 10 mile limit was reasonable commuting distance and was not arbitrary" (*McClelland v. Paris Public Schools,* 1988, p. 908). It should be noted, however, that while residency requirements have been upheld in many jurisdictions, a number of states have statutory provisions prohibiting school districts from imposing such requirements (McCarthy, Cambron-McCabe, & Thomas, 1998).

Health and Physical Requirements

Most states and school boards have adopted health and physical requirements for teachers. The courts have recognized that such requirements are necessary to protect the health and welfare of students and other employees. Accordingly, the courts have upheld the release or reassignment of employees in instances where their failed eyesight, hearing, or other physical condition made it impossible for them to meet their contractual duties. The courts have also upheld school districts in requiring medical examinations to determine employees' fitness to perform their duties. In fact, in *Harris v. Board of Education of Columbus, Ohio* (1992), the court said the duty the administration owed to the school and the district provided sufficient grounds to require the medical examination of a 69-year-old teacher in relation to his dsyphonia (voice strain), diabetes, and heart-related problems.

While the courts have upheld school districts' imposition of health and physical requirements, they are concerned that such requirements not be arbitrarily applied, be specific to the position, and not violate state and federal laws intended to protect the rights of the handicapped. For example, Section 504 of the Rehabilitation Act of 1973, which protects otherwise qualified handicapped individuals from discrimination, served as the basis for a 1987 U.S. Supreme Court ruling that overturned the dismissal of an Arkansas teacher with tuberculosis (*School Board of Nassau County v. Arline,* 1987). The Court concluded that persons suffering from the contagious disease of tuberculosis had a physical impairment that justified their being considered handicapped persons within the meaning of the Rehabilitation Act. Accordingly, discrimination based solely on fear of contamination is to be considered discrimination against the handicapped. The Supreme Court instructed the lower court to determine if the teacher posed a "significant risk" that would preclude her from being "otherwise qualified" and if her condition could reasonably be accommodated by the district. Ultimately the court found the teacher posed little risk, was otherwise qualified, and she was reinstated with back pay.

The decision in *Arline* and the provisions of Section 504 have been relied on by plaintiff teachers in cases involving AIDS. In the lead case, *Chalk v. U.S.*

How would you respond to being assigned to team with a colleague who has a contagious disease?

District Court Cent. Dist. of California (1988), the U.S. District Court relied heavily on the significant risk standard articulated in *Arline* to determine when a contagious disease would prevent an individual from being "otherwise qualified." In applying the "significant risk of communicating" standard in this instance, the court found that the overwhelming consensus of medical and scientific opinion regarding the nature and transmission of AIDS did not support a conclusion that Chalk posed a significant risk of communicating the disease to children or others through casual social contact.

A major federal statute impacting on health and physical requirements for school district employees is the Americans With Disabilities Act of 1990, which prohibits employment discrimination against "qualified individuals with a disability." Such a person is defined as one who "satisfies the requisite skill, experience, education, and other job-related requirements of the [position] . . . and who, with or without reasonable accommodation, can perform the essential functions" of the position. While the law does not require the hiring or retention of unqualified persons, it does prohibit specific actions of employers that adversely affect the employment opportunities of disabled persons (e.g., inquiring into a disability or requiring a medical examination before an offer is made, or writing job descriptions that include nonessential job functions), and it does require employers to make "reasonable accommodation" for a known mental or physical disability.

An area of current dispute in regard to health and physical requirements for school employees involves mandatory testing for AIDS or alcohol or drug use. To date the courts have held that mandatory urine and blood tests that are not part of a routine medical examination required by law or agreed to by the employee violate the Fourth Amendment prohibition against unreasonable searches unless there is an "individualized reasonable suspicion" of a condition that imperils the proper functioning of the teacher or the well-being of others. However, where an employee's history or job duties implicate student safety (e.g., driving a school bus), he or she may be required to undergo testing without violating the Fourth Amendment (Valente, 1998).

The Employment Contract

The general principles of contract law apply to the teacher employment contract. That is, in order for the contract to be valid, it must contain the basic elements of (1) offer and acceptance, (2) legally competent parties, (3) consideration (compensation), (4) legal subject matter, and (5) agreement in form required by law. In addition, the employment contract must meet the specific requirements of applicable state law.

The authority to contract lies exclusively with the school board. Although the superintendent or other officials may screen candidates and recommend employment, only the school board is authorized to enter into contracts, and only when it is a legally constituted body. That is, contracts issued when a quorum of the board is not present, or at an illegally called meeting of the board (e.g., adequate notice is not given), are not valid.

In order to be enforceable, a contract must pertain to a legal subject matter (i.e., a contract for the purchase of illegal substances or the performance of illegal services is not enforceable). Also, the contract must be in the proper form required by law. In most states this means the contract must be in writing and signed. However, unless so required by state law, an oral agreement that contains all the legal requirements of a contract can be legally binding on both parties (McCarthy, Cambron-McCabe, & Thomas, 1998).

The employee's rights and obligations of employment are derived from the contract. The courts have held that all valid rules and regulations of the school board, as well as all applicable state statutes, are part of the contract, even if not specifically included. Accordingly, employees may be required to perform certain tasks incidental to classroom activities, regardless of whether the contract specifically mentions them. These have included such activities as field trips, playground and cafeteria duty, supervision of extracurricular activities, and club sponsorship. Teachers cannot, however, be required to drive a bus, perform janitorial duties, or perform duties unrelated to the school program.

Tenure

Tenure is "the status conferred upon teachers who have served a probationary period . . . which then guarantees them continual employment until retirement, subject to the requirements of good behavior, financial necessity, and in some instances good periodic evaluations" (Sperry, Daniel, Huefner, & Gee, 1998, p. 1041). Tenure is a creation of statute designed to maintain permanent and qualified instructional personnel. Most state statutes specify the requirements and procedures for obtaining tenure, which normally include the satisfactory completion of a probationary period of three years. During the probationary period the teacher is usually issued a one-year contract that, subject to satisfactory service and district finances, is renewable at the end of each of the probationary years prior to tenure.

However, satisfactory completion of the probationary period does not guarantee tenure. In most states school districts are not required to give the reasons for a nonrenewal of a contract during the probationary period or to provide a hearing on the decision not to renew. However, most states do require that the probationary teacher be given timely notice of intent to nonrenew. And, in all cases, if the district attempts to break the contract of a probationary teacher during the term of the contract, the teacher must be given, at a minimum, a notice of dismissal and a hearing on the causes. In some states tenure is automatically awarded at the end of the probationary period unless the school board notifies the teacher that he or she will not be rehired, while in other states official action of the school board is necessary for the awarding of tenure.

Tenure statutes normally specify the grounds for dismissal of a tenured teacher as well as the procedures that must be followed in the dismissal. The dismissal protection afforded tenured teachers compared to nontenured teachers is perhaps the major benefit of obtaining tenure. Tenure status gives teachers the security of practicing their profession without threat of removal for arbitrary, capricious, or political motivations. In fact, the courts have said that the granting of tenure in effect awards the teacher with a *property right* to continued employment that cannot be taken away without due process of law.

Does a tenure system protect incompetent teachers? What is your response to proposals that the tenure system be abolished?

However, the awarding of tenure does not guarantee permanent employment. The teacher may be dismissed for disciplinary reasons (for cause) or because declining enrollments, financial exigencies, or other circumstances necessitated a reduction in force. The granting of tenure also does not guarantee the right to teach in a particular school, grade, or subject area. Subject to due process requirements, teachers may be reassigned to any position for which they are certified.

Legal Responsibilities of Teachers

In addition to the terms and conditions of employment disclosed in the preceding section, other requirements may be made as a condition of teacher employment as long as they do not violate teacher rights or state or federal law. Some requirements, such as those related to providing reasonable care and maintaining discipline, are discussed later in this chapter. Requirements related to two topics, reporting child abuse and use of copyrighted materials, are discussed here. These topics have become increasingly important to educators in the last decade.

Reporting Child Abuse and Neglect

As discussed in Chapter 10, teachers are among those professionals named in state statutes as being required to report suspected child abuse and neglect. State reporting statutes apply not only to suspected parental abuse but also to suspected abuse by school employees. Under most state supporting statutes, failure to report abuse may result in the teacher being found criminally liable, with penalties as high as a year in jail and a fine of $1,000. A civil suit claiming negligence also may be brought against the teacher for failure to report child abuse. In addition, school districts may also impose disciplinary measures against employees for failure to follow required reporting statutes (McCarthy, Cambron-McCabe, & Thomas, 1998). Because of the serious consequences of failure to report child abuse—to the child, the teacher, and possibly the district (the district could be required to pay monetary damages if liability is found)—most school boards also have adopted policies affirming the responsibility of district employees to report child abuse and detailing the procedures to be followed when abuse is suspected. Such policies are also intended to protect employees against false charges of child abuse.

State statutes that require teachers to report suspected child abuse do not demand that reporters be absolutely sure that the child has been abused, only that there be "reasonable cause to believe" that the child is subject to abuse or neglect. Under all state statutes, school employees who report suspected child abuse or neglect are immune from civil and criminal prosecution if the report was made in good faith, and in many states good faith is presumed and the person challenging the reporter would have to prove that the reporter acted in bad faith.

Observing Copyrights

Copyright laws are designed to protect the author or originator of an original work from unauthorized reproduction or use of the work. Because of their widespread use of print and nonprint material in the classroom, it is important that teachers be

Teachers are responsible for prohibiting unauthorized use of copyrighted computer software in their classes.

knowledgeable about, and comply with, federal copyright laws. The *fair use doctrine* allows the nonprofit reproduction and use of certain materials for classroom use without permission of the copyright owner if each copy bears the copyright notice and meets the tests of brevity, spontaneity, and cumulative effect outlined in the Guidelines for Classroom Copying presented in Figure 12.1.

The increasing use of instructional technology has brought to light a number of issues related to use of copyrighted nonprint materials, namely, television programs, videotapes, and computer software. In 1981 Congress issued Guidelines for Off-the-Air Recording of Broadcast Programming for Educational Purposes. The guidelines provide that a nonprofit educational institution may tape broadcast television programs for classroom use if requested by an individual teacher. Programs also may be taped at home by the teacher. All copies must include the copyright notice on the program. During the first 10 days after taping,

Figure 12.1: Guidelines for Classroom Copying

1. A single copy may be made of any of the following for your own scholarly research or use in teaching:

   A. A chapter from a book;

   B. An article from a periodical or newspaper;

   C. A short story, short essay, or short poem;

   D. A chart, graph, diagram, drawing, cartoon or picture from a book, periodical, or newspaper.

2. Multiple copies (not to exceed in any event more than one copy per pupil in a course) may be made for classroom use or discussion, provided that each copy includes a notice of copyright and that the following tests are met:

   A. Brevity Test

   (i) Poetry: (a) a complete poem if less than 250 words and if printed on not more than two pages, or (b) from a longer poem, an excerpt of not more than 250 words.
   (ii) Prose: (a) Either a complete article, story, or essay of less than 2,500 words, or (b) an excerpt from any prose work of not more than 1,000 words or 10 percent of the work, whichever is less, but in any event a minimum of 500 words.
   (iii) Illustration: One chart, graph, diagram, drawing, cartoon or picture per book or per periodical issue.
   (iv) "Special" works in poetry, prose, or in "poetic prose" that combine language with illustrations and are less than 2,500 words in their entirety may not be reproduced in their entirety; however, an excerpt of not more than two of the published pages of such special work and containing not more than 10 percent of the words may be reproduced.

   B. Spontaneity Test

   (i) The copying is at your instance and inspiration, and
   (ii) The inspiration and decision to use the work and the moment of its use for maximum teaching effectiveness are so close in time that it would be unreasonable to expect you would receive a timely reply to a request for permission.

   C. Cumulative Effect Test

   (i) The coping of the material is for only one course in the school in which the copies are made.
   (ii) Not more than one short poem, article, story, essay or two excerpts may be copied from the same author, nor more than three from the same collective work or periodical volume during one class term.
   (iii) There cannot be more than nine instances of multiple copying for one course during one class term.

   [These limitations do not apply to current news periodicals and newspapers and current news sections of other periodicals.]

3. Copying cannot be used to create or to replace or substitute for anthologies, compilations, or collective works.

4. There can be no copying of, or from, "consumable" works (e.g., workbooks, exercises, standardized tests and test booklets and answer sheets).

5. Copying cannot substitute for the purchase of books, publishers' reprints, or periodicals.

6. Copying cannot be directed by a higher authority.

7. You cannot copy the same item from term to term.

8. No charge can be made to the student beyond the actual cost of the photocopying.

Source: Excerpt from Report of the House Committee on the Judiciary (House Report No. 94–1476).

the material may be shown once by the individual teacher and may be repeated only once for purposes of instructional reinforcement. Additional use is limited to viewing for evaluating the program. After 45 days the tape must be erased or destroyed. All other off-the-air recording (except for the purpose of time shifting for personal use) is illegal unless the program is recorded from educational television. These recordings may be shown for a period of seven days after the broadcast, but must then be erased or destroyed. The taping of television programs telecast by cable or satellite providers does not fall under these guidelines because they are not free to the public. Before taping any programs carried by cable or satellite, the particular station or network should be contacted to determine their taping guidelines (Botterbusch, 1996).

The copying of computer software and material on the Internet and World Wide Web has become a major area of copyright infringement. The high cost of software, combined with limited school budgets, has resulted in numerous cases of unauthorized copying of software. In 1980 the copyright law was amended to include software. According to the amendments, one archival or backup copy can be made of the master program; making multiple copies, even for educational purposes, would be a violation of the fair use principle. However, teachers and school districts can negotiate license agreements with a software company that would allow for multiple use of a particular program at a substantial savings over purchasing multiple copies. In the use of copyrighted software, as in the use of any copyrighted material, teachers are required to obey both the letter and the spirit of copyright laws and adhere to any relevant school board policies or guidelines. In the case of materials found on the Internet or World Wide Web, educators should remember that even if the materials are not registered with the copyright office, they still are protected by copyright laws and should not be considered in the public domain unless specifically stated (Botterbusch, 1996).

Teacher Dismissal

Grounds for Dismissal

The statutory provisions regarding teacher dismissal "for cause" vary among the states both in terms of the specified grounds for dismissal as well as the legal requirements for dismissal. The behaviors that would justify dismissal apply equally to tenured and nontenured teachers. The reasons for dismissal most frequently cited in statutes are immorality, incompetency, and insubordination. Among the other commonly mentioned reasons are neglect of duty, unprofessional conduct, unfitness to teach, and the catch-all, "other good and just cause." Most challenges to dismissals center around two primary issues: (1) whether the conduct in question fit the statutory grounds for dismissal, and (2) if so, whether the school board presented the facts necessary to sustain the charge. The burden of proof in justifying a dismissal lies with the school board and must be supported by sufficient evidence to justify the dismissal. In addition, as will be discussed in the next section, in any dismissal, the school board must provide the teacher with all the due process required by state statute, school board policy, or negotiated agreement.

Immorality. Although immorality is the most frequently cited ground for dismissal in state statutes, they normally do not define the term or discuss its application to specific conduct. As a consequence, these tasks have been left to the courts. A review of cases challenging dismissals related to immorality shows that they generally have been based on one or more of the following categories of conduct: (1) sexual conduct with students; (2) sexual conduct with nonstudents; (3) homosexuality; (4) making sexually explicit remarks or talking about sex unrelated to the curriculum; (5) distribution of sexually explicit materials to classes; (6) use of obscene, profane, or abusive language; (7) possession and use of controlled substances; (8) other criminal misconduct; and (9) dishonesty.

Should teachers be held to a higher standard of conduct than other professionals? Why or why not?

While acknowledging that the concept of immorality "is subject to ranging interpretations based on shifting social attitudes [and therefore] must be resolved on the facts and circumstances of each case" (*Ficus v. Board of School Trustees of Central School District,* 1987, p. 1,140), some standards have evolved from the cases in this area and are often applied to other cases involving dismissal for immorality. The first is the exemplar standard. While not as universally accepted today as in the past, the courts do recognize that there are "legitimate standards to be expected of those who teach in the public schools" (*Reitmeyer v. Unemployment Compensation Board of Review,* 1992, p. 508—teacher dismissed for distribution of racist "joke sheet" to coworkers). Second, in most jurisdictions there must be a connection between the out-of-school conduct of the teacher and the teacher's ability to teach, or the conduct must have an adverse effect on the school relationship or be the subject of public notoriety. The exceptions to the principle that the behavior must affect teaching performance or become the subject of notoriety have been made most often in regard to notoriously illegal or immoral behavior, including sexual conduct with minors.

Since the facts of no two cases are exactly the same, the connection may exist in one case involving a particular conduct but not in another. For example, the courts also have held that conviction of a felony or misdemeanor, including possession of illegal drugs, does not necessarily, in and of itself, serve as grounds for dismissal. Again, the circumstances of each case are important, especially the effect on the school, students, and coworkers. Thus, the courts might not uphold the dismissal of a teacher solely because he or she once was indicted for possession of a small amount of marijuana, but they probably would support a firing based on evidence of a widely publicized conviction, combined with testimony that the teacher's criminal behavior would undermine his or her effectiveness as a teacher (Fischer, Schimmel, & Kelly, 1995). Similarly, some courts have overturned the dismissal of homosexual and bisexual teachers based only on their private conduct, when no conviction of law had taken place. In Washington, a high school teacher was dismissed after admitting to his assistant principal that he was a homosexual. Although it was not the teacher but school officials who then publicized his homosexual status, the court accepted the officials' testimony that his continued presence would interfere with the orderly operation of the school (*Gaylord v. Tacoma School District No. 10,* 1977).

While cases involving alleged immoral conduct must be settled on a case-by-case basis, the courts have agreed on the factors to be considered in determining if the alleged conduct renders the teacher unfit to teach. These factors include (1) the age and maturity of the teacher's students, (2) the likelihood that the teacher's conduct will have an adverse effect on students or other teachers, (3) degree of anticipated adversity, (4) proximity of the conduct, (5) extenuating or aggravating circumstances surrounding the conduct, (6) likelihood that the conduct would be repeated, (7) underlying motives, and (8) the chilling effect on the rights of teachers (*In Re Thomas*, 1996).

Incompetency. Those conditions or behaviors that have been sustained most successfully as constituting *incompetence* fall into five general categories: (1) inadequate teaching, (2) lack of knowledge of the subject matter, (3) poor discipline, (4) physical or mental incapacity, and (5) willful neglect of duty. As with dismissals for alleged immorality, in dismissals for incompetence the courts require that there be an established relationship between the employee's conduct and the operation of the school. Additionally, the standard against which the teacher is measured must be one used for other teachers in a similar position, not some hypothetical standard of perfection, and the conduct must not be an isolated incident but a demonstrated pattern of incompetence. Most jurisdictions also require that before termination a determination be made as to whether or not the behavior in question is remedial, a notice of deficiency be given, and a reasonable opportunity to remediate be provided.

Insubordination. Regardless of whether or not it is specified in statute, *insubordination* is an acceptable cause for dismissal in all states. Insubordination involves the *persistent* and *willful* violation of a reasonable rule or direct order from a recognized authority. The rule must not only be reasonable, but it must be clearly communicated and cannot be an infringement upon the teacher's constitutional rights. For example, rules that limit what teachers can say or write may in some cases violate their First Amendment right to free speech. Normally, unless the insubordinate act is severe, a single action is insufficient grounds for dismissal.

In cases involving insubordination it is not necessary to establish a relationship between the insubordinate action(s) and teaching effectiveness. Among the actions that have been held to constitute insubordination are unauthorized absence from duty, abuse of sick leave, refusal to follow established policies and procedures, inappropriate use of corporal punishment, refusal to meet with superiors, encouraging students to disobey school authority, refusal to perform assigned nonteaching duties, failure to acquire required approval for use of instructional materials, and refusal to cease extemporaneous prayer and the reading of Bible stories.

Procedural Due Process

In keeping with the Fourteenth Amendment, if the dismissal of a teacher involves either a property or liberty right, *procedural due process* must be provided. As previously noted, teachers that are tenured have a "property right" to continued employment. Nontenured teachers do not have a property right claim to due

*Should non-
tenured teachers
be given the
same due
process as
tenured teachers
in nonrenewal of
contracts? Why
or why not?*

process unless they are dismissed during the contract year or unless the dismissal action impairs a fundamental constitutional right, creates a stigma, or damages the employee's reputation to the extent that it forecloses other employment opportunities. Nontenured teachers may also establish a *liberty interest* claim if the nonrenewal decision was made to retaliate for the teacher's exercise of one of his or her fundamental liberties.

Once it has been established that a school district action requires procedural due process, the central issue becomes what process is due. In arriving at its decision, the court will look to the procedural due process requirements in state statutes, state agency or school board regulations, or employment contracts to determine both their propriety and the extent to which they were followed.

Generally the courts have held that an employee facing a severe loss such as termination of employment must be ensured the following procedural elements:

1. notice of charges
2. the opportunity for a hearing
3. adequate time to prepare a rebuttal to the charges
4. the names of witnesses and access to evidence
5. a hearing before an impartial tribunal
6. the right to representation by legal counsel
7. the opportunity to introduce evidence and cross-examine witnesses
8. a decision based solely on the evidence presented and the findings of the hearing
9. a transcript or record of the hearing
10. the opportunity to appeal (McCarthy, Cambron-McCabe, & Thomas, 1998)

Notice must not merely be given, it must be timely (on or before an established date) and in sufficient specificity to enable the employee to attempt to remediate or to prepare an adequate defense. A formal hearing as practiced in courts is not required, but the hearing must provide the employee a full and fair opportunity to rebut all charges. Table 12.1 lists some Supreme Court cases affecting teachers' rights in matters of employment and in matters inside and outside the classroom.

Teacher Rights Outside the Classroom

School boards in this country have historically considered it their right, indeed their responsibility, to control the personal as well as the professional conduct of teachers. School boards have sought to regulate teachers' dress, speech, religion, and association. However, in the last quarter of the twentieth century, teacher activism, court decisions, and enlightened legislators and school boards have greatly expanded the rights of teachers.

Freedom of Expression

In the landmark U.S. Supreme Court decision regarding freedom of expression in the public schools, *Tinker v. Des Moines* (1969), the Court ruled that neither teachers nor students shed their constitutional rights to freedom of speech or expression

Table 12.1: Selected U.S. Supreme Court Cases Affecting Teachers' Rights

Case	Decision
Indiana *ex rel.* Anderson v. Brand (1938)	Tenure statutes provide qualifying teachers with contractual rights that cannot be altered by the state without good cause.
Keyishian v. Board of Regents (1967)	Loyalty oaths that make mere membership in a subversive organization grounds for dismissal are unconstitutionally overboard.
Pickering v. Board of Education (1968)	Absent proof of false statements knowingly or recklessly made, teachers may not be dismissed for exercising the freedom to speak on matters of public interest.
Board of Regents v. Roth (1972)	A nontenured teacher does not have a property right to continued employment and can be dismissed without a statement of cause or a hearing as long as the employee's reputation or future employment have not been impaired.
Perry v. Sindermann (1972)	Teachers may not be dismissed for public criticism of superiors on matters of public concern.
Cleveland Board of Ed. v. Le Fleur (1974)	School board policy requiring that all pregnant teachers take mandatory leave is unconstitutional.
Hortonville Joint School District No. 1 v. Hortonville Education Association (1976)	A school board may serve as the impartial hearing body in a due process hearing.
Washington v. Davis (1976)	To sustain a claim of discrimination an employee must show that the employer's action was a deliberate attempt to discriminate, not just that the action resulted in a disproportionate impact.
Mount Healthy City School District v. Doyle (1977)	To prevail in a First Amendment dismissal case school district employees must show that the conduct was protected and was a substantial and motivating decision not to renew the contract, and the school board must prove that it would have reached the same decision in the absence of the protected conduct.
United States v. South Carolina (1978)	Use of the National Teachers Examinations both as a requirement for certification and as a factor in salary determination serves a legitimate state purpose and is not unconstitutional despite its disparate racial impact.
Connick v. Myers (1983)	The First Amendment guarantee of freedom of expression does not extend to teachers' public comments on matters of personal interest (as opposed to matters of public concern).
Cleveland Board of Education v. Laudermill (1985)	A teacher who can be dismissed only for cause is entitled to an oral or written notice of charges, a statement of the evidence against him or her, and the opportunity to present his or her side prior to termination.
Garland Independent School District v. Texas State Teachers Association (1986)	Teachers can use the interschool mail system and school mailboxes to distribute union material.
Wygant v. Jackson Board of Education (1986)	Absent evidence that the school board has engaged in discrimination or that the preferred employees have been victims of discrimination, school board policies may not give preferential treatment based on race or ethnicity in layoff decisions.
School Board of Nassau County v. Arline (1987)	Persons suffering from contagious diseases are considered handicapped persons, and discrimination against them based solely on fear of contamination is considered unconstitutional discrimination against the handicapped.

when they enter the schoolhouse gate. However, this does not mean that teachers or students are free to say or write anything they wish. Rather, in reviewing cases involving expression, the courts attempt to balance the rights of the individual against the harm caused to the schools.

In the lead case involving teachers' freedom of expression, Marvin Pickering, a high school teacher in Illinois, was terminated after writing a letter to the newspaper severely criticizing the superintendent and school board for their handling of school funds. On appeal the U.S. Supreme Court (*Pickering v. Board of Education,* 1968) overturned his dismissal and ruled that teachers, as citizens, do have the right to make critical public comments on matters of public concern. The Court further held that unless the public expression undermines the effectiveness of the working relationship between the teacher and his or her superior or coworkers, the employee's ability to perform his or her duties, or the orderly operation of the schools, such expression may not furnish grounds for reprisal. Finding that the issue of school board spending is an issue of legitimate public concern, that Pickering's statements were not directed at people he normally worked with, nor that there was any disruption of the operation of the schools (in fact, the letter had been greeted with apathy by everyone but the board), the Supreme Court overturned Pickering's dismissal.

If, however, the public comment is not related to matters of public concern, it is not protected. The U.S. Supreme Court ruled in *Connick v. Myers* (1983) that free expression is not protected when a public employee "speaks not as a citizen upon matters of public concern, but instead as an employee upon matters only of personal interest" (p. 147). Thus, comments related to political advocacy and policies governing the welfare of students or the school district have been found to be matters of public concern, while comments or complaints about individual work assignments, unfavorable performance evaluations, conditions of employment, or relations with superiors generally have been found to be matters of private grievance, not public concern (McCarthy, Cambron-McCabe, & Thomas, 1998).

Even if expression does involve a matter of public concern, it still is not protected if the impact of the expression undermines the effectiveness of working relationships or is disruptive to the normal operation of the schools. For example, the Fourth Circuit upheld the dismissal of a teacher who wrote and circulated a letter to fellow teachers objecting to a delay in receiving summer pay, complaining about budgetary management, and encouraging teachers to stage a "sick-out" during final examination week. The court ruled that any First Amendment interest inherent in the letter was outweighed by the public interest in having public education provided by teachers loyal to that service (i.e., not causing a disruption of exams by a sick-out that was in violation of district policy and the teachers contract and professionally questionable behavior), and by the employer interest "in having its employees abide by reasonable policies adopted to control sick leave and maintain morale and effective operation of the schools" (*Stroman v. Colleton County School District,* 1992, p. 159).

What actually constitutes disruptive speech was not defined by the *Pickering* court. However, a subsequent Supreme Court decision held that public employers need not prove that the speech actually caused a material disruption, only that at

Teachers have the right to participate in demonstrations.

the time of the employer's disciplinary action the employer "reasonably believed" the speech would be disruptive (*Waters v. Churchill,* 1994). The effect of the *Waters* decision, together with *Connick,* is to make it "more difficult for public employees to succeed in claims that adverse employment actions have impaired their First Amendment expression rights than was true in the decade following *Pickering*" (McCarthy, Cambron-McCabe, & Thomas, 1998, p. 275).

Right to Organize, Bargain Collectively, and Strike

The associational rights of teachers have been greatly expanded in the last quarter-century. The courts have ruled that teachers have the right of free association, and unjustified interference with this right by school boards violates the Fourteenth Amendment. In fact, the Supreme Court has sanctioned the use of the school mail for dissemination of union literature, as well as the right to engage in discussion of union activities during nonclass time (*Texas State Teachers' Association v. Garland Independent School District,* 1986).

   Although teachers have a right to form or join a union or professional association, whether they have a right to engage in collective bargaining depends on state law. About 40 states have passed laws permitting school boards to engage

Should teachers be denied the right to strike? What would you do if your professional association called for a strike when state law forbids teachers to strike?

in collective bargaining with teacher groups. The collective bargaining laws vary widely. Some states require school boards only to "meet and confer" with the teacher organization. Other statutes are much more detailed, specifying the topics to be negotiated (typically, salary, leaves of absence, job benefits, and transfers) and the procedures to be followed if an impasse occurs in negotiations (Fischer, Schimmel, & Kelly, 1995).

Despite the recognition of the right of teachers to organize, the right to strike has not been recognized by the courts and is denied by about half the states. In those states where strikes are allowed, they usually are allowed only after the requirements for impasse resolution have been met and only after the school board has been notified of the intent to strike. When teachers strike in violation of state law or without having met the requirements of the law, the school board may seek an injunction to prohibit the strike. Violation of a court order or an injunction ordering strikers back to work may result in a contempt of court decree and fine or imprisonment. Moreover, those who engage in illegal strikes may be subject to economic sanctions (e.g., withholding of raises or fines) or disciplinary actions, including dismissal (*Hortonville Joint School District No. 1 v. Hortonville Education Association,* 1979).

Political Activity

Teachers have the right to engage in political activities and hold public office; however, restrictions may be placed on the exercise of this right. For example, teachers may discuss political issues and candidates in a nonpartisan manner in the classroom and even wear political buttons, badges, or armbands to class. However, they may not make campaign speeches in the classroom or otherwise take advantage of their position of authority over a captive audience to promote their own political views. Political activity in the schools that would cause divisiveness among the faculty or otherwise be disruptive also may be restricted if the school can demonstrate it is necessary to meet a compelling public need to protect efficiency and integrity in the school.

The authority of school boards to restrict teachers' political activities outside the school setting is far less than their authority to restrict activities in the schools. The courts have upheld teachers' rights to support candidates of their choice, display political buttons and stickers, and participate in demonstrations. In addition, the courts generally have upheld the right of teachers to run for and hold public office. However, the courts also have indicated that if the time and activities associated with running for or holding office interfere with the performance of teaching duties, the teacher may be required to take a leave of absence or even resign. Also, the courts have found the holding of certain political offices (e.g., school board member in the employing school district) to present a conflict of interest and therefore forbid the joint occupancy of both positions.

If you felt strongly that a particular candidate would be in the best interest of your community or state, how would you work for his or her election? Would you consider running for public office as an "education candidate" in order to improve education?

Academic Freedom: Teacher Rights in the Classroom

Academic freedom refers to the teacher's freedom to discuss the subject matter discipline and to determine the most appropriate instructional materials and teaching strategies without unwarranted restrictions. Academic freedom is not without limits. For example, teachers do not have the ultimate right to determine course content or select textbooks; that authority belongs to the school board. The school board may also require that teachers receive prior approval for the use of supplementary materials. Teachers also do not have the right to ignore prescribed content or to refuse to follow the designated scope and sequence of content or materials, even if the refusal is for religious reasons.

Although teachers have limited freedom in determining the content of the curriculum, they have greater freedom in choosing the particular strategies to teach the prescribed content. In reviewing school board attempts to restrict teachers' methodologies, the courts consider a number of factors, including

> the adequacy of notice that use of specific teaching methodologies will result in disciplinary action, the relevance of the method to the course of study, the support for the strategy or materials by the teaching profession, and the threat of disruption posed by the method. The judiciary also has considered community standards in assessing challenges to various teaching methods. However, if a particular strategy is instructionally relevant and supported by the profession, it will probably survive judicial review even though it might offend some parents. (McCarthy, 1989, p. 260)

In a case in point, a Texas teacher was discharged for failure to obey a school board warning that she refrain from using a role-playing simulation to teach about post–Civil War American history (*Kingsville Independent School District v. Cooper,* 1980). Parents had complained that the simulation aroused strong feelings about racial issues. When the teacher refused to obey the district's directive "not to discuss Blacks in American history," her contract was not renewed. The Fifth Circuit Court of Appeals reinstated the teacher and awarded back pay and attorney's fees, finding that the district violated her constitutional rights by basing the nonrenewal on classroom discussions that were protected by the First Amendment.

If, however, the teacher is discussing, showing, or distributing material that is lewd or not relevant, or using a teaching method that is not supported by the profession, the teacher may be sanctioned. This was the case when a teacher was dismissed for refusing to stop using a classroom management technique she had developed called "Learnball," which included a sports format, dividing the class into teams, and a system of rewards that included radio playing and shooting foam basketballs in class. The teacher not only continued to use the technique, but advocated its use by others, and in connection with his advocacy publicly criticized the school system. While acknowledging the teacher's First Amendment right to advocate Learnball and to criticize school officials, the court ruled that the teacher had "no constitutional right to use Learnball in the classroom" (*Bradley v. Pittsburgh Board of Education,* 1990).

Book Banning. Currently, perhaps the most contested academic freedom issue involves attempts to censor the curriculum by excluding certain offerings (e.g., evolution, sex education, and values clarification) or materials deemed vulgar, offensive, or that promote secular humanism. The courts typically have supported the school board in the face of parental attempts to censor the curriculum or ban certain books from the school library. However, when it is the school board itself that advocates censorship, judicial support is not as easily won. This is because the courts traditionally have recognized the authority of the school board to determine the curriculum, select texts, purchase books for the library, approve the use of supplementary materials, and perform a host of other curriculum-related activities. Nonetheless, in a number of instances the courts have found that specific censorship activities violated the teacher's right to academic freedom or students' First Amendment rights to have access to information. While acknowledging that the banning of books and materials on the basis of obscenity or educational unsuitability is permissible, the courts in these cases have held that censorship motivated primarily by the preferences of school board members or to suppress particular viewpoints or controversial ideas contained in the book, or for narrow partisan political purposes, is not permissible (LaMorte, 1996).

The controversy regarding who controls instructional and curricular matters, teachers or the school board, is likely to continue, as are parental attempts to exert greater control over the curriculum. Until definitive guidance is provided by the Supreme Court, resolution will continue on a case-by-case basis, attempting to balance the teacher's interest in academic freedom against the school board's interest in promoting an appropriate educational environment.

Tort Liability of Teachers

A *tort* is defined as a civil wrong that leads to injury to another (criminal wrongs are not torts) and for which a court will provide a remedy in the form of an action for damages. To protect both school district employees and school board members against financial loss resulting from a tort suit, many school districts purchase liability insurance. Many educators also participate in liability insurance programs through their professional organizations.

The most common category of torts in education is *negligence*. Basically, negligence can be defined as a failure to do (or not do) what a reasonable and prudent person would have done under the same or similar circumstances, resulting in injury to another. Before an educator can be found guilty of negligence, four elements must be proved:

1. The educator had a duty to provide an appropriate standard of care to another individual (student, coworker, the public).
2. The educator failed in his or her duty to provide the reasonable standard of care.
3. There is a causal relationship between the negligent action and the resultant injury (i.e., the action was the *proximate cause* of the injury).
4. There is a physical or mental injury resulting in actual loss.

Standard of Care and Duty
Although teachers have the responsibility of providing an appropriate standard of care for their students, the standard of care expected is not the same for all

teachers and all students. Teachers of younger children are held to a higher standard of care than teachers of more mature students. A higher standard of care also is required of teachers of the physically or mentally handicapped, as well as of physical education and vocational and industrial arts teachers because of the inherent dangers in the activities involved.

Reasonableness Doctrine. In determining whether the educator failed to provide the appropriate standard of care, the courts compare the teacher's actions with those of the hypothetical "reasonable and prudent" teacher—one with average intelligence and physical attributes, normal perception and memory, and possessing the same special knowledge and skills as others with his or her training and experience—not some "ideal" or "super" teacher.

What impact does the potential for negligence suits have on you as a prospective or practicing teacher?

Foreseeable Doctrine. A related element is whether the hypothetical reasonable teacher could have foreseen, and thus prevented, the injury. The actions of the teacher are compared with those of the reasonable teacher to determine negligence.

Proximate Cause

Even in situations in which the teacher has failed in his or her recognized duty to provide a reasonable standard of care, liability will not be assessed unless it can be shown that the teacher's action was the proximate cause of the injury, that is, that the injury would not have occurred had it not been for the teacher's conduct. In some cases an intervening event, such as the negligent act of a third party, may relieve the teacher of liability. Because each case brings with it a set of circumstances distinct from all others, the determination of proximate cause must be made on a case-by-case basis.

Educational Malpractice

Historically, most educational liability litigation has involved pupil injuries. In the last two decades, however, a new topic of negligence litigation called *educational malpractice* has emerged and become the focus of concerned discussion in both the educational and legal communities. As in medical malpractice, the term is concerned with some negligence on the part of the professional. In general, there are three kinds of educational malpractice suits: (1) instructional malpractice suits concerned with students who have received certificates or diplomas and do not possess basic academic skills, (2) suits involving misdiagnosis or improper educational placement, and (3) suits involving the failure of school personnel to protect students known to be at risk for suicide or harm to another.

In regard to the first kind of suit, the courts have continued to reject student claims that they have a right to a predetermined level of achievement in return for compulsory school attendance. In the seminal case in this area, *Peter W. v. San Francisco Unified School District* (1976), Peter W. was awarded a high school diploma even though he was functionally illiterate. Peter W. sued the district for negligence in allowing him to graduate. The courts dismissed the case, finding no certainty that a causal relationship existed between the defendants' conduct and

Peter W.'s injuries. In *Peter W.* and a similar action in New York, *Donohue v. Copiague Union Free Schools* (1979), the courts noted that allowing such suits would require the courts to intervene in matters of educational policy and to become entangled in educational questions—actions judged inappropriate for the courts and likely to flood the courts with similar suits.

In the lead case concerned with placement malpractice, *Hoffman v. Board of Education of the City of New York* (1979), plaintiff Hoffman was examined by a school psychologist upon entry to kindergarten using the Stanford-Binet intelligence test, which, in part, requires verbal responses. Hoffman had a severe speech defect. The psychologist recommended that he be placed in a class for the mentally retarded, but also that he be reexamined in two years. No reexamination took place for 13 years, and then only at his mother's request. This examination showed him to be of normal intelligence. Hoffman sued and was awarded $750,000 in damages by the jury. A New York Court of Appeals later overturned the award, stating that it was unwilling to

> substitute its judgment for the professional judgment of the board of education as to the type of psychometric devices to be used and the frequency with which such tests are to be given. . . . To do so would open the door to an examination of the propriety of each of the procedures used in the education of every student in our school system. (p. 320)

Although other cases involving alleged negligence in diagnosis and placement have been equally unsuccessful (see, e.g., *Brantley v. District of Columbia,* 1994; *Suriano v. Hyde Park Cent. School District,* 1994), the courts have recognized that there might be cases in which defendants knowingly violated statutes related to special education placements or intentionally misplaced students that would be actionable under tort law (see, e.g., *B. M. by Berger v. State of Montana,* 1985).

The third category of educational malpractice, which might more appropriately be termed "professional malpractice" (Valente, 1998), is based on the case law related to the medical profession, which says that despite patient or client confidentiality, these professionals have a duty to warn and attempt to protect those at risk for harm. In the first case of this kind, *Eisel v. Board of Education of Montgomery* (1991), two school counselors were found negligent in failing to communicate to a parent a student's suicidal statements made to other students and told to them. The counselors had questioned the student about the statements, but when she denied them, they did nothing further. The court ruled that "school counselors have a duty to use reasonable means to prevent a suicide when they are on notice of a child or adolescent student's suicidal intent" (p. 456).

Teacher Rights: Employment Discrimination and Sexual Harassment

Employment Discrimination

School districts and their employees are prohibited by the Fourteenth Amendment and numerous state and federal statutes from engaging in practices that intentionally discriminate against employees or students on the basis of race, sex, age, religion, national origin, or handicapping condition. To be successful in a claim of employment *discrimination* under the Fourteenth Amendment, the employee must prove that the district's action constituted a deliberate intent to discriminate, not just that the action resulted in a disproportionate impact (*Washington v. Davis,* 1976). Because of the difficulty in proving intentional discrimination, most cases alleging discrimination are brought under Title VII or one of the other civil rights statutes detailed in Table 11.1.

Two types of employment discrimination claims are typically brought under Title VII: disparate treatment, which requires that the plaintiff prove that he or she was treated less favorably than others by some employment practice or policy, and *disparate impact,* which requires that the plaintiff show that an employment practice or policy results in a disparate impact on a protected class. If the employer answers the challenge by claiming the policy or practice is job related and consistent with a business necessity, the employee can still prevail by showing that the district could have accomplished its goal by less discriminatory means. For example, a female applicant for a high school biology teaching position was successful in a sex discrimination suit on the basis that the district's requirement that applicants also have the ability to coach varsity softball had a disparate impact on women *(Civil Rights Division v. Amphitheater Unified School District, 1983).* The court rejected the district's business necessity defense because the district was unable to demonstrate that less discriminatory alternatives had been attempted.

Sexual Harassment

Sexual harassment is considered a form of sex discrimination prohibited under Title VII. According to Title VII, sexual harassment occurs when unwelcome advances or requests for sexual favors are made a condition of being hired, receiving a raise or promotion, or any other benefit of employment *(quid pro quo harassment),* or where verbal or physical conduct is sufficiently severe or pervasive as to unreasonably interfere with an individual's work performance or creates an intimidating, hostile, or offensive work environment *(hostile environment harassment).*

The courts have traditionally held that under the legal principal of agency employers can be held vicariously liable for negligence and sexual harassment committed by employees. As a result, employers were sometimes held liable in instances in which they neither condoned nor even knew of the acts of the employee. While not abandoning this position, in two recent cases the Supreme Court said that in cases that involved a supervisor engaging in what heretofore would have been called *quid pro quo* harassment (the court did not like these labels), the employer will still be held strictly liable. But in cases of hostile environment harassment, the employer will not be liable if it can prove (1) it had a sexual policy in place designed to prevent and effectively address allegations of sexual harassment, and (2) the harassed employee did not follow the procedures in the policy to file a complaint or to seek help (*Burlington Industries v. Ellerth,* 1998 and *Faragher v. Boca Raton,* 1998).

Equal Opportunity and Affirmative Action

The legal principle of *equal opportunity,* whether equal employment opportunity or equal educational opportunity, is founded in antidiscrimination legislation. Equal opportunity requires that school districts and other agencies develop policies and procedures to ensure that the rights of employees and students are protected, and that they are given equal treatment in employment practices, access to programs, or other educational opportunities.

Affirmative action goes beyond equal opportunity. The principle of affirmative action holds that ensuring nondiscrimination is not enough; what is needed are affirmative steps to recruit, hire, and retain individuals who are underrepresented in the workplace or the classroom. Many school districts have adopted affirmative action plans that set forth their intended goals in these areas and their intended actions to achieve these goals.

What should school districts do to increase the number of women in administrative positions?

The U.S. Supreme Court, in *Regents of the University of California v. Alan Bakke* (1978), ruled against the establishment of firm quotas that designate a predetermined number of "slots" only for minorities, resulting in so-called *reverse discrimination.* However, the Court has upheld the voluntary adoption of goals and race-conscious remedies in hiring practices that are designed to bring balance to the composition of the workforce or student body. Nonetheless, as the U.S. Supreme Court ruled in *Wygant v. Jackson Board of Education* (1986), which overturned a Michigan school district's collective bargaining agreement that released white employees with greater seniority than black employees in order to preserve the percentage of minority teachers employed prior to the layoffs, affirmative action plans must be designed to remedy location-specific past discrimination, not general societal discrimination. That is, there must be evidence that remedial action is necessary, and second, the plan must be "narrowly tailored" to remedy the past discrimination (see also, *Taxman v. Board of Education of Piscataway,* 1996, retention of equally qualified black teacher over white teacher to preserve racial diversity overturned by Third Circuit Court of Appeals).

Student Rights and Responsibilities

Traditionally, it was accepted that school officials had considerable authority in controlling student conduct. Operating under the doctrine of *in loco parentis* (in place of a parent), school authorities exercised almost unlimited and usually unchallenged discretion in restricting the rights of students and in disciplining students. However, beginning in the late 1960s students increasingly challenged the authority and actions of school officials. Subsequent court decisions have broadened the scope of student rights and, at the same time, have attempted to maintain a balance between the rights of students and the rights and responsibilities of school officials (see Figure 12.2 and the discussion of mandated community service on p. 412).

Figure 12.2: Balancing the Rights of Students and the Responsibilities of School Officials

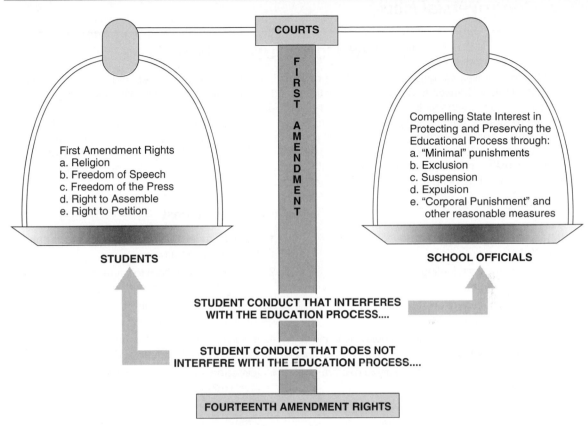

Source: From *The Schools, the Courts, and the Public Interest* by J. C. Hogan. Copyright © 1974, 1985 by Lexington Books, an imprint on Macmillan, Inc.

Student Discipline

Although the *in loco parentis* doctrine has been weakened in recent years, school officials do have the authority—and in fact the duty—to establish reasonable rules of student conduct designed to protect students and employees, as well as rules necessary to establish and maintain a climate conducive to learning. The authority and responsibility to establish rules of conduct carries with it the authority to discipline students for violations of these rules. The severity of the violation will determine the nature of the discipline and the due process required. Because state compulsory attendance laws give students a property right to attend school, if disciplinary action involves exclusion from school or the removal of the student from the classroom for even a minimal period of time,

Controversial Issues

Mandated Community Service

National leaders as well as national organizations have called upon all citizens to become, as one initiative is called, "Volunteers in Service to America." The National and Community Service Act, which was passed in 1993, encouraged the schools to become involved by providing grants to support K–12 school-based community service programs. Since that time numerous schools and school districts have moved to establish voluntary community service programs, while a number of others, as well as the state of Maryland, have made community service a requirement for high school graduation. While there is little opposition to the schools establishing volunteer community service programs, in those locations where community service has been made mandatory, it has been the subject of considerable debate.

Arguments For

1. It helps prepare students for responsible citizenship.
2. It reduces students' feeling of alienation and builds self-esteem.
3. It has a positive affect on students' grades, attendance and motivation.
4. It promotes a feeling of social responsibility and capacity to empathize.
5. It provides students the opportunity to explore career interests or abilities.
6. It provides scarce resources to community service projects and organizations.

Arguments Against

1. It takes students' time away from much needed academic programs.
2. It exposes the school to unnecessary liability for students' injury or harm.
3. It requires considerable staff resources to administer and monitor the program.
4. It violates the 13th Amendment's prohibition against involuntary servitude.
5. It interferes with parents' right to direct the moral education of their children.
6. In some students it will build resentment and destroy their spirit of volunteerism.

some due process is required, even if in the latter instance it is only informally providing the student the opportunity to give his or her side of the story.

Suspensions and Expulsions

Short-term *suspensions* usually are defined as exclusions from school for periods of time of 10 days or less; *expulsions* (i.e., long-term suspensions) are for periods of time in excess of 10 days. While a teacher or administrator may initiate an expulsion proceeding, normally only the school board can expel the student. Because of the severity of expulsions, state statutes and school board regulations usually detail the grounds for expulsion as well as the procedures that must be followed. Grounds for expulsion typically include theft or vandalism of school property, possession or use of alcohol or drugs, causing or attempting to cause injury to another, and engaging in any behavior forbidden by law. In addition, the Gun Free Schools Act of 1994 requires any school receiving federal funds to expel for one year any student bringing a firearm to school. (This can be mitigated on a case-by-case basis by the local superintendent.) The procedures that must be followed in expelling a student from school usually include the right to

1. A written notice specifying the charges, the time and place of the hearing, and the procedures to be followed at the hearing
2. A hearing before an impartial tribunal
3. A cross-examination of witnesses and a presentation of witnesses and evidence to refute adverse evidence
4. Representation by legal counsel or other adult representation
5. A written statement of the findings/recommendations of the hearing body that demonstrated the decision was based on the evidence presented
6. A written or taped record of the hearing if appeal is to be made
7. A clear statement of the right to appeal

In contrast to the detailed statutory guidelines pertaining to expulsions, in *Goss v. Lopez* (1975), the U.S. Supreme Court ruled that for short-term suspensions of less than 10 days the student need only be given oral or written notice of the charges, an explanation of the evidence, and the opportunity to rebut the charges before an objective decision maker. However, the Court did recognize that there might be situations that would require more detailed procedures, such as situations in which the facts are disputed and not easily resolved, as well as emergency situations in which the safety of persons or property is threatened, where no due process is required prior to disciplinary action. However, even in these situations due process must be followed as soon as possible after the danger of harm has passed. While *Goss* specified only the basics of due process that must be followed for short-term suspensions, state laws may, and often do, require additional procedures.

What effect, if any, does the weakening of the doctrine of in loco parentis *and the apparent expansion of student rights have on the willingness of educators to discipline disobedient or disruptive students?*

One month after *Goss,* the Supreme Court handed down another decision that had further impact on student exclusion cases. In *Wood v. Strickland* (1975), the Court held that students may sue school board members for monetary damages under the Civil Rights Act of 1871 if their constitutional rights are violated. In this case, two girls were suspended from school without a hearing for spiking the punch at a school party. The Supreme Court clarified its *Wood* decision in *Carey v. Piphus* (1978). The Court said that in order to collect damages when their rights have been violated, students must show that they have sustained an actual injury. Otherwise, they are entitled to recover only the nominal damage amount of $1.

Special considerations are involved in the suspension or expulsion of children with disabilities. The Supreme Court has held that disruptive handicapped students can be suspended for up to 10 days, but that they cannot be summarily suspended while waiting an expulsion hearing (*Honig v. Doe,* 1988). Expulsions or long-term suspension would be a change in placement and cannot take place until the necessary procedural requirements under the IDEA have been satisfied and an alternative placement has been agreed upon.

Corporal Punishment

Although the U.S. Supreme Court has said that corporal punishment is not prohibited by the Eighth Amendment, as noted in the previous chapter, if the punishment is excessive, a student may have an assault and battery claim, and the administrator or teacher administering the corporal punishment may be found liable under tort law for the injuries sustained. However, punishment administered in a "priviledged manner" is not a tort. Punishment is said to be priviledged when it serves a reasonable purpose and is reasonable in its method and degree of force. This includes a consideration of the nature of the infraction; the age, sex, and physical and mental condition of the student; and the instrument employed (Valente, 1998).

Half the states prohibit corporal punishment (Dayton, 1994). In a number of others, corporal punishment is prohibited by school board policy. In the states and school districts where corporal punishment is permitted, school board policies will normally dictate the conditions under which corporal punishment can be administered. Most such policies require that the principal rather than the teacher administer the punishment and that another adult be present.

Search and Seizure

The issues surrounding search and seizure of students have increased in recent years, along with the concern about drugs and weapons in the schools. The Fourth Amendment protection against unreasonable search and seizure has been interpreted as requiring law enforcement officials to have probable cause that a crime has been committed and to obtain a search warrant before conducting a search. Prior to 1985, some courts held school officials to the same standard. However, in *New Jersey v. T.L.O.* (1985), the Supreme Court ruled that school officials' interest in maintaining discipline in the schools was sufficient to justify their being held to a lesser standard than probable cause. Rather, school officials may conduct a warrantless search if it passes the two-pronged "reasonableness test": (1) there is "individualized" reasonable cause or suspicion that the search will reveal evidence of a violation of the law or school rules, and (2) the scope of the search is reasonably related to the objective of the search and is not "excessively intrusive" in light of the age and sex of the child and the nature of the alleged infraction.

The court in *T.L.O.* did not say that an individualized suspicion is an *absolute* requirement for a reasonable search. Exceptions may exist where the privacy interests are minimal or the object of the search is very serious. For example, in *Thompson v. Carthage School District* (1996), the Eighth Circuit Court upheld a search of all male students in grades 6–12 based on a report that a weapon was being concealed by a student. The court ruled that the search was minimally intrusive and justified in light of the need to uncover a dangerous weapon. On the other hand, a search of all students in an art class for a pair of allegedly stolen sneakers was not upheld by the court. The court said that deviation from the individualized suspicion requirement is only justified in special circumstances, such as protecting students from weapons or drugs (*DesRoches ex rel. DesRoches v. Caprio,* 1997).

In determining whether a particular search is reasonable, some courts have distinguished between school property, such as lockers, and personal property. These courts have held that while a student may have exclusive use of a locker in regard to other students, the possession is not exclusive in regard to school officials who retain control of the lockers. Other courts have said that students have the same expectation of privacy regarding a locker as they do a wallet or purse. Schools or school districts can minimize the expectation of privacy by notifying students in the student handbook that lockers are subject to inspection.

The use of drug-sniffing dogs is currently one of the most unsettled issues in the area of student searches. In *Doe v. Renfrow* (1981), the Seventh Circuit Court viewed the use of dogs as preliminary to the search itself and legal, provided the dogs were used to sniff particular students, not all students or random groups. An opposing conclusion was reached by the Fifth Circuit in *Horton v. Goose Creek Independent School District* (1982), which ruled that the use of drug-detecting dogs to sniff students without individualized suspicion was an unconstitutional invasion of the student's privacy. However, the *Horton* court did agree that the use of dogs in sniffing lockers and cars does not constitute a search and is permissible.

Strip searches, because of their intrusive nature, are carefully scrutinized and most often disallowed by the courts. However, they will be allowed if they meet the *T.L.O.* reasonableness standard, particularly in regard to the scope of the search. In a case in point, the Court upheld the partial strip search of a student suspected of being under the influence of marijuana. The student was said to be "giggling and acting in an unruly fashion" and had dilated pupils and bloodshot eyes. A school nurse conducted a cursory medical assessment of the student as well as a search that required the student to remove his under jersey, shoes and socks, and empty his pockets. The court held that there was a reasonable basis for the search given the subject's behavior and that the search was not excessively intrusive (*Bridgman v. New Trier High School District,* 1997).

What would be some examples of student conduct that would constitute "reasonable suspicion" for you to institute a search for drugs?

Perhaps the most controversial current issue in the area of student searches is drug testing of students. Thus far, the courts have invalidated blanket drug testing of the general student population on the basis of the individualized suspicion standard (*Anable v. Ford,* 1985; *Brooks v. E. Chambers Consolidated School District,* 1989). However, the question of "suspicionless" random drug testing of students who wish to participate in extracurricular activities has yielded the opposite result. In *Vernonia School District v. Acton* (1995) the Supreme Court found a school district's policy requiring student athletes to submit to a random urinalysis was not unreasonable under the Fourth Amendment. The Court not only agreed with the district's contention that the policy was justified based on its interest in preventing injuries and deterring drug use, but also noted that the testing procedure used was no more intrusive than the students' daily undressing in the locker room. The Court also noted that there are "special needs," in this case the need to eradicate drugs from the schools, which support the reasonableness of the search.

The *Acton* "special needs" argument has been used in subsequent decisions to support random searches with metal detectors. For example, in *State of Florida v. J. A.* (1996), the Court referenced *Acton* in ruling that in student search cases

Table 12.2: Selected U.S. Supreme Court Cases Affecting Students' Rights

Case	Decision
Tinker v. Des Moines (1969)	School officials cannot limit students' rights to free expression unless there is evidence of a material disruption or substantial disorder.
Goss v. Lopez (1975)	For suspensions of less than 10 days, the student must be given an oral or written notice of charges, an explanation of the evidence against him or her, and the opportunity to rebut the charges before an objective decision maker.
Wood v. Strickland (1975)	Students may sue school board members for monetary damages under the Civil Rights Act of 1871.
Ingraham v. Wright (1977)	Corporal punishment does not constitute cruel and unusual punishment under the Eighth Amendment and does not require due process prior to administration.
Board of Education, Island Trees Union Free School District v. Pico (1982)	Censorship by the school board acting in a narrowly partisan or political manner violates the First Amendment rights of students.
Pyler v. Doe (1982)	The denial of a free public education to undocumented alien children violates the equal protection guarantees of the Fourteenth Amendment.
Bethel School District v. Fraser (1985)	School boards have the authority to determine what speech is inappropriate and need not tolerate speech that is lewd or offensive.
New Jersey v. T.L.O. (1986)	School officials are not required to obtain a search warrant or show probable cause to search a student, only reasonable suspicion that the search will turn up evidence of a violation of law or school rules.
Hazelwood School District v. Kuhlmier (1988)	School officials may limit school-sponsored student speech as long as their actions are related to a legitimate pedagogical concern.
Honig v. Doe (1988)	Disruptive handicapped children may be expelled but must be kept in their current placement until an official hearing is held.
Franklin v. Gwinnett (1992)	The sexual harassment of a student may be a violation of Title IX for which monetary damages can be sought.
Vernonia School District v. Acton (1995)	Special needs can justify "suspicionless" random searching of students.

the court must "strike a balance between the school child's legitimate expectations of privacy and the school's equally legitimate need to maintain an environment in which learning can take place" (p. 316). Table 12.2 lists some Supreme Court decisions affecting students' rights.

Freedom of Expression

In 1965, several students in Des Moines, Iowa, were suspended after wearing black armbands to school to demonstrate their opposition to the Vietnam War. The wearing of armbands was prohibited by a school district policy, which had been adopted to prevent possible disturbances after it was learned that students planned to wear the armbands. The suspended students filed suit, and the decision by the Supreme Court (*Tinker v. Des Moines,* 1969) has become a landmark case not only in student expression, but also in the broader area of student rights.

In finding for the students, the Court said that students have the freedom to express their views by speech or other forms of expression so long as the exercise of this freedom does not cause "material disruption," "substantial disorder," or invade the rights of others. According to the Court:

> In order for the State in the person of school officials to justify prohibition of a particular expression of opinion, it must be able to show that its action was caused by something more than a mere desire to avoid the discomfort and unpleasantness that always accompany an unpopular viewpoint. . . . undifferentiated fear or apprehension of disturbance is not enough to overcome the right to freedom of expression. (pp. 508 509)

The "material and substantive disruption" standard articulated in *Tinker* has been applied to numerous student expression cases that have followed. Subsequent rulings have clarified that while the fear of disruption must be based on fact, not intuition (*Butts v. Dallas Independent School District,* 1971), school officials need not wait until a disruption has occurred to take action. If school officials possess sufficient evidence on which to base a "reasonable forecast" of disruption, action to restrict student expression is justified (*Dodd v. Rambis,* 1981).

Disruptive Speech

Freedom of expression does not include the right to use lewd and offensive speech, even if it does not cause disruption. At a high school assembly, Matthew Fraser nominated a classmate for a student council office using what the Court described as "an elaborate, graphic, and explicit sexual metaphor." Fraser was suspended for two days. Lower courts held his suspension to be a violation of his rights to free speech and stated that his speech was not disruptive under the *Tinker* guidelines. The Supreme Court, however, went beyond *Tinker's* concern with the effect of the students's speech to the content of the speech, and concluded that the school board has the authority to determine what speech in the classroom or in school assembly is inappropriate, and that lewd or offensive speech or conduct that are inconsistent with the "fundamental values" of public education need not be tolerated (*Bethel School District No. 403 v. Fraser, 1986*).

Student Publications

Although students have the right to publish and distribute literature published both on and off campus, school officials can enact reasonable rules as to the time, place, and manner of distribution. However, until recently, the courts have been careful to emphasize that in cases in which school policies require faculty or administrative approval prior to publication, censorship is only justified if the material is libelous, obscene, or likely to cause material and substantial disruption. In addition, the procedures and standards for review must be clearly articulated. Unpopular or controversial content, or content critical of school officials, has been considered insufficient justification for restricting student expression. This standard was applied to school-sponsored as well as to nonsponsored publications.

In a 1988 case, however, the Supreme Court awarded significant discretion to school authorities in censoring school-sponsored publications. In this case, *Hazelwood School District v. Kuhlmeier,* a school principal deleted two articles from a school newspaper, one dealing with pregnant students and their sexual histories and use or nonuse of birth control, and the other on the impact of divorce on students, which included quotes from a student condemning her father. According to the principal, he was not concerned with the content of the articles, but felt that they were not well written by journalistic standards (e.g., did not maintain student anonymity or give the father a chance to defend himself). Believing that there was not enough time before the publication deadline to make the needed changes in the articles, he deleted the two articles.

The Supreme Court decision said that school officials "do not offend the First Amendment by exercising editorial control over the style and content of student speech in school-sponsored expressive activities so long as their actions are reasonably related to legitimate pedagogical concerns." Such concerns were described as "speech that is ungrammatical, poorly written, inadequately researched, biased or prejudiced, vulgar or profane, or unsuitable for immature audiences."

In making its decision, the Court made a distinction between personal expressions by students and those activities that students, parents, and the public might reasonably assume bear the "imprimatur of the school." In the latter category, the Court included not only school-sponsored publications but "theatrical productions and other expressive activities." The effect of the *Hazelwood* decision has been to allow school officials greater discretion in determining what is inappropriate student speech and expression. When read together, the *Tinker, Bethel,* and *Hazelwood* decisions present three principles for assessing the First Amendment rights of students:

> First, vulgar or plainly offensive speech (Fraser-type speech) may be prohibited without a showing of disruption or substantial interference with the school's work. Second, school sponsored speech (Hazelwood-type speech) may be restricted when the limitation is reasonably related to legitimate educational concerns. Third, (person) speech that is neither vulgar nor school-sponsored (Tinker-type speech) may only be prohibited if it causes a substantial and material disruption of the school's operation. (*Pyle v. South Hadley School Community,* 1994, p. 166).

Student Appearance as Symbolic Speech

The U.S. Supreme Court has not provided any guidance in the area of student appearance, but the majority of lower courts have recognized that students have either a liberty right or a right of expression that can be violated by appearance regulations that are unduly vague or restrictive. And, as is true for other forms of expression, the courts will not uphold appearance regulations unless the district can show a compelling interest in having such a regulation, such as the disruptive effects of the appearance on the educational process or for health and safety reasons. However, schools have been successful in prohibiting dirty, scant, or revealing clothing; excessively tight skirts or pants; clothing displaying obscene

Increased gang activity has led to increased efforts to prohibit the wearing of gang apparel.

pictures, sexually provocative slogans, or vulgar and offensive language; clothing caricaturing school administrators as being drunk; loose clothing in shop areas; attending the school prom dressed in clothing of the opposite sex; or other dress deemed likely to cause a material or substantial disruption to school operations.

An issue of recent concern regarding student dress is the wearing of clothing, jewelry, or other symbols of gang membership. Schools have responded to the increased gang activity on campus by enacting stricter dress codes. The courts have held that schools may prohibit students from wearing specific clothing or other symbols of gang membership if it can be shown that a gang problem exists and that in fact a relationship exists between the particular item(s) prohibited and the public policy goal of curbing gang activity on campus (e.g., *Colorado Independent School District v. Barber,* 1995). However, if no gang problem exists or if a relationship between the items and gang activity cannot be established, the school district policy will not be upheld. The dress code of a California school district for elementary, middle, and secondary students prohibited the wearing of clothing identifying any college or professional sports teams. However, testimony showed that gang members were, in fact, wearing Pendleton shirts; Nike shoes; white T-shirts; baggy, dickie, or black pants; and that there was negligible gang

Did the elementary and secondary schools you attended have dress codes or regulations regulating student appearance? How did you respond to them at the time? Do you now feel they served any educational purpose?

activity at the middle school and no gang activity at the elementary level. Absent a rational relationship between the dress code and the activity it aimed to curtail, the Court did not support the code as it related to elementary and middle school students, and found the prohibition against the wearing of clothing with insignia of professional and college sports teams to be in violation of students' First Amendment rights to free expression (*Jeglin v. San Jacinto Unified School District,* 1993).

Student dress codes will also not be upheld if they lack clarity or do not provide sufficient clarity so that students know what expression is prohibited. In *Stephenson v. Davenport Community School District* (1997), a student, under threat of expulsion, underwent laser surgery to remove a two-year-old tattoo of a cross from between her thumb and index finger. She later sued for damages because the procedure left a scar. The circuit court ruled in her favor and held that the school district's policy which prohibited "gang-related activities such as display of colors, symbols, signals, signs, etc." was too vague to put the student on notice that the tattoo would fall within the scope of the policy.

Sexual Harassment of Students

As noted in Chapter 10, as many as 80% of the students in the public schools have been victims of some form of sexual harassment. As with employees, students can be victims of *quid pro quo* harassment if the conditioning of some benefit is on the granting of sexual favors. More often, however, students are the victims of hostile environment harassment. In *Franklin v. Gwinnett* (1992), which involved the sexual harassment of a student by a teacher, the Supreme Court recognized that sexual harassment, if sufficiently severe, persistent, or pervasive, can create a hostile environment for the victim that limits the student's ability to benefit from, or participate in, an educational program or activity in violation of Title IX. In such a case, the Court ruled, the student can sue for damages under Title IX. The Supreme Court later ruled, however, that the school district is only liable for damages if the employee's supervisor knew about the harassment and failed to take action to stop it (*Gebster v. Lago Vista Independent School District,* 1998).

As a K–12 student were you ever sexually harassed by a peer? How did it make you feel? Did a teacher or other school officer take any action?

When the sexual harassment of a student comes from peers, which is the type of sexual harassment most students experience, the guidance from the courts is less clear. In 1996 the Supreme Court let stand a decision by the Fifth Circuit that said school districts were not liable for student-to-student sexual harassment unless the school intended to discriminate by treating complaints of sexual harassment from males and females differently (*Rowinsky v. Bryan Independent School District,* 1997). However, contrary decisions have been reached by other courts who have reasoned that Title VII hostile environment principles apply to cases in which school officials knew of the harassment and failed to act (see, e.g., *Doe v. University of Illinois,* 1998). This is also the position taken by the U.S. Department of Education's Office of Civil Rights (OCR) in its 1997 guidelines, *Sexual Harassment Guidance: Harassment of Students by School Employees, Other Students, or Third Parties.* The OCR not only defined what sexual harassment is, and what it is not—a kiss on the cheek by a first grader—but specified the conditions under which a school will be held liable for student-to-student sexual harassment: (1) a hostile environment exists, (2) the school knew or should have known of the harassment, and (3) the school failed to take immediate and appropriate action to stop the harassment. Teachers can play a major role in preventing sexual harassment if they adopt a no tolerance policy for all forms of harassment and discrimination, take all complaints seriously, and strictly comply with all school district policies regarding sex discrimination and sexual harassment.

Students With AIDS

The initial response by school districts to AIDS-infected children was to exclude them from the school setting and provide home instruction or separate facilities for their instruction. More recently, in part as a result of more information and education on how the disease is transmitted, and in part as a result of court decisions, AIDS-infected children are being provided greater access to the classroom. The courts have held that children infected with the AIDS virus are protected from discrimination by Section 504 of the Rehabilitation Act and by the Individuals With Disabilities Act. Most states and school districts have adopted policies regarding the admission and instruction of infected children modeled after guidelines issued by the National Centers for Disease Control (CDC). These policies recommend that children with AIDS be allowed to attend public schools unless they have open lesions, cannot control their bodily functions, or display negative behavior practices such as biting, in which case they might still be allowed to attend school, but in a more restrictive environment. The CDC also recommends that the determination of whether individual students pose a "significant risk" should be made on a case-by-case basis by a team composed of health and educational personnel. State policies also provide guidelines for handling body fluids and other procedures designed to protect fellow students and personnel in the school, as well as steps to protect the privacy of victims and to educate both school district personnel and parents.

Student Records

For every student who attends the public schools, various records are kept by school authorities. Questions about the contents of these records, and who has access to them, have been the source of serious contention over the years. Until the passage of the Family Educational Rights and Privacy Act, also known as the Buckley Amendment, in 1974, parents often were denied access to these records, while they were open to various nonschool personnel (e.g., employers). The Buckley Amendment sought to redress this situation by:

1. Requiring school districts to establish procedures for accessing student records and informing parents, guardians, and eligible students (over 18 years old) of their rights under the law.
2. Requiring written permission from parents or eligible students before disclosing personally identifiable information contained in the records with

Professional Reflections

"Amid the pile of papers to grade, attendance to record, grades to calculate, meetings to attend, and reports to fill out, teachers sometimes lose sight about what is really important in teaching—students. Teachers affect the lives of their students. We all have those special students whose lives we know we have impacted. However, we often don't realize where our influence extends."

Patricia Randolph, Teacher of the Year, Nebraska

"Classroom management is about mutual respect, not public humiliation or retribution. Always allow a student to 'save face' and make up for the wrong done. Use the 3F's . . . Fair, Firm, and Friendly."

Denise Bryan, Teacher of the Year, South Dakota

anyone other than educators or officials in the school district who have a legitimate educational interest; officials of a school to which the student is transferring; persons who have obtained a court order; persons for whom the information is necessary to protect the health or safety of the student or other individuals in an emergency; or in connection with financial aid for which the student has applied.

3. Providing a complaint and investigation mechanism for alleged violations.
4. Providing for the loss of federal funds to districts found not in compliance with the law.

When students become 18 years old or enroll in a postsecondary institution, they must be allowed to see the record if they so desire.

What kind of information would you record in your personal notes that you would not record in a student's official record?

Although the Buckley Amendment guarantees parents and eligible students access to records, this does not mean that records must be produced anytime or anywhere on demand. School officials can adopt rules that specify reasonable time, place, and notice requirements for reviewing. Neither does this law give parents the right to review the personal notes of teachers and administrators if these records are in their sole possession and not shared with anyone except a substitute teacher.

Parental rights under the Buckley Amendment are not limited to custodial parents. Unless prohibited by court order, a separated parent who is not the custodial parent or guardian has the same right of access to the student's record as does the custodial parent.

After reviewing the record, if the parents (or the eligible student) believes that information contained in the record is inaccurate, misleading, or in violation of the rights of the student, he or she can request that the information be amended. If school officials refuse, the parents or eligible student must be advised of his or her right to a hearing. If the hearing officer also agrees that the record should not be amended, the parents or student is entitled to place a statement of explanation or objection in the record.

Summary

The educational process takes place in an environment in which the rights of teachers and students are constantly being balanced against the rights and responsibilities of school officials to maintain a safe and orderly environment conducive to learning. Although the rights of both teachers and students have been greatly expanded in the last quarter-century, they do not include the right to say, publish, or teach whatever one feels or believes. The courts continue to uphold the rights and responsibilities of school districts to limit teacher conduct that has a negative impact on performance in the classroom, that is unrelated to the course of study, or that is materially or substantially disruptive. Teachers also have the responsibility to comply with various statutory requirements related to terms of employment, copyright, and so on, and to provide a reasonable standard of care for their students. When they do not comply with these statutory requirements or when they breach the standard of care, they can be subjected to a variety of disciplinary actions both within and outside the school system. While every situation is unique, certain legal principles have been established that can provide direction in many situations. It is imperative that teachers not only be knowledgeable about these principles, many of which are broadly discussed in this chapter, but that they become familiar with applicable laws and school board policy in their state and district.

In the next chapter, we will discuss a topic that sometimes is not given sufficient attention in teacher preparation programs—the governance structure of the public schools. Yet, as you will see, the way schools are organized, administered, and financed has a vital impact on the teacher and the educational program.

Key Terms

Academic freedom

Affirmative action

Discrimination

Disparate impact

Educational malpractice

Equal opportunity

Expulsion

Fair use doctrine

Hostile environment harassment

Incompetence

In loco parentis

Insubordination

Liberty interest

Negligence

Procedural due process

Property right

Proximate cause

Quid pro quo harassment

Reverse discrimination

Suspension

Tenure

Tort

Discussion Questions

1. What action should be taken against Marty Robinson if an examination of Johnny Avery's back shows no marks? Should students be encouraged to "be on the lookout" for and report suspicions of physical and sexual abuse among their peers? How could this be done?

2. What limits can be placed on teachers expressing themselves on political issues in the classroom? Outside the classroom?

3. Describe the "reasonable teacher" guideline as it relates to tort liability.

4. What should be the role of the schools in confronting the AIDS epidemic?

5. To what extent should teachers, administrators, and school board members be held liable for the education, or lack of education, received by the students under their control?

6. What are the statutory requirements in your state regarding student expulsions? Student suspensions?

7. How does the doctrine of *in loco parentis* serve to give students expectations about the care given them in the schools? How does the doctrine serve to define the teacher's right to control and supervise students?

Internet Resources

1. **www.law.cornell.edu/topics/education.html**
   This site provides an overview of education law and recent U.S. Supreme Court and circuit court decisions involving education.

2. **www.montanabar.org/directory/sections/school**
   School Law News, a publication of the School Law Section of the State Bar of Montana, provides a discussion of current issues and cases in education law.

3. **www.nsba.org/cosa/whatsnew/lowercourts.htm**
   This is the site for the National School Board Association Council of School Attorneys' "What's New in the Courts," an analysis of recent court cases concerning the schools.

4. **www.lawsource.com/also**
   American Law Sources On-line provides links to all on-line sources of American law that are available without charge.

5. **www.findlaw.com**
   Find Law provides links to law firms, cases and codes, the federal courts, as well as its "Law Crawler" search engine.

6. **gsul.gsu.edu/metaindex/**
   Meta-index for Legal Research provides links to judicial opinions, legislation, federal regulations, people in law, and other legal sources.

7. **web.lexisnexis.com/universe**
   Lexis Nexis Academic Universe provides links to a wide range of legal reference information.

8. **www.ilrg.com**

The Internet Legal Resources Guide provides links to 4,000 web sites, including law journals, law outlines, law schools, and selected U.S. and state courts.

9. **www.lawcrawler.com**

Law Runner: A Legal Research Tool, a search engine powered by Alta Vista, facilitates a more efficient search of Alta Vista by searching only law sites.

References

Ambach v. Norwick, 441 U.S. 68 (1979).

Anable v. Ford, 653 F. Supp. 22 (W. D. Ark, 1985), modified, 663 F. Supp. 149 (W. D. Ark. 1985).

B. M. by Berger v. State of Montana, 649 P. 2d 425 (Mont. 1982), *aff'd remanded,* 698 P.2d 399 (Mont. 1985).

Bethel School District No. 403 v. Fraser, 106 S. Ct. 3159 (1986).

Botterbusch, H. R. (1996). *Copyright in the age of new technology.* Bloomington, IN: Phi Delta Kappa Educational Foundation.

Bradley v. Pittsburgh Board of Education, 913 F. 2d 1064 (3d Cir. 1990).

Brantley v. District of Columbia, 640 A.2d 181 (D. C. App. 1994).

Bridgman v. New Trier High School District, 128 F. 3d 1146 (7th Cir. 1997).

Brooks v. E. Chambers Consolidated School District, 730 F.Supp. 759 (S. D. Tex. 1989).

Burlington Industries v. Ellerth, No. 97-569 S. Ct. (1998).

Butts v. Dallas Independent School District, 436 F. 2d 728 (5th Cir. 1971).

Carey v. Piphus, 435 U.S. 247 (1978).

Chalk v. U.S. District Court Cent. Dist. of California, 840 F. 2d 701 (9th Cir. 1988).

Civil Rights Division of the Arizona Department of Law v. Amphitheater Unified School District No. 10, 680 P. 2d 517 (Ariz. 1983).

Colorado Independent School District v. Barber, 901 S.W.2d 447 (Tex. 1995).

Connick v. Myers, 461 U.S. 138 (1983).

Dayton, J. (1994). Corporal punishment in public schools: The legal and political battle continues. *West's Education Law Quarterly, 3,* 448–459.

DesRoches ex rel. DesRoches v. Caprio, 974 F. Supp. 542 (E. D. Va. 1997).

Dodd v. Rambis, 535 F. Supp. 23 (S.D. Ind. 1981).

Doe v. University of Illinois, 138 F. 3d 653 (7th Cir. 1998).

Doe v. Renfrow, 631 F. 2d 91 (7th Cir. 1980), *cert. denied,* 451 U.S. 1022 (1981).

Donohue v. Copiague Union Free Schools, 407 N.Y.S. 2d 874 (App. Div. 1978), *aff'd,* 391 N.E. 1352 (N.Y. 1979).

Eisel v. Board of Education of Montgomery County, 597 A. 2d 447 (Md. 1991).

Faragher v. Boca Raton, No. 97-282 S. Ct. (1998).

Ficus v. Board of School Trustees of Central School District of Green County, 509 N.E. 2d 1137 (Ind. App.1 Dist. 1987).

Fischer, L., Schimmel, D., & Kelly, C. (1995). *Teachers and the law* (3rd ed.). New York: Longman.

Franklin v. Gwinnett, 503 U.S. 60 (1992).

Gaylord v. Tacoma School District No. 10, 559 P. 2d 1340 (Wash. 1977).

Gebster v. Lago Vista Independent School District, 118 S. Ct. 1989 (1998).

Goss v. Lopez, 419 U.S. 565 (1975).

Harris v. Board of Education of Columbus, Ohio, 798 F. Supp. (S. D. Ohio 1992).

Hazelwood School District v. Kuhlmeier, 108 S. Ct. 562 (1988).

Hoffman v. Board of Education of the City of New York, 400 N.E. 2d 317 (1979).

Honig v. Doe, 198 S. Ct. 592 (1988).

Horton v. Goose Creek Independent School District, 677 F. 2d 471 (5th Cir. 1982).

Hortonville Joint School District No. 1 v. Hortonville Education Association, 225 N.W.

2d 658 (Wis. 1975), rev'd on other grounds and remained, 426 U.S. 482 (1976), *aff'd,* 274 N.W. 2d 697 (Wis. 1979).

Ingraham v. Wright, 430 U.S. 651 (1977).

In Re Thomas, 926 S. W. 2d 163 (Mo. App. 1996).

Jeglin v. San Jacinto Unified School District, 827 F.Supp. 1459 (C.D. Cal. 1993).

Kingsville Independent School District v. Cooper, 611 F. 2d 1109 (5th Cir. 1980).

LaMorte, M. W. (1996). *School law: Cases and concepts* (5th ed.). Boston: Allyn and Bacon.

McCarthy, M. (1989). Legal rights and responsibilities of public school teachers. In M. C. Reynolds (Ed.), *Knowledge base for the beginning teacher* (pp. 255–266). New York: Pergamon Press.

McCarthy, M. M., Cambron-McCabe, N. H., & Thomas, S. B. (1998). *Public school law: Teachers' and students' rights* (4th ed.). Boston: Allyn and Bacon.

McClelland v. Paris Public Schools, 742 S.W. 2d 907 (Ark. 1988).

New Jersey, Petitioner v. T.L.O., 105 S. Ct. 733 (1985).

Peter W. v. San Francisco Unified School District, 131 Cal. Rptr. 854 (Cal. App. 1976).

Pickering v. Board of Education, 391 U.S. 563 (1968).

Pyle v. South Hadley School Community, 861 F. Supp. 157 (D. Mass. 1994), *vacated,* 55 F.3d 20 (1st Cir. 1996).

Regents of the University of California v. Alan Bakke, 438 U.S. 265 (1978).

Reitmeyer v. Unemployment Compensation Board of Review, 602 A. 2d 505 (Pa.Comwlth. 1992).

Rowinsky v. Bryan Independent School District, 80 F.3d 1006 (5th Cir. 1996), *cert. denied,* 117 S. Ct. 165 (1997).

School Board of Nassau County v. Arline 107 S. Ct. 1129 (1987).

Sperry, D. J., Daniel, P. T. K., Huefner, D. S., & Gee, E. G. (1998). *Education law and the public schools: A compendium* (2nd ed.). Norwood, MA: Christopher-Gordon.

State of Florida v. J. A., 679 So.2d 316 (1996), *cert. denied* 118 S. Ct. 98 (1997).

Stephenson v. Davenport Community School District, 110 F.3d 1303 (8th Cir. 1997).

Stroman v. Colleton County School District, 981 F. 2d 152 (4th Cir. 1992).

Suriano v. Hyde Park Cent. School District, 611 N.Y.S.2d 20 (App. Div. 1994).

Taxman v. Board of Education of Township of Piscataway, 91 F.3d 1547 (3d Cir. 1996).

Texas State Teachers' Association v. Garland Independent School District, 777 F. 2d 1046 (5th Cir. 1985), *aff'd,* 107 S. Ct. 41 (1986).

Thompson v. Carthage School District, 87 F.3d 979 (8th Cir. 1996).

Tinker v. Des Moines Independent Community School District, 393 U.S. 503 (1969).

United States Department of Education, Office of Civil Rights. (1997). *Sexual harassment guidance: Harassment of students by school employees, other students or third parties.* Washington, DC: Author.

Valente, W. D. (1998). *Law in the schools* (4th ed.). New York: Merrill.

Vernonia School District v. Acton, 115 S. Ct. 2386 (1995).

Washington v. Davis, 426 U.S. 229 (1976).

Waters v. Churchill, 511 U.S. 661 (1994).

Wood v. Strickland, 420 U.S. 308 (1975).

Wygant v. Jackson Board of Education, 106 S. Ct. 1842 (1986).

Chapter 13

We may have reached the time when the public will not grant us more money for public instruction unless we can show greater efficiency in spending the dollars which have already been voted for school use.

NASSP *Fifth Yearbook,* 1921

Governance and Financing of Elementary and Secondary Schools

▶ *A school board election is scheduled in a few months in the school district in which Mr. Rodriguez lives and works as a teacher. At a parent–teacher meeting at the school, a parent asks about the functions and desirable qualities of school board members in the community. As a new teacher in the district, Mr. Rodriguez is asked to be a panelist at a public forum on school board selection. His assignment is to indicate why he decided to work in the district and what he thinks are some needs of the district.*

How would you contrast the role of a teacher with that of a school board member? What levels of education and other qualifications should be required of school board members?

How active should teachers be in school board elections? Should the teachers' association endorse specific candidates? What are some possible implications of teachers endorsing candidates for the school board?

What information does Mr. Rodriguez need about the district to prepare for the meeting?

The purpose of this chapter is to increase your understanding of how schools are financed and governed and related issues. Teachers will be more effective in their daily work if they understand the organization, administration, and financing of public education; issues surrounding the governance of education; and ways in which the structure affects the work of teachers. Throughout your career as an educator you will be asked to explain how schools are governed, to justify educational funding, and to explain how funds are expended. Since education is the nation's largest industry with the largest public expenditure except for defense, a high level of public interest is to be expected and justified. As you read and discuss this chapter and undertake the related activities, consider the following objectives and their impact upon you in your future role as a teacher. After reading the chapter, you should be able to:

- Discuss the impact that school-site decision making might have on the roles and responsibilities of the classroom teacher.
- Determine the number and different types of local school districts in your state.
- Describe the roles of the local school board and the superintendent of schools.
- Differentiate between the role of the local superintendent of schools and that of the chief state school officer.
- Discuss the role of the federal government in elementary and secondary education.

- Identify the effect of federal programs on local school district decisions about educational programs.
- Describe the three goals of school finance programs.
- Compare the goals of the various state school finance programs.
- Identify the major local, state, and federal revenue sources.
- Discuss the role of private education in America.

Consistent with the checks and balances inherent in the American governmental system, the governance system for public elementary and secondary education also has its checks and balances. Among the nations of the world, the United States is unique in the emphasis placed on decentralization and local participation in the conduct of public elementary and secondary education. Each state establishes the governance system for its schools, provides for the funding of the schools, and establishes various minimum standards for school operation. The primary concerns of the federal government are funding for the educational needs of special populations, national research priorities, and data gathering and reporting.

In the following overview of the governance and financing structure for public elementary and secondary education in the United States, initial attention is given to the overall governance structure of public education. Following this overview of governance, the discussion focuses on state school finance programs and revenues for schools. The chapter concludes with a brief discussion of private education and current issues related to governance and finance of the public schools.

The Context of the Public Schools

Public elementary and secondary education has been referred to as a state responsibility, a local function, and a federal concern. These principles are illustrated in both the governance structure and the financial structure of the public schools. Even though education is not referred to in the federal Constitution, an education clause can be found in each state's constitution. In many ways the provisions are similar; however, some states have chosen to express the function in somewhat different ways. References are made to an efficient system of schools, a common system of schools, a general and uniform system of schools, or a thorough and efficient system of schools. The technical wording of these provisions has become critical during the past 25 years as state systems for financing schools have been challenged in the courts.

Among the states, there are great similarities in the organization and financing of schools. For example, the grade structure of kindergarten through grade 12 is found in all states. Statutes and regulations for teacher licenses do not vary greatly among the states; usually, only limited additional study is required to receive a license in another state. Textbooks are published for a national market. The recently developed national curriculum standards provide another example of the similarities rather than the differences in public elementary and secondary schools among the states. All states except Hawaii have local school districts to operate schools and rely on state and local tax sources to fund schools.

Organization for Education

The complexity of the educational enterprise is awesome. For example, one person in five either attends or is employed in the nation's public elementary and secondary schools. Rather than a single monolithic system of schools like a large corporation, the American educational delivery system operates through 50 separate state educational agencies with instruction being provided by over 14,000 local school districts in about 80,000 schools. Operational *policies* are set by governors, state legislatures, state boards of education, and local *school boards.* Governors and legislators not only face the public policy challenge of determining the funding system for the schools, but also are expected to provide adequate and equitable financing for this system of schools.

Support for elementary and secondary education is the largest single item in the budgets of many state and local governments. Expenditures for public elementary and secondary schools are approaching $300 billion annually. While funds come from a combination of local, state, and federal sources, the majority of the money comes from state and local taxes. Federal funds are targeted for special programs or conditions and provided less than 7% of the expenditures for public elementary and secondary schools in 1997–98. Figure 13.1 shows the national average sources of funding for education from each of the three levels of government.

Unlike governmental functions such as national defense, interstate commerce, and international relations, which have a heavy federal orientation, the governmental structure for the public schools has evolved as a combination of state and local powers and responsibilities. Rather than being the source of centralized educational policies and decisions about the operation of public elementary and

Figure 13.1: Sources of Funds for Public Elementary and Secondary Schools, 1995–96

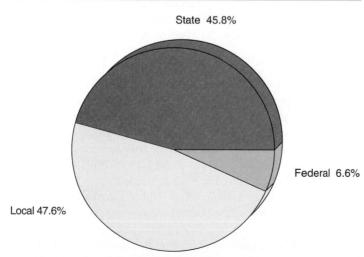

Source: U.S. Department of Education. (1997). National Center for Education Statistics, Common Core of Data, "National Public Education Survey." Washington DC: U.S. Department of Education.

secondary schools, the federal government has a very limited role. The current structure has been reinforced by the various recommendations and actions associated with educational reform in the 1980s and 1990s. In the quest for educational improvement, state legislative actions have resulted in increased duties, responsibilities, and expectations being placed on local school districts.

Education at the Local Level

Public education in the United States is a highly decentralized endeavor. States have provided for the creation of local school districts that are responsible for the actual operation of schools. Their sole purpose is to operate elementary and secondary schools. Even though there are state requirements and national goals, local school districts and individual schools have great freedom in organizing their programs and the teaching/learning environment. These freedoms are being expanded with the emphasis on decentralization and site-based decision making. The primary functions of local school districts are to:

- Adopt policies and regulations for the operation of schools.
- Within the context of state guidelines, adopt the curriculum for the schools.
- Serve as linkages between community patrons and the schools and provide periodic reports about the schools.
- Provide the human and material resources needed to operate schools.
- Take the necessary steps to provide and maintain adequate facilities for instruction.
- Provide the *state department of education* and other agencies with required information about the schools.

Local school districts and their governing bodies, local school boards, are often the targets of criticism, but they appear to be permanent features in the structure of American government. Citizens place a high value on this opportunity to participate in educational decision making. In a variety of ways, these citizens determine the direction that the schools will take.

School Boards

State statutes provide for the selection of lay citizens to serve on school boards that govern the operation of school districts. The legal power of lay citizens to control public education through a system of local school boards is a unique feature of the American educational system. In principle, school boards represent all the people; members are chosen as stewards with a public trust. There is no time or place for personal agendas. Through the schools, these lay citizens help build the future of the nation (American Association of School Administrators, 1946).

What should be the qualifications of local school board members?

School boards are either appointed or elected. In most cases, there are no educational requirements for school board membership. Members come from all walks of life. People seek appointment or election to school boards for a variety of reasons. The only prerequisite may be that the board member be a resident of the school district.

The primary function of the local school board is to set the policies under which the schools will operate. Before making decisions, the board has a responsibility to consider the beliefs, values, and traditions of the community. However, boards typically rely on the counsel and recommendations of the superintendent. As they serve, board members must function as a group, for they only have power and authority when the board is in session (Orlosky, McCleary, Shapiro, & Webb, 1984).

Other functions of the school board include budget adoption, approval of expenditures, approval of the school's organizational pattern, employment of personnel, and issuance of contracts. These legal functions are in addition to the role of the school board in informing the community. Community support is especially critical because of the role of the *local property tax* in financing schools in many states and the importance of maintaining a strong base of citizen support for the public schools. As enrollments increased and as school districts became more complex organizations, the need for full-time professional leadership and management became evident, and the position of *superintendent of schools* became a full-time position. The typical administrative organization in many school districts is illustrated in Figure 13.2.

What powers should local school board members in making decisions about school programs?

Superintendent of Schools

Each school district has a chief administrator, typically referred to as the superintendent. As the role and responsibilities of the superintendent of schools have evolved, the job has become chief executive officer of the local school district. Typically, educational program and related responsibilities of the superintendent include planning, staffing, coordinating, budgeting, administering, evaluating, and reporting. The superintendent's primary responsibility is to work with the local school board and the school district's staff to improve educational programs in the district.

When compared with private business, in many ways the local school board functions like the board of directors of a corporation. The superintendent of schools, the counterpart of the chief executive officer of the corporation, is responsible for the day-to-day operation of the enterprise, the schools (Campbell, Cunningham, Nystrand, & Usdan, 1985).

What should be the qualifications of the local superintendent of schools?

In contrast to an earlier time when the superintendent on occasion was a part-time teacher, today's superintendent has a full-time position and may view the job as a career. School superintendents typically come from the ranks of teachers. Today, specialized training in educational administration beyond the master's degree is typically required for licensing or certification. Many states require the equivalent of two years of graduate work. A national study group proposed requiring the doctorate in educational administration for permanent certification (National Policy Board, 1989); however, significant changes have not occurred. Among local school districts, there appears to be some interest in nontraditional career paths for persons with leadership potential who have demonstrated in other fields that they possess the management and leadership skills required to be a successful superintendent of schools. Some school districts have looked to private sector executives and retired military officers in recent years. Examples of this practice in large school districts may be found in San Diego, Seattle, and Washington, D.C.

Figure 13.2: Local Education Governance

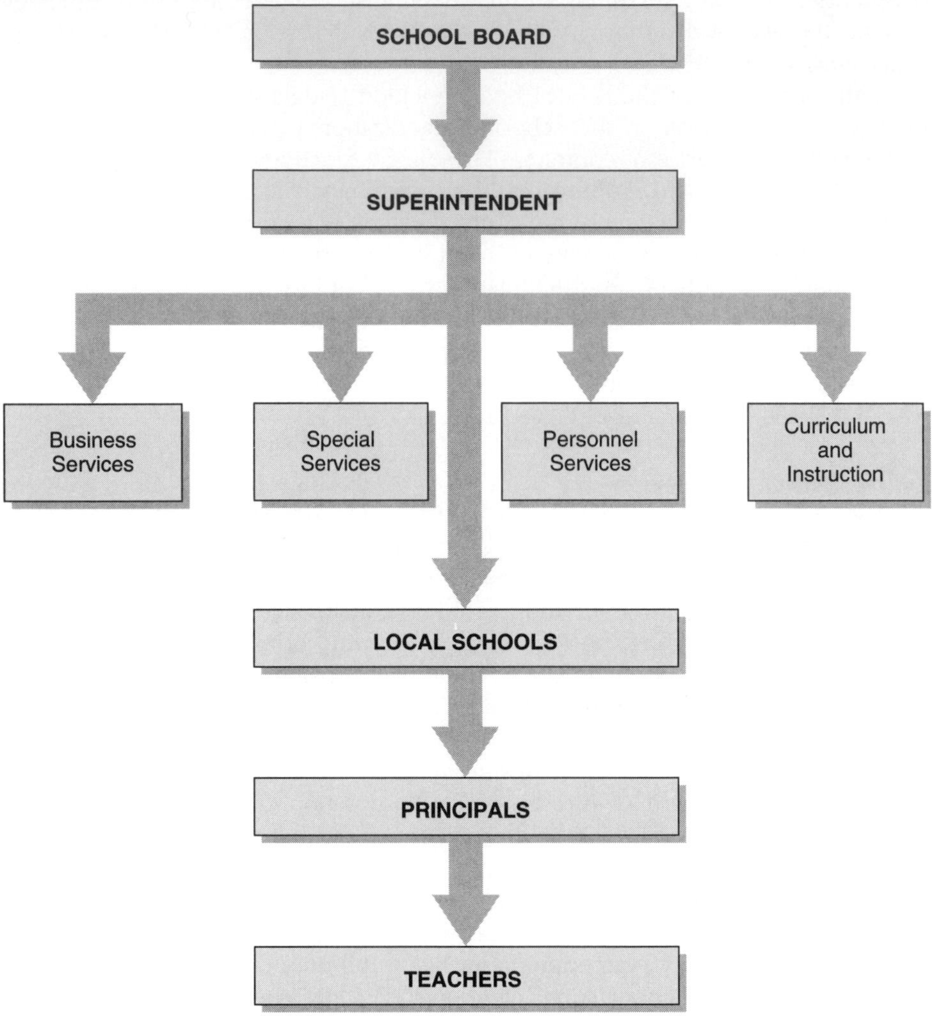

Building Principal

The key participant with the primary responsibility for the success or failure of the educational program in each local school is the *building principal*. Successful administration of a school requires that the principal exercise leadership as well as practice effective management and planning skills. Historically, principals have been teachers and may serve as an assistant principal before becoming a principal. Some have viewed the principalship as a career and others have considered the job to be a stepping stone to a position such as assistant superintendent or superintendent. Recently, a new career pattern has emerged. The principalship has come to be viewed as a career opportunity with a unique set of skills and professional opportunities. One reason for this change in perception is that decentralized decision making will require that the principal develop an expanded set of human relations as well as technical and planning skills. The principal will spend much more time planning and working with, rather than directing, faculty members and community patrons.

Pattern of School Districts in the States

Among the states, the number of school districts varies greatly and is associated with differences in educational opportunity for students. The number of school districts in each state is shown in Table 13.1. As indicated in the table, excluding Hawaii and the District of Columbia, the number of school districts in a state ranges from 17 in Nevada, 19 in Delaware, and 24 in Maryland to over 900 in California, Illinois, and Texas. Other states with relatively few school districts include Florida, Louisiana, New Mexico, Utah, and West Virginia.

Table 13.1: Number of School Districts by State, 1995–96

State	Total Number of Districts	State	Total Number of Districts
50 States and D.C.	14,367	Missouri	525
Alabama	127	Montana	465
Alaska	55	Nebraska	653
Arizona	214	Nevada	17
Arkansas	311	New Hampshire	164
California	999	New Jersey	582
Colorado	176	New Mexico	89
Connecticut	166	New York	709
Delaware	19	North Carolina	119
District of Columbia	1	North Dakota	234
Florida	67	Ohio	611
Georgia	180	Oklahoma	548
Hawaii	1	Oregon	233
Idaho	112	Pennsylvania	500
Illinois	905	Rhode Island	36
Indiana	292	South Carolina	95
Iowa	383	South Dakota	173
Kansas	304	Tennessee	138
Kentucky	176	Texas	1,044
Louisiana	66	Utah	40
Maine	228	Vermont	251
Maryland	24	Virginia	132
Massachusetts	248	Washington	296
Michigan	593	West Virginia	55
Minnesota	383	Wisconsin	426
Mississippi	153	Wyoming	49

Source: U.S. Department of Education, National Center for Education Statistics, (1997). Common Core of Data, "National Public Education Survey." Washington, DC: U.S. Department of Education.

Data in the table indicate that the number of school districts in a state is not related to either the total enrollment or geographic size of the state. For example, California, Illinois, and Texas all have over 900 school districts, but Florida has 67 districts. Another example is that Montana has 465 districts and Wyoming has 49 districts. Montana has less than two times the enrollment of Wyoming, but nine times as many districts.

Southeastern states tend to have the fewest school districts. In several states, school districts are organized on a county unit basis where the county and school district have the same boundary. States in the Midwest and Great Plains tend to have more districts because the civil township was a beginning point for their school districts. However, in the 1950s and 1960s, several states took action to consolidate small school districts so that educational opportunities for students would be enhanced. Since 1950, the number of school districts in the nation has been reduced from 100,000 to less than 15,000. The number of school districts has little relationship to the number of schools in a state. For the nation, the number of public schools totals about 80,000. The number of schools in a school district may be the result of enrollment changes, population shifts, topographical conditions, or tradition.

As they organized their school districts, states created different types of school districts. The most common pattern of school district organization is the unit school district that provides educational programs for students in kindergarten through grade 12. However, a few states (Arizona, California, Illinois, Montana, New Jersey, and Vermont) permit the operation of separate high school districts serving grades 9 through 12 and elementary districts serving students in kindergarten through grade 8. The original rationale for separate high school and elementary districts may have been that this arrangement would increase the high school offerings available to students, but the benefits of the K–12 unified school districts seem to outweigh the disadvantages. Educational program planning and sequencing can be handled more efficiently, and students can be assisted in making the transition from elementary to high school.

A major problem with the multiple types of districts is that neither the elementary nor the high school district is held accountable for the educational outcomes of students as they attempt to make the transition into high school. Another critical consideration is the lack of articulation or coordination between the elementary schools and the high schools. Courses and programs may not be coordinated, and students may experience difficulty in making the transition from grade 8 to grade 9.

The Myth of Local Control

Since their origin in colonial days, local school districts always have been subject to the control of state legislatures. Local school districts have two kinds of powers, stated and implied. Stated powers are explicit in actions of the state legislature or provisions of the state constitution. Implied powers are implicit, but are required to carry out the stated powers or the assigned functions. An example of these implied powers is the authority of the school district to purchase chalk and custodial cleaning materials. The likelihood of these items being mentioned specifically in state statutes is slim, but they fall under the category of implied powers because they are necessary for the effective operation of schools.

To illustrate the various ways in which the states have retained control over public education, local school districts only have the taxing powers that have been granted by the state. In some states, school districts do not have the authority to adopt budgets and set tax rates; they must submit their budgets to municipal or county governments for review and final approval before finalizing their fiscal plans for the school year. On the other hand, state legislatures have granted to state boards of education such powers as setting minimum standards for teacher licensing or certification, minimum graduation requirements, minimum length of school day, and minimum number of school days in a year.

The recent interest in education reform and *accountability* has resulted in state legislatures and state boards of education imposing a variety of additional requirements on local school districts. Examples include graduation requirements, entrance examinations for teachers, school and school district report cards, content standards for disciplines, standardized tests, and "no pass, no play" requirements for participants in high school interscholastic activities. Statutes have authorized intervention and takeover of underperforming schools in several states. Because of the emphasis on student performance on standardized tests, the term "high-stakes testing" has been used in referring to the education accountability system of incentives, recognition, and interventions.

Local School District Planning and Budgeting

Public elementary and secondary schools are labor-intensive endeavors. Personnel costs represent the majority of expenditures in local school budgets. About 70% of the typical school district's expenditures are for instructional services, with 50% being for classroom instruction. Funds for administrator salaries at both the central office and the building level account for about 10% of the total. Figure 13.3 shows the percentage of the budget allocated for the various major functions in the typical local school district.

The concept of *strategic planning* has become an important component in the program planning and funding decisions of local school districts. Starting with the school district's or the school's mission statement supported by goals and objectives, funding priorities are linked to resource allocations to ensure that budgetary decisions are compatible with program priorities. However, strategic planning by a school district does not automatically result in participative decision making. If the planning process is to be from the bottom up, teachers will be active participants. They will be members of the school working committee and possibly also of various subcommittees. However, if the planning process is to be top down, opportunities for broad-based teacher participation will be limited.

Site-Based Management

As the smallest management unit of the school district, the local school is the most critical unit in the educational delivery system. One focus of the education reform movement in the 1980s was the emphasis on decentralized or school-site

What kinds of decisions should be made at the school site?

Figure 13.3: Percent of Total Current Expenditures by Function for 1996–97

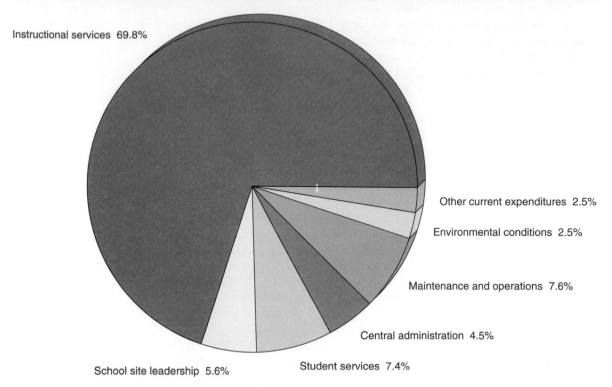

Instructional services 69.8%

Other current expenditures 2.5%

Environmental conditions 2.5%

Maintenance and operations 7.6%

Central administration 4.5%

School site leadership 5.6%

Student services 7.4%

Source: Protheroe, N. (1997). ERS—Local school budget profile study. *School Business Affairs, 63*(10), 42–49.

decision making as a way to increase teacher morale, improve the management of schools, and raise student performance. A key element was perceived to be greater control of resources at the school site level. To achieve this new pattern of operation, the reform movement has called for greater flexibility in school decision making and increased involvement of school faculties, parents, and community leaders.

Models for involvement and decision making include school-site budgeting as well as school-level decision making. A recent survey (NEA Research, 1997) reported that a significant percentage of teachers were involved in decision making in their schools. In 1996, over three fourths (75.5%) of the respondents indicated that their schools were involved in some type of school reform. Over two fifths of the respondents (42.5%) reported that they had participated in curriculum committees. Slightly over half (51%) participated in other committees such as budget and personnel. Much obvious progress has been made in teacher participation in site-based decision making when these percentages are compared with 35.3% in 1971.

One potential problem with school-level decision making is the lack of open communication between the central office and the school site. Steps should be taken to ensure that school-level personnel do not invest major amounts of time and energy and then find that their proposals have been ignored or rejected without explanation.

Calls for greater teacher participation in school-level decisions have been operationalized as school-site decision making. Complete decentralization in decision making is not possible because local schools, as part of a school district within a state system of education, are subject to statutes, policies, and regulations from the school district and the state. However, there seems to be a consensus that schools are more successful when teachers have a voice in decisions about their working conditions and the operation of the local school.

Decentralization does not ensure parental and staff participation in decision making. A principal can still make decisions without staff or community participation; however, this latter management style is not consistent with the principles of decentralized decision making. An underlying assumption is that teachers should be heavily involved in planning, discussing, and making the final decisions. This process also is viewed as an opportunity to increase parental participation in schools by involving parents in critical aspects of school-site decision making.

Education at the State Level

The legal principle of education being a state responsibility contributes to state educational agencies playing a key role in the development of the structure and delivery system for public elementary and secondary education. Each state has a state-level administrative agency whose primary functions include:

- Implementing the state board of education's broad policies for the operation of the state's public elementary and secondary schools.
- Monitoring the schools in accordance with legislative mandates.
- Being an advocate for public education.
- Providing the state legislature and citizens with information about the schools.
- Providing technical assistance to the schools.
- Collecting data about the schools.
- Disbursing state funds for the operation of local school districts.

Should educational standards be consistent among the states?

This state-level governance structure typically includes a *state board of education* as the policy-making body, a state administrative agency typically referred to as the state department of education, and a *chief state school officer* who serves as executive officer of the state board of education and as administrator of the state department of education. Figure 13.4 reflects the state-level administrative organization in many states.

State Boards of Education

State boards of education have various responsibilities. These boards usually are charged with adopting regulations and monitoring local school districts to ensure implementation of the constitutional and statutory mandates related to the operation of the state system of schools. Their directives and mandates are related to

Public elementary and secondary education is a responsibility and function of state government. State constitutional provisions and legislative actions prescribe how schools will be governed and financed. Most states utilize a system of local school districts to operate schools.

What should be the qualifications of members of the state board of education?

policy formulation and enforcement within the context of the state's statutory provisions. Examples include graduation requirements for high school students and mandated curricular offerings in schools. Advisory functions are related to leadership, encouragement, and interactions with local school districts. Among the important state board functions are providing the state legislature with timely reports about the schools, proposing changes in statutes, proposing new initiatives and programs, and presenting and serving as an advocate for the budget for state support of schools. Most state boards are not responsible for the direct operation of educational institutions or schools; rather, their concern is with the overall direction of the state's schools.

Virtually all states have a state board of education, but they differ in composition, method of selection, relationship with the chief state school officer, and functions. For example, in Florida, the cabinet consisting of the state's elected officials also serves as the state board of education. The state superintendent of public instruction is elected and is a member of the cabinet. This is in contrast to Texas, where members of the state board are elected on a population-based district basis. In other states, members of the state board of education are appointed by the governor, sometimes with the consent of the state legislature.

Figure 13.4: State Education Governance

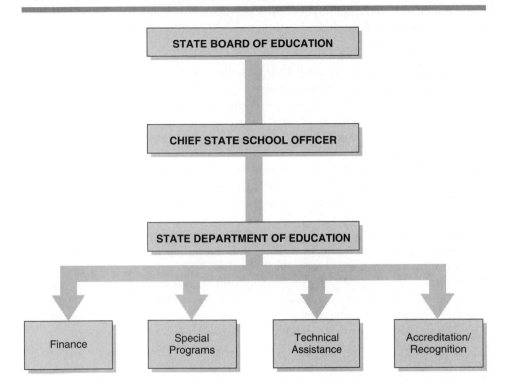

Chief State School Officer

Each state has either constitutional or statutory provisions for a chief state school officer; the person often is referred to as the superintendent of public instruction or the commissioner of education. In most instances, responsibilities are limited to elementary and secondary education, but in a few states the person also has responsibilities for higher education.

The professional status of the position is improving, but in several states required qualifications are either unstated or very broad. This is especially true in those states where the chief state school officer is elected. In states where the chief state school officer is appointed, the tendency is to select a person with professional training and experience in educational administration. Over 30 of the 50 chief state school officers are appointed either by the governor or the state board of education. The others are elected on a popular basis statewide (Campbell, Cunningham, Nystrand, & Usdan, 1985).

What should be the qualifications of the chief state school officer?

State Secretaries of Education

Recently, several states have adopted the federal cabinet system with a *secretary of education* who is responsible to the governor. Usually, the statutory provisions related to the chief state school officer and the state board of education have not been greatly altered by the creation of this cabinet position, and the state department of education has remained in place. The primary duties of the secretary of education have been related to long-range planning and budgeting rather than to administering the state department of education or monitoring schools.

The Federal Government and Public Education

As noted in Chapter 6, the absence of mention of education in the federal Constitution and the reservation of this function to the states should not be interpreted as indicating a lack of interest in education by the nation's founders. When the Constitution was being written, several states already had provided for education in their state constitutions and leaders in those states did not want the federal government to interfere with those provisions. In addition, private and church-related schools were numerous in some states and some persons may have supported this option for providing education (Grieder, Pierce, & Jordan, 1969).

Federal Role and Involvement

The emphases of current federal education programs are threefold. First, the major portions of the funds are for programs and services for special populations; these include funding for programs to serve students with disabilities, educationally disadvantaged youth, financially needy college students, and vocational education students. Recent amendments to federal education legislation have granted local school districts greater flexibility in administering these programs.

The second emphasis area is educational statistics and research. Since the creation of the first Department of Education in 1867, the one continuing role of the federal education agency has been data gathering and reporting. Even though education is a state function, there is an interest in national information about the educational enterprise. Rather than each individual state gathering and reporting data in the state's format, it has been more cost-effective for the function to be performed by a federal education agency, the National Center for Education Statistics. Reporting of consistent and comparable data can be enhanced and information can be provided for international comparisons.

A third emphasis has been research and demonstration projects. Since the creation of the Cooperative Research Program in 1957, the federal government has funded educational demonstration and research projects. The rationales for federal support of educational research and demonstration projects are similar to those for data gathering and reporting. Cost-effectiveness will be improved by central funding of national research priorities and disseminating this information for better-informed educational decision making. These programs often are funded through competitive grants; demonstration projects also are conducted by local school districts or state educational agencies.

U.S. Department of Education

For more than 130 years, some type of federal agency for education has been in existence. Starting in 1867 with the creation of a Department of Education without cabinet status, various federal agencies have had responsibility for education. The chronology suggests an uncertainty in the federal commitment to education. For example, in 1869 the title was changed to Office of Education, in 1870 to Bureau of Education, and in 1929 back to Office of Education (Grieder, Pierce, & Jordan, 1969). That designation was retained until the creation of the Department of Education in 1980, when education was given cabinet status. Until the creation of the Department of Education with a secretary of education, the federal education agency had been administered by a commissioner of education.

Secretary of Education

The first secretary of education, Shirley Hufstadler, was a federal judge at the time of appointment. The second, Terrel Bell, was a former U.S. commissioner of education, chief state school officer in Utah, local superintendent, and college professor. Next was William Bennett, a former college professor appointed to the position from another federal position; after him, Lauro Cavazos, a university president at the time of appointment. In 1991, President Bush nominated Lamar Alexander, former governor of Tennessee, to succeed Cavazos as secretary of education. President Clinton's appointment as secretary of education was William Riley, former education reform governor of South Carolina.

Some secretaries of education have viewed the position as an opportunity to ensure that all students have access to educational programs and services. Others have tried to maintain and expand federal educational programs and services. Some have viewed the position as a "bully pulpit" from which to improve education by promoting different education reforms.

Financing of Education

In addition to establishing the governance structure for education, state legislatures also establish the basic structure for financing public elementary and secondary schools. The state enacts the funding system for schools and sets the taxing and spending powers of local school districts. This includes the state's method for funding schools, the types of taxes that may be used, and the tax rate that may be levied.

Methods of financing public elementary and secondary schools and funding levels per pupil differ in a variety of ways both within and among states. However, two basic legal principles guide the financing of the public schools in the United States. First, education is a responsibility of the state level of government. Second, in the design and implementation of the state school finance program, the state has an equal responsibility to each pupil (Jordan & Lyons, 1992). Adhering to these principles has been difficult because the states have chosen to let the local school districts, with their wide differences in enrollment, taxable wealth, and citizen aspirations, administer and deliver education.

Public Policy Goals in School Finance

State systems for financing schools are imperfect and full of educational and political compromises. Public policy decisions about how schools should be

Many communities whose students have complex educational needs do not have sufficient funds for their schools because of the heavy reliance on the local property tax as a major source of funds for schools.

financed are made with three goals in mind: *equity, choice,* and *adequacy* (Jordan & Lyons, 1992). Of these goals, equity is the most important. The problem with equity is that the majority may not be able to agree that equity has been attained, but they can agree that equity has not been attained as long as large disparities in per-pupil expenditures exist.

Equity

The concept of equity refers to the equal treatment of persons in equal circumstances. For students, this means an equal opportunity for education. For taxpayers, this means equal tax rates on similar property in districts with different levels of taxable wealth per pupil. The problem is that equity may not result in adequate or sufficient funds for schools; it may only result in equal treatment.

Horizontal equity assumes that students who are alike should be treated the same way. *Vertical equity* assumes that groups of students with different educational and service needs should be treated differently, and also that those with similar needs in different districts should have similar access to educational programs and services.

Choice

In the 1990s, the term *choice* has been used to refer to two different goals. One is local control of funding decisions. Traditionally, local school boards have been permitted to choose the level of funding for the schools. In some cases, equity and choice have come into conflict because a district's freedom to choose the level of funding has resulted in inequitable treatment of taxpayers and students. Currently, choice also is being used to refer to the power of parents to select the school that their child will attend. There have not been enough experiences with this type of choice to indicate the impact on equity to either students or taxpayers.

Adequacy

Adequacy refers to the extent to which the funding level for programs and learning opportunities is sufficient to provide the programs and services needed by students. Factors affecting adequacy include quality of staff, sufficient materials, and skill levels of teachers.

State School Finance Programs

The history of state school finance programs can be traced to about 1900, when Ellwood Cubberley contended that the state had a responsibility to address the unfairness of a school finance system that relied almost exclusively on the local property tax to finance schools. As a result of his efforts, state school finance *equalization* models were developed in the early decades of the twentieth century; prior to that time, state funds were limited and typically were distributed on a *flat-grant* basis irrespective of differences in local wealth or educational need. The forerunner of today's commonly used state school finance programs can be traced to that period.

Of the five major models or funding approaches, three are equalization models: equalized foundation grants, equalized reward for tax effort, and *full state funding*. The other two models are flat grants and *categorical funding*.

To equalize access to funds for education, states have enacted statutes designed to compensate for the differences in taxable wealth among local school districts. The most frequently used approach is equalized foundation grants. About two thirds of the states use a school finance formula that can be classified as a foundation program (Gold, Smith, & Lawton, 1995).

Although state school finance laws originally were developed to assist schools in the poorer rural areas, it is the urban school districts that now require additional help. They have two types of additional burdens. One is *educational overburden,* which refers to the relatively larger number of pupils in city schools who require high-cost educational programs and the higher costs of instructional goods and services in urban areas. A related problem is *municipal overburden,* which refers to the need for a greater range of social services in urban areas that must be paid for by the same taxpayers who support the schools.

Foundation Programs

The major state school finance programs are illustrated in Table 13.2. The Strayer-Haig model, typically referred to as the *foundation plan,* provides the difference between a fixed amount per pupil and the amount the district can collect locally through a uniform tax rate (Strayer & Haig, 1923). For example, if the foundation plan provides for $4,000 per pupil and the yield from a prescribed local tax rate for a school district raises $2,500 per pupil, the state payment would be $1,500 per pupil. If the prescribed local tax rate raises $1,000 per pupil, the state payment would be $3,000 per pupil. However, if the prescribed local tax rate raises $5,000 per pupil, the state would make no payment to the local school district. The different amounts of state payments illustrate the ways in which equalization can be operationalized so that state and local revenues provide a foundation of funds. In

Of the three public policy goals for school finance, which do you think is most important?

Table 13.2: Current Funding Approaches

Description	Who Uses It?	Problems
Strayer-Haig Equalization Funding Model (foundation plan)		
Developed in 1920s by George D. Strayer and Robert M. Haig at Columbia University. Provides difference between district's need and amount collectible locally. Uniform tax rate applied to assessed value of property in school district. Entitlement based on funds required to ensure a minimum per pupil or per teacher; minimum determined by legislature. Adjusted to recognize additional funds needed for concentration of pupils with special needs.	Used in some form in over two thirds of the states.	Keeps funding at a minimum level; insufficient to support an adequate educational program. State does not participate in efforts to provide funds beyond minimum.
Power Equalization (effort oriented)		
Developed in 1922 by Harlan Updegraff at University of Pennsylvania. Local school officials choose level of funding. Tax revenues in district "equalized" by state allocations. Any excess raised in a district sent to state treasury.	About one sixth of states used it in some form in the late 1990s.	No assurance of funding at an adequate level.
Full State Funding		
No local taxes collected.	Used only in Hawaii.	No local choice permitted.
Flat grants		
State provides uniform amount per student; funds available for any legal educational purpose.	Originally most common form of state support. May be used with an equalization program to ensure that wealthy school districts receive some funds.	Funds do not generally go to area of greatest need.
Categorical Funding		
State funds are allocated for specific purpose (e.g., bilingual education, in-service programs for teachers, instructional materials, etc.).	Often used to encourage specific programs that are not mandated by state law.	Typically allocated irrespective of district's wealth.

terms of the previously discussed school finance goals, equity and adequacy can be achieved if the foundation amount per pupil is sufficiently high.

Foundation programs have been criticized because funding may be at a minimum level and not be sufficient to support an adequate educational program. This inability to meet the adequacy criterion has a stifling effect because the state typically does not provide funds beyond the minimum level. In terms of other school finance goals, student and taxpayer equity can be attained, but choice will be dependent upon the discretion granted to local school districts.

Power Equalization Programs

Under *power equalization* formulas, local school officials choose the level of funding they desire for their schools. Revenues raised by taxes in the district are "equalized" by state allocations (Updegraff, 1922). This differs from the foundation plan in which the state sets the target amount per pupil or per teacher. In 1994–95, six states were using the power equalization concept as the primary funding method (Gold, Smith, & Lawton, 1995).

In states using power equalization funding programs, the local school board sets a tax rate and the state then guarantees a specified amount per unit of tax rate (Coons, Clune, & Sugarman, 1970). For example, if the state guarantees $50 per pupil per penny of tax rate and a penny in district A raises $30 per pupil, the state would provide $20 per pupil per penny of tax rate. If a one-penny tax rate raises $10 in district B, the state would provide $40 per pupil per penny of tax rate. Under this option, the state does not provide a foundation funding level, but allocates funds in relation to the tax rates selected in local school districts.

In terms of the previously discussed school finance goals, taxpayer equity and local district choice can be achieved, but there is no assurance that the level of funding will be adequate or sufficient. In addition, this option may not treat students equitably in their access to an appropriate education.

Full State Funding

Full state funding for public schools occurs when no local tax revenues are collected for support of schools. All funds for schools come from state-level taxes (Morrison, 1930). This model is used only in Hawaii, which has just one school district for administrative management of all state schools (Gold, Smith, & Lawton, 1995). A single teacher's salary schedule is in effect for all schools on the islands.

Under full state funding, students and taxpayers are treated equally, but attainment of adequacy will be dependent upon the funding level. No opportunity for local district choice is available.

What kind of school finance program is used to fund schools in your state?

Flat Grants

Originally the most common form of state payment to school districts, flat grants have now been replaced by foundation or equalization programs. Under the flat-grant program, states provide a uniform amount per student, and the funds may be used for any legal educational purpose (Cubberley, 1905). Several states still include a low-level flat-grant program when enacting an equalization program to provide some state funds to high-wealth schools that might not receive funds under the equalization program. In the early 1990s, only two states were using the flat grant as the primary funding method (Gold, Smith, & Lawton, 1995).

Under the flat grant, students and taxpayers are treated equitably, but attainment of adequacy will be dependent upon the funding level. Choice is sacrificed unless the flat grant can be supplemented.

Categorical Funding

Categorical funding means that state funds are allocated for a specific educational purpose (e.g., bilingual education, education of handicapped pupils, pupil transportation, in-service programs for teachers, or instructional materials). Most states have some type of categorical funding for special programs, but this is not the principal method for funding schools.

In categorical programs, students and taxpayers are treated equally, but attainment of adequacy will be dependent upon the funding level. Students not in the program will not be treated equitably. Choice will be sacrificed unless other funding is available.

State programs for the education of disadvantaged youth have been enacted in about half of the states. In 1997, the New Mexico legislature took a somewhat different approach when it included an at-risk index in the state's funding formula. (The concept of at-risk youth has been discussed in Chapter 10.) Under the New Mexico program, each district receives an allocation based on its index of need; components of the index of need include measures of student poverty, English proficiency, student dropouts, and student mobility. Districts have the freedom to make a local determination of the best program for their at-risk youth. The New Mexico funding formula uses a neural network computer program to determine the magnitude of the district's need, and funds are allocated using an index multiplier in the calculation of the district's funding through the state school finance formula. Students are not labeled as being at-risk; thus, the program can focus funds on prevention as well as remediation (Jordan, Jordan, Moak, & Kops, 1996).

State Spending and Enrollment Differences

In 1998–99, among the 50 states and the District of Columbia, current per-pupil expenditures ranged from $10,153 in New Jersey to $3,732 in Utah and $4,528 in Mississippi. The 1998–99 national average was $6,407 per pupil. Data for each state are presented in Table 13.3.

What is the range in per pupil expenditures among school districts in your state?

Among the 50 states, the estimated number of pupils in 1998–99 ranged from 5,536,406 in California and 3,748,167 in Texas to 94,411 in Wyoming and 105,565 in Vermont. The 12 states with more than 1 million pupils accounted for over 59% of the slightly less than 45 million pupils.

Sources of Revenue for Schools

Funds for public elementary and secondary schools come from the various taxes levied by local, state, and federal governments. As indicated previously, the

Table 13.3: Estimated Membership and Current Expenditures per Pupil by State, 1998–99

State	Fall 1999 Student Membership	Current Expenditures	Rank
50 States and D.C.	46,349,803	$6,407	—
Alabama	758,816	$4,786	45
Alaska	134,374	$8,607	4
Arizona	829,252	$4,599	48
Arkansas	455,647	$4,596	49
California	5,828,938	$5,856	29
Colorado	699,135	$5,766	30
Connecticut	544,690	$9,427	2
Delaware	113,167	$7,434	10
District of Columbia	71,889	$8,386	5
Florida	2,335,124	$5,585	35
Georgia	1,401,291	$5,594	34
Hawaii	187,395	$5,569	33
Idaho	245,100	$4,634	47
Illinois	2,022,108	$7,077	13
Indiana	989,134	$6,589	20
Iowa	502,571	$6,253	24
Kansas	469,850	$5,800	31
Kentucky	646,092	$5,866	28
Louisiana	753,722	$5,698	36
Maine	219,741	$6,652	19
Maryland	837,250	$6,972	16
Massachusetts	964,358	$8,083	6
Michigan	1,692,700	$7,139	11
Minnesota	857,900	$6,934	17
Mississippi	502,382	$4,528	50
Missouri	921,391	$5,529	38
Montana	161,023	$5,869	27
Nebraska	291,010	$6,332	23
Nevada	311,063	$5,371	42
New Hampshire	194,512	$7,046	14
New Jersey	1,293,840	$10,153	1
New Mexico	328,753	$5,692	32
New York	2,852,000	$9,192	3
North Carolina	1,245,608	$5,509	39
North Dakota	113,929	$5,504	40
Ohio	1,849,685	$6,185	25
Oklahoma	626,674	$5,167	43
Oregon	543,176	$6,357	21
Pennsylvania	1,818,090	$7,700	9
Rhode Island	154,485	$8,001	7
South Carolina	644,150	$5,572	37
South Dakota	141,561	$4,936	44
Tennessee	908,885	$4,773	46

(continues)

Table 13.3: *(continued)*

State	Fall 1998 Student Membership	Current Expenditures	Rank
Texas	3,900,488	$5,488	41
Utah	477,061	$3,732	51
Vermont	105,442	$6,680	18
Virginia	1,125,735	$6,031	26
Washington	999,628	$6,352	22
West Virginia	296,332	$6,978	15
Wisconsin	888,245	$7,765	8
Wyoming	94,411	$7,097	12

Source: U.S. Department of Education, National Center for Education Statistics. (1999, April). *Early estimates of public elementary and secondary education statistics: school year 1998–99.* Washington, DC: U.S. Department of Education, p. 9.

proportion of revenues from each source varies both among and within states. The principal source of local revenue for schools is the *ad valorem* tax on real property or, in common terminology, the local property tax. This tax is levied on the value of land, residences, apartment buildings, commercial buildings, railroads, and utilities. On average, over 90% of all local tax revenues for schools come from taxes on real property. State sales and income taxes are the principal sources of state revenues for schools. All states have either sales or income taxes, and many have both. The taxes are levied on retail sales and on personal and business income.

A majority of the states raise some amount of revenue through lotteries. The proceeds typically become a part of the state's general fund, but education often benefits. (See the Historical Note on page 451.)

Equity in school finance is achieved through a balanced system of state and local taxes and a state funding program that recognizes differences in educational needs among students and school districts.

Historical Note

The Lotteries and Education

The use of lotteries, both for settling disputes and as games of chance, has been traced to 3500 B.C. When the English colonists came to the New World, they brought with them a tradition of private and public lotteries. Colonial churches and governments made use of the lottery. Benjamin Franklin and other leading citizens of Philadelphia sponsored a lottery to raise money to buy a battery of cannons for the city. The Continental Congress used a lottery to generate funds to support the troops. In the 1790s, lotteries were used to help finance the construction and improvement of Washington, D.C.

Lotteries were also used by various educational institutions. Dartmouth, Harvard, Kings College (Columbia University), Pennsylvania, Princeton, and William and Mary are among the colonial colleges that benefited from lotteries. From the signing of the Constitution to the Civil War, some 300 elementary and secondary schools and 47 colleges were beneficiaries of lotteries (Ezell, 1960).

Unfortunately, as the use of lotteries grew, so did the abuses and irregularities associated with them. In the second and third quarters of the nineteenth century, state after state passed antilottery bills, and by 1878 all states except Louisiana prohibited lotteries. Louisiana's "Golden Octopus" lotteries, so called because they reached into every state and large city in the nation, had also died by the end of the century.

The first modern government-operated lottery in the United States was instituted in 1964 by the state of New Hampshire as a means of generating revenues for education. In 1967, New York started a lottery. Within the next decade, a dozen other states joined the list of those operating lotteries. Today, 30 states operate lotteries and in about 20 states, education is beneficiary of part or all of the lottery proceeds.

The principal source of federal revenue for education is the federal income tax, but federal funding for elementary and secondary education has been limited. A major advantage of the federal income tax is that it relies on the entire nation as the taxpaying base.

Differences Among States in Sources of Revenue

In school year 1996–97, excluding Hawaii and the District of Columbia, the percentage of the total revenues for schools that came from local tax sources ranged from 90.3% in New Hampshire to 21.5% in Alabama. The percentage from state tax sources ranged from 69.0% in Alabama to 6.6% in New Hampshire. The percentage from the federal government ranged from 13.5% in Mississippi to 3.0% in New Hampshire. The national average was 44.2% from local sources, 48.9% from state sources, and 6.9% from federal sources. Data for each state are presented in Table 13.4.

What kinds of state taxes are collected in your state? How do the taxes compare with those in other states?

Sources for Nontax Revenues

An effect of the recent court cases seeking greater equity in school funding has been the development of greater reliance on nontax sources of funding for schools. The pressures for greater equity have been countered by local citizens'

Table 13.4: Percentage Distribution of Revenues for Public Elementary and Secondary Schools, by Source and State, School Year 1995–96

State	Local & Intermediate	State	Federal
50 States and D.C. Average	45.8	47.5	6.6
Alabama	29.5	61.3	9.2
Alaska	22.8	66.1	11.1
Arizona	46.8	44.1	9.0
Arkansas	31.5	60.0	8.5
California	35.4	55.8	8.9
Colorado	50.9	43.8	5.3
Connecticut	58.3	38.0	3.7
Delaware	26.7	66.6	6.7
District of Columbia	91.9	0.0	8.1
Florida	44.0	48.6	7.4
Georgia	41.3	51.9	6.8
Hawaii	2.4	89.8	7.8
Idaho	28.6	64.3	7.1
Illinois	66.6	27.3	6.1
Indiana	40.6	54.3	5.2
Iowa	45.9	49.0	5.1
Kansas	37.3	57.3	5.4
Kentucky	26.4	65.3	8.3
Louisiana	37.6	50.3	12.1
Maine	47.5	47.0	5.6
Maryland	56.9	38.2	4.9
Massachusetts	57.0	38.3	4.7
Michigan	27.1	66.8	6.1
Minnesota	37.5	58.2	4.3
Mississippi	28.5	57.8	13.7
Missouri	53.8	40.2	6.0

creativity in finding other sources of funding for schools, including participation or user fees for school activities, formation of nonprofit educational foundations at the school or school district level, and local profit-making activities.

Participation fees are becoming a significant source of revenues in many school districts. Increased reliance on fees to participate in school activities conflicts with the court cases that are seeking greater equity in funding and equality of access to educational programs and services. For example, athletes are being required to purchase their equipment. In some instances, local school officials provide waivers for those students unable to pay the fees, but the effect is that poor children will have less opportunity to participate in many school activities. The basic question may be whether the activity is considered a necessary part of the school program or a truly extracurricular activity being provided under the sponsorship of the school. If the activity is a basic part of the school program, charging a participation fee might be considered discriminatory because a poor student is denied access to the program.

Table 13.4 *(continued)*

State	Local & Intermediate	State	Federal
Montana	41.5	48.6	9.9
Nebraska	62.8	31.6	5.6
Nevada	63.5	32.0	4.5
New Hampshire	89.7	7.0	3.3
New Jersey	58.0	36.6	3.4
New Mexico	13.9	73.9	12.2
New York	54.4	39.7	5.8
North Carolina	28.3	64.5	7.2
North Dakota	46.3	42.1	11.5
Ohio	53.0	41.7	6.3
Oklahoma	31.3	59.3	9.3
Oregon	39.4	54.1	6.5
Pennsylvania	54.6	39.8	5.6
Rhode Island	53.4	41.5	5.1
South Carolina	39.8	52.9	8.3
South Dakota	60.4	29.7	9.8
Tennessee	43.4	47.9	8.6
Texas	49.9	42.9	7.2
Utah	34.8	58.6	6.7
Vermont	67.5	27.8	4.7
Virginia	63.6	31.1	5.3
Washington	26.2	68.0	5.8
West Virginia	28.9	63.0	8.0
Wisconsin	52.8	42.9	4.3
Wyoming	42.6	51.3	6.2

Note: Details may not add to total due to rounding.

Source: U.S. Department of Education. (1997). National Center for Education Statistics, Common Core of Data, "National Public Education Survey." Washington DC: U.S. Department of Education.

Another source of nontax revenues for schools is local school or local school district educational foundations. Some school districts have created these nonprofit foundations to provide funds for programs and services that cannot be supported from tax funds. As a result of state restrictions on local school spending and court actions seeking greater equity in funding for public education, schools have been forced to curtail programs and services. In an effort to find alternative ways to fund and maintain programs, some local schools have formed educational foundations that can receive tax-deductible gifts from parents, interested citizens, and businesses.

The Courts and School Finance

Since 1970, state programs for financing the public schools have been challenged in over 40 states (Underwood, 1997; Verstegen & Whitney, 1997). Litigation has been initiated in both federal and state courts. The issues are related to contentions that the state is failing to provide "equal protection" for students because the state system for financing education has resulted in unequal levels of spending among school districts, and the differences in spending are related to differences in wealth among districts. In this context, wealth refers to assessed value of taxable real property per student.

In *San Antonio v. Rodriguez* (1973), the U.S. Supreme Court rejected the argument that education is a constitutionally protected right and that equal treatment is required in providing education under the U.S. Constitution. After the decision, some observers thought that the number of legal actions would diminish, but the number of cases in state courts suggests a continuing interest in challenging state school finance programs. The effect of *Rodriguez* was to base challenges of existing state school finance programs on the technical provisions of the state constitutions rather than on provisions in the U.S. Constitution.

These state-level legal challenges have been initiated because of the interaction of two conditions—the use of the local property tax as a major source of revenue for schools and the wide differences in taxable wealth per pupil among local school districts. As a result of these conditions, tax rates to provide an equal level of funding for education and per-pupil spending vary among school districts. This condition is viewed as being unfair to both taxpayers and students. Depending on the district, taxpayers must be taxed at different rates to provide the same level of support. The result is that students in poor districts are at a disadvantage relative to students in other districts with greater wealth or higher tax rates.

Trends in the court decisions are difficult to determine. Of the decisions that have been issued by state supreme courts, a slight majority of the decisions have held the state system to be unconstitutional. In the decisions that have upheld the existing funding systems, education has been viewed as an important government service, but not a fundamental right under which each student in the state would be guaranteed equal treatment. In most instances, the courts have been critical of the financing systems but have indicated that the problem should be resolved by legislative actions rather than judicial decisions (McCarthy, 1994).

In the decisions that have declared state school finance programs to be unconstitutional, the courts have held that the current system was unfair to both taxpayers and students. Unequal tax burdens were considered to be in violation of the equal protection provisions of the state constitution, and differences in expenditures per pupil were found to be in violation of the equal protection provisions of the state constitutions or the technical language of the state constitution pertaining to education or taxation (Underwood, 1997; Verstegen & Whitney, 1997).

Should the federal government be more or less active in controlling education. In what ways?

Litigation has been active in California and New Jersey for most of the past 25 years. In the 1990s, courts in Alabama, Arizona, Missouri, and Texas ruled that the states' school finance systems were in violation of the state constitutions' equal protection and/or education clause. The concerns were related to different levels of spending and differences in the access that students had to educational programs, materials, equipment, facilities, and related opportunities. The state's responsibility to provide each child with equal access to an education has been upheld (Underwood, 1997).

Federal Aid for Elementary and Secondary Schools

Consistent with the concept that education is a state responsibility and a local function, the federal government has played a limited role in the financing of elementary and secondary education. Less than 7% of the total expenditures for elementary and secondary education comes from federal revenue sources. Even though its role has been limited, the federal government's involvement in education has been influential in providing programs for special needs youth.

Education of Special Needs Youth

Of the federally funded elementary and secondary education programs, the largest is for the Title I programs for the education of disadvantaged pupils. The funding level for this program was about $7.4 billion annually in 1998 for programs in local school districts (Sack, 1998). As discussed in Chapter 9, the intent of the program is to improve educational programs for disadvantaged pupils from low income homes. These programs are funded completely by the federal government and would not be continued if the federal funds were terminated.

Federal funds and regulations for education of children with disabilities under Public Law 94–142, as amended first by the Americans With Disabilities Act and later by the Individuals With Disabilities Education Act (IDEA), represent a different type of major federal initiative. Under the statute and resulting regulations, local school districts have to provide eligible pupils who have disabilities with a free and appropriate education irrespective of the level of federal funds. About 7% of the total school-age population has been classified as disabled and in need of special education programs and services. Funds for this federal program reached about $4.5 billion in 1998 (Sack, 1998). While this seems to be a significant amount, this funding level, as well as the $7.4 billion in federal funds for the education of disadvantaged pupils, should be placed in the context of the estimated $282 billion in expenditures for public elementary and secondary education in 1997–98. (See Chapter 9 for a more detailed discussion of P.L. 94–142 and of the ADA and the IDEA.)

Other federal programs for special-needs youth include the bilingual and migrant education programs; the budget for these programs was $354 million in 1998. These funds are provided to local school districts for programs to serve youth with limited English proficiency and school-age youth from migrant worker families (Sack, 1998).

The federally funded Head Start program for low income preschool children typically is not operated by public school districts, but is an important program. Funding for this program in 1998 was $4.3 billion (Portner, 1998). Obviously, this program is important in efforts to attain the national goal of readiness for school.

Federal funds have been provided for vocational education since the enactment of the Smith Hughes Act in 1917. This program was started in response to the need for trained workers following World War I. Since that time, the emphasis of vocational education has shifted as the nation's economy and job needs have changed. In 1994 the federal government provided about $1 billion to support vocational education, representing about 10% of the total spending for public school vocational education programs (Sack, 1998).

Through careful analysis of local conditions and adaptation of research findings to local schools, teachers and administrators can work together to attain school improvement goals.

Another long-standing federal program is impact aid to school districts for the education of youth residing with parents who live and/or work on federal property or are active duty uniformed military personnel. Funding for this program in 1998 was $808 million (Sack, 1998).

Educational Research and Assessment

As the federal government has provided more funds for elementary and secondary education programs, interest in federal funds for a national research program has increased. Currently, federal research funds for education are administered through the Office for Educational Research and Improvement in the Department of Education. The actual level of federal funding for educational research efforts is difficult to determine because research programs are funded by a variety of federal agencies, including the National Science Foundation, Department of Energy, Department of Defense, and Department of Labor.

School Reform

Funding for school reform has been limited to relatively small amounts for limited purposes, but $491 million was appropriated in 1998 for the Goals 2000: Educate America Act. Funds under this program are to be used for grants to state and local school reform efforts (Sack, 1998).

Private Education

In contrast to public education being provided through a range of school districts with multiple schools, private education typically is provided through a system of independent schools. As individually controlled schools, they have been created for a variety of reasons including college-prep programs, religious instruction, and family values.

With the rising level of concern about a variety of educational issues, interest in the private school alternative is being expressed by a wide spectrum of parents. The private school option is not new; it has provided an alternative to public education in the United States since the colonial period. However, these schools take different forms in response to parents who want their children to have broader educational opportunities, who seek a more rigorous or more restrictive environment for their children, or who desire a more permissive environment than the public schools can provide. This pattern of diverse aspirations has contributed to the development of private schools noted more for their differences than their similarities. They include traditional church-related schools, schools associated with evangelical groups, private traditional day schools, and "free" schools in which students can pursue individual interests. Some of these interest groups may select the *charter school* option if parents do not think that state requirements for charter schools are too restrictive.

Schools operated for profit make up a growing sector of the private school market. *Proprietary schools* have been an educational option since the colonization of America, but recently their numbers have been increasing. Their popularity has been attributed to parents being attracted to the high standards that many espouse, the extras (e.g., before- and after-school remediation and counseling and a wide variety of extracurricular activities), in-depth education, and smaller class size. Proprietary schools represent only 1% of all elementary and secondary schools. Concerns have been related to the lack of accountability for these schools and to some of their advantages because they are not subject to the same regulations as the public schools. If these schools increase in popularity, the impact on the composition of the student body in the public schools could be significant. Financial support for the public schools could deteriorate if upper income families opt out of the public schools. The attention of educators and policy makers to these issues likely will increase if the number of proprietary schools continues to grow (Bridgman, 1988).

What kinds of control should state legislatures and/or state agencies exercise over private schools?

Private School Enrollments

The proportion of elementary and secondary school students in private schools has changed little over the past 10 years. The percentage was 12% in 1987 and 11% in 1997. The majority (84%) of private school students attend church-related, or *parochial schools,* and about 51% of those students attend Roman Catholic schools. Declining enrollments in Roman Catholic-affiliated schools appear to have been reversed; enrollments in these schools have increased slightly in the past two years to over 2.5 million students (U.S. Department of Education, 1998a). However, the number of Catholic schools has declined from a high of 14,296 in 1965 to 8,243 in 1996 (Russo & Rogus, 1998). Non-Catholic enrollment increases have been largely in schools operated by evangelical and fundamentalist Christian denominations. During the past two decades, minority enrollments in private schools have increased, particularly in Catholic-affiliated schools in urban areas.

The percentage of minority enrollments in Catholic-affiliated schools more than doubled from 1970–71 to 1993–94, from 10.8% to 24.7% (Lawton, 1994). This trend takes on special significance, considering that achievement differences between white students and minority students are less in private schools than in public schools. Smaller differences in student achievement between white and minority students at all socioeconomic levels in type of program enrollments (e.g., college preparatory, vocational, and general education) have been found in the Catholic-affiliated schools. In addition, more than 85% of private school students graduate from high school as compared to 73% of public school students (Orstein, 1989). These observations suggest the need for a careful study of the differences between public and private schools and their student bodies to identify ways in which the success rates of all students might be improved (Hispanic Policy Development Project, 1987).

In spite of the recent private school enrollment growth in some sectors, projections suggest that the overall percentage of American students enrolled in private elementary and secondary schools will remain stable for the next several years. However, if states and/or the federal government provide vouchers to students or direct funding for the general operation of nonpublic schools, the percentage of students enrolled in these schools might increase dramatically.

Current Issues in Organizing and Financing of Education

Concerns about the role of education in the development of youth and the importance of an educated populace in a democracy are being expressed in a variety of ways. The challenge confronting public school advocates is to generate and maintain citizen support for the funds required to provide quality education into the next century. Maintaining public support for public elementary and secondary schools is becoming more difficult because of a series of interactive social and economic developments.

Changes in the Population

The American population is becoming younger and older at the same time; that is, both the proportion of the population that is of school age and the proportion that is elderly or retired are increasing. Further, youth who comprise the increases in the school-age population tend to be educationally disadvantaged because they often live in urban areas, are poor, and come to school with limited English-speaking ability. Consequently, providing these youth with an adequate education requires more funds.

Competition for Funds

In addition to the need for more funds to support education, competition for scarce public funds will come from the elderly population that is in need of a variety of services, including better health care and other social services. Many of the elderly are on fixed incomes and must have some type of public assistance for medical and other essential social services. Reconciling these two social pressures will be a formidable challenge to public policy makers.

Special Needs Students

Special needs students often are as diverse as other students. In addition to children with disabilities, special needs youth also include those who are at risk of not completing school. Policy makers are involved in different but interrelated issues concerning the education of special needs youth. One is the extent to which children with disabilities should be included in the regular classroom. Issues include the benefits or disservice to regular children and children with disabilities, and the ability of the classroom teacher to meet the needs of all students. A second issue is the challenge to secure adequate funding for specialized programs and services that will increase the likelihood that at-risk youth will remain in, and profit from, school. A third issue is that state funding for the full range of special needs youth often is not sufficient, and local districts with fiscal constraints must reduce programs for regular students to provide programs and services for special needs students.

Equity in State Funding Systems

A continuing issue is the extent to which a state's school funding system should reduce the disparities in educational opportunity for pupils among districts and move the state toward providing an adequate program for all pupils. Local school officials seek predictable and relatively stable levels of funding for schools to facilitate orderly budgetary and educational planning. Taxpayers seek stability in their tax rates so that they can plan their businesses. From a different perspective, local school officials seek a state system for financing schools that will respond to changing economic and demographic conditions. As the number of pupils increases and as costs for services and materials increase, pressures for equity in state school finance systems likely will increase.

Education Reform

As noted elsewhere in this text, the 1980s were characterized by broad-based calls for reform of public elementary and secondary education. The principal justification for the various school reform reports has been the need to improve America's competitive position in the world economy. Many of the early reform recommendations were additive (i.e., they call for increased requirements for graduation, longer school days and years, and higher teacher salaries), requiring

Professional Reflections

"Kind words often fall on deaf, de-sensitized ears. But words preceded by love in action, are not only received, but returned with love and respect. *The goal is not to get students to like us.* The goal is to invest our time, energy, and interest in our youth . . . for it is the long-term investment that yields the greatest return."

Kay A. Long, *Teacher of the Year, Oklahoma*
Keith Robinson, *Teacher of the Year, Iowa*

additional funds. Additional state and federal funds for the implementation of reforms have been limited. With the passage of the Goals 2000: Educate America Act, the education reform movement has entered a new phase, with the adoption of national goals for education and the development of curricular standards for subject matter areas and assessment systems to determine the extent to which standards are attained.

Accountability

Concerns also are being expressed about accountability in terms of the performance and responsiveness of schools. At least 40 states have enacted legislation designed to inform policy makers and the public about student/school performance with rewards/incentives and penalties. Various factors are used to measure performance, but the most common variable is student/school performance on standardized tests. Some have advocated that funding for schools be based on pupil performance. However, local school officials seek a level of stability in funding that might be threatened if performance fluctuates. Caution has been advocated because reducing state aid to an underachieving school district would mean that the district would have less to spend on programs even though its need would be greater. One result appears to be that an underperforming school can expect some type of intervention to improve student performance.

Charter Schools

Considerable attention has been given to development of charter schools; 33 states had some type of charter school legislation in 1998. These schools have been advocated as a way to provide parents and students with a public school that is under the control of the parents or the person holding the school's charter. Even though the number of charter schools is increasing each year, they provide an alternative for a relatively small number of students. The number of schools is in the single digits in several states, but some states, such as Arizona, are predicted to have 200 or more charter schools in operation by the turn of the century. Some schools have been formed by parents; others have been formed by teachers and private entrepreneurs. Some have taken a conservative route in their program; others have taken a liberal route. The common element appears to be a dissatisfaction with the available public schools. The unanswered questions

Controversial Issues

Charter Schools

One of the most evident outcomes of the school reform movement has been the emergence of charter schools. These schools are public schools in which state and school district controls typically have been relaxed. Parents and teachers have a greater voice in school decisions. After a somewhat modest beginning, numbers are increasing rapidly. Over 30 states have charter schools in some form. Impetus for the state legislation authorizing charter schools has come from a variety of sources: parents seeking a particular curricular emphasis in the schools, teachers wanting relief from state and district requirements so that they can address the educational needs of at-risk students, and parents desiring a specific type of school environment.

Opinions about charter schools are divided; some view the schools as the panacea of all the wrongs in education; others view the schools as being divisive and leading to separatism based on personal values and philosophies of parents. Some of the typical pros and cons for charter schools are listed below:

Pros

1. Provide parents and students with a choice in the public school system.

2. Permit each school to determine its philosophy and curricular emphasis with a coherent academic mission and high standards.

3. Increase the heterogeneity of students in schools by attracting private school students into the charter schools.

4. Have an image of being smaller and safer than the typical public school.

5. Develop a positive attitude among students about schoolwork and teachers.

6. Give teachers greater freedom and the challenge of starting and designing a program for a new school.

7. Have been given operational and programmatic freedom in return for a results-based accountability.

Cons

1. Are so diverse in their purpose and control that a *common* charter school cannot be described.

2. Fail to enroll a diverse student population or to provide a hospitable environment for students with special needs.

3. Can ignore the National Education Goals and national content standards in developing their program.

4. Are often controlled by national for-profit firms that impose standardized programs with limited local school choice.

5. Fail to provide teachers with the same salaries and fringe benefits they receive in the public schools.

6. Have encountered fiscal accountability and management problems in the use of public funds.

7. Do not have the perceived independence because they are still a part of the public education system and susceptible to changes in local and state requirements.

are whether or not the initial success can be maintained and whether or not student achievement gains can be demonstrated (Schneider, 1998).

Summary

State governmental and organizational structures for schools differ in some ways, but the general pattern is consistent. Greater differences can be found in the patterns of school finance and the range in the proportion of funds that comes from state and local revenue sources. The organizational structure of American education is constantly undergoing changes. The balance between school-site decision making and uniform state standards for school performance likely will be one of the focal points for discussion in the early years of the next century. As pressures for accountability increase, reporting and monitoring requirements likely will increase.

The annual cost of public elementary and secondary education, the largest item in some state and local budgets, will approach $300 billion by the turn of the century. This outlay is viewed as an investment because education contributes trained workers who support the economy through the purchase of consumer goods. The challenge is to find the funds needed and to distribute them in an equitable manner.

In terms of state provision for education, one challenge will be to develop school finance programs that provide for an acceptable balance between the conflicting goals of equity, adequacy, and choice. A second challenge will be to raise the revenues for the programs in a fair and equitable manner to ensure that all students have access to an appropriate educational program.

Providing adequate funds for education will become more difficult. More older citizens and an increased number of educationally disadvantaged students will be competing for scarce public funds. While state programs look for stability in funding, local school officials seek a system that will respond to changes. The responses will depend on whether policy makers view funds for education as an expenditure or an investment.

With this background on school organization, administration, and finance, you have a context in which to place the discussion of school curriculum in the following chapter.

Key Terms

Accountability
Adequacy
Building principal
Categorical funding
Chief state school officer
Choice
Educational overburden
Equalization
Equity
Flat grants

Foundation plan
Full state funding
Horizontal equity
Local property tax
Municipal overburden
Parochial school
Policies
Power equalization
Proprietary schools
School board

Secretary of education
Site-based management
State board of education
State department of education

Strategic planning
Superintendent of schools
Vertical equity

Discussion Questions

1. How do the duties and responsibilities of school board members differ from those of teachers?

2. How does education being a state function affect the powers of citizens to determine programs in local schools?

3. What qualifications should a person have to hold membership on a local school board, to be a principal, or to be a superintendent?

4. What kinds of responsibilities should teachers have in the administration of an individual school?

5. In what ways are private schools and their students different from public schools and their students?

6. How does the per-pupil funding level for schools in your state compare with the level in other states?

7. What programs should the federal government finance?

8. Given the reduced rate of economic growth, shortage of funds for public services, and increased demand for public services, what should be the priority—funding for education or health care, funding for children with special needs, funding for regular children, or funding for all children?

Internet Resources

1. See Appendix

2. **nces.ed.gov**
   The National Center for Education Statistics produces a variety of reports and publications, including the annual *Condition of Education* and *Digest of Education Statistics,* which contain a vast collection of education statistics.

3. **www.eric.uoregon.edu**
   The ERIC Clearinghouse on Education Management provides publications and links to a wide range of topics of concern to educational practitioners, policy makers, and interested others.

4. **www.ecs.org**
   The home page for the Educational Commission of the States provides access to reports and policy studies on a range of current issues in education as well as links to other educational organizations and sites.

5. **www.nsba.org**
   The home page of the National School Boards Association provides access to numerous publications by the organization as well as information and links to "Issues," federal agencies, the U.S. Congress, the White House, and more.

6. **www.nassp.org, //www.naesp.org and //aasa.org**
Learn more about the role of the principal and other administrators at the home pages of the National Association of Secondary School Principals, the National Association of Elementary School Principals, and the American Association of School Administrators.

7. **www.ncrel.org/sdrs/sitemap.htm**
The home page of Pathways to School Improvement provides access to a number of topics (and related links) discussed in this chapter, including charter schools, organization and management issues, and school finance (under "Critical Issues").

References

American Association of School Administrators. (1946). *School boards in action.* 24th yearbook. Arlington, VA: American Association of School Administrators.

Bridgman, A. (1988). Private, for-profit schools: Where they stand. *Education Digest, 23*(6), 10–13.

Campbell, R. F., Cunningham, L. L., Nystrand, R. O., & Usdan, M. D. (1985). *The organization and control of American schools* (5th ed.). Columbus, OH: Merrill.

Coons, J. E., Clune, W. H., III, & Sugarman, S. D. (1970). *Private wealth and public education.* Cambridge, MA: Belknap Press.

Cubberley, E. P. (1905). *School funds and their apportionment.* New York: Teachers College, Columbia University.

Ezell, J. S. (1960). *Fortune's merry wheel, the lottery in America.* Cambridge, MA: Harvard University Press.

Gold, S., Smith, D., & Lawton, S. (1995). *Public school finance programs of the United States and Canada, 1993–94.* Albany: American Educational Finance Association, Center for the Study of the States, State University of New York.

Grieder, C., Pierce, T. M., & Jordan, K. F. (1969). *Public school administration.* New York: Ronald Press.

Hispanic Policy Development Project. (1987). Policy remedies. *The Research Bulletin, 1*(2), 9.

Jordan, K. F., Jordan, T. S., Moak, L. M., & Kops, G. C. (1996). *Final report to the Public School Funding Formula Task Force.*

Santa Fe, NM: New Mexico Legislature, Office of the Legislative Council.

Jordan, K. F., & Lyons, T. S. (1992). *Financing public education in an era of change.* Bloomington, IN: Phi Delta Kappa Educational Foundation.

Lawton, M. (1994, April 13). Catholic schools record increase in enrollment for 2nd straight year. *Education Week, 13,* p. 5.

McCarthy, M. (1994). The courts and school finance reform. *Theory into Practice, 33*(2), 89–97.

Morrison, H. C. (1930). *School revenue.* Chicago: University of Chicago Press.

National Policy Board. (1989). *Report of the National Policy Board.* Charlottesville, VA: Curry School of Education, University of Virginia.

NEA Research. (1997). *Status of the American public school teacher, 1995–96: Highlights.* Washington, DC: National Education Association.

Orlosky, D. E., McCleary, L. E., Shapiro, A., & Webb, L. D. (1984). *Educational administration today.* Columbus, OH: Merrill.

Orstein, A. C. (1989). The growing non-public school movement. *Educational Horizons, 67*(71), 74.

Portner, J. (1998, February 11). Budget highlights child care, juvenile justice. *Education Week,* pp. 24–25.

Russo, C. J., & Rogus, J. F. (1998). Catholic schools; Proud past, promising future. *School Business Affairs, 64*(6), 13–16.

San Antonio Independent School District v. Rodriguez. 411 U.S. 1. (1973).

Sack, J. (1998, February 11). Budget plan emphasizes new efforts. *Education Week,* pp., 1, 26.

Schneider, A. (1998). Charting the charter school movement. *School Business Affairs,* *64*(6), 17–23.

Strayer, G. D., & Haig, R. M. (1923). *The financing of education in the state of New York.* Report of the Educational Finance Commission 1. New York: Macmillan.

Underwood, J. (1997). *Interpretation of state education clauses as of November 1, 1997.* Oxford, OH: Miami University.

Updegraff, H. (1922). *Rural school survey in New York state: Financial support.* Ithaca, NY: Author.

U.S. Department of Education, National Center for Education Statistics. (1998). *Common core of data.* Washington, DC: U.S. Department of Education.

Verstegen, D. A., & Whitney, T. (1997). From courthouses to schoolhouses: Emerging judicial theories of adequacy and equity. *Educational Policy, 11*(3), 330–352.

Part Six

Curriculum and Instruction

Chapter 14

The young man taught all he knew and more; the middle-age man taught all he knew; the old man taught all that his students could understand.

The School Curriculum: Development and Design

➤ *As a new teacher, Mary Sherman has found that there is some community controversy over who should control the curriculum in the public schools; this question also is receiving considerable attention in local school board meetings and parent teacher meetings. The community has not been able to reach consensus. Mary has read a recent Phi Delta Kappa poll of teachers that indicates that the teachers felt that they should have the greatest influence on what is taught in the schools. In reviewing the national content standards that have been adopted by the state for the major subject areas, Mary found that the national professional organizations had been deeply involved in the development of the standards. The state also has recently adopted a statewide assessment program designed to determine the extent to which the students have attained the standards. Mary has also seen national polls that report that parents feel that the school's curriculum needs to be changed to meet today's needs and that they should be given a greater role in determining its direction.*

What steps should the local teachers' organization take to address these apparently conflicting positions? What effects will the content standards and the statewide assessment program have on Mary's role as a teacher and what she teaches in the classroom? What are the implications for the academic freedom and academic responsibility of the public school classroom teacher?

The *curriculum* in the nation's elementary and secondary schools is undergoing significant changes with the adoption of content standards and statewide assessment systems. In this chapter the concept of curriculum is explored from its many perspectives, ranging from curriculum as content to curriculum as experiences. This chapter provides information to help you to:

- Review the sociopolitical forces that influence curriculum policy making and design.
- Contrast the technical production process of curriculum development with the critical theorist process of curriculum development.

- Compare the subject-centered and student-centered patterns of curriculum organization.
- Describe the hidden curriculum and its effects on schooling.

The term *curriculum* is a complex and evasive notion. Curriculum theorists do not agree on any one definition. Broadly defined, curriculum is said to be all the educational experiences of students that take place under the auspices of the school. Yet how we conceive of curriculum is important because our conception of curriculum reflects and shapes how we think about, study, and act on the education provided to students (Cornbleth, 1988).

In this chapter, various concepts of the curriculum will be examined. First, the influence of a number of sociopolitical forces on curriculum policy making and design will be reviewed. Specific attention will be given to the impact of the *national goals for education.* Next, the curriculum development process will be summarized. Last, the major patterns of intended curricular organization or design will be described, followed by a discussion of the unintended, or hidden, curriculum.

Forces Influencing the Curriculum

Decisions about the curriculum are not made in a vacuum by teachers, administrators, and curriculum specialists. They take place in the context of a particular community, state, and nation at a particular time. At different times various professional, political, social, economic, and religious forces have attempted to influence the curriculum. Their motives, methods, strengths, and successes have varied (Tietelbaum, 1998).

As noted in the following discussion, concerns about student performance and international competitiveness have contributed to a much more active national interest in education. These interests may contribute to greater uniformity in curricular content and student assessment. In this section, the influence of the following forces on curriculum are briefly discussed: parent and community groups, teachers, local school boards, state governments, the federal government, national committees and reports, professional organizations, national goals and standards, standardized tests, and textbooks.

Parent and Community Groups

Because of their vested interest in the local school and their proximity to local decision makers, parents and community groups have the potential for exercising tremendous influence on the curriculum. For example, in recent years parent groups active in the areas of special education and gifted education have had great success in promoting educational programs for these groups. Parents often serve on textbook adoption committees or education committees at the local, state, or national level. Parent Teacher Associations, band boosters, and other special interest groups are often active in supporting special programs or influencing legislation and supporting tax or spending referenda. Other groups bring pressure on school boards and school officials to include or not to include curriculum material on sex education, substance abuse, suicide, ethnic or women's studies, and religion. Currently, certain fundamentalist groups are bringing pressure on local

Should parents have the ultimate decision as to what their children are taught? Why or why not?

Various interest groups are concerned about the content of textbooks and instructional materials. Schools need to respect this public interest while retaining an appropriate level of professional autonomy.

school boards, state boards of education, political decision makers, and the textbook industry to rid our schools of all material and teaching that promotes secular humanism and ignores religion (see Chapter 11).

Parents in general also have concerns about the extent to which the curriculum needs to be changed to meet current expectations. In the 1998 Phi Delta Kappa poll, 53% of the parents said that they wanted more say in their school's curriculum (Rose & Gallup, 1998). The potential for conflict emerges when this finding is compared with the following finding about teacher attitudes concerning the curriculum.

Teachers

Historically, teachers have had a significant impact on the curriculum of a school, but recently developed national content standards and student access to technology are changing the role of teachers. They once were the primary source of knowledge in the classroom and were perceived to have the knowledge and skills to determine what was to be taught. They participated in the development of curriculum guides and related materials. This traditional position assumed that students had little to offer in terms of knowledge that would be of value in the classroom. Rather than assuming that they know where to begin instruction without any assessment of student knowledge, the new teacher of the twenty-first century will assume responsibility for dignifying student knowledge and insights, working

What role should teachers have in deciding what is to be taught? What role should teachers have in determining how to teach what is to be taught?

cooperatively with peers, searching for interdisciplinary and multidisciplinary learning opportunities, and promoting better transitions between elementary, middle, and high schools (Sheeran & Sheeran, 1996).

With the enactment of state accountability and assessment programs and the adoption of content standards, teachers have less control over what is to be taught and when. Teachers will retain the academic freedom to determine how to teach, but their freedom to determine what to teach or when to teach certain content will be restricted because of the adoption of content standards and state assessment programs. Conflicts may emerge as the accountability movement and national content standards become institutionalized, for teachers in a recent survey thought that they should have the most influence in deciding what is taught in the public schools (Langdon, 1997).

Local School Boards

Local school boards make a host of curriculum decisions about the content and learning opportunities that are provided for students. Within the limits of state authority, local boards decide what electives will be offered, which textbooks and other instructional materials will be purchased, which curriculum guides are to be followed, what teachers will be hired, how the budget will be spent, and how to respond to innumerable other issues that directly or indirectly influence the curriculum. It is the local school board that most often feels the pressure of parents and special interest groups, for this body decides such matters as whether a new program will be piloted, whether such courses as sex education will be offered, or whether a program for the hearing-impaired will be offered by the district.

In recent years, increasing concern has been expressed regarding the extent to which the local school board represents all constituencies in the community. One concern is that local boards are influenced too much by small but vocal groups of parents or concerned citizens. Another concern is the elitist composition of boards of education. Except for rural school boards, most school boards tend to be composed of a disproportionate number of white male professionals or businesspersons (Spring, 1998).

State Governments

As the level of government with legal responsibility for education, the state obviously has an interest in curricular matters. The state's influence over the curriculum is exercised in several ways. First, state statutes often mandate that certain subjects be included in the curriculum. Some states also specify what cannot be taught (e.g., communism). The state's impact on the curriculum has been particularly evident in the aftermath of the reform reports of the 1980s. The reports called for more state requirements as well as for the decentralization of decision making. In response, the states have taken a more active role in prescribing the curriculum for local schools (Elmore & Fuhrman, 1994).

A major recommendation of many of the reform reports was that students be required to take an increased number of basic courses in English, social studies,

What are the backgrounds and occupations of members of the school board in your community? How representative are they of the members of the local community?

What are the subject requirements for high school graduation in the state in which you plan to teach?

Figure 14.1: Minimum High School Graduation Requirements, 1980 and 1996

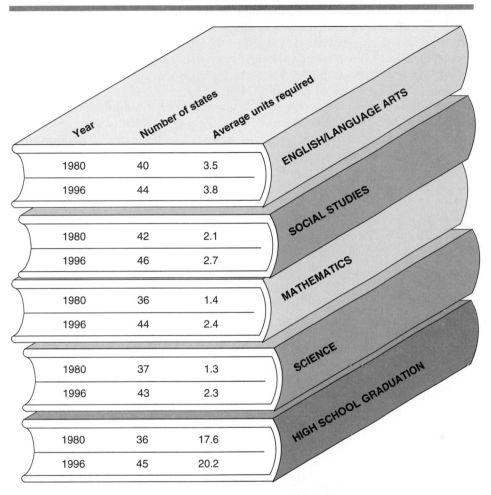

Year	Number of states	Average units required	
			ENGLISH/LANGUAGE ARTS
1980	40	3.5	
1996	44	3.8	
			SOCIAL STUDIES
1980	42	2.1	
1996	46	2.7	
			MATHEMATICS
1980	36	1.4	
1996	44	2.4	
			SCIENCE
1980	37	1.3	
1996	43	2.3	
			HIGH SCHOOL GRADUATION
1980	36	17.6	
1996	45	20.2	

Source: National Center for Education Statistics. *Digest of Education Statistics 1997.* Washington, DC: U.S. Department of Education. Figure style reprinted with permission from *The American School Board Journal.* Copyright, 1989. The National School Boards Association. All rights reserved.

mathematics, and science (see Table 14.1). In response, 42 states increased minimum high school graduation requirements during the period 1980 to 1996. Mathematics requirements were increased in 41 states, science requirements in 34 states, English/language arts in 19 states, and social studies in 26 states (Medrick, Brown, & Henke, 1992; U.S. Department of Education, 1996; U.S. Department of Education, 1997a). Figure 14.1 provides a comparison of the number of states with specific subject area requirements for graduation and the average number of units required in 1980 and 1996. Despite the increase in graduation requirements, the majority of the states still do not require as many credits as recommended by the first, and perhaps the foremost, reform report, *A Nation at Risk*, which recommended a minimum of four credits of English and three credits each of social studies, mathematics, and science. In six states, the number of credits required for graduation was left to the discretion of local school boards. However, 15 states in 1996 had statutes or regulations related to the awarding of an advanced diploma to students who had taken more rigorous courses in high school (U.S. Department of Education, 1997a).

Another example of the role of state government is found in the adoption of content standards for different subject areas. By 1997, 48 states were developing common standards in the core academic subjects, and 42 states were developing or had developed assessments to measure student progress toward those standards. Other evidence of progress included that the percent of students taking the core courses recommended in *A Nation at Risk* had increased from 14% in 1982 to 53% in 1994 (U.S. Department of Education, 1997b).

Accompanying the movement to increase high school graduation requirements, 18 states have imposed a minimum competency test that must be passed before a diploma will be awarded. In four additional states, plans are underway to initiate a minimum competency test that must be passed before a diploma is awarded (Associated Press, 1998). This development is consistent with a projected trend for the next century that the high school diploma will be replaced by achievement goals (Lemonick, 1992).

In addition to statutory requirements, the state influences the curriculum through the state board of education which, in many states, is authorized to decide upon curriculum requirements, review curriculum proposals, promulgate curricular guidelines, and establish teacher certification requirements. Yet another state entity, the state department of education, also influences the curriculum through leadership, instructional resources and support, and publication of curriculum guides that are provided to local school districts. State curriculum guides often detail the goals and objectives, competencies, and instructional activities for every subject at every grade level. (See Chapter 13 for a discussion of the roles and responsibilities of state boards and departments of education.)

Another important way in which the state influences the curriculum is through the textbook adoption and selection process. Books are adopted on the basis of state-mandated criteria. In many states, local school districts cannot purchase textbooks unless they are on a state adoption list. In some states, such as California, the state adoption committee determines the approach and perspective a text must have in order to be approved.

The Federal Government

The federal government's influence over the curriculum does not come from mandating that certain courses or programs of study be taught, but from providing support for specific initiatives and drawing attention to certain perceived national problems and issues. For example, as noted in previous chapters, when the launching of the Sputnik spacecraft by the Soviet Union in 1957 caused fear that the United States was falling behind in the space race, the federal government did not respond by mandating more mathematics or science offerings, or higher graduation requirements, but by passing the National Defense Education Act. This act provided financial encouragement to schools to upgrade their mathematics, science, and foreign language offerings. In later years, the National Science Foundation became instrumental in curricular revision in mathematics.

Vocational education is an area that has been heavily influenced by federal legislation. In fact, it was federal legislation that often set the course for, or at least stimulated, state action, and state programs often paralleled federal programs in vocational education. Federal legislation in other areas, including compensatory education, bilingual education, sex equity, career education, adult education, and environmental education, has also tended to direct attention in the curriculum to areas deemed important at the federal level. The federal government also influences curriculum development by virtue of the support given to research in certain areas, which has the effect of promoting curriculum reform in these areas.

National Committees and Reports

As was discussed in several other sections of this text, it has been a practice in this country throughout this century for select national committees to be formed to study and make recommendations regarding some aspect of education. The curriculum impact of some of these committees has been profound. For example, the *Cardinal Principles of Secondary Education,* issued by the NEA Commission on the Reorganization of Secondary Education in 1918, played a major role in the establishment of the comprehensive high school.

The most recent series of national committees and reports contain a number of observations and recommendations directed at the curriculum. The first wave of these reports tended to look at a number of things that were alleged to be "wrong" with the nation's schools, the curriculum being one of them. Required courses, their number and content, and minimum skills and competencies are all addressed by the reports. A second wave of reports, appearing at the end of the 1980s, focused more directly on specific academic components of the curriculum and are noted in the next section. The curriculum recommendations of the major reports in the first wave are summarized in Table 14.1.

How much voice should parents have in the adoption of textbooks?

The various reports appear to be having a significant impact on education policy. For example, the effect of their support for the "new basics" is evident. They can also be credited with the increased attention given to homework, mastery learning, and competency testing. Some of the recommendations, such as merit pay, the extended day, and the extended year have not been widely adopted. It is safe to say, however, that these reports have received more publicity and have been the subject of more discussion by professional educators, educational decision makers, and lay citizens than any educational event in the past quarter-century. They have provided the impetus for the *National Goals for Education,* federal funding for the development of content standards, and expansion of the National Assessment of Educational Progress.

Table 14.1: Curriculum Recommendations from Selected Education Reform Reports

Reform Report	Recommendations
A Nation at Risk (The National Commission on Excellence in Education)	• Significantly more time should be devoted to learning the "new basics"—English, mathematics, science, social studies, computer science, and, for the college-bound, a foreign language. • Elementary schools should provide a sound base in English language development and writing, computational and problem-solving skills, science, social studies, foreign language, and the arts. • Foreign languages should be started in the elementary grades. • All students seeking a diploma should be required to complete four years of English; three years each of mathematics, science, and social studies; and one-half year of computer science.
Making the Grade (Twentieth Century Fund Task Force)	• The federal government should clearly state that the most important objective of elementary and secondary education in the United States is the development of literacy in the English language. • A common core should include the basic skills of reading, writing, and calculating; technical capability in computers; training in science and foreign languages; and knowledge of civics.
Action for Excellence (Education Commission of the States Task Force on Education for Economic Growth)	• The academic experience should be more intense and more productive. Courses in all disciplines must be enlivened and improved. The goal should be both richer substance and greater motivational power—elimination of "soft," nonessential courses, more enthusiastic involvement of students in learning, encouragement of mastery of skills beyond the basics, e.g., problem solving, analysis, interpretation, and persuasive writing. • Educators, business and labor leaders, and other interested parties should clearly identify the skills that the schools are expected to impart to students for effective employment and citizenship.

Professional Organizations

In addition to their individual influence, educators historically had influence over the curriculum through their collective association in professional organizations. Both the National Education Association and the American Federation of Teachers, the two largest organizations, attempt to influence public policy about curriculum through full-time lobbying efforts directed at the state and national legislatures. These and other influential professional organizations, such as the National Council of Social Studies, National Council for Teachers of Mathematics, National Science Teachers Association, International Reading Association, Association for Supervision and Curriculum Development, and American Association of School Administrators, influence the profile and direction of the school curriculum as they set national agendas and goals and raise their collective voices.

The second wave of school reform reports, concerned with curriculum and emanating primarily from these professional organizations, is an example of their involvement and attempt to provide direction for the school curriculum. Directed at the core subjects of mathematics, science, language arts, and social studies,

Table 14.1: *(continued)*

Reform Report	Recommendations
American High School Study (Ernest L. Boyer, Carnegie Foundation)	• In elementary schools, the focus should be on communication skills. All high school students should complete a basic English course with an emphasis on writing. The high school core should stress the spoken word. • Required courses in the student's core should be increased from one half to two thirds of the total required for graduation. The core would include three units of English; two and a half units of history; two units each of science, mathematics, and foreign language; one unit of civics; one half unit each of technology and health; a seminar on work; and a senior independent social issues project. • In the last two years of high school, students should enroll in a cluster of electives and explore career options. • A service requirement involving school or community volunteer work should be added.
A Place Called School (John Goodlad)	• There should be a better balance in the curriculum of the school and the student. The individual curriculum should be devoted to up to 18% language and literature; up to 18% mathematics and science; up to 15% each to society and social studies, the arts, and the vocations; and the remaining 10% to guided individual choice.
The Paideia Proposal (Mortimer Adler)	• There should be a common curriculum for all students involving: (a) acquisition of knowledge through didactic instruction in three subject areas: language, literature, and fine arts; mathematics and natural sciences; history, geography, and social sciences; (b) the development of intellectual skills in linguistics, mathematics, and science through coaching, exercise, and practice; and (c) the enlargement of understanding, insight, and aesthetic appreciation through the Socratic discussion of books and other works of art and participation in artistic activities such as music, drama, and the visual arts. • The only elective in the 12 years of school should be for a second language.

these reports have focused on essential knowledge and skills, called for more rigorous content, and encouraged the development of critical thinking skills. Marzano (1998) identified the following curriculum reports as the most official sources of essential sources of knowledge for the indicated subject areas:

- American Association for the Advancement of Science—*Science for All Americans* (1989)
- Center for Civics Education—*National Standards for Civics and Government* (1994)
- Consortium of National Arts Education Association—*National Standards for Arts Education: What Every Young American Should Know and Be Able to Do in the Arts* (1994)
- Geography Education Standards Project—*Geography for Life: National Geography Standards* (1994)
- Joint Committee on National Health Education Standards—*National Health Education Standards: Achieving Health Literacy* (1995)
- National Association for Sports and Physical Education—*Moving into the Future: National Standards for Physical Education* (1995)
- National Association for the Advancement of Science–*National Science Education Standards* (1996)

- National Association for the Advancement of Science—*Benchmarks for Science Literacy* (1993)
- National Center for History in the Schools—*National Standards for History: Basic Edition* (1996)
- National Council of Teachers of English—*The English Coalition Conference: Democracy Through Language* (1989)
- National Council of Teachers of Mathematics—*Curriculum and Evaluation Standards for School Mathematics* (1989)
- National Council for the Social Studies—*Expectations of Excellence: Curriculum Standards for Social Studies* (1994)
- National Commission on Social Studies in the Schools—*Charting a Course: Social Studies for the 21st Century* (1989)
- National Research Council—*Everybody Counts: A Report to the Nation on the Future of Mathematics Education* (1989)
- National Science Teachers Association—*Essential Changes in Secondary Science: Scope, Sequence, and Coordination* (1989)
- National Standards in Foreign Language Education Project—*Standards for Foreign Language Learning: Preparing for the 21st Century* (1996)
- The English Language Arts—*Standards in Practice: Grades K–2* (Crafton, 1996); *Standards in Practice: Grades 3–5* (Sierra-Perry, 1996); *Standards in Practice: Grades 6–8* (Wilhelm, 1996); *Standards in Practice: Grades 9–12* (Smagornsky, 1996)
- The Secretary's Commission on Achieving Necessary Skills—*What Work Requires of Schools: A SCANS Report for America 2000* (1991)
- The World of Work—*Workplace Basics: The Essential Skills Employers Want* (Carnevale, Gainer & Meltzer, 1990)

Some observers have expressed reservations about the extent to which these standards might become a *de facto* national curriculum. They represent the best thinking of expert panels in response to inquiries from teachers about what essential elements in a subject students should acquire. They are not national or federal mandates but are guidelines to encourage curriculum development to promote higher student achievement. States and local school districts can determine the extent to which the standards will be used and the amount of time devoted to teaching for the standards. Not only will their influence be determined by their level of usage in local school district curriculum development, but also their influence will be determined by the degree to which textbook publishers and achievement developers rely on the standards as they develop materials (Kellough, 1997).

National Goals and Standards

As a result of the adoption of the *National Goals for Education* by the National Governors' Association (1990) and the enactment of the Goals 2000: Educate America Act, increased attention is being given to national goals and standards for education. The adoption of national education goals by the president and the nation's governors represents the first time that political leaders have made a comprehensive formal statement about goals for the public schools. As listed in Chapter 7, the goals originally focused on readiness for school; retention of students in school; student performance; good citizenship; adult literacy; and a safe, drug-free environment for teaching and learning. The goals were expanded to eight with the enactment of the Goals 2000: Educate America Act; the new goals are related to parent participation and teacher preparation. The provisions of the Goals 2000: Educate America Act and earlier federal legislation provide for the appointment of two national bodies to develop and oversee the national goals and national standards: the National Goals Panel and the National Education Standards and Improvement Council.

The function of the National Goals Panel is to review and certify education standards and assessments. The work of this oversight group is being coordinated with the National Education Standards and Improvement Council, whose mission is to provide support and quality control for the several standards-setting efforts that have been funded by the U.S. Department of Education (Olson, 1994a). Even though these two bodies and the standards from the professional organizations do not have the legal status of requirements on the schools, they represent a much more active role of the federal government in education than has existed previously. These standards likely will be reflected in curriculum development and revision efforts and also in textbook revisions. The standards have a special status and high credibility as a result of their having been developed by the appropriate national professional organization with federal funding. They also have served as a resource for the states as they have adopted content standards.

Questions have been raised about the extent to which national goals and standards for public elementary and secondary education threaten state and local control of education (Pitsch, 1994). The concept of national goals and standards appears to conflict with the traditional position that education is a local function, a state responsibility, and a national concern. However, various writers have emphasized that the goals and standards are "national" in terms of being important to the nation's citizens rather than "federal" in terms of being mandates from the federal government. In view of the press for accountability at the state level, the content standards likely will be used by state education agencies, local school districts, and publishers of textbooks and instructional materials as they revise and update curriculum guides, instructional materials, and textbooks (Kellough & Kellough, 1999).

Should schools have the discretion of ignoring the National Goals for Education and the national content standards?

Standardized Tests

The impact of national standardized tests on the entire educational enterprise in the last two decades has been nothing short of overwhelming. All states except Nebraska and Iowa require tests at different grades. Iowa has a voluntary program in which most school districts participate; and Nebraska reportedly plans to introduce statewide tests (Associated Press, 1998). Students, schools, and school districts are praised or prodded based on test results. Interest in student performance on standardized tests is high in the 32 states and 34 large-city school districts in which accountability systems are based in part on students' test scores (Olson, 1998).

Students are admitted to postsecondary institutions, private elementary and secondary schools, and specialized programs in the public schools based on their

Student performance on standardized tests continues to be the subject of public debate.

test results. Many scholarships are based entirely or in part on test results. Teachers, programs, and schools are considered more or less effective based on test results. The admission of prospective teachers and administrators into degree or certification programs, or their later certification, is determined by test results. Practicing teachers and administrators are tested in some states. Many accountability or merit pay plans include test results as output indicators.

To a large extent, these tests function as "gatekeepers of knowledge" (Spring, 1998). Test developers decide what knowledge most merits testing. Although within any discipline there is usually considerable debate as to what knowledge is of most worth, in the end it is often the viewpoint of the test makers that gives direction to the curriculum. While not necessarily advocating "teaching to the test," school boards, administrators, and teachers themselves seek to ensure that the schools' curriculum "prepare[s] students to do well on the test." If test scores are down in a certain curriculum area, district resources and instruction may be redirected to that area. Increasingly, individual students and their families invest in tutorial books, computer software, and seminars in an attempt to raise test scores.

Standardized tests can play an important role in providing the standards and data needed for curriculum assessment, but their limits must be recognized. Educators, policy makers, and parents should keep in mind that the only thing that most of the tests measure is achievement; they do not measure other desired outputs of the learning experience. Nor do they measure whether individual teachers or schools are achieving their own instructional goals. Thus, to allow the concern about national standardized tests to dictate the curriculum would be a serious error.

This is particularly true in light of the concerns expressed by many educators and psychologists that some tests are biased against females, minorities, and those from lower socioeconomic strata. Although the testing industry has taken steps to rid tests of their blatant white, male, middle-class biases, test analyses continue to reveal content that discriminates against certain populations. An overreliance on items that assume experiences or knowledge not common to certain gender, racial, and ethnic groups illustrates the type of content that causes test bias. Rather than being a measure of student performance, much of the variability in state scores can be accounted for by such demographic variables as number of parents in the home, level of parental education, type of community, and poverty rates for children ages 5–17. The test data may be more an index of educational challenge than a measure of educational performance (Robinson & Brandon, 1994). Although the decision to administer most tests is not within the authority of teachers, they can play a role in examining tests for bias and in ensuring that results are properly interpreted, communicated, and utilized.

In addition to the previously discussed concerns about national testing, this issue also has been raised in reference to assessment of the *National Goals for Education*. The national goals and standards movement has emphasized the importance of focusing student assessment efforts on observable behaviors and levels of student performance. Some interest groups (Committee for Economic Development, 1994; Olson, 1994b) have called for either the federal government or state governments to develop assessment programs to measure the extent to which students attain the new content standards. However, others have expressed reservations about the capacity of available tests, the potential misuse of testing information, and the ability of a test to determine the extent to which an individual is capable of applying knowledge in addressing problems outside the classroom (Stecklow, 1997). These comments, in the context of the two federal panels and the efforts to develop national standards, suggest an expanded and more active role for the federal government in influencing school curricular content and state and local assessment practices and policies. However, President Clinton has been stymied by Congress in his push for national tests in reading and mathematics (Associated Press, 1998).

Textbooks

In the course of his or her educational career a student may be exposed to hundreds of textbooks. In the classroom, students spend at least two thirds of their time using textbooks. Teachers rely heavily on textbooks for instructional content, organization, and evaluation. Without question, textbooks and other published instructional materials influence what is taught and learned in the classroom. Textbook publishers are commercial enterprises with a profit motive, so they are responsive to marketplace economic pressures. By virtue of their influence in

What is the textbook adoption process in your state?

determining what content is included and how it is portrayed, textbooks, textbook publishers, and state adoption policies have an impact on not only the knowledge base of students, but also their attitudes and beliefs (Apple, 1998). It is because they recognize the powerful influence of textbooks that religious and other special interest groups have been so vocal and persistent in their attempts to influence not only textbook adoption decisions but also the textbook industry itself.

In addition to the previously discussed concerns about content expressed by some religious groups, textbooks have also been criticized for being too "hard" on American institutions and activities, and presenting an inadequate portrayal of women, minorities, and other groups. That is, women and minorities are often portrayed in traditional and lower status roles or are given limited coverage. The elderly and handicapped often are excluded from narrative discussion or pictures and illustrations.

Given the potential influence of textbooks and the unresolved concerns about their content, it is important that teachers be sensitive to textbook treatment of cultural diversity, gender differences, and special populations. Teachers should actively participate in the textbook selection process. Unfortunately, teachers often have not received training in the evaluation of instructional material or are not given sufficient time to thoroughly review the textbooks under consideration. Ultimately, the influence that textbooks have on the curriculum is determined by the care taken in their selection and how they are used in the classroom.

Curriculum Development

The curriculum development and planning literature is replete with models, paradigms, and "steps," which all can be categorized according to two perspectives: the technical production perspective and the critical perspective. The technical production perspective has dominated thought on curriculum planning for 40 years. The newer critical perspective takes issue with the very assumptions underlying the technical production perspective and advocates critical reflection on all assumptions in discussions about the curriculum (Posner, 1998).

Technical Production Perspective

The technical production perspective views curriculum planning as a rational and technical process that can be accomplished by objective decision making. Further, curriculum planning is presumed to be a production-oriented enterprise in which the planner objectively and, if possible, scientifically establishes the means to obtain the desired educational outcomes. The technical production model has been popular for so long because it is congruent with the prevailing assumption that education is a production process in which individual learning is the primary product (Posner, 1998).

The technical production perspective is best represented by the work of Ralph Tyler (1949). Tyler's rationale for curriculum planning is organized around four steps. First, the planners must determine what educational purposes (aims and objectives) the school(s) should pursue. As discussed in Chapters 3 and 4, there are widely varying schools of thought about the purpose of education, and these are translated into curriculum and instructional practice.

After deciding on the educational objectives, as a second step planners must decide those learning experiences that are likely to attain these purposes. Once developed, possible experiences must be checked to see if they give students the opportunity to acquire the behavior stated in the objectives and if they lead to the effect intended (Walker & Soltis, 1986).

In the third step, planners must decide how the learning experiences can be organized effectively. Here, attention must be given to the *continuity* and *sequence* of experiences. Consistent with Piaget's theory that cognitive development is gradual (progressing through four levels) and that any subject can be taught in some form to any student at any stage of development, continuity is concerned with the reiteration of major curriculum elements so that skills can be practiced and developed. Sequencing aims at ensuring that successive experiences build on preceding ones. The concepts of continuity and sequence, which Tyler refers to as vertical organizational dimensions, also correspond to Bruner's concept of the spiral curriculum, which, as explained in Chapter 7, proposes that concepts and topics be treated at progressive grade levels in increasing complexity and detail.

The effective organization of experiences also involves the *integration* of skills and knowledge across disciplines. Tyler refers to integration as the horizontal dimension of curriculum organization. As the fourth step in the Tyler model, the planner must develop a means of evaluating whether the stated purposes are being attained by the selected learning experiences. Tyler (1949) viewed curriculum planning as a continuous process whereby

> as materials and procedures are developed, they are tried out, their results appraised, their inadequacies identified, and suggested improvements indicated. The process involves replanning, redevelopment and then reappraisal. In this continuing cycle, the curriculum and instructional program can be continuously improved over the years. (p. 123)

Figure 14.2 provides a graphic depiction of Tyler's curriculum planning cycle.

Critical Perspective

In sharp contrast to the technical production perspective is the critical perspective, which rejects the notion that curriculum planning can be an objective, value-free process. Rather, this perspective argues that curriculum decisions are essentially ideological and sociopolitical. As some critical theorists point out, the very decisions about what the objectives should be, what knowledge is of most value, how the curriculum will be organized and delivered, to whom it will be delivered, and how it will be evaluated involve assumptions and values that reinforce the existing power and social structure. For example, because of the relationship between evaluators and employers, if it were known to an evaluator that the administration of a district had been active in initiating a particular curriculum and had fought hard to secure financial support for the program, the evaluator would probably feel great pressure to discover results not unfavorable to the program.

Figure 14.2: The Tyler Planning Cycle

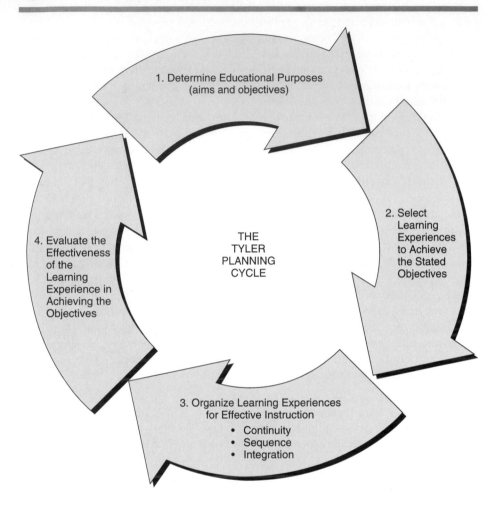

Each of these perspectives is important in curriculum development. Knowing how to develop a curriculum involves technique. Being able to identify the assumptions underlying curriculum discussions requires a curriculum conscience. Curriculum planning without technique is incompetent, and without curriculum conscience, is ungrounded (Posner, 1998).

Patterns of Curriculum Organization

Decisions about how the curriculum should be organized involve choices about what content to study and how this content will be presented to the students.

Controversial Issues

The Subject-Centered and Student-Centered Curricula

The debate between the essentialists and others who support the subject-centered curriculum and the progressives and others who support a student-centered curriculum has continued unabated for almost a decade and appears likely to continue into the next century. Among the arguments the proponents of each orientation give are the following:

Arguments for the Subject-Centered Curriculum

1. Introduces learners to the cultural heritage.
2. Gives teachers a sense of security by specifying what their responsibilities are for developing given skills and knowledge.
3. Reduces repetition or overlap between grade levels or different sections of the same class.
4. Increases the likelihood that learners will be exposed to knowledge and develop skills in an orderly manner.
5. Permits methodical assessment of pupil progress; assumes that knowledge is the only measurable outcome of learning experiences.
6. Facilitates cooperative group planning by educators in allocating the scope and sequence of learning experiences.

Arguments for the Student-Centered Curriculum

1. Releases the teacher from the pressure to follow a prescribed scope and sequence that invariably does not meet all learners' needs.
2. Has a positive influence on learners as they find that instruction is varied to meet individual needs and purposes.
3. Encourages teacher judgment in selecting the content deemed most suitable for a group of learners.
4. Increases the likelihood that content has relevance to learners.
5. Modifies instruction to accommodate developmental changes and behavioral tasks as individual differences are identified and monitored.
6. Allows much more latitude for creative planning by the individual teacher.

What other arguments can you think of for the subject-centered or student-centered curriculum?

Source: Shane, H. G., & Tabler, M. B. (1981). Educating for a new millennium (pp. 79–80). Bloomington, IN: Phi Delta Kappa. Reprinted with permission.

Although there are many different structures that reflect alternative perspectives about the nature of the curriculum, these alternatives can be classified as being either subject centered or student centered. The subject-centered perspective is the older, more traditional, and most common. It views the curriculum as a program of studies or collection of courses that represents what students should know. The second perspective focuses on the needs and interests of the student and the process by which learning takes place.

The subject-centered and student-centered perspectives are the two ends of a continuum of curricular design. In this section six alternative curriculum designs along this continuum are examined: subject-area design, integrated design, core curriculum design, student-centered design, constructivism and social reconstruction design. Various components of the different curriculum organizations are compared in Table 14.2.

The Subject-Area Design

The *subject-area curriculum* design is the oldest and most common organization plan for the curriculum. This design views the curriculum as a group of subjects or body of subject matter. The subject matter to be included in the curriculum is that which has survived the test of time. It is also that which is perceived to be of most value in the development of the intellect—said by supporters to be the primary purpose of education. The subject-area curriculum is consistent with the essentialist philosophy of education.

The subject-area design has its roots in classical Greece. In this country William T. Harris, superintendent of schools in St. Louis, Missouri, in the 1870s and U.S. commissioner of education from 1886 to 1906, is credited with establishing this design, which has been the dominant curriculum organization for over a century. Harris viewed the curriculum as the means by which the student is introduced to the essential knowledge and values of society and transformed into a reasoning and responsible citizen. The curriculum of the elementary school was to include the fundamentals, which Harris called the "five windows of the soul": mathematics, geography, literature and art, grammar, and history. In the high school, concentration was on the classics, languages, and mathematics (Cremin, 1962). Electives in languages, fine arts, and industrial arts were to be used to develop specific skills or meet special interests (Ellis, Mackey, & Glenn, 1988).

Modern spokespersons for the subject-area curriculum include Arthur Bestor, Mortimer Adler, Robert Hutchins, Allan Bloom, and E. D. Hirsch. They have been joined in their call for a return to fundamentals and a curriculum of basic studies by supporters of the back-to-basics movement. There is no universal agreement on the operational description of the back-to-basics movement. Sadker and Sadker (1997) have indicated that some of the common elements are:

1. Majority of the school day in elementary school spent on reading, writing, and arithmetic.
2. Heavy secondary school emphasis on English, science, mathematics, and history.
3. More authority to teachers including the authority to use corporal punishment.
4. Instructional procedures that stress drill, homework, and frequent testing.
5. Textbooks that reflect patriotism and do not include material that challenges traditional values.
6. Elimination of electives, frills, and innovations and such social services as guidance, sex education, humanistic education, and peace education.

7. Promotion from grade to grade based on demonstrated proficiency on specific examinations.

Those who criticize the subject-area curriculum claim that it ignores the needs, interests, and experiences of students and discourages creativity on the part of both students and teachers. Another major criticism of the subject-area curriculum is that it is fragmented and compartmentalized. The subject-area curriculum is also faulted for failing to adequately consider both individual differences and contemporary social issues. The primary teaching methods of the subject-area curriculum are lecture and discussion. Rote memorization and recitation are required of students.

The subject-area curriculum has remained the most popular and dominant curriculum design for four basic reasons. First, most teachers, especially secondary school teachers, are trained in the subject areas. Secondary school teachers usually think of themselves as American history teachers, biology teachers, English teachers, or whatever. Second, organizing the school by subject matter makes it easy for parents and other adults to understand a student's education since most adults attended schools that were organized by subject matter. Third, the subject-area organization makes it easy for teachers to develop curriculum and goals: the content provides the organization and focus needed in planning. Finally, textbooks and other instructional materials are usually developed for subject-area use (Ellis, Mackey, & Glenn, 1988). Because the subject-area design has been so dominant in this country, it is possible to go into schools from Seattle to Key West and find much the same curriculum.

The Integrated Design

The *integrated curriculum* design emerged as a response to the multiplication of courses resulting from the subject-centered design. In this design emphasis remains on subjects, but in place of separate courses in history, geography, economics, political science, anthropology, and sociology, for example, an integrated course in social studies might be offered. By this approach, it is claimed, knowledge is integrated in a way that makes it more meaningful to the learner. The integrated design also provides greater flexibility to the teacher in choosing subject matter.

Among the more common integrated courses are language arts, which has taken the place of separate courses in reading, writing, spelling, speaking, grammar, drama, and literature; mathematics, which integrates arithmetic, geometry, and algebra; general science, which includes botany, biology, chemistry, and geology or earth science; and the previously mentioned social studies. Although the integrated design usually combines separate subjects within the same discipline, in some instances content from two or more branches of study have been integrated into a new field of study. Futuristics, which integrates knowledge from mathematics, sociology, statistics, political science, economics, education, and a number of other fields, is one such new field of study.

The integrated curriculum has been widely accepted at the elementary level. Where once a number of separate subjects were taught for shorter periods of time, the typical elementary curriculum is now more likely to integrate these subjects into "subject areas" that are taught in longer blocks of time. Jacobs (1997) has indicated that the process of integrating curricula has matured into a workable and formidable force in high school reform. This approach is in sharp contrast with the past tendency to polarize the curriculum into separate disciplines. She contends that the question is no longer whether the curriculum should be integrated but rather when and in what format.

The Core Curriculum Design

The definition of a *core curriculum* has changed significantly since it was first advanced in the 1930s. Originally, the core curriculum was proposed as an interdisciplinary approach of relating one subject to another in the study of everyday situations of interest and value to students. The content of the core was taught in an extended block of time centered around defining and solving problems of concern to all students. Attention was directed to the study of culture and fundamental social values. Typical core courses dealt with how to earn a living, social relations, or life adjustment. As described at the time, the core curriculum was said to be

> made up of those educational experiences which are thought to be important for each citizen in our democracy. Students and teachers do not consider subject matter to be important in itself. It becomes meaningful only as it helps the group to solve the problems which have been selected for study. (MacConnell et al., cited in Goodlad, 1987, p. 10)

Different interpretations of the core concept have emerged in the last decade, primarily as a result of the national reports of the early 1980s. Alternately, the concept of a core curriculum is used to refer to the required minimum "subjects and topics within subjects that all students in a given system are required to or expected to learn" (Skilbeck, 1989, p. 198) or, more broadly, "the comprehensive body of common learnings deemed necessary for all" (Goodlad, 1987, p. 11).

What impact have the back-to-basics movement and other interest groups had on your discipline?

The support for the "new core" came from the same disillusionment with American education that fed the back-to-basics movement that began in the 1970s. The curriculum was said to be lacking in rigor, to contain too many "frills" and soft courses, and to inadequately prepare students to effectively participate and contribute to our increasingly technological and global society. Serious deficits in mathematics, science, and languages also were noted.

The response of some of the national studies was to recommend a core of subjects to be taken by all students. As seen in Table 14.1, the National Commission on Excellence recommended 13.5 units in "the Five New Basics"; Boyer proposed a "core of common learning" consisting of 14.5 units; and others wanted less specific, but still identifiable, cores. To others the concept of a core is more reminiscent of the core curriculum espoused by the progressive educators of the 1930s, 1940s, and early 1950s. For example, although Goodlad (1983) in *A Place Called School* "deliberately and reluctantly" defined a core in conventional terms, he subsequently has joined that body of educators who recognize that increasingly the expectations of schooling are broad and transcend mere academic outcomes. What is needed is not a core of subjects to be taken by all students but a core curriculum consisting of the domains of human experience and thought that should be encountered by all students. The American Association for Supervision and Curriculum Development (ASCD), like Boyer, refers to a core of common learning to help ensure that "all students are provided the curriculum content and learning experiences most appropriate to their future lives" (Cawelti, 1989, p. 33).

Yet many educators are concerned that it is not possible to have a core curriculum for all students and still maintain quality. Others are concerned about the impact of a universal core requirement on the schools' ability to meet the needs of different populations, including those interested in vocational preparation. Probably all agree that the task of defining the proper core will be among the most challenging professional tasks facing educators.

The Student-Centered Design

The concept of the student-centered curriculum has its roots in the efforts of Rousseau, Pestalozzi, and Froebel (see Chapter 6). In the United States, the concept was revived by the progressive education movement. There are a number of variations of the student-centered curriculum, including the experience- and activity-centered curriculum and the relevant curriculum. The emphasis of all student-centered curricula is on the student's freedom to learn and on activities and creative self-expression.

Whereas the traditional curriculum is organized around the teaching of discrete subject matter, in the student-centered curriculum students come to the subject matter out of their own needs and interests. The student-centered curriculum focuses on the individual learner and the development of the whole student. The scope of the student-centered curriculum is as broad as all of human life and society. The goal of the curriculum is to motivate and interest the student in the learning process. To achieve this goal, the curriculum encompasses a wide range of activities, including field geography, nature study, number concepts, games, drama, storytelling, music, art, handicrafts, other creative and expressive activities, physical education, and community involvement projects.

Student-centered designs are often criticized for being too broad and for being so inclusive as to be nonfunctional (Portelli, 1987). They are also criticized for being too permissive and for their lack of attention to subject matter mastery. Modern proponents (e.g., John Holt, Herbert Kohl, and Elliot Eisner) counter that the student-centered curriculum enhances learning because it is based on the needs and interests of the learner. Student-centered curricula have operated in numerous districts and schools throughout this century, primarily at the elementary level. However, they have never been seriously considered at the secondary level.

The Constructivism Design

The major theme of *constructivism* is that learning is an active process in which students construct new ideas or concepts based on their current and past knowledge and experiences (Bruner, 1960). Students select the desired information, transform those ideas into hypotheses, and make decisions based on this new

Table 14.2: Patterns of Curriculum Organization

Curriculum Design	Philosophical Orientation	Curriculum Focus	Proponents
Subject-centered	Essentialism	A group of subjects or subject matter that represent the essential knowledge and values of society that have survived the test of time.	Bestor Adler Hutchins
Integrated	Experimentalism	The integration of two or more subjects, both within and across disciplines, into an integrated course.	Broudy Silberman Sarason
Core curriculum	Perennialism	A common body of curriculum content and learning experience that should be encountered by all students; the Great Books.	Goodlad Boyer
Student-centered	Progressivism	Learning activities centered around the interests and needs of the child, designed to motivate and interest the child in the learning process.	Dewey Holt Kohl Eisner
Constructivism	Critical theory Existentialism Pragmatism Social reconstructionism	Learning activities which encourage students to construct their own meaning based on current and past knowledge and experience.	Derrida Foucault Rorty
Social reconstructionist	Social reconstructionism	Critical analysis of the political, social, and economic problems facing society; future trends; social action projects designed to bring about social change.	Counts Rugg Bramald Shane

knowledge. The students then adjust their understanding of reality to include this new information. The role of the teacher is to engage the student in an active dialogue, translate information into the student's current sphere of understanding, and encourage the student to discover the needed information and the principles. The subject curriculum should be designed so that students can integrate this new knowledge with previously learned information (San Diego State University, 1996).

Building on prior knowledge, individuals construct their own view of the world through experiences within their physical and social environment. Students link their prior knowledge to the new knowledge in a continuous, active process that raises their thinking skills. In this context, constructivism and core curriculum have similar qualities because both require the reorganization of existing knowledge to make room for new knowledge (Appalachian Rural School Initiative [ARSI], 1998).

Students learn more in a responsible and stimulating learning environment.

Both constructivism and student-centered design emphasize experiences, are activity centered, and are relevant. Students have the freedom to learn and create information; the curriculum is centered on their needs and interests. Individual students have the final responsibility for their learning (ARSI, 1998).

The Social Reconstruction Design

The *social reconstruction curriculum* design is based on the belief that through the curriculum the school can and should effect social change and create a more equitable society. As discussed in Chapter 7, the social reconstruction movement in education emerged in the 1930s and had its origin in the progressive education movement. In 1932, in his book *Dare the Schools Build a New Social Order?*, George Counts (1969) proposed that the schools involve students in a curriculum designed to reconstruct society. Modern reconstructionists such as Theodore Brameld continue to advocate that the schools become the agents of social change and improvement.

The major assumption underlying the social reconstruction curriculum is that the future is not fixed, but is amenable to modification and improvement. Accordingly, the social reconstruction curriculum seeks "to equip students with tools (skills) for dealing with changes about them. So equipped, the student can meet an unknown future with attitudes and habits of action" (Wiles & Bondi, 1998, p. 355). The primary goal of the curriculum according to the social reconstructionist view is to engage students in a critical analysis of society at every level so that they can improve it.

The social reconstruction design combines classroom learning with application outside the school. Teachers and students join in inquiry. Instruction is often carried on in a problem-solving or inquiry format (Wiles & Bondi, 1998).

What kinds of instructional materials should be used in a social reconstruction curriculum? How difficult would it be to obtain the materials?

Curriculum Contrasts

In practice, most schools do not adopt a strictly subject-centered or student-centered design, but use variations of both in their curriculum organization. Historically, elementary schools have tended to be more student centered in their orientation and secondary schools more subject centered. Ultimately, the choice of curriculum design reflects philosophical orientation. The major arguments in support of the subject-centered and student-centered curricula are summarized on page 485.

The Hidden Curriculum

What impact might the hidden curriculum have on your role as a beginning teacher?

Perhaps even more important than the formal curriculum is the informal or *hidden curriculum*. This concept was briefly mentioned in Chapter 8 in regard to the socialization role of the school. Schools teach students more than is in the formal curriculum; they are influenced by the implicit things in the school that send them messages about what they ought to be doing and thinking. Teachers help shape the hidden curriculum in the classroom by sending signals about what is considered to be important. For example, the social studies teacher may be sending an unintended message if he or she admonishes students to read the front page of the newspaper, but is seen only reading the sports pages (Armstrong, Henson, & Savage, 1997). The message may be unintended and may not be reflected in the school catalog, but a powerful message is communicated to students. Other examples may be found in student elections and contests; the informal unplanned learnings may send a variety of messages to students (Sadker & Sadker, 1997).

Professional Reflections

"Remember that the core of education is children. Children are each unique, and so the purpose of education is to meet the needs of those individual children in any way we can. Curriculum is a vehicle, not an end."

Jacqueline Collier, Teacher of the Year, Ohio

"Communicate with parents about the good things that are happening in your classroom. One of the best things I've ever done is to send a postcard home to every child at least once each quarter."

Darla Mallein, Teacher of the Year, Kansas

The hidden curriculum includes the norms and values that undergird the formal curriculum. Even though the hidden curriculum is not taught directly or included in the objectives of the formal curriculum, it impacts on both students and teachers. Evidence of the hidden curriculum may be found in textbooks and other curriculum materials and in the norms and values of the school. The hidden curriculum includes the organizational structure of the classroom and the school as well as the ways in which students and teachers interact with each other (Gollnick & Chinn, 1998).

The hidden curriculum includes the *null curriculum;* these are the things that are consciously excluded because they are controversial, because of insufficient funds, because educators are uninformed, or because relevant materials are nonexistent (Eisner, 1994). The null curriculum, like all areas of the hidden curriculum, does not have the same impact on all students. Differences are found even within the same school or classroom in what certain students have the opportunity to learn.

In recent years increasing attention has been focused on the hidden curriculum as more has been learned about the strength of its influence. Particular concern exists about its negative influence. For example, the lessons of the hidden curriculum tend to promote conformity and in the process may stifle creativity and independent thinking. The hidden curriculum also teaches students to avoid conflict and change. Through the hidden curriculum, bias and stereotyping of race, gender, and class are reproduced and reinforced (Gollnick & Chinn, 1998).

The Curriculum Cycle

Throughout the twentieth century, the curriculum in America's schools has shifted between a subject-centered orientation and a student-centered orientation. The first two decades of the century were dominated by the progressive movement and its student centeredness. In the wake of World War I came a more conservative political posture and a renewal of interest in a more orderly academic curriculum. Out of the social upheaval of the Great Depression emerged a more liberal voice that championed concern for the individual. In the 1950s, Conant's study of secondary schools, which underscored the need for greater attention to academic studies, was reinforced by the Soviet launching of Sputnik, and a curriculum reform movement was initiated aimed at strengthening mathematics, science, and foreign language offerings and providing greater rigor in all disciplines. The Great Society of the 1960s drove the cycle in the opposite direction. The open school and alternative school movements were the most visible reflections of the increased attention being focused on students. By the late 1970s many of the curricular innovations of the previous decade had disappeared, and again a call was heard for a return to the basic academic subjects and an elimination of the frills. This mood dominated the 1980s and the 1990s.

At the turn of the century, the curricular reform cycle appears to be responding to the interest in national goals and performance standards. The unknown is the degree of attention that will be given to values education, decision-making and critical thinking skills, development of self-esteem, and the individuality of students. For those who are concerned about the direction of the curriculum cycle, the consolation is that the cycle is short and directions change (McDaniel, 1989).

Summary

The decade of the 1990s has seen the school reform movement focus its attention on the curriculum in an effort to achieve what increasing core requirements and expenditures had not been able to do—increase student performance. The increased attention on the curriculum has served not only to highlight the controversy about various curriculum orientations, but also to emphasize the sociopolitical context within which curriculum decisions are made.

The 1990s have brought a shift in the dominant curriculum orientation. The conservative, subject-centered approach that was emphasized by the first wave of reform reports is giving way to a more balanced approach that incorporates greater concern for national goals and performance standards. The involvement of various professional educational associations and the nation's governors in the reform arena should bring new force to curriculum change.

A curriculum standing alone is of little value. Not until it is implemented does it take on meaning. The process by which it is implemented, termed instruction, is discussed in the following chapter, along with the emerging issues and trends in curriculum and instruction.

Key Terms

Constructivism

Continuity

Core curriculum

Curriculum

Hidden curriculum

Integrated curriculum

Integration

Null curriculum

Sequence

Social reconstruction curriculum

Subject-area curriculum

Discussion Questions

1. As a new teacher like Mary Sherman, how would you respond to the parent who is critical of the school's curriculum?

2. How would you define the terms *curriculum* and *hidden curriculum?* Should the lessons of the hidden curriculum be incorporated into the formal curriculum? If not, how can they be dealt with by the teacher? Should they be dealt with?

3. Which of the agencies or groups discussed in this chapter has had the most influence on the curriculum in your district in the last five years?

4. How will the national goals and standards movement impact on the professional life of the individual teacher?

5. Who should have the most input on textbook content? The author? The publisher? The user?

6. Which of the curricular designs discussed in this chapter is most consistent with your philosophy of education as identified in Chapters 3 and 4?

7. Describe the curriculum that would best prepare students for the twenty-first century.

Internet Resources

1. See Appendix.

2. **www.ascd.org**
The home page of the Association for Supervision and Curriculum Development provides information about the organization, its products and services (including HireEd, a on-line job bank and résumé posting service), and links to other curriculum-related sites.

3. **www.ed.gov/nationaltests/**
Maintained by the U.S. Department of Education, this site provides discussion of the status and results of the voluntary national tests of 4th-grade reading and 8th-grade mathematics.

4. **www.mcrel.org/standards-benchmarks/**
This is McRel's compendium and searchable database of standards and benchmarks in all content areas.

5. **putwest.boces.org/standards.html**
This page gives an annotated list of sites with K–12 educational standards and curriculum framework documents by state, subject area, and organizations, with links to related sites at U.S. government, other nations, and more.

6. **www.ncrel.org/sdrs/areas/issues/ envrnmnt/stw/sw100.htm**
The Web page of Developing an Applied and Integrated Curriculum provides a detailed discussion of curriculum integration with numerous embedded links.

References

Appalachian Rural School Initiative (ARSI) Web Site. (1998). *Constructivism key points.* McConnelsville, OH: Todd Spence, ARSI Teacher Partner. http://www.mnp.net/arsi/cons/strategies.htl.

Apple, M. (1998). The culture and commerce of the textbook. In L. Beyer & M. Apple (Eds.), *The curriculum: Problems, politics and possibilities* (pp. 157–176). Albany: State University of New York Press.

Apple, M. (1988). *Hidden curriculum.* In R. A. Gorton, G. T. Schneider, & J. C. Fisher (Eds.), *Encyclopedia of school administration* (p. 137). Phoenix, AZ: The Oryx Press.

Armstrong, D., Henson, K., & Savage, T. (1997). *Teaching today: An introduction to education.* Upper Saddle River, NJ: Merrill.

Associated Press. (1998, August 25). Standardized tests become the norm. *Las Vegas Review Journal,* p. 6A.

Bruner, J. (1960). *The process of education.* Cambridge, MA: Harvard University Press.

Carnevale, A., Gainer, J., & Meltzer, A. (1990). *Workplace basics: The essential skills employers want.* San Francisco: Jossey-Bass.

Cawelti, G. (1989). Designing high schools for the future. *Educational Leadership, 47*(1), 33.

Committee for Economic Development. (1994). *Putting learning first: Governing and managing the schools for high achievement.* New York: Author.

Cornbleth, C. (1988). Curriculum in and out of context. *Journal of Curriculum and Supervision, 3,* 85–96.

Counts, G. S. (1969). *Dare the schools build a new social order?* New York: John Dey.

Crafton, L. (1996). *Standards in practice: Grades K–2.* Urbana, IL: National Council of Teachers of English.

Cremin, L. A. (1962). *The transformation of the school.* New York: Alfred A. Knopf.

Eisner, E. (1994). *The educational imagination* (3rd ed.). New York: Macmillan.

Ellis, A., Mackey, J., & Glenn, A. (1988). *The school curriculum.* Boston: Allyn and Bacon.

Elmore, R., & Fuhrman, S. (1994). Educational professionals and curriculum governance. In R. Elmore & S. Fuhrman (Eds.), *The governance of curriculum* (pp. 210–215). Alexandria, VA: Association for Supervision and Curriculum Development.

Gollnick, D., & Chinn, P. (1998). *Multicultural education in a pluralistic society.* Upper Saddle River, NJ: Prentice-Hall.

Goodlad, J. (1983). *A place called school.* New York: McGraw-Hill.

Goodlad, J. (1987). A new look at an old idea: Core curriculum. *Educational Leadership, 44*(4), 10.

Jacobs, H. (1997). Designing with rigor: Crafting interdisciplinary high school curricula. *The High School Magazine, 4*(3), 32–37.

Kellough, R. (1997). *A resource guide for teachers.* Upper Saddle River, NJ: Merrill.

Kellough, R., & Kellough, N. (1999). *Secondary school teaching: A guide to methods and resources.* Upper Saddle River, NJ: Merrill.

Langdon, C. (1997). *The fourth Phi Delta Kappa poll of teachers' attitudes toward the public schools.* Bloomington, IN: Phi Delta Kappa.

Lemonick, M. D. (1992, Fall). Tomorrow's lesson: Learn or perish. *Time.* Special edition, 59–60.

Marzano, R. (1998). What are the general skills of thinking and reasoning and how do you teach them? *Clearing House, 71*(5), 268–273.

McDaniel, T. R. (1989). Demilitarizing public education: School reform in the era of George Bush. *Phi Delta Kappan, 71,* 15–18.

Medrick, E., Brown, C., & Henke, R. (1992). *Overview and inventory of state requirements for course work and attendance.* NCES 92–663. Washington, DC: National Center for Education Statistics, U.S. Department of Education.

National Governors' Association. (1990). *National Goals for Education,* Washington, DC: Author.

Olson, L. (1994a, August 3). Clinton expected to name standards board this month. *Education Week,* pp. 13, 28.

Olson, L. (1994b, September 17). "Fuzzy" talk on standards imperils reform. *Education Week,* pp. 14, 12.

Olson, L. (1998, February 11). The push for accountability gathers steam. *Education Week,* pp. 1, 21.

Pitsch, M. (1994, October 19). Critics target Goals 2000 in schools "war." *Education Week,* pp. 1, 21.

Portelli, J. P. (1987). On defining curriculum. *Journal of Curriculum and Supervision, 2,* 354–367.

Posner, G. (1998). Models of curriculum planning. In L. Beyer & M. Apple (Eds.), *The curriculum: Problems, politics and possibilities* (pp. 79–100). Albany: State University of New York Press.

Robinson, G., & Brandon, D. (1994). *NAEP test scores: Should they be used to compare and rank state educational quality?* Arlington, VA: Educational Research Service.

Rose, L., & Gallup, A. (1998). The 30th annual Gallup Poll of the public's attitudes toward the public schools. *Phi Delta Kappan, 80*(1), 41–56.

Sadker, M., & Sadker, D. (1997), *Teachers, schools and society.* New York: McGraw-Hill.

San Diego State University (SDSU). (1996). *Constructivism.* San Diego, CA: http://edweb.sdsu.edu/courses/edtec540/Perspective/learn.html.

Sheeran, T., & Sheeran, M. (1996). Schools, schooling, and teachers: A curriculum for the future. *NASSP Bulletin, 80*(500) 47–56.

Sierra-Perry, M. (1996). *Standards in practice: Grades 3–5.* Urbana, IL: National Council of Teachers of English.

Skilbeck, M. (1989). Revitalizing the core curriculum. *Journal of Curriculum and Supervision, 4,* 198.

Smagornsky, P. (1996). *Standards in practice: Grades 9–12.* Urbana, IL: National Council of Teachers of English.

Spring, J. (1998). *American education: An introduction to social and political aspects* (6th ed.). New York: Longman.

Stecklow, S. (1997, September 2). Apple polishing: Kentucky's teachers get bonuses, but some are caught cheating. *The Wall Street Journal,* pp. A1, A2.

Tietelbaum, K. (1998). Contestation and the curriculum: The efforts of American socialists, 1900–1920. In L. Beyer & M. Apple (Eds.), *The curriculum: Problems, politics and possibilities* (pp. 34–57). Albany: State University of New York Press.

Tyler, R. W. (1949). *Basic principles of curriculum and instruction.* Chicago: University of Chicago Press.

U.S. Department of Education. (1997b). *National standards for academic excellence.* Washington, DC: Author.

U.S. Department of Education, National Center for Education Statistics. (1996). *Digest of education statistics.* Washington, DC: Author.

U.S. Department of Education, National Center for Education Statistics. (1997a). *Digest of education statistics.* Washington, DC: Author.

Walker, D. E., & Soltis, J. F. (1986). *Curriculum and aims.* New York: Teachers College Press, Columbia University.

Wilhelm, J. D. (1996). *Standards in practice: Grades 6–8.* Urbana, IL: National Council of Teachers of English.

Wiles, J., & Bondi, J. (1998). *Curriculum development* (5th ed.). New York: Merrill.

Chapter 15

*All education is a continuous dialogue—questions and
answers that pursue every problem to the horizon.*

William O. Douglas
Wisdom, October 1956

Instructional Practices in Effective Schools

➤ *David Crowley is a beginning teacher in a school that has a high percentage of students on free or reduced-priced lunches, large numbers of students from single-parent households, low parental participation in school functions, high teacher turnover, low student attendance, and low levels of student performance on standardized tests for over a decade. The school has been identified as a "target for improvement" by the accountability unit in the state department of education; this classification makes the school eligible to apply for a $100,000 grant for school improvement. The principal has appointed David to a study committee composed of staff members and parents; the charge is to recommend a school improvement model that might be used to "reinvent" the school.*

Review the school improvement models in this chapter and list the pros and cons of each model for this type of school. Of the different approaches for organizing instruction, which approach do you think David should suggest for this type of school? What additional information would he need to make a recommendation?

Instructional practices differ among schools, and exciting discussions are underway about the goals and objectives of education and the ways in which teachers and students interact. Increasing attention is being given to discussions about the characteristics of effective schools. As you study, observe, and analyze the practices found in today's classrooms and schools, this chapter should provide you with information that will help you to:

- Describe the difference between educational goals and instructional objectives.
- Relate the ways in which district goals, objectives, and outcomes will affect how a teacher organizes instruction and works with students.
- Discuss methods of organizing for instruction.
- Differentiate between mastery learning and powerful learning.

- Compare and contrast four different teaching strategies.
- Discuss the assumptions about student learning in the different models for school improvement.
- Identify your personal learning style.
- Discuss the characteristics of effective schools.

Schools for All

The organization of America's schools and the ways that teachers work with students in the classroom are extensions of the overarching goals of American education. The public schools and the classrooms are the arena in which the goal of free public instruction for all citizens is achieved.

This chapter reviews various instructional practices associated with good teaching and the characteristics of different school improvement models. Rather than advocating a particular approach, the focus is on different techniques and approaches that teachers and schools may use for different purposes with different groups of students. First, attention is given to the importance of instructional goals and objectives in schools. The second section contains a discussion of how schools and classrooms may be organized for instruction. Teaching strategies are discussed in the third section, followed by an overview of the concepts of mastery learning and powerful learning. The concluding section contains a discussion of school improvement models.

Instructional Goals and Objectives

How can a teacher demonstrate democratic principles in the classroom?

An overarching goal of American public education, and thus of states, school districts, and individual schools, has been to provide free public instruction for all citizens. This goal, together with more specific educational and instructional goals, should guide school districts and schools as they select educational and instructional objectives. The interaction between educational goals and objectives is discussed in the following paragraphs.

Educational Goals

In making decisions about education, the first issue is to decide what to teach. To make that decision, educators and policy makers need clearly defined goals and objectives for instruction and information about the roles and responsibilities of learners in relation to the specific goals and objectives.

Educational goals are ideals you intend to reach or your accomplishment targets. They may be goals for you as a teacher, goals for your students, or joint goals (Kellough & Kellough, 1999). Examples of goal statements are:

- The learner will develop basic math skills.
- The learner will develop an appreciation of poetry.
- The learner will develop an understanding of World War II.

Educational goals are general statements about directions toward which we want learning outcomes to lead; *educational objectives* are more specific. Rather than identifying specific skills, educational goals describe characteristics or attributes of what society considers to be a well-educated person. Goals are to be the result or cumulative effect of a series of learnings. Obviously, as defined, goals

Figure 15.1: Criteria for Educational Objectives

1. The place or condition for learning is established. Specific references should be made to the activity in which the goal is to be attained, i.e., test, game, laboratory experiment, recital, or report on an activity.
2. The learner's behavior is stated in measurable and observable terms. The types of evidence need to be stated clearly, i.e., completion of a specific test or experiment, completion of a recital, or submission of a written report.
3. The minimally acceptable level of performance is stated. Examples include the desired percentage of correct responses on the test, the maximum number of permissible errors in the recital, and the desired length of the report and number of permissible grammatical errors.

Source: Kourilsky, M., & Quaranta, L. (1987). *Effective teaching: Principles and practice.* Glenview, IL: Scott, Foresman.

designate the desired outcome of instruction but lack the specificity to actually implement an instructional sequence (Kellough & Kellough, 1999). That is where educational objectives come into play.

Educational Objectives

An *educational objective* is a clearly defined, observable, and measurable student behavior that indicates learner progress toward the achievement of a particular educational goal. Educational objectives also are referred to as instructional or behavioral objectives. An educational objective should meet the criteria listed in Figure 15.1.

Educational or instructional objectives are used to operationalize educational goals. Reference is often made to a more specific term, *behavioral objectives.* Unlike other types of educational objectives, behavioral objectives force the teacher to describe the learning outcomes from the learner's viewpoint. Behavioral objectives answer the questions How do you know the learner has learned? and What is the learner to do to prove he/she has learned? (Jacobsen, Eggen, & Kauchak, 1999; Mager, 1997). Examples of behavioral objectives are shown in Figure 15.2.

Figure 15.2: Examples of Educational or Behavioral Objectives

1. The student provides the correct answer for 90% or more of the items on the test.
2. The student places 50% or more of the arrows within six inches of the center of the target.
3. The student dissects the frog and correctly identifies and labels each part of the frog stipulated in the exercise.
4. The student is present for all rehearsals, arrives on time for the recital, and is error-free in the recital.
5. The student prepares a 10-page report on an activity with five or fewer spelling errors and no incomplete sentences.

Figure 15.3: Levels of Bloom's Taxonomy

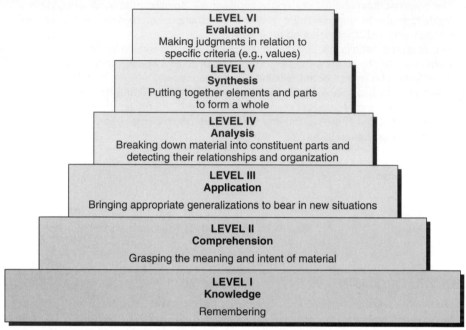

Source: Kourilsky, M., & Quaranta, L. (1987). *Effective teaching: Principles and practice.* Glenview, IL: Scott, Foresman.

Taxonomies of Educational Objectives

In the development of educational objectives, a taxonomy or classification system is needed. Benjamin S. Bloom has developed a widely used hierarchy of levels of intellectual behavior referred to in the literature as *Bloom's Taxonomy of Educational Objectives* (Bloom, 1956). The levels are listed in Figure 15.3. This hierarchy is helpful in delineating the increasingly complex levels of the intellectual process. It is also important when planning instruction to incorporate activities from the full range of levels in students' learning experiences to stimulate and develop their intellectual skills. This is especially true relative to helping students master what is popularly referred to as higher order thinking skills (HOTS). The higher order thinking skills in Bloom's Taxonomy are analysis, synthesis, and evaluation.

Goals and objectives become the structure that schools and teachers use in determining how they will organize for instruction. As indicated in the following section, several different approaches are used.

Organizing for Instruction

Teachers and principals can be creative in organizing schools and students. Typically, students are treated as members of a group, but the group does not have to

Table 15.1: Types of Instruction

Type of Instruction	Teacher's Role	Typical Activity
Group instruction	Provides formal instruction Monitors class activity	American history: Teacher gives formal lecture on historical facts.
Cooperative learning	Sets the stage for learning Facilitates groups of students Organizes the structure of the classroom	U.S. presidents: Class is divided into teams of three or four students. Each team is responsible for conducting research on one U.S. president.
Individualized instruction	Acts as resource person Guides and monitors student's learning	Reading: Each student is assigned a different short story according to his/her reading ability.
Independent instruction	Negotiates topics and assignments with students Consults and advises students Evaluates student's learning activities	English: Each student consults individually with the teacher and is given a special essay topic.
Mastery learning	Provides formal instruction Administers formative tests Provides feedback to students	Math: students work progressively through the basic math facts (e.g., addition before subtraction).

include the entire class; students may be clustered into smaller groups with similar interests or instructional needs. An alternative to group instruction is cooperative learning in which the teacher encourages students to work together in addressing problems; the teacher provides the initial leadership in defining the activity and functions as a resource person for the process. Another alternative is individualized instruction in which the teacher works with each student on a one-to-one basis diagnosing, prescribing, and evaluating progress. Independent learning can be viewed as an extension of individualized instruction, but the responsibility of the student is increased and the teacher is not as closely involved with the student. Additional descriptions of each of these types of instruction are found in the following discussion. Table 15.1 summarizes the principal types of instruction with brief information about the teacher's role and an example of a typical activity.

Group Instruction

Much classroom teaching can be classified as *group instruction*. The teacher either views all students in the room as members of a single group or divides the class into subgroups. In the first instance, the setting is teacher dominated. Various instructional strategies may be used, but individualization often is sacrificed in an effort to accommodate the needs and interests of the group.

When subgroups are used, the role of the teacher changes. Major portions of the teacher's time are spent planning, coordinating, and monitoring the activities of the subgroups. For the groups to function, students must assume more responsibility for their learning. The capacity of the group to teach itself is enhanced because students typically are assigned to subgroups on the basis of special needs or interests.

How can a teacher work with a group of students and still individualize instruction?

Cooperative learning provides an opportunity for students to learn by working together with the teacher serving as a resource person. These experiences provide a model for lifelong learning.

A major challenge for the teacher in group instruction is to develop ways to organize teaching/learning activities for the entire group, while at the same time recognizing individual differences among students. Thus, in planning the group activities, the teacher also must be sensitive to the needs of individual students.

Cooperative Learning

In *cooperative learning,* students work in small groups rather than as individuals. This teamwork fosters the development of an interdependence and helps students develop social skills. The groups often are considered to be heterogeneous in terms of contribution and/or classroom performance, and students have the opportunity to learn from their peers. The result of this interaction is a higher noise level in the classroom, sometimes referred to as the "busy hum of learning." Since the group often is the unit that is evaluated, students are rewarded for helping one another. Rather than being in competition with each other, they have a reduced likelihood of failure and an increased probability of success because of the combined resources of the group. Depending on the specific content, teachers can vary their instructional approach. The teacher still has responsibility for setting the stage and working with students, but students work in groups rather than as individuals (Orlich, Harder, Callahan, & Gibson, 1998).

The positive effects of cooperative learning in elementary and secondary schools appear to be associated with two essential elements—group goals and individual accountability (Slavin, 1989). By working together, students have the opportunity to exercise leadership and also reap the benefits of other indicators of group success. As individuals, they are responsible for their personal performance and achievement. Peer tutors and support groups can be especially useful in breaking down some of the barriers found in multicultural schools.

For several reasons, the use of cooperative learning as the organizing scheme in the classroom is likely to increase. First, research findings are positive. Students who have had good experiences in cooperative learning are more willing to participate in the instructional approach and will have a higher level of confidence as they become involved. Second, the likelihood of cooperative learning becoming more commonplace also is enhanced because this approach is frequently employed in preservice and inservice education for teachers. Last, and possibly most important, students and teachers seem to enjoy this method of organizing the classroom for instruction (Slavin, 1989).

Equity in the treatment and expectations of students is one problem with cooperative learning; teachers tend to have high expectations of high-status students and low expectations of low-status or disadvantaged students. The challenge is to make cooperative learning a positive experience for all students. Because of the complexities of cooperative learning, the experience can be positive for all students if the teacher recognizes individual differences and has mixed expectations of competence from all students. For this to be successful, the teacher must convince the student of three things:

1. The cooperative task requires many different intellectual abilities.
2. No one student will have all of these abilities.
3. Every student will have some of these abilities (Cohen, 1998).

Individualized Instruction

Individualizing instruction for each student is a worthy but difficult goal. Traditionally, schools have been organized to provide instruction for groups of students. When the group approach is not successful in addressing the specific instructional needs of a few students, *individualized instruction* often is used as an alternative. The teacher assumes the role of a resource person who guides and monitors the student's learning rather than providing formal instruction in a traditional class setting.

Individualized instruction also may be used to cope with teaching and/or learning differences in the classroom. The approach can be especially effective as teachers work with gifted and talented students or slow learners in the same classroom.

What different teaching styles have you encountered in your schooling?

Independent Learning

In this organizational option, topics or assignments are negotiated between the student and the teacher on an individual basis. Then students assume personal responsibility for their learning; the role of the teacher is to facilitate the process. The teacher functions first as a consultant/adviser to the student and later as an evaluator of the student's learning activities.

Rather than being an option restricted to gifted and talented students, *independent learning* can be used with most students. As they work independently, students learn to set goals, plan their learning, and assume personal responsibility for their programs. Students thus assume an increased level of responsibility for their own schooling. The teacher's responsibilities are different with different students. Success is measured by the extent to which the student completes the topics or assignments in a timely manner at the predetermined level of quality.

A range of student-centered teaching methodologies may be used in independent learning. They include programmed instruction, self-paced instruction, contract learning, and performance-based instruction, which are often collectively labeled personalized systems of instruction (PSI). These methodologies are individually based, student-paced instructional models in which students learn independently of their classmates. PSI may be an appropriate mode of instruction if the teacher is guided by the following assumptions: (1) students are not homogeneous; (2) as they mature, students' heterogeneity increases; and (3) most students will learn best if allowed to learn at their own pace (Guskey, 1985).

A classroom operating exclusively under a PSI format is a rarity. One of the greatest potential problems with the PSI format is that, once established, the system can run so smoothly that teachers feel they have nothing to do and end up behind their desks. Rightfully, under this mode of instruction, the teacher is liberated to work individually with students. Another potential problem is that administrators accustomed to the more traditional teacher-centered forms of instruction have difficulty evaluating both PSI instruction and the teacher using the methodology. A final problem is how to orient students effectively so that they can work independently and sustain their self-motivation.

Models of Instruction

Historically, teachers have used different strategies, tactics, or methods depending on their personal talents, the content to be taught, and the interests and abilities of the students. As discussed in Chapter 1, teaching is often described as an art. This does not imply that teachers operate without design or planning; rather, it underscores the need for teachers to understand and be able to use a variety of strategies as they work with students.

How will you as a teacher determine the instructional strategy that you will use in the classroom?

Teaching has also been described as a craft or an applied science (Tom, 1984). In fact, it may be inappropriate to assume that teaching should take a single form. In a recent survey of teachers, about 95% of the respondents indicated that they made some use of a variety of teaching methods in addition to lecturing; examples included cooperative learning and hands-on experiences (NEA Research, 1997). Adler (1984) refers to three types of teaching: didactic instruction, coaching, and Socratic questioning. In didactic teaching, students acquire knowledge by becoming actively engaged in instruction through question and answer strategies. Coaching calls on the teacher to prepare the student for exhibiting a skill in public. Socratic questioning does not assume that the teacher or the student knows all the answers; the goal is to develop an understanding of ideas and values. Adler's ideal teacher possesses a blend of instructional skills, judgment about student understanding of the material, expertise on the subject matter, and the capacity to communicate effectively with individuals and groups (Duke, 1984).

Traditional patterns in which teachers may select their teaching strategy on the basis of personal preference are being challenged. Historically, teachers and schools have tended to assume that all children learn in the same way and thus teachers could be free to select the teaching strategy of their choice. In their efforts to work with at-risk youth, educators have come to recognize that each student has special talents and abilities that can be addressed in each classroom. If teachers are to be successful in working with all students, they will need to have the skills to recognize and respond to the diverse abilities and needs of students. This assumes that teachers and schools will have the means needed to reconstruct their teaching practices and environment to provide meaningful learning opportunities for all students. The challenge is to discover the strengths of each student and gear the learning opportunities to the abilities, interests, and experiences of the child.

This recognition of individual differences and strengths can be traced to the research of Howard Gardner (1993) at Harvard University, which led to the proposition that children have multiple intelligences. His research focused on the symbol-using capabilities of children and the breakdown of cognitive capacities in individuals suffering from brain damage. He concluded that different kinds of symbols involve separate psychological processes; this led to the conclusion that human cognitive competence is pluralistic rather than unitary (Haggerty, 1995).

Based on Gardner's research, a wider and more universal set of competencies has been identified to encompass the realm of human cognition. The result was the identification of the following set of seven intelligences:

- Linguistic intelligence refers to the use of words orally and in writing and the manipulation of language structure. These persons have highly developed auditory skills and like to use words to express themselves. They excel in the academic environment.
- Logical mathematical intelligence is the capacity to use numbers and reasoning in logical patterns and relationships. These persons enjoy work with data, mathematical problems, and strategy games.
- Spatial intelligence refers to the use of pictures and images with a sensitivity to color, line, shape, and form and their interrelationships. These persons tend to think in pictures and are visual learners.
- Bodily-kinesthetic intelligence is the expression of ideas and feelings through the use of one's body. Using physical skills such as coordination, balance, and dexterity, these persons like to move around, act things out, and touch persons during the discussion. They prefer to communicate through demonstration.
- Musical intelligence uses musical forms as a means of expression, perception, and transformation of thoughts. These persons are sensitive to environmental and musical sounds, and often hum or sing while they work.

- Interpersonal intelligence refers to perceiving and making distinctions in the words, intentions, motivations, and feelings of others. These persons like to work in groups and serve as mentors.
- Intrapersonal intelligence is the use of self-knowledge and the ability to adapt on the basis of that knowledge. These persons tend to be independent and self-directed; they are intuitive and often introverts (Armstrong, 1994).

The assumption undergirding this theory of multiple intelligences is that each person possesses all seven intelligences and can develop all to competency. Each is interwoven into the complex fabric of an individual. Thus, there is no single expression of intelligence (Gardner, 1993).

The development and acceptance of the *multiple intelligences theory* has direct implications for teachers. The assumption is that all students are born, to varying degrees, with the seven areas of intelligence. It becomes critical that teachers respect and nurture each student's special interests and talents. When teachers develop the skills required to recognize this perspective in their practice, classrooms will become friendlier places for all students. The result is that the teacher strives to meet the needs of each student in a personalized way (Rea & Warkentin, 1997). One implication is that each classroom should have a series of learning centers in which students have access to the equipment and supplies that will enable them to use their particular intelligence in solving problems (Armstrong, 1994).

Models of instruction may be grouped into six categories: expository, demonstration, inquiry or discovery, critical thinking, mastery learning, and powerful learning. Rather than selecting a single method of instruction, the effective teacher should be familiar with, and understand, how to use a variety of methods in response to different teaching/learning opportunities. Summary information on the models of instruction is presented in Table 15.2. The table summarizes the roles of teachers and students, strengths and weaknesses of each model, needed resources, and evaluation procedures.

Expository Instruction

Expository instruction, a teacher-centered method, conveys information. The most common forms of expository instruction are formal lecture, informal lecture, and teacher-led discussion. Expository instruction is considered appropriate when (1) all students need to know an essential body of knowledge and (2) the students are relatively homogeneous in their ability and knowledge of the topic.

In expository instruction, the teacher controls and directs the learning process. The teacher also determines the methods of presentation, the pace of instruction, the quantity of supervised practice or reinforcement, and the form of student evaluation. The student is expected to listen, read, and answer questions as the teacher directs.

If expository instruction is to be effective, the teacher should keep in mind that students differ in their levels of competence and that expository instruction requires more extensive and detailed daily lesson planning. Some would contend that lectures virtually need to be scripted. The structure and direction of the lecture or discussion should be obvious to the learner. Further, even with extensive preparation and a quality presentation, the teacher must realize that portions of the information contained in a lecture will have to be repeated or retaught (Barone, 1989; Cuban, 1989).

Demonstration Instruction

In demonstration instruction, the student learns through doing and/or observing. This method includes laboratory experiments, dramatizations, constructions, recitations, and exhibitions. Demonstration instruction is assumed appropriate when (1) the student's level of understanding will be enhanced by observing or working with a functioning model or guide, and (2) the student has sufficient background and maturity to understand the value or relevance of the demonstration. The teacher plans, organizes, and usually conducts the demonstration.

Properly conducted and supervised, this methodology can be most effective; however, the learner must have sufficient prior knowledge to benefit from the demonstration. For this reason, demonstration instruction is often preceded by expository instruction. The teacher's ability to teach skills is critical to the effectiveness of this methodology. The teacher must be capable of conducting the demonstration effectively. For example, the teacher who "cannot carry a tune" is not the teacher who should sing the scale in a vocal music class. The demonstration should relate directly to the specific instructional objectives; if it does not, the demonstration may be merely an effort to entertain students. Preparation and concerns about all students being able to see the demonstration are critical elements in demonstration instruction (Kellough & Kellough, 1999).

Inquiry Instruction

Inquiry instruction was first made popular in America by John Dewey at the beginning of this century. (See Chapter 7 for additional discussion.) Subsequently, other authors have referred to this method of instruction as problem solving, the inductive method, creative thinking, the scientific method, or conceptual learning. The underlying presumption is that students would prefer seeking knowledge than having it provided to them through demonstrations and textbook readings. As the concept has developed, the ultimate form of inquiry instruction occurs when students recognize and identify the problem as well as decide the process and reach the conclusion (Kellough & Kellough, 1999).

The relationships between constructivism and inquiry instruction are very strong. In inquiry instruction, the assumption is that students construct their knowledge. The teacher, the classroom, the school, and the community provide the setting and support that will encourage students through process. Because of differences among students, knowledge is constructed through different processes and patterns of thinking. Through engagement in the learning process, the learner becomes active and assumes responsibility for acquiring and applying knowledge (Orlich, Harder, Callahan, & Gibson, 1998).

Reflective thinking or inquiry instruction takes place when a person is faced with a problem or forced choice. Students generate ideas and then identify ways to test the ideas. The five phases of the inquiry cycle are identification or

Table 15.2: Models of Instruction

	Teacher's Role	*Student's Role*	*Strengths*
Expository instruction	• Teacher-centered • Controls and directs the learning process • Determines methods of presentation	• Follow the leader • Listens, reads, and answers teacher-directed questions	• Best method for students grouped homogeneously by ability
Demonstration instruction	• Plans, organizes, and conducts the demonstration	• Observes, listens and participates as directed	• Retention is enhanced by active participation
Inquiry or discovery instruction	• Guides the learning process • Stimulates and challenges learners	• Student-centered activities • Self-directed critical thinking and problem solving	• Encourages higher order thinking skills • Challenges gifted/talented students
Critical thinking	• Facilitates the learning process • "Nondirected" • Stimulates and challenges learners • Empowers students	• Finds out information for themselves • Asks questions, rather than being asked questions	• Encourages higher order thinking skills and problem solving
Mastery learning	• Identifies content and predetermined outcomes that are expected of all students • Modifies and adapts instruction to learning preferences of students	• Demonstrates mastery of the learning units	• Enables teachers to address the special needs of students • Provides students with success at each stage in learning process
Powerful learning	• Identifies learning opportunities based on students' life experiences	• Constructs meaning in school activities from their own experiences	• Consistent with what is known about learning • Builds on student interests

recognition of the problem, application of thought or exploration of the problem, organization and analysis of the data, identification of a tentative conclusion, and testing of the conclusion (Kellough & Kellough, 1999). Each phase is part of well-designed inquiry instruction. The sequence of the inquiry process is illustrated in Figure 15.4. The activity is student centered; the most common forms are oral and written student reports and nonmathematical problem-solving activities. In contrast to other forms of instruction or teaching, the "transmission of the accumulated knowledge and wisdom of a culture" is not the primary role of inquiry instruction (Skinner, 1965). Students use the process to develop a better understanding of current knowledge and create new knowledge.

Table 15.2: *(continued)*

Weaknesses	Resources	Evaluation
• Principles not consistent with meeting the needs of individual students	• Filmstrips • Films • Slides • Video tapes • Guest speakers	• Standardized tests • Teacher-written criterion-referenced tests
• Students must have prior knowledge to benefit from demonstration	• Science labs • Computer labs • Drama classrooms • Specialized materials	• Written exams • Student products (e.g., lab reports, computer programs discussion, etc.)
• Takes a sophisticated learner to really be effective	• Topics and ideas for exploration • Research tools	• Oral and written student reports • Standardized tests that focus on higher order thinking skills and problem solving
• Many teachers find this method difficult	• Topics and ideas for exploration • Research tools	• Standardized tests that focus on higher order thinking skills and problem solving • Open-ended questions
• Students will attain mastery at different rates • Mastery of the content of one unit does not necessarily ensure transfer to future learning	• Learning packets for each unit • Corrective/remedial instructional materials • Instructional materials	• Administration of formative tests until students demonstrate mastery
• Need for teachers to respond to students' differences in life experiences, learning rates, and styles	• Materials related to complex and authentic problems in the life experiences of students	• Evidence of the development of the skills required to solve problems

Successful inquiry instruction is dependent upon the effective interaction of sophisticated students and teachers in a supportive learning environment. Students and teachers must be comfortable with the challenges and the freedoms associated with the student-centered dimensions of the inquiry process. Successful inquiry instruction in today's educational environment requires that students have easy access to research tools and educational technology and be free to use them at their own pace.

Critical Thinking Instruction

When the development of *critical thinking* is the instructional goal, the student becomes more active and responsible and the teacher becomes less dominant.

Figure 15.4: The Inquiry Cycle

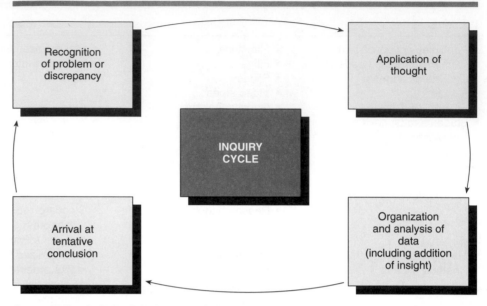

Source: Kellough, R. D., & Kellough, N. G. (1999). *Secondary school teaching: A guide to methods and resources.* Columbus, OH: Merrill.

The teacher organizes and provides direction for student learning, but the student is an active rather than passive participant. The teacher is no longer the center of activity. In both the critical thinking and the inquiry models, the teacher is a guide, facilitator, stimulator, even a cheerleader who challenges learners. In essence, the teacher abdicates his/her position and empowers students. However, the teacher often assumes the role of the devil's advocate and forces students to defend and explain their positions.

Analytical or higher order thinking skills are the central elements in the process of critical thinking. Students who become critical thinkers can view problems in different dimensions and consider problems in a larger context. They seek maximum information before deciding on a course of action. Rather than finding quick and simple solutions to complex problems, critical thinkers not only examine the particular problem as an individual issue but also consider it in the larger dimension of related issues (Ellis, Mackey, & Glenn, 1988). Teachers and students become active in identifying and seeking solutions to problems. The process of critical thinking is illustrated in Figure 15.5.

The problems associated with this mode of instruction are primarily an outgrowth of teachers' experiences as students; teachers tend to teach as they were taught. For this reason, teachers often have difficulty adapting to change. Most teachers were taught by expository instruction; to teach and help students learn differently requires a totally new orientation. Few teachers have observed, let alone experienced, critical thinking or inquiry instruction as methods of learning.

Figure 15.5: The Process of Critical Thinking

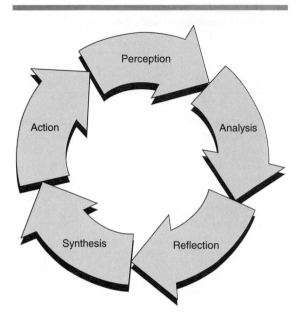

Mastery Learning

Mastery learning is based on a set of assumptions about both the content and the process of learning. Mastery learning assumes a uniform set of predetermined expected outcomes that all students are expected to master and assumes that learning is a sequential linear process. However, the teacher will find that students differ in their learning styles. Some will be primarily verbal learners, others will be primarily visual learners, and others may be primarily kinesthetic learners. The challenge to the teacher is to recognize and respond to the different learning styles and preferences of the students (Kellough & Kellough, 1999).

Mastery learning is a process for teaching and learning advocated by Benjamin S. Bloom of the University of Chicago. The basic assumptions of mastery learning are that (1) mastery learning is possible for all students if the learning units are small enough; (2) for quality learning to occur, the instruction rather than the students must be modified and adapted; (3) some students will take longer to attain mastery than others; (4) most learning outcomes can be observed or measured; (5) most learning units are sequential and logical; and (6) students can experience success at each phase of the instructional process. Thus, the concepts from one unit are built upon and extended by the next unit. Mastery learning is generally taught through group instruction and therefore is primarily teacher centered. Table 15.3 shows the major differences between mastery learning and other systems of instruction (Kellough & Kellough, 1999).

The mastery learning instructional format assumes that the teacher presents the learning unit and then administers what is called the first formative test. The purpose of the test is to check learning progress and provide the students with

How do the different modes of instruction affect the role and responsibility of the student, affect the teacher?

Table 15.3: Major Differences Between Mastery Learning and Personalized Systems of Instruction

| | Model | |
Characteristic	Mastery Learning	Personalized Systems of Instruction
Basis of instruction	Group	Individual
Pace of instruction	Teacher, determined	Student determined
Primary source of instruction	Teacher, supplemented by materials	Materials, supplemented by the teacher
Standard of mastery	80–90%	100%
Number of retake tests per unit	One	As many as needed for mastery
Correctives	New and different approach	Repetition of original material
Major applications	Elementary and secondary levels	College level

feedback and suggestions to help them overcome any difficulties they are experiencing. Following the test, students who have not mastered the material are provided corrective work for a few class periods. Then a second parallel test is administered to ensure that the students have achieved mastery before the class moves on to the next learning unit. Students who demonstrated mastery on the first formative test are given enrichment activities during the corrective phase of instruction. Figure 15.6 illustrates the mastery learning instructional process.

Mastery learning enables the teacher to address the special needs of students in multicultural environments. Critics, however, assert that the process has been oversimplified, that mastery of the individual units does not necessarily transfer to future learning, and that students cannot be expected to learn and achieve at the mastery level indefinitely.

Powerful Learning

As an alternative to mastery learning, the concept of *powerful learning* has evolved from Henry Levin's work on "accelerated schools" (Levin, 1996; Levin, 1997). An underlying assumption is that the educational experiences provided to gifted students work best for all students. The challenge is to create situations that encompass the best that is known about learning and about the children in the school. If students see meaning in their lessons and perceive connections between the activities and their lives, the concept assumes that they will become active learners and build on their own strengths.

Powerful learning assumes that students, who bring different life experiences to the learning setting, should become active learners and build upon their strengths. The assumption is (1) that students can, and should, differ in the degree to which they attain or exceed mastery, and (2) that learning is a random interactive process that may occur in spurts.

Figure 15.6: The Mastery Learning Instructional Process; (a) Instructional Sequence and (b) Achievement Distribution Curve in a Mastery Learning Classroom

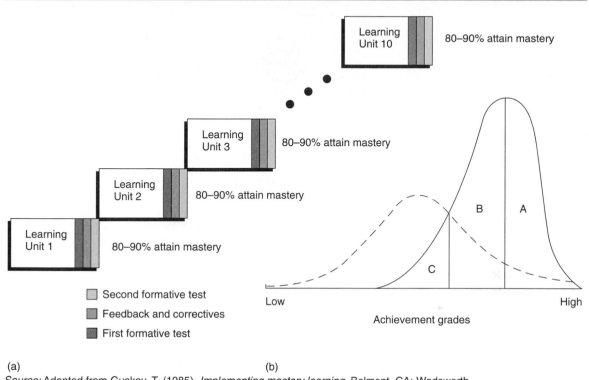

(a)   (b)

Source: Adapted from Guskey, T. (1985). *Implementing mastery learning.* Belmont, CA: Wadsworth.

Learning experiences are considered to have three dimensions. The first dimension is what is learned; this includes the content or curricular knowledge and beliefs about one's abilities and relationships to the world. The second is how the content is learned through various opportunities and forms of instruction. The third is the context in which learning experiences come together to provide a setting for the what and how. These include time and resources, flexibility of schedule, and the environment (Hopfenberg, Levin, & Associates, 1993).

The concept of powerful learning is consistent with the constructivism view of learning and with brain research about learning. Students are active participants as they construct meaning from their own experiences and the prior knowledge in their various intelligences (Gardner, 1993). Students will learn at different rates and in different ways as they draw upon their personal abilities, knowledge, and experiences in the process of solving problems. Under these assumptions, students learn best when they are provided with complex, complete, and authentic problems.

Powerful learning occurs when teachers and the school make use of knowledge about what students like, need, and want to learn; how students learn best;

**Figure 15.7: Components of
Powerful Learning**

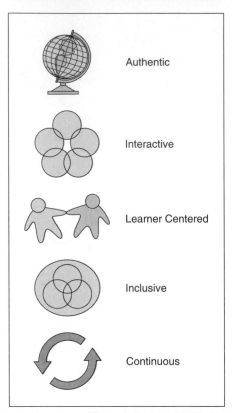

Authentic

Interactive

Learner Centered

Inclusive

Continuous

Source: National Center for the Accelerated Schools Project. (1997). *Training packet.* Stanford, CA: Stanford University, p. 3.

and the contexts that best support and promote their learning. The concept assumes that these three dimensions are totally and necessarily integrated. For the concept of powerful learning to become a reality, schools will be required to make modifications in curricular content, time on task, and mode of instruction.

As illustrated in Figure 15.7, powerful learning has five components. First, it is authentic because it builds upon student interests; the topic can emerge from questions that have relevance to the lives of students. Second, it is interactive in that it builds upon strengths of resources in the school community. Third, it is learner centered in that the focus changes in response to student interests. Fourth, through a variety of teaching and learning methods, powerful learning is inclusive and builds on strengths and interests of all students. Fifth, it is continuous in that there is no end to a topic; students are empowered to guide the learning as they raise and explore the answers to additional questions (National Center for the Accelerated Schools Project, 1997).

If teaching and learning are active, participative processes, students will develop the higher order thinking skills needed to acquire and integrate knowledge in solving problems.

Relationships Between Learning and Teaching

Various proposals to reform, reinvent, and restructure schools as ways to improve education have come from both public and private sources. Many of the recommendations have focused on the mandates and admonitions designed to change school operation or programs as a means to improve student performance. Major emphasis has been placed on modifying the structure or the decision-making process. However, one of the problems with education reform is that the simplistic prescriptions are not consistent with what educational research says about teaching and learning. After a decade of school reform recommendations, questions are being raised about whether sufficient attention is being given to the most critical consideration—the relationship between how teachers teach and how children learn. Marzano (1992) indicated that the challenge is to base school reform decisions on what is known about how children learn.

Students vary greatly in their learning styles. The complexity of this concept is illustrated by the following definition of learning style that was developed by the National Task Force on Learning Style and Brain Behavior:

> Learning style is that consistent pattern of behavior and performance by which an individual approaches educational experiences. It is the composite of characteristic cognitive, affective, and physiological behaviors that serve as relatively stable indicators of how a learner perceives, interacts with, and responds to the learning environment. It is formed in the deep structure of neural organization and personality [that] molds and is molded by human development and the cultural experiences of home, school, and society. (Cited in Parkay & Stanford, 1995, p. 336)

Each student's learning style is determined by the interaction of hereditary and environmental influences. Some learn best through seeing; others learn best by hearing. Some need structure and directions; others need independence and freedom. Some need total silence; others can function in a noisy environment. The critical point is that there is no one correct view of learning style to guide teachers in their decision making (Parkay & Stanford, 1995). The Historical Note on page 519 describes the work of Polingagsi Qöyawayma with Hopi students which emphasized the importance of adapting teaching to the learning styles and experiences of the students.

McCarthy (1997) has identified four separate learning styles. The *imaginative learner* perceives information concretely and processes it reflectively. The *analytical learner* perceives information abstractly and processes it reflectively. The *common sense learner* perceives information abstractly and processes it actively. The *dynamic learner* perceives information concretely and processes it actively. The challenges for the teacher are to recognize that each classroom likely will have one or more of each type of learner and to provide instruction that will be meaningful to each student.

Curriculum development work by Dunn (1995) contributed to the identification of distinct differences in the ways that students responded to materials. Some liked to work alone, and others preferred working in groups or with the teacher. He identified four variables that affected a student's learning style:

- Learning environment
- Emotional support
- Peer interaction
- Personal and physical preferences

School Improvement Models

The education reform movement in the 1980s and 1990s challenged many of the traditional assumptions about the learning potential of disadvantaged youth and the power of the school to affect student performance. Following the initial work in the 1970s on the concept of effective schools, educational researchers worked

Historical Note

Polingaysi Qöyawayma

Polingaysi Qöyawayma (1892–1990) was an innovator in shaping American Indian education in the United States and preserving the cultural traditions of the Hopi Indians. (Her English name was Elizabeth White.) As one of nine children in a traditional Hopi family, she was educated by missionaries, taught in schools operated by the Bureau of Indian Affairs, and was influential in Indian education because of her emphasis on the importance of basing education on the content and examples from the lives of students.

After having first been hidden by her mother to avoid attending the BIA school in which the Hopi language could not be spoken and students were given English names, Polingaysi became curious and followed her sister to school. When she heard about an opportunity to attend school in "the land of the oranges," she persevered until her parents reluctantly gave their permission. She rode in a wagon to Winslow, Arizona, and took the train to the Sherman Indian Institute in Riverside, California. She was there for four years without returning home. Upon her return, she attempted to become a missionary to the Hopis, but found neither success nor fulfillment because of the conflict with traditional Hopi beliefs.

Polingaysi then became a teacher in the BIA schools. Very soon, she became concerned because the teaching materials, illustrations, and photographs were not within the life experiences of Indian students. To provide a more realistic educational environment, she took the students into the natural surroundings and used Hopi legends, songs, and stories. Students translated these stories into English. Polingaysi's goal was to blend the best of the Hopi culture with the best of the white man's culture and to retain the essence of good from this blend. After initial skepticism, her supervisors began to support her teaching efforts. With the appointment of John Collier as Commissioner of Indian Affairs, Polingaysi found unexpected support for her teaching methods. She was chosen to demonstrate her teaching methods at a summer institute for BIA teachers. The focus was on starting the teaching/learning process by basing teachings on what students already know rather than utilizing a totally new set of experiences. If teachers and students met on mutual ground, students tended to come out of their shells and become active learners. In her life as a teacher, Polingaysi learned to meet criticism with serenity and to appreciate the good in both the Hopi and non-Hopi ways of life.

Source: Reyhner, J. (1994). Polingaysi Qöyawayma. In M.S. Seller (Ed.), *Women educators in the United States, 1820–1993* (pp. 397–402). Westport, CT: Greenwood Press.

---

for two decades to identify the conditions that contribute to differences in effectiveness among schools (Edmonds, 1979; Edmonds, 1982; Westbrook, 1982; Clark, Lotto, & Astuto, 1984). The typical characteristics of effective schools are summarized in Figure 15.8.

A school's culture often is not listed among the correlates of effective schools, but this condition can be a positive or negative influence on the learning environment. Thus, school culture will play an important role in school reform and improvement efforts. The elements that make up school culture are diverse and complex; they range from the quality and quantity of the interactions among staff members to the noise levels in the halls and cafeteria, and from the physical environment of the school to student and faculty feelings about the safety of the school. No single factor determines a school's culture; the interaction of multiple factors

Figure 15.8: Characteristics of an Effective School

Strong administrative leadership
- Principal has a clear vision about the desired direction of the school.
- Principal has a commitment to improvement of instruction.
- Principal encourages participative decision making.
- Principal serves as a buffer for teachers so that they can devote maximum time to working with students.

Safe and orderly environment
- Working conditions support the efforts of teachers to address specific problems of their students.
- Environment is conducive to teaching and learning.

Emphasis on instruction in the basic skills
- The school has a commitment to the basic skills as instructional goals.
- Basic skills are the foundation for higher order thinking skills.

High teacher expectations of students
- Teachers set high performance standards for students.
- Teachers provide specific instructions and are sensitive to individual differences.
- Teachers use clear and appropriate rewards to recognize student work.

Monitoring and reporting student performance
- Systematic methods are used to assess student progress.
- Curriculum is aligned across subject areas and grades.
- Curriculum, desired outcomes, and assessment activities all match.

Necessary resources to meet objectives
- Sufficient personnel and materials are available in the school.
- Sufficient time is provided for instructional planning, staff development, and adapting new innovations.
- Opportunities are provided for professional growth.

Culture of the school
- Positive human interactions exist among students and teachers.
- Continuous growth and development of students and teachers is encouraged.
- State-of-the-art instructional practices and strategies are provided for teaching and learning.

either facilitates or hinders teaching and learning (Freiberg, 1998). However, school leaders (principals, teachers, and parents) can take actions to improve the culture of a school. Peterson and Deal (1998) contend that the common elements in schools with strong, positive cultures include:

1. A shared sense of purpose among the staff with high commitment to teaching.
2. Underlying norms of collegiality, improvement, and hard work.
3. The use of rituals and traditions to celebrate student accomplishment, teacher innovation, and parental commitment.
4. An informal network that provides and maintains a social web of information, support, and history.
5. A prevailing attitude in the school of success, joy, and humor. (Peterson & Deal, 1998)

From the early research on effective schools, various educational researchers began to devote their energies to the design and development of several school improvement models. Their initial efforts were underway when state legislatures began to enact legislation that called for improvement in school and student performance and greater accountability in the public schools. There seems to be general agreement that implementation of many school reforms requires a change in the ways that schools operate. The challenge is for schools to become more effective as they are confronted with changes in the composition of their student bodies and the world scene, as well as changes in educational programs and output expectations. National attention is being drawn to the importance of America's public schools providing an education that will help all students attain the national standards including those who are disadvantaged and at risk of school failure. A variety of program and school reform approaches are available to help schools respond to the challenge (Herman & Stringfield, 1997). As schools examine and review the different models to determine the extent to which they have been effective and appropriate for the school, two critical questions in selecting a model are:

1. Is the model appropriate for the specific needs and conditions of the school community?
2. What commitment and/or resources must be provided to implement the model successfully?

The following school improvement models are externally developed models. Among them, the common expectation is that the school will implement the model in a manner consistent with the model's philosophy and design.

Comer Model (School Development Program)

Developed by Professor James Comer and his colleagues at the Yale Child Study Center, the *School Development Program* is a schoolwide restructuring project to address the needs of the whole child, including school-based health services, parent involvement, and teacher participation in restructuring the school's programs. A central component of this model is a school management and governance team composed of the principal, teachers, parents, a mental health specialist, and support personnel; this group is responsible for development of the school's master plan. Since the model focuses on the personal, social, and academic growth of students, nonacademic gains are also relevant. Like many of the other school improvement models, this program was initially developed in elementary schools (Comer, 1988, 1996).

Planning time for the various working teams is a critical component. Experience also suggests that facilitators and other specialists are needed to support the model. In addition, the success of the program appears to depend upon the degree to which it is fully implemented (Comer, 1996; 1997). In 1997, the Comer School Development Program was operating in 600 schools in 60 school districts (Herman & Stringfield, 1997).

Success for All

How does the role of the teacher and learner change among the different school improvement models?

The *Success for All* program calls for a schoolwide restructuring designed to ensure that students begin with success in the early grades and then maintain success through the elementary years. Developed by Professor Robert Slavin at Johns Hopkins University, this program assumes a research-based preschool program; full-day kindergarten; beginning reading programs for 90 minutes per day with the integration of phonics and whole language in a set sequence of activities; homogenous reading groups that are regrouped on a periodic basis; one-on-one tutoring with an integration of the regular curriculum in grades 1–3; cooperative learning in intermediate reading, writing/language arts, and mathematics; family support services to increase parent involvement and address home-based problems; and a part-time or full-time facilitator to coordinate the program and provide training and technical assistance (Slavin, Madden, Karweit, Dolan, & Wasik, 1992).

In its design, this program relied on a strong research base; data indicate that the program helped children learn to read and enjoy reading. The success of the program appears to depend upon the extent to which school staff make a commitment to the key components and periodically revisit that decision. Secure supplemental funding on a multiyear basis is deemed to be critical to the success of the program. In 1994, the program was being implemented in 400 schools in 26 states (Slavin, Karweit, & Wasik, 1994).

Paideia Program

The central concept of the *paideia* approach is that high academic achievement is expected of all students. Developed by Mortimer Adler (1984) in *The Paideia Proposal: An Educational Manifesto,* the goals of the program are acquisition of knowledge, development of intellectual skills, and enlarged understanding of ideas and values. Classes are heterogeneous and use original sources, including but not limited to the "Great Books." The goals of the program are addressed through three instructional approaches:

1. *Didactic instruction.* Teacher lectures provide opportunities for students to acquire knowledge.
2. *Coaching.* Students work at their own pace with one-on-one instruction from the teacher.
3. *Small-group seminars.* The teacher serves as a facilitator using the Socratic method of questioning to explore issues.

Implementation of this program requires schoolwide restructuring and a reorganization of the school schedule to accommodate the different instructional approaches. In some instances, teachers have had difficulty in addressing the range of student abilities. Even though teachers have indicated that students had become more proficient in critical thinking and self-expression, only limited data are available on the program's effect on traditional assessments such as standardized tests. In 1993, the program was reaching more than 5,000 students in grades K–12 in 23 Chicago schools (Herman & Stringfield, 1997).

Coalition of Essential Schools

The evolution of this model, which was developed by Professor Ted Sizer of Brown University; is traced in a trilogy (Sizer, 1984, 1992, & 1997). In contrast to many of the other approaches, which were designed for elementary schools, this model was initially designed for high schools. However, elementary schools are currently involved in the program. The initial focus of this approach was on the triangle of learning between teacher, student, and subject matter. The model has evolved from classroom to school-based change as developers of the approach came to recognize that effective school reform requires fundamental changes in the school as an institution. This model is referred to as the *Coalition of Essential Schools (CES).*

The CES model assumes the acceptance of the following set of common principles:

1. Schools should have an intellectual focus with simple goals that apply to all students.
2. Teaching and learning should be personalized with students-as-workers and teachers-as-coaches.
3. Diplomas should be awarded on demonstration of mastery.
4. The tone of the school should stress high expectations.
5. In their work, principals and teachers should view themselves as generalists first and as teachers second.
6. In the operation of the school, teacher load should be 80 or fewer students, and per-pupil cost should not exceed traditional school costs by more than 10%. (Sizer, 1992)

Implementation may pose a problem with traditional teachers, for this approach is less structured. The focus of instruction changes from the teacher to the student. Common planning periods help teachers work together more productively and also provide an opportunity to address problems. Experience with the model suggests that limiting the costs to 10% more than traditional schools has not been possible, and no high school had achieved the 80:1 student-to-teacher ratio in daily student contacts. Since in this model each school's goals are distinct, the CES philosophy is not supportive of using traditional norm-referenced tests or other readily standardized measures (Sizer, 1992).

Accelerated Schools

The concept of *Accelerated Schools* originated in a research project conducted by Professor Henry Levin and his associates at Stanford University. Their research led them to conclude that remediation was more a part of the problem than the solution in working with at-risk youth. The concept of Accelerated Schools includes the concept of powerful learning, classroom transformation, effective principals, and effective schools. Accelerated Schools share a set of values, beliefs, and attitudes that contribute to a culture for growth, creativity, and accelerated learning. These values undergird every aspect of the Accelerated Schools' philosophy, process, and daily practices. The three basic principles of Accelerated Schools are

Which of the school improvement models do you find most appealing, why?

unity of purpose, school community empowerment coupled with responsibility, and building on strengths. Teachers, parents, support staff, and students are involved in the transformation process that leads to the development of an Accelerated School. In the transformation process, terms such as participation, community collaboration, experimentation, trust, and risk taking become actions leading to the creation of an Accelerated School (Hopfenberg, Levin, & Associates, 1993).

As the concept has developed over the past 12 years, a high priority has been the creation of a system that builds capacity for effective implementation. The project uses a coaching model in which a trained coach from the local district, the school principal, and an internal facilitator function as a team to provide the leadership for implementation in the school. The team is trained in several sessions over the year and meets monthly with other teams to review implementation and develop strategies to address problems.

Interest in the concept of Accelerated Schools appears to be increasing. Starting with two schools in 1986–87, about 1,000 schools were in the program in 1997–98 in 40 states with 13 regional centers (Levin, 1998).

Reading Recovery

Reading recovery is a preventive tutoring program developed by Marie Clay, a New Zealand child psychologist. Rather than being a whole-school program, this program focuses on first grade students who are having difficulties in the development of their reading skills. The American version of this program is different from the New Zealand program because American students are exposed to reading a year later than are students in New Zealand. The principles underlying this program are that (1) reading takes place in a child's mind, (2) reading and writing are interconnected, and (3) children learn to read by reading. The program's target group is first grade students in the bottom 20% of those having difficulty in reading. Six reading and writing skills are tested—letter identification, word test, concepts about print, writing vocabulary, dictation, and text reading level (Hiebert, 1994).

How does the focus of the school improvement models compare with your school experiences?

Under the program, the child starts with familiar works to establish a base level for instruction. The school tutoring sessions (generally 30 minutes daily) follow a set format with the student moving to more progressive levels of difficulty. Materials are sent home with pupils so that parents can help the child practice words and skills. When a student achieves a 90% level of accuracy, he/she is graduated from the program.

Critical concerns about the program included the importance of adopting the entire program, teachers' acceptance of the program, training burden on the lead teachers, parent participation in the program, teacher expertise, and broad-based teacher acceptance of the program. In 1993, the program was operating in 201 sites in the United States (Hiebert, 1994).

Conclusions

The general conclusions from the research findings and on-site observations of various school reform models are that

- Disadvantaged children are capable of achieving levels of performance that meet and exceed the national average.
- Implementation of school reform programs can best be achieved when the strengths of the selected program match the schools needs and assets.
- In choosing a program for a particular school, careful consideration should be given to whether the selected program is likely to work with the school's teachers and administrators. Each program needs a supportive and accepting environment to be successful.
- A school's ability to obtain and maintain sufficient fiscal support is critical to the implementation of any new program.
- Ongoing access to program-specific technical support is a critical element to long-term success.
- Programs that concentrate on the lower grades tend to be more successful than those that are spread evenly over all elementary grades or in secondary schools.
- Whole school programs appear to be more successful than pullout programs.
- Externally designed programs appear to achieve more consistent implementation than locally developed programs.
- The range in cost among various programs can be great. Start-up costs and continued funding requirements are among the factors that should be considered in program selection. (Herman & Stringfield, 1997, pp. 125–130)

Educational Uses of Technology

With the introduction of each new technological innovation, various observers have predicted that technology would revolutionize education. Some advancements have occurred, but technology has not been the panacea for the problems of education. One hurdle to the expanded use of technology in the classroom has been that teachers have failed to recognize the ways in which technology can be used to increase their efficiency in the classroom. Rather than restricting the teacher, technology empowers the teacher by giving students and teachers access to additional information. Technology provides teachers with the opportunity to change the ways that they teach and enhance learning opportunities for students. For example, by using technology efficiently, teachers can devote greater portions of their time to preparation of learning experiences for students. Also, instructional units can be prepared and stored so that students can access the information at their convenience (McGrath, 1998).

Rather than presenting information and issuing instructions in the traditional format, teachers using technology can place a greater emphasis on small group learning activities rather than on formal lectures. Diverse students working together can share learning experiences. The teacher can devote more time to working with individual students and addressing their particular problems. As an alternative to live lectures, the teacher can use a videotape for group instruction. As teachers become more proficient in the use of technology, they can devote more of their time to addressing individual needs, gathering materials, and structuring learning opportunities for students. The teacher then functions more as a

Figure 15.9: Creative Uses of Technology in the Classroom

1. Technology increases student motivation, and motivated students are more receptive, more engaged, and more likely to learn.
2. Technology promotes cooperation and collaboration among students and good teachers can capitalize on these opportunities. Cooperative learning approaches with technology give students with different talents a chance to excel.
3. In classrooms with computers, conversations between teachers and students and among students themselves become deeper and more probing.
4. Technology use encourages teacher-as-facilitator approaches.
5. Technology promotes a "balance of power" between the teacher and his or her students.
6. With technological tools, students show more persistence in solving problems.
7. Technology encourages varied methods of assessment.
8. Despite all the challenges of a one-computer/one Internet-connection classroom, even this classroom environment enables good teachers to work effectively with diverse students.
9. Technology fosters increased and improved oral and written communication.
10. Technology enables opportunities for more depth of understanding, but the breadth of the curriculum is still problematic.
11. Technology provides increased opportunities for thematic, interdisciplinary explorations; teachers can use these interdisciplinary connections to further engage and excite students.
12. Technology makes classroom activities "feel" more real-world and relevant, and students often take these activities more seriously.

Source: McGrath, B. (1998), Partners in learning: Twelve ways technology changes the teacher-student relationship. *T.H.E. Journal, 25*(9), 58–61.

guide or facilitator in working with individual students or groups of students in the teaching/learning process. However, before teachers can begin to maximize the integration of technology into their classrooms, they must become comfortable with the technology, explore the data sources that can enrich and enhance their current instruction, develop ways to integrate the technology into their lesson plans, conduct trial runs with lessons in their classrooms, and assess and refine their efforts (McGrath, 1988). The ways in which technology changes the relationship between students and teachers are listed in Figure 15.9.

The *information superhighway* is providing many public schools in all parts of the nation with access to data and information; however, implementation will require significant investments in both hardware and software as well as orientation and staff development for teachers (Pearlman, 1994). The public policy challenge will be to ensure that all students and teachers have access to this valuable resource.

Teacher use of technology is affected by the length of time that the teacher has had access to the technology. There appears to be a lag between the date that equipment is commercially available and the date that teachers have ready access to the recently developed equipment. In a 1996 survey, 80% or more of the teachers indicated that they had ready access to such equipment as video

How does access to technology affect the role and responsibility of the student, affect the teacher?

Teacher effectiveness can be enhanced by providing and encouraging the effective use of instructional technology to improve instruction and expand teaching and learning opportunities.

cassette players, television monitors, computers, instructional videotapes, and standard software. The survey indicated that teachers did not have ready access to some of the newer technologies (see Figure 15.10). These conditions illustrate some of the challenges faced by schools and teachers as they attempt to prepare students for a future driven by technology (NEA Research, 1997).

As more teachers who have had experience with technology as students enter the classroom, the classroom uses of technology likely will expand. A recent national survey of classroom teachers reported that 71.8% of the respondents had made some effort to go beyond the basics and include computer literacy in their school's program (NEA Research, 1997). Currently, some districts have automated many of the menial routine classroom tasks so that teachers can devote more time to working directly with students. This permits teachers to use their time more efficiently. The greater challenge is for all teachers, and especially those in isolated settings with limited resource materials, to recognize and use the resources available in the rapidly expanding information superhighway. Rather than being limited to print materials available in the local school, teachers now can use resources from throughout the world in planning their lessons and developing instructional materials for students. The mere availability of hardware

Figure 15.10: Percent of Teachers With Selected Teaching Resources Available at Work Site, 1996.

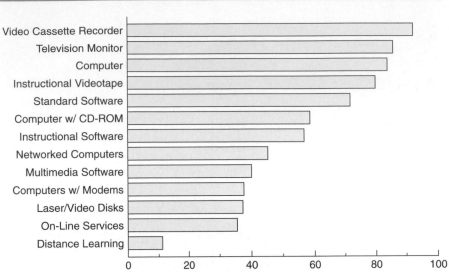

Source: NEA Research. (1997). *NEA today: Status of the American public school teacher, 1995–96.* Washington, DC: National Education Association.

and software, however, will not result in high usage levels for technological resources. Teachers will need support from their administrators, time, guidance, and the freedom to experiment with different approaches (McGrath, 1998).

Technology can be used in a variety of ways in the classroom. Grabe and Grabe (1996) have identified five themes that describe the different uses of technology in classrooms.

1. The integration of technology into content-area instruction in which the technology is secondary to the content
2. The use of technology tools such as word processing or spreadsheets
3. The use of technology to promote a more active role for students
4. The use of technological resources to facilitate an integrated or multidisciplinary approach
5. The use of technology to encourage students to interact and become involved in group work

As illustrated in these themes, technology can be used in a variety of ways to provide direct support for the instructional process as well as to encourage the social growth and development of students and the development of group process skills.

Student uses of computers can be grouped into two broad applications—tutorial and tool. Using the computer as a tutor in drill and practice empowers both the student and teacher by reducing the need for direct personal contact and providing opportunities for students to progress at different rates. The

Through the use of modern technology in many of today's classrooms, teachers can provide students with access to a wide range of learning resources and activities.

teacher and the student can access data related to individualized, self-paced learning, as well as student progress. Another tutorial application, simulation, provides the student with the potential to maximize the computer's capabilities and expand learning opportunities. The student can write the instructions and use the computer to solve problems. The student develops higher order thinking skills by becoming involved in the orderly progression of steps involved in addressing a problem. A major benefit of simulation is that efforts to address problems are made in a safe and artificial setting. The results of the simulation can then be used in determining the options to be considered in real-life situations.

Tool applications provide opportunities for students to expand their learning opportunities, improve their performance, and develop skills that will enhance their abilities as independent learners. Word processing software makes it much easier to teach writing as a process in which a student writes, revises, and rewrites until satisfied with the effort. The result is a better-written product without excessive effort. Spreadsheets take the drudgery out of hand calculations of data. The challenge is to ensure that students not only develop a sufficient level of basic competency in their mathematical skills and an understanding of numbers, but also develop an understanding of alternative formulas as tools for problem solving. By accessing on-line databases, students can gain access to

Professional Reflections

"Discover new ways to deliver the content so that each and every student experiences learning. Teaching is an art that requires a generous dose of creativity and imagination. Teaching is also a science that requires assessments and accountabilities."

Peggy J. Woods, Teacher of the Year, Arizona

"The most successful instructor teaches by example. . . your character. . . honesty and integrity must be woven into your instruction."

Robert Foor-Hogue, Teacher of the Year, Maryland

national and international databases and explore information in libraries, public agencies, and private sources throughout the world. Students can build their own databases for class projects or continuing learning opportunities. Massive databases can be transmitted electronically for students to use in class projects. With the federal emphasis on creating an information superhighway, classrooms and homes throughout the nation will have immediate access to information formerly available only in a few large research libraries or governmental agencies.

Summary

The overall goal of education, free public instruction for all, is attained through the selection of educational goals and the implementation of instructional objectives for meeting the goals. These goals and objectives help teachers to determine how to organize for instruction. Teachers may use a variety of organizational options as they work with students, and may vary the strategies to recognize differences in students. Technology has the potential to provide teachers and students with opportunities to increase instruction capacity, but effective use of technology requires knowledgeable implementation. Various school improvement models have been developed to address the educational needs of at-risk youth.

In the next chapter, the focus is on social, political, and educational issues that affect projections for the future. The principal concern is the different forces that will impact on schools and teachers as they seek to serve an increasingly diverse and multicultural pupil population.

Key Terms

Accelerated Schools

Analytical learner

Bloom's Taxonomy of Educational
  Objectives

Coalition of Essential Schools (CES)

Common sense learner

Cooperative learning

Critical thinking

Demonstration instruction
Dynamic learner
Educational goals
Educational objectives
Expository instruction
Group instruction
Imaginative learner
Independent learning
Individualized instruction

Information superhighway
Inquiry instruction
Mastery learning
Multiple intelligences theory
Powerful learning
Reading recovery
Reflective thinking
School Development Program
Success for All

Discussion Questions

1. In addition to serving on the study committee, what other appropriate roles might David play in the selection of a school improvement model for a low-performing school?

2. What are the most important goals of American public education?

3. How will a well-designed system of goals, objectives, and outcomes affect the ways in which a teacher organizes instruction and works with students?

4. How does the role of the teacher change in the various ways in which schools and classrooms may be organized for instruction?

5. How can the teacher determine if certain strategies would be more appropriate with particular subjects or students?

6. How will the interest in national goals and standards for American education affect the daily activities of teachers in the classroom?

7. How can the characteristics of the effective schools concept be made more relevant in suburban, rural, and inner-city schools?

8. What are the strengths and weaknesses of the various school improvement models?

9. Given the importance of educational leadership in developing an effective school, what actions can teachers take when the principal fails to provide active instructional leadership for the school?

10. How have schools changed in their day-to-day operation and decision-making styles compared to early days in American education discussed in Chapter 6?

Internet Resources

1. See Appendix.

2. **www.iste.org**
   The home page for the International Society for Technology in Education provides technology curriculum standards, curriculum resources, projects, articles, and links to technology-related sites.

3. **www.iteawww.org**

The home page for the International Technology Education Association, a professional organization of technology teachers, has numerous technology resource links.

4. **www.essentialschools.org**

The home page for the Coalition of Essential Schools provides information on its philosophy, projects, publications, schools, centers that work with Essential Schools, and more.

5. **metalab.unc.edu/edweb/ edref.mi.th.html**

The Theory of Multiple Intelligences and its eight faculties—and the possibility of a ninth—are discussed in detail with links to related sites.

6. **www.stanford.edu/group/asp**

The home page for The Accelerated Schools Project provides detailed in-

formation about the project and how to become a school, as well as information on the Powerful Learning Project.

7. **www.sonoma.edu/cthink/**

The home page of the Critical Thinking Community provides information about critical thinking theory and practice as well as a number of techniques for teaching critical thinking.

8. **www.ed.gov/pubs/or/ consumerguides/success.html**

A *Consumer Guide* produced by the U.S. Department of Education, Office of Research, discusses the principles, goals, and elements/components of the Success for All program, with examples of successful programs.

References

Adler, M. (1984). *The Paideia program: An educational manifesto.* New York: Macmillan.

Armstrong, T. (1994). *Seven kinds of smart.* New York: Putnam Books.

Barone, T. (1989). Ways of being at-risk: The case of Billy Charles Barnett. *Phi Delta Kappan, 71,* 147–151.

Bloom, B. (1956). *Taxonomy of educational objectives 1: Cognitive domain.* New York: David McKay.

Clark, D., Lotto, L., & Astuto, T. (1984). Effective schools and school improvement. *Educational Administration Quarterly, 20*(3), 41–86.

Cohen, E. (1998). Making cooperative learning equitable. *Educational Leadership, 56*(1), 18–21.

Comer, J. (1988). Educating poor minority children. *Scientific American, 259,* 42–48.

Comer, J. (1996). *Rallying the whole village: The*

Comer process for reforming education. New York: Teachers College Press.

Comer, J. (1997). *Waiting for a miracle: Why schools can't solve our problems—and how we can.* New York: Dutton.

Cuban, L. (1989). The "at-risk" label and the problem of school reform. *Phi Delta Kappan, 70,* 780–784.

Duke, D. L. (1984). *Teaching: The imperiled profession.* Albany: State University of New York.

Dunn, R. (1995). *Strategies for educating diverse learners.* Bloomington, IN: Phi Delta Kappa Educational Foundation.

Edmonds, R. (1979). Some schools work and more can. *Social Policy, 9*(5), 28–32.

Edmonds, R. (1982). Programs of school improvement: An overview. *Educational Leadership, 40*(3), 5–11.

Ellis, A. K., Mackey, J. A., & Glenn, A. D.

(1988). *The school curriculum.* Boston: Allyn and Bacon.

Freiberg, H. (1998). Measuring school climate: Let me count the ways. *Educational Leadership, 56*(1), 22–26.

Gardner, H. (1993). *Multiple intelligences.* New York: Harper Collins.

Grabe, M., & Grabe, C. (1996). *Integrating technology for meaningful learning.* Boston: Houghton Mifflin.

Guskey, T. (1985). *Implementing mastery learning.* Belmont, CA: Wadsworth.

Haggerty, B. (1995). *Nurturing intelligences.* New York: Addison Wesley.

Herman, R., & Stringfield, S. (1997). *Ten promising programs for educating all children.* Arlington, VA: Educational Research Service.

Hiebert, E. (1994). Reading recovery in the United States: What difference does it make to an age cohort? *Educational Researcher, 23*(9), 15–25.

Hopfenberg, W., Levin, H., & Associates. (1993). *The accelerated schools: Resource guide.* San Francisco: Jossey-Bass.

Jacobsen, D., Eggen, P., & Kauchak, D. (1999). *Methods of teaching: Promoting student learning.* Columbus, OH: Merrill.

Kellough, R., & Kellough, N. (1999). *Secondary school teaching: A guide to methods and resources.* Upper Saddle River, NJ: Merrill.

Levin, H. (1996). Accelerated schools after eight years. In L. Schauble & R. Glaser (Eds.), *Innovations in learning: New environments for education.* Mahwah, NJ: Lawrence Erlbaum Associates.

Levin, H. (1997). Raising school productivity: An x-efficiency approach. *Economics of Education Review, 16*(3), 303–311.

Levin, H. (1998). *Research background on accelerated schools: Work in progress.* Stanford, CA: Accelerated Schools Project, Stanford University.

Mager, R. (1997). *Preparing instructional objectives: A critical tool in the development of effective instruction* (3rd ed.). Atlanta, GA: The Center for Performance, Inc.

Marzano, R. (1992). *A different kind of classroom: Teaching with dimensions of learning.*

Alexandria, VA: Association for Supervision and Curriculum Development.

McCarthy, B. (1997). A tale of four learners: 4MAT's learning styles. *Educational Leadership, 54*(6), 47–51.

McGrath, B. (1998). Partners in learning: Twelve ways technology changes the teacher-student relationship. *T.H.E. Journal, 25*(9), 58–61.

National Center for the Accelerated Schools Project. (1997). *What is powerful learning?* Stanford, CA: Accelerated Schools Project, Stanford University.

NEA Research. (1997). *Status of the American public school teacher, 1995–96: Highlights.* Washington, DC: National Education Association.

Orlich, D., Harder, R., Callahan, R., & Gibson, H. (1998). *Teaching strategies: A guide to better instruction.* Boston: Houghton Mifflin.

Parkay, F. W., & Stanford, B. H. (1995). *Becoming a teacher* (3rd. ed.). Boston: Allyn and Bacon.

Pearlman, R. (1994 May 25). Can K-12 education drive on the information superhighway? *Education Week,* p. 48.

Peterson, K., & Deal, T. (1998). How leaders influence the culture of schools. *Educational Leadership, 56*(1), 28–30.

Rea, D., & Warkentin, R. (1997). *Investing in our youth: Pooling community resources.* New York: McGraw-Hill.

Sizer, T. R. (1984). *Horace's compromise.* Boston: Houghton Mifflin.

Sizer, T. R. (1992). *Horace's school.* Boston: Houghton Mifflin.

Sizer, T. R. (1997). *Horace's hope.* Boston: Houghton Mifflin.

Skinner, B. (1965). Why teachers fail. *Saturday Review, 67,* 101.

Slavin, R. (1989). Research on cooperative learning: Consensus and controversy. *Educational Leadership, 47*(4), 52–54.

Slavin, R., Karweit, N., & Wasik, S. (1994). *Preventing early school failure: Research, policy, and practice.* Boston: Allyn and Bacon.

Slavin, R., Madden, L., Karweit, N., Dolan, L., & Wasik, S. (1992). *Success for all: A relentless approach to prevention and early intervention in elementary schools.* Arlington, VA: Educational Research Service.

Tom, A. (1984). *Teaching as a moral craft.* New York: Longman.

Westbrook, J. (1982). *Considering the research: What makes an effective school?* Austin, TX: Southwest Educational Development Laboratory.

Part Seven

Projections for the Future

Chapter 16

For the future to be bright, it must be lit by the lamp of learning—the true Olympic torch.

William A. Henry III (1992)

Education for the New Millennium

➤ *It was midday on August 17, 2020, Cheryl Woo sat down at her networking console (home/work/school station) and started her interactive video system. In moments, she was connected with the Tate Gallery in London and the Louvre in Paris. She checked the computer menu and accessed a printout of the works of Rodin. In seconds she retrieved a series of holograms. Now she could put the finishing touches on the multimedia project she was completing for summer session credit from Cambridge University. Next, she accessed the Worldwide Electronic Bulletin Board and sent a message to her classmate Donna, who was finishing her summer term at the Sorbonne.*

Cheryl's younger brother Todd was downstairs working with his keyboard emulator. Physically handicapped since birth, Todd had very limited mobility but was able to control his computer by merely gazing at the terminal screen.

A red light flashed across the center wall accompanied by a subliminal sound. It was their mother, Dr. Audrey Woo, who was calling while en route home from Singapore where she consulted with the World Congress of Biomedical Scientists the day before. She was calling from Concorde II to tell Cheryl and Todd that she expected to arrive home by the dinner hour. She also reminded Cheryl to reprogram SRV3, their household robot, so that dinner would be ready when she arrived.

What type of individual would be most suited for teaching in the year 2020? Do you anticipate that you will still be teaching in the year 2020? Why or why not?

Each person has a vision and a dream of the world of tomorrow. Rather than being an endless cycle of repetition of the past, the future is a journey into the unknown. The one constant is change. As we enter the information age, we will learn to live with and capitalize on the explosive increases in knowledge, the expanding capacity of technology, the growing potential for travel, and the ways that electronic advancements give us access to cultures throughout the world (Henry, 1992).

This chapter examines projected technological advances and societal trends for the next century and their potential impact on education. These trends include projected demographic, socioeconomic, and demographic changes and their implications for education. Trends and challenges confronting education are identified, and questions and issues are raised about the future of the schools in the context of these trends. The information in the chapter will enable you to:

- Discuss what schools must do to meet the needs of school-age youth.
- Describe how the future economy may influence the educational enterprise.
- Discuss the changing workplace and the worker of the future.
- Identify how schools can accommodate the changing workplace.
- Describe how schools can accommodate the lifestyles of the families of tomorrow.
- Speculate on how technological advances might influence schools and learning.

As you study the material in this chapter, give special attention to the potential impact that these developments will have on schools and classrooms and on the expectations of education. One of the challenges confronting teachers is to help their students understand the need to become active learners throughout their lives. As students become discriminating consumers, they will look for linkages between yesterday and today. This will become an additional challenge for teachers. If students are to maximize their potential, they will need to develop a vision of an emerging world that is much different from the one they are experiencing.

How should schools and school programs respond to the shrinking world and development of a global society?

We live in a global society that continues to experience unprecedented change. These changes have included transitions from an agricultural world to an industrial world and, during the twentieth century, to an information-oriented world. What will the world of the twenty-first century look like? What will its educational system look like? Numerous hypotheses attempt to answer these questions. One way to glimpse the education of the next millennium is to study projected societal trends. The Historical Note below discusses an early futurist's attempt to answer similar questions.

The quality of the nation's educational system is the key to America's maintaining its leadership position in the world economic community. In an earlier era when nations were isolated, disparities in the quality of education among nations were of little concern so long as each nation produced sufficient goods and services for its economy. However, that luxury no longer exists with the

 Historical Note

Nostradamus—Astrologer, Physician, and Futurist

Nostradamus (Michel de Nostredame) was born in 1503 at St. Remy in Provence and died in 1566. An astrologer, physician, and adviser to Henry II and Charles IX, as well as Catherine de Medici, Nostradamus was well known for his predictions of the future. In 1555 and in subsequent years he published 10 "Centuries" or books, each containing 100 rhymed quatrains of predictions of the future. For example, he predicted with accuracy the fatal death of Henry II, the decline of the Catholic Church, and the details of the French revolution and the Napoleonic period.

During his lifetime, futuristic prophecy was considered taboo and was condemned. As a result, he was forced to disguise his prophecies by using symbolism, hidden meanings, and terminology from several languages including French, Spanish, Portuguese, Italian, Latin, Greek, and Hebrew.

The fame of Nostradamus continued beyond his lifetime. Generations of followers have regarded his quatrains as serious prophetic messages. For example, several contemporary commentators have alleged that he foresaw World War II in great detail. As we anticipate the next millennium, Nostradamus enthusiasts will no doubt be particularly interested in his predictions and visions for tomorrow.

Source: Cavendish, R. (Ed.). (1983). *Man, myth and magic.* New York: Marshall Cavendish.

emergence of a global economy and free trade. In a world that relies on an educated workforce with technological understanding and specialized skills, America's educational system must improve if the nation is to continue to be a world economic power. A skilled workforce will be essential to prevent the export of high-paying jobs. This need for a skilled workforce extends beyond production workers, for the nation also will need scientists and engineers to respond to the need for additional progress in research and development.

The challenge is greater than merely devoting attention to the basic skills and good work habits. To meet the demands of a more diverse student body, educational personnel will need to be well versed in a variety of forms of multicultural, multiethnic, and bilingual education. The research on mentoring and modeling behavior tells us that teachers, administrators, support personnel, and school governing bodies will need to be sensitive to the problems and values of students from different cultural and linguistic backgrounds. Schools will need to be sensitive to the importance of role models for all youth.

In the following discussion, initial attention is given to socioeconomic and demographic changes that will influence education in the twenty-first century. Areas of interest include the changing demographics of the population, the transformation of the economy, and the shrinking world, or globalization. Also discussed are the effects of technological advances on the operation of schools and the simultaneous movements toward nationalization and decentralization in education.

Changing Demographics

The changing demographics in the United States have implications for the full range of social services including education. Overall, the population of the United States is projected to increase by 50% between 1995 and 2050; however, the annual rate of increase is expected to decline from 1.05% for 1990–95 to 0.63% for the decade of 2040 to 2050. The population will progressively become older. The proportion of the population 65 and over is projected to increase from 13% in 1995 to 20% by 2050. The proportion of the population 85 and over is expected to increase from 1.4% in 1995 to 4.6% by 2050. The proportion of the population from 18 to 44 years of age is projected to decrease from about 42% in 1995 to about 34% by 2050; just under 70% of the 1995 population was in the traditional wage earning years (18–64) compared to about 60% in 2050. The proportion of the population under 18 years is projected to increase from about 20% in 1995 to about 22% in 2050. ("How We're Changing," 1997). As the proportions of the population over 65 and under 18 increase and the proportion from 18 to 65 years of age decreases, the demand for social services will be increasing at the same time that the proportion of persons in their productive years will be decreasing. Figure 16.1 shows projections on the aging of the population.

The Hispanic-origin sector of the population is projected to be the fastest growing. Projections suggest that this sector will double its 1990 number by 2015

Figure 16.1: Distribution of the Population by Age (1995 to 2050: middle-series projections)

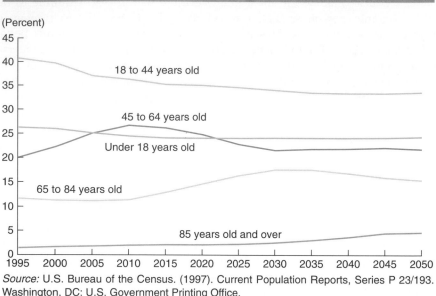

Source: U.S. Bureau of the Census. (1997). Current Population Reports, Series P 23/193. Washington, DC: U.S. Government Printing Office.

and quadruple its 1990 number by 2050. As the percent of the population that is white declines from 75.7% in 1990 to 52.5% in 2050, the percent of the population that is of Hispanic origin is projected to increase from 9.0% in 1990 to 22.5% in 2050. Projections for the African American sector of the population call for a slower rate of growth from 12.3% in 1990 to 15.7% in 2050. These shifts will be occurring from 2030 to 2050, when the population is projected to grow more slowly than ever before in the nation's history (Day, 1997). The data are illustrated in Figure 16.2.

Educational attainment levels have continued to rise for several years. In March 1995, 82% of all adults 25 and over had completed at least high school, and 23% had earned a bachelor's degree or more. As would be expected, the high school completion rate was higher for the younger age groups and decreased as the age groups became older (87.4% for the 25 to 29 group and 60.4% for the 75 and older group). The pattern of school completion for men and women was about the same for high school completion, but males had attained more post-high school education. Sizeable differences remain in the completion rates among whites, African Americans, and persons of Hispanic origin. Among whites, 83% had completed high school; the percentages for African Americans was 74% and the percentage for persons of Hispanic origins was 53%. Progress in the high school completion rates for African Americans ages 25 to 29 years was evident with the percentages increasing from 81% in 1985 to 87% in 1995; the rate for this group of whites was 87% for both years (Day & Curry, 1997; "How We're Changing," 1997).

Figure 16.2: Percent of the Population, by Race and Hispanic Origin: 1990, 2000, 2025, and 2050 (Middle-series projections)

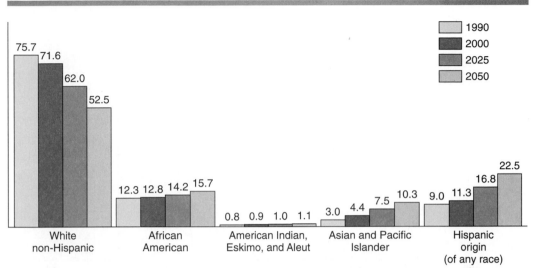

Source: U.S. Census Bureau, *Current Population Reports*. Washington, DC: U.S. Department of Commerce. Last Revised: 9 May, 1997.

Modest progress in household income was reported from 1994 to 1995. Real median household income showed an increase for the first time in six years—from $33,178 to $34,076 (2.7%). For 1995, the proportion of the population in poverty was 13.8% compared to 14.5% in 1994. A further decline was noted in 1996 when the proportion was 13.7%. In 1996, for whites, the proportion of the population in poverty was 11.2%; for African Americans, 28.4%; for Hispanics, 29.4%; and for Asians and Pacific Islanders, 14.5%. The poverty data were less favorable for persons of school age (see Figure 16.3). Children under 18 years represent 40% of the poverty population compared to about 25% of the total population. Of even greater interest are data that reported a poverty rate of 23.7% for related children under age six in a household ("How We're Changing," 1997).

The previous data about the poverty rates for school-age youth become of special interest in light of the various research studies that have emphasized the importance of preschool experiences to the success of children in school. This is especially important for single-parent families. The proportion of children under 18 years living in a single-parent household grew from 12% in 1970 to 27% in 1995. The proportion of white children in one-parent households was 21% compared to 56% for African American children and 33% for Hispanic children. If adequate preschool programs were available, the impact of this household pattern might be less severe. However, between 1988 and 1991, the proportion of preschoolers in organized childcare facilities declined from 26% to 23%. Historically, family day-care programs have been a consistent source of childcare arrangements providing 23% of all arrangements in 1977 and 1988; however, this

Figure 16.3: Percent of Population in Poverty, 1996

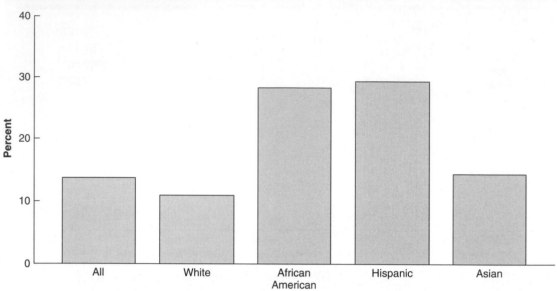

Source: U.S. Bureau of the Census. (1997). Current Population Reports, Series P 23/193. Washington, DC: U.S. Government Printing Office.

proportion fell to 18% in 1991 and remained at that level in 1993 ("How We're Changing," 1997). Thus, the schools likely will be confronted with increasing numbers of disadvantaged youth with special needs (Day & Curry, 1997).

Of possible interest to those who question the merits of public education would be the following summary points:

- Educational attainment is higher for the employed than for the unemployed.
- In professional specialty occupations, 75.5% had completed a bachelor's degree or higher compared to 23% for the total population.
- Earnings for the population 18 years and over were higher at each progressively higher level of education, ranging from $15,011 for a person who did not complete high school to $63,317 for a person with an advanced degree.
- Educational attainment levels were lowest in the South; the proportion of the population completing high school ranged from 79.3% in the South to 85.2% in the Midwest. The West was highest for the completion of some college (55.6%) and the Northeast and Midwest were highest for completion of a bachelor's degree or more (26.6% and 25.9%) (Day & Curry, 1997).

Educational Implications

These demographic changes will have multiple effects. Pressures for public service programs for the elderly and for school-age children will increase. Additional funds will be required to provide day-care programs for the increasing

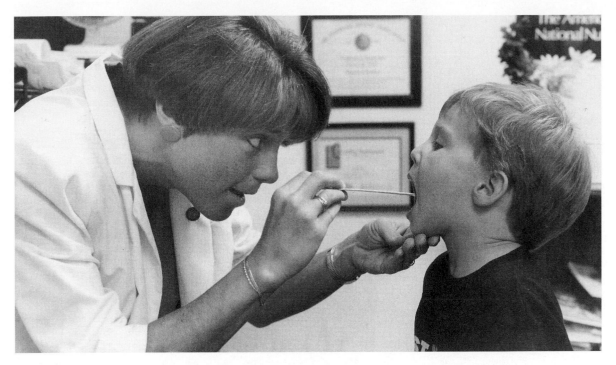

Policymakers are recognizing the importance of adequate healthcare to a child's success in school and are proposing that the full range of social services be available in schools.

number of youth with two working parents. At the same time, pressures will increase for various support programs for the increasing numbers of the elderly. Both groups will need medical services, recreational programs, and educational programs.

In a more immediate context, state legislatures and state departments of education are placing increased emphasis on accountability and student performance. Schools are being called upon to reduce dropout rates and address the educational needs of all students. Various states are initiating special programs for at-risk youth. As discussed in Chapters 13 and 15, governance systems for schools are being decentralized, and schools are changing instructional models to address the needs of at-risk youth. Schools will need more resources to provide meaningful programs for a more heterogeneous student body. Special programs will be needed to help many students develop proficiency in English.

As the population increases in urban areas, heavier demands will be made on the limited resources of older inner-city school districts. In the 1950s and 1960s, many of these districts had the reputation that they provided exemplary education programs. For a variety of reasons, these districts do not enjoy the same reputation as we enter the next century. In addition, these districts have the highest numbers of at-risk youth (Casserly, 1998).

What are the advantages and disadvantages of one-stop social service programs in which social and medical services are available in local schools?

The aging American population presents a variety of social problems and opportunities.

Because the numbers of day-care programs have been declining, schools will be asked to develop or expand before-school and after-school programs and supervision for school-age children whose parents are working. The need for safe, affordable, and quality care for infants and children whose parents are working continues to plague families, in particular poor families. Numerous legislators continue to work toward the development and implementation of a comprehensive childcare policy at the national level.

What implications does elimination of mandatory retirement at age 70 have for education and the teaching profession?

The extraordinary growth of our elderly population is not without economic and educational consequences. The increase in funds required to meet the Social Security and medical needs of tomorrow's elderly population will probably have a negative effect on the financing of education. Not only will there be competition for limited resources, but an aged population that does not have children enrolled in school may be less supportive of education. The challenge will be to renew the interest and support that this group has for education. On a more positive note, a significant number of these senior citizens may take advantage of occupational and postsecondary educational opportunities to prepare for second careers or enhance avocational opportunities. Tomorrow's postsecondary institutions may witness an entirely new group of students in their schools, the septuagenarians.

Economic Transformation

The structure of the American economy is undergoing significant changes as the emphasis on quantity of production shifts to an emphasis on reduction of costs; the goal is to produce the same or more volume at lower costs. In a variety of industries, jobs are being shifted to developing countries because of a cheaper labor supply. The days of lifetime employment by one company appear to be more a memory of yesterday than an expectation for the future. Many will be employed in jobs that will be vulnerable to changing job requirements due to continually advancing technology. Most persons can look forward to multiple employers and multiple jobs in their lifetime. As a result, retraining of employees will become commonplace, and the worker who is most receptive to retraining will be the most valued employee of tomorrow (Carnevale, 1992).

In addition to efficient and economical production, performance in the new economy is being measured by five additional standards. The first is quality, or the matching of products and services to human needs while maintaining standards in production. The second is variety, or providing choices in response to diverse needs. The third is customization, an extension of variety, in which goods and services are tailored to individual clienteles. The fourth is convenience, in which user-friendly products and services are delivered in ways that satisfy customers. The fifth is timeliness, which is accomplished by innovations, continuous improvement, and quick development of new applications (Carnevale, 1992). Information processing, rapid transportation, and technology all are critical resources in efforts to meet these five standards.

The unknown about the future of the American economy is the effect of changing economic relations among nations. Free trade agreements have the potential of lowering tariff barriers among nations and opening new markets for America's goods. The unknown is the effect that these agreements will have on manufacturing jobs in the American economy. These events are taking place when the major economic trend in jobs is the shift from an industrial/manufacturing-based economy to a service/information/technology-based economy. By 2005, experts estimate that service workers and administrative support workers will comprise more than one third of the nation's workforce. Job creation will be greatest in health, education, childcare, protective services, computer systems analysis, and government occupations (Leftwich, 1994). This major shift will have profound implications on expectations of education to prepare persons to enter this future workforce.

Rather than being isolated events, political decisions, economic conditions, and technological advancements are having profound implications for the changing workforce. Similarly, the changing workforce will influence the trends of tomorrow in significant ways. The structure of jobs will continue to evolve throughout the coming decades. About 25% of the jobs in 2005 will be in human services, and some of these jobs, such as childcare and home health care, pay little more than a minimum wage (Leftwich, 1994). Approximately 45% of the workforce is currently involved in information processing as a result of computer

Figure 16.4: Female and Minority Participation in the Workforce, With Projections: 1970–2005.

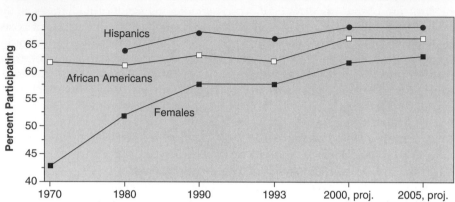

Source: U.S. Bureau of the Census. (1994). *Statistical abstract of the United States 1994.* Washington, DC: U.S. Government Printing Office.

technology. The dilemma is that wages for many of these newly created jobs are not as high as those in the industrial manufacturing economy.

The age and gender composition of the workforce will continue to change. More women will enter and remain in the workforce (see Figure 16.4). Minorities (see Figure 16.4) and elderly workers will soon constitute the majority of tomorrow's workforce. It is estimated that this trend will continue beyond the turn of the century. As the age increases at which a person can receive maximum Social Security benefits, the workforce will include much older and more experienced employees.

Educational Implications

As the nature of the American economy shifts, skills that once were demanded only of the white-collar elite are being required of all workers (Carnevale, 1992). These new skills can be grouped into six categories. The first is the academic basics, including reading, writing, and computation. The second is adaptability skills such as learning to learn, creative thinking, and problem solving. Personal considerations are emphasized in the third group of skills; these self-management skills include self-esteem, goal setting, motivation, employability, and career development. The fourth group includes social skills such as interpersonal relations, negotiation, and teamwork. Another group focuses on communication skills such as listening and oral communication. Consistent with the human emphasis in these skills, the last group of influencing skills includes organizational effectiveness and leadership. These skills reflect the changing workplace and the changing values of management. Many of these skills are required in workplaces that emphasize total quality management and customer satisfaction.

Students in the next millennium will need to be able to process information about complex systems, think holistically and abstractly, and above all, be creative. The powerful learning concept discussed in Chapter 15 has special relevance in this context. In short, higher cognitive skill development will be a necessary component of education. Since tomorrow's economic forecast emphasizes a shift to a service-oriented global society, we probably will experience more active involvement of students in service/learning experiences. Volunteerism in hospitals, museums, and community service across the globe will become an integral aspect of the teaching/learning process. This movement toward community service has already been incorporated into high school completion requirements in many states.

The discouraging news for students looking forward to employment is that some of the fastest growing occupations pay low wages. However, for students and for education, the encouraging news is that there is a positive correlation between education and earnings. As noted earlier in this chapter, income levels are higher for persons in occupations that require higher levels of education (Day & Curry, 1997).

The challenge to education is to recognize the cultural and occupational changes that are associated with the emergence of the technological information age. Most recent changes in education have been timid improvements to improve on the margin that are not consistent with the massive changes that are taking place in the American economy. The social contracts that once existed between heavy industry employees such as autoworkers and steelworkers and their employers no longer exist. At one time, education could be content to train people for specific trades or professions. Today, however, much of the technical training is being assumed by the employer; in 1996 an estimated $60 billion was spent on corporate training (Keeley, 1997). (This should be placed in the context of the $220+ billion spent in the public schools during the same period.)

Given the pace of change in the workplace, employers have come to recognize that corporate training is the only practical way to keep a workforce in tune with the changing times. In this context, the emphasis shifts from career training to lifelong learning. Employers are willing to make the investment in corporate training because the additional skills make the employees more valuable to the firm.

For schools, the challenge is to package learning experiences for students that incorporate the latest developments in technological and educational innovations. Students can work in small groups, and learning can become an interactive and positive experience. Students then move beyond the mastery of materials to learning to learn through searching for information, finding the patterns in the information, and discerning the value and relevance of the information to a particular problem or issue. The technology and the information exist; the missing element is student development and students' understanding of how they can work together in groups. They will need to determine what they know, question what they believe, identify weak arguments, and apply this knowledge to particular problems or issues (Keeley, 1997).

Globalization

One of the most challenging trends projected for the future is the emergence of global interdependence. As our nation enters the twenty-first century, we no longer have the luxury of geographical and economic isolation from other nations. International economic competition, international politics, and the interaction among peoples and nations emphasize the importance of students being informed about the world. Relationships among nations will be based more on cooperation than confrontation. Competition among nations in the twenty-first century will be played out using the weapons of commerce—growth rates, investments, imports, and exports—not aggression or war. Through the United Nations, efforts will be made to address worldwide environmental problems that cannot be addressed piecemeal (Nelan, 1992). International trade agreements, which provide other evidence of global interdependence, will grow in size and number.

Schwahn and Spady (1998) contend that education's current and future consumers reside in a global marketplace that is characterized as being:

- extraordinarily dynamic and driven by technologies that are obsolete upon arrival;
- client centered and flexible or facing extinction;
- filled with limitless challenge and opportunity for the able, adept, and motivated, but increasingly limited for others;
- an arena with an exploding knowledge base and limitless access; and
- a society that is becoming more diverse and unequal and more divided about how to address its problems.

Advances in telecommunication satellites and fiber optics, which already have provided almost instantaneous communication between nations, are eroding the meaning of nationality, ethnicity, and national boundaries (Henry, 1992). These advanced telecommunication technologies make it possible for us to expand our knowledge of the world in significant ways. In short, we have the capability of creating a new twenty-first century world citizen.

As the economic system of the United States becomes increasingly linked to the economic systems of other nations, the English language probably will emerge as the global language. Naisbitt and Auburdene (1990) contended that more than 1 billion individuals around the globe currently spoke English; two thirds of all scientific papers were published in English; and an increasing number of Chinese were mastering English. As international boundaries become more permeable and a global identity emerges, the mastery of English in addition to other languages will be an asset.

In the coming decade we will witness the expansion and merger of multinational corporations and industries in unprecedented numbers. These new industries will reflect a more cooperative model of doing business, compared to the competitive model that has persisted for decades. We also will experience more collaborative projects and joint ventures between countries in manufacturing, marketing, banking, law, agriculture, research and development, science and technology, education, medicine, and the arts.

Educational Implications

As the world shrinks, schools will need to rethink their curriculum and plan for a global society. Developing an understanding of our fellow world citizens will require study of such areas as differences among nations. Case (1993) identified five affective and cognitive elements essential for a global perspective— open-mindedness, anticipation of complexity, resistance to stereotyping, recognition of different points of view, and nonchauvinism. Case indicates that these elements are intertwined and cannot be taught in isolation. Thus, a global perspective emerges from the interaction of the elements. An understanding of language and cultural differences is an essential part of developing an overall global understanding.

Global issues change over time with the expansion of knowledge, changes in political alignments, economic shifts, and advancements in transportation and

What implications do changes in the global economy have for you as a teacher?

Learning is an active process in which children develop human relations skills as well as develop an appreciation for, and understanding of, their peers.

communication. Accordingly, schools of tomorrow will have to continually re-design and reconceptualize their view of the world and the curriculum. In place of the classical curriculum that features the history and culture of Western civilization, we will need a new interdisciplinary approach that focuses on world cultures, world history, world geography, and the humanities, taught from a global perspective. Rather than consisting of a set of accepted premises, instruction should emphasize different points of view; comparisons of different times, geographical areas, and cultures; and the possible impact of alternative actions. A critical consideration in this area is to balance the presentation of different frames of reference and points of view (Case, 1993).

Preparing the world citizen for the information age will necessitate different instructional strategies, new learning methods, and the application of technology to the schools. Schools no longer will be defined by their four walls. Rather, geographic and cultural boundaries will be penetrated, and the students of the future will have an opportunity to experience other cultures firsthand.

Different approaches may be used in selecting materials and working with students in these areas. Issues and concepts often overlap. Additional attention needs to be given to refinement of materials and processes of instruction. Few would question the critical importance of students having a broader perspective of the world, but the wide differences in the values of different cultures present a challenge for the teacher in organizing and presenting materials.

Technology and Education

Technology's current or potential impact on education is not illustrated by large-scale programs such as the space program and scientific or medical research. The range of effects likely will accrue through the speed with which students in school access and process information and data to achieve a better understanding among peoples and nations. We are living in a shrinking world in which some children can sit in their own homes or in schoolrooms and communicate with others throughout the world. Opportunities and access that previously have been restricted to economically privileged youth are becoming available to a much broader range of the population.

Economically powerful interests are seeking to refine the means and redefine the ends of public schooling according to their visions of a technology-driven economy. The issue is whether the interest is in the use of technology to serve education or an effort to use the educational system to serve the technological enterprise. These efforts and interests have to be considered in the context of the failure of recent education reformers to overcome the historical, cultural, bureaucratic, and pedagogical barriers to technological innovation in the classroom (Noble, 1998).

The introduction of technology into schools should not be viewed as an independent introduction of computers or fiber optic cables. Rather, the technology interests represent new forces in educational decision making, forces that are supported by extensive research and development, and forces that receive encouragement from outside the traditional educational community. The challenge confronting educators and the public at large is to recognize this possibility of schooling being colonized in the service of technology. Of special interest is the potential for neglect of the education of the whole student in favor of instructional delivery systems that are dedicated to a high performance economy (Noble, 1998).

Great progress has been made in the introduction of telecommunication in the public schools, but much remains to be done. In 1996, 65% of the schools had access to the Internet, an increase of 15 percentage points in two consecutive years. Internet access was available to 61% of all public elementary schools and 77% of the secondary schools. The access problem was evident in that higher rates were found in large schools and suburban schools. Schools with high levels of students in poverty were less likely to have Internet access; access was available to 53% of the schools in which 71% or more of the students were eligible for the free or reduced-price lunch program (Statistics in Brief, 1997).

America's classrooms are critical components in the effort to provide all youth with access to technology and empower them so that they can use technology to advance in their education and careers. In his State of the Union address in 1996, President Clinton focused attention on the need to provide every classroom in America with connections to the information superhighway and with state-of-the-art computers, current software, and well-trained teachers. To achieve these goals, the president announced four goals to bring about technology literacy for students (Gibbons & Young, 1997):

Goal 1: All teachers in the nation will have the training and support they need to help students learn using computers and the information superhighway.

Goal 2: All teachers and students will have access to modern multimedia computers in their classrooms.

Goal 3: Every classroom will be connected to the information superhighway.

Goal 4: Effective software and on-line learning resources will be an integral part of every school's curriculum.

Technological developments provide opportunities to expand the instructional capacities of teachers and learning opportunities for students. Educators and policy makers face a series of opportunities and challenges as they search for effective uses of technology in learning and instruction, and for the fiscal resources required to implement technology in schools. The challenge is for schools to use technology as a tool that will open the doors to new ways of learning. Technology has the potential to enhance opportunities for student growth so that students can become independent learners.

The challenge for decision makers is to create a vision that recognizes the potential uses of technology in education so that schools become informed and discriminating users of technology rather than captives of the latest fad. A second challenge is for teachers to view technology as a tool to improve current and future learning for all students. As this occurs, the traditional fears that the human element will be displaced by technology will be replaced by a recognition that human capacities can be enhanced by the use of technology. Finally, technological tools are effective only to the degree that the users are trained and informed as to their potential. Installation of instructional technology in a school is expensive in terms of both dollars and staff time; therefore, decisions to acquire technology should include sufficient resources to train both student and teacher users (Gibbons & Young, 1997).

Educational Implications

Information technologies have had a significant impact on America's offices, factories, and stores, but schools have been only minimally affected by technological advancements. A presidential committee of national experts on technology has reported that the potential of technology to transform schools in important ways provides ample justification for immediate and widespread incorporation of technology in K–12 schools. *Report to the President on the Use of Technology to Strengthen K–12 Education in the United States,* a 1997 report to President Clinton (Gibbons & Young, 1997), charted a direction for the future of technology in America's schools; the report's principal recommendations are shown in Figure 16.5.

The range of curricular uses of technology will be limited only by the creativity and resources of the software developers and classroom teachers. Examples include video writing assignments in language arts, micro-based laboratories (MBLs) in science, microcomputer simulations, and computer-based experiences. Applications also can be found in database management software for organizing student research projects in a variety of subjects, synthesizers in music, computer graphics in art, *CD-ROM* (compact disc, read-only memory) laser disk systems in science, voice-activated keyboards, and interactive television (Lemonick, 1992). Through exploratory learning, students can direct their own learning and develop higher order thinking skills as they use technology to identify and solve problems. Video exploratory applications will enable them to bridge the traditional boundaries of disciplines in learning exercises (Means, Blando, Olson, &

What effect have technological advances had on your education?

Figure 16.5: Strategic Recommendations of the President's Committee of Advisors on Science and Technology, Panel on Educational Technology

1. Focus on learning *with* technology, not *about* technology.
2. Emphasize content and pedagogy, not just hardware.
3. Give special attention to professional development.
4. Engage in realistic budgeting.
5. Ensure equitable, universal access.
6. Initiate a major program of experimental research.

Source: Gibbons, J., & Young, J. (1997). *Report to the President on the use of technology to strengthen K-12 education in the United States.* Washington, DC: President's Committee of Advisors on Science and Technology.

Middleton, 1993). As a greater emphasis is placed on development and enhancement of thinking and communication skills, *electronic books* and CD-ROMs may replace many of the print materials that have been the principal source of information for the past few centuries. New techniques for teaching and learning can emerge from language learning software (Gibbons & Young, 1997).

Possibly some of the most advanced applications may be found in special education. Technological advances in the hardware domain have greatly enhanced the educational experiences for individuals with disabilities. The applications can be grouped into input/output (I/O) devices and assistive devices. I/O devices are components of computer systems that permit a user to command and control the processing of data or the outcomes. Examples of input devices include modified keyboards, graphics tables, and optical character readers. Examples of output devices include braille displays, synthesized speech, and telecommunication devices for the deaf. In addition, numerous assistive devices such as environmental control systems and voice-output communications aids (VOCA) exist. Environmental control systems permit persons with physical disabilities to control lamps, appliances, and telephones. VOCAs enable students who cannot speak clearly to communicate by inputting messages into a computer that then converts the messages into synthesized speech (Steinhoff, Babbitt, & Jordan, 1999; Viadero, 1997).

As illustrated in the previous discussion, technology can contribute to major changes in the instructional process and in the role of the teacher. The Stevens Institute of Technology's Center for Improved Engineering and Science Education has observed a variety of positive effects of technology in the classroom (McGrath, 1998).

1. A renewal effect on teachers who had lost their enthusiasm for teaching
2. Tech-savvy teachers who maximize the use of technology in the classroom to help their students develop retrieval skills and engage them in solving real-world problems
3. The development of curiosity in disaffected students as they become familiar with the power of technology
4. The emergence of reticent students as they become active participants in a group problem-solving effort

As suggested, technology will effect changes in the roles of both teachers and students. Rather than being primarily dispensers of information, teachers will become managers of information and mentors or guides for students in their quest for information. Students will become active learners who seek and find information to supplement the efforts of the teacher. Students and teachers will both become empowered with access to this additional resource.

To achieve curriculum integration and planning, the entire instructional staff needs to develop a basic understanding of the potential and limitations of technology as an instructional resource. While teachers will need to develop an understanding of the multiple uses of technology, this will not occur immediately. Teachers need time, guidance, support, and flexibility to understand the potential of technology as a tool to improve teaching and learning (McGrath, 1998).

Technology has the potential for expanding curricular opportunities and affecting classrooms in a variety of ways. Various national efforts have been made to expand the use of technology. Instructional television via satellite transmission brings outstanding instructors into classrooms in isolated areas. Both teachers and students have the opportunity to learn through this activity. Media such as videotapes may be used repeatedly to enhance the understanding of complex concepts. Significant advancements have been made in information retrieval systems through telephone linkages between computers. For example, a teacher can access research information (e.g., the ERIC system) related to the improvement of teaching and learning. The development of the compact disc and international electronic network technology brings to each student's desktop computer instantaneous access to information in libraries and other depositories throughout the world.

Given the pace at which knowledge about information processing and retrieval is expanding, the challenge for both teachers and students will not be to learn specific subject content, but to learn how to learn. By the time schools identify what technical information or skills to teach, the content often is obsolete. When confronted with a problem in the technological age, the student will not be expected to recall from memory the necessary information; rather, the student will be expected to secure the desired information by using various data retrieval systems. The challenge will be for students to become critical and informed consumers of information.

If educational technologies are to reduce the gulf between the achievement of advantaged and disadvantaged students, concerted efforts will be required to ensure that all students have access to and use of information technologies. Some progress has been made in reducing the unequal access of students to computers in schools, but the largest problem is found in the access that students have to computers in their homes (Gibbons & Young, 1997).

The challenges in the use of technology in the schools are illustrated by the ways in which schools and teachers were using telecommunications in schools in 1996. Greatest usage was to access information (74%) and for record keeping within the school or school district (67%). Other lower usage levels were communication with parents (22%), distance learning (22%), teaching (20%), professional development (16%), and curriculum development (15%). If telecommunications are to impact teaching and learning, significant increases will be required in the last three areas (Statistics in Brief, 1997).

How can schools continue to secure the funds required to maintain state-of-the-art technology?

One issue emerging from the $5 billion investment in educational technology is the absence of data on the technology's effectiveness. Too many policy decisions are based on anecdotal information rather than on a careful analysis of comprehensive information (Fatemi, 1997). However, the anecdotal reports include many examples of the merits of technology as a tool to enhance teaching and learning (Trotter, 1997). Issues related to the cost benefits of technology were addressed in the presidential committee's call for careful research on the ways that computing and networking technologies can be used to improve educational outcomes and the ratio of benefits to costs (Gibbons & Young, 1997).

Private Contractors for Public Education

One of the most controversial developments in public education in the 1990s was the emergence of private for-profit firms as potential contractors for the operation of individual schools and entire school districts. Private providers are not new in public education; for decades, many school districts have contracted for pupil transportation, food services, and custodial services. In addition, in the past few years, new private firms have been formed that contract to provide remedial assistance for groups of students or to provide components in the instructional program.

For-profit firms seeking contracts can be classified into two groups. One is the private firm that contracts with the school district to provide a specific service such as custodial services, transportation, or food service. The main rationales for contracting to provide these support services are that cost reduction is achieved through competition and private delivery of services, that the district can avoid unionized employees with high fringe benefits, and that schools can benefit by the introduction of private management techniques. Perhaps the most significant efforts are illustrated by such firms as Marriott and ARA who have contracted to provide school food service programs and school bus services throughout the nation.

The second group includes contractors who assume responsibility for the complete operation of a school, several schools in a district, or the complete school district. These efforts have not expanded at the anticipated rate. These relatively new entrepreneurs include a variety of firms such as Alternative Public Schools (Nashville); Brittannica Learning Centers, Edison Project (New York); Educational Alternatives, Inc. (EAI) (Minneapolis); Huntington Learning Centers (Oradell, NJ); Josten's Learning (Minneapolis); Kumon Educational Institute (Fort Lee, NJ); Ombudsman Educational Services (Libertyville, IL); and Sylvan Learning Group (Columbia, MD). These groups have different interests ranging from the complete operation of one or more schools, the provision of special programs, or operation of the entire school district (McLaughlin, 1995).

Considerable attention has been focused on EAI and the Edison Project. EAI's contracts in Baltimore and Hartford were not renewed, but EAI has recently contracted to operate 12 charter schools in Arizona. The Edison Project is focusing its efforts on contracts for the operation of individual schools (Bushweller, 1997; Harrington-Lueker, 1996). For a variety of reasons, the success of these efforts continues to be rather limited.

The Edison Project has been a well-publicized effort; its stated purpose was to invent, develop, and operate 1,000 new schools. These schools will be privately operated on a for-profit basis; the annual expenditures are to be equivalent to the per-pupil expenditures in public schools. Seed money for the effort has come from various private communications and electronic firms, but only a few contracts have been signed. Brodinsky (1993) noted that the momentum for this effort appeared to have been reduced with the election of President Clinton in 1992.

Educational Implications

Privatization has the potential of impacting the educational system in two primary areas—staffing and program emphasis. From the staffing perspective, both of the major teachers' organizations have expressed concerns about privatization. Their reservations may be related to one of the reasons for privatization of services in both public and private enterprises—the desire to reduce employee costs and avoid restrictive employee relations statutes or contractual commitments related to hiring, job security, and fringe benefits.

Much of the interest in privatization can be traced to low student performance in schools serving disadvantaged communities. As the private firms work to improve performance, they likely will focus their efforts on specific learning activities that will improve student performance in the desired areas. Thus, one issue is the extent to which student enrichment activities and supplemental programs are sacrificed in the quest for improved student performance in the basic skills. However, if privatization extends to suburban schools with a different clientele, the contractor likely will encounter a different set of interests in those communities.

How might the focus of privatization efforts in suburban schools differ from the current focus on improving student performance in urban schools?

In contrast to traditional public schools that are expected to respond to a variety of external pressures (often without additional resources), these entrepreneurial efforts can restrict their programs to the provisions of the contract. The emergence of the private alternative may result in public schools reexamining their staffing structures, program offerings, and school calendars. School officials may be forced to review such items as student activities, teacher tenure, and year-round schools. As in the private sector of the economy, this new source of competition may force the public schools to subject their operation to a serious critique and may contribute to an honest and open discussion of how private contractors can work with the public schools to enhance the education of all students (DeBlois, 1997).

The public policy dilemma is whether public school regulations and rules should apply to private contractors to ensure that they are held to the same level of accountability as schools being operated in the traditional manner (Clark, 1995). Private providers do not become involved in operating schools or school districts because of altruistic motives; they view this field as an important component in the service economy and as an opportunity for market expansion. Given the values of the private providers, they likely will behave in the same manner as any entrepreneur—by responding to the interest of the client.

Centralization and Decentralization of Education

Public policy pressures for reform of public elementary and secondary education in the 1980s and 1990s were paradoxical. Simultaneous pressures developed for both the centralization and decentralization of education. The traditional governance structure of local school boards has been characterized as unresponsive to the changing needs of students and society. Pressures for national standards for curriculum content and student assessment were accompanied by calls for decentralized decision making, teacher empowerment, and parental choice.

By 2010, historians may view the development and endorsement of the national goals for education by the National Governors' Association in 1990 as the first step in the nationalization of public education in the United States. This action contributed to federal education reform proposals being presented by both the Bush and Clinton administrations, and the eventual enactment of the Goals 2000: Educate America Act in 1994. National organizations and state departments of education have developed content standards for the various subjects taught in the schools. States have enacted accountability legislation that relies heavily on student performance on nationally norm-referenced tests; in 1997, 45 states had some type of educational indicator system in place (Dowling, Jordan, Jordan, & Weiner, 1998).

Much of the impetus for the decentralization movement can be traced to the school reform reports and the subsequent actions of state legislatures. In contrast to the nationalization movement that is projected as being voluntary even though the public pressures for participation likely will be great, the decentralization movement has been mandatory in some states, such as the requirement for school-site decision making in Kentucky (Kentucky Education Reform Act, 1990). Other decentralization efforts are illustrated in the legislation authorizing the creation of charter schools in 33 states (Schneider, 1998). Typically, charter school legislation is accompanied by some efforts to decrease state regulatory authority over these schools. The potential effect of these movements is national standardization of some facets of education such as curriculum and assessment, but opportunities for diversification in structure and decision making in local schools. The unknown is whether this seemingly intellectual contradiction will contribute to the improvement of education for youth.

Educational Implications

As one considers the changes in education since the school reform reports, a clear distinction can be made between a federal educational system and a national education system. Support for a federal system is receiving virtually no support from the Congress, the Executive Branch, or the professional education community. However, there do appear to be high levels of interest in national education goals, national curriculum content standards, national certification of teachers, and voluntary national tests for high school completion.

States and localities have taken great pride in their individuality and have valued local control, but structural differences are not great among the nation's schools. Grade levels are the same; graduation requirements are rather similar; basic curricular offerings do not vary greatly; and teacher qualifications permit the interstate movement of teachers. Thus, the major differences resulting from education reform may well be in the acceptance and ratification of the national goals and standards, and the process to be used in assessing the degree to which schools are achieving the national goals and standards. The critical issues then

What components of the educational system should be common among the states, what components might be different?

become the participants in, and the process for, developing and adopting the goals and standards, assessment techniques, and expected performance levels. As this process moves forward, one challenge will be to ensure that alignment exists between the school's curriculum and textbooks and the state's content standards and assessment process. If schools are to be evaluated by the performance of their students on standardized tests, this alignment becomes critical. This should not be interpreted as suggesting that teachers should teach for the test, but does imply that teachers should ensure that adequate consideration is given to the content standards.

The public policy dilemma confronting state and national leaders likely will be what action should be taken when students in localities, states, or nations do not perform at expected levels. For example, if the national standards are not attained, will legislation be enacted that will be punitive on the underperforming states, local school districts, schools, teachers, or students? Legislation in 23 states authorizes a state agency to initiate some type of takeover action when a school is underperforming (Reinhard, 1998). The dilemma is that state officials may not have the political will to do the unpopular act of taking over a local school (Johnson, 1998).

What specific changes in your role as a teacher do you foresee as a result of the focus on national goals and content standards?

One major effect of the decentralization and school reform movements has been the reduction of the discretion of local school boards with the increased state regulation and requirements for schools. In addition, budget and personnel powers have been transferred to individual schools. The interaction of national standards and decentralization provide professional educators with the opportunity to have greater influence and authority over education. The unanswered questions are:

- Will the interests of the advocates for individual disciplines be balanced against the broader collective needs of education at the national level?
- Will a sufficient number of teachers and parents have the time and energies required for successful decentralization and charter schools?

The thrust of the various education reforms suggests the possibility that the true professionalization of teaching may have begun. Significant advances are being made in certification standards for teachers, content standards for students, and efforts to reform teacher preparation and licensing. As noted in Chapter 2, both the AFT and the NEA are advocating a more active role of the profession in policing itself and also are stressing the importance of staff development activities.

Coping with the Future

As an educator, you will enter an educational environment that is in constant flux as policy makers enact legislation requiring education reforms in such areas as performance standards, accountability, and student assessment. These requirements are being imposed during a period when the economic and political interactions among nations demonstrate that the world is shrinking. The increasingly rapid pace of advancements in basic knowledge, transportation, and communication makes it impossible to teach the concepts and facts that will influence the characteristics of the world that your students will experience as adults.

Because of the rapid rate of change and the development of technology, you will not be able to teach the future as a course. Instead, your challenge will be to prepare your students for continued learning in a world that cannot be projected with a high degree of certainty. One approach is to recognize the relationships between different subjects and search for ways to sensitize students to the interactions. For example, a combined science and social studies unit could focus on the anticipated impact of the greenhouse effect on the natural ecological balance of the future and its relationship to economic development. Students could identify problems and probe for underlying cause-and-effect relationships. The application of such a problem-analysis approach in a secondary school might include an exploration of the moral and ethical considerations of genetic engineering. Such an approach emphasizes the power of the individual or group to alter the environment.

One challenge will be to help students develop an optimistic perspective by focusing on the positive and empowering capabilities of the human race. Rather than disseminating mere facts and information, instruction could involve inquiries into hypothetical simulations or scenarios and the development of alternative solutions. The application of an open-ended, inquiry-based methodology in a secondary school might include the development of exploratory predictions of the future through attitude surveys and brainstorming techniques. This methodology might be best suited for courses in journalism, political science, history, or sociology. Students could project themselves into a variety of probable future scenarios and extrapolate creative solutions to problems. The major goal is to teach creative thinking skills so that students can cope with the ever-changing world.

Professional Reflections

"Some of the responsibility of the future of this great nation rests upon the work you do in the classroom. Even though you will not wield a scalpel or command any army, your words, actions, and the very essence that makes you unique will leave a mark on each child whose life you touch."

Kay Brost, Teacher of the Year, Montana

"It is important for teachers to recognize, admire, and respect everyone's talents, then provide an opportunity for all students to be active participants in their own learning."

Carol Banaszynski, Teacher of the Year, Wisconsin

As a teacher, your challenge is to prepare students so that they can cope with the complexity of change. In spite of the uncertainty of the future, there is much we can do to aid our students in preparing for it by helping them develop the skills needed to analyze, clarify, generalize, and make critical judgments. In addition, the study of the future offers numerous creative opportunities for imagining and designing the best possible alternatives and visions for tomorrow.

Summary

Projecting the future is never without its risks. A number of societal trends are so marked, however, that there is reason to believe that they will extend into the next century. Each of these trends will affect education in significant ways. Two of the trends that will affect education the most are the growing minority student body and the aging population. Both have the potential of placing a heavy financial burden on the economy, which in turn may have a deleterious effect on the financing of education. As discussed in Chapter 13, the great debate of this and future decades may concern the competition between the needs of youth and those of the aging population.

The educational implications of technology are limitless, but technology is not the panacea for all of the ills of education. A total redesign of the educational enterprise, including the curriculum, may be necessary for technology to be most effective.

The complexity of tomorrow's world requires a certain type of knowledge and skill that enables one to adapt to and cope with ongoing change. A futures curriculum can help develop the necessary skills to cope with the uncertainty of the future.

Key Terms

CD-ROM   Electronic book

Discussion Questions

1. If you were asked to write an essay describing elementary and secondary schools in 2020, what would be your principal points relative to developments in the educational program, student-teacher interactions, types of instruction, school calendar, and use of technology?

2. Much of the conjecture about the future centers around global interdependence. What effect will the recently signed international trade agreements have on the need for various educational programs and services?

3. What elementary, secondary, and post-secondary curriculum recommendations would you advance to best prepare the world citizen for tomorrow's global society?

4. It is hypothesized that the technology of the future, in particular electronic technologies, will have a profound impact on the school. Design a home/work/school station of the future that integrates the use of advanced technology in your subject matter discipline.

5. In 1970 the renowned psychologist Carl R. Rogers wrote an essay entitled "From Interpersonal Relationships: U.S.A. 2000" for a symposium sponsored by the Esalen Institute. In his essay he discussed such topics as relationships between men and women,

between parents and children, and among individuals in the workplace, as well as religion as interpersonal living. If you were invited to write an essay on "Interpersonal Relationships in the Next Millennium," what key points would your essay include?

6. In 1966, John R. Platt wrote the following for the American Association for the Advancement of Science: "A lifetime ago we made the transformation to education for a living. It is time now to make the transformation to education for wholeness, for delight, and for diversity" (p. 1139). What do you think Platt meant by this statement? Does the quote still apply for the future (i.e., the year 2010)? If yes, how? If no, why not?

Internet Resources

1. See Appendix.

2. **www.census.gov**
   The home page for the U.S. Bureau of the Census provides access to a warehouse of demographic and economic information with video enhancements.

3. **www.wfs.org/wfs/index.htm**
   The home page for the World Future Society, a nonprofit educational and scientific organization dedicated to exploring how social and technological developments shape the future, provides information about the society and numerous links to other future related sites, as well as ongoing and updated predictions for the future.

4. **www.mars2030.net/maini.htm**
   This is the homepage for the Mars Millennium Project, a cooperative venture

of the U.S. Department of Education, NASA, the National Endowment for the Arts, and the J. Paul Getty Trust. It is a learning project designed to get students to think about the future by designing a community for the planet Mars.

5. **www.edutechnet.com**
   The Education Technology Network web site provides commentaries, products, information, best practices, and links to other sites related to the use of technology in education.

6. **www.alumni.caltech.edu/~jamesf/ nfaqs.htm**
   This site provides brief answers to questions about the life and prophecies of Nostradamus.

References

Brodinsky, B. (1993). How "new" will the "new" Whittle American School be? A case study in privatization. *Phi Delta Kappan, 74,* 540–547.

Bushweller, K. (1997). Education Ltd.: Wall Street eyes school privatization. *The American School Board Journal, 184*(3), 19–21.

Carnevale, A. (1992). Skills for the new world order. *The American School Board Journal, 179*(5), 28–30.

Case, R. (1993). Key elements of a global perspective. *Social Education, 57,* 318–325.

Casserly, M. (1998). Urban school funding inequities cited. *Urban Educator, 7*(4), 1–2.

Clark, R. (1995). At a minimum. *The American School Board Journal, 182*(1), 31–32.

Day, J. (1997). *National population projections.* Washington, DC: U.S. Department of Commerce, Census Bureau.

Day, J., & Curry, A. (1997). *Educational attainment in the United States: March 1997.* Washington, DC: U.S. Department of Commerce, Current Population Reports, Population Characteristics.

DeBlois, R. (1997). Public vs. private: Time for an honest discussion that could benefit all schools. *NASSP Bulletin, 81*(589), 90–98.

Dowling, J., Jordan, T., Jordan, K., & Weiner, L. (1998) *Incentives, recognition, and interventions for the New Mexico accountability program.* Santa Fe, NM: New Mexico State Department of Education.

Fatemi, E. (1997, November 5). *Education Week* technology report cites lack of data. *Education Week,* p. 3.

Gibbons, J., & Young, J. (1997). *Report to the President on the use of technology to strengthen K–12 education in the United States.* Washington, DC: President's Committee of Advisors on Science and Technology.

Harrington-Lueker, D. (1996). The high-flyer falls. *The American School Board Journal, 183*(4), 26–33.

Henry, W. A. III. (1992, Fall). Ready or not, here it comes. *Time.* [Special edition], 34.

How We're Changing. (1997). *Demographic state of the nation.* Washington, DC: U.S. Department of Commerce, Current Population Reports, Special Studies, Series P23–193.

Johnson, R. (1998, January 28). Mich. schools get reprieve on sanctions. *Education Week,* pp. 1, 17.

Keeley, L. (1997). Designing for an educational revolution. *Educom Review, 32*(6), 12–14.

Kentucky Education Reform Act. (1990). Frankfort: General Assembly of the Commonwealth of Kentucky.

Leftwich, K. (1994). Job outlook 2005: Where to find the good jobs. *Vocational Education Journal, 69*(7), 27–29.

Lemonick, M. D. (1992, Fall). Tomorrow's lesson: Learn or perish. *Time* [Special edition], 59–60.

McGrath, B. (1998). Partners in learning: Twelve ways technology changes the teacher-student relationship. *T.H.E. Journal, 15,* (9), 58–61.

McLaughlin, J. (1995). Private education and private enterprise: Where's this new relationship going? *School Administrator, 52*(7), 7–13.

Means, B., Blando, J., Olson, K., & Middleton, T. (1993). *Using technology to support education reform.* Santa Monica, CA: SRI International.

Naisbitt, J., & Auburdene, P. (1990). *Megatrends 2000: Ten new directions for the 1990s.* New York: William Morrow.

Nelan, B. W. (1992, Fall). How the world will look in 50 years. *Time* [Special edition], 37.

Noble, D. (1998). The regime of technology in education. In L. Beyer & M. Apple (Eds.), *The curriculum: Problems, politics and possibilities.* (pp. 267–283). Albany: State University of New York Press.

Platt, J. R. (1966). Diversity. *Science, 154,* 1139.

Reinhard, B. (1998, January 14). Racial issues cloud state takeovers. *Education Week,* pp. 1, 18.

Rogers, C. R. (1970). From interpersonal relationships: USA 2000. In M. Dunston and P. W. Garden (Eds.), *Worlds in the making: Probes for students of the future* (pp. 320–325). Englewood Cliffs, NJ: Prentice-Hall.

Schneider, A. (1998). Tracking the charter school movement. *School Business Affairs, 64*(6), 17–23.

Schwahn, C., & Spady, W. (1998). *Total leaders: Applying the best future-focused change strategies to education.* Arlington, VA: American Association of School Administrators.

Statistics in Brief. (1997). *Advanced telecommunications in U.S. public elementary and sec-* *ondary schools, fall 1996.* Washington, DC: U.S. Department of Education, Office of Educational Research and Improvement, National Center for Education Statistics.

Steinhoff, C., Babbitt, B., & Jordan, T. (1999). The hardware domain. In J. Lindsey (Ed.), *Computers and exceptional individuals.* Austin, TX: Pro-Ed.

Trotter, A. (1997, November 10). Taking technology's measure. *Education Week: Technology Counts,* pp. 6–11.

Viadero, D. (1997, November 10). Special Assistance. *Education Week: Technology Counts,* p. 14.

Appendix

The following sites on the World Wide Web are general reference sites for education where additional information about many of the topics discussed in this text may be found. These sites can serve as springboards to many other related sites.

1. **www.ed.gov**
   The home page for the U.S. Department of Education provides thousands of full-text publications, searchable collections, and links to education sites, as well as to ERIC, the world's largest education database.

2. **www.ed.gov/programs.html**
   This site lists the state departments of education for each state and their agencies and programs.

3. **www.ecs.org**
   The home page of the Education Commission of the States is a source for information and reports on educational issues of national concern.

4. **www.rrnet.com/~gleason/ k12.html**
   This site provides links to the home pages of school districts across the nation.

5. **www.edweek.org**
   Educational Week is a weekly publication that presents research, discussion, and statistics on issues of current interest to the education community as well as to policy makers and the general public.

6. **www.eric.syr.edu**
   The Educational Resources Information Center (ERIC) provides access to almost one million articles, research studies, and research summaries on a wide range of topics in education.

7. **www.schoolmatch.com**
   This site provides a comprehensive directory of public schools, as well as statistics about elementary and secondary schools, students, and resources.

8. **www.ccsso.org**
   The home page for the Council of Chief State School Officers provides access to status reports on various education practices and policies among the states.

9. **www.ed.gov/newsletters.html**
   The Office of Educational Research and Improvement (OERI) is the primary research and statistics arm of the U.S. Department of Education and supports 20 national research and development centers, 10 regional education labs, 16 ERIC clearinghouses, the National Library of Education, and more.

In addition to the sites listed, we encourage you to use your search engine(s) to locate material on specific topics of interest. A good tutorial on how to navigate the Web and use search engines can be found at **www.webteacher.org/winnet/ indextc.html.**

Education-specific search engines include:
www.education-world.com
www.education-index.com
www.excite.com/education
www.lycos.com/education
www.webcrawler.com/career_and_ education
www.yahoo.com/education/k_12

Glossary

Academic freedom. The teacher's freedom to determine the most appropriate instructional materials and the most appropriate teaching strategies without censorship, interference, or fear of reprisal.

Academy. A type of private secondary school operating in the 1800s, designed to teach subjects useful in trade and commerce.

Accelerated schools. Originated in a research project conducted by Professor Henry Levin and his associates at Stanford University, the concept is based on three basic principles: unity of purpose, school community empowerment coupled with responsibility, and building on the strengths of teachers, parents, support staff, and students.

Accountability. A concept in which the schools and teachers are held responsible for the accomplishment of expressed educational goals.

Acculturation. The process of becoming conditioned to the cultural patterns of the dominant group.

Acquired immune deficiency syndrome (AIDS). A serious health condition caused by a virus that destroys the immune system and leaves the body incapable of fighting disease.

Activity curriculum. A curriculum that is determined to a large extent by student interest and that emphasizes self-expression through games, singing, or other creative and spontaneous activities.

Adequacy. The extent to which funding for programs and learning opportunities is sufficient.

Administrative law. The formal regulations and decisions of state or federal agencies.

Aesthetics. The branch of philosophy concerned with values in beauty, especially in the fine arts.

Affirmative action. Affirmative steps to recruit and hire, or recruit and retain, individuals from groups who are underrepresented in the workplace or the classroom.

Alternative certification. State provisions or regulations for awarding a teaching license to a person who has not followed the traditional teacher education program; exceptions typically are related to completion of a concentrated professional education sequence, teaching internships or prior experience, or credits for work experience.

Alternative schools. Schools that offer specialized programs and learning experiences not normally found in the public schools, or that provide greater individual attention for students who are not making normal progress.

Amalgamation. A form of diversity that supports the "melting pot" notion and envisions American culture as emerging from the best elements of many cultures.

Analytical learner. A person who perceives information in an abstract form and processes that information in a reflective manner.

Apparent reality. The reality made up of day-to-day experiences and life events.

Assimilation. A response to population diversity that requires conformity to a single model, which is largely defined by traditional British political, social, cultural, and religious institutions.

At risk. A term used to describe students who are achieving below grade-level expectations or are likely to experience educational problems in the future, as well as students who are likely to experience physical and mental health problems.

Authentic assessment. A form of evaluation based on the cooperation between the student and teacher, student and student, teacher and administrator or supervisor, and community and teacher.

Axiology. The branch of philosophy concerned with the nature of values.

Back-to-basics movement. A revival of essentialism begun in the 1970s and echoed in education reform reports of the 1980s that emphasizes the three Rs, a core curriculum, and more rigorous academic program requirements.

Behavioral objectives. Action-oriented statements that indicate specific behaviors or knowledge that students are expected to learn or demonstrate upon completion of an instructional sequence.

Behaviorism. An educational theory predicated on the belief that human behavior can be explained in terms of responses to external stimuli. The basic principle underlying behaviorism in education is that behaviors can be modified in a socially acceptable manner through the arrangement of the conditions for learning.

Bibliotherapy. The use of books as a therapeutic intervention.

Bilingual education. Instruction to non-English-speaking students in their native language while teaching them English.

Bloom's Taxonomy of Educational Objectives. List and organizing scheme containing expected learnings for students.

Board certified. Certification awarded by the assessment board of a profession acknowledging the recipient's qualifications in specified areas.

Building principal. The person responsible for the administration and management of a school.

Burnout. Physical or emotional exhaustion caused by long-term stress.

Career ladder. A career development plan that provides differential recognition and rewards for teachers at steps of the plan, which coincide with increased experience and expertise.

Carnegie unit. A measure of clock time associated with a high school course used to award credit toward high school graduation.

Cartesian method. A process proposed by Descartes that involves the derivation of axioms upon which theories can be based by the purposeful and progressive elimination of all interpretations of experience except those that are absolutely certain.

Categorical funding. The practice of state funding of specific educational programs or activities (e.g., bilingual education, education of handicapped pupils, pupil transportation, or in-service programs).

Categorical imperatives. Universal moral laws that guide our actions and behaviors.

CD-ROM. A compact disc with read-only memory used for the storage of audio, visual, and textual data.

Certification. The authorization of an individual by the state to teach in an area where the state has determined he or she has met established state standards.

Charity (pauper) schools. Schools in colonial New England designed for children who could not afford to attend other fee-charging schools.

Charter schools. Publicly supported schools established upon the issuance of a charter from the state, local school board, or other entity and designed to provide greater autonomy to individual schools and greater choice in educational programs to parents and students.

Chief state school officer. The elected or appointed executive officer of the state department of education, responsible for elementary and secondary education, and sometimes for higher education; often referred to as the superintendent of public instruction or the commissioner of education.

Child abuse. The repeated mistreatment or neglect of a child, which can result in physical, emotional, verbal, or sexual injury or harm.

Child benefit theory. The legal theory that supports providing state aid to private education when the aid benefits the private school child rather than the private school itself.

Child neglect. Child abuse that includes an unwillingness to provide for the basic needs of the child.

Child (student)-centered curriculum. Curriculum designed with the child's interest and needs at the center of the learning process; learning takes place through experience and problem solving.

Chlamydia infection. One of the most prevalent sexually transmitted diseases that affects young women.

Choice. Power or authority of (1) a local school board to select the instructional program and level of funding to be provided students in the school district, or (2) parents to select the school that their child attends.

Classical conditioning. A type of behaviorism that demonstrates that a natural stimulus that produces a certain type of response can be replaced by a conditioned stimulus.

Cluster suicides. A series of suicides that are closely related in time and place.

Coalition of Essential Schools (CES). Developed by Professor Ted Sizer of Brown University, the Coalition of Essential Schools is based on the concept of a triangle of learning between teacher, student, and subject matter. The model assumes that effective school reform requires fundamental changes in the school as an institution.

Code of ethics. A set of professional standards for behavior of members of a profession.

Cognitive styles. The alternative processes by which learners acquire knowledge.

Common schools. Publicly supported schools started during the mid-1800s attended in common by all children.

Common sense learner. One of four learning styles related to the perceiving and processing of information. The common sense learner perceives information abstractly and processes it actively.

Compensatory education. Special educational programs designed to overcome the educational deficiencies associated with the socioeconomic, cultural, or minority group disadvantages of youth.

Competency testing. Testing designed to assess basic skills and knowledge.

Comprehensive high school. A public secondary school that offers curricula in vocational education, general education, and college preparation.

Constitution. A written contract for the establishment of a government; the highest level of law.

Constructivism. (See Postmodern constructivism).

Continuity. The repetition of major curriculum elements to ensure that skills can be practiced and developed.

Cooperative learning. Instructional system that assumes that students will study and work together in a supportive relationship rather than competitively.

Core curriculum. A curriculum design that emphasizes the required minimum subjects and topics within subjects that all students are expected to learn.

Cosmology. The branch of philosophy concerned about the nature of the universe or cosmos.

Crisis intervention team. Volunteer teachers, counselors, administrators, social workers, school nurses, and school psychologists who network with each other and identify the student who appears to be overwhelmed by stress, or displays suicidal gestures or suicidal threats.

Critical literacy. A type of curriculum that challenges all unequal power relationships and denounces any form of exclusion.

Critical theory. A set of principles that reflects the melding of the philosophies of Kant, Hegel, Freud, and Marx.

Critical thinking. The process of thinking and problem solving that involves the examination and validation of assumptions and evidence and the application of logic to the formulation of conclusions.

Cultural literacy. An assumed body of knowledge about which persons should be able to demonstrate mastery if they are to function at an optimal level in society.

Cultural pluralism. A form of diversity that emphasizes the multiple cultures in the larger society.

Culture. The behavioral patterns, ideas, values, religions and moral beliefs, customs, laws, language, institutions, art, and all other material things and artifacts characteristic of a given people at a given period of time.

Curriculum. All the educational experiences of students that take place in the school.

Dame school. The elementary school in the New England colonies, usually held in a kitchen or living room and taught by women with minimal education.

Deductive logic. Logic that deduces concrete applications from a general principle or general rule.

De Facto **segregation.** Segregation existing as a matter of fact, regardless of the law.

De Jure **segregation.** Segregation sanctioned by law.

Demonstration instruction. Instructional technique in which students learn through doing and/or observing.

Desegregation. The abolition of racial, ethnic, or gender segregation.

Discrimination. Showing bias or prejudice in the treatment of individuals because of their race, ethnicity, gender, or handicapping condition.

Disparate impact. The situation that exists when a policy or practice has a differential impact on individuals in a protected class.

Dropout. A pupil who leaves school for any reason except death, before graduation or completion of a program of studies and without transferring to another school or institution.

Dynamic learner. One of four learning styles related to the perceiving and processing of information. The dynamic learner perceives information concretely and processes it actively.

Ebonics. A dialect or form of speech communication known as Black English which is spoken primarily by African Americans in urban areas.

Educational foundations. Charitable or not-for-profit entities established to receive and/or distribute funds that can be used to enrich the educational opportunities for students.

Educational goals. Broad general statements of desired learning outcomes.

Educational malpractice. Failure on the part of an education professional to render a reasonable amount of care in the exercise of his/her duties with resultant injury or loss to another.

Educational objective. A clearly defined, observable, and measurable student behavior that indicates learner progress toward the achievement of a particular educational goal.

Educational overburden. A condition that exists in many urban districts because of the relatively larger number of pupils in these districts who require high-cost educational programs and the fact that the costs of goods and services to provide instruction are higher.

Electronic books. Content formerly available only through print material that can be accessed through commercially available CD-ROM and other software as well as through on-line networks.

Emergency (temporary) certificate. A certificate issued to a person who does not meet the specified degree, course, or other requirements for regular certification; issued with the presumption that the recipient teacher will obtain the necessary credentials for regular certification.

Eminent domain. The right of the government to take private property for public use.

Emotional abuse. Nonphysical abuse such as blaming, rejecting, or withholding security and affection.

Employee services. A benefit designed to help the employee to enjoy an improved lifestyle or meet certain obligations at a free or reduced cost (e.g., credit unions, employee assistance programs, childcare).

Enculturation. The process of learning about one's culture.

English as a Second Language (ESL). A form of bilingual education in which standard English is taught to limited-English-proficient students.

Epistemology. The branch of philosophy concerned with the investigation of the nature of knowledge.

Equalization. A model for the distribution of financial aid to education in inverse proportion to school district wealth.

Equal opportunity. A legal principle that when applied to education requires school districts and other agencies to develop policies and procedures to ensure that the rights of employees and students are protected and that they are given equal treatment in employment practices, access to programs, or other educational opportunities.

Equity. The equal treatment of persons/students in equal circumstances.

Essentialism. An educational theory that focuses on an essential set of learnings that prepare individuals for life, by concentration on the culture and traditions of the past.

Ethics. The branch of philosophy concerned with the study of the human conduct and what is right and wrong or good and bad.

Ethnic group. A subgroup of the population distinguished by having a common heritage (language, customs, history, etc.).

Existentialism. A philosophic belief that focuses on personal and subjective existence; the world of choice and responsibility is primary.

Expository instruction. A teacher-centered instructional method designed to convey information through formal lecture, informal lecture, and teacher-led discussion.

***Ex post facto* law.** A law passed after the fact or after the event.

Expulsion. Exclusion of students from school for periods of time in excess of 10 days.

Fair use doctrine. The rules that govern the reproduction and use of copyrighted materials.

Fiber optics. Land-based transmission lines that can transmit large quantities of data and information at rapid speeds.

Flat grants. A method for allocation of educational funds based on the allocation of a uniform amount per student, per teacher, per classroom, or other unit.

Formative evaluation. Form of evaluation designed to provide feedback while an activity is underway to improve the manner in which the activity is conducted.

Foundation plan. State school finance system that provides a base amount per pupil to local school districts from a combination of state and local tax sources with the amount of state funds

per pupil received by a local school district being in inverse relation to the fiscal capacity per pupil of the local school district.

Full state funding. A school finance system whereby all funds for the support of the public schools come from the state and from state-level taxes.

Gender equity. In education, this term refers to the concepts of equal treatment and equal opportunity for all students, regardless of their gender.

Grammar school. A secondary school, originating in ancient Rome and continuing into the nineteenth century, which emphasized a classical education; forerunner of the high school; in current usage, an elementary school.

Great Books. The great works of the past, including literature, philosophy, history, and science, which represent absolute truth according to perennialist theory.

Group instruction. An instructional system in which teachers divide the class into groups of students (often five to eight students) and structure instruction and learning activities for this smaller number of students.

Hermeneutics. The art or science of the interpretation of lived experience.

Hidden curriculum. The rules, regulations, rituals, and interactions that are part of the everyday life of the school.

Home schooling. The education of children in the home; a form of private education.

Horizontal equity. In the financing of schools or the treatment of individuals, the principle that states that those who are alike should be treated the same; the equal treatment of equals.

Hornbook. A wooden board on which a sheet of parchment was placed and covered with a thin sheath of cow's horn; used in colonial New England primary schools.

Hostile environment harassment. Verbal or physical conduct of a sexual nature that interferes with an individual's work performance.

Human immunodeficiency virus (HIV). Any of several retro viruses that cause AIDS.

Humanism. The dominant philosophy of the Renaissance that emphasized the importance of human beings and promoted the literature and art of classical Rome and Greece.

Humanistic education. An educational program reflecting the philosophy of humanism.

Idealism. The oldest philosophic belief which views the world of the mind and ideas as fundamental.

Imaginative learner. One of four learning styles related to the perceiving and processing of information. The imaginative learner perceives information concretely and processes it reflectively.

Incentive pay. Paying teachers more for different kinds or amounts of work (e.g., master teacher plans or career ladder plans).

Inclusion. Serving students with a variety of abilities and disabilities in the regular classroom with appropriate support services.

Incompetence. Lack of legal qualification, inability or capacity to discharge the required duty. In regard to teachers, incompetence falls into four general categories: (1) inadequate teaching, (2) poor discipline, (3) physical or mental incapacity, and (4) counterproductive personality traits.

Independent learning. A range of student-centered teaching methodologies that include programmed instruction, self-paced instruction, contract learning, and performance-based instruction.

Indirect compensation. Payments or fringe benefits that employees receive in addition to payments in the form of money; classified as either employee benefits or employee services, such as health and life insurance, long-term disability protection, or leaves with pay.

Individualized education program (IEP). A program designed by a team of educators, parents, and at times the student to meet the unique needs of the child for whom it is developed.

Individualized instruction. Instructional system in which teachers work with students on a one-on-one basis and structure instruction and learning activities for each student.

Inductive logic. Logic that begins with a combination of facts and from those facts a general principle or rule is formulated.

Infant school. A type of public elementary school introduced in the United States in the nineteenth century to prepare children aged four to seven for elementary school.

Information superhighway. A series of electronic networks for communication and information sharing that are potentially accessible by telecommunication links to all schools, homes, and offices.

In loco parentis. In the place of a parent.

Inquiry instruction. A problem-oriented instructional system in which students assume major responsibility for designing and structuring their learning activities and teachers serve as resource persons and facilitators.

Insubordination. The persistent and willful violation of a reasonable rule or direct order from a recognized authority.

Integrated curriculum. A curriculum design that combines separate subjects from within the same discipline, and in some instances content from two or more branches of study.

Integrated studies. A component of the teacher education program that includes on- and off- campus clinical, laboratory, and practicum experiences.

Integration. The coordination of skills and knowledge across disciplines in the curriculum.

Intelligence quotient (IQ). A number intended to indicate an individual's level of mental development or intelligence.

Interstate reciprocity. A mutual agreement between states that allows teachers who are certified in one state to be eligible for certification in another.

Intervention programs. Programs or strategies directed at providing assistance to children and adolescents who are already at risk.

Junior college. An educational institution that offers courses for two years beyond high school. These courses may transfer to a four-year institution or may be complete career or vocational programs.

Junior high school. An intermediate school between elementary and high school that includes grades 7 and 8 or 7, 8, and 9.

Learning disability. Having a disorder or delayed development in one or more of the processes of thinking, speaking, reading, writing, listening, or doing arithmetic operations.

Least restrictive environment. The educational setting that enables the handicapped child to have an educational experience most like that of a nonhandicapped child.

***Lemon* test.** A tripartite test used by the courts to evaluate claims under the establishment clause. Asks three questions: Does the action or policy (1) have a primarily secular purpose, (2) have the primary effect of advancing or inhibiting religion, or (3) foster an excessive entanglement between the state and religion?

Liberty interest. The right to a fundamental constitutional liberty (speech, press, etc.).

Life adjustment education. An educational program, popular in the mid-twentieth century, which focused on youth who did not attend college, rejected traditional academic studies, and stressed functional objectives such as vocation and health.

Limited open forum. The condition said to exist when schools provide noncurriculum student groups the opportunity to meet on school premises during noninstructional time.

Linguistic minority. Nonnative English speakers and others who are native speakers of English, but have been exposed to another language in the home since birth.

Local property tax. A tax on real property (land and buildings) levied by a local governmental unit such as a school district.

Logical positivism (logical empiricism). The view that no proposition can be considered scientifically valid unless it can be verified on logical or empirical grounds.

Lyceum. A voluntary organization sponsoring programs, demonstrations, and lectures for the education and information of its members.

Magnet school. A school offering specialized and unique programs designed to attract students from throughout the district, thereby promoting racial integration.

Mainstreaming. The placing of handicapped children, to the maximum extent possible, into the regular classroom where they have contact with nonhandicapped children.

Major depression. A serious depression with persistent symptoms that typically last for at least two or more weeks.

Mass media. Television, popular music, movie, music video, radio, newspaper, and magazine industries.

Master teacher. A teacher who is given special status, pay, and recognition, but remains in the classroom as a role model for other teachers, or is released from a portion of the regular classroom assignment to work with other teachers in a supportive, nonsupervisory role.

Mastery learning. An instructional system in which the desired learning and performance levels are identified and teachers work with students until they attain the desired level of performance.

Mentoring. Formal and informal relationships between a beginning teacher and an experienced teacher(s) that are sources of information and support for the beginning teacher.

Metaphysics. The branch of philosophy concerned with the nature of reality and existence.

Monitorial school. A school where one teacher taught a lesson to a group of older students, called monitors, who then each taught the lesson to a larger group of younger students.

Multicultural education. An educational strategy that provides for students whose cultural and linguistic backgrounds may prevent them from succeeding in the traditional school setting, which historically reflects the dominant Anglo-Saxon culture.

Multiple intelligences theory. Developed by Howard Gardner at Harvard University, the concept of multiple intelligences assumes that human cognitive competence is pluralistic rather than unitary.

Municipal overburden. A burden caused by the need for a greater range of social services in urban areas that must be paid for by the same taxpayers who support the schools.

National Assessment of Educational Progress (NAEP). A series of tests mandated by Congress and administered nationally in reading, mathematics, and science.

Naturalism. A philosophic or educational philosophy that emphasizes the natural world, the freedom of the individual, and the development of that which is natural in humans.

Negligence. A failure to do (or not to do) what a reasonable and prudent person would do under the same or similar circumstances, the result of which is injury to another.

Neo-Thomism. A traditional philosophy that bridges the dualism of idealism and realism and emphasizes the existence of God, which can be known by both faith and reason.

New basics. A curriculum composed of English, mathematics, science, social studies, computer sciences, and foreign languages for those aspiring to college.

Nongraded school. A school in which grade divisions are eliminated for a sequence of two or more years.

Normal school. Institutions established in the 1800s for the purpose of training teachers.

Null curriculum. Those things that are not included in the formal curriculum because of their controversial nature, because they represent different values, or because of the lack of resources or information.

Object lesson. An instructional activity that centers on concrete materials within the child's experience and involves discussion and oral presentation.

Ontology. The branch of metaphysics that is concerned about the nature of existence and what it means for anything "to be."

Open classroom. An architectural design for elementary schools popular during the 1960s that consisted of large, open instructional spaces not divided into traditional walled classrooms.

Operant conditioning. A type of behaviorism in which any response to any stimulus can be conditioned by immediate reinforcement or reward.

Paideia. The general body of knowledge that all educated individuals should possess.

Parochial school. A private elementary or secondary school supported or affiliated with a church or religious organization.

Perennialism. An educational theory that focuses on the past, namely the universal truths and such absolutes as reason and faith. Perennialists believe the purpose of the school is to cultivate the rational intellect and search for the truth.

Phenomenology. The study of the consciousness and experiencing of phenomena in philosophy.

Philosophical analysis. The process of systematic questioning of assumptions, values, theories, procedures, and methods designed to help formulate and clarify beliefs about teaching and learning.

Philosophy of education. The theory of philosophic thought that defines our views about the learner, the teacher, and the school.

Plenary. Absolute, as the power of the state legislature to enact any legislation controlling the schools that is not contrary to the federal Constitution or the state constitution.

Policies. Guidelines or principles for action adopted by a local school board to provide direction for administrative rules and regulations used in administering a local school district.

Postmodern constructivism. A theory of learning which states that learners construct their own knowledge and meaning based on their prior experiences within a social context.

Postvention programs. Strategies or programs designed to help the school return to normal in the aftermath of a crisis, which include grief counseling, support groups, interacting with the media, and follow-up care.

Power equalization. A state school finance system in which the governing board of each local school district determines its spending level per pupil. For each unit of local tax rate, the state will provide sufficient funds to ensure a guaranteed amount; state funds will be in inverse relation to the fiscal capacity per pupil of the local school district.

Powerful learning. Based on Henry Levin's work with at-risk youth, the concept of powerful learning assumes that if students see meaning in their lessons and perceive connections between the activities and their lives, they will become active learners and will build on their own strengths even though they will differ in the degree to which they attain or exceed mastery, and will learn at different rates.

Pragmatism. A philosophy that focuses on the things that work; the world of experience is central.

Premack principle. The principle that states that because organisms freely choose to engage in certain behaviors rather than others, providing access to the preferred activities will serve as a reinforcement for engaging in nonpreferred activities.

Prevention strategies. Strategies including programs, activities, and services designed to reduce the occurrence of at-risk behaviors in children and adolescents.

Procedural due process. The process by which individuals are provided fair and equitable procedures in a matter affecting their welfare (procedural due process) and are protected from unfair deprivation of their property.

Profession. An occupation involving relatively long and specialized preparation on the level of higher education and governed by its own code of ethics.

Professional development. Activities designed to build the personal strengths and creative talents of individuals and thus create human resources necessary for organizational productivity.

Programmed instruction. A teaching method that enables individual students to answer questions about a unit of study at their own rate, checking their own answers and advancing only after answering correctly.

Progressivism. A theory of education that is concerned with "learning by doing" and purports that children learn best when pursuing their own interests and satisfying their own needs.

Project method. An instructional methodology that attempts to make education as "life-like" as possible through the use of educative activities that are consistent with the child's own goals.

Property right. The right to specific real or personal property, tangible and intangible; e.g., the right to continued employment or the use of one's name.

Proprietary school. A school operated by an individual, group, or corporation for profit to serve the educational needs of a particular clientele.

Protective factors. Personal attributes, family factors, and community factors that guard against maladaptive behavior.

Proximate cause. The primary act or mission that produces an injury and without which the injury would not have occurred. A standard used to determine a teacher's liability in the cause of an injury.

***Quid pro quo* harassment.** Making a benefit of employment conditional upon the receipt of sexual favors.

Rate bill. A tuition fee based on the number of children paid by the parents during the mid-1800s.

Reading recovery. A preventive tutoring program developed by Marie Clay, a New Zealand child psychologist. Reading recovery focuses on first grade students who are having difficulties in the development of their reading skills. The principles underlying this program are that (1) reading takes place in a child's mind, (2) reading and writing are interconnected, and (3) children learn to read by reading.

Realism. A philosophy in which the world of nature and physical matter is superior to the world of ideas. Matter exists whether the mind perceives it or not.

Real reality. A form of reality that includes the realm of ideas, eternal truths, and perfect order in the philosophy of idealism.

Reflective thinking. Thinking that is characterized by deliberate inquiry into all assumptions, claims of knowledge, evidence, and one's own thought processes.

Religious realism. The interface of the secular ideas of Aristotle and Christian teachings of

St. Augustine. Neo-Thomism is also called religious realism.

Resiliency. Having developed the necessary coping mechanisms despite overwhelming hardships and obstacles.

Restructuring. A buzzword of the 1990s, connoting a number of prescriptions for education: parental choice, year-round schools, longer school days and years, recast modes of governance, alternative funding patterns, and all-out commitments to technology.

Reverse discrimination. Discrimination or bias against members of one class in an attempt to correct past discrimination against members of another class.

Scholasticism. The philosophy of Thomas Aquinas that serves as the foundation for Catholic education and holds that man is a rational being who possesses both a spiritual nature and a physical nature, that truth can be arrived at through the deductive process, and that when reason fails, man must rely on faith.

School board. As created by the state, the governing body for a local school district, with members generally selected by popular vote.

School culture. Social interactions of the students and adults in the school environment and the ways in which their behavior is influenced by the official rules and established mores of the school.

School Development Program. Developed by James Comer and his colleagues at the Yale Child Study Center, the School Development Program is a schoolwide restructuring project to address the needs of the whole child, including school-based health services, parent involvement, and teacher participation in restructuring the school's programs. A central component of the model is a school management and governance team composed of the principal, teachers, parents, a mental health specialist, and support personnel who are responsible for development of the school's master plan.

School effectiveness. The level at which students are performing in the basic skills.

Scientific method. The systematic reporting and analysis of what is observed and retesting of hypotheses formulated from the observations.

Secondary school. A program of study that follows elementary school, such as junior high school, middle school, or high school.

Secretary of education. The executive officer of the U.S. Department of Education; a member of the president's cabinet.

Secular humanism. Allegedly a faith that denies God, deifies man, and glorifies reason.

Sense realism. The belief that learning must come through the senses.

Separatism. A form of diversity that suggests that by maintaining a separatist position, minority groups can build strength, maintain their identity, and gain power.

Sequence. The arrangement of learning experiences in a curriculum to ensure that successive experiences build upon preceding ones.

Seven liberal arts. The curriculum that includes the trivium (grammar, rhetoric, and logic) and the quadrivium (arithmetic, geometry, music, and astronomy).

Sex bias. The biased behavior that results from believing in sex role stereotypes.

Sex discrimination. Any action that denies opportunities, privileges, or rewards to a person or persons because of their gender, in violation of the law.

Sexism. Discrimination against an individual on the basis of gender, in particular, discrimination and prejudicial stereotyping of females.

Sex role stereotyping. The attribution of specific behaviors, abilities, personality characteristics, and interests to a given gender.

Sexual abuse. Contact or interaction between a child and an adult when the child is being used for the sexual stimulation of the perpetrator or another person.

Sexually transmitted diseases (STDs). Diseases such as gonorrhea or chlamydia infection that are transmitted sexually.

Single salary schedule. A salary schedule for teachers that provides equivalent salaries for equivalent preparation and experience.

Site-based management. Delegation by a school board of certain decision-making responsibilities about educational programs and school operations to individual schools. Usually provides that teachers, parents, and the principal serve as the decision-making group.

Skinheads. Neo-Nazi gang members.

Social class. A social stratum in which the members share similar characteristics, such as income, occupation, status, education, etc.

Socialization. The process by which persons are conditioned to the customs or patterns of a particular culture.

Social mobility. The movement upward or downward among social classes.

Social reconstruction curriculum. A curriculum design that aims to engage students in a critical analysis of society and prepare them to effect change and create a more equitable society.

Social reconstructionism. An educational theory that advocates change, improvement, and the reforming of the school and society.

Social selection. A position that suggests that schools serve the wealthy and powerful at the expense of the poor.

Society. A group of persons who share a common culture, government, institutions, land, or set of social relationships.

Socioeconomic status. The social and economic standing of an individual or group.

Socratic Method. A dialectical teaching method employed by Socrates using a questioning process based on the student's experiences and analyzing the consequences of responses, leading the student to a better understanding of the problem.

Spiral curriculum. Curriculum in which a subject matter is presented over a number of grades with increasing complexity and abstraction.

Stare decisis. Let the decision stand; a legal rule that states that once a court has laid down a principle of law as applicable to a certain set of facts, it will apply it to all future cases in which the facts are substantially the same and that

other courts of equal or lesser rank will similarly apply the principle.

State board of education. A state agency charged with adopting regulations and monitoring local school districts to ensure implementation of the constitutional and statutory mandates related to the operation of the state system of schools.

State department of education. The operating arm for the administration of state education activities and functions.

Statutory law. The body of law consisting of the written enactments of a legislative body.

Strategic planning. A planning process that involves the establishment of a mission statement, the specification of goals and objectives, and the linking of funding priorities to the accomplishment of program priorities.

Student-to-student sexual harassment. A form of sexual abuse that includes being verbally harassed or touched, pinched, or grabbed in a sexual gesture by a classmate or peer.

Subculture. A group of people distinguished by ethnic, racial, religious, geographic, social, economic, or lifestyle traits.

Subject-area curriculum. A curriculum design that views the curriculum as a group of subjects or a body of that subject matter which has survived the test of time.

Subject-centered curriculum. Curriculum designed with the acquisition of certain knowledge as the primary goal. The learning process usually involves rote memorization, and learning is measured using objective test scores.

Success for All. Developed by Professor Robert Slavin at Johns Hopkins University, this program assumes a research-based preschool program; full-day kindergarten; beginning reading programs with the integration of phonics and whole language; homogenous reading groups; one-on-one tutoring with an integration of the regular curriculum in grades 1–3; cooperative learning in intermediate reading, writing/language arts, and mathematics; family support services; and a facilitator to coordinate the program and provide training and technical assistance.

Suicide gesture. A behavior that suggests a willingness to commit suicide.

Suicide ideation. Thoughts about suicide.

Suicide threat. An expression of an intention to commit suicide.

Sunday schools. Educational programs of the later 1700s and early 1800s offering the rudiments of reading and writing on Sunday to children who worked during the week.

Superintendent of schools. The chief executive officer of the local school district whose educational program and related responsibilities include planning, staffing, coordinating, budgeting, administering, evaluating, and reporting. This person informs and works with the local school board.

Suspension. Exclusion of students from school for a period of time of 10 days or less.

Tabula rasa. Literally, blank slate: applied to the concept of the human mind which says that children come into the world with their minds a blank slate.

Tax benefits. Tax deductions and tax credits designed to benefit patrons and nonpublic schools.

Teachers' institute. A teacher training activity begun in the nineteenth century, lasting from a few days to several weeks, where teachers met to be instructed in new techniques, informed of modern materials, and inspired by noted educators.

Tenure. The status conferred on teachers who have served a specific period that guarantees them continuation of employment, subject to the requirements of good behavior and financial necessity.

Theory. A hypothesis or set of hypotheses that have been verified by observation or experiment, or a general synonym for systematic thinking or a set of coherent thoughts.

Theory of education. Systematic thinking or generalization about schooling.

Tort. A civil wrong that leads to injury to another and for which a court will provide a remedy in the form of an action for damages.

Vernacular schools. Elementary schools originating in Germany in the sixteenth century that offered instruction in the mother tongue or vernacular, and a basic curriculum of reading, writing, mathematics, and religion.

Vertical equity. The assumption that groups that have different needs should be treated differently and also that those within each group should be treated in the same way.

Voucher. A grant or payment made to a parent or child to be used to pay the cost of the child's education in a private or public school.

Whole-child movement. An educational movement emphasizing totality of the child as the composite of the social, emotional, physical, and mental dimensions.

White flight. The exodus of middle and upper class white families from urban school districts to avoid desegregation.

Author Index

Subject Index